Cases for Contemporary Strategy Analysis

Cases for Contemporary Strategy Analysis

Kent E. Neupert
University of Houston

Joseph N. Fry
The University of Western Ontario

First published 1996

Blackwell Publishers, Inc.
238 Main Street
Cambridge, Massachusetts 02142

Blackwell Publishers Ltd.
108 Cowley Road
Oxford OX4 1JF
UK

Library of Congress Cataloging-in-Publication Data

Neupert, Kent E.
    Cases in contemporary strategy analysis / Kent E. Neupert, Joseph N. Fry.
        p.   cm.
    Includes bibliographical references and index.
    ISBN 1-55786-929-4 (pbk.)
    1. Strategic planning—Case studies. 2. Decision-making—Case studies. I. Fry, Joseph N. II. Title.
HD30.28.N478   1996
658.4′012—dc20   95-51324
                                                                                                              CIP

British Library Cataloguing in Publication Data

A CIP catalogue record for this book is available from the British Library.

Typeset in 11 pt. on 13 Sabon by AM Marketing

Printed in the United States of America

This book is printed on acid-free paper

Contents

Prince Edward Island Preserve Co. is a producer and marketer of specialty food products. In August 1991, company president Bruce McNaughton was contemplating future expansion. Two cities were of particular interest: Toronto and Tokyo. At issue was whether consumers in both markets should be pursued, and if so, how. The choices available for achieving further growth included mail order, distributors, and company controlled stores.

Coral Divers Resort is a scuba diving resort in the Caribbean. Revenues have flattened in recent years and are down in 1995. To remedy the decline, the resort is considering a shift in strategy to focus its orientation. In determining what to do, the manager of Coral Divers Resort must consider the resources and capabilities required to shift from their current market to a new market focus.

This case focuses on the successful evolution of Wal*Mart's remarkably successful discount operations and describes the company's more recent attempts to diversify into other businesses. The company has entered the warehouse industry with its Sam's Clubs and the grocery business with its Supercenters, a combination supermarket and grocery store. Wal*Mart experienced a drop in the value of its stock price in early 1993, which it has not made up.

This note illustrates an industry that is losing its competitive advantages due to globalization. The industry in Malaysia had enjoyed the benefits of large tin resources (the major raw material in pewter) as well as a cheap labor force; consequently it had become one of the major players in the world pewter industry. This result is evidenced by Royal Selangor International, a Malaysian pewter company that had taken advantage of the country's resources to become one of the leading pewter companies in the world.

The 3M operating committee is meeting in world headquarters in St. Paul, Minnesota, to consider a proposal to rationalize the North American production and distribution of "SCOTCH-BRITE" hand scouring pads. Two 3M plants, one in the U.S. and one in Canada, are competing for a regional product mandate.

Logitech was one of three companies that dominated the global market for pointing devices for computers. While Logitech had captured a large share of the original equipment manufacturer (OEM) mouse market, Microsoft was the clear leader in terms of industry standards and dollar share of the retail market. KYE, with a strong presence in Europe, was poised to compete aggressively in North America. Faced with the intensifying competition and eroding margin, Logitech was considering the introduction of an innovative line of ergonomic mice, which promised to change the competitive dynamics of the industry.

Following a recent acquisition, a small Mexican owned travel agency, Bancomer Travel Services, must be transformed into a branch office of Rosenbluth International (RI), which was known worldwide for its exceptional customer service and expertise in corporate travel management. The success of RI's agencies was linked to the company's unique set of service philosophies and values.

Cast North America, a large international shipping company with major operations centers in Montreal and Antwerp, Belgium, and head office in Bermuda, provides Blue Bow container shipping services to North American and European firms. While providing door-to-door service, the company keeps track of the thousands of documents daily through a sophisticated international telecommunications network, which includes land circuits, undersea cable circuits, and satellite links. Its sophisticated private international communications network is viewed as a strategic resource which provides a critical competitive advantage. The case describes Cast's network evolution and differences between North American and European telecommunications situations, and highlights key decisions regarding network expansion that the company must make in the near future.

The Executive Vice-President of Quadra Logic Technologies (QLT) was thinking over the firm's latest opportunity to commercialize a product. The small company's research group had come up with a drug which, when combined with laser technology, could be used in the treatment of cancer. QLT must decide how to market the new product, whether to go it alone or with someone else, or whether they should wait to introduce the product.

This case explores the evolution of the corporate strategy of Sharp Corporation, Japan. Sharp Corporation, a second-tier assemble of TV sets and home appliances, gradually and consistently improved performance by developing expertise in electronic device technologies such as specialized ICs and LCDs and used these technologies to develop innovative end products. As a result, the company was regarded as a world leader in opto-electronics and was becoming a premier comprehensive electronics company.

In mid-1986, the new Sears catalogue contained a twenty-page section called Elements. This section bore a striking resemblance to the format of an IKEA catalog and the furniture being offered was similar to IKEA's knocked-down self-assembly product line. The head of IKEA's North American operations wondered how serious Sears was about its new initiative and what, if anything, IKEA should do in response.

In the summer of 1994, executives at British Airways (BA) were reviewing their investment in faltering USAir and its implications for BA's global-leadership strategy. Following many setbacks, BA had purchased 25 percent of USAir's equity for U.S.$400 million in early 1993 to secure a marketing partner and access to a route structure in the United States. Now, sixteen months later with USAir still not profitable, BA's options varied from severing the marketing relationship and writing-off the investment to injecting further cash.

Perdue Farms, Inc. is a highly successful company that has transformed itself from a simple chicken grower into the fourth largest, vertically integrated poultry company in the U.S. Its hallmark is unyielding quality, an attribute that Frank Perdue used to differentiate his product and build brand recognition. The key issue is whether the firm can continue adequate growth as a regional poultry producer or whether it must become national – and international – and begin to diversify in earnest.

In January 1993, the Vice President of International Operations for Neilson International, a division of William Neilson Limited, was assessing a recent proposal from Sabritas, a division of Pepsico Foods in Mexico, for a joint venture to launch Neilson's brands in the Mexican market. Recent attempts to expand into several foreign markets, including the U.S., had taught them valuable lessons. Although it was now evident that they had world class products to offer global markets, their competitive performance was being constrained by limited resources. Pepsico's joint branding proposal would allow greater market penetration than Neilson could afford. But, at what cost?

In 1990, the chairman and CEO of Imasco Limited was reviewing an acquisition proposal from one of its operating units, Hardee's Food Systems, to purchase the Roy Rogers Restaurant chain. While he was inclined to support the proposal, he wanted to carefully weigh its broader impact for Imasco as a whole. The probable price of $390 million represented a substantial commitment of funds, at a time of slowing growth in the U.S. fast food business.

Grupo Industrial Saltillo, S.A. de C.V. (GISSA), is a Mexican conglomerate which was started as and remains a family-owned company. In 1991, the dynamic economic and political context poses several questions that influence the future of GISSA. Can GISSA achieve its growth and quality aspirations given its closely-held status and the current state of Mexican markets? How diversified can GISSA remain if NAFTA is established and new competitors enter GISSA's markets? What relative emphasis should GISSA give to its production for domestic markets and export markets? What outsiders or partners, if any, should GISSA seek to help prepare for increased competition? These and other challenges confront GISSA as the del Bosque family considers how to survive in an economy on the brink of massive change.

In August 1992, the Business Development Manager for GE Canada, met with executives from GE Supply, a U.S.-based distribution arm of GE. The purpose of the meeting was to discuss new business opportunities in energy efficiency, an industry that focused on the reduction of energy usage through the installation of energy-efficient technologies. He had recently gained pre-qualification for GE Canada to bid in a $1 billion program to install energy-efficient technologies in all Federal Government buildings. GE Supply executives were interested in the program but felt it would be more efficiently run through a division of GE Supply, rather than as a locally managed Canadian venture.

Preface

Managers face complex business decisions. While the questions of in which industry to compete, what products and services to offer, and how to be competitive? have long confronted managers, today's rapid technological changes and increasingly international marketplace compound the decisions. A contemporary approach to sorting through these challenges incorporates the recognition of distinct resources and capabilities that firms command. This approach helps managers to better understand how to compete in today's marketplace.

This casebook is designed to provide an application of the view that strategy is the quest for superior profitability through competitive advantage. The underlying premise of this approach is that building and defending a position of advantage against competitors requires effectively deploying a firm's resources and capabilities within its environment. To do so requires the analysis of the firm's industry environment and the analysis of its resources and capabilities.

The cases in this collection were selected because they represent the decisions faced by managers in today's dynamic business environment. All of the cases are based on real situations involving decisions faced by managers. Each case was chosen specifically for its facilitation of analysis and discussion of business decisions using contemporary concepts of resources and capabilities. In addition, the cases were chosen to illustrate the universality of these decisions. Seventeen different industries in nine different countries around the world are presented for analysis. Many of the products and services are global. While not positioned as an international casebook, the collection was assembled to illustrate that the same decisions are faced by managers around the world.

While the cases in this collection were assembled to accompany Robert M. Grant's *Contemporary Strategy Analysis: Concepts, Techniques, Applications*, published by Blackwell, the collection is robust enough to stand with other texts. The Western Business School at the University of Western Ontario is the second largest publisher of management cases in the world. It has a long tradition of the case method. A unique strength of Western Business School cases is that the cases present the reader with important management decisions. This allows the reader to work through the situation as the manager has done. While many cases only present a detached discussion of management issues, Western cases raise the level of involvement by focusing on a decision. The question of what to do is placed with the reader.

The cases are grouped under the general headings of "Fundamentals of Strategic Management," "The Analysis of Industry and Competition," "The Analysis of Competitive Advantage," and "Corporate Strategy." In this sequence, the cases match well with the text chapters in *Contemporary Strategy Analysis*. This matching is only a suggestion as the cases are rich enough to be used with several topics.

The casebook is suitable for MBA and undergraduate audiences. The level of analysis and discussion can be determined by the instructor. The information contained in the case is sufficient as to not require outside research. All of the cases have been thoroughly classroom tested in undergraduate, MBA, and executive programs around the world.

Acknowledgments

We would like to thank a number of colleagues and institutions for their contributions to this project.

Paul W. Beamish, Western Business School
Julian Birkinshaw, Norwegian School of Economics
S. P. Bradley, Harvard Business School
David J. Collis, Harvard Business School
Terry Deutscher, Western Business School
S. Foley, Harvard Business School
J. Michael Geringer, California Polytechnic University-San Luis Obispo
Sumantra Ghoshal, London Business School
Robert M. Grant, Georgetown University
Jean M. Hanebury, Texas A&M University-Corpus Christi
Sid L. Huff, Western Business School
C. B. Johnston, Western Business School
John Kamauff, Western Business School
Donald J. Lecraw, Western Business School
Barbara L. Marcolin, University of Calgary
Kerry McLellan, Director, Applied Business Research
Allen J. Morrison, Thunderbird, The American Graduate School of International Business
T. Noda, Harvard Business School
Kenneth J. Rediker, University of Houston
George Rubenson, Salisbury State University
Adrian Ryans, Western Business School
Ronald J. Salazar, Idaho State University
Frank M. Shipper, Salisbury State University
Brock Smith, University of Victoria
Roderick E. White, Western Business School

Research Associates and Assistants

David Ager
R. Azimah Ainuddin
Sara Allen
Alan Andron
Charlotte Butler

Gayle Duncan
Miguel Leon Garza
D. B. Lanning
Gary Loveman
Douglas Reid
Kathleen Ryans
Ingrid Taggart
Shari Ann Wortel

We would like to thank Cecelia Ottenweller at the University of Houston and Jeannette Weston and Sue O'Driscoll at the Western Business School for their generous help in bringing this project together. We also want to thank Paul Beamish and the faculty and staff at the Western Business School for their encouragement and support, and to Harvard University and INSEAD for their assistance. Finally, thanks are due Rolf Janke and Mary Beckwith at Blackwell Publishers for their encouragement and assistance. Without them, this book would not have been possible.

Kent E. Neupert
Houston, Texas

Joseph N. Fry
London, Ontario

Case Analysis

This section has been adapted from Mark C. Baetz and Paul W. Beamish, *Strategic Management,* Second Edition (Homewood, IL: Irwin, 1990), pp. 13–28. Used with permission of the authors. The original chapter incorporated material from Arthur A. Thompson and A. J. Stricklin, *Strategic Management: Concepts and Cases* (Plano, TX: Business Publications, 1984), pp. 272–289.

CASE ANALYSIS IN MANAGEMENT EDUCATION

The purpose of case analysis in management education is to allow the student practice at being a manager. A case describes the events and organization circumstances surrounding a particular situation and puts the reader in the shoes of the decision maker by describing the situation and the decision faced by the manager. A case may concern an industry, an organization, or a unit of the organization. The organizations described may be profit seeking or not-for-profit organizations. Case studies generally contain information regarding the relevant industry and its characteristics, the organization's history and development, its products and markets, and the backgrounds and personalities of the key players in the organization. It also presents information on the organization's production facilities, the work environment, the organizational structure, the marketing approach, and relevant financial, accounting, sales, production, and market information.

The student's goal is to analyze and assess the situation described, and to determine what, if any, actions need to be taken. As an analyst, the student should evaluate the situation from a managerial perspective. Questions to be asked include: What factors have contributed to the situation? What problems are evident? How serious are they? What analysis is needed to determine solutions? What feasible recommendations can be offered? What facts and figures support my position?

The cases in this book are not intended to be examples of right or wrong, or good or bad management. The organizations described were not selected because they are the best or worst in their industries. They were selected because they described a decision-making situation encountered by a manager. The students should try to understand the situation and decide what they would do under similar circumstances.

WHY USE CASES IN MANAGEMENT EDUCATION

Lectures are generally a passive and one-way method of communication. Listening without doing does little to prepare someone for encountering management situations. Many have suggested that there is no collection of ready-made answers. Each situation has unique aspects requiring its own diagnosis and understanding prior to judgment and action. Cases provide students of management with an important and valid kind of daily practice in wrestling with management problems.

The case method is *learning by doing*. The pedagogy of the case method of instruction is predicated on the benefits of acquiring managerial "experience" by means of simulated management exercises, i.e., cases. The best justification for cases is that few students come into direct contact with a wide range of companies and real-life managerial situations. Cases offer a viable substitute by bringing a variety of industries, organizations, and management problems into the classroom and permitting students to assume the manager's role. Management cases, therefore, provide students with a kind of experiential exercise in which to test their ability to apply textbook knowledge about management.

OBJECTIVES OF THE CASE METHOD

The use of the case method is intended to accomplish four student-related goals:[1]

1. You are able to apply textbook knowledge about management into practice.
2. You act less as a receiver of facts, concepts, and frameworks and more as one who diagnoses problems, analyzes and evaluates alternatives, and develops workable plans of action.
3. You learn to work out answers and solutions for yourself, instead of relying on a professor or textbook.
4. You gain exposure to a range of firms and managerial situations, which might otherwise take years to experience, thereby offering you a basis for comparison as you begin or continue your own management career.

With these as the objectives, students should be less bothered by the question, "What is the answer to the case?" In contrast to textbook statements of fact and purported definitive lecture notes, students often find that discussions and analyses of managerial cases do not produce any hard answers. Instead, issues are discussed pro and con. Various alternatives and approaches are evaluated. Usually, a good argument can be made for more than one course of action. If the class concludes without a clear consensus on what to do and which way to go, some students may feel frustrated because they are not told "what the answer is" or "what the company actually did."[2]

However, cases where answers are not clear-cut are quite realistic. Organizational problems whose analysis leads to a definite, single path solution are likely to be so oversimplified and rare as to be trivial or lacking practical value. In reality, several feasible courses of action may exist for dealing with the same set of circumstances. Also, in real life, when a manager makes a decision or selects a particular course of action, there is no peeking at the back of the book to see if you have chosen the best thing to do. No book of "right" answers exists. In fact, the true test of management action is results. The important thing for a student to understand in case analysis is that it is the managerial exercise of identifying, diagnosing, and recommending that counts, not the discovering of a right answer or finding what actually happened.

Simply put, the purpose of management cases is not to learn authoritative answers to specific managerial problems but to become skilled in the process of designing workable action plans through evaluation of the prevailing circumstances. The goal is not for you to guess what the instructor is thinking or what the organization did, but to support your views against the countervailing views of the group or to join in the discovery of different approaches and perspectives. Therefore, in case analysis you are expected to bear the strains of thinking actively, of making managerial assessments which may be vigorously challenged, of offering your analysis, and of proposing action plans. This is how you are provided with meaningful practice at being a manager.

Analyzing the case yourself is what initiates you in the ways of thinking "managerially" and exercising responsible judgment. At the same time, you can use cases to test the rigor and effectiveness of your own approach to the practice of management and begin to evolve your own management philosophy and management style.

PREPARING A CASE FOR CLASS DISCUSSION

Given that cases rest on the principle of learning by doing, their effectiveness depends upon *you* making *your* analysis and reaching *your* own decisions and then in the classroom participating in a collective analysis and discussion of the habits. If this is your first experience with the case method, you may need to adjust your study habits. Since a case assignment emphasizes student participation, the effectiveness of the class discussion depends upon each student having studied the case beforehand. Consequently, unlike lecture courses which have no imperative of specific preparation before each class and where assigned readings and reviews of lecture notes may be done at irregular intervals, *a case assignment requires conscientious preparation before class*. After all, you cannot expect to get much out of hearing the class discuss a case with which you are totally unfamiliar.

Unfortunately, though, there is no nice, neat, proven procedure for conducting a case analysis. There is no formula, fail-safe, step-by-step technique that we can recommend beyond emphasizing the sequence: identify, evaluate, consider alternatives, and recommend. Each case is a new situation and has its own set of issues, analytical requirements, and action alternatives.

A first step in understanding how the case method of teaching/learning works is to recognize that it represents a radical departure from the lecture/discussion classroom technique. To begin with, members of the class do most of the talking. The instructor's role is to solicit student participation and guide the discussion. Expect the instructor to begin the class discussion with such questions as: What is the organization's strategy? What are the strategic issues and problems confronting the company? What is your assessment of the company's situation? Is the industry an attractive one to be in? Is management doing a good job? Are the organization's objectives and strategies compatible with its skills and resources? Typically, members of the class will evaluate and test their opinions as much in discussions with each other as with the instructor. But irrespective of whether the discussion emphasis is instructor-student or student-student, members of the class carry the burden for analyzing the situation and for being prepared to present and defend their analyses in the classroom. Thus, you should expect an absence of professorial "here's how to do it," "right answers," and "hard knowledge for your notebook"; instead, be prepared for a discussion involving your size-up of the situation, what actions you would take, and why you would take them.[3]

Begin preparing for class by reading the case once for familiarity. An initial reading should give you the general flavor of the situation and make possible preliminary identification of issues. On the second reading, attempt to gain full command of the facts. Make some notes about apparent organizational objectives, strategies, policies, symptoms of problems, root problems, unresolved issues, and roles of key individuals. Be alert for issues or problems that are lurking beneath the surface. For instance, at first glance, it might appear that an issue in the case is whether a product has ample market potential at the current selling price; on closer examination, you may see the root problem is that the method being used to compensate salespeople fails to generate adequate incentive for achieving greater unit volume. Strive for a sharp, clear-cut size-up of the issues posed in the case situation.

To help diagnose the situation, put yourself in the position of some manager or managerial group portrayed in the case and get attuned to the overall environment facing management. Try to get a good feel for the condition of the company, the industry, and the economics of the business. Get a handle on how the market works and on the nature of competition. This is essential if you are to come up with solutions which will be both workable and acceptable in light of the prevailing external constraints and internal organizational realities. Do not be dismayed if you find it impractical to isolate the problems and issues into distinct categories which can be treated separately. Very few significant strategy management problems can be neatly sorted into mutually exclusive areas of concern. Furthermore, expect the cases (especially those in this book) to contain several problems and issues, rather than just one. Guard against making a single, simple statement of the problem unless the issue is very clear-cut. Admittedly, there will be cases where issues are well defined and the main problem is figuring out what to do, but in most cases, you can expect a set of problems and issues to be present, some of which are related and some of which are not.

Next, you must move toward a solid evaluation of the case situation based on the information given. Developing an ability to evaluate companies and size up their situations is the core of what strategic analysis is all about. The cases in this book, of course, are all strategy related, and they each require some form of strategic analysis, that is, analysis of how well the organization's strategy has been formulated and implemented.

Uppermost in your efforts, strive for defensible arguments and positions. Do not rely upon just your opinion; support it with evidence! Analyze the available data and make whatever relevant accounting, financial, marketing, or operations calculations are necessary to support your assessment of the situation. Crunch the numbers! If your instructor has provided you with specific study questions for the case, by all means make some notes as to how you would answer them. Include in your notes all the reasons and evidence you can muster to support your diagnosis and evaluation.

Last, when information or data in the case is conflicting and/or various opinions are contradictory, decide which is more valid and why. Forcing you to make judgments about the validity of the data and information presented in the case is both deliberate and realistic. It is deliberate because one function of the case method is to help you develop your powers of judgment and inference. It is realistic because a great many managerial situations entail conflicting points of view.

Once you have thoroughly diagnosed the company's situation and weighed the pros and cons of various alternative courses of action, the final step of case analysis is to decide what you think the company needs to do to improve its performance. Draw up your set of recommendations on what to do and be prepared to give your action agenda. This is really the most crucial part of the process; diagnosis divorced from corrective action is sterile. But bear in mind that proposing realistic, workable solutions and offering a hasty, ill-conceived "possibility" are not the same thing. Don't recommend anything you would not be prepared to do yourself if you were in the decision-maker's shoes. Be sure you can give reasons why your recommendations are preferable to other options which exist.

On a few occasions, some desirable information may not be included in the case. In such instances, you may be inclined to complain about the lack of facts. A manager, however, uses more than facts upon which to base his or her decision. Moreover, it may be possible to make a number of inferences from the facts you do have. So be wary of rushing to include as part of your recommendations the need to get more information. From time to time, of course, a search for additional facts or information may be entirely appropriate, but you must also recognize that the organization's managers may not have had any more information available than that presented in the case. Before recommending that action be postponed until additional facts are uncovered, be sure that you think it will be worthwhile to get them and that the organization can afford to wait. In general, though, try to recommend a course of action based upon the evidence you have at hand.

Again, remember that rarely is there a "right" decision or just one "optimal" plan of action or an "approved" solution. Your goal should be to develop what you think is a pragmatic, defensible course of action based upon a serious analysis of the situation and appearing to you to be right in view of your assessment of the facts. Admittedly, someone else may evaluate the same facts in another way and thus have a different right solution, but since several good plans of action can normally be conceived, you should not be afraid to stick by your own analysis and judgment. One can make a strong argument for the view that the right answer for a manager is the one that he or she can propose, explain, defend, and make work when it is implemented. This is the middle ground we support between the "no right answer" and "one right answer" schools of thought. Clearly, some answers are better than others.

THE CLASSROOM EXPERIENCE

In experiencing class discussion of management cases, you will, in all probability, notice very quickly that you will not have thought of everything in the case that your fellow students have. While you will see things others did not, they will see things you did not. Do not be dismayed or alarmed by this. It is normal. As the old adage goes, "Two heads are better than one." So it is to be expected that the class as a whole will do a more penetrating and searching job of case analysis than will any one person working alone. This is the power of group effort, and one of its virtues is that it will give you more insight into the variety of approaches and how to cope with differences of opinion. Second, you will see better why sometimes it is not managerially wise to assume a rigid position on an issue until a full range of views and information has been assembled. And, undoubtedly, some-where along the way, you will begin to recognize that neither the instructor nor other students in the class have all the answers, and even if they think they do, you are still free to present and hold to your own views. The truth in the saying "there's more than one way to skin a cat" will be seen to apply nicely to most management situations.

For class discussion of cases to be useful and stimulating, you need to keep the following points in mind:

1. The case method enlists a maximum of individual participation in class case discussion. It is not enough to be present as a silent observer; if every student took this approach, then there would be no discussion. (Thus, do not be surprised if a portion of your grade is based on your participation in case discussions.)

2. Although you should do your own independent work and independent thinking, don't hesitate to discuss the case with other students. Managers often discuss their problems with other key people.

3. During case discussions, expect and tolerate challenges to the views expressed. Be willing to submit your conclusions for scrutiny and rebuttal. State your views without fear of disapproval and overcome the hesitation of speaking out.

4. In orally presenting and defending your ideas, strive to be convincing and at your most persuasive. Always give supporting evidence and reasons.

5. Expect the instructor to assume the role of extensive questioner and listener. Expect to be cross-examined for evidence and reasons by your instructor or by others in the class. Expect students to dominate the discussion and do most of the talking.

6. Although discussion of a case is a group process, this does not imply conformity to group opinion. Learning respect for the views and approaches of others is an integral part of case analysis exercises. But be willing to "swim against the tide" of majority opinion. In the practice of management, there is always room for originality, unorthodoxy, and unique personality.

7. In participating in the discussion, make a conscious effort to contribute rather than just talk. There is a big difference between saying something that builds the discussion and offering a long-winded, off-the-cuff remark that leaves the class wondering what the point was.

8. Effective case discussion can occur only if participants have the facts of the case well in hand; rehashing information in the case should be held to a minimum except as it provides documentation, comparisons, or support for your position. In making your point, assume that everyone has read the case and knows what "the case says."

9. During the discussion, new insights provided by the group's efforts are likely to emerge. Don't be alarmed or surprised if you and others in the class change your mind about some things as the discussion unfolds. Be alert for how these changes affect your analysis and recommendations (in case you are called on to speak).

10. Although there will always be situations in which more technical information is imperative to the making of an intelligent decision, try not to shirk from making decisions in the face of incomplete information. Wrestling with imperfect information is a normal condition managers face and is something you should get used to doing.

PREPARING A WRITTEN CASE ANALYSIS

From time to time, your instructor may ask you to prepare a written analysis of the case assignment. Preparing a written case analysis is much like preparing a case for class discussion, except that your analysis, when completed, must be reduced to writing. Just as there was no set formula for preparing a case for oral discussion, there is no iron-clad procedure for doing a written case analysis. With a bit of experience, you will arrive at your own preferred method of attack in writing up a case, and you will learn to adjust your approach to the unique aspects that each case presents.

Your instructor may assign you a specific topic around which to prepare your written report. Common assignments include:

1. Identify and evaluate company X's corporate strategy.
2. In view of the opportunities and risks you see in the industry, what is your assessment of the company's position and strategy?
3. How would you size up the strategic situation of company Y?
4. What recommendation would you make to company Z's top management?
5. What specific functions and activities does the company have to perform especially well in order for its strategy to succeed?

Alternatively, you may be asked to do a comprehensive written case analysis. It is typical for a comprehensive written case analysis to emphasize four things:

1. Identification.
2. Analysis and evaluation.
3. Discussion of alternatives.
4. Presentation of recommendations.

You may wish to consider the following pointers in preparing a comprehensive written case analysis.[4]

Identification It is essential that your paper reflect a sharply focused diagnosis of strategic issues and key problems and, further, that you demonstrate good business judgment in sizing up the company's present situation. Make sure you understand and can identify the firm's strategy. You would probably be well advised to begin your paper by sizing up the company's situation, its strategy, and the significant problems and issues which confront management. State problems/issues as clearly and precisely as you can. Unless it is necessary to do so for emphasis, avoid recounting facts and history about the company (assume your professor has read the case and is familiar with the organization).

Analysis and Evaluation Very likely, you will find this section the hardest part of the report. Analysis is hard work! Study the tables, exhibits, and financial statements in the case carefully. Check out the firm's financial ratios, its profit margins and rates of return, and its capital structure and decide how strong the firm is financially. Exhibit 1 contains a summary of various financial ratios and how they are calculated. Similarly, look at marketing, production, managerial competencies, and so on, and evaluate the factors underlying the organization's successes and failures. Decide whether it has a distinctive competence and, if so, whether it is capitalizing upon it. Check out the quality of the firm's business portfolio.

Check to see if the firm's strategy at all levels is working and determine the reasons why or why not. Appraise internal strengths and weaknesses and assess external opportunities and threats; do a "SWOT" analysis. (That means you'll check for *Strengths, Weaknesses, Opportunities,* and *Threats.*) See Exhibit 2 for suggestions about what to look for. Decide whether a competitor analysis is needed to clarify competitive forces. You may want to draw up a strategic group map and/or do an industry analysis. Decide whether and why the firm's competitive position is getting stronger or weaker. Try to decide whether the main problems revolve around a need to revise strategy, a need to improve strategy implementation, or both.

In writing your analysis and evaluation, bear in mind:

1. You are obliged to offer supporting evidence for your views and judgments. Do not rely upon unsupported opinions, over-generalizations, and platitudes as a substitute for tight, logical argument backed up with facts and figures.
2. If your analysis involves some important quantitative calculations, you should use tables and charts to present the data clearly and efficiently. Don't just tack the exhibits on at the end of your report and let the reader figure out what they mean and why they were included. Instead, in the body of your report, cite some of the key numbers and summarize the conclusions to be drawn from the exhibits, and refer the reader to your charts and exhibits for more details.
3. You should indicate that you have command of the economics of the business and the key factors which are crucial to the organization's success or failure. Check to see that your analysis states on what the company needs to concentrate in order to achieve higher performance.
4. Your interpretation of the evidence should be reasonable and objective. Be wary of preparing a one-sided argument which omits all aspects not favorable to your conclusion. Likewise, try not to exaggerate or overdramatize. Endeavor to inject balance into your analysis and to avoid emotional rhetoric. Strive to display good business judgment.

Discussion of Alternatives   There are typically many more alternatives available than a cursory study of the case reveals. A thorough case analysis should include a discussion of all major alternatives. It is important that meaningful differences exist between each alternative. In addition, the discussion of alternatives must go beyond the following:

- Do nothing.
- Something obviously inappropriate.
- The alternative to be recommended.

Each alternative discussed should be analyzed in terms of the associated pros and cons.

Recommendations   The final section of the written case analysis should consist of a set of definite recommendations and a plan of action. Your set of recommendations should address all of the problems/issues you identified and analyzed. If the recommendations come as a surprise or do not follow logically from the analysis, the effect is to weaken greatly your suggestions of what to do. Obviously, your recommendations for action should offer a reasonable prospect of success. State what you think the consequences of your recommendations will be and indicate how your recommendations will solve the problems you identified. Be sure that the company is financially able to carry out what you recommend. Also check to see if your recommendations are workable in terms of acceptance by the persons involved, the organization's competence to implement them, and prevailing market and environmental constraints. Unless you feel justifiably compelled to do so, do not qualify or hedge on the actions you believe should be taken.

Furthermore, state your recommendations in sufficient detail to be meaningful with some definite nitty-gritty details. Avoid such unhelpful statements as "the organization should do more planning" or "the company should be more aggressive in marketing its product." State specifically what should be done and make sure your recommendations are operational.

For instance, do not stop with saying, "The firm should improve its market position." Continue on with exactly how you think this should be done. And, finally, you should say something about how your plan should be implemented. Here you may wish to offer a definite agenda for action, stipulating a timetable and sequence for initiating actions, indicating priorities, and suggesting who should be responsible for doing what. For example, "Manager X should take the following steps:

1. _____
2. _____
3. _____
4. _____"

A key element in the recommendation summary is to assess the financial implications of each recommendation. Any proposed strategy must be feasible, which means, among other things, that the organization must be able to afford it. In addition, when there are major uncertainties, particularly in the medium to long term, contingency plans should be specified, that is, "If such and such transpires, then do X."

In preparing your plan of action, remember there is a great deal of difference between being responsible, on the one hand, for a decision that may be costly if it proves in error and, on the other hand, expressing a casual opinion as to some of the courses of action that might be taken when you do not have to bear the responsibility for any of the consequences. A good rule to follow in making your recommendations is to avoid recommending anything you would not yourself be willing to do if you were in management's shoes. The importance of learning to develop good judgment in a managerial situation is indicated by the fact that while the same information and operating data may be available to every manager or executive in an organization, the quality of the judgments about what the information means and what actions need to be taken do vary from person to person.[5] Developing good judgment is thus essential.

It should go without saying that your report should be organized and written in a manner that communicates well and is persuasive. Great ideas amount to little unless others can be convinced of their merit – this takes effective communication.

KEEPING TABS ON YOUR PERFORMANCE

Every instructor has his or her own procedure for evaluating student performance, so, with one exception, it is not possible to generalize about grades and the grading of case analyses. The one exception is that grades on case analyses (written or oral) almost never depend entirely on how you propose to solve the organization's difficulties. The important elements in evaluating student performance on case analyses consist of

1. the care with which facts and background knowledge are used
2. demonstration of the ability to state problems and issues clearly
3. the use of appropriate analytical techniques
4. evidence of sound logic and argument
5. consistency between analysis and recommendations, and
6. the ability to formulate reasonable and feasible recommendations for action.

Remember, a hard-hitting, incisive, logical approach will almost always triumph over a seat-of-the-pants opinion, emotional rhetoric, and platitudes.

One final point. You may find it hard to keep a finger on the pulse of how much you are learning from cases. This contrasts with lecture/problem/discussion courses where experience has given you an intuitive feeling for how well you are acquiring substantive knowledge of theoretical concepts, problem-solving techniques, and institutional practices. But in a case course, where analytical ability and the skill of making sound judgments are less apparent, you may lack a sense of solid accomplishment, at least at first. Admittedly, additions to one's managerial skills and powers of diagnosis are not as noticeable or as tangible as a loose-leaf binder full of would-be lecture notes. But this does not mean they are any less real or that you are making any less progress in learning how to be a manager.

To begin with, in the process of hunting around for solutions, very likely you will find that considerable knowledge about types of organizations, the nature of various businesses, the range of management practices, and so on has rubbed off. Moreover, you will be gaining a better grasp of how to evaluate risks and cope with the uncertainties of enterprise. Likewise, you will develop a sharper appreciation of both the common and the unique aspects of managerial encounters. You will become more comfortable with the processes whereby objectives are set, strategies are initiated, organizations are designed, methods of control are implemented and evaluated, performance is reappraised, and improvements are sought. Such processes are the essence of strategic management, and learning more about them through the case method is no less an achievement, even though there may be a dearth of finely calibrated measuring devices and authoritative crutches on which to lean.

Notes

1. Charles I. Gragg, "Because Wisdom Can't Be Told," in *The Case Method at the Harvard Business School,* ed. M. P. McNair (New York: McGraw-Hill, 1954), p. 11. as reported in Mark C. Baetz and Paul W. Beamish, *Strategic Management,* Second Edition (Homewood, IL: Irwin, 1990), pp. 13–28.
2. Ibid., pp. 12–14; and D. R. Schoen and Philip A. Sprague, "What Is the Case Method?" in McNair, *The Case Method at the Harvard Business School,* pp. 78–79. as reported in Mark C. Baetz and Paul W. Beamish, *Strategic Management,* Second Edition (Homewood, IL: Irwin, 1990), pp. 13–28.
3. Schoen and Sprague, "What is the Case Method?" p. 80. as reported in Mark C. Baetz and Paul W. Beamish, *Strategic Management,* Second Edition (Homewood, IL: Irwin, 1990), pp. 13–28.
4. For additional ideas and viewpoints, see Thomas J. Raymond, "Written Analysis of Cases," in McNair, *The Case Method at the Harvard Business School,* pp. 139–163. Raymond's article contains an actual case, a sample analysis of the case, and a sample of a student's written report on the case, as reported in Mark C. Baetz and Paul W. Beamish, *Strategic Management,* Second Edition (Homewood, IL: Irwin, 1990), pp. 13–28.
5. Gragg, "Because Wisdom Can't Be Told," p. 10. as reported in Mark C. Baetz and Paul W. Beamish, *Strategic Management,* Second Edition (Homewood, IL: Irwin, 1990), pp. 13–28.

Exhibit 1 A Summary of Key Financial Ratios, How They Are Calculated, and What They Show

Profitability Ratios		
Ratio	How Calculated	What It Shows
1. Gross profit margin	$$\frac{\text{Sales} - \text{Cost of goods sold}}{\text{Sales}}$$	An indication of the total margin available to cover operating expenses and yield a profit.
2. Operating profit margin	$$\frac{\text{Profit before taxes and before interest}}{\text{Sales}}$$	An indication of the firm's profitability from current operations without regard to the interest charges accruing from the capital structure. (Helps to assess impact of different capital structures.)
3. Net profit margin	$$\frac{\text{Profit after taxes}}{\text{Sales}}$$	Aftertax profits per dollar of sales. Subpar-profit margins indicate that the firm's sales prices are relatively low or that its costs are relatively high or both.
4. Return on total assets	$$\frac{\text{Profits after taxes}}{\text{Total assets}}$$ OR $$\frac{\text{Profits after taxes} + \text{interest}}{\text{Total assets}}$$	A measure of the return on total investment in the enterprise. It is sometimes desirable to add interest to aftertax profits to form the numerator of the ratio since total assets are financed by creditors as well as by stockholders; hence, it is accurate to measure the productivity of assets by the returns provided to both classes of investors.
5. Return of stockholders' equity (or return on net worth)	$$\frac{\text{Profits after taxes}}{\text{Total stockholders' equity}}$$	A measure of the rate of return on the stockholders' investment in the enterprise.
6. Return on common equity	$$\frac{\text{Profits after taxes} - \text{Preferred stock dividends}}{\text{Total stockholders' equity} - \text{Par value of preferred stock}}$$	A measure of the rate of return on the investment which the owners of common stock have made in the enterprise.
7. Earnings per share	$$\frac{\text{Profits after taxes} - \text{Preferred stock dividends}}{\text{Number of shares of common stock outstanding}}$$	The earnings available to the owners of common stock.

Exhibit 1   A Summary of Key Financial Ratios, How They Are Calculated, and What They Show *(continued)*

Liquidity Ratios		
Ratio	How Calculated	What It Shows
1. Current ratio	$\dfrac{\text{Current assets}}{\text{Current liabilities}}$	The extent to which the claims of short-term creditors are covered by assets expected to be converted to cash in a period roughly corresponding to the maturity of the liabilities.
2. Quick ratio (or acid-test ratio)	$\dfrac{\text{Current assets} - \text{Inventory}}{\text{Current liabilities}}$	A measure of the firm's ability to pay off short-term obligations without relying upon the sale of its inventories.
3. Inventory to net working capital	$\dfrac{\text{Inventory}}{\text{Current assets minus Current liabilities}}$	A measure of the extent to which the firm's working capital is tied up in inventory.

Leverage Ratios		
Ratio	How Calculated	What It Shows
1. Debt-to-assets ratio	$\dfrac{\text{Total debt}}{\text{Total assets}}$	A measure of the extent to which borrowed funds have been used to finance the firm's operations.
2. Debt-to-equity ratio	$\dfrac{\text{Total debt}}{\text{Total stockholders' equity}}$	Another measure of the funds provided by creditors versus the funds provided by owners.
3. Long-term debt-to-equity ratio	$\dfrac{\text{Long-term debt}}{\text{Total stockholders' equity}}$	A widely used measure of the balance between debt and equity in the firm's long-term capital structure.
4. Times-interest-earned (or coverage) ratios	$\dfrac{\text{Profits before interest and taxes}}{\text{Total interest charges}}$	A measure of the extent to which earnings can decline without the firm becoming unable to meet its annual interest costs.
5. Fixed-charge coverage	$\dfrac{\text{Profits before taxes and interest} + \text{lease obligations}}{\text{Total interest charges} + \text{lease obligations}}$	A more inclusive indication of the firm's ability to meet all of its fixed-charge obligations.

Exhibit 1   A Summary of Key Financial Ratios, How They Are Calculated, and What They Show   *(continued)*

Activity Ratios		
Ratio	How Calculated	What It Shows
1. Inventory turnover	$$\frac{\text{Sales}}{\text{Inventory of finished goods}}$$	When compared to industry averages, it provides an indication of whether a company has excessive or inadequate finished-goods inventory.
2. Fixed-assets turnover	$$\frac{\text{Sales}}{\text{Fixed assets}}$$	A measure of the sales productivity and utilization of plant and equipment.
3. Total-assets turnover	$$\frac{\text{Sales}}{\text{Total assets}}$$	A measure of the utilization of all the firm's assets. A ratio below the industry average indicates the company is not generating a sufficient volume of business given the size of its asset investment.
4. Accounts-receivable turnover	$$\frac{\text{Annual credit sales}}{\text{Accounts receivable}}$$	A measure of the average length of time it takes the firm to collect the sales made on credit.
5. Average collection period	$$\frac{\text{Accounts receivable}}{\text{Total sales/365}}$$ OR $$\frac{\text{Accounts receivable}}{\text{Average daily sales}}$$	The average length of time the firm must wait after making a sale before it receives payment.

Other Ratios		
Ratio	How Calculated	What It Shows
1. Dividend yield on common stock	$$\frac{\text{Annual dividends per share}}{\text{Current market price per share}}$$	A measure of the return to owners received in the form of dividends.
2. Price-earnings ratio	$$\frac{\text{Current market price per share}}{\text{Aftertax earnings per share}}$$	Faster growing or less risky firms tend to have higher price-earnings ratios than slower growing or more risky firms.
3. Dividend-payout ratio	$$\frac{\text{Annual dividends per share}}{\text{Aftertax earnings per share}}$$	The percentages of profits paid out as dividends.
4. Cash flow per share	$$\frac{\text{Aftertax profits + Depreciation}}{\text{Number of common shares outstanding}}$$	A measure of the discretionary funds over and above expenses available for use by the firm.

Exhibit 1 A Summary of Key Financial Ratios, How They Are Calculated, and What They Show *(continued)*

	Other Ratios	
Ratio	How Calculated	What It Shows
5. Break-even analysis	$$\frac{\text{Fixed costs}}{\text{Contribution margin/unit}}$$ (selling price/unit – variable cost/unit)	A measure of how many units must be sold to begin to make a profit; to demonstrate the relationship of revenue, expenses, and net income.

Exhibit 2 The SWOT Analysis – with Suggestions of What to Look For

Internal	
Strengths	Weaknesses
Adequate financial resources?	No clear strategic direction?
Well thought of by buyers?	Obsolete facilities?
An acknowledged market leader?	Lack of managerial depth and talent?
Well-conceived functional area strategies?	Missing any key skills or competencies?
Access to economies of scale?	Poor track record in implementing strategy?
Insulated (at least somewhat) from strong competitive pressures?	Plagued with internal operating problems? Falling behind in R&D?
Proprietary technology?	Too narrow a product line?
Cost advantages?	Weak market image?
Product innovation abilities?	Below-average marketing skills?
Proven management?	Unable to finance needed changes in strategy?
Other?	Other?

External	
Opportunities	Threats
Serve additional customer groups?	Likely entry of new competitors?
Enter new markets or segments?	Rising sales of substitute products?
Expand product line to meet broader range of customer needs?	Slower market growth? Adverse government policies?
Diversify into related products?	Growing competitive pressures?
Add complementary products?	Vulnerability to recession and business cycle?
Vertical integration?	Growing bargaining power of customers or suppliers?
Ability to move to better strategic group?	Changing buyer needs and tastes?
Complacency among rival firms?	Adverse demographic changes?
Faster market growth?	
Other?	Other?

Exhibit 3   Format for Strategic Analysis Report[1]

Strategic analysis of: _____ (case or company)

EXTERNAL ENVIRONMENT

MACROENVIRONMENT

Political:

- ○ Regulation
- ○ Trade barriers
- ○ Change in tax laws/incentives
- ○ Other...

Summary:

Legal:

- ○ Anti-trust
- ○ Equal pay/employment
- ○ Environmental protection
- ○ Health & safety
- ○ Other...

Summary:

Economic:

- ○ Interest rates
- ○ Recession (aggregate demand)
- ○ Energy prices
- ○ Other...

Summary:

MICROENVIRONMENT

Industry – Competitive Analysis:

Define the (primary) industry in which this firm competes

Key segmentation variables:

- ○ Identify the industry segment in which your firm competes

Power of suppliers:

Factors affecting relative bargaining power (high or low threat?)

- ○ What proportion of the value of our product(s) is provided by suppliers?
  Cost of goods sold/Sales

---

[1]This material was prepared by Jeff W. Trailer, Ph.D. It has been adapted for this section.

Exhibit 3   Format for Strategic Analysis Report *(continued)*

Strategic analysis of: _____ (case or company)

- O Price sensitivity
    - Cost of purchases relative to total costs
    - Profitability of suppliers vs. buyers
    - Importance of the product to the quality of buyer's quality

- O Bargaining power
    - Size and concentration of buyers relative to suppliers
    - Buyer's switching costs
    - Buyer's information
    - Buyer's ability to backward vertically integrate
        - Risk of owning obsolescent technology
        - Related experience in making the supplies
        - Is owning non-complementary assets required?

  Summary:

Power of buyers: (high or low threat?)

- O Factors affecting relative bargaining power
    - Price sensitivity
        - Size of purchase(s) relative to total discretionary income of the buyer
        - Profitability of buyers vs. suppliers
        - Importance of the product to the buyer's quality requirements

- O Bargaining power
    - Size of the purchase relative to the supplier's total sales
    - Buyer's switching costs
    - Buyer's information
    - Buyer's ability to backward vertically integrate
        - Risk of owning obsolescent technology/locations
        - Related experience with the product
        - Is owning non-complementary assets required?

  Summary:

Potential new entrants: (high or low threat?)

- O Factors creating barriers to entry in industry
    - capital requirements
    - economies of scale
    - economies of scope
    - excess plant capacity
    - access to channels of supply/distribution
    - government and legal barriers
    - other...

- O Factors creating barriers to mobility
    - Identify resources which prevent other firms in your industry from entering your segment

  Summary:

Exhibit 3   Format for Strategic Analysis Report *(continued)*

Strategic analysis of: _____ (case or company)

Potential substitutes: (high or low threat?)

- ○ Examples of most likely substitutes for this industry or segment

- ○ Factors affecting demand elasticity
     Product's proportion of total cost
     Relative price performance differences (differentiation)
     Switching costs
       time required to learn to use new product
       ease of obtaining product, parts, repair/service
       other...

  Summary:

Level of rivalry: (high or low threat?)

- ○ Factors affecting rivalry power
     Similarity of strategies
       Geographic regions covered
       Price ranges

- ○ Concentration ratio/relative market share
     horizontal integration (merging with competitors)
     unused capacity/demand growth
     barriers to exit

  Summary:

SUMMARY: Which of five forces is our greatest strength, greatest threat?

INTERNAL ENVIRONMENT

BUSINESS STRATEGY

Organizational Goals/Mission:

- ○ Is the firm successful?
    - Describe the organization's mission
    - What are the organization's values?
    - What are the organization's goals?
    - Is the firm's performance meeting or exceeding the goals of the firm?

- ○ Which is the dominant goal currently: growth, profitability, survival?

- ○ To what extent has the firm been successful in achieving that goal?

Summary of the internal environment:

Exhibit 3   Format for Strategic Analysis Report *(continued)*

Strategic analysis of: _____ (case or company)

Competitive advantage: (what is the profit margin?)

Differentiation:
○ Describe the ways in which the firm differentiates its products/services.
    For each of the major differentiation advantages, estimate how vulnerable the differentiation tactics are to imitation/substitution
    • Durability
        Obsolescence
        Depletion of the resource
    • Mobility
        Transaction costs
        Firm-specific resources
    • Replicability
        Causal ambiguity/Uncertain imitability
        Organizational routines
    • Appropriability
        Relative bargaining power
        Embeddedness of resources

Summary:

Low cost:
○ Describe the ways in which the firm keeps its costs competitive
    Keep the entire activity-cost chain in mind

○ Estimate how vulnerable the low cost tactics are to imitation/substitution
    • Durability
        Obsolescence
        Depletion of the resource
    • Mobility
        Transaction costs
        Firm-specific resources
    • Replicability
        Causal ambiguity/Uncertain imitability
        Organizational routines
    • Appropriability
        Relative bargaining power
        Embeddedness of resources

Summary:

Summary of competitive advantage:

Exhibit 3   Format for Strategic Analysis Report *(continued)*

Strategic analysis of: _____ (case or company)

Volume expansion strategy: (what is the market share?)

(Discuss in terms of the Product-Market Matrix)

    Market penetration: (same product, same market)
      Identifying new customers in current market
      Selling more to current customers

    Market development: (same product, new market)
      Geographic expansion

    Product development: (new product, same market)
      Narrow vs. Broad segment scope
        Similar key success factors
          Economies of scope
      Add-on/complementary products

    Diversification: (new product, new market)
      Potential for coinsurance effect (non-core business)
      Potential as future "core" business (escape route)
        Growth potential
        Barriers to entry
      BCG matrix: resource allocation assessment

Strategic Profit Model:

  Overview
    Briefly describe what you found in each section

  Liquidity (and Coverage): (is survival at stake?)
    Are we able to meet our current obligations?
      If not, this is our number one concern!
    Where are we most vulnerable?
    Summary:

  Operating Efficiency:
    How efficiently are we managing our resources?
      ROA, Sales/PE, Sales/Employees, Sales/WC, etc.
    What are our strengths?
      Relative to past performance
      Relative to competitors/industry
    What are our weaknesses?
    Summary:

  Leverage:
    Is our capital structure helping or hurting us?
      Why?

Exhibit 3 Format for Strategic Analysis Report *(continued)*

Strategic analysis of: _____ (case or company)

STRATEGIC PERFORMANCE ASSESSMENT

Performance Indicator	19_____	19_____	19_____	Industry
Return on Equity	_____	_____	_____	_____
Net Profit Margin	_____	_____	_____	_____
Sales Growth	_____	_____	_____	_____
Market Share	_____	_____	_____	_____
Bankruptcy Prediction (Z-Score)	_____			

(Be sure to include a discussion of the data above)

REVIEW AND SUMMARY OF RECOMMENDATIONS

Should summarize all previously mentioned recommendations

Each recommendation should be tied clearly to one of the following:
1. weaknesses: a current problem
2. vulnerabilities: will be a problem if not addressed
3. opportunities: new tactic, a bit risky, but targets high rewards

ADDITIONAL NOTES:

Strong or Weak, Opportunity or Threat:

When beginning a discussion, take a stand (ex: this is a strength)

Explain why:
Relative to others
Trend is improving/worsening

Summary: Identify the important items in the group
Why are these important?

1

Prince Edward Island Preserve Co.

In August, 1991, Bruce MacNaughton, president of Prince Edward Island Preserve Co. Ltd. (P.E.I. Preserves), was contemplating future expansion. Two cities were of particular interest: Toronto and Tokyo. At issue was whether consumers in either or both markets should be pursued, and if so, how. The choices available for achieving further growth included mail order, distributors, and company controlled stores.

BACKGROUND

Prince Edward Island Preserve Co. was a manufacturing company located in New Glasgow, P.E.I. which produced and marketed specialty food products. The company founder and majority shareholder, Bruce MacNaughton, had realized that an opportunity existed to present P.E.I. strawberries as a world class food product and to introduce the finished product to an "up-scale" specialty market. With total sales in the coming year expected to exceed $1.0 million for the first time, MacNaughton had made good on the opportunity he had perceived years earlier. It had not been easy, however.

MacNaughton arrived in P.E.I. from Moncton, New Brunswick in 1978. Without a job, he slept on the beach for much of that first summer. Over the next few years he worked in commission sales, waited tables in restaurants, and then moved to Toronto. There he studied to become a chef at George Brown Community College. After working in the restaurant trade for several years, he found a job with "Preserves by Amelia" in Toronto. After six months, he returned to P.E.I. where he opened a restaurant. The restaurant was not successful and MacNaughton lost the $25,000 stake he had accumulated. With nothing left but 100 kg. of strawberries, Bruce decided to make these into preserves in order to have gifts for Christmas 1984. Early the following year, P.E.I. Preserves was founded.

The products produced by the company were priced and packaged for the gift/gourmet and specialty food markets. The primary purchasers of these products were conscious of quality and were seeking a product which they considered tasteful and natural. P.E.I. Preserves felt their product met this standard of quality at a price that made it attractive to all segments of the marketplace.

Over the next few years as the business grew, improvements were made to the building in New Glasgow. The sense of style which was characteristic of the company was evident from the beginning in its attractive layout and design.

Table 1.1

Operation	Year Opened				
	1985	1989	1990	1991	Projected 1992
New Glasgow – Manufacturing and Retail	X	X	X	X	X
Charlottetown – Restaurant (Perfect Cup)		X	X	X	X
New Glasgow – Restaurant (Tea Room)			X	X	X
Charlottetown – Retail (CP Hotel)				X	X
Toronto or Tokyo?					X

In 1989 the company diversified and opened "The Perfect Cup," a small restaurant in P.E.I.'s capital city of Charlottetown. This restaurant continued the theme of quality, specializing in wholesome, home-made food featuring the products manufactured by the company. The success of this operation led to the opening in 1990 of a small tea room at the New Glasgow location. Both of these locations showcased the products manufactured by the P.E.I. Preserve Co.

In August 1991, the company opened a small (22 sq. meter) retail branch in the CP Prince Edward Hotel. MacNaughton hoped this locale would expand visibility in the local and national marketplace, and serve as an off-season sales office. P.E.I. Preserves had been given very favorable lease arrangements (well below the normal $275 per month for space this size), and the location would require minimal financial investment. As Table 1.1 suggests, the company had experienced steady growth in its scope of operations.

MARKETPLACE

Prince Edward Island was Canada's smallest province, both in size and population. Located in the Gulf of St. Lawrence, it was separated from Nova Scotia and New Brunswick by the Northumberland Strait. The major employer in P.E.I. was the various levels of government. Many people in P.E.I. worked seasonally, in either farming (especially potato), fishing, or tourism. During the peak tourist months of July and August, the island population would swell dramatically from its base of 125,000. P.E.I.'s half million annual visitors came "home" to enjoy the long sandy beaches, picturesque scenery, lobster dinners, arguably the best tasting strawberries in the world, and slower pace of life. P.E.I. was best known in Canada and elsewhere for the books, movies, and (current) television series about Lucy Maud Montgomery's turn-of-the-century literary creation, Anne of Green Gables.

P.E.I. Preserves felt they were competing in a worldwide market. Their visitors were from all over the world, and in 1991 they expected the numbers to exceed 100,000 in the New Glasgow location alone. New Glasgow (population 200) was located in a rural setting equidistant (15 km.) from Charlottetown and P.E.I.'s best known North Shore beaches. In their mailings they planned to continue to promote Prince Edward Island as "Canada's Garden Province" and the "little jewel it was in everyone's heart!" They had benefitted, and would continue to benefit, from that image.

MARKETING

Products

The company had developed numerous products since its inception. These included many original varieties of preserves as well as honey, vinegar, mustard, and tea (repackaged). The company had also added to the appeal of these products by offering gift packs composed of different products and packaging. With over 80 items, it felt that it had achieved a diverse product line and efforts in developing new product lines were expected to decrease in the future. Approximately three quarters of total retail sales (including wholesale and mail order) came from the products the company made itself. Of these, three-quarters were jam preserves.

With the success of P.E.I. Preserves, imitation was inevitable. In recent years, several other small firms in P.E.I. had begun to retail specialty preserves. Another company which produced preserves in Ontario emphasized the Green Gables tie-in on its labels.

Price

P.E.I. Preserves were not competing with "low-end" products, and felt their price reinforced their customers' perception of quality. The eleven types of jam preserves retailed for $5.89 for a 250 ml jar, significantly more than any grocery store product. However, grocery stores did not offer jam products made with such a high fruit content and with champagne, liqueur, or whisky.

In mid-1991, the company introduced a 10 percent increase in price (to $5.89) and, to date, had not received any negative reaction from customers. The food products were not subject to the 7 percent National Goods and Services Tax or P.E.I.'s 10 percent Provincial Sales Tax, an advantage over other gift products which the company would be stressing.

Promotion

Product promotion had been focused in two areas – personal contact with the consumer and catalogue distribution. Visitors to the New Glasgow location (approximately 80,000 in 1990) were enthusiastic upon meeting Bruce, "resplendent in the family kilt," reciting history, and generally providing live entertainment. Bruce and the other staff members realized the value of this "Island Touch" and strove to ensure that all visitors to New Glasgow left with both a positive feeling and purchased products.

Visitors were also encouraged to visit the New Glasgow location through a cooperative scheme whereby other specialty retailers provided a coupon for a free cup of coffee or tea at P.E.I. Preserves. In 1991, roughly 2000 of these coupons were redeemed.

Approximately 5,000 people received their mail-order catalogue annually. They had experienced an order rate of 7.5 percent with the average order being $66. They hoped to devote more time and effort to their mail order business in an effort to extend their marketing and production period. For 1991–92, the order rate was expected to increase by as much as 15 percent because the catalogue was to be mailed two weeks earlier than in the previous year. The catalogues cost $1 each to print and mail.

In addition to mail order, the company operated with an ad-hoc group of wholesale distributors. These wholesalers were divided between Nova Scotia, Ontario, and other locations. For orders as small as $150, buyers could purchase from the wholesalers' price list. Wholesale prices were on average 60 percent of the retail/mail order price. Total wholesale trade for the coming year was projected at $150,000, but had been higher in the past.

Danamar Imports was a Toronto-based specialty food store supplier which had previously provided P.E.I. Preserves to hundreds of specialty food stores in Ontario. Danamar had annually ordered $80,000 worth of P.E.I. Preserves at 30 percent below the wholesale price. This arrangement was amicably discontinued in 1990 by MacNaughton due to uncertainty about whether he was profiting from this contract. P.E.I. Preserves had a list of the specialty stores which Danamar had previously supplied, and was planning to contact them directly in late 1991.

Over the past few years, the company had received numerous enquiries for quotations on large scale shipments. Mitsubishi had asked for a price on a container load of preserves. Airlines and hotels were interested in obtaining preserves in 28 or 30 gram single-service bottles. One hotel chain, for example, had expressed interest in purchasing 3,000,000 bottles if the cost could be kept under $0.40 per unit. (Bruce had not proceeded due to the need to purchase $65,000 worth of bottling equipment, and uncertainty about his production costs.) This same hotel chain had more recently been assessing the ecological implications of the packaging waste which would be created with the use of so many small bottles. They were now weighing the hygiene implications of serving jam out of multi-customer use larger containers in their restaurants. They had asked MacNaughton to quote on $300,000 worth of jam in two-liter bottles.

FINANCIAL

The company had enjoyed a remarkable rate of growth since its inception. Sales volumes had increased in each of the six years of operations, from an initial level of $30,000 to 1990's total of $785,000. These sales were made up of $478,000 from retail sales (including mail order) of what they manufactured and/or distributed, and $307,000 from the restaurants (the Tea Room in New Glasgow, and Perfect Cup Restaurant in Charlottetown.). Exhibits 1.1 and 1.2 provide Income Statements from these operations, while Exhibit 1.3 contains a consolidated balance sheet.

This growth, although indicative of the success of the product, has also created its share of problems. Typical of many small businesses which experience such rapid growth, the company had not secured financing suitable to its needs. This, coupled with the seasonal nature of the manufacturing operation, had caused numerous periods of severe cash shortages. From Bruce's perspective, the company's banker (Bank of Nova Scotia) had not been as supportive as it might have been. (The bank manager in Charlottetown had last visited the facility three years ago.) Bruce felt the solution to the problem of cash shortages was the issuance of preferred shares. "An infusion of 'long term' working capital, at a relatively low rate of interest, will provide a stable financial base for the future," he said.

At this time, MacNaughton was attempting to provide a sound financial base for the continued operation of the company. He had decided to offer a preferred share issue in the amount of $100,000. These shares would bear interest at the rate of eight percent cumulative

Exhibit 1.1 P.E.I. Preserve Co. LTD. (Manufacturing and Retail) Statement of Earnings and Retained Earnings

	Year ended January 31, 1991 (Unaudited)	
	1991	1990
Sales	$478,406	$425,588
Cost of sales	217,550	186,890
Gross margin	260,856	238,698
Expenses		
Advertising and promotional items	20,632	6,324
Automobile	7,832	3,540
Doubtful accounts	1,261	—
Depreciation and amortization	11,589	12,818
Dues and fees	1,246	2,025
Electricity	7,937	4,951
Heat	4,096	4,433
Insurance	2,426	1,780
Interest and bank charges	5,667	17,482
Interest on long-term debt	23,562	9,219
Management salary	29,515	32,600
Office and supplies	12,176	10,412
Professional fees	19,672	10,816
Property tax	879	621
Rent	—	975
Repairs and maintenance	6,876	9,168
Salaries and wages	70,132	96,386
Telephone and facsimile	5,284	5,549
Trade shows	18,588	12,946
	249,370	242,045
Earnings (loss) from manufacturing operation	11,486	(3,347)
Management fees	—	7,250
Loss from restaurant operations – Schedule 2	3,368	—
Earnings before income taxes	8,118	3,903
Income taxes	181	1,273
Net Earnings	7,937	2,630
Retained earnings, beginning of year	9,290	6,660
Retained earnings, end of year	$ 17,227	$ 9,290

and would be non-voting, non-participating. He anticipated that the sale of these shares would be complete by December 31, 1991. In the interim he required a line of credit in the amount of $100,000, which he requested to be guaranteed by the Prince Edward Island Development Agency.

Exhibit 1.2   P.E.I. Preserve Co. LTD. Schedule of Restaurant Operations (Charlottetown and New Glasgow)

Year ended January 31, 1991
(Unaudited)

| | SCHEDULE 2 |
	1991
Sales	$306,427
Cost of sales	
Purchases and freight	122,719
Inventory, end of year	11,864
	110,855
Salaries and wages for food preparation	42,883
	153,738
Gross margin	152,689
Expenses	
Advertising	2,927
Depreciation	6,219
Electricity	4,897
Equipment lease	857
Insurance	389
Interest and bank charges	1,584
Interest on long-term debt	2,190
Office and supplies	2,864
Propane	2,717
Rent	22,431
Repairs and maintenance	3,930
Salaries and wages for service	90,590
Supplies	12,765
Telephone	1,697
	156,057
Loss from restaurant operations	$ 3,368

Projected Sales for the Year Ended January 31, 1992 were:

New Glasgow Restaurant	$ 110,000
Charlottetown Restaurant	265,000
Retail (New Glasgow)	360,000
Wholesale (New Glasgow)	150,000
Mail Order (New Glasgow)	50,000
Retail (Charlottetown)	75,000
Total	$1,010,000

Exhibit 1.3 P.E.I. Preserve Co. LTD. Balance Sheet

As of January 31, 1991
(Unaudited)

	1991	1990
Current assets		
Cash	$ 5,942	$ 592
Accounts receivable		
Trade	12,573	6,511
Investment tax credit	1,645	2,856
Other	13,349	35,816
Inventory	96,062	85,974
Prepaid expenses	2,664	6,990
	132,235	138,739
Grant receivable	2,800	1,374
Property, plant, and equipment	280,809	162,143
Recipes and trade name, at cost	10,000	10,000
	$425,844	$312,256
Current liabilities		
Bank indebtedness	$ 2,031	$ 9,483
Operating and other loans	54,478	79,000
Accounts payable and accrued liabilities	64,143	32,113
Current portion of long-term debt	23,657	14,704
	144,309	135,300
Long-term debt	97,825	99,679
Deferred government assistance	54,810	—
Payable to shareholder, non-interest bearing,		
no set terms of repayment	43,373	49,687
	340,317	284,666
Shareholders' equity		
Share capital	55,000	5,000
Contributed surplus	13,300	13,300
Retained earnings	17,227	9,290
	85,527	27,590
	$425,844	$312,256

OPERATIONS

Preserve production took place on-site, in an area visible through glass windows from the retail floor. Many visitors, in fact, would videotape operations during their visit to the New Glasgow store, or would watch the process while tasting the broad selection of sample products freely available.

Production took place on a batch basis. Ample production capacity existed for the $30,000 main kettle used to cook the preserves. Preserves were made five months a year, on a single shift, five day per week basis. Even then, the main kettle was in use only 50 percent of the time.

Only top quality fruit was purchased. As much as possible, P.E.I. raw materials were used. For a short period the fruit could be frozen until time for processing.

The production process was labor intensive. Bruce was considering the feasibility of moving to an incentive-based salary system to increase productivity and control costs. Because a decorative cloth fringe was tied over the lid of each bottle, bottling could not be completely automated. A detailed production cost analysis had recently been completed. While there were some minor differences due to ingredients, the variable costs averaged $1.25 per 250 ml bottle. This was made up of ingredients ($.56), labor ($.28), and packaging ($.20/bottle, $.11 /lid, $.03/label, and $.07/fabric and ribbon).

Restaurant operations were the source of many of Bruce's headaches. The New Glasgow restaurant had evolved over time from offering 'dessert and coffee/tea' to its present status where it was also open for meals all day.

Management

During the peak summer period, P.E.I. Preserves employed forty-five people among the restaurants, manufacturing area, and retail locations. Of these, five were managerial positions (see Exhibit 1.4). The company was considered a good place to work, with high morale and limited turnover. Nonetheless, most employees (including some management) were with the company on a seasonal basis. This was a concern to McNaughton who felt that if he could provide year round employment, he would be able to attract and keep the best quality staff.

Carol Rombough was an effective assistant general manager and bookkeeper. Maureen Dickieson handled production with little input required from Bruce. Kathy MacPherson was in the process of providing, for the first time, accurate cost information. Natalie Leblanc was managing the new retail outlet in Charlottetown, and assisting on some of the more proactive marketing initiatives Bruce was considering.

Bruce felt that the company had survived on the basis of word-of-mouth. Few follow-up calls on mail-order had ever been done. Bruce did not enjoy participating in trade shows – even though he received regular solicitations for them from across North America. In 1992, he planned to participate in four retail shows, all of them in or close to P.E.I. Bruce hoped to be able eventually to hire a sales/marketing manager but could not yet afford $30,000 for the necessary salary.

The key manager continued to be MacNaughton. He described himself as "a fair person to deal with, but shrewd when it comes to purchasing. However, I like to spend enough money to ensure that what we do – we do right." Financial and managerial constraints meant that Bruce felt stretched ("I haven't had a vacation in years.") and unable to pursue all of the ideas he had for developing the business.

THE JAPANESE CONSUMER

MacNaughton's interest in the possibility of reaching the Tokyo consumer had been formed from two factors: the large number of Japanese visitors to P.E.I. Preserves, and the fact that the largest export shipment the company had ever made had been to Japan. MacNaughton

Exhibit 1.4   Key Executives

President and General Manager – Bruce MacNaughton, Age 35

Experience:	Seventeen years of "front line" involvement with the public in various capacities;
	Seven years of managing and promoting Prince Edward Island Preserve Co. Ltd;
	Past director of the Canadian Specialty Food Association.
Responsibilities:	To develop and oversee the short-, mid-, and long-term goals of the company;
	To develop and maintain quality products for the marketplace;
	To oversee the management of personnel;
	To develop and maintain customer relations at both the wholesale and retail level;
	To develop and maintain harmonious relations with government and the banking community.

Assistant General Manager – Carol Rombough, Age 44

Experience:	Twenty years as owner/operator of a manufacturing business;
	Product marketing at both the wholesale and retail level;
	Personnel management;
	Bookkeeping in a manufacturing environment;
	Three years with the Prince Edward Island Preserve Co. Ltd.
Responsibilities:	All bookkeeping functions (i.e. Accounts Receivable, Accounts Payable, Payroll);
	Staff management – scheduling and hiring;
	Customer relations.

Production Manager – Maureen Dickieson, Age 29

Experience:	Seven years of production experience in the dairy industry;
	Three years with the Prince Edward Island Preserve Co. Ltd.
Responsibilities:	Oversee and participate in all production;
	Planning and scheduling production;
	Requisition of supplies.

Consultant – Kathy MacPherson, Certified General Accountant, Age 37

Experience:	Eight years as a small business owner/manager;
	Eight years in financial planning and management.
Responsibilities:	To implement an improved system of product costing;
	To assist in the development of internal controls;
	To compile monthly internal financial statements;
	To provide assistance and/or advice as required by management.

Store Manager – Natalie Leblanc, Age 33

Experience:	Fifteen years in retail
Responsibilities:	To manage the retail store in the CP Hotel;
	Assist with mail order business;
	Marketing duties as assigned.

had never visited Japan, although he had been encouraged by Canadian federal government trade representatives to participate in food and gift shows in Japan. He was debating whether he should visit Japan during the coming year. Most of the information he had on Japan had been collected for him by a friend.

Japan was Canada's second most important source of foreign tourists. In 1990, there were 474,000 Japanese visitors to Canada, a figure which was expected to rise to 1,000,000 by 1995. Most Japanese visitors entered through the Vancouver or Toronto airports. Within Canada, the most popular destination was the Rocky Mountains (in Banff, Alberta numerous stores catered specifically to Japanese consumers). Nearly 15,000 Japanese visited P.E.I. each year. Excluding airfare, these visitors to Canada spent an estimated $314 million, the highest per-capita amount from any country.

The Japanese fascination with Prince Edward Island could be traced to the popularity of Anne of Green Gables. The Japanese translation of this and other books in the same series had been available for many years. However, the adoption of the book as required reading in the Japanese school system since the 1950s had resulted in widespread awareness and affection for "Anne with red hair" and P.E.I.

The high level of spending by Japanese tourists was due to a multitude of factors: the amount of disposable income available to them, one of the world's highest per person duty-free allowances (200,000 yen), and gift-giving traditions in the country. Gift giving and entertainment expenses at the corporate level are enormous in Japan. In 1990, corporate entertainment expenses were almost ¥5 trillion, more than triple the U.S. level of ¥1.4 trillion. Corporate gift giving, while focused at both year end (seibo) and the summer (chugen), in fact, occurred throughout the year.

Gift giving at the personal level was also widespread. The amount spent would vary depending on one's relationship with the recipient; however, one of the most common price points used by Japanese retailers for gift giving was offering choices for under ¥2000.

The Japanese Jam Market

Japanese annual consumption of jam was approximately 80,000 tons. Imports made up 6–9 percent of consumption, with higher grade products (¥470 or more per kilo wholesale CIF) making up a third of this total. Several dozen firms imported jam, and utilized a mix of distribution channels (see Exhibit 1.5). Prices varied, in part, according to the type of channel structure used. Exhibit 1.6 provides a common structure. Import duties for jams were high – averaging about 28 percent. Despite such a high tariff barrier, some firms had been successful in exporting to Japan. Excerpts from a report on how to access Japan's jam market successfully are contained in Exhibit 1.7.

CANADIAN WORLD

In Spring 1990, P.E.I. Preserves received its biggest ever export order: $50,000 worth of product was ordered (FOB New Glasgow) for ultimate shipment to Ashibetsu, on the northern Japanese island of Hokkaido. These products were to be offered for sale at Canadian World, a new theme park scheduled to open in July 1990.

In 1981, Japan's first theme park was built outside Tokyo. Called Tokyo Disneyland, in 1989 it had an annual revenue of $815 million, 14.7 million visitors, and profits of $119

Exhibit 1.5 Jam Distribution Channel in Japan

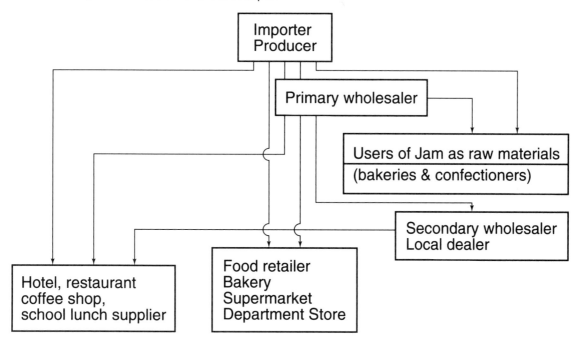

Source: Access to Japan's Import Market, Tradescope, June 1989.

Exhibit 1.6 Example of Price Markups in Japan

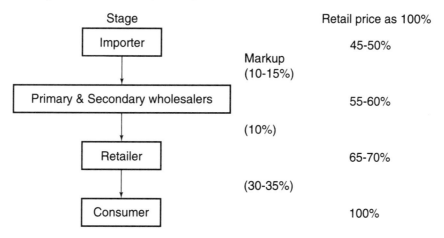

Source: Access to Japan's Import Market, Tradescope, June 1989.

million. Not surprisingly, this success has spawned a theme park industry in Japan. Over the past decade, twenty parks with wide-ranging themes have opened. Another sixteen were expected to open in 1991–92.

The idea to construct a theme park about Canada was conceived by a Japanese advertising agency hired by the Ashibetsu city council to stop the city's declining economy. The city's

Exhibit 1.7 The Japanese Jam Market

To expand sales of imported jam or to enter the Japanese market for the first time it is necessary to develop products after precise study of the market's needs. Importers who are making efforts to tailor their products to the Japanese market have been successfully expanding their sales by 10 percent each year. Based on the analysis of successful cases of imported jam, the following factors may be considered very important.

Diversification of consumer preferences: Strawberry jam occupies about 50 percent of the total demand for jam and its share is continuing to rise. Simultaneously, more and more varieties of jam are being introduced.

Low sugar content: European exporters have successfully exported low sugar jam that meets the needs of the Japanese market. Jam with a sugar content of less than 65 percent occupies a share of 65–70 percent of the market on a volume basis.

Smaller containers: Foreign manufacturers who stick to packaging products in large-sized containers (650g, 440g, 250g), even though their products are designed for household use, have been failing to expand their sales. On the other hand, foreign manufacturers who have developed products in smaller containers (14g, 30g, 42g) specifically for the Japanese market have achieved successful results.

Fashionable items: Contents and quantity are not the only important aspects of jam. The shape and material quality of the containers and their caps, label design and product name can also influence sales. It is also important that the label not be damaged in any way.

Development of gift items: Sets of various types of imported jams are popular as gift items. For example, there are sets of 10 kinds of jam in 40g mini-jars (retail price ¥2,000) sold as gift sets.

Selection of distribution channel: Since general trading companies, specialty importers, and jam manufacturers each have their own established distribution channels, the selection of the most appropriate channel is of the utmost importance.

Source: Access to Japan's Import Market, Tradescope, June 1989.

population had decreased from 75,000 in 1958 to 26,000 in 1984 due principally to mine closures.

With capital investment of ¥750,000,000, construction started in mid-1989 on forty-eight of the 156 available hectares. The finished site included six restaurants, eighteen souvenir stores, sixteen exhibit event halls, an outdoor stage with 12,000 seats, and twenty hectares planted in herbs and lavender.

The theme of Canadian World was less a mosaic of Canada than it was a park devoted to the world of Anne of Green Gables. The entrance to the Canadian World was a replica of Kensingston Station in P.E.I. The north gateway was Brightriver Station, where Anne first met with Matthew. There was a full scale copy of the Green Gables house, Orwell School where you could actually learn English like Anne did, and so forth. Canadian World employed fifty-five full-time and 330 part-time staff. This included a high school girl from P.E.I. who played Anne – complete with (dyed) red hair – dressed in Victorian period costume.

In late August 1991, Canadian World still had a lot of P.E.I. Preserves' products for sale. Lower than expected sales could be traced to a variety of problems. First, overall attendance at Canadian World had been 205,000 in the first year, significantly lower than the expected 300,000. Second, the product was priced higher than many competitive offerings. For reasons unknown to Canadian World staff, the product sold for 10 percent more than expected (¥1200 vs ¥1086).

Wholesale price in P.E.I.	$3.50
Freight ($4.20/kilo, P.E.I. to Hokkaido)	.80
Duty (28% of wholesale price + freight)	1.20
Landed cost in Japan	5.50
Importer's Margin (15%)	.83
Price to Primary Wholesaler	6.33
Wholesaler Margin (10%)	.63
Price to Retailer	6.96
Canadian World mark up (30%)	2.09
Expected retail price	$9.05
Exchange (Cdn. $1.00 = 120 yen)	¥1086

Third, the product mix chosen by the Japanese buyers appeared to be inappropriate. While it was difficult to locate any of the company's remaining strawberry preserves in the various Canadian World outlets which carried it, other products had not moved at all. Canadian World personnel did not have a tracking system for product-by-product sales. Fourth, the company's gift packs were not always appropriately sized or priced. One suggestion had been to package the preserves in cardboard gift boxes of three large (250 ml) or five small (125 ml) bottles for eventual sale for under ¥2000.

An increasing portion of all of the gifts being sold at Canadian World were, in fact, being made in Japan. Japanese sourcing was common due to the high Japanese duties on imports, the transportation costs from Canada, and the unfamiliarity of Canadian companies with Japanese consumer preferences.

THE TOKYO MARKET

With ten million residents, Tokyo was the largest city in Japan and one of the most crowded cities anywhere. Thirty million people lived within 50 km of Tokyo's Imperial Palace. As the economic center of the nation, Tokyo also had the most expensive land in the world – U.S. $150,000 per square meter in the city center. Retail space in one of Tokyo's major shopping districts would cost $75–160 per square meter or $1600–3400 per month for a shop equivalent in size to that in the CP Prince Edward Hotel. Prices in the Ginza were even higher. In addition to basic rent, all locations required a deposit (guarantee money which would be repaid when the tenant gave up the lease) of at least $25,000. Half of the locations available in a recent survey also charged administrative/maintenance fees (5–12% of rent), while in about one-third of the locations a "reward" (gift) was paid by tenants to the owner at the time the contract was signed. For a small site it might amount to $10–15,000.

THE TORONTO MARKET

With three million people, Toronto was Canada's largest city and economic center. It contained the country's busiest airport (fifteen million people used it each year) and was a popular destination for tourists. Each year, roughly twenty million people visited Toronto for business or vacation.

MacNaughton's interest in Toronto was due to its size, the local awareness of P.E.I., and the high perceived potential volume of sales. The company did not have a sales agent in Toronto.

The Toronto market was well served by mass market and specialty jam producers at all price points. Numerous domestic and imported products were available. Prices started as low as $1.00 (or less) for a 250 ml bottle of high sugar – low fruit product. Prices increased to $2.00–$2.50 for higher fruit, natural brands and increased again to $3.00–$3.50 for many of the popular branded imports. The highest priced products such as P.E.I. Preserves, were characterized by even higher fruit content, highest quality ingredients, and a broader selection of product offerings.

The specialty domestic producers were from various provinces and tended to have limited distribution areas. The specialty imports were frequently from France or England. The Canadian tariff on imports was 15 percent for most countries. From the United States, it was 10.5 percent and declining.

The cost of retail space in Toronto varied according to location, but was slightly lower than that in Tokyo. The cost of renting 22 square meters would be $100 per square meter per month (plus common area charges and taxes of $15 per square meter per month) in a major suburban shopping mall, and somewhat higher in the downtown core. Retail staff salaries were similar in Toronto and Tokyo, both of which were higher than those paid in P.E.I.

Future Directions

MacNaughton was the first to acknowledge that, while the business had been "built on gut and emotion, rather than analysis," this was insufficient for the future. The challenge was to determine the direction and timing of the desired change.

2

Coral Divers Resort

Jonathon Greywell locked the door on the equipment shed and began walking back along the boat dock to his office. He was thinking about the matters that had weighed heavily on his mind during the last few months. Over the years, Greywell had established a solid reputation for the Coral Divers Resort as a safe and knowledgeable scuba diving resort. It offered not only diving, but a beachfront location. As a small, but well regarded all-around dive resort in the Bahamas, many divers had come to prefer his resort over other crowded tourist resorts in the Caribbean.

However, over the last three years, revenues had flattened out and, for 1995, bookings were off 10 percent for the first half of the year. Greywell felt he needed to do something to increase business before things got worse. He wondered if he should add some specialized features to distinguish Coral Divers Resort from others.

One approach was to focus on family outings. He had met with Theresa Detchemendy and Deborah Baratta from Rascals in Paradise, a travel agency that specializes in family diving vacations. They had offered to help him convert his resort to the same speciality. They had shown him industry demographics indicating that families are a growing market segment (see Exhibit 2.1). They had made suggestions as to what changes would need to be made at the resort. Deborah had even offered to create menus for children and to show the cook how to prepare the meals.

Another potential strategy for the Coral Divers Resort was adventure diving. Other resort operators in the Bahamas were offering adventure-oriented deep-depth dives, shark dives, and night dives. The basic ingredients for adventure diving, reef sharks in the waters near New Providence and famous deep water coral walls, were already in place. However, either strategy, family or adventure, would require changes and additions to his current operations. Greywell was not sure which, if either, of the changes was worth the time and investment. He could choose a third option which was to try to improve upon what he was already doing.

SCUBA DIVING INDUSTRY OVERVIEW

Scuba Diving Overview

Skin diving Skin diving is an underwater activity of ancient origin in which a diver swims freely, unencumbered by lines or air hoses. Modern skin divers use three pieces of basic

Exhibit 2.1   U.S. Population Demographics and Income Distribution: 1970, 1980, and 1990

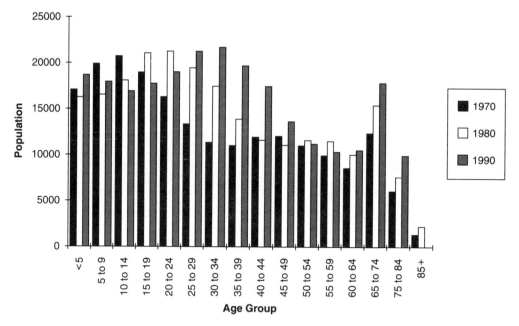

*numbers are in the thousands

*from the American Almanac, 1944-1955, from US Bureau of Census

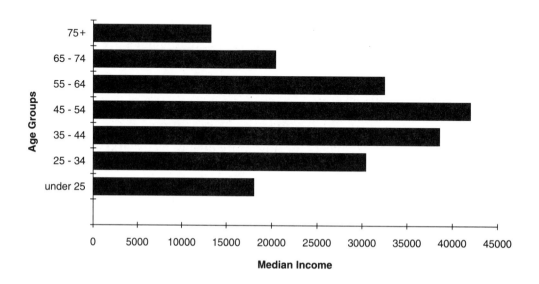

*from The Official Guide to the American Marketplace, 1992

equipment: a face mask for vision, webbed rubber fins for propulsion, and a snorkel tube for breathing just below the water's surface. The snorkel is a plastic tube shaped like a *J* and fitted with a mouthpiece. When the opening of the snorkel is above water, a diver will be able to breathe. For diving to greater depths, the breath must be held, otherwise water will enter the mouth through the snorkel.

Scuba diving   Scuba diving provides a diver with time to relax and explore the underwater world without having to surface for their next breath. Scuba is an acronym for Self-Contained Underwater Breathing Apparatus. While attempts to perfect this type of apparatus date from the early twentieth century, it was not until 1943 that the most famous scuba gear, Aqualung, was invented by the Frenchmen Jacques-Yves Cousteau and Emil Gagnan. The Aqualung has made recreational diving possible for millions of nonprofessional divers. Scuba diving is also called free diving, because the diver has no physical connection with the surface. Although some specially trained commercial scuba divers descend below 100 m (328 ft) for various kinds of work, recreational divers rarely go below a depth of 40 m (130 ft) because of increased risk of nitrogen narcosis, a type of intoxication similar to drunkenness, or oxygen toxicity, which causes blackouts or convulsions.

The scuba diver wears a tank that carries a supply of pressurized breathing gas, either air or a mixture of oxygen and other gases. The heart of the breathing apparatus is the breathing regulator and the pressure-reducing mechanisms that deliver gas to the diver on each inhalation. In the common scuba gear used in recreational diving, the breathing medium is air. As the diver inhales, a slight negative pressure occurs in the mouthpiece, which signals the valve that delivers the air to open. The valve closes when the diver stops inhaling, and a one-way valve allows the exhaled breath to escape as bubbles into the water. When using a tank and regulator, a diver can make longer and deeper dives and still breathe comfortably.

Along with scuba gear and its tanks of compressed breathing gases, the scuba diver's essential equipment includes a soft rubber mask with a large faceplate; a soft rubber diving suit for protection from cold water; long, flexible, swimming flippers for the feet; buoyancy compensator (known as a BC); weight belt; waterproof watch; wrist compass; and diver's knife.

Certification Organizations[1]

There are several international and domestic organizations that train and certify scuba divers. PADI (Professional Association of Diving Instructors), NAUI (National Association of Underwater Instructors), SSI (Scuba Schools International), and NASDS (National Association of Scuba Diving Schools) are the most well known of these organizations. Of these, PADI is the largest certifying organization.

PADI   PADI is the largest recreational scuba diver training organization in the world. PADI, founded in 1967, has issued more than 5.5 million certifications since it began operation. Since 1985, seven of every ten American divers and an estimated 55 percent of all divers around the world are trained by PADI instructors using PADI's instructional programs. Presently PADI certifies well over half a million divers internationally each year and has averaged a 12 percent increase in certifications each year since 1985. In 1994, PADI

International issued 625,000 certifications, more than in any other single year in company history.

PADI's main headquarters are in Santa Ana, California. Its distribution center is in the U.K., and it has seven local area offices in Australia, Canada, Japan, New Zealand, Norway, Sweden, and Switzerland, with professional and member groups in 175 countries and territories. PADI is made up of four groups: PADI Retail Association, PADI International Resort Association, Professional Members, and PADI Alumni Association. The association groups emphasize the "Three E's" of recreational diving: Education, Equipment, and Experience. By supporting each facet, PADI provides holistic leadership to advance recreational scuba diving and snorkel swimming to equal status with other major leisure activities, while maintaining and improving the excellent safety record PADI has experienced. PADI offers seven levels of instruction and certification ranging from entry level to instructor (see Exhibit 2.2).

NAUI   NAUI first began operation in 1960. The organization was formed by a nationally recognized group of instructors known as the National Diving Patrol. Since its beginning, NAUI has been active worldwide, certifying sport divers in various levels of proficiency from basic skin diver to instructor. In addition, NAUI regularly conducts specialty courses for cave diving, ice diving, wreck diving, underwater navigation, and search and recovery.

Industry Demographics[2]

Scuba diving has grown regularly in popularity, especially in recent years. For the period 1989–1994, increases in the number of certifications averaged over 10 percent per year. The total number of certified divers worldwide is estimated to be over 10 million. Of these newly certified scuba divers, approximately 65 percent are male and 35 percent are female. Approximately half are married. Approximately 70 percent of them are between the ages of 18 and 34, while about 25 percent are between 35 and 49 (see Exhibit 2.3). They are generally well educated with 80 percent having a college education. Overwhelmingly, they are employed in professional, managerial, and technical occupations. Their average annual household income is $75,000. Forty-five percent of divers travel most often with their families. Another 40 percent travel with friends or informal groups.

Divers are attracted to diving for various reasons: Seeking adventure and being with nature are the reasons cited most often (over 75 percent for each). Socializing, stress relief, and travel also are common motivations. Two-thirds of divers travel overseas on diving trips once every three years, while 60 percent travel domestically on dive trips each year. On average, divers spend $2,816 on dive trips annually, with an average equipment investment of $2,300. Aside from upgrades and replacements, the equipment purchase could be considered a one-time cost. Warm water diving locations are generally chosen two to one over cold water diving sites. Cozumel, the Cayman Islands, and the Bahamas are the top three diving destinations outside the continental U.S. for Americans.

According to a consumer survey, the "strongest feelings" divers associate with their scuba diving experiences are "excitement" and "peacefulness." In a recent survey, the two themes drew an equal number of responses. However, there seems to be very distinct differences in the two responses. One suggests a need for stimulation, while the other suggests relaxation

Exhibit 2.2 PADI Certification Overview

PADI CERTIFICATION OVERVIEW*

Open Water Diver: This is a fully credited entry level scuba diver, and at the time of certification would be classed as a novice diver with a suggested maximum depth of not more than 60 feet, until he or she has gained experience.

Advanced Open Water Diver: This diver has gained additional experience in night diving, deep diving, underwater navigation, and two other specialty areas. When the student has completed this course, he or she will have completed at least nine training dives under Instructor supervision.

Advanced Plus Open Water Diver: This diver has gained additional experience in night diving, deep diving, underwater navigation, and six other specialty areas. This program also includes a First Aid and CPR component and an introduction to advanced diving academics. When this course is completed the student will have completed at least thirteen training dives under Instructor supervision. A student has the option of taking either of the two advanced programs. Either one will give the credit necessary to move to the next level.

Rescue Diver: This is a fully trained Rescue diver capable of providing assistance to another in distress while diving.

Divemaster: This is the first professional level. Divemasters are trained to plan, organize, and supervise other divers or groups of divers. They also act as instructional assistants to PADI instructors.

Assistant Instructor: Assistant Instructors are trained to plan, organize, and supervise other divers or groups of divers, just like Divemasters. They also act as instructional assistants to PADI Instructors. Assistant Instructors can independently teach skin diving.

Open Water Scuba Instructor: This is a fully certified Instructor who can certify a student from Open Water up to Assistant Instructor.

Specialty Instructor: Certified to teach a specific diving subject in a detailed program. There are 17 different PADI specialty programs.

Master Diver Trainer: This is an Open Water Instructor with five specialties. This is a recognition award given to an instructor. It does not give them any additional authority.

Instructor Development Course (IDC) Staff Instructor: This Instructor assists in the training of new Instructors under the supervision of a PADI Course Director.

Course Director: This is the highest PADI instructional level. This person trains new PADI Instructors. All new Instructors are evaluated by PADI after the Course Director has trained the individual.

*Adapted from PADI information release.

and escape. Visual gratification ("beauty") is another strong motivation for divers. The feelings "freedom, weightlessness, and flying" were also popular responses.

Under PADI regulations, twelve is the minimum age for certification by the majority of scuba training agencies. At age twelve, the child can earn a Junior Diver certification. The Junior Diver meets the same standards as an Open Water diver but generally must be accompanied on dives by a parent or other certified adult. At age fifteen, the Junior Diver certification can be upgraded by an instructor to Open Water status. This upgrade may require a skills review and evaluation. Pre-dive waiver and release forms require the signature of a parent or guardian until the minor turns eighteen.

Exhibit 2.3   Diver Demographics: PADI 1991 Survey

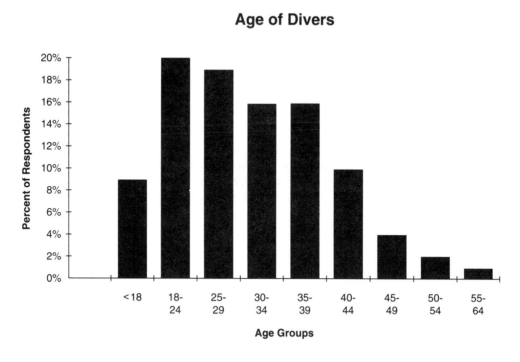

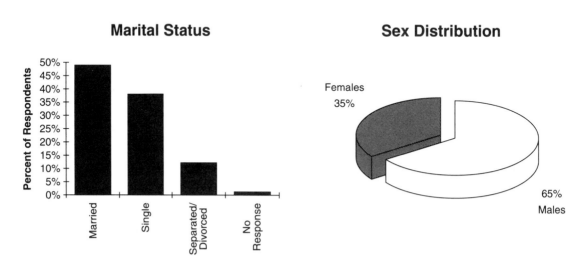

*information taken from the PADI 1991 Diver Survey Results and Analysis, Preliminary Draft

A cautious approach to young divers is based on the concept of readiness to dive. An individual's readiness to dive is determined by physical, mental, and emotional maturity. Physical readiness is easiest to assess: Is the child large and strong enough to handle scuba equipment? An air tank and weight belt can weigh over 40 pounds, although most dive shops can provide equipment specially sized for smaller divers. Mental readiness refers to whether the child has the academic background and conceptual development to understand diving physics and perform the arithmetic required for certification. The arithmetic understanding focuses on allowable bottom time, which requires factoring in depth, number of dives, and length of dives. Emotional readiness is the greatest concern. Will the junior diver accept the responsibility of being a dive buddy? Divers never dive alone and dive buddies are supposed to look out for and rely on each other. Do they comprehend the safety rules of diving and willingly follow them? Most dive centers accept students from age twelve, but the final determination of readiness to dive rests with the scuba instructor. Instructors are trained to evaluate the readiness of all students prior to completion of the course work and will only award a certification to those who earn it, regardless of age.

DIVING IN THE BAHAMAS[3]

New Providence Island is best known for its major population center, Nassau. Nassau's early development was based on its superb natural harbor. Now, as the capital of the Bahamas, it is the seat of government and is also home to 400 banks, elegant homes, ancient forts, and a wide variety of duty-free shopping. It also has the island's most developed tourist infrastructure with resort hotels, casinos, cabaret shows, and cruise ship docks. Nassau is the nation's most populous and cosmopolitan city. More than two-thirds of the population of the Bahamas live on New Providence. Most of these 150,000 people live in or near Nassau on the northeast corner of the island.

With thousands of vacationers taking resort courses (introductory scuba courses taught in resort pools), Nassau has become known as a destination that is as good for an exploratory first dive as it is for more advanced diving. There are many professional dive operations in the Nassau/Paradise Island area. While all offer resort courses, many also offer a full menu of dive activities designed for the more advanced and experienced diver. Within a thirty-minute boat ride are shipwrecks, beautiful shallow reefs, and huge schools of fish.

In contrast to the bustle of Nassau, the south side of New Providence Island is quieter and more laid back. While large tracts of pine trees and rolling hills dominate the central regions, miles of white sand beach surround the island. At the west end of the island is Lyford Cay, an exclusive residential area. Nearby, the winding canals of the Coral Harbour area offer easy access to the sea. While golf and tennis are available, the primary attraction is good scuba diving and top quality dive operators.

The southwest side of the island has been a favorite spot for Hollywood filmmakers to use as an underwater set. The "Bond Wrecks" are popular diving destinations for divers and operators. The Vulcan Bomber used in *Thunderball* has aged into a framework draped with colorful gorgonians and sponges. The freighter known as the *Tears of Allah*, where James Bond eluded the tiger shark in *Never Say Never Again,* remains a popular dive attraction in just forty feet of water. The photogenic appeal of this wreck has improved with age as more and more marine life congregates on this artificial reef.

There are other more natural underwater attractions. Shark Wall and Shark Buoy are popular shark feed dive spots. Drop-off dives like Tunnel Wall feature a network of crevices and tunnels beginning in thirty feet of water and exiting along the vertical wall at seventy or eighty feet. Southwest Reef offers magnificent high profile coral head in only fifteen to thirty feet of water, with pristine Elkhorn and Staghorn formations and schooling grunts, squirrelfish, and barracuda. A favorite of the shallow reef areas is Goulding Cay, where broad stands of Elkhorn coral reach nearly to the surface.

TYPES OF DIVING

A wide array of diving activities are available in the Bahamas. These include shark dives, wreck dives, wall dives, reef dives, drift dives, night dives, and so forth. Illustrative examples follow.

Shark Diving

The top three operators of shark dives in the Caribbean are in the Bahamas. While shark diving trips vary with the operators running them, there is at least one common factor in the Bahamas. The primary shark present in Bahamian shark dives is the Caribbean reef shark (*Carcharhinus perezi*). When the dive boat anchors at the customary feed site, the sound of the motor and the anchor hitting the bottom act as a dinner bell. Even before the divers are in the water, the sharks gather for their handouts.

Long Island in the Bahamas was the first area to promote shark feeds on a regular basis. This method began twenty years ago and has remained relatively unchanged. The feed is conducted as a frenzy. Sharks circle as divers enter the water. After the divers position themselves with their backs to a coral wall, the feeder enters the water with a bucket of fish. This is placed in the sand in front of the divers and from there the action develops quickly. At Walker's Cay, in Abaco, the method is similar except for the number and variety of sharks in the feed. While Caribbean reef sharks make up the majority, lemon sharks, bull sharks, hammerhead sharks, and other species also appear.

The shark feed off Freeport, Grand Bahama is a highly-organized event. It attracts primarily Caribbean reef sharks, fed either by hand or off the point of a polespear. The divers are arranged in a semi-circle with safety divers guarding the viewers as the feeder is positioned at the middle of the group. The energy is very well controlled, with food being distributed from a large neoprene-covered PVC pipe. If the sharks become unruly, the food is withheld until they calm down. The sharks then go into a regular routine of circling, taking their place in line and advancing to receive the food. Although the sharks come within touching distance, the vast majority of divers resist the temptation to reach out.

Shark Wall, on the southwest side of New Providence, is a pristine drop-off decorated with masses of colorful sponges along the deep water abyss known as the Tongue of the Ocean. Divers position themselves along sand patches among the coral heads in about fifty feet of water as Caribbean reef sharks and an occasional bull or lemon shark cruise midwater in anticipation of a free handout. During the feeding period, the bait is controlled and fed from a polespear by an experienced feeder. There are usually six to twelve sharks present, ranging from four to eight feet in length. Some operators make two dives to this site, allowing divers to cruise the wall with the sharks in a more natural way before the feeding dive.

The Shark Buoy, also on the southwest side of New Providence, is tethered in 6,000 feet of water. Its floating surface attracts enmasse a wide variety of ocean marine life such as dolphinfish, jacks, rainbow runners, and silky sharks. The silky sharks are typically small, three to five feet long, but swarm in schools of six to twenty, with the sharks swimming up to the divemasters' hands to grab the bait.

From the operator's standpoint, the only special equipment needed for shark dives is a chain mail diving suit for the feeder's protection, some type of feeding apparatus, and intestinal fortitude. The thrill of diving among sharks is the main attraction for the divers. For the most part, the dives are safe, with only the feeder taking an occasional nick from an excited shark.

Wreck Diving

Wreck diving is divided into three levels: non-penetration, limited penetration, and full penetration. Full penetration and deep wreck diving should be done only by divers who have completed rigorous training and have extensive diving experience. Non-penetration wreck diving refers to recreational diving on wrecks without entering an overhead environment that prevents direct access to the surface. Divers with open water certification are qualified for this type of diving without further training as long as they are comfortable with the diving conditions and the wreck's depth. Limited penetration wreck diving is defined as staying within ambient light and always in sight of an exit. Full penetration wreck diving involves an overhead environment away from ambient light and beyond sight of an exit. Safely and extensively exploring the insides of a wreck involves formal training and mental strength. On this type of dive, the first mistake could be the last.

Wall Diving

In a few regions of the world, island chains, formed by volcanos and coral, were altered by movements of the earth's crustal plates. Extending approximately due east-west across the central Caribbean Sea is the boundary between the North American and the Caribbean crustal plates. The shifting of these plates has created some of the most spectacular diving environments in the world, characterized by enormous cliffs, 2000 to 6000 feet high. At the cliffs, known as walls, the diver experiences the overwhelming scale and dynamic forces that shape the ocean more than in any other underwater environment. It is on the walls that a diver is most likely to experience the feeling of free motion, or flying, in boundless space. Many of the dives in the Bahamas are wall dives.

Reef Diving

Reefs generally are made up of three areas: a reef flat, a lagoon or bay, and a reef crest. The depth in the reef flat averages only a few feet with an occasional deeper channel. The underwater life on a shallow reef flat may vary greatly in abundance and diversity within a short distance. The reef flat is generally a protected area, not exposed to strong winds or waves, making it ideal for novice or family snorkelers. The main feature distinguishing bay and lagoon environments from a reef flat is depth. Caribbean lagoons and bays may reach depths of sixty feet, but many provide teaming underwater ecosystems in as little as fifteen to twenty feet. This is excellent for underwater photography and ideal for families or no decompression stop diving. The reef's crest is the outer boundary that shelters the bay and flats from the full force of the ocean's waves. Since the surging and pounding of the waves is too strong for all but the most advanced divers, most diving takes place in the protected bay waters.

FAMILY DIVING RESORTS

The current average age of new divers is thirty-six. As the median age of new divers has increased, families have become a rapidly growing segment of the vacation travel industry. Many parents are busy and do not spend as much time with their children as they would prefer. Many parents who dive would like to have a vacation that would combine diving and spending time with their children. In response to increasing numbers of parents travelling with children, resort operators have added amenities ranging from babysitting services and kids' camps to dedicated family resorts with special facilities and rates. The resort options available have greatly expanded in recent years. At all-inclusive self-contained resorts, one price includes everything: meals, accommodations, daytime and evening activities, and watersports. Many of these facilities offer special activities and facilities for children. Diving is included or available nearby.

For many divers, the important part of the trip is the quality of the diving, not the quality of the accommodations. But for divers with families, the equation changes. Children, especially younger children, may find it difficult to do without a comfortable bed, television, or VCR, no matter how good the diving promises to be. Some resorts, while not dedicated to family vacations, do make accommodations for divers with children. Condos and villas are an economical and convenient vacation option for divers with children. The additional space of this type of accommodation allows for bringing along a babysitter. Having a kitchen on hand makes the task of feeding children simple and economical. Most diving destinations in the Bahamas, Caribbean, and Pacific offer condo, villa, and hotel-type accommodations. Some hotels organize entertaining and educational activities for children while parents engage in their own activities.

As the number of families vacationing together has increased, some resorts and dive operators have started special promotions and programs. On Bonaire, part of the Netherland Antilles, August has been designated Family Month. During this month, the island is devoted to families, with a special welcome kit for children and island-wide activities including "eco-walks" at a flamingo reserve, snorkeling lessons, and evening entertainment for all ages. In conjunction, individual resorts and restaurants offer family packages and discounts. Similarly, in Honduras, which has very good diving, a resort started a children's dolphin camp during summer months. While diving family members are out exploring the reefs, children between ages eight and fourteen spend their days learning about and interacting with a resident dolphin population. The program includes classroom and in-water time as well as horseback riding and paddle boating.

One travel company, Rascals in Paradise (1-800-U-RASCAL), specializes in family travel packages. The founders, Theresa Detchemendy and Deborah Baratta, are divers, mothers, and travel agents who have developed innovative packages for diving families. Theresa says, "The biggest concern for parents is their children's safety, and then what the kids will do while they're diving or enjoying an evening on the town." The Rascals people have worked with a number of family-run resorts all over the world to provide daily activities, responsible local nannies, and child-safe facilities with safe balconies, playgrounds, and children's pools.

They have also organized Family Weeks at popular dive destinations in Belize, Mexico and the Cayman Islands. Family Week packages account for over 50 percent of Rascals' bookings each year. On these scheduled trips, groups of three to six families share a teacher/

escort who brings along a fun program tailored for children and serves as activities director for the group. Rascals Special Family Weeks packages are priced based on a family of four (two adults and two children, age 2–11) and include a teacher/escort, one babysitter for each family, children's activities, meals, airport transfers, taxes, services, and cancellation insurance (see Exhibit 2.4). For example, in 1995, a seven-night family vacation at Hotel Club Akumal on the Yucatan coast was US$2080–$3100 per family.[4] Rascals also packages independent family trips to fifty-seven different condos, villas, resorts, or hotels which offer scuba diving. An independent family trip would not include a teacher/escort (see Exhibit 2.5). A seven-night independent family trip to Hotel Club Akumal ran US$624–$1779[5] in 1995.

Rascals' approach is unique in the travel industry, as they personally select the resorts with which they work. "We try to work with small properties so our groups are pampered

Exhibit 2.4 Rascals in Paradise 1995 Pricing Guide:* Rascals Special Family Weeks

Destination	Duration	Price	Notes
BAHAMAS			
South Ocean Beach	7 nights	$3120–$3970	Lunch not included.
Small Hope Bay	7 nights	$3504	Scuba diving included. Local host only.
MEXICO			
Hotel Buena Vista	7 nights	$2150–$2470	
Hotel Club Akumal	7 nights	$2080–$3100	Lunch and airport transfer not included.

*Prices are based on a family of four with two adults and two children aged 2–11. All packages include the following (except as noted): Accommodations, Rascals escort, meals, babysitter, children's activities, airport transfers, taxes & services, and a $2500 cancellation insurance per family booking. Airfares are not included.

Exhibit 2.5 Rascals in Paradise 1995 Pricing Guide:** Independent Family Trips

Destination	Duration	Price	Notes
BAHAMAS			
South Ocean Beach	7 nights	$1355–$1771	
Small Hope Bay	7 nights	$2860–$3560	All meals, bar service, babysitter, and diving included.
Hope Town Harbour Lodge	7 nights	$962–$1121	
Treasure Cay	7 nights	$875–$1750	
Stella Maris, Long Island	7 nights	$1547–$2597	
MEXICO			
Hotel Buena Vista	7 nights	$1232–$1548	All meals included.
Hotel Club Akumal	7 nights	$624–$1779	
Hotel Presidente	7 nights	$1120–$1656	
La Concha	7 nights	$655–$963	
Plaza Las Glorias	7 nights	$632–$1017	

**Prices are based on a family of four with two adults and two children aged 2–11. Rates are per week (7 nights) and include accommodations and applicable taxes. These rates are to be used as a guide only. Each booking is quoted separately and will be dependent on season, type of accommodation, ages, number of children, and meal and activity inclusions. All prices are subject to change. Some variations apply. Airfares are not included.

and looked after," says Detchemendy. "The owners are often parents and their kids are sometimes on the property. They understand the characteristics of kids." Typically, Detchemendy and Baratta visit each destination, often working with the government tourist board in identifying potential properties. If the physical structure is already in place, it is easy to add the resort to the Rascals booking list. If modifications are needed, the two sit down with the management and outline what needs to be in place so the resort can be part of the Rascals program.

Rascals evaluates resorts on several factors: (1) is the property friendly toward children and does it want them?; (2) how does the property rate in terms of safety?; (3) what are the facilities and is there a separate room to be used as a Rascals Room?; (4) does the property provide babysitting and child care by individuals who are screened and locally known? A successful example of this approach is Hotel Club Akumal in Akumal, Mexico. Detchemendy and Baratta helped the resort expand its market reach by building a family-oriented resort and being part of the Rascals program. Baratta explained "In that case, we were looking for a place close to home, with a multi-level range of accommodations that offered something other than a beach, that was family-friendly, and not in Cancun. We found Hotel Club Akumal, but they didn't have many elements in place, so we had to work with them. We established a meal plan, an all-inclusive product and designated activities for kids. We went into the kitchen and created a children's menu and we asked them to install a little kids' playground that's shaded." The resort became one of their most popular family destinations.

Rascals offers two types of services to resort operators interested in creating family vacations. One is a consulting service. For a modest daily fee plus expenses, Baratta or Detchemendy, or both, conduct an on-site assessment of the resort. This usually takes one or two days. They will provide a written report to the resort regarding needed additions or modifications to the resort to make it safe and attractive for family vacations. Possible physical changes might include: the addition of a Rascals room, child-safe play equipment, and modifications to existing buildings and structures, such as rooms, railings, and docks to prevent child injuries. Rascals always tries to use existing equipment or equipment available nearby. Other non-structural changes include: the addition of educational sessions, play-times, and other structured times for entertaining children while their parents are diving. The report also includes an implementation proposal. Then after implementation, the resort could decide whether or not to list with the Rascals for bookings.

Under the second option, Rascals provides the consulting service at no charge to the resort. However, they ask that any requests for family bookings be referred back to Rascals. Rascals then also lists and actively promotes the resort through its brochures and referrals. For resorts using the Rascals booking option, Rascals provides premiums such as hats and T-shirts, in addition to the escorted activities. This attention to the family was what differentiated a Rascals resort from other resorts. Generally, companies who promise packages receive net rates from the resorts which are 20–30 percent lower than "rack" rates. Rascals, in turn, promotes these special packages to the travel industry in general and pays a portion of their earnings out in commissions to other travel agencies.

Rascals tries to work with its resorts to provide packaged and prepaid vacations. This approach creates a win-win situation for the resort managers and the vacationer. A package, or all-inclusive vacation, is a cruise-ship approach. It allows the inclusion of many activities in the package. For example, such a package might include seven nights' lodging, all meals, baby-sitting, children's activities, and scuba diving. This approach allows the vacationer to know, up-front, what to expect. Moreover, the cost is included in one set price, so the family will not have to pay for each activity as it came along. The idea is to remove the surprises and make the stay enjoyable. It also allows the resort operator to bundle activities together, providing more options than might otherwise be offered. As a result, the package approach is becoming popular with both resort owners and vacationers.

In its bookings, Rascals requires prepayment of trips. This results in higher revenues for the resort since all activities are paid for in advance. Ordinarily, resorts on their own might only require a two or three night room deposit. The family would pay for other activities or services as they were used and for the rest of the room charge upon leaving. While vacationers might think they have a less expensive trip this way, in fact, pre-paid activities are generally cheaper than a la carte activities. Moreover, a la carte activities potentially yield lower revenues for the resort. Rascals promoted prepaid vacations as a win-win, low stress approach to travel. Rascals has been very successful with the resorts it lists. Fifty percent of their bookings are repeat business, and many inquiries are based on word of mouth referrals. All in all, Rascals provides a link to the family vacation market segment that the resort might not have otherwise. It is common for resorts listed by Rascals to average annual bookings of 90 percent.

CORAL DIVERS RESORT

Coral Divers Resort has been in operation ten years. Annual revenues have grown to $550,000. Profits generally have been in the 2 percent range (see Exhibit 2.6). While not making them rich, the business has provided an adequate income for Greywell and his wife, Margaret, and their two children, ages seven and five. However, business has begun to drop after three years of flat revenues. From talking with other operators, Greywell understood that resorts with strong identities and reputations for quality service are doing well. Greywell thinks that the Coral Divers Resort has not distinguished itself on any particular aspect of diving or as a resort.

The Coral Divers Resort property is located on a deep water channel on the southwest coast of the island of New Providence in the Bahamas. The property occupies three acres and has beach access. There are six cottages on the property, each having a kitchenette, a full bath, a bedroom with two full-size beds, and a living room with two sleeper sofas. Four of the units have recently been renovated with new paint, tile floors, microwave, color TV, and VCR. The two other units range from "adequate" to "comfortable." Greywell tries to use the renovated units primarily for families and couples, while putting groups of single divers in the other units. Also on the property is a six-unit attached motel-type structure (see Exhibit 2.7). Each of these units has two full-size beds, a pull-out sofa, sink, refrigerator, microwave, and TV. The resort has the space and facilities on the property for a kitchen and dining room, but the space has not been used. However, there is a small family-run restaurant and bar within walking distance.

Greywell has three boats, which can carry from eight to twenty passengers each. Two are forty-foot fiberglass V-hull boats powered by a single diesel inboard with a cruising speed of 18 knots and protected cabin with dry storage space. The third is a thirty-five-

Exhibit 2.6   Coral Divers Resort

	Income Statement (US$) as of June 30		
	1994	1993	1992
Revenues			
Diving and lodging packages	523,160	523,670	521,820
Day diving	14,680	15,360	14,980
Certifications	6,165	7,240	7,120
Lodging	2,380	1,600	1,200
Miscellaneous	2,534	1,645	1,237
Total Revenues	548,919	549,515	546,357
Expenses			
Advertising and promotional	15,708	15,240	13,648
Boats, maintenance and fuel	29,565	31,024	29,234
Depreciation and amortization	126,851	129,752	103,759
Dues and fees	3,746	4,024	3,849
Duties and taxes	9,574	11,458	17,231
Goods purchased for resale	931	1,584	5,429
Insurance	36,260	34,890	32,780
Interest and bank charges	2,376	2,697	2,975
Interest on long-term debt	19,690	20,782	21,875
Management salary	31,600	31,600	31,600
Office and supplies	12,275	12,753	11,981
Professional fees	11,427	10,894	10,423
Repairs and maintenance	15,876	12,379	9,487
Salaries and wages	196,386	194,458	191,624
Telephone and fax	7,926	7,846	7,689
Trade shows	4,523	4,679	14,230
Vehicles, maintenance and fuel	12,753	12,064	11,567
Total expenses	537,467	538,124	519,381
Earnings (loss) from operations	11,452	11,391	26,976
Retained earnings, beginning of year	48,385	36,994	3,518
Retained earnings, end of year	59,837	48,385	30,494

Note: Bahama$1 = US$1

foot covered platform boat. Greywell also has facilities for air dispensing, equipment repair, rental and sale, and tank storage.

Coral Divers Resort, affiliated with PADI and NAUI, has a staff of eleven, which includes four scuba diving instructors. Greywell, who works full-time at the resort, is certified as a diving instructor by both PADI and NAUI. The three other diving instructors have various backgrounds. One is a former U.S. Navy SEAL working for Coral Divers as a way to gain resort experience. One is a local Bahamian whom Greywell has known for many years. The third is a Canadian who came to the Bahamas on a winter holiday and never left. There are two boat captains and two mates. Given the size of the operation, the staff is scheduled to provide overall coverage, with all of the staff rarely working at the same time. In addition, there is a housekeeper, a groundskeeper, and a person who minds the office and store. Greywell's wife, Margaret, works at the business on a part-time basis, taking care of

Exhibit 2.6 Coral Divers Resort *(continued)*

	Balance Sheet (US$) as of June 30		
	1994	1993	1992
ASSETS			
Current assets:			
Cash	5,643	2,592	15,592
Accounts receivable	11,603	8,660	20,259
Inventories	5,519	6,861	19,013
Prepaid expenses	11,404	2,854	15,041
Total current assets	34,169	20,967	69,905
Property, plant and equipment	1,131,000	1,131,000	961,000
Less: Accumulated depreciation	506,100	377,400	428,700
Total fixed assets	624,900	753,600	532,300
Total assets	659,069	774,567	602,205
LIABILITIES			
Current liabilities			
Bank loan	16,542	102,272	2,263
Accounts payable and accrued liabilities	16,891	47,236	15,041
Mortgage payable	25,203	25,985	25,892
Current portion of long-term liabilities	32,856	31,586	34,001
Total current liabilities	91,492	207,079	77,197
Long-term exclusive of current portion	462,861	476,224	449,635
Total liabilities	554,353	683,303	526,832
SHAREHOLDERS' EQUITY			
Share capital	44,879	44,879	44,879
Retained earnings	59,837	48,385	30,494
Total shareholders' equity	104,716	93,264	75,373
Total liabilities and shareholders' equity	659,069	776,567	602,205

administrative activities such as accounting and payroll. The rest of her time is spent looking after their two children and their home.

Greywell's typical diving day at Coral Divers begins around 7:30 a.m. He opens the office and reviews the activities list for the day. If there are any divers that need to be picked up at the resorts in Nassau or elsewhere on the island, the van driver needs to leave by 7:30 a.m. to be back for the 9 a.m. departure. Most resort guests began to gather around the office and dock about 8:30. By 8:45, the day's captain and mate begin loading the diving gear for the passengers.

The boat leaves the Coral Divers' dock at 9 a.m. Morning dives are usually "two tank dives," that is, two dives utilizing one tank of air each. The trip to the first dive site takes about twenty to thirty minutes. Once there, the captain explains the dive, the special attractions of the dive, and tells everyone when they are expected back on board. Most dives last about forty-five minutes. A divemaster always accompanies the divers on the trip down. The divemaster's role is generally to supervise the dive. The divemaster is responsible for the safety and conduct of the divers while they are under water.

Exhibit 2.7 Coral Divers Resort 1995 Pricing Guide†

		Family Dive Vacations	
Destination	Duration	Price	Notes
BAHAMAS			
Coral Divers Resort	7 nights	$1355–$1455	Standard accommodations, continental breakfast, and daily two tank dive included.
Coral Divers Resort	7 nights	$1800–$1950	Deluxe accommodations, continental breakfast, and daily two tank dive included.

†Prices are based on family of four with two adults and two children aged 2–11. Rates are per week (7 nights) and include accommodations and applicable taxes. Rates will be dependent on season, type of accommodation, ages, and number of children. All prices are subject to change. Airfares are not included.

		Non-Family Dive Vacations†	
Destination	Duration	Price	Notes
BAHAMAS			
Coral Divers Resort	7 nights	$600–$700	Standard accommodations, continental breakfast, and daily two tank dive included.
Coral Divers Resort	7 nights	$800–$900	Deluxe accommodations, continental breakfast, and daily two tank dive included.

†Prices are single prices based on double occupancy. Rates are per week (7 nights) and include accommodations and applicable taxes. Rates will be dependent on season and type of accommodation. All prices are subject to change. Airfares are not included.

Once divers are back on board, the boat moves to the next site. Greywell tries to plan dives at sites near each other. For example, the first dive might be a wall dive in sixty feet of water, while the second would be a nearby wreck forty feet down. The second will also last about forty minutes. If things go well, the boat will be back at the resort by noon. This allows for lunch and sufficient surface time for divers who might be going back out in the afternoon. Two morning dives are part of the resort package. Whether the boat goes out in the afternoon depends on whether enough non-resort guest divers have contracted for afternoon dives. If they have, Greywell is happy to let resort guests ride and dive free of charge. If there are not enough outside paying divers, there are no afternoon dive trips, and the guests are on their own to swim at the beach, go sightseeing, or just relax.

GREYWELL'S OPTIONS

Greywell's bookings run 90 percent of capacity during the high season (December through May) and 50 percent during the low season (June through November). Ideally, he wants to increase the number of bookings for the resort and dive businesses during both seasons. Adding additional diving attractions could increase both resort and dive revenues. Focusing on family vacations could increase revenues since families would probably increase the number of paying guests per room. Breakeven costs were calculated based on two adults sharing a room. Children provide an additional revenue source since the cost of the room is covered by the adults and children under 12 incur no diving related costs. However, either strategy, adding adventure diving to his current general offerings or adjusting the focus of the resort to encourage family diving vacations, would require some changes and cost money. The question became whether the changes would increase revenue enough to justify the costs and effort involved.

Emphasizing family diving vacations would probably require some changes to the physical property of the resort. Four of the cottages have already been renovated. The other two also would need to be upgraded. This would run $10,000 to $20,000 each depending on the amenities added. The Bahamas have duties up to 50 percent which causes renovation costs involving imported goods to be expensive. The attached motel-type units also would need to be spruced up at some point. Greywell has the space and facilities for a kitchen and dining area, but has not done anything with it. The Rascals in Paradise people have offered to help set up a children's menu. He could hire a chef or cook and do it himself or offer the concession to the nearby restaurant or someone else. He would also need to build a play structure for children. There is an open area with shade trees between the office and the cottages that would be ideal for a play area. Rascals provides the teacher/escort for the family vacation groups. It would be fairly easy to find babysitters for the children as needed. The people, particularly on this part of the island, are very family-oriented and would welcome the opportunity for additional income. From asking around, it seems that $5 per hour is the going rate for a sitter. Toys and other play items could be added gradually. The Rascals people have said that, once the program is in place, he could expect bookings to run 90 percent capacity annually from new and return bookings. While the package prices are competitive, the attraction is in group bookings and the prospect of a returning client base.

Adding adventure diving would be a relatively easy thing to do. Shark Wall and Shark Buoy are less than an hour away by boat. Both of these sites offered sharks that were already accustomed to being fed. The cost of shark food is $10 per dive. None of Greywell's current staff are particularly excited about the prospect of adding shark feeding to his or her job description. But these staff members could be relatively easily replaced. Greywell could probably find an experienced divemaster who would be willing to lead the shark dives. He would also have to purchase a special chain mail suit for the feeder at a cost of about $10,000. While there are few accidents during the feeds, Greywell would rather be safe than sorry. His current boats, especially the forty footers, are adequate for transporting divers to the sites. The other shark dive operators might not be happy about having him at the sites, but there was little they could do about it. Shark divers are charged a premium fee. For example, a shark dive costs $100 for a two tank dive, compared to $25 to $75 for a normal two tank dive. Greywell figures that he could add shark dives to the schedule on Wednesdays and Saturdays without taking away from regular business. He needs a minimum of four divers on a trip at regular rates to cover the cost of taking out the boat. Ten or twelve divers is ideal. Greywell can usually count on at least eight divers for a normal dive, but he does not know how much additional new and return business he can expect from shark diving.

A third option is for Greywell to try to improve his current operations and not add any new diving attractions. This would require him to be much more cost efficient in his operations. Actions such as strictly adhering to the minimum required number of divers per boat policy, along with staff reductions might improve the bottom line by 5 to 10 percent. He would need to be very attentive to materials ordering, fuel costs, and worker productivity in order to realize any gains with this approach. However, he is concerned that by continuing as he has, Coral Divers Resort would not be distinguished as unique from other resorts in the Bahamas. He does not know what would be the long term implications of this approach.

As Greywell reached the office, he turned to watch the sun sink into the ocean. The water was calm. He could smell the food his wife was cooking. He had a few things yet to finish in the office in preparation for the guests arriving tomorrow, and the question of what to do about the business lingered in his mind.

NOTES

1. Information on certifying agencies is drawn from materials published by the various organizations.
2. This section draws from results of surveys conducted by Scuba diving organizations and publications for the years 1991–1993.
3. Based on information drawn from *The Islands of the Bahamas: 1994 Dive Guide,* published by the Bahamas Ministry of Tourism, Commonwealth of the Bahamas, in conjuction with The Bahama Diving Association.
4. Lunch and airport transfer are not included. Prices reflect seasonal fluctuations and are subject to change. Airfares are not included.
5. Based on a family of four with two adults and two children age 2–11. Rates are to be used as a guide only. Each booking is quoted separately and will be dependent on season, type of accommodation, ages and number of children, meal and activity inclusions. All prices are subject to change. Some variations apply. Airfares are not included.

Exhibit 2.8   A Canadian Vacation Comparison: Diving in Nassau vs. Skiing in Whistler/Banff

Nassau – 7 Nights*	January 5–11 (CAN$)			February 16–22 (CAN$)		
	Dbl/Person	Child	Family (3)	Dbl/Person	Child	Family (3)
Alba Tours – British Colonial	1077	667	2821	1217	717	3151
Alba Tours – Radisson Cable Beach	1237	667	3141	1367	717	3451
Alba Tours – Nassau Beach	1137	667	2941	1367	717	3451
Cdn Holidays – Radisson Cable Beach	1247	707	3201	1397	707	3501
Cdn Holidays – Paradise – Paradise	1177	707	3061	1297	707	3301
Cdn Holidays – Atlantis/Paradise Island	1377	707	3461	1687	707	4081
Sunquest – Crystal Palace	1227	727	3181	1477	727	3681
Air Canada – British Colonial Beach	1167	737	3071	1287	737	3311
Air Canada – Radisson Cable Beach	919	737	2575	1437	737	3611
Air Canada – Carnival's Crystal Palace	1277	737	3291	1657	737	4051
Air Canada – Holiday Inn Pirate's Cove	1287	737	3311	1477	737	3691
Air Canada – Comfort Suites	1287	737	3311	1487	737	3711
Average cost	$1,201.33	$711.17	$3,113.83	$1,429.50	$723.67	$3,582.67

*includes quotes for select hotels only
*includes transportation and accommodations (some taxes may be additional) and estimated cost for five two tank dives (CAN337.50)

Exhibit 2.8   A Canadian Vacation Comparison: Diving in Nassau vs. Skiing in Whistler/Banff
(continued)

Ski Vacation – 7 Nights*	January 5–11 (CAN$)			February 16–22 (CAN$)		
	Dbl/Person	Child	Family (3)	Dbl/Person	Child	Family (3)
Air Canada – Whistler – Crystal Lodge	1355	555	3265	1475	555	3505
Air Canada – Whistler – Delta	1553	555	3661	1611	555	3777
Air Canada – Whistler – Chateau Whistler	1645	555	3845	1739	555	4033
Air Canada – Whistler – Village Inns	1243	555	3041	1515	555	3585
Air Canada – Whistler – Timberline Lodge	1315	555	3185	1619	555	3585
Air Canada – Banff Springs Hotel	1221	469	2911	1403	469	3275
Air Canada – Banff – The Inns of Banff	1079	469	2627	1209	469	2887
Air Canada – The Rocky Mountain	1253	469	2975	1327	469	3123
Air Canada – Banff – Caribou Lodge	1065	469	2599	1167	469	2803
Air Canada – Banff – Voyager Inn	1019	469	2507	1085	469	2639
Cdn Holidays – Whistler – Westbrook	1310	546	3166	1439	546	3424
Cdn Holidays – Whistler – Listel Hotel	1077	546	2700	1269	546	3084
Cdn Holidays – Whistler – Delta	1350	658	3358	1367	658	3392
Cdn Holidays – Whistler – Mountainside	1166	1166	3498	1172	1172	3516
Cdn Holidays – Whistler – Blackcomb	1269	546	3084	1434	546	3414
Cdn Holidays – Banff – Swiss Village	757	573	2087	824	573	2221
Cdn Holidays – Caribou Lodge	817	573	2207	858	573	2289
Cdn Holidays – Banff – Charlton's	825	454	2104	897	454	2248
Cdn Holidays – Banff – Douglas Fir	936	573	2445	925	573	2423
Cdn Holidays – Banff – Banff Springs Hotel	957	573	2487	1063	573	2699
Average	$1,161	$566	$2,888	$1,270	$567	$3,107

*includes quotes for select hotels only
*includes transportation, accommodations and lift passes; some taxes may be additional
*Air Canada Vacations include 4 lift passes/person; Cdn holidays includes 5 lift passes/person
*do not include airfare

Exhibit 2.9 A US Vacation Comparison: Diving in The Caymans/Cozumel vs. Skiing in Vail/
Breckenridge/Winter Park

7 Nights	January 5–11 (US$)			April 16–22 (US$)		
	Dbl/Person	Child	Family (3)	Dbl/Person	Child	Family (3)
Cayman Islands						
7 Mile Beach Resort	1099	free	1998	949	free	1698
Seaview Hotel	899	free	1628	799	free	1428
Hyatt Regency	1499	free	2856	1299	free	2198
Radisson	1299	free	2398	1149	free	1998
Cozumel						
Casa del Mar	899	free	1648	799	free	1248
Suites Colonia	799	free	1538	719	free	1278
Average cost	$933	free	$2,011	$952	free	$1,641

*includes quotes for select hotels only

Exhibit 2.9 A US Vacation Comparison: Diving in The Caymans/Cozumel vs. Skiing in Vail/
Breckenridge/Winter Park *(continued)*

Ski Vacation – 7 Nights*	January 5–11 (US$)			February 16–22 (US$)		
	1 to a Room	2 to a Room	3 to a Room	1 to a Room	2 to a Room	3 to a Room
Vail						
United Vacations – Evergreen Lodge	967	589	522	1935	1109	890
United Vacations – Holiday Inn	1023	617	512	1753	1018	804
United Vacations – Lion Square Lodge	1156	684	571	1858	1071	853
United Vacations – Lodge at Vail	2766	1489	1215	1928	1106	890
United Vacations – Lodge Tower	1191	701	596	1928	1106	890
United Vacations – Roost Lodge	694	463	391	1137	710	587
Mountain Vacations – Evergreen Lodge	1050	1050	1050	1283	1283	1283
Mountain Vacations – Beaver Creek	1015	1015	1015	1304	1304	1304
Breckenridge						
United Vacations – Breckenridge Hilton	607	397	327	1028	626	492
United Vacations – The Village Hotel	831	509	402	1343	783	597
United Vacations – Fireside Inn	845	516	465	1056	640	545
Mountain Vacations – Beaver Run Resort	852	852	852	965	965	965
Mountain Vacations – Lodge at Breckenridge	768	768	768	839	839	839
Winter Park						
Mountain Vacations – Timber Run	724	724	724	801	801	801
Mountain Vacations – Vintage Resort	709	709	709	857	857	857
United Vacations – Beaver Village Hotel	420	298	(n/a)	655	445	(n/a)
United Vacations – Raintree Inn	798	522	430	998	652	536
United Vacations – Inn at Silvercreek	525	298	(n/a)	830	533	(n/a)
Average	$945	$678	$659	$1,250	$880	$821

*includes quotes for select hotels only
*includes lodging and lift passes; some taxes may be additional
*Mountain vacations include rental cars
*does not include airfare

3

Wal*Mart Stores, Inc.

This case was prepared by Sharon Foley under the direction of Stephen P. Bradley as the basis for class discussion rather than to illustrate either effective or ineffective handling of an administrative situation. Reprinted by permission of the Harvard Business School.

Copyright © 1994 by the President and Fellows of Harvard College. Harvard Business School case 794-024.

In Forbes magazine's annual ranking of the richest Americans, the heirs of Sam Walton held spots five through nine in 1993 with $4.5 billion each. Sam Walton, the founder of Wal*Mart Stores, Inc., who died in April 1992, had left his fortune to his wife and four children. Wal*Mart was a phenomenal success with a twenty-year average return on equity of 33 percent, and compound average sales growth of 35 percent. At the end of 1993, Wal*Mart had a market value of $57.5 billion, and its sales per square foot were nearly $300, compared to the industry average of $210. It was widely believed that Wal*Mart had revolutionized many aspects of retailing, and it was well known for its heavy investment in information technology.

David Glass and Don Soderquist faced the challenge of following in Sam Walton's footsteps. Glass and Soderquist, CEO and COO, had been running the company since February 1988, when Walton, retaining the chairmanship, turned the job of CEO over to Glass. Their record spoke for itself – the company went from sales of $16 billion in 1987 to $67 billion in 1993, with earnings nearly quadrupling from $628 million to $2.3 billion. At the beginning of 1994, the company operated 1,953 Wal*Mart stores (including 68 supercenters), 419 warehouse clubs (Sam's Clubs), 81 warehouse outlets (Bud's), and four hypermarkets. During 1994, Wal*Mart planned to open 110 new Wal*Mart stores, including five supercenters, and twenty Sam's Clubs, and to expand or relocate approximately seventy of the older Wal*Mart stores (65 of which would be made into supercenters), and five Sam's Clubs. Sales were forecast to reach $84 billion in 1994, and capital expenditures were expected to total $3.2 billion. Exhibit 3.1 summarizes Wal*Mart's financial performance 1984-1993. Exhibit 3.2 maps Wal*Mart's store network.

The main issue Glass and Soderquist faced was how to sustain the company's phenomenal performance. Headlines in the press had begun to express some doubt: "Growth King Running Into Roadblocks," "Can Wal*Mart Keep Growing at Breakneck Speed?" and "Wal*Mart's Uneasy Throne." In April 1993, the company confirmed in a meeting with analysts that 1993 growth in comparable store sales would be in the 7 to 8 percent range, the first time it had fallen under 10 percent since 1985. Sellers lined up so quickly that the New York Stock Exchange temporarily halted trading in the stock. From early March through the end of April 1993, the stock price fell 22 percent to 26 5/8, destroying nearly $17 billion in market value. With supercenters and international expansion targeted as the prime growth vehicles, Glass and Soderquist had their work cut out for them.

Exhibit 3.1 Wal*Mart Stores, Inc., Financial Summary 1983 to 1993 (US$ Millions)

	1983	1984	1985	1986	1987	1988	1989	1990	1991	1992	1993
Operating Results											
Net Sales	4,667	6,401	8,451	11,909	15,959	20,649	25,811	32,602	43,887	55,464	67,345
Sam's Club	37	221	778	1,678	2,711	3,829	4,841	6,579	9,430	12,339	14,749
McLane	–	–	–	–	–	–	337	2,513	2,911	3,977	–
License Fees and Other Income	36	52	55	85	105	137	175	262	403	501	641
Cost of Goods Sold	3,418	4,722	6,381	9,053	12,282	16,057	20,070	25,500	34,786	44,175	53,444
Operating, SG&A Expenses	893	1,181	1,485	2,008	2,599	3,288	4,070	5,152	6,664	8,321	10,333
Interest Cost	35	48	57	87	114	136	138	169	266	323	517
Taxes	161	231	276	396	441	488	832	752	945	1,172	1,358
Net Income[a]	196	271	327	450	628	837	1,076	1,291	1,608	1,995	2,333
Financial Position											
Current Assets	1,006	1,303	1,764	2,353	2,905	3,831	4,713	6,415	8,575	10,196	12,115
Net Property P&E & Capital Leases	628	870	1,303	1,676	2,145	2,662	3,430	4,712	6,434	9,793	13,175
Current Liabilities	503	689	993	1,340	1,744	2,066	2,645	3,990	5,004	6,754	7,406
Long-term Debt	41	41	181	179	186	184	185	740	1,722	3,073	6,156
Long-term Oblig. Under Capital Leases	340	450	595	764	867	1,009	1,087	1,159	1,556	1,772	1,804
Shareholders' Equity	738	985	1,278	1,690	2,257	3,008	3,966	5,366	6,990	8,759	10,752
Share Information ($)											
Net Income Per Share	.09	.12	.15	.20	.28	.37	.48	.57	.70	.87	1.02
Dividends Per Share	.01	.01	.02	.02	.03	.04	.06	.07	.09	.11	.13
Book Value Per Share	.33	.44	.57	.75	1.00	1.33	1.75	2.35	3.04	3.81	4.68
End of Year Stock Price	2.25	2.38	4.00	5.88	6.5	7.66	11.25	15.12	29.5	32.0	25.0
Financial Ratios[b] (%)											
Return on Assets	16.5	16.4	14.8	14.5	15.5	16.3	16.9	15.7	14.1	12.9	11.3
Return on Shareholders' Equity	40.2	36.7	33.3	35.2	37.1	37.1	35.8	32.6	30.0	28.5	26.6
Number of Stores											
Discount Stores	642	745	859	980	1,114	1,259	1,399	1,568	1,714	1,850	1,953
Sam's Wholesale Clubs	3	11	23	49	64	105	123	148	208	256	419
Supercenters	–	–	–	–	–	–	3	5	6	30	88
Number of Associates (000)	62	81	104	141	183	223	271	328	371	434	528

Source: Wal*Mart annual reports, Value line, Bloomberg, Salomon Bros.
[a]Columns may not total due to rounding.
[b]On beginning of year balances.

Exhibit 3.2 Store and Distribution Center Locations, January 1994

#W Denotes the number of Wal*Mart
   discount stores in that state (total 1,953)

#S Denotes the number of Sam's Clubs in
   that state (total 419)

#SU Denotes the number of Supercenters in
   that state (total 68)

▲ Distribution Center

◆ McLane Distribution Center

✪ Wal*Mart Home Office and 3 Wal*Mart
   Distribution Centers

Source: Wal*Mart Annual Report.

DISCOUNT RETAILING

Discount stores emerged in the United States in the mid-1950s on the heels of supermarkets, which sold food at unprecedentedly low margins. Discount stores extended this approach to general merchandise by charging gross margins 10 to 15 percent lower than those of conventional department stores. To compensate, discount stores cut costs to the bone: fixtures were distinctly unluxurious, in-store selling was limited, and ancillary services, such as delivery and credit, were scarce.

The discounters' timing was just right, as consumers had become increasingly better informed since World War II. Supermarkets had educated them about self-service, many categories of general merchandise had matured, and TV had intensified advertising by manufacturers. Government standards had also bolstered consumers' self-confidence, and many were ready to try cheaper, self-service retailers, except for products that were big-ticket items, technologically complex, or "psychologically significant."

Discount retailing burgeoned as a result, and many players entered the industry at the local, regional, or national levels. Sales grew at a compound annual rate of 25 percent from $2 billion in 1960 to $19 billion in 1970. During the 1970s, the industry continued to grow at an annual rate of 9 percent, with the number of new stores increasing 5 percent annually; during the 1980s, it grew at a rate of 7 percent, but the number of stores increased by only 1 percent; and during the 1990s, it grew 11.2 percent, with the number of stores increasing by nearly 2 percent. This trend toward fewer new store openings was attributed to a more cautious approach to expansion by discounters, who placed increasing emphasis on the refurbishment of existing stores. In 1993, discount industry sales were $124 billion, and analysts predicted that they would increase about 5 percent annually over the next five years.

Of the top ten discounters operating in 1962 – the year Wal*Mart opened for business – not one remained in 1993. Several large discount chains, such as King's, Korvette's, Mammoth Mart, W.T. Grant, Two Guys, Woolco, and Zayre, failed over the years or were acquired by survivors. As a result, the industry became more concentrated: whereas in 1986 the top five discounters had accounted for 62 percent of industry sales, in 1993 they accounted for 71 percent, and discount store companies that operated fifty or more stores accounted for 82 percent. Exhibit 3.3 shows the top discounters in 1993.

WAL*MART'S DISCOUNT STORES

History of Growth

Providing value was a part of the Wal*Mart culture from the time Sam Walton opened his first Ben Franklin franchise store in 1945. During the 1950s, the number of Walton-owned Ben Franklin franchises increased to fifteen. In 1962, after his idea for opening stores in small towns was turned down by the Ben Franklin organization, Sam and his brother Bud opened the first "Wal*Mart Discount City Store," with Sam putting up 95 percent of the dollars himself.[1] For years, while he was building Wal*Marts, Walton continued to run his Ben Franklin stores, gradually phasing them out by 1976. When Wal*Mart was incorporated on October 31, 1969, there were eighteen Wal*Mart stores and fifteen Ben Franklins.

By 1970, Walton had steadily expanded his chain to thirty discount stores in rural Arkansas, Missouri, and Oklahoma. However, with continued rapid growth in the rural

Exhibit 3.3 Top 15 Discount Department Stores by 1993 Sales (US$ Millions)

Chain		Sales			Number of Stores			Average Store Size
		1993	1992	% Change	1/94	1/93	1/92	(000 Sq. Ft.)
Wal*Mart[a]	AR	44,900	38,200	17.5	1,953	1,850	1,720	84
Kmart	MI	26,449	25,013	5.7	2,323	2,281	2,249	110
Target	MN	11,743	10,393	13.0	554	506	483	110
Caldor	CT	2,414	2,128	13.5	150	136	128	99
Ames[c]	CT	2,228	2,316	(3.8)	308	309	371	50
Bradlees	MA	1,880	1,831	2.7	126	127	127	71
Venture	MO	1,863	1,718	8.4	104	93	84	100
Hills[d]	MA	1,766	1,750	0.9	151	154	154	67
ShopKo	WI	1,739	1,683	3.3	117	111	109	74
Family Dollar	NC	1,297	1,159	12.0	2,105	1,920	1,759	7
Rose's[e]	NC	1,246	1,404	(11.3)	172	217	217	43
Dollar General	TN	1,133	921	23.0	1,800	1,617	1,522	6
Value City[f]	OH	842	798	5.5	75	73	53	60
Jamesway[g]	NJ	722	856	(15.6)	94	108	122	59
Pamida	NE	659	625	5.4	173	178	178	27

Source: Discount Store News, July 4, 1994, Value Line.
[a]Sales are for discount stores and Bud's, but not supercenters.
[b]Sales are for US Kmart stores only.
[c]Acquired Zayre in 1989, filed for Chapter 11 protection in 1990, and emerged from Chapter 11 in 1992.
[d]Emerged from Chapter 11 in 10/93.
[e]In Chapter 11.
[f]Fiscal year ended 7/31/93.
[g]In Chapter 11.

south and midwest, the cost of goods sold – almost three-quarters of discounting revenues – rankled. As Walton put it, "Here we were in the boondocks, so we didn't have distributors falling over themselves to serve us like competitors in larger towns. Our only alternative was to build our own warehouse so we could buy in volume at attractive prices and store the merchandise."[2] Since warehouses cost $5 million or more each, Walton took the company public in 1972 and raised $3.3 million.

There were two key aspects to Walton's plan for growing Wal*Mart. The first was locating stores in isolated rural areas and small towns, usually with populations of 5,000 to 25,000. He put it this way: "Our key strategy was to put good-sized stores into little one-horse towns which everybody else was ignoring."[3] Walton was convinced that discounting could work in small towns: "If we offered prices as good or better than stores in cities that were four hours away by car," he said, "people would shop at home."[4] The second element of Walton's plan was the pattern of expansion. As David Glass explained, "We are always pushing from the inside out. We never jump and then backfill."[5]

In the mid-1980s, about one-third of Wal*Mart stores were located in areas that were not served by any of its competitors. However, the company's geographic growth resulted in increased competition with other major retailers. By 1993, 55 percent of Wal*Mart stores faced direct competition from Kmart stores, and 23 percent from Target, whereas 82 percent of Kmart stores and 85 percent of Target stores faced competition from Wal*Mart.[6] Wal*Mart penetrated the West Coast and northeastern states, and by early 1994, operated in 47 states, with stores planned for Vermont, Hawaii, and Alaska. Exhibit 3.4 compares Wal*Mart's performance with that of its competitors.

Sam's Legacy

When Sam Walton died in April of 1992 at the age of seventy-four after a long fight with cancer, his memorial service was broadcast to every store over the company's satellite system. Walton had a philosophy which drove everything in the business: he believed in the value of the dollar and was obsessed with keeping prices below everybody else's. On buying trips, his rule of thumb was that trip expenses should not exceed 1 percent of the purchases, which meant sharing hotel rooms and walking instead of taking taxis.

Walton instilled in his employees (called associates) the idea that Wal*Mart had its own way of doing things, and tried to make life at the company unpredictable, interesting, and fun. He even danced the hula on Wall Street in a grass skirt after losing a bet to David Glass, who had predicted that the company's pretax profit would be more than 8 percent in 1983. Walton said that, "Most folks probably thought we just had a wacky chairman who was pulling a pretty primitive publicity stunt. What they didn't realize is that this sort of stuff goes on all the time at Wal*Mart."[7]

Walton spent as much time as possible in his own stores and checking out the competition. He was known to count the number of cars in Kmart and Target parking lots, and tape-

Exhibit 3.4 Overall Corporate Performance of Discounters, Ranked by ROE (%)

Chain	Five Year Average[a]			1993 or Latest 12 Months		
	Return on Equity[b]	Sales Growth[c]	Earnings Per Share Growth	Return on Sales	Return on Capital[d]	Debt to Capital Ratio[e]
Wal*Mart	31.2	28.2	25.0	3.5	17.3	40.3
Venture	28.7	6.8	15.4	2.5	16.7	31.1
Family Dollar	21.5	14.4	23.6	4.9	22.5	0.0
ShopKo	18.7	9.7	12.1	2.5	9.5	45.2
Dollar General	16.1	8.7	37.3	4.1	21.9	2.6
Dayton Hudson[f]	15.8	10.5	12.1	1.8	8.1	56.9
Kmart	13.8	8.1	NM	1.9	8.5	39.5

NM: Not meaningful, i.e. the company lost money in more than one year.
[a]Five-year growth rates are based on the latest fiscal year-end results.
[b]ROE = EPS/shareholders' equity per share at the start of the fiscal year. The five-year average is calculated using a modified sum-of-the-years method which gives greater importance to recent results.
[c]Sales and earnings growth rates are calculated using the least squares method which adjusts for sharp fluctuations and closely reflects the average rate of growth.
[d]Forbes defines a firm's total capitalization as long-term debt, common and preferred equity, deferred taxes, investment tax credits and minority interest in consolidated subsidiaries.
[e]Debt to total capital is calculated by dividing long-term debt, including capitalized leases, by total capitalization.
[f]Parent of Target stores.
Source: "Annual Report on American Industry," Forbes Magazine, January 3, 1994.

measure shelf space and note sale prices at Ames. Walton knew his competitors intimately and copied their best ideas. He got to know Sol Price, who created Price Club, and then redid the concept as Sam's Club.

To Walton, the most important ingredient in Wal*Mart's success was the way it treated its associates. He believed that if you wanted the people in the stores to take care of the customers, you had to make sure that you were taking care of the people in the stores. There was one aspect of the Wal*Mart culture that bothered Walton from the time Wal*Mart became really successful. "We've had lots and lots of millionaires in our ranks," he said, "and it just drives me crazy when they flaunt it. Every now and then somebody will do something particularly showy, and I don't hesitate to rant and rave about it at the Saturday morning meeting. I don't think that big mansions and flashy cars are what the Wal*Mart culture is supposed to be about – serving the customer."[8]

Walton described his management style as "management by walking and flying around." Others at Wal*Mart described it as "management by wearing you down" and "management by looking over your shoulder." On managing people, Walton said, "You've got to give folks responsibility, you've got to trust them, and then you've got to check up on them." Wal*Mart's partnership with its associates meant sharing the numbers – Walton ran the business as an open book and maintained an open-door policy. Wal*Mart aimed to excel by empowering associates, maintaining technological superiority, and building loyalty among associates, customers, and suppliers.

Merchandising

Wal*Mart merchandise was tailored to individual markets and, in many cases, to individual stores. Information systems made this possible through "traiting," a process which indexed product movements in the store to over a thousand store and market traits. The local store manager, using inventory and sales data, chose which products to display based on customer preferences, and allocated shelf space for a product category according to the demand at his or her store. Wal*Mart's promotional strategy of "everyday-low prices" meant offering customers brand name merchandise for less than department and specialty store prices. Wal*Mart had few promotions. While other major competitors typically ran 50 to 100 advertised circulars annually to build traffic, Wal*Mart offered thirteen major circulars per year. In 1993, Wal*Mart's advertising expense was 1.5 percent of discount store sales, compared to 2.1 percent for direct competitors.[9] In addition, Wal*Mart offered a "satisfaction guaranteed" policy, which meant that merchandise could be returned to any Wal*Mart store with no questions asked.

Wal*Mart was very competitive in terms of prices, and gave its store managers more latitude in setting prices than did "centrally priced" chains such as Caldor and Venture. Store managers priced products to meet local market conditions, in order to maximize sales volume and inventory turnover, while minimizing expenses. A study in the mid-1980s found that when Wal*Mart and Kmart were located next to each other, Wal*Mart's prices were roughly 1 percent lower, and when Wal*Mart, Kmart, and Target were separated by four to six miles, Wal*Mart's average prices were 10.4 percent and 7.6 percent lower, respectively. In remote locations, where Wal*Mart had no direct competition from large discounters, its prices were 6 percent higher than at locations where it was next to a Kmart.

Competitive changes in discount retailing were reflected in Wal*Mart's decision to change its marketing slogan from "Always the low price-Always," (which Wal*Mart had used when building its chain by offering better prices than small-town merchants), to "Always low prices-Always." See Exhibit 3.5 for a pricing study between Wal*Mart, Kmart, and Bradlees in suburban New Jersey. By the early 1990s, there was, typically, a 2 to 4 percent pricing differential between Wal*Mart and its best competitors in most markets: in seven pricing surveys conducted between 1992–1993, Wal*Mart's prices were 2.2 percent below Kmart's on average, and 3 percent below on items priced at all stores. Compared to Target in six surveys, Wal*Mart's prices were 3.7 percent lower on average, and 4.1 percent lower on items priced at all stores. And compared to Venture, the lowest cost regional operator, Wal*Mart's prices were 3.9 percent and 4.7 percent lower, respectively. With other regional competitors, Wal*Mart's price advantage was far greater: 21.4 percent with Caldor on average, and 28.8 percent with Bradlees.[10]

Wal*Mart was known for its national brand strategy, and the majority of its sales consisted of nationally advertised branded products. However, private label apparel made up about 25 percent of apparel sales at Wal*Mart. Wal*Mart gradually introduced several other private label lines in its discount stores, such as Equate in health and beauty care, Ol' Roy in dog food, and Sam's American Choice in food. In 1992, a year after it was introduced, there were about forty items in the line, consisting of such products as cola, tortilla chips, chocolate chip cookies, and salsa. Sam's Choice, which was considered the company's premium-quality line, offered an average 26 percent price advantage over comparable branded products, with the range of the advantage being 9 to 60 percent.[11] The line was also sold in Sam's Clubs (in larger club packs) and in supercenters.

In an effort to replace foreign-sourced goods sold at Wal*Mart stores with American-made ones, Wal*Mart developed its "Buy American" program, and in 1985, invited U.S. manufacturers by letter to participate in it. By 1989, the company estimated it had converted or retained over $1.7 billion in retail purchases that would have been placed or produced offshore, and created or retained over 41,000 jobs for the American work force.

Store Operations

The company leased about 70 percent of Wal*Mart stores and owned the rest. In 1993, Wal*Mart's rental expense was 3 percent of discount store sales, compared to an average 3.3 percent for direct competitors.[12] An average Wal*Mart store, which covered 80,000 square feet, with newer units at about 100,000 square feet, took approximately 120 days to open. Construction costs were about $20 per square foot. Starting in the 1980s, Wal*Mart did not build a discount store at a location where it could not be expanded at a later date. In early 1990, 45 percent of Wal*Mart stores were three years old or less, and only 15 percent were more than 8 years old, compared to 10 percent and 85 percent for Kmart, respectively. Sales per square foot of $300 compared with Target at $209 and Kmart at $147. A Wal*Mart store devoted 10 percent of its square footage to inventory, compared with an industry average of 25 percent. Its operating expenses were 18.1 percent of discount store sales in 1993, versus the industry average of 24.6 percent. See Exhibit 3.6 for the average economics of the discount industry.

The majority of Wal*Mart stores were open from 9 a.m. to 9 p.m. six days a week, and from 12:30 p.m. to 5:30 p.m. on Sundays. Some, including most of the supercenters, were

Exhibit 3.5 Wal*Mart Discount Stores – Comparative Pricing Study, Berlin, New Jersey, January 1993

Items Priced	Size	Prices			Avg. Price	Variance from Avg. Price (%)		
		Wal*Mart	Kmart	Bradlees		Wal*Mart	Kmart	Bradlees
HEALTH AND BEAUTY AIDS								
Crest Toothpaste (Regular)	8.4 oz.	1.24	1.24	2.29	1.59	-0.22	-0.22	0.44
Noxzema Skin Cream	10 oz.	2.68	2.79	3.59	3.02	-0.11	-0.08	0.19
Tampax	24 Ct.	3.46	3.59	4.49	3.85	-0.10	-0.07	0.17
Preparation H	1 oz.	3.59	3.68	3.99	3.75	-0.04	-0.02	0.06
Tylenol Extra Strength	60 tablets	4.64	5.2	4.99	4.94	-0.06	0.05	0.01
Old Spice After Shave	4.75 oz	4.42	4.42	5.19	4.68	-0.05	-0.05	0.11
Oil of Olay Facial Cleanser	2.5 oz.	5.52	5.58	8.49	6.53	-0.15	-0.15	0.30
Pepto-Bismol	8 oz.	3.58	2.64	3.99	3.40	0.05	-0.22	0.17
Vaseline	3.5 oz.	1.54	1.54	1.79	1.62	-0.05	-0.05	0.10
Johnson & Johnson Baby Powder	24 oz.	2.93	2.97	3.99	3.30	-0.11	-0.10	0.21
HOUSEHOLD CHEMICALS & CONSUMABLES								
Lysol Disinfectant	38 oz.	2.45	2.43	3.99	2.96	-0.17	-0.18	0.35
Woolite	18 oz.	3.59	3.39	3.87	3.62	-0.01	-0.06	0.07
Easy-Off Oven Cleaner	16 oz.	2.73	2.69	3.29	2.90	-0.06	-0.07	0.13
Cascade Dishwasher Powder	50 oz.	2.27	2.29	3.29	2.62	-0.13	-0.12	0.26
Fantastik Spray Cleaner	22 oz.	1.97	1.87	2.29	2.04	-0.04	-0.08	0.12
Reynolds Wrap	75 sq. ft.	3.79	3.89	4.59	4.09	-0.07	-0.05	0.12
Glad Trash Bags	50 ct.	5.38	5.58	6.99	5.98	-0.10	-0.07	0.17
HOME HARDLINES								
GE Light Bulbs	60 watt/4 pk	1.34	1.67	2.29	1.77	-0.24	-0.05	0.30
Duracell Batteries	AA 2 pk.	1.44	1.45	2.71	1.87	-0.23	-0.22	0.45
Kodak Gold 200 Film	24 exp.	2.68	3.27	4.29	3.48	-0.17	-0.06	0.23
Presto Salad Shooter		22.59	22.94	34.99	26.84	-0.16	-0.15	0.30
SPORTING GOODS								
Wilson Tennis Balls	3 pk.	2.96	2.38	2.49	2.61	0.13	-0.09	-0.05
Coleman Lantern		17.94	19.97	29.99	22.63	-0.21	-0.12	0.33
AUTOMOTIVE								
Valvoline Motor Oil 1OW30	1 qt.	0.64	0.91	1.49	1.06	-0.22	-0.16	0.38
Champion Spark Plugs	4 regular	3.92	5.12	5.99	5.01	-0.22	0.02	0.20

Exhibit 3.5 Wal*Mart Discount Stores – Comparative Pricing Study, Berlin, New Jersey, January 1993 (continued)

Items Priced	Size	Prices			Avg. Price	Variance from Avg. Price (%)		
		Wal*Mart	Kmart	Bradlees		Wal*Mart	Kmart	Bradlees
PAINT & HARDWARE								
WD40	12 oz.	1.74	1.97	2.99	2.23	-0.22	-0.12	0.34
Rustoleum	12 oz.	2.94	2.94	3.09	2.99	-0.02	-0.02	0.03
Thompson's Water Seal	1 gal.	9.47	9.98	9.99	9.81	-0.03	0.02	0.02
Stanley Power Lock 16' x 3/4"		11.97	9.94	9.99	10.63	0.13	-0.07	-0.06
Black & Decker Drill	.5" drive	43.97	44.96	44.99	44.64	-0.02	0.01	0.01
FOOD								
Planters Peanuts	16 oz.	2.38	2.37	3.69	2.81	-0.15	-0.16	0.31
Oreo Cookies	16 oz.	1.64	1.79	1.99	1.87	-0.02	-0.04	0.06
STATIONERY								
Crayola 64		1.96	2.05	2.15	2.05	-0.05	0.00	0.05
Scotch Tape	22.2 yds.	0.94	0.95	1.19	1.03	-0.08	-0.07	0.16
Average Variance						-9.46%	-8.31%	17.77%
Percent Items Priced Below Average						91.0%	85.0%	6.0%

Source: Solomon Brothers, Inc., January 1993.

Exhibit 3.6   Economics of the Discount Industry, 1993 (% of sales)

	Wal*Mart	Wtd. Avg. of Direct Competitors	Kmart[a]	Target[a]	F.Meyer	Caldor	Bradlees	Venture	ShopKo
Sales ($Mil.)	48,620	18,730[b]	28,039	11,743	2,979	2,414	1,881	1,863	1,737
	100.0	100.00	100.0	100.0	100.0	100.0	100.0	100.0	100.0
COGS	75.1	72.8	72.4	75.3	68.7	71.7	67.6	74.7	71.9
Gross Profit	24.9	27.2	27.6	24.7	31.3	28.3	32.4	25.3	28.1
Op. Expenses	18.1	24.6	25.2	20.7	27.2	24.5	30.1	21.1	24.2
Other income[c]	0.7	1.3	1.4	0.7	0.4	0.2	0.7	0.2	0.7
Op. income	7.5	3.9	3.8	4.8	4.6	4.1	3.0	4.3	4.6

Source: Goldman Sachs, casewriter estimates.
[a]Discount stores and supercenters only.
[b]Weighted by estimated 1993 sales.
[c]Includes license fees.

open twenty-four hours. Customers walking into a Wal*Mart store were met by a "People Greeter," an associate who welcomed them and handed out shopping carts. Sales were primarily on a self-service, cash-and-carry basis. Customers could also use Visa, MasterCard, the Discover card, or a lay-away plan available at each store.

Wal*Marts were generally organized with thirty-six departments offering a wide variety of merchandise, including apparel, shoes, housewares, automotive accessories, garden equipment, sporting goods, toys, cameras, health and beauty aids, pharmaceuticals, and jewelry.

Electronic scanning of Uniform Product Codes (UPC) at the point of sale, which began in Wal*Mart stores in 1983, was installed in nearly all Wal*Mart stores by 1988, two years ahead of Kmart. Store associates used hand-held bar code scanning units to price-mark merchandise. These scanners, which utilized radio frequency technology, communicated with the store's computerized inventory system to ensure accurate pricing and improve efficiency. Many stores used shelf labeling, rather than product price tags. A system to track refunds and check authorizations helped reduce shrinkage – a euphemism for pilferage or shoplifting – by identifying items that were stolen from one Wal*Mart store and submitted for refund at another.

Electronic scanning and the need for improved communications between stores, distribution centers, and the head office in Bentonville, Arkansas, led to the installation of a satellite system in 1983. The satellite allowed sales data to be collected and analyzed daily, and enabled managers to learn immediately what merchandise was moving slowly, and thus avoid overstocking and deep discounting. It was later also used for video transmissions, credit card authorizations, and inventory control. At an individual Wal*Mart store, daily information, such as sales by store and department, labor hours, and inventory losses, could be compared to the results for any time period, for any region, or for the nation. From 1987 to 1993, Wal*Mart spent over $700 million on its satellite communications network, computers, and related equipment.

Table 3.1 Sales by Product Category, 1993 (% of sales)

Category	Wal*Mart	Industry Average[a]
Softgoods (apparel, linens, fabric)	27	35
Hardgoods (hardware, housewares, auto supplies, small appliances)	26	24
Stationery and candy	11	9
Sporting goods and toys	9	9
Health and beauty aids	8	7
Gifts, records, and electronics	8	9
Pharmaceuticals	7	2
Shoes	2	2
Jewelry	2	2
Miscellaneous (pet supplies)	0	2

[a]Column does not total to 100 due to rounding.
Source: Wal*Mart 10K, *Discount Merchandiser*, June 1994.

Distribution

Wal*Mart's two-step hub-and-spoke distribution network started with a Wal*Mart truck bringing the merchandise to a distribution center, where it was sorted for delivery to a

Wal*Mart store usually within forty-eight hours of the original request. The merchandise replenishment process originated at the point of sale, with information transmitted via satellite to Wal*Mart headquarters or to supplier distribution centers. About 80 percent of purchases for Wal*Mart stores were shipped from its own twenty-seven distribution centers – as opposed to 50 percent for Kmart. The balance was delivered directly from suppliers, who stored merchandise for Wal*Mart stores and billed the company when the merchandise left the warehouse. A technique known as "cross-docking" was being introduced to transfer products directly from in-bound vehicles to store-bound vehicles, enabling goods to be delivered continuously to warehouses, repacked, and dispatched to stores often without ever sitting in inventory. By early 1994, roughly 10 percent of Wal*Mart's merchandise was "cross-docked" at four distribution facilities that were equipped for it. In 1993, analysts estimated Wal*Mart's cost of inbound logistics, which was part of cost of goods sold, to be 3.7 percent of discount store sales, compared to 4.8 percent for its direct competitors.[13]

Each store received an average of five full or partial truckloads a week, and because Wal*Mart stores were grouped together, trucks could resupply several on a single trip. Returned merchandise was carried back to the distribution center for consolidation, and since many vendors operated warehouses or factories within Wal*Mart's territory, trucks also picked up new shipments on the return trip. Roughly 2,500 people drove Wal*Mart's fleet of more than 2,000 trucks, which ran 60 percent full on backhauls. A store could select one of four options regarding the frequency and timing of shipments, and more than half selected night deliveries. For stores located within a certain distance of a distribution center, an accelerated delivery plan was also available, which allowed merchandise to be delivered within 24 hours.

A typical distribution center spanned one million square feet, and was operated twenty-four hours a day by a staff of 700 associates. It was highly automated and designed to serve the distribution needs of approximately 150 stores within an average radius of 200 miles. When orders were pulled from stock, a computerized "pick to light" system guided associates to the correct locations. In 1993 Wal*Mart expanded its distribution network to service its growing number of stores by opening million-square-foot distribution centers in Wisconsin, Pennsylvania, Arizona, and Utah.

VENDOR RELATIONSHIPS

Wal*Mart was known as a no-nonsense negotiator. When vendors visited the company's headquarters in Bentonville, they were not shown to buyers' offices, but into one of about forty interviewing rooms equipped with only a table and four chairs. Wal*Mart eliminated manufacturers' representatives from negotiations with suppliers at the beginning of 1992, at an estimated savings of 3 to 4 percent (a matter the reps tried unsuccessfully to take to the Federal Trade Commission). The company made it a practice to call its vendors collect, and centralized its buying at the head office, with no single supplier accounting for more than 2.4 percent of its purchases in 1993. It also restricted sourcing to vendors who limited work weeks to sixty hours, provided safe working conditions, and did not employ child labor.

In Wal*Mart's early days, a powerful supplier, such as Procter and Gamble (P&G), would dictate how much it would sell and at what price. But over time, as Wal*Mart grew, its relationships with some suppliers evolved into partnerships, a key element of which was sharing information electronically to improve performance. P&G was one of the first manufacturers to link up with Wal*Mart by computer, dedicating a team of seventy based in Bentonville to manage its products for Wal*Mart. By 1993, Wal*Mart had become P&G's largest customer, doing about $3 billion in business annually, or about 10 percent of P&G's total revenue.

The installation of electronic data interchange (EDI) enabled an estimated 3,600 vendors, representing about 90 percent of Wal*Mart's dollar volume, to receive orders and interact with Wal*Mart electronically. The program was later expanded to include forecasting, planning, replenishing, and shipping applications. Wal*Mart used electronic invoicing with more than 65 percent of its vendors, and electronic funds transfer with many. By the late '80s, selected key suppliers, including Wrangler and GE, were using vendor-managed inventory systems to replenish stocks in Wal*Mart stores and warehouses. Wal*Mart transmitted sales data to Wrangler daily, which it used to generate orders for various quantities, sizes, and colors of jeans, and to plan deliveries from specific warehouses to specific stores. Similarly, Wal*Mart sent daily reports of warehouse inventory status to GE Lighting, which it used to plan inventory levels, generate purchase orders, and ship exactly what was needed when it was needed. As a result, Wal*Mart and its vendors benefited from reduced inventory costs and increased sales. Beginning in 1990, Wal*Mart's "retail link" also gave more than 2,000 suppliers computer access to point-of-sale data, which they used to analyze the sales trends and inventory positions of their products on a store-by-store basis. In 1993, Wal*Mart's information systems expense was 1.5 percent of discount store sales, compared with 1.3 percent for direct competitors.[14]

Each Wal*Mart department also developed computerized, annual strategic business planning packets for its vendors, sharing with them the department's sales, profitability, and inventory targets, macroeconomic and market trends, and Wal*Mart's overall business focus. The packets also specified Wal*Mart's expectations of them, and solicited their recommendations for improving Wal*Mart's performance as well as their own. The planning packet for one department ran to sixty pages.

However, not all of Wal*Mart's supplier relationships were successful. A case in point was Gitano. Wal*Mart accounted for 26 percent of Gitano's sales of $780 million in 1991, and pushed the company hard to improve its record of greater than 80 percent on-time and defect-free deliveries. Its failure to do so despite great effort resulted in a $90 million loss from restructuring and inventory write-downs in 1992, sending its stock price to $3 per share from $18 within a year.[15]

Human Resource Management

Wal*Mart was recognized as one of the 100 best companies to work for in America. It employed 528,000 full- and part-time staff and was the largest employer after the federal government and General Motors. The company was non-unionized, and 30 percent of its staff worked part-time. Wal*Mart's culture stressed the key role of associates, who were motivated by more responsibility and recognition than their counterparts at other retail chains. Information and ideas were shared: at individual stores, associates knew the store's sales, profits, inventory turns, and markdowns. According to Glass, "There are no superstars at Wal*Mart. We're a company of ordinary people overachieving."[16] Suppliers recognized associates as being totally committed to the company: "Wal*Mart is a lean operation managed by extremely committed people," said an executive at a leading manufacturer. "It's very exciting being anywhere near these people. They live to work for the glory of Wal*Mart. This may sound like B.S., but it's incredible. Our production, distribution, and marketing people who visit Wal*Mart can't believe it."[17]

Training at Wal*Mart was decentralized. Management seminars were offered at the distribution centers rather than at the home office, exposing store managers to the distribution network. And before a store opened, new associates were trained by ten to twelve assistant managers brought in from other stores. In addition, Wal*Mart instituted many programs to involve the associates in the business. In the "Yes We Can Sam" suggestion program, associates suggested ways to simplify, improve, or eliminate work. More than 650 suggestions were implemented in 1993, resulting in an estimated savings of over $85 million. Wal*Mart also began to emphasize the "store within a store" in 1986 in order to support, recognize, and reward associates in the management of their area of merchandise responsibility. Under the program, department managers became store managers of their own "store within a store," and area sales in many instances exceeded $1 million.

Finally, the "shrink incentive plan" provided associates yearly bonuses if their store held shrinkage below the company's goal. Shrinkage cost was estimated to be approximately 1.7 percent of Wal*Mart discount store sales in 1993, compared to an average 2 percent for direct competitors.[18]

Managers and supervisors were compensated on a salaried basis, with incentive compensation based on store profits. Store managers could earn more than $100,000 a year. Assistant managers who earned $20,000 to $30,000 annually were relocated on average every twenty-four months in order to meet the company's growth demands. For instance, an Oklahoman who managed a store in California, moved eight times in ten years with the company.[19] Other store personnel were paid an hourly wage with incentive bonuses awarded on the basis of the company's productivity and profitability. Part-time associates who worked at least twenty-eight hours per week received health benefits.

Profit sharing was available to associates after one year of employment. Based on earnings growth, Wal*Mart contributed a percentage of every eligible associate's wages to his or her profit-sharing account, whose balance the associate could take upon leaving the company either in cash or Wal*Mart stock. The company added $727 million to employee profit-sharing plans since 1988, or 8 percent of net income, 80 percent of which was invested in Wal*Mart stock by a committee of associates. Under profit sharing some employees had made sizable gains. One general office associate's $8,000 grew to $228,000 between 1981 and 1991. An hourly associate who earned the minimum wage of $1.65 an hour when he started in 1968 took $200,000 in profit sharing when he retired in 1989 earning $8.25 an hour. A Wal*Mart truck driver in Bentonville who joined the company in 1972 had $707,000 in profit sharing in 1992.[20] Wal*Mart also offered an associate stock ownership plan for the purchase of its common stock, matching 15 percent of up to $1,800 in annual stock purchases. About 60 percent of Wal*Mart associates participated in the stock purchase plan.

The recent drop in value of Wal*Mart stock was the highest-profile problem facing Glass and Soderquist. "There is a lot of pressure on management to perform," explained Soderquist. "We have a lot of responsibility to our associates. Right now, we think the stock represents a great buying opportunity. All we have to do is work hard, and the stock will take care of itself."[21] During a companywide satellite broadcast aimed at explaining to associates why Wal*Mart stock was down, Soderquist pointed out that most people were not planning to sell their stock the next day, and assured them that the price of the stock would in time reflect the company's performance.

MANAGEMENT

The Wal*Mart management team, with only a few exceptions, consisted of executives in their 40s and 50s who had started working for the company after high school or college. David Glass, president and CEO, was one of the few who started his career outside of Wal*Mart, working for Consumers Markets in Missouri after college. He joined Wal*Mart in 1976 as executive VP of finance and went on to become its chief financial officer. In 1984, Walton had engineered a job switch between Glass, then the CFO, and Jack Shewmaker, the president. Glass was known as an operationally oriented executive and was an important contributor to Wal*Mart's sophisticated distribution system. Don Soderquist, Wal*Mart's chief operating officer since 1987, joined the company in 1980, after leaving his job as president of Ben Franklin Variety Stores in Chicago.

Glass's administrative style, like Walton's, emphasized frugality. "He is one of the tightest men on the face of the earth," said a Wal*Mart executive VP.[22] Glass rented subcompact cars and shared hotel rooms with other Wal*Mart executives when he traveled. At headquarters, he paid a dime for his cup of coffee like everyone else. This didn't mean he wasn't a very rich man – his 1.5 million Wal*Mart shares were worth $82 million in 1992. Since suffering a heart attack in 1983, however, Glass tried to limit his long hours and late nights at the office.

Glass was on the road two or three days a week visiting stores. Since visiting each one once a year was impossible, he used the company satellite to talk to employees across the country. Fifteen regional vice presidents operating from Bentonville spent about 200 days a year also visiting stores. They managed a group of eleven to fifteen district managers, who in turn were each in charge of eight to twelve stores. The visits to stores each week began early on Monday morning, when regional VPs, buyers, and fifty to sixty corporate officers boarded the company's fleet of fifteen aircraft. They tried to return to Bentonville on Wednesday or Thursday "with at least one idea which would pay for the trip." The fact that Wal*Mart did not operate regional offices was thought to save the company about 2 percent of sales each year.[23]

The weekly merchandise meeting occurred on Friday morning. Glass said that in the meetings he would "force [the group] to talk about how individual items are selling in individual stores."[24] According to him, "We all get in there and we shout at each other and argue, but the rule is that we resolve issues before we leave."[25] Guests were often invited to the meeting, including GE CEO Jack Welch, who observed: "Everybody there has a passion for an idea, and everyone's ideas count. Hierarchy doesn't matter. They get eighty people in a room and understand how to deal with each other without structure. I have been there three times now. Every time you go to that place in Arkansas, you can fly back to New York without a plane."[26]

The next morning at 7, Wal*Mart's entire management team and general office associates, along with friends and relatives, assembled in the auditorium for the Saturday meeting, which combined informal entertainment with no-nonsense business for the purpose of sharing information and rallying the troops. Don Soderquist, often dressed in blue jeans and a bright flannel shirt, ran through regional results, market share data, and weekly and quarterly numbers for the divisions, and regional VPs reported on the performance of new stores. A huge billboard flashed the savings that customers were said to have obtained from shopping at Wal*Mart since 1962: roughly $12 billion as of June 1993. However, no accomplishment was too small, and cheers went up for a variety of reasons: stock ownership among associates was up, three associates had ten-year anniversaries, or the week's special item was selling well in selected Wal*Mart stores. Guests included former NFL quarterback Fran Tarkenton, country singer Garth Brooks, and comedian Jonathan Winters. On Monday morning, decisions were implemented in the stores, and the process began again.

Diversification

In the early 1980s, Wal*Mart began testing several new formats beyond the original retail store. Wal*Mart opened the first three Sam's warehouse clubs in 1983, and soon after, the first dot Deep Discount Drugstore in Iowa, and Helen's Arts and Crafts store in Missouri, named after Sam Walton's wife. Wal*Mart sold its three Helen's stores in 1988, and its fourteen dot's stores in 1990.

In 1987, Wal*Mart opened its first supercenter, and two of four Hypermart USA stores, borrowing the hypermarket concept from France where it originated in the 1960s. A hypermarket was a combination grocery and general merchandise store of over 220,000 square feet, which carried 20,000 to 30,000 items, and had gross margins of 13 to 14 percent. Based on the learning from its experiment with hypermarkets, Wal*Mart dropped the format in favor of the smaller supercenters.

In 1991, Wal*Mart acquired Western Merchandisers – a wholesale distributor of music, videos, and books – and Phillips Companies, which operated twenty grocery stores in Arkansas. Wal*Mart also developed a chain of close-out stores called Bud's, named for Sam Walton's older brother. A Bud's store, which generated $6 to $7 million in annual sales, was housed in a former Wal*Mart discount store when the discount store outgrew its site. About 20 percent of Bud's merchandise was Wal*Mart surplus, and the rest was close-out, damaged, or over-run goods shipped directly from vendors.

Sam's Clubs

Warehouse clubs, which were pioneered by Price Club in the 1970s, used high-volume, low-cost merchandising, minimized handling costs, leveraged their buying power, and passed the savings on to members, with gross margins of 9 to 10 percent. A limited number of stock-keeping units (SKUs) resulted in a high inventory turnover rate. Inventory was financed essentially through trade accounts payable (as much as 80 to 90 percent in some cases), resulting in minimal working capital needs. Membership fees comprised about two-thirds of operating profits. The first Sam's Club opened in the early 1980s, and within four years, Sam's sales had surpassed Price Club's, making it the largest wholesale club in the country. By 1993, Sam's was nearly twice the size of Price Club.

The operating philosophy at Sam's Club was to offer a limited number of SKUs (about 3,500 compared to nearly 30,000 for a full-size discount store) in pallet-size quantities in a no-frills, warehouse-type building. Name brand merchandise at wholesale prices was offered to members (70 percent of whom were businesses) for use in their own operations or for resale to their customers. Sam's was run by a separate team of managers than the discount stores, and would often locate next to a Wal*Mart. Together the stores would generate sales of $80 to $140 million a year. Although the Discover card was accepted, Sam's was mostly a cash-and-carry operation. Both business and individual members paid an annual membership fee of $25. A valid state/city tax permit or current business license was required to join. Individual members came from groups such as the federal government, schools and universities, utilities, hospitals, credit unions, and Wal*Mart shareholders. Sam's Clubs operated seven days a week, and unlike Wal*Mart stores, received about 70 percent of their merchandise via direct shipments from suppliers, and the rest from the company's distribution centers.

Sales at Sam's Club rose 19.5 percent in 1993 (compared with 31 percent in 1992), the highest of the national warehouse club chains (see Exhibit 3.7 for the top warehouse clubs by volume). Industry analysts estimated Sam's Club's gross margin at 9.4 percent in 1993, its expense ratio at 8.4 percent, and operating margin at 3 percent, down from 32 percent in 1992.[27] Sam's sales accounted for 39 percent of the industry's volume in 1993 – up from 36 percent in 1992. However, for the first time, comparable store sales in Sam's Clubs were down 3 percent in 1993 as compared to 1992. Sales in the warehouse club industry were projected to grow to $40.5 billion in 1994 – up from $37.5 billion in 1993, when most of the growth had come from clubs "filling in" their existing markets, rather than entering new regions. Sam's chose to cannibalize its own sales by opening clubs close to one another in many markets, rather than give competitors any openings.

Overcapacity had generated intense competition within the industry, and its consolidation was expected to continue. In 1991 Wal*Mart acquired The Wholesale Club, which operated

Exhibit 3.7   Top Warehouse Clubs by 1993 Sales (US$ Millions)

Chain		Sales 1993	1992	1991	Number of Stores 1993	1992	1991	Average Store Size (000 Sq. Ft.)
Sam's Club	AR	14,749	12,339	9,430	319	256	208	120
Price Club[a]	CA	7,648	7,320	6,598	96	81	69	117
Costco	WA	7,506	8,500	5,215	122	100	82	115
Pace[b]	CO	4,000	4,358	3,646	100	114	87	107
BJ's Wholesale Club	MA	2,003	1,787	1,432	52	39	29	116
Smart & Final	CA	637	765	663	135	129	116	16
Mega Warehouse Foods	AZ	409	293	248	46	22	15	10
Warehouse Club	IL	215	233	250	10	10	10	100
Wholesale Depot	MA	150	200	100	11	8	4	64
Source Club[c]	MI	–	10	NA	7	3	0	100
Industry Total		37,517	33,805	27,582	898	762	620	–

Source: Discount Store News, July 4, 1994, and July 5, 1993, company annual reports.
[a]Price Club and Costco merged in October 1993. Fiscal year ended 8/29/93.
[b]Kmart sold 14 Pace Clubs to Wal*Mart for its Sam's Club division in June 1993, and 91 additional ones in January 1994, and closed the rest.
[c]Meijer announced in December 1993 that it planned to close its 7 Source Clubs in order to free up resources for its supercenters.

twenty-eight outlets in the Midwest, and began remodeling the units and incorporating them into the Sam's Club network. In October 1993, Price Co. and Costco Wholesale Corp. merged to form the 206-store PriceCostco Inc. chain. By the end of 1993, Sam's Club acquired ninety-nine of Kmart's 113 Pace clubs, giving Sam's entry into Alaska, Arizona, Rhode Island, Utah, and Washington, and expanding its presence in the massive California retail market. For Kmart, the sale marked a major step in its plan to shed specialty store businesses and focus on its core discount stores.

Supercenters

A supercenter was a combination supermarket and discount store averaging 120,000 to 130,000 square feet in size. Unlike supermarkets which carried a large assortment of products, supercenters offered limited package sizes and brands in order to keep costs low. In addition, they often contained bakeries, delis, and convenience shops such as portrait studios, photo labs, dry cleaners, optical shops, and hair salons. A Wal*Mart supercenter was staffed by about 450 associates, 70 percent of whom worked full-time. There were about thirty cash registers at a central checkout area, with stores open twenty-four hours, seven days a week. At the beginning of 1993, Wal*Mart had thirty supercenters in operation, with sales of $1 billion, and by the end of the year, had sixty-eight supercenters, with sales of $3.5 billion.

The grocery section of a supercenter competed for food sales with supermarkets, independent food stores, discount retailers, and warehouse clubs. Food retailing was a $380 billion industry in 1993, made up of local and regional operators, rather than national chains (see Exhibit 3.8 for the financial position of the ten major supermarket chains). Independent stores accounted for 42 percent of supermarket sales two decades before and only 29 percent

Exhibit 3.8 Top 10 Supermarkets by 1993 Sales (US$ Millions)

| Chain | | Sales | | | 5-Yr. Average[a] | | 1993 | |
		1993	1992	% Change	ROE	Sales Growth	ROS	Gross Margin
Kroger	OH	22,384	22,145	1.1	NE	4.5	0.7	23.6
Safeway Stores	CA	15,214	15,152	0.4	NE	NM	0.6	27.2
American Stores	UT	14,400	14,500	(0.7)	14.2	5.3	1.3	26.4
Albertson's	ID	11,284	10,174	10.9	24.0	10.8	2.9	24.7
Winn-Dixie	FL	10,832	10,337	4.8	23.2	3.8	2.2	22.6
A&P	NJ	10,384	10,499	(1.1)	4.7	2.7	def	30.8
Food Lion	NC	7,610	7,196	5.8	28.5	19.3	1.4	19.6
Publix[b]	FL	6,800	6,800	3.0	NA	NA	NA	NA
Ahold USA	NJ	6,615	6,323	4.6	22.1	6.8	NA	NA
Vons	CA	5,075	5,596	(9.3)	14.4	10.9	0.8	27.2

Sources: Stores, July 1994, Forbes Magazine, January 3, 1994, Value Line, company annual reports.
NE: Negative.
NM: Not meaningful, i.e. the company lost money in more than one year.
NA: Not available.
def: Deficit
[a]1993 or latest five years.
[b]Privately held company.

in 1992. Operating margins within the industry were extremely low – a typical supermarket was lucky to squeeze out a 2 percent profit margin (see Exhibit 3.9 for supermarket versus supercenter profitability). Specialty departments, such as bakeries, seafood shops, floral boutiques, and deli sections, increased customer traffic and offered higher margins of 35 to 40 percent. In 1993, discount retailers and warehouse clubs sold nearly $20 billion in food, up from $16.3 billion in 1992, and about 15 percent of supermarkets sold general merchandise as well as food. These combination supermarkets, or "superstores," ranged in size from 45,000-65,000 square feet, with about 25 percent of the space devoted to non-food merchandise. Supermarket companies were opening a higher percentage of combination stores over conventional units. Sales of general merchandise (including health and beauty aids) in combination supermarkets nearly doubled from $6.4 billion in 1985 to $12.2 billion in 1993, and the number of stores increased 42 percent from 2,667 to 3,786. Non-supermarket sales of food, which accounted for 5 percent of total food sales in 1993, were predicted to double by 1996.[28]

The supercenter format had produced impressive growth, with sales in 1993 increasing to $14.6 billion from $11.8 billion in 1992. Meijer and Fred Meyer continued to lead the field in sales and store count, respectively, though analysts expected them to remain regional. See Exhibit 3.10 for a list of the top supercenter chains. Food, which typically accounted for 40 percent of sales, was the key ingredient in a successful discount/grocery operation because of its powerful traffic draw. Profits generally came from higher-margin general merchandise. Kmart had nineteen combination outlets, known as Super Kmarts at the end of 1993. It planned to open an additional fifty-five Super Kmarts in 1994, and saw the potential for several hundred more over the next several years. The company was shifting much of its investment in remodeling old Kmart stores into building new Super Kmarts, each of which usually replaced one or more traditional discount stores in a market. Kmart supplied its supercenters through two food wholesalers, Fleming and Super Valu, and had no plans to build a food distribution network. Recently, Target had also announced that it would open supercenters in 1995.

Exhibit 3.9   Supercenter Profitability

	Average Supermarket (40,000 Sq. Ft.)	Wal*Mart Supercenter (150,000 Sq. Ft.)
Investment		
Fixtures	$1,400,000	$2,100,000
Working Capital	500,000	2,000,000
Pre-opening Expenses	200,000	600,000
Total Investment	$2,100,000	$4,700,000
Projected Operating Statistics		
Sales	$20,000,000	$50,000,000
EBIT	700,000	3,100,000
EBIT Margin	3.5%	6.2%
EBIT/Investment	33.3%	66.0%

Source: Supermarket News, May 4, 1992.

Exhibit 3.10 Top 10 Supercenter Chains by 1993 Sales (US$ Millions)

Chain		Sales 1993	1992	1991	Number of Stores 1/94	1/93	1/92	Average Store Size (000 Sq. Ft.)
Meijer	MI	5,480	5,043	4,400	75	69	65	200
Wal*Mart[a]	AR	3,500	1,500	600	68	34	10	173
Fred Meyer	OR	2,932	2,809	2,702	97	94	94	137
Smitty's	AZ	678	650	580	28	26	24	105
Bigg's	OH	500	449	350	7	7	6	200
Super Kmart Centers	MI	500	313	255	17	4	6	165
Big Bear Plus	OH	290	280	190	12	12	9	120
Twin Valu	MN	115	110	110	3	2	2	80
Laneco	PA	115	110	100	16	15	14	80
Holiday Mart	HI	100	100	100	3	3	3	100

Sources: Discount Store News, July 4, 1994; company annual reports.
[a]Includes four Hypermart USAs.
[b]Includes Smitty's and Xtra supermarket chain.

Wal*Mart was testing several sizes of supercenters, covering 116,000 square feet, 136,000 square feet, 167,000 square feet, and the largest, which combined a grocery section of 60,000 square feet with a discount section of 130,000 square feet. The grocery section offered about 17,000 SKUs of food (including a newly introduced "Great Value" private label line of about 500 items), and the discount section about 60,000 SKUs of nonfood items. According to industry analysts, Wal*Mart supercenters were "looking for a profit equal to or greater than $50 per square foot, which is not even approached by any other leading retailer except Toys 'R' Us."[29] Wal*Mart's first supercenters were located in small towns in Arkansas, Missouri, and Oklahoma, where they replaced the oldest Wal*Mart discount stores, drawing customers from up to sixty miles around, and capitalizing on Wal*Mart's familiarity and low-price image.

In 1990, Wal*Mart purchased McLane Company, a Texas retail grocery supplier, to service its supercenters and Sam's Clubs. In 1993, McLane had sixteen distribution centers which supplied convenience and grocery stores across the country. Its warehouses in Arkansas and Texas, which opened in 1993, were each 760,000 square feet in size, and capable of supplying eighty to ninety supercenters. In 1993, McLane's sales increased 37 percent to nearly $4 billion. Industry analysts estimated the distributor's gross margin to be 9 percent in 1993, its expense ratio 7.5 percent, and operating margin 1.5 percent.[30]

It remained uncertain how easy it would be for Wal*Mart to gain market share in the supermarket industry as compared to discount retailing. The ability of supercenters to undercut small-town supermarkets was reduced by the 1 to 2 percent margins on which the industry already operated. Several chains had begun to feature larger package sizes in an effort to combat the warehouse clubs, and most had private label lines, which carried higher margins, and were attractively packaged and priced lower than name brands. Also, established grocery-store chains were defending their market-share: Supermarkets General planned to expand its 147-store Pathmark chain's supercenters in the northeast, and Cincinnati-based Kroger, which had more than 1,270 stores and competed head-to-head with

Wal*Mart in a half-dozen areas, had earmarked $130 million for information technology to reduce distribution and other costs.[31]

International Expansion

Wal*Mart's perspective on future growth was decidedly global. Glass believed that Wal*Mart could not overlook the emerging world economy, and told store executives at a recent regional meeting that if they didn't think internationally, they were working for the wrong company.[32] However, management was uncertain whether Wal*Mart's formats would be successful outside the U.S. In 1992, Wal*Mart formed a joint venture with Mexico's largest retailer, Cifra S.A., to test several retail formats in Mexico, its first international market, and by late 1994, anticipated operating sixty-three stores in metropolitan areas such as Mexico City, Monterrey, and Guadalajara – which included twenty-two Sam's Clubs, and eleven Wal*Mart supercenters – with plans to have more than 100 stores there by the end of 1995. Price/Costco and Kmart also operated in Mexico with local retail partners – by late 1994, Price/Costco planned to have eleven warehouse clubs, with additions expected in 1995, and Kmart planned to open five stores.

In March 1994, Wal*Mart expanded into Canada, purchasing 122 Woolco stores from Woolworth Corp. (with sales-per-square-foot of $72), and immediately began to convert them to its own format – remerchandising and renovating them, and retraining nearly 16,000 Woolco staff members. Wal*Mart also gave Canadian companies the opportunity to supply local stores under a "Buy Canada" program, provided they complied with its standards for service, on-time delivery, and price. Together with the newly acquired Pace Clubs in the U.S., the Woolco stores added $900 million to sales in the first quarter of 1994, but produced no profits.

Wal*Mart planned to enter South America in 1995, with its first stores in Brazil and Argentina, the continent's largest consumer markets, where its competitors would be the European-based retailers, Carrefour and Makro. And in Asia, with Kmart planning to open two stores in Singapore in 1994, analysts believed that Wal*Mart was looking closely at ventures in Hong Kong, as a precursor to expanding into China's vast and highly regulated markets. It would compete in China with the roughly 280,000 government-owned enterprises that controlled 40 percent of retail sales, estimated to reach $188 billion in 1994. Analysts believed Wal*Mart's potential international sales alone to be $100 billion.[33]

OUTLOOK FOR THE FUTURE

Glass and Soderquist acknowledged that the current Wal*Mart was a different company from the one Sam Walton had left. Its enormous size and the stagnant economy of the early 1990s presented challenges that Walton had not faced. There was additional pressure on Glass because he followed a popular company founder. "You can't replace a Sam Walton," said Glass, but he has prepared the company to run well whether he's there or not.[34] Glass's top priority was to maintain as much communication as possible with Wal*Mart associates.

Several public challenges also confronted Wal*Mart as it entered 1994: Growing opposition groups in small towns accused Wal*Mart of forcing local merchants out of business. In Vermont, plans to build the state's first Wal*Mart had been tied up in court for over two years. And, in 1993, three independent pharmacies successfully sued Wal*Mart for pricing pharmaceutical items below-cost in its supercenter in Conway, Arkansas. The company was ordered to stop selling below-cost, and planned to appeal what it termed an "anticonsumer" decision. A similar suit was pending in another part of Arkansas. (Wal*Mart had lost a pricing case in 1986 in Oklahoma, and settled out of court during its appeal, agreeing to raise prices in the state.) Moreover, Target was blasting Wal*Mart's price comparisons in ads that claimed that Wal*Mart's prices were often wrong, noting that "this never would have happened if Sam Walton were alive." Wal*Mart retorted that it still maintained and followed Sam Walton's policies, and that Target was simply wrong.

Glass summed up the new challenges facing Wal*Mart: "For a lot of years, we avoided mistakes by studying those larger than we were – Sears, Penney, Kmart. Today we don't have anyone to study. . . . When we were smaller, we were the underdog, the challenger. When you're number one, you are a target. You are no longer the hero."[35]

NOTES

1. Two other large discounters also got their start in 1962: Kmart and Target.
2. *Forbes,* August 16, 1982, p. 43.
3. Sam Walton with John Huey, *Sam Walton, Made in America* (New York: Bantam Books, 1992).
4. *Business Week,* November 5, 1979, p. 145.
5. *Ibid.,* p. 146.
6. George C. Strachan, "The State of the Discount Store Industry," Goldman Sachs, April 6, 1994.
7. Walton, *Made in America.*
8. *Ibid.*
9. Management Ventures, Inc.
10. Strachan, "Discount Industry."
11. Emily DeNitto, "In Dry Grocery, Wal*Mart Sees Selective Success," *Supermarket News,* May 4, 1992.
12. Management Ventures, Inc. Includes lease, rent, and depreciation.
13. Management Ventures, Inc.
14. Management Ventures, Inc.
15. *Business Week,* December 21, 1992.
16. Wendy Zellner, "OK, So He's Not Sam Walton," *Business Week,* March 16, 1992.
17. *Supermarket News,* May 4, 1992.
18. Management Ventures, Inc.
19. Bill Saporito, "A Week Aboard The Wal*Mart Express," *Fortune,* August 24, 1992.
20. Walton, *Made in America.*
21. Jay L. Johnson, "We're All Associates," *Discount Merchandiser,* August 1993.
22. Zellner, *Business Week,* March 16, 1992
23. *Ibid.*
24. *Ibid.*
25. *Fortune,* August 24, 1992.
26. Bill Saporito, "What Sam Walton Taught America," *Fortune,* May 4, 1992.
27. Strachan, "Discount Industry."
28. *Discount Merchandiser,* April 1994.
29. Wendy Zellner, "When Wal*Mart Starts a Food Fight, It's a Doozy," *Business Week,* June 14, 1993.
30. Strachan, "Discount Industry."
31. Zellner, *Business Week,* June 14, 1993.

32. *Discount Store News,* June 20, 1994.
33. *Ibid.,* September 5, 1994.
34. Zellner, *Business Week,* March 16, 1992.
35. Ellen Neuborne, "Growth King Running into Roadblocks," *USA Today,* April 27, 1993.

4

A Note on the Malaysian Pewter Industry

May 3, 1994, was another hot and humid afternoon in Kuala Lumpur (KL), the capital city of Malaysia. About five km from the city, several busloads of tourists arrived at the largest pewter factory in Malaysia, reputedly the largest in the world. The factory, operated by Royal Selangor International Sdn Bhd[1] (RSI), was a major attraction for foreign visitors to KL. At RSI, the pewter alloy was handcrafted into high-quality, aesthetic products such as decorative household utensils, giftware items, and souvenirs. They were sold under the brand name – Royal Selangor pewter (RS pewter).

At the conclusion of the short factory tour, visitors at the RSI facility were given the opportunity to make purchases from among the many products in the showroom. A few visitors, seeing the crowds and knowing that pewter was made mostly of locally abundant tin, could not help wondering whether investment opportunities existed in the Malaysian pewter industry. For them, at issue was the need to assess how attractive the industry was, and whether export opportunities existed.

HISTORICAL PERSPECTIVES OF THE INDUSTRY

Pewter is an alloy of tin. During the Middle Ages, the composition of pewter ranged from 65 to 75 percent tin, 20 to 30 percent lead, and small amounts of copper. English pewter was then considered the finest pewter as it contained 75 percent tin and only two to three percent lead.

The lead content in the pewter alloy caused pewter items to tarnish easily, giving it an unappealing appearance. Lead could also separate easily from the alloy to contaminate drinks or food contained in pewter containers such as beer mugs, plates, and bowls. The toxic nature of lead caused alarm among pewter consumers and subsequently affected the demand for pewter utensils.

In the 1770s, English pewterers invented a new pewter alloy named Britannia metal which contained tin, copper, and antimony as a replacement for lead. This alloy then became the standard pewter alloy. High quality pewter was set to contain 84 percent tin with variable amounts of antimony and copper. Since tin was abundant in Malaysia, Malaysian pewter was able to exceed the standard by producing finer quality pewter with 97 percent tin and very small amounts of copper and antimony. Tin used in Malaysian pewter is refined (Malaysian) Straits Tin which is 99.85 percent pure. Although the tin content determined the quality of pewter, copper and antimony had to be added to make tin, a soft and brittle metal, harder and malleable.

The use of pewter dated back to at least the time of the Roman Empire. Artifacts found in ancient Egyptian tombs indicated the existence of pewter since 1300 B.C. The use of pewter utensils had flourished during medieval Europe. Although these utensils were used initially by the richer households to replace wood and coarse pottery, pewter had then become the most common material suitable for daily use by most households. Some of the most common utensils made of pewter were tankards, plates, bowls, dishes, flagons, and spoons.

At that time, pewter guilds were formed to ensure the credibility of the pewterer and his products. The guilds regulated the quality of metal used, checked on prices and wages, and organized apprenticeships. An apprenticeship could last for at least seven years before the apprentice could become a pewterer and set up his own business. A pewterer usually used marks called touches or touchmarks to identify the maker and to guarantee the quality of his work. Pewter guilds were known to have been established in Germany, Sweden, France, and England. In the 1980s, the guilds were replaced by new organizations such as the Association of British Pewter Craftsmen, the Gutegemeinschaft Zinngart of Germany, and the Belgian Pewter Association. In North America, the American Pewter Guild was founded in 1958 to actively promote trade in the region.[2]

By the end of the 17th century, throughout Europe and America, pewter's popularity as tableware began to decline steadily as new materials such as glass, porcelain, and good quality earthenware became more favored. While most pewter items had simple and dull designs, the new materials were more appealing with their brightly colored and decorative designs. Nevertheless, the pewter industry persisted and pewterers began to manufacture pewter items for decorative purposes.

Pewter also had a history of use in Japan when it was introduced into the country from China over 1,000 years ago. This was evidenced by a 1,200 year-old pewter piece currently displayed at an ancient treasure house at Nara Perfecture in Japan. During the early days, pewter was a highly valued material used for making utensils for the nobility in the imperial courts. In particular, pewter ware was used to keep sake (Japanese wine) warm. The tin content was believed to "soften" the flavor of the wine, and this practice is common even today among those with a refined sense of taste. A similar belief was prevalent among the German pewter users who said that beer tasted better when drunk from a pewter mug.

THE INDUSTRY IN MALAYSIA

The pewter industry began during the nineteenth century when Malaysia (then known as Malaya) was ruled by the British. The British had exploited the large tin resources in the country to meet the demand for tin by British industries. Over the years, as the tin industry expanded, Malaysia became the world's largest tin producer. In 1960, the country's annual tin production peaked at 70,000 tonnes and employed approximately 40,000 people.

Apart from the abundance of the raw tin for the foreign pewter industry, there was also a small demand from England for finished pewter products (particularly pewter tankards, wine goblets, and flower vases). The local demand for pewter was almost negligible since the use of pewter was not in the tradition of the local population. In addition, pewter was not highly regarded because it was made mostly of tin, a cheap and abundant local resource in the country. As such, interest in pewter-making was nonexistent. As well, the skills in pewter-making had always been confined to the pewterer and passed down to family members. Thus, the pewter industry could not easily expand.

Among the first pewterers who capitalized on the small demand for Malaysian pewter was an immigrant pewtersmith from China who set up a pewter business in the tin-rich state of Selangor. The Chinese had used pewter items such as incense burners and joss-stick holders, but these were limited mostly to ceremonial purposes. The business, established in 1885, was later known as Selangor Pewter Sdn Bhd and today, as Royal Selangor International (RSI). It has since become the leading pewter company in the country and synonymous with the Malaysian pewter industry. In 1993, RSI captured 75 percent of the Malaysian market and was one of the largest pewter manufacturers in the world.

When the British rule ended in 1957, there was continued demand for Malaysian pewter from the former British residents. Consequently, local pewter companies began exporting their products to England. As these companies gained experience in the export market, they started to explore other markets in Europe where traditionally, there was a strong demand for pewter. By the 1970s, the pewter industry in Malaysia was export driven and local companies were producing quality pewter products that met the tastes and preferences of their customers overseas. Locally, pewter was positioned as a high-end gift item.

In 1985, the Malaysian economy was hit by a recession caused by its excessive dependence on the export of commodities such as tin, rubber, and palm oil. A ten-year Industrial Master Plan was implemented to diversify into the manufacturing sector. Several industries were identified for development via a pragmatic foreign investment policy. Consequently, there was an influx of foreign companies and expatriates to the country which led to increased demand for pewter products. In 1987, increased living standards and purchasing power among the local population after the recession further boosted the demand for pewter gifts and souvenirs.

The rapid growth of the Malaysian economy in the late 1980s could not, however, overcome the consistent deficits in the country's balance of payments. In 1990, the government undertook programs to develop the tourism industry in Malaysia. A "Visit Malaysia Year" campaign in 1990 resulted in a marked increase of tourist arrivals to the country. Tourists had since become a major market for the pewter industry in Malaysia. Tourists were attracted to Malaysian pewter souvenirs because pewter was considered a national heritage and a local handicraft.

In 1993, the retail sales of pewter in Malaysia were estimated at about RM40 million[3] (equal to approximately U.S.$16 million). Although there was an increase in the local demand, there were only six Malaysian companies known to be actively involved in the manufacture of pewter. This included a recent entrant to the industry, JS Pewter Sdn Bhd (JS). The excess demand had encouraged new entrants to the industry, but their presence was short-lived. The owner of JS explained:

At least two other companies established in KL in 1992 had left the industry. Although these companies were knowledgeable about the market, they lacked the skills in pewter-making. Basically, pewter making is still a handicraft industry which requires skillful hands to ensure high quality products. In addition, new pewter companies must be able to produce products that are comparable in quality to that of RS pewter and subsequently compete on price. Although buyers tend to be price sensitive, sometimes they are not willing to give up on quality for a small difference in price.

(Exhibit 4.1 describes the processes involved in making pewter.)

The Product

Malaysian pewter companies offered a wide selection of pewter products. In 1993, RSI produced more than 1,000 different items ranging from designer pewter collections to pewter sets and small pewter souvenirs.

The aesthetic value of pewter seemed to be a very important factor in determining the success of a product. Thus, it was common for pewter companies to employ in-house designers to create new designs and refine the existing ones. RSI employed a team of 15 designers to design the company's standard and custom-made products. Investments were also made in engaging well-known designers in other industries such as jewelry and fashion apparel to design pewter collections.

In the early 1970s, RSI began to penetrate foreign markets in a planned and aggressive fashion. It took a multidomestic approach in terms of the design of its pewter products. The company developed designs that suited the tastes and preferences of the market within a specific country. For example, wine goblets of the Roemer design were produced for the German market and Oxford-styled goblets for the Australian market. In recent years, although RSI continued to produce pewter designs according to cultural tastes, such as the sake sets for the Japanese and the four seasons oriental design for the Chinese, these products were marketed on a global basis.

RSI was very aggressive in the development of new product designs with at least four new product lines being introduced each year. In January 1993, RSI introduced a collection of figurines based on the mythical fantasy of unicorns and sorcerers which was launched in Australia, Hong Kong, and Singapore. About three months later, the Meridian Collection comprised of a shaving kit crafted from pewter with a combination of leather and sailcloth was launched. Shortly after that, a range of pewter desk accessories known as the "corporate jungle," featuring letter openers, book ends, and business card holders with animal designs, was introduced. Another product line introduced within the year was a collection created by a controversial fashion designer from Japan, Junko Koshino. In this collection, pewter plates, picture frames, and trays were finished with wood grain pattern which appeared simple, yet was considered a dramatic innovation using pewter.

Large capital investments in design and product development were beyond the financial capability of the other local companies. Occasionally, these companies would capitalize on RSI's designs and produce a similar range of products, and subsequently, compete on price. Others catered to special orders and custom-made designs. A pewterer commented, "A pewter company could take advantage of a new product design for at most, six months. Designs can easily be copied by the other companies and vice versa. Unless some new form of technology was used for a particular design of a pewter item, a company could not sustain its advantage based solely on a particular design for a very long period of time."

In response to the demand for pewter souvenirs, the local pewter companies turned to designs reflecting Malaysian culture in the form of local landmarks, people in traditional

Exhibit 4.1   The Methods of Making Pewter.

There are two main methods of making pewter: casting and spinning. Cast pewter was usually preferred to spun pewter because cast pewter was made from molten pewter and was thought to be of the best quality. Spun pewter, made from thin pewter sheets, was light and considered to be of lower quality. However, spun pewter was easier to mass produce than cast pewter and was gaining in popularity as improvements in quality, designs, and finishes were made.

CASTING

The two methods of casting commonly used in the Malaysian pewter industry were die casting and casting by centrifugal force in a rubber mold. The traditional method of pewter-making in Europe was die casting, using a gun-metal (bronze) mold. Pewter companies in Malaysia had instead used steel molds in casting pewter.

In die casting, a pewter maker poured molten pewter from a ladle into a pre-heated steel mold. The mold was held at an angle and molten pewter was ladled into the mold and the pewter maker slowly held the mold upright as it was filled. This technique required skill and experience to know exactly at which angle to hold the mold as the molten pewter was poured. This was to ensure that the molten pewter flowed smoothly to obtain a smooth hardened pewter with minimal rough edges.

Although the casting was done by hand, the process took only a few seconds as the molten pewter inside the mold solidified within seconds. The hardened pewter was removed from the steel cast and rough edges were scraped before the pewter was ready for polishing. Polishing removed a layer of pewter oxide left on the surface and was usually done using a fine grade sandpaper or against a buffing wheel. The pewter was rotated on a lathe as the craftsman peeled off the thin coating on the pewter. This process required steady hands as a sharp steel blade was used to peel off the coating while it was rotated.

The different parts of a pewter product were cast separately, polished, and then joined by soldering. These pieces included appendages such as handles, spouts, or hinges to be attached to a pewter mug or pitcher. Soldering pewter was especially difficult because of its low melting point. Thus, this process required skill and experience to ensure that neat joints were made. In a well-soldered piece, the joints were almost invisible to the naked eye. The final product was then polished with a soft flannel and with a dried stone leaf (a wild tropical leaf with fine, abrasive texture) to achieve a satin sheen. Other finishes included shiny, sandblast, and stained or antique.

Major pewter companies included a quality control check as the final stage of the production process. Items that did not pass the quality check were melted down into the molten mass.

Another casting technique used in pewter making in Malaysia was centrifugal casting. This method used two halves of a flat circular mold which were clamped together. The upper half of the mold had a central hole from which channels ran into cavities which were to be filled with molten pewter. The mold was rotated at very high speed on a turntable as molten pewter was poured in. A few seconds later the pewter hardened and was removed from the mold. This technique had the advantage of using the less expensive rubber mold but its use was limited to the production of small items such as figurines and keychains. Large and hollow-ware items such as vases and mugs could not be produced by this technique.

SPINNING

In this process, a circular pewter alloy sheet was placed in a lathe, pressure was exerted by a spinning tool, and the pewter was forced into the required shape. This method required skilled craftsmen to model the metal as it was spun but it was a more efficient method than die casting, particularly in making hollow cylindrical items such as vases, tumblers, and pitchers. The spun product was finished on the lathe or given a satin or polished finish by high speed polishing using a greased mop. A different mop was used for each type of finish. Compared to casting, the spinning method was faster, more efficient, and was used to make the cheapest pewter mugs.

dresses, and various scenes of Malaysian life. These designs were inscribed on the flat surface of a pewter plate, keychain, or the handle of a letter opener. There were also pewter figurines of Malaysian people, and local landmarks and scenes carved out of pewter.

Pewter Substitutes

A major and continuing challenge faced by Malaysian pewter companies was the threat of substitute products. In place of pewter gifts, a customer had a wide range of gift products ranging from handcrafted jewelry to textiles, electronic gadgets, ceramics, crystal, porcelain, wood-based products, glassware, and earthenware products. Within the fabricated metal product category, pewter had to compete with silver, brass, and even gold and gold-plated products.

Pewter as a Malaysian souvenir was only one of many Malaysian handicrafts which reflected the local culture and national heritage of the country. Malaysian batik, a fabric handpainted with attractive designs, appealed to many tourists. Batik prices ranged widely, due in part to the fabric used. Batik could be made from relatively cheap cotton material or the best quality Italian, Chinese, or Korean silk. These batik materials were sewn into traditional dresses, shirts, ties, handkerchiefs, and purses.

On a global perspective, another potential pewter substitute was a pewter-look-alike alloy made of statesmetal which was used by companies in the USA to produce souvenir and gift items. Some of these items, which went under the name Armetale, looked like pewter, but were much more scratch resistant. One company, Carson Industries Inc., produced about 100 different items and the product range appeared to be quite similar to the range of pewter products offered by most pewter companies. There were letter openers, picture frames, candle holders, wind chimes, and even art nouveau design trays made of this pewter-like alloy. These items were available in gift outlets that carried various other giftware products. At a glance, both retailers and customers could easily be fooled by these products because they looked very much like pewter since they were given a stained, antique finish.

The Pewter Market

The Malaysian market for pewter consisted of several groups – corporate purchasers, tourists, and the gift market. Corporate purchasers included private companies, government departments, associations, sports and recreation clubs, and non-profit organizations. Engraved pewter plates were popular among corporate purchasers as gifts for foreign visitors and long-serving employees, while pewter trophies were common as prizes in competitive events.

Increased prosperity among Malaysian companies led to increased demand for high-end gift items. There was a tendency for these companies to give high-end gifts and souvenirs to their valued customers. For example, at the launch of a new car model in the local market, the local distributor of a Japanese automobile company switched from plastic to pewter keychain souvenirs for its new car purchasers.

To meet the demand from corporate purchasers, prompt delivery, quality, and competitive prices seemed to be the key success factors. As the leader in the market, RSI had set the industry standard for quality and price of pewter products. RSI was also an efficient producer and paid particular attention to prompt delivery. For a May 1993 special order, RSI formed a special team to run additional shifts for several days to meet the delivery of an order of

7,000 tankards within eight days. Smaller companies that offered competitive prices but were not able to deliver on time would not pose much competition to RSI.

Another major market segment in the Malaysian pewter market consisted of tourists and foreign visitors (participants in international conferences and sporting events, and corporate guests). This segment was characterized by impulse buying, although there were some foreign purchasers who had planned their purchase prior to their visit to Malaysia. It was common for foreign visitors to request a visit to the pewter factory or a pewter outlet to make their purchase. They seemed to possess awareness of the product from sources within their own country. Such visitors usually ended up making large purchases which sometimes required the pewter company to make special shipments back to their home country.

Although there were some items which seemed to be a bargain when bought in Malaysia, the price difference of others was not significantly large. See Exhibit 4.2 for a comparison of RSI's prices in Malaysia and prices of similar items in Canada. Nevertheless, there was a wider selection of items in the RSI's showrooms in Malaysia compared to the very limited range of RS pewter displayed in gift shops overseas.

Generally, tourists preferred low to medium-priced pewter souvenirs with cultural motifs to commemorate their visit to Malaysia. Such items were also favorites among Malaysians who purchased pewter as gifts for foreign friends and acquaintances. Among the local population, pewter was positioned as high-end gifts and was popular for special occasions – birthdays, weddings, and anniversaries. Favorite items were vases, picture frames, potpourri containers, and jewelry boxes.

The Export Market

Since the 1960s, the export market had been a major market for Malaysian pewter companies. The most common markets among these companies were Singapore, Japan, Australia, and the USA. RSI exported about 60 percent of its production directly to 20 countries and about 15 percent more was exported indirectly through foreign visitors.

Exhibit 4.2 RSI'S Retail Prices in Malaysia and Canada for Selected Items (in C$)

Product	Prices in Malaysia	Prices in Canada
Erik Magnusson Collection		
Candlestand	34.00	39.00
Bowl (small)	120.00	125.00
Large coffee pot	207.00	275.00
Gerald Benney Collection		
Bowl (5.75 cm high)	37.00	45.00
Coffee pot (122 cl)	235.00	275.00
Tankard, mirror finish (45cl)	46.00	85.00
Water goblet (23 cl)	30.00	45.00
Hip flask (9.5 cl)	44.00	55.00
Sugar bowl (9.5 cm high)	55.00	85.00
Vase (15 cm high)	22.00	28.00
Vase (20 cm high)	27.00	35.00
Picture frame	22.00	32.00

Source: Royal Selangor, Retail Price Lists.

Although the pewter industry was not identified as one of the priority industries for development under the Industrial Master Plan, a pewter company could enjoy many privileges provided to any manufacturing concern. These privileges were in the form of tax allowances for capital expenditure in the expansion of a production facility or in R&D activities.

Additional incentives were available for companies that exported and promoted their products overseas. Incentives in the form of tax deductions were given to companies that incurred expenses for overseas advertising, market research in foreign countries, maintenance of sales offices, and participation in trade or industrial exhibitions. The availability of such incentives coupled with the high demand for pewter in foreign countries had encouraged Malaysian pewter companies to emphasize the export market.

Another factor that induced Malaysian companies to export was the reduced tariff rates resulting from most favored nation (MFN) status. Consequently, Malaysian pewter was more competitive in certain foreign markets than pewter from countries that did not enjoy the MFN privilege. However, in markets such as Canada, Malaysian pewter would be less competitive than pewter imports from the USA. Even before the implementation of NAFTA, the import duty for American pewter was only 9.1 percent compared to 10.2 percent imposed on Malaysian pewter imports.

RSI had established sales offices in its major foreign markets while the smaller companies like JS would usually sell their products on a free-on-board basis. The importer would take the responsibility to make arrangements to ship the products into a particular country and bear the costs of freight and handling and the insurance charges. An importer from Canada explained:

> The easiest way to import 500 pieces of Christmas ornaments, each weighing 20 grams and priced at C$4, from a pewter company in Malaysia is to appoint a broker who makes further arrangements with an agent in Malaysia. The agent picks up the package from the Malaysian producer and has it transported to Canada either by sea or by air. Shipment by sea will take about 3 1/2 weeks to reach Vancouver but only 5 days to reach Toronto by air. The costs involved to transport it by air include – C$75 for freight and handling charges in Kuala Lumpur, C$55 for airport terminal handling in Toronto, $80 for customs clearance charges, $204 for import duty based on a rate of 10.2 percent of C$2,000, and the federal 7 percent Goods and Services Tax charge which is added to all goods sold in Canada.

Marketing Practices

Pricing   As the leader in the Malaysian pewter industry, RSI set the prices of Malaysian pewter. RSI's products were sold at standard prices throughout the country to maintain the perception of high quality and to ensure that retailers did not undercut prices or give unnecessary discounts. The other pewter companies based their pricing on RSI's prices, and subsequently priced slightly lower to ensure a share in the market. This pricing strategy guaranteed their continued existence in the industry. While RSI enjoyed large mark-ups, the smaller companies were willing to accept smaller profit margins. RSI's keychain with Malaysian cultural motifs was retail priced at RM20 while JS's wholesale price was RM10 and retail priced at RM15. The cost of producing such an item was estimated at only RM6.

In the export markets, RSI's prices had to be competitive in view of the large variety of products offered by local pewter companies as well as those from other foreign companies.

For example, in Canada, a RS pewter photo frame was retail priced at C$31.95 compared to an equivalent item with almost similar design made by Seagull, retail priced at C$33.95. However, an almost similar pewter item made in Korea was retail priced at only C$24.95.

A retailer commented, "Pewter is now produced in many countries and not limited to tin-producing countries. In fact, there are pewter companies in Belgium that operate tin mines in African countries to supply the raw material to their manufacturing facilities in Belgium. In addition, customers are not too particular about the pewter brand. For example, a customer looking for a letter opener made of pewter would settle for one that was made in Thailand with an antique finish priced at C$29.95 rather than RSI's shiny letter opener displayed in a nice wooden box priced at C$39.95."

Distribution   RSI had established more than forty pewter showrooms in the major cities and main towns throughout Malaysia. These places were the best markets because of the large concentration of government departments, institutions, private companies, and tourist attractions. These showrooms were equipped with engraving facilities and RSI employees conducted pewter-making demonstrations for tourists.

At the showrooms, the pewter items were displayed on open racks where customers were able to take a closer look at the design and material. Once a customer decided on an item he/she wished to buy, a brand new item was presented to the customer. Most customers were amazed to see the difference between the item on display and the fresh new item in the box. Due to constant handling by various customers, the pewter on display on open racks tended to lose its lustre and shine unless fingerprints were wiped off immediately. In fact, a special cleaning agent was available for the long-term maintenance of pewter.

In places within Malaysia where RSI had not established its own showroom, the company appointed more than 250 authorized retailers, particularly giftware outlets and book stores, to carry its products. In such outlets, pewter brands other than RS pewter were also available. In these outlets, buyers were able to compare RSI's products with those of the other pewter companies. In comparing the products, price-conscious buyers who were not too concerned over brand image would usually settle for products other than RS pewter.

In foreign markets, RSI had established its own representative offices and outlets in Australia, Singapore, Hong Kong, Japan, Switzerland, and Denmark. There were about 2,500 agents and distributors of RS pewter overseas. Currently, many international exclusive shops carried RSI's products. They included Harrods in London, Ilum Bolighus in Denmark, Birks of Canada, Myer of Australia, and Mitsukoshi of Japan. The other Malaysian pewter companies had also ventured into foreign markets in their own small way, mainly through foreign agents.

There was a significant advantage for pewter companies that established their own retail outlets or distributed their products through appointed retailers which sold exclusively the products of a particular pewter company. While competition could be increasingly intense when pewter of competing companies was displayed side by side, the shelf space available for each company was also very limited. These companies were not able to provide a wide selection of their products. On the contrary, a retail shop would be able to accommodate a larger shelf space to display the products of only one particular company that had appointed it as the retailer for a specific location.

Promotion   To obtain international exposure, it was common for pewter companies to participate actively in trade shows and exhibitions, particularly in international gift fairs. Numerous fairs were held in major cities all over the world throughout the year. These fairs were the Toronto Gift Fair, the Birmingham Fair, Formland Fair in Denmark, the Frankfurt International Gift Fair, and the Sydney Gift Fair. Fairs provided new and existing companies with the opportunity to promote their products to leading retailers in the giftware industry.

RSI had made heavy investments in export promotion by consistent participation in international trade fairs. For the last ten years, RSI maintained a permanent stand at the spring and autumn international fairs in Frankfurt; this meant paying an annual rental for about ten days of use in a year when the fair was on. As one RSI manager had said, "This seemed like a very expensive investment but we were able to enhance our image as a serious exporter to international business people. These fairs had acted as a springboard for our new products."

Participation in trade shows and exhibitions also helped companies to evaluate their own positions in the industry. Pewter companies took advantage of these occasions to keep up with the designs of their competitors and to seek new ideas in designing their own products. Since a design was not company specific, pewter companies could easily imitate the designs of each other's best selling items.

In the 1970s, in view of the positioning of pewter as high-end gifts and souvenirs, RSI decided to invest in the design of a suitable package to accompany the image of the product it contained. The other Malaysian companies were quite content to use ordinary boxes and simple plastic sleeves to package their smaller products. Usually, the cost of packaging was included in the price of most pewter items.

THE MALAYSIAN PEWTER COMPANIES

Besides RSI, the largest pewter company in Malaysia, there were four other pewter companies that sold pewter under their own specific brands. These companies were Penang Pewter & Metal Arts Sdn Bhd (Penang pewter), Oriental Pewter Sdn Bhd (Oriental pewter), Zatfee (M) Sdn Bhd (Tumasek pewter), and Selex Corporation (Selwin pewter), a subsidiary of RSI. JS, a new pewter company in Malaysia, sold generic pewter which was used for custom-made products for marketing agents or individual orders.

Apart from RSI, the other Malaysian companies were niche players and were less well-known among the Malaysians. They had established their own markets within the locality where they operated. Penang Pewter and Oriental Pewter catered to markets in the northern states of Peninsular Malaysia (Penang and Perak), JS in Melaka, and Zatfee and Selex in KL and Selangor. These companies had also ventured into the export markets. The following segment describes RSI as the leader in the industry, depicts JS as the new entrant, and provides brief accounts of some of the other Malaysian pewter companies.

Royal Selangor International

RSI, established more than 100 years ago, operated as a family business with a paid-up capital of RM16 million. The company had grown dramatically in the late 1980s. In 1988, RSI's profits doubled from RM1.0 million in 1987 to RM2.2 million in 1988. The number doubled again in 1989 when profits jumped to RM4.9 million. In the following years, growth averaged about 14 percent.

RSI was a major consumer of local tin, using about 250 metric tons of the commodity annually. RSI produced its own pewter alloy by melting tin ingots and adding copper and antimony to the molten metal. In 1993, the Malaysian tin industry experienced a dramatic decline when its annual tin production dropped to 10,000 tonnes and employment in the tin industry slipped to only 2,300 people. Although RSI was a major consumer of tin, the decline in the tin industry would not significantly affect the profitability of the company. RSI's manager commented, "Even if the tin output in Malaysia had declined, tin is readily available from the international commodity market. Furthermore, our products are many times value-added. Thus, the price of the commodity has no direct effect on our costs."

RSI had positioned itself in the market as a producer of high quality pewter products. In 1991, the company was conferred the use of 'Royal' in its name by the ruler of the State of Selangor, where RSI was established. According to RSI's manager, the name change from Selangor Pewter to Royal Selangor was a move toward exclusivity. RSI predicted that over the next twelve years, more than twelve million pieces of its pewter items would be exported to various parts of the world, accounting for about 60 percent of the company's total production.

RSI's products were sold in more than twenty countries and were particularly successful in Europe, Canada, Australia, and Hong Kong. RSI had won several international awards for the design and quality of its products and its innovative packaging. Locally, RSI enhanced its image by winning non-pewter-related awards such as Best Employer of the Handicapped Award given by the Ministry of Welfare Services, Malaysia in 1982 and 1985.

In 1993, RSI employed about 1,000 workers in its pewter factory. The workers were highly skilled in performing specific tasks such as casting the molten pewter, soldering parts of an item together, and creating hammered finishes on pewter mugs. While RSI operated a modern factory, traditional methods of craftsmanship were retained where most of the individual tasks were done by hand.

Industry observers commented that as an established pewter company, RSI had invested large amounts of money in training its craftsmen in specific skills. While this was to ensure that these workers became more productive as they became more skillful, such specialization served two other important purposes. First, specialization helped to deter new entrants. Craftsmen specializing in casting would not be skillful in the other aspects of pewter making. Thus, it would be difficult for them to take advantage of their skills and entrepreneurial spirit to set up their own pewter business. This had prevented the entry of new competitors into the industry.

Secondly, since there were very few pewter companies, RSI could further ensure its leadership by maintaining a strong bargaining power with its skilled workers. These workers were skillful in a particular craft which had very limited use in other industries. Thus, their mobility was limited to jobs in other pewter companies which might not be able to offer better deals.

JS Pewter

JS was established in January, 1993 by C.Y. Tay and his two brothers. Tay's brothers were former employees of RSI. They were employed as factory workers for more than ten years and had acquired the skills of pewter-making.

JS had a paid-up capital of RM100,000. During the first year of operation the company incurred a loss, but Tay was positive that JS would be able to recover its losses that year. Tay attributed the losses to JS's lack of experience in the industry. He said, "Last year, we were still new and had to sell cheap and provide better terms to our customers. We are slowly gaining their trust, and when we get ourselves established, only then can we seek for better deals."

Upon entering the industry, JS had positioned itself as a niche player by catering to small corporate and special orders. Tay believed that JS was filling a gap in the industry by taking jobs which RSI would have turned down. "JS was willing to accept small orders of even less than 100 pieces which RSI would not be willing to fill. We were not competing for the same business as RSI. Our target customers were those who could not afford RSI's products and were not particular about the RSI brand. We used RSI's price for a similar item as a guide and priced our products 30 to 40 percent lower."

JS operated a factory in Melaka, about 200 km from its sales office in KL. The factory was a rented shop measuring twenty feet by fifty feet. Rental and energy charges amounted to about RM2,000 per month. Other overheads included insurance premiums and capital investments on a casting machine costing about RM50,000. JS did not produce its own pewter alloy, but purchased pewter bars from local metal-based companies. In 1994, the price of a pewter bar containing 97 percent tin and weighing 4 kg was RM72. Tay said that the price of pewter bars had not changed much since he ventured into the business.

JS used the less expensive rubber-mold production process. Since JS catered to specific orders, the rubber mold could be discarded once an order had been fulfilled. Rubber molds were cheaper but their application was limited to the production of figurines and smaller items such as key holders. JS charged RM300 for the cost of making a mold for an order of less than 500 pieces. JS had not ventured into the production of large and hollow items such as mugs and vases which required the use of steel molds.

JS employed ten workers who were paid a monthly salary of RM300 to RM400 depending on their skills and experience. The factory operated daily from nine to five, six days a week. During busy periods, JS had to pay overtime at more than double the daily wage of the workers. On average, a worker earned up to RM500 to RM600 per month on overtime. Tay said:

> We have only ten workers and our factory is still very small to cope with large orders. Although we would like to take advantage of scale economies by filling large orders for few clients, it would be too risky to be dependent on a few large orders. At this stage, we are trying to develop a wide customer base and gain experience in producing a wide range of products.

JS also employed two sales personnel – one to handle sales in KL, the other to establish markets in Melaka. Melaka was a major tourist attraction known for its historical sites, including the remains of a Portuguese fortress and buildings of Dutch architecture, preserved to retain the state's heritage. In 1994, Melaka had also joined in the country's pace of industrialization and undertook various activities to woo local and foreign investors to the state. By the end of 1993, rents in Melaka had increased 100 percent and employment in the low income sectors such as construction had to depend on immigrants mainly from Indonesia, the Philippines, and Bangladesh.

Other Malaysian Pewter Companies

Penang Pewter & Metal Arts was one of the better known pewter companies. The company catered to markets in Penang, an island off the northern coast of peninsular Malaysia. Penang, known as the Pearl of the Orient, was a major tourist attraction in Malaysia because of its beaches. In recent years, the state had developed industrial parks to attract foreign investment which further boosted the demand for pewter in the area. Locally, Penang was the major geographical market for Penang pewter although the products were readily available in gift outlets in major cities, particularly KL. With a complement of about 100 workers, the company produced a wide range of pewterware which was exported to markets such as Australia, Singapore, Japan, and USA.

Zatfee produced a wide range of pewter under the brand name, Tumasek pewter, which was exported to Canada, USA, and Japan. The company had expanded gradually from ninety employees in 1987 to 200 in 1993. In 1993, the company increased its global market penetration by entering new markets such as Australia, Hong Kong, Korea, New Zealand, and Singapore. Zatfee's annual turnover of RM1.5 million in 1987 had grown to RM6.5 million in 1993.

Oriental Pewter was located in Perak, formerly another tin-rich state in Malaysia. With a workforce of about 100 employees, the company produced modern and unique pewterware which was exported to Canada, New Zealand, Singapore, Australia, UK, and Japan.

GLOBAL COMPETITION

The export market had always been the thrust of the Malaysian pewter industry. However, in recent years, the world market had become increasingly competitive with the emergence of pewter companies even in countries where tin was an unknown metal. For example, the pewter industry had flourished in Sweden, and pewter was manufactured in Korea, Taiwan, and Belgium. Exhibit 4.3 gives a list of countries known to have tin deposits.

Pewter companies had initiated the establishment of pewter-making concerns in Taiwan and Korea to take advantage of the relatively cheap and skilled labor in these countries. Thailand and Indonesia seemed to have the potential for the establishment of a competitive pewter industry in view of the presence of large tin deposits and a cheap workforce. Pewter

Exhibit 4.3   Estimates of Tin Deposits in Selected Countries

Country	1987–1990 average (in tonnes)
Australia	8,000
Brazil	31,500
Canada	3,500
Germany	3,900
Indonesia	10,700
Malaysia	32,800
Portugal	100
South Africa	1,400
Thailand	16,000
United Kingdom	4,000

Source: IMD & World Economic Forum, The World Competitiveness Report, 1992.

was at present manufactured in Thailand, while PT Tambang Timah, an Indonesian tin producer, was planning to set up a pewter plant which would consume at least half of its tin supplies for the production of high value-added pewter products. See Exhibit 4.4 for hourly compensations of the workforce in fabricated metal industries in selected countries.

In Sweden, the pewter industry began about 150 years ago. At present, there was a strong market demand, particularly for pewter trophies. Prizes for most sporting events such as yachting, skiing, ice hockey, and swimming were made of pewter and Swedish sportsmen were known to have built a collection of pewter trophies. Other pewterware produced by the Swedish pewter companies included household items, jewelry, and gifts.

Scandiapresent was the largest pewter manufacturer in Sweden and was noted for its antique-finished pewter. Another company was Arktis Smedgen, formed in 1980, and employing four craftsmen; it produced a range of pewterware with engraved patterns. AB Harryda Adelmetallsmide produced the Harryda Tenn pewter products such as tankards, bowls, and goblets with a shiny finish.

Other pewter companies in Sweden included AB Koppar & Tennsmide, Jokkmok Tenn AB Sigurd Ahman, Metallum AB, and several other companies which mostly operated as small concerns employing four to eight craftsmen. Metallum AB in Stockholm, set up in 1988, produced small pewter gifts and jewelry; it was also the agent in Sweden for the supply of pewter sheets and ingots from a UK supplier, George Johnson & Company (Birmingham) Limited.

In the UK, where the pewter industry had a long history, there was a high concentration of pewter companies in Sheffield. Of fourteen pewter manufacturers in the UK, two were located in London, three in Birmingham, one in Glasgow, and the rest in Sheffield. Sheffield pewter, noted for its highly polished and hammered finishes, was distributed in large retail outlets as an exclusive product, usually displayed in glass cases. The product line was, however, quite narrow, limited to tankards, mugs, and hipflasks.

Canada was one of the countries that produced pewter and had quite a large retail market. In 1994, Seagull Pewter and Silversmiths Ltd (Seagull) was one of the most successful

Exhibit 4.4   Hourly Compensation in Fabricated Metal Products, 1990

Country	U.S.$
Belgium	15.07
Brazil	1.12
Canada	15.90
Germany	19.88
Korea	3.94
Portugal	2.90
South Africa	3.05
Sweden	20.31
Taiwan	3.80
United Kingdom	11.84
United States	14.98

Source: IMD & World Economic Forum, The World Competitiveness Report 1992.
Note: The hourly compensation in Indonesia, Malaysia, and Thailand was estimated at U.S.$1.60, U.S.$3.30, and U.S.$3.00, respectively.

Canadian pewter companies. Exhibit 4.5 gives a brief description of Seagull to provide an insight into the operations of a pewter company in a foreign country. Seagull had recently grown rapidly to become one of the top ten pewter manufacturers in North America and represented major competition to the Malaysian pewter companies in the global market.

There were at least eight other Canadian pewter manufacturers. They were located in Nova Scotia (Amos Pewterers), Newfoundland, Quebec (Val David's pewter), New Brunswick (Aitkens Pewter), Ontario (Morton-Parker Ltd), Alberta, and British Columbia (Boma Manufacturing Ltd). Currently, in the Canadian market, the products of Malaysian pewter

Exhibit 4.5 Seagull Pewterers & Silversmiths Limited (Seagull)

Seagull, located in Pugwash, Nova Scotia, was established in 1979 by a husband and wife team, John Caraberis and Bonnie Bond, who were seeking a more peaceful lifestyle and a less expensive place to live. In a town with a population of 1,000 people, they expanded their original basement operation to a six-thousand-square-foot factory ten years later. Their business line had developed from silver and pewter jewelry to pewter giftware. Currently, Seagull produced 1,000 different items and was constantly adding new products and refining existing ones.

Seagull employed 100 pewter makers, designers, and sales representatives. The company had a wide product line of pewter giftware ranging from picture frames, letter openers, and mugs to a large selection of Christmas ornaments. The Caraberis' ranked their company's pewter line as the broadest in North America.

The business was booming at Seagull, and for most of the year, the workers worked two separate shifts (ten-hour days, four days a week). Several methods were employed to produce different pewter products. Jewelry was hand-made from twisted pewter wire and thin pewter plates. Seagull's hollowware was made by spinning while a majority of its other items were made in rubber-casts. In rubber casting, original items were designed and several copies of the models were made by hand. These models were then used to make several thousand rubber molds. The company used over 400 molds a week and each mold lasted for between 100 and 200 casts.

Seagull was very aggressive in promoting its products and claimed to have a total of 10,000 accounts spread across every state and province in North America. The accounts included independent retail shops, tourist shops, country and craft shops, and jewelry stores. Aggressive selling was undertaken by Seagull's twelve sales representatives and strengthened by dozens of other giftware distributors. In 1988, the U.S. accounted for about 70 percent of Seagull's total sales and the company was looking for opportunities in Australia, Japan, and Europe, particularly Germany.

In the Canadian market, Seagull would appoint an exclusive retailer who carried only Seagull pewter together with a range of giftware, except pewter from other companies. Seagull pewter would occupy a corner of the retail gift outlet where a wide selection of the pewter items was displayed in open racks. Customers were able to handle the product without having to seek assistance from the salesperson. Items purchased were taken off the rack and packed in boxes or plastic sleeves for the smaller items. Seagull's pewter bookmark was retailed at C$7, a keychain at C$13, a photo frame at C$34, and a Christmas ornament at C$8.

For the past several years, Seagull had invested heavily in giftware design to ensure that its product line was current, comprehensive, and consumer-oriented. "Given the giftware industry which typically launches two product lines a year, that can be hectic. The development of new products does not require new technology but is very demanding and takes a lot of work and money," said Caraberis.

The owners of Seagull Pewter had also attributed the company's success to their active participation in trade shows. Seagull attended and displayed its products at forty to fifty shows throughout North America each year, at show locations such as Boston, Washington, D.C., New York, Dallas, Kansas City, Toronto, Montreal, Edmonton, and Halifax. "We're a little more rigorous in getting out there in the marketplace for a small business. You've got to be there to build up your reputation, to build up your clientele," explained Caraberis.

companies such as Tumasek pewter, Oriental pewter, RS pewter, and Selwin pewter faced intense competition from the local and foreign pewter companies.

To understand the global nature of supply on the retail side, the experience in Stratford, Ontario, is illustrative. Stratford was a small town with a major tourist attraction due to its Shakespearean Festival. In Stratford, only the Touchmark Shop carried RS pewter and Selwin pewter. Although RS pewter and Selwin pewter were among Touchmark's best selling items, there was intense competition from pewter made in Brazil (John Sommers pewter), Thailand, Belgium (Riskin pewter), and England (Sheffield pewter), and the locally produced pewter, particularly Boma pewter and Lindsay Claire pewter. A salesperson at Touchmark commented, "Pewter was an impulse item; thus, customers looked for items that had appealing designs and were reasonably priced. Only customers who had prior knowledge of pewter were conscious of pewter brands and their country of origin."

Seagull pewter was sold exclusively at three large gift shops in Stratford: Bradshaws, La Crafe, and Christmas and Country Gift Shop. Bradshaws, however, had on display a very small selection of pewter made in Korea and Metzke pewter from the USA. Since these shops did not carry pewter of other manufacturers, Seagull pewter occupied a relatively large shelf space and purchasers could not make a spontaneous comparison in terms of product design and price with competitors' products.

Touchmark was reported to have sold more than C$500 worth of pewter per month during the summer season. On the contrary, at about the same time, the retailer of a large gift shop in Kitchener complained that the pewter items were selling more slowly than the rest of the other gifts such as crystal, silver, and porcelain. As a result, the shop had a limited range of products, mainly Riskin pewter and John Sommers pewter from Brazil.

FUTURE OUTLOOK

Based on the current situation in the pewter industry in Malaysia, RSI's leadership in the industry was indisputable and was expected to remain so for the next decade at least. RSI had been a family-owned business and there were no immediate plans for the company to go public. Such a strategy shielded the company from acquisition threats and leakages of trade secrets. Although RSI had conquered a major share of the Malaysian pewter market, RSI together with the other Malaysian pewter companies faced a major challenge from existing and emerging pewter companies all over the world. At issue for the new entrants was whether they could compete globally by emphasizing efficient production and targeting the low to medium-priced giftware market segment. But was this realistic? And overall, was this an attractive industry for investment?

NOTES

1. Sdn Bhd is an abbreviation for Sendirian Berhad which means Private Limited.
2. Brett, Vanessa. 1981. *Phaidon guide to pewter*. Lausanne: Elsevier Publishing.
3. The Malaysian currency is the Ringgit Malaysia (RM). On December 31, 1993, U.S.$1.00 = RM2.73.

5

A Note on the U.S. Cable TV Industry

"They want a recommendation in a week." Carol Dixon looked again at the last line of the urgent message she had just received through the intercompany electronic mail system. It was March 11, 1994. She had worked at Pigot, da Silva (a medium-sized New York investment bank) for five years, after receiving an MBA from a prestigious Canadian business school. During this time, Dixon had conducted many detailed industry studies for Pigot, da Silva's clients – but had rarely received a request of this magnitude.

"Our client is considering whether to make an offer to Rogers Communications for Maclean Hunter's U.S. cable assets," the message from Dixon's boss began. "Acquiring a cable company is a way for them to diversify. Consequently, they don't know how to put a value on the Maclean Hunter cable business. They do know what Rogers paid, but they need us to go beyond the obvious – anyone can analyze the financial statements. I want you to prepare a brief report that tells them what factors will be of most importance in deciding the value of the U.S. cable TV industry of the future. Then suggest an appropriate price and cash flow multiple for the Maclean Hunter assets. Confidentiality is important, and as always, time is of the essence."

CATV OPERATIONS

Cable television (CATV) systems originated in the early days of television when many smaller and remote communities could not receive television broadcast signals with simple home antennas. By the late 1960s, CATV systems had spread to many communities in the U.S. where broadcast signals were not easily received, including parts of major cities where signal reflections and shadowing by large buildings interfered with signal reception quality.

The advent of satellite-based signal transmission created the present-day CATV industry, since it led to the creation of a wide range of new channels that bypassed and competed with traditional broadcast networks. In addition, rulings by the U.S. Supreme Court legalized the provision of pay-TV services such as Home Box Office. The CATV operators added new channels that served specialized subscriber niches with dedicated news, music, and sports broadcasts. By 1990, the Cable Facts Book listed more than 100 such channels in operation, including ten pay-TV and ten pay-per-view services. Since then, the number of these services has grown, and specialty channels such as ESPN and CNN have become key sources of entertainment and information.

The explosion of new channels resulted in rapid growth in demand for cable services. Exhibit 5.1 shows the growth that occurred in the industry in selected years from 1976 to 1993. The coaxial cables of CATV operators passed approximately 95 percent of homes in the U.S.,[1] and by the end of 1993, the industry served 56.3 million subscribers or 62 percent of American homes with potential access to cable service. About 90 percent of these homes received more than thirty channels. As a result of this ready availability of service, plus the predominance of television as an entertainment medium, cable operators generated total industry revenues in 1993 of $22.8 billion. Average cable company operating margins were 46 percent[2] and the size of an average monthly bill sent to a cable subscriber in 1993 was $33.84.

In most communities there were three principal categories of programming, each with a different fee structure:

Basic Programming   This category included all the channels that cable subscribers received by paying a basic monthly fee. The basic package included the signals of the major broadcast networks, which were essentially free to the cable operator who also carried the advertising that was associated with them. The cable operators paid a monthly fee to receive each satellite channel, usually $0.20 to $0.25 per subscriber. However, the satellite networks and the cable operators also sold advertising time in competition with the networks. These revenues were $3 billion in 1993.

Exhibit 5.1   History of Cable and Pay-TV Subscribers and Revenues

Averages for Year	Basic Subscribers (mil.)	% Change
1976	11.0	–
1981	21.5	22.9
1986	38.2	7.6
1991	52.6	4.1
1992	54.3	3.3
1993	56.3	3.7

At Year End	Homes Passed (mil.)	Basic Subscribers (mil.)	Full Pays (mil.)	Mini Pays (mil.)	Pay TV Homes (mil.)	Basic Subscribers as % of Homes Passed	Full Paying Subscribers as % of Basic
1976	23.1	11.8	1.0	–	n/a	51.1	8.5
1981	41.8	23.0	15.5	–	13.8	55.0	67.4
1986	69.4	39.7	32.1	–	20.7	57.2	80.9
1991	88.4	53.4	39.9	3.2	24.0	60.4	74.7
1992	90.6	55.2	40.7	3.7	24.7	60.9	73.7
1993	92.9	57.4	41.5	4.8	26.4	61.8	72.3

Exhibit 5.1 History of Cable and Pay-TV Subscribers and Revenues *(continued)*

Year	Basic Revenues (mil.)	Pay TV Revenue (mil.)	PPV Revenue (mil.)	Home Shopping Revenues (mil.)	Install Revenue (mil.)	Ad Revenue (mil.)	Misc. Revenue (mil.)	Revenues from Sources (mil.)	Total Revenues per Subscribers per Month	% Change
1976	$ 851	$ 65	n/a	n/a	$ 13	n/a	$ 3	$ 932	$ 7.06	—
1981	2,061	1,317	n/a	n/a	67	$ 17	173	3,656	14.17	16.7
1986	4,891	3,872	$ 37	$ 23.0	253	192	472	10,144	22.13	5.5
1991	11,414	4,943	378	81.0	269	721	951	19,463	30.86	4.8
1992	12,433	4,980	404	90.0	278	852	1,004	21,044	32.30	4.6
1993	13,552*	4,633	512	128.4	289	984	1,123	22,863	33.84	4.8

All amounts are U.S.$.
* Weighted average basic rate of $20.06/month used to calculate full year revenues, representing 8 months of unregulated basic rates, and 4 months of the FCC rolled-back rate.
Reprinted from *Cable TV Investor*, March 31, 1994, with the permission of Paul Kagan Associates, Inc., Carmel, CA.

Pay Channels   For an additional monthly fee, which averaged $5.70 in 1993, subscribers could receive a pay channel using a set-top decoder. There were only a small number of these channels, and they all offered movies as their chief programming fare. Typically, a cable system would pay 50 percent of the monthly subscriber fees to the satellite network for pay channels. The satellite system would, in turn, pay half of what it received to the owners of the program rights. To offer a full schedule, a pay channel needed to show 300 movies per year. Although 80 percent or more of subscribers to basic services opted for at least one pay channel, a continuing problem for CATV operators was subscriber churn, a situation that occurred when a subscriber dropped their subscription to one channel and switched to another (usually because of the kinds of movies that were available).

Pay-per-view (PPV) channels: PPV channels were a more recent innovation, and as such, they were not available to a large percentage of U.S. cable subscribers. PPV channels required subscribers to pay for each program they viewed either by credit card or by telephoning in an order (the fee would be added to their cable bill). PPV rates were similar to the rental price of a movie (approximately $3–4). Once placed, an order could not be cancelled. A subscriber wishing to order PPV programming had to have an addressable set-top decoder box attached to his or her television. This box cost $100–$150, and a rental fee for the decoder box was built into a subscriber's monthly bill. PPV had been successful only with major athletic events such as heavyweight boxing. Estimated CATV revenues for PPV in 1993 were $512 million, an increase of more than 25 percent over the previous year. During the 1990s, the average home in those cable service areas supporting PPV ordered 3.5 PPV features each year.

CATV operators were concerned that delays in receiving hit movies were harming cable revenues. They claimed they needed to show movies before the movies had reached video stores. For that to happen, the distribution system would have to change. Movie distribution was tightly controlled by the studios that owned movie rights. Each year between 300–400 movies were produced; only 20–25 would ever become major box office successes. To maximize their returns, the studios normally launched a movie in stages. First, exhibition would occur in theatres, accompanied by an intensive domestic and international promotional campaign. At this point, individual theatre admission would cost from $7–8 per patron. When theatre revenues slowed, the studios permitted distribution through video stores. Video rental charges were in the range of $3–5, but could be seen by a large number of people during the rental period. After six weeks or so of video store distribution, movies were made available to PPV, and then to pay channels (meaning that the customer incurred no additional cost beyond the cost of the pay service), and, eventually, were released to major network broadcasters which distributed the signal free-of-charge to viewers.

CABLE TELEVISION SYSTEM TECHNOLOGY

A typical cable distribution system was designed to transmit the same information, one way, to many locations within a defined service area and required a considerable amount of capital. However, most of the signal distribution equipment was readily available in competitive markets within the U.S., and was only somewhat differentiable on performance. Support wire and system electronics were imported from Taiwan, Mexico, and other countries, but were not considered to offer differentiable performance.

The architecture of a CATV system began with the headend, which received video signals from transmission sources such as satellites, or from a super-trunk line connected to another headend. Main lines, called trunks, then carried the signals into a community. The length of a trunk was limited by the number of amplifiers needed to boost television signals since signals weakened due to losses in the cable. Feeder lines branched off the trunks. Each feeder line typically served 200–400 homes. Individual homes were connected to the feeder line by drops. See Exhibit 5.1 for a typical cable system configuration.

This "tree and branch" configuration was a very economical way of distributing the same information to many subscribers. New cable systems were estimated to cost approximately $300 per subscriber, with feeder lines and drops accounting for more than 75 percent of the cost. However, this amount varied between cable systems according to the density of the market served, the total size of the installed system, and the proportion of aerial to underground cable in each system's design. Some analysts estimated that the cost breakdown for a new cable system plant was as follows: headend (6 percent); trunk network (19 percent); feeder or distribution network (55 percent); subscriber drop and house wiring (20 percent).

Cable operators have traditionally rebuilt their plant approximately every 10–15 years and upgraded electronics every seven years. They used coaxial cable to distribute signals from the headend to the home. The measure of the carrying capacity of a cable system was bandwidth – more bandwidth meant that more signals could be carried. Most early cable systems had the capacity to provide 35 channels using P1 cable, which had a bandwidth of several hundred megahertz.[3]

TECHNOLOGY TRENDS

Industry experts believed that plant investment in the 1990s would concentrate on replacing traditional tree-and-branch coaxial cable systems with more sophisticated systems using optical fiber, which was generally more suitable for high-speed data transmission and advanced video communications. When combined with switching capabilities at the headend and digital signal compression, this type of system could distribute a wide range of new services including video-on-demand and certain telephone-like services. And, by partitioning the system, a cable operator could divide an operating area into a collection of clusters and be able to segment program offerings accordingly. It was considered theoretically possible to segment program offerings and commercials to the level of the individual household.

Exhibit 5.1   A Typical Cable System Configuration

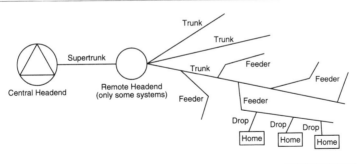

The National Cable Television Association estimated that the CATV industry would spend more than $18 billion in the years 1994–2004 for upgrades to plant and equipment, with more than 60 percent of the existing CATV systems slated to be rebuilt. All of the trunk and most of the feeder lines scheduled for construction during this period were expected to use optical fiber.

INDUSTRY MARKET STRUCTURE AND REGULATION

CATV operated in a highly regulated environment in which the FCC had the ultimate authority to set rules and standards. In cable's early days, the FCC was concerned that CATV networks remain independent of both telephone companies and large broadcast networks. Thus, the FCC prohibited both types of companies from owning cable systems in their operating areas.

The FCC began regulating rates at the time of cable's inception. Since cable companies operated as legal monopolies within their service areas, the FCC felt that rate regulation was needed to counterbalance the CATV operator's potential to overcharge or underservice a market. Another force behind industry regulation was the apparent absence of readily available substitutes. At the time the FCC established a regulatory framework for CATV, there were insufficient alternatives available to customers who desired clear signal reception and a large number of viewing choices. Consequently, the FCC did not consider it possible for customers to switch CATV service providers and used regulation as a means of ensuring that CATV carriers focused on delivering promised service at reasonable prices.

A main objective of the 1984 Cable Communications Policy Act was to decentralize much of the control of the cable industry to the municipal level and to give operators more freedom to set rates. Municipalities were empowered to grant franchises for terms of between five and fifteen years. Most municipalities preferred shorter terms so as to improve the accountability of CATV operators.

Obtaining a franchise involved navigating a lengthy, cumbersome process involving competitive bidding and often, aggressive lobbying. A bidder's local reputation and experience in other communities were significant factors in winning franchises. Prospective franchise holders had to submit detailed tenders that described the number and type of channels that would be offered, make guarantees about signal quality, planned system extensions and improvements, and the franchise fee they would pay. Such fees ranged between 3–5 percent of revenues. Municipalities frequently insisted that cable operators make time available to local groups for community programming.

If the cable franchisee lived up to the terms of the agreement, the Act provided some level of legal protection so that the franchise could not be arbitrarily withdrawn at renewal time. However, competitive bidding for franchises at renewal time was common and the winner was usually expected to make major investments to upgrade a system to meet the demands of the municipality. Common subscriber complaints were related to the quality of the video signal, the number of system outages experienced, and the number and type of channels offered. It was generally felt in the industry that subscribers were virtually powerless to demand new services until it was close to franchise renewal time.

Recent court rulings had found that local franchises could no longer be offered on an exclusive basis. As a result, by 1991, approximately 50 cities had competing cable systems, twice as many as in 1989. In competitive situations, a second system would "overbuild" the first by installing cables along the same route or right-of-way as the first system. When overbuilding occurred, it usually preceded intense competition between the rivals in price, advertising, service give-aways, and service expansion.

In the 1990s, rates were essentially deregulated, except for those covering some rural areas. The rationale was that CATV was no longer a natural monopoly, that other forms of entertainment were broadly available and they acted to keep cable rates competitive, that customers had a choice of whether or not to subscribe, and that customers had a choice between service providers. However, the FCC retained a broad power to order rate rollbacks. Exhibit 5.2 shows how cable rates evolved between 1976 and 1993.

The population density of a carrier's served area had an important influence on the value of the carrier's system. Analysts and carriers assumed a density of twenty homes passed per mile in rural areas, eighty homes passed per mile in suburban areas, and several hundred homes passed per mile in urban areas. During the 1980s, many cable companies were acquired by other, larger operators. Some systems were selling for upwards of $2,500 per subscriber. This was considerably higher than the average system's undepreciated book value of plant and equipment of approximately $465 per subscriber. These larger companies were called MSOs (multiple systems operators), because they operated several cable systems that were usually not geographically adjacent and thus were not run as a single system from a signal distribution standpoint. Exhibit 5.3 lists the top cable MSOs in the U.S.

MSOs benefitted in significant ways from industry consolidation. First, it was easier to raise money to fund system upgrades and expansions. Second, an MSO had greater bargaining power in dealing with satellite program providers and could offer more to attract potential advertising revenue. Scale economies were possible in administration, government relations, and franchise negotiations. As a result, the larger MSOs had cash flows often in excess of 50 percent of revenues. However, cumulative industry debt was high. Most of the larger MSOs had diversified into other areas of entertainment or information distribution within the U.S. and internationally.

Exhibit 5.2 Cable Rates

Year	Basic Cable Rate	% Change	Full Pay TV Rate	Mini-Pay TV Rate	Total Pay TV Rate Change
1976	$ 6.45	–	$ 7.71	–	–
1981	7.99	3.9	8.92	–	3.5%
1986	10.67	9.7	10.31	–	0.6
1991	18.10	7.9	10.27	$1.50	(0.3)
1992	19.08	5.4	10.17	1.50	(0.8)
1993	19.39*	1.6	9.11	2.75	1.6

* Weighted average basic rate of $20.06/month used to calculate full year revenues, representing 8 months of unregulated basic rates, and 4 months of the FCC rolled-back rate.
Reprinted from *Cable TV Investor*, March 31, 1994, with the permission of Paul Kagan Associates, Inc., Carmel, CA.

Exhibit 5.3 Top 50 Cable System Operators As of December 31, 1993

Company	Basic Subscribers (000)	Expanded Basic (000)	Pay Units (000)	Mini Pay (000)	Homes Passed (000)	Basic/ Homes Passed	Pay/Basic	Pay/Homes Passed
						Percentage Ratios		
1. Tele-Comm. Inc. (1,2,e)	10,406	9,288	6,362	3,704	17,425	59.7	61.1	36.5
2. Time-Warner Cable (3)	7,215	2,141	4,558		12,012	60.1	63.2	37.9
3. Continental Cablevision (4)	3,149		2,615		5,637	55.9	83.1	46.4
4. Comcast Cable (2,5)	2,648		1,812		4,219	62.8	68.4	42.9
5. Cablevision Systems	2,148		3,940		3,563	60.3	183.4	110.6
6. Cox Cable Communications	1,784	1,754	1,206	42	2,838	62.9	67.6	42.5
7. Newhouse Broadcasting	1,384	560	1,009	22	1,940	71.3	72.9	52.0
8. Cablevision Ind. (e)	1,328		697		1,957	67.9	52.5	35.6
9. Times Mirror Cable	1,274	1,230	703		2,069	61.6	55.2	34.0
10. Jones Spacelink	1,263	1,198	1,031	3	2,163	58.4	81.6	47.6
11. Adelphia Communications	1,244	27	555	53	1,758	70.8	44.6	31.6
12. Viacom	1,094	1,065	718		1,730	63.3	65.6	41.5
13. Sammons Communications	1,072	1,036	607		1,592	67.4	56.6	38.1
14. Falcon Cable TV	1,055	183	369	8	1,287	81.9	35.0	28.6
15. Century Communications (e)	945		539		1,653	57.2	57.0	32.6
16. Crown Media	857	484	518		1,572	54.5	60.4	33.0
17. Colony Communications	787		467		1,222	64.4	59.3	38.2
18. TeleCable Corporation	717	583	647		992	72.2	90.3	65.2
19. Scripps Howard	702	702	600		1,159	60.5	85.5	51.7
20. Lenfest Communications (6,7)	658	646	500		1,025	64.2	76.0	48.8
21. InterMedia Ptrs. (6) #	632		386		1,030	61.4	61.0	37.5
22. KBLCOM (8)	605	513	488		1,198	50.5	80.7	40.7
23. TKR Cable (2,6)	602		496		898	67.1	82.4	55.3
24. Prime Cable	557	435	475		1,190	46.9	85.3	40.0
25. Post-Newsweek Cable	482	442	279	22	693	69.6	57.9	40.3
26. TCA Cable (e)	473	283	241	4	645	73.5	50.9	37.4
27. Wometco Cable Corporation	452	444	268		783	57.7	59.4	34.3
28. Tele-Media	426	42	156		611	69.8	36.5	25.5
29. Maclean Hunter	425		378		751	56.6	89.0	50.3
30. Multimedia Cablevision	417	394	323		694	60.1	77.4	46.5
31. Rifkin & Associates	380		219		536	70.9	57.5	40.8
32. Triax Communications	370		193		562	65.8	52.0	34.2
33. Western Communications (e)	323		149		434	74.6	46.0	34.3
34. C-TEC	258	247	176		417	62.0	68.2	42.3
35. Columbia International (6)	249		193	10	399	62.6	77.2	48.4
36. Service Electric	242		80		342	70.7	33.1	23.4
37. SBC Media Ventures (9)	233	226	195	40	395	59.0	83.8	49.5

Exhibit 5.3 Top 50 Cable System Operators As of December 31, 1993 *(continued)*

Company	Basic Subscribers (000)	Expanded Basic (000)	Pay Units (000)	Mini Pay (000)	Homes Passed (000)	Percentage Ratios Basic/ Homes Passed	Pay/Basic	Pay/Homes Passed
38. Greater Media	227	218	198		373	60.7	87.4	53.1
39. Harron Communications	223	174	150	4	330	67.5	67.2	45.4
40. Media General	220	201	164	24	324	68.1	74.5	50.7
41. U.S. Cable Corporation	209	198	119		348	60.0	57.1	34.3
42. MultiVision	208	74	153		357	58.4	73.2	42.7
43. Garden State Cable	192		152		284	67.7	79.3	53.7
44. Sutton Capital Association	183	176	171		273	67.0	93.2	62.5
45. Armstrong Utilities	181		97		229	79.2	53.5	42.3
46. Bresnan Communications *,#	174	167	85	24	267	65.0	49.2	32.0
47. Simmons Communications	169	163	64	1	243	69.6	38.1	26.5
48. Northland Communications	158	155	44		214	73.8	28.0	20.7
49. Summit Comm. Group	157	150	93		235	66.9	59.3	39.6
50. Blade Communications	149	148	88		237	62.7	59.4	37.2

Reprinted from *Cable TV Investor*, March 31, 1994, with the permission of Paul Kagan Associates, Inc., Carmel, CA.

1. TCI counts include 100% of UA partnerships (13% owned by TCI) but do not include 80% BRESNAN, 70% TKR Cable I, II and III, Liberty spinoff interests or international holdings. Net owned basic subscribers number 10,701,000; total gross TCI owned/affiliated basic subscribers total 15,206,000.
2. Includes STORER split-off subscribers: TCI – 609,000; Comcast – 927,500; TKR – 265,788.
3. Time-Warner Cable counts include: 100% Paragon, 937,715 basic subscribers (50% owned); 100% of other affiliated systems, 400,000.
4. Continental counts include 34% of Insight (52nd largest cable company).
5. Pro rata 40% Garden State Cablevision (76,888), Comcast subscriber count would be 2,724,888.
6. Partially owned by Liberty Media: TKR 50%; Lenfest 50%; Intermedia 3%; Columbia 30%; and other various % of non-listed cable holdings. Total Liberty net subscribers: 938,580.
7. Lenfest counts reflect 40% equity in Garden State Cable (43rd largest cable operator).
8. Paragon (50% owned by Houston Industries) included at 100% in Time-Warner count. Pro rata 50% Paragon, Houston Industries has 1,073,451 subscribers, ranking it as the 14th largest operator.
9. SBC Ventures is Southwestern Bell's cable operating company – acquisition of Hauser Communications complete by 12/31.
Count reflects a recent sale or acquisition.
* Owned in part by TCI.
e Estimate by Paul Kagan Associates.

FUTURE SERVICES

Most analysts believed that CATV was a mature product in the markets it served. Future growth was expected to come from a range of enhanced services.

Pay per view   This service was still unavailable in most parts of the U.S., but availability was expected to grow steadily.

Enhanced pay per view (EPPV)   The additional channels needed to offer EPPV could be obtained by upgrading the amplifiers on the system to take advantage of the full capacity of coaxial cable (up to 150 channels). Such new equipment was not expected to cost more than $150 per subscriber.

Impulse pay per view (IPPV)   IPPV was an enhancement that would make it possible for customers to place PPV orders closer to airtime. Digital signals were not required, although they would make IPPV function more efficiently. IPPV would normally be installed along with EPPV, but the stand-alone installation cost for IPPV was expected to be $20 per subscriber.

High Definition TV (HDTV)   This service would require CATV companies to add digital capabilities to the existing coaxial cable network. The set-top decoder needed to convert digital signals was expected to cost approximately $450 at the time of introduction, although it was widely believed that the $250 threshold would be the level at which most operators would earn an adequate return on their investment. The cost of the digital converter was expected to account for between 60–70 percent of the total investment required to introduce HDTV as measured on a per-subscriber basis. However, the lack of an agreement on a common HDTV standard meant that this service was not expected to generate much revenue in the medium term.

Video on Demand (VOD)   This system was expected to offer customers an opportunity to order any one of a range of available videotapes for immediate viewing. It was highly likely that VOD would require the installation of a sophisticated new network with additional bandwidth, incorporating optical fiber from the headend to the feeder, plus switching and digital compression to handle the demand and bandwidth requirements of such a service. The cost of an upgrade had been estimated by industry experts to be approximately $1,350 per subscriber ($400 for fiber to the feeder, $500 for switching, $450 for digital compression and conversion). One CATV operator had conducted a study of VOD and discovered that customers would purchase an average of 2.5 movies per month, at $3–4 per showing, selected from an available play list of eighty movies.

   VOD service would compete against the $15 billion video rental business, but as executives in the video rental business knew, most of these annual revenues were earned on rentals of older titles (not on rentals of current movies) and increasingly, on rentals of sophisticated video games. Video rental company executives believed that VOD would be viable at the earliest by 2002–2004, and even then, would only be capable of offering 100 movies on-line at any one time. However, Blockbuster Entertainment Corporation, a leading U.S. video rental chain, had announced plans to develop a VOD service in conjunction with Viacom, a cable company, and eventually had plans to merge with Viacom.

Telephony   Industry executives believed that the U.S. Congress would soon pass legislation allowing CATV companies to offer local exchange telephone service within their cable service areas. Cable companies would then be able to offer local telephone services to their customers, most likely at a discount to prevailing telephone company rates, although it was expected that there would be no extraordinary prohibitions preventing the telephone companies from lowering their rates to forestall customer churn. In return, telephone companies would be permitted greater freedom to distribute video services, including television signals, over their lines. It was not clear what additional expenditure CATV companies would need to make to offer local loop telephone service, although the experience of some UK cable companies involved in telephony since January, 1991 was expected to be quite valuable in helping estimate capital requirements. More than 300,000 British households depended on their cable carriers for telephone service, and some of these carriers were owned by U.S. CATV networks. Many U.S. cable companies planned to rebuild their plant to handle local telephone calls and data transmission.

Catalogue Shopping   Mail-order catalogue shopping in the U.S. was a $70 billion business in 1993, although it represented only a small fraction of the overall $2.1 trillion spent at all U.S. retail locations. More than $200 million alone was sold to consumers who placed orders through modems which connected them to on-line databases. Via cable, catalogue shopping was expected to present customers with "virtual" catalogs, which could be updated rapidly. Orders could be placed using touchpads connected to a cable converter or via the telephone.

Catalogue shopping offered customers two main benefits: cost savings and convenience. Since the costs of intermediate distribution outlets would be eliminated, it would be possible for home shopping services to be profitable on low margins, below the 8–10 percent usually earned by the most aggressive price competitor, warehouse clubs. One area where home shopping was felt to have strong potential was in grocery purchasing, which was consistently identified in studies as the type of shopping least liked by Americans. Conceivably, cable operators offering home grocery shopping services could charge food manufacturers a stocking fee to feature their products in a virtual supermarket catalogue. One analyst estimated that sales of $100 billion through cable could be possible ten years after the introduction of a catalogue shopping service.

Other Information Services   The American public was beginning to become increasingly interested in a set of information services, including electronic mail and remote database access, that was being referred to as the "information highway." Because of the bandwidth requirements for data transfer, cable television networks could conceivably serve to connect subscribers with data resources stored in remote computers. However, such access would likely be routed from the headend to the remote site using telephone lines or through a private or public data transmission service. Some level of upgrade to the cable network would be required to make interactive communications possible, although it would be difficult to estimate the cost of the necessary hardware and software. However, once in place, an interactive network would make it possible for a broad range of applications to be offered by cable carriers, including burglar and fire alarm services and remote energy management.

COMPETITION

Other than industry rivals, historically, CATV operators had no competition for video direct access to households. One exception that was expected to become more important as a technology was direct broadcast satellite (DBS). Viewers who purchased a DBS system could receive signals directly using a satellite receiving dish. Although widely used in Europe and Japan, DBS was not popular in the U.S. except in those areas where conventional cable service was not available. Where cable was available, it was almost always less expensive than DBS. In cities, it was often impractical to use DBS given the size of satellite dish that was required.

However, new DBS technology was threatening to make satellite broadcasting more competitive. A new company owned by MSOs planned to launch a satellite network that would deliver 80 channels of service to customers anywhere in the U.S. beginning in June, 1994. Moreover, the satellite dish needed to receive television signals from a satellite would be only a few feet in diameter – considerably smaller than the dishes used to date. However, DBS had one critical flaw – it did not have enough bandwidth to offer video-on-demand service. Nevertheless, it did present a viable alternative to CATV, although the price of hardware (estimated to be $700–800 for a satellite receiver and decoder) meant that customers would incur significant switching costs if they ceased relying on their local CATV operators for signals.

Other potential competitors included the local telephone operating companies, including the Regional Bell Operating Companies (RBOCs). The RBOCs held more than 75 percent of the local exchange service market in the U.S. They were individually quite large, and had combined 1993 revenues of more than $84 billion.

The telephone companies had lobbied vigorously in Washington to be allowed to be freed from the restrictions set down in federal law, FCC rulings, and in the 1984 "Consent Decree" that had prohibited their entry into other businesses. In the early 1990s, regulations had been relaxed somewhat to permit the telephone companies to offer information services such as home banking and shopping. In October, 1991 the FCC issued a Notice of Proposed Rule that would allow local telephone companies to carry "video dial tone." This meant they could carry video programs provided by third parties, but would not be allowed to program or edit programs themselves.

Traditionally, telephony used twisted pair copper wire to carry signals in two directions. But twisted pair had a relatively small bandwidth, since voice telephony could be delivered using as little as 6 MHz. This meant that the telephone companies would have to use a different system to transmit video signals, especially if they chose to offer interactive services. A new technology was proposed by Bellcore (the RBOC standards-setting and technology planning group) called Asymmetrical Digital Subscriber Loop (ADSL). ADSL promised to provide one digital video channel to each subscriber's home using the existing twisted pair telephone line. The subscriber could switch this channel at the TV set to select a program. The signal would be of VCR-grade quality, and while this was not up to the level of signal quality provided by a good CATV carrier, it did present a viable alternative to cable. Moreover, the RBOCs already had an installation and customer service infrastructure in place, along with extensive expertise in both operating addressable networks and providing services that relied on switching technology. While the deployment of ADSL would require a considerable capital expenditure on the part of the RBOCs, estimated at $750–$1,500 per subscriber, it seemed certain that they would offer cable service in selected markets within a few years.

RBOCs could also offer video on demand (VOD), but only at costs per subscriber that were higher than those for comparable CATV-based services, since the RBOCs would need to install optical fiber lines with large bandwidths right to each customer's home. Deploying fiber to the home was estimated to cost between $2,000–$3,000 per subscriber, although the RBOCs could use combinations of fiber and coaxial cable to reduce their costs somewhat. Upgrading the switches in the telephone system to handle multimedia products was expected to add another $500 per subscriber, but it was believed that these costs would drop as technologies improved. While the RBOCs at first appeared to be uncompetitive in VOD service, it was expected that they planned to install additional VOD-like capabilities to provide customers with other multimedia services such as improved video conferencing and Internet access. The business savings associated with the successful introduction of multimedia services to business telephone customers could result in system growth and increased volume, making VOD a more economic proposition due to the realization of potential scope economy effects.

On August 24, 1993, a federal judge in Virginia struck down sections of the Cable Act that prevented telephone companies from operating cable systems in their local market. This decision had the effect of making cable companies potential targets for acquisition by RBOCs, especially as RBOC revenues were growing at only 2–3 percent each year. On October 13, 1993, Bell Atlantic announced its plans to acquire 100 percent of TCI, America's largest cable operator, in the country's largest such transaction ($32.6 billion). This was equivalent to 11.75 times the annualized latest three-month cash flow for TCI, or an estimated $2,350 per subscriber. Less than two months later, Canada's BCE Telecom International announced that it had acquired 30 percent of Jones Intercable as its first step in taking complete ownership of the company in a deal that was to be completed over eight years, and at an estimated cost of $2,089 per subscriber.

At least one CATV CEO was reported as saying that the RBOCs wanted to enter other areas of service, including cable, to protect their own local telephone service franchise from competition. Such competition could come from CATV companies if regulatory barriers were lowered and additional capital investments were made by these companies to provide telephone service. Most cable companies had spare bandwidth, and, with the introduction first of digital compression and then of optical fiber cable, the additional capacity needed for telephony would be readily available. Some CATV executives even felt that the RBOCs were also interested in acquiring CATV networks outside their own operating areas, and then using these acquisitions to offer local telephone service and, thus, competing with other RBOCs.

MACLEAN HUNTER CABLE

The Offer

At the end of 1993, Maclean Hunter Cable was the twenty-ninth largest operating cable company in the U.S. Maclean Hunter Cable was part of Maclean Hunter Ltd., a Canadian cable and publishing firm which had, on February 2, 1994, received an unsolicited offer from Rogers Communications, Inc. to purchase all its shares. On February 11, the Rogers board announced they would offer C$17 a share plus a right to receive a payment if Rogers sold Maclean Hunter's U.S. cable operations for more than C$1.5 billion. The deadline for acceptance of this offer was March 15. The Maclean Hunter board rejected this offer, claiming it to be insufficient. After prolonged negotiations, Rogers and Maclean Hunter announced on March 8 that a take-over deal had been concluded. Rogers would pay C$17.50 for Maclean Hunter shares, and shareholders would lose any right to claim a portion of the proceeds from the sale of the U.S. cable assets. The total value of the take-over was C$3.1 billion, including bridge financing of C$2 billion. Rogers had indicated that it would sell Maclean Hunter's U.S. cable assets to repay C$1.5 billion of the loan. The estimated cost of these cable assets to Rogers was C$1,082 million (C$2,192 per subscriber), or eleven times the cable assets' cash flow. See Exhibit 5.4 for a valuation of each company's main lines of business.

History

During the 1980s, there was intense competition for cable franchises within the U.S. The rivalry was so strong that this period was often referred to as "the franchise wars." Two factors contributed to the rivalrous climate. First, a number of very large U.S. media conglomerates had realized the enormous financial potential of the cable business and decided to gain entry by applying their resources to the task of winning franchises. Second, the number of major urban areas without cable service had diminished considerably. It was felt by 1983 or 1984 that all of the most attractive franchises had been awarded. This type of shortage helped increase the value of existing franchises, including those held by Maclean Hunter.

Despite the risks and costs that the company faced as a result of shifts in the competitive environment, Maclean Hunter remained intent on expanding its American cable TV holdings in the 1980s, partly because it had reached the limits of growth in the smaller Canadian market. Average penetration in the U.S. market was only 45 percent of homes passed, meaning that significant system expansion was still possible. As well, the regulatory climate in the U.S. had shifted toward market-based mechanisms. Ancillary services were often lightly regulated. The proliferation of channels further fragmented the U.S. market, meaning that advertisers had to increasingly rely on cable to deliver their messages to target audiences.

Maclean Hunter made every effort to capitalize on its strengths during the 1980s. It decided to pursue new opportunities through the franchising route rather than engage in acquisitions (an increasingly popular tactic among U.S. cable operators), because it felt that managing cable systems was a firm-specific advantage. To benefit from this advantage, Maclean Hunter had to build its own system from the ground up. The acquisition route was also unattractive, because the company found the asking price of existing systems excessive in view of weak fundamentals. The asking price of seven to ten times cash flow was too high, since most acquisition targets required a significant investment to bring them up to Maclean Hunter's standards.

The company's strategy was to build state-of-the-art systems so that subscribers could be assured of receiving new services as they were developed. The basic cable package was continually expanded, and arrangements made with the programmers of the latest and best pay-TV services, so they could be offered to customers at attractive rates. Considerable attention was given to local origination programming, and strong local management teams

Exhibit 5.4 Companies' Valuation for Main Lines of Business

	Assets (C$ millions)	1994 Cash Flow Multiple	Cash Flow Value (C$ millions)
Maclean Hunter			
Cable	$229	10.7x	$2,450
Periodicals	16	9.5	152
Business Forms	55	9.0	495
Newspapers	21	10.5	221
Broadcast	9	9.5	86
Communications Services	6	8.0	48
Subtotal/Average	$336	10.3x	$3,452
Net Debt			(187)
Private Market Value			(C$) 3,265
Fully Diluted Shares (millions)	179.0		
Private Market Value/Share			(C$) $18.24
Rogers Communications			
Cable	$228	9.5x	$2,736
Cellular	377*	14.0	5,278
Radio	12	8.0	96
Long Distance	31*	25.0	775
Subtotal/Average	$708	12.5x	$8,885
21% of Canadian Satellite Communications			35
25% of Teleglobe			123
80% of Cantel Paging			49
Canadian Home Shopping Network			20
Total Assets			$9,112
Net Debt			(1,846)
Private Market Value			(C$) $7,266
Fully Diluted Shares (millions)	202.1		
Private Market Value/Share			(C$) $35.95

*Calculated using present values of 1996 cash flows, discounted at 10%.
Reprinted from *Cable TV Investor*, February 28, 1994, with the permission of Paul Kagan Associates, Inc., Carmel, CA.

were given a high degree of autonomy to respond to local market needs. These policies cemented Maclean Hunter's reputation as a leading cable operator.

The company continued to focus its efforts on winning suburban systems. Not only did Maclean Hunter find the bidding process to be less costly than in the cities, but believed that suburban franchises offered advantages that urban franchises did not. For instance, some suburban franchises had a population density that was on par with those in nearby cities. Since building a state-of-the-art plant in suburban locations could be done more rapidly and at a lower cost than an upgrade within a city, a suburban cable system could be activated sooner. This had the effect of more rapidly generating cash, a consideration that was of prime importance to a financially-conservative company like Maclean Hunter. The company also found that suburban communities were more homogeneous, meaning that programming requirements were simpler and less expensive. Eventually, Maclean Hunter began bidding for franchises in a number of U.S. cities, rather than concentrating on building up contiguous systems. The primary reason was the need for additional revenue, and Maclean Hunter accepted the need to manage each system as a separate entity.

At the time of the Rogers acquisition, Maclean Hunter had 499,000 subscribers in New Jersey, Michigan, and Florida. The company was considered to be one of the leading cable operators in the U.S., offering its customers a wide variety of channels delivered through technologically advanced distribution systems. Moreover, the company's U.S. operations were profitable and relations with municipalities were for the most part harmonious. However, some industry analysts felt that the company's U.S. cable operations had not been upgraded sufficiently to justify a high cash flow multiple if sold.

THE FCC AND RATE ROLL-BACKS

On May 3, 1993, the FCC released a 475-page manual implementing the Cable Act of October 3, 1992. This Act was intended to force cable companies that had been overcharging customers to reduce their rates and was rooted in a congressional drive to re-regulate cable television as part of a four-year effort to curb escalating cable charges. The FCC published cable rate benchmarks and new reporting that required operators to provide the FCC with extensive information about rate-setting procedures, and it also ordered the cable companies to roll back rates by $2 per month per subscriber beginning in September, 1993. Rates were frozen at the new lower level. Further rate increases would be tied to changes in a GNP-fixed-weight price index plus some portion of a CATV operator's expenses.

The effect of the roll-back on the U.S. cable industry was to immediately reduce forecast revenues by an estimated $2 billion. For an average operator, this roll-back would reduce revenues by 7.4 percent, cash flow by 15.7 percent, and cash flow margin by more than 4 percent (from 46.5 percent to 42.3 percent). The cost of FCC compliance monitoring, estimated by the FCC chairman at $28 million, would be passed on to the industry through a supplemental assessment. One of the effects of the roll-back was to reduce the amount of cash that had been used to expand the broadband network and to offer more programming.

On February 22, 1994, the FCC unanimously voted to reduce rates a further 7 percent. The FCC chairman, Reed Hundt, indicated that the combined roll-backs would affect 90 percent of all cable systems and save consumers $3 billion. In effect, operators were required to reduce their September, 1992 rates by 17 percent and then compare these rates to new FCC benchmarks. Systems whose rates would fall below the new benchmark after making the 17 percent deduction were entitled to a phased implementation of rate reductions following an FCC cost study. A typical cost study took a year to complete. Small cable operators (those with less than 15,000 subscribers) also qualified for phased roll-backs. Basic cable service would be permitted to earn a maximum ROA of 11.5 percent. Industry executives were concerned that FCC rate unpredictability would make it difficult to properly value cable holdings in the future.

CAROL DIXON'S EVALUATION

After reviewing published analysts' reports (selected comments are given in Exhibit 5.5) and conducting her own background research, Dixon reached some tentative conclusions about the direction of the cable industry in the U.S. These are summarized in Exhibit 5.6.

As she saw it, setting a final price involved weighing industry-wide uncertainties with some potential consequences of the acquiring firm's strategy. Key uncertainties included:

Standards: Despite an abundance of discussion about new services such as video on demand, there were no accepted technical standards in existence that would permit either the CATV industry or the RBOCs to move beyond the concept stage. Dixon worried that the U.S. Congress was considering a bill that would set a deadline for the industry to establish standards. Her concern was that if the deadline was not met, then the FCC could make standards decisions that the industry would have to live with for a long time. Many interests wanted a say in setting standards: the telephone companies and database operators saw standards as a way to steer the future of the industry to naturally favor their key competencies. Other interested companies, including Microsoft, Apple, and General Instrument (suppliers of set-top descramblers and other in-home cable equipment) wanted the CATV industry to set its own standards, but wanted to keep some of their own technological breakthroughs private, thereby limiting the number of open standards that could be readily emulated. The delay in confirming standards also served to increase uncertainty about the future, since the costs of new technologies kept changing and would remain estimates at best until careful designs based on new standards had been completed and production volumes for new equipment became known.

Software Alliances: While cable signals were sent via hardware, consumer acceptance of new services was going to be decided by the quality of the interface presented by each cable operator. Therefore, many executives in the CATV industry felt that the presence or absence of existing or prospective alliances with software companies would have a long-term effect on a CATV company's ability to build a customer base for new, enhanced services.

Open Access: Dixon's key concern centered around mandated access to the cable network. Would legislation oblige networks to carry any and all traffic according to published rate schedules (especially important for data, telephony, and some entertainment services), or could the cable carrier decide what it would carry and at what price? The answer to this question would determine where the cable carriers would be positioned on the emerging "infotainment" industry value chain.

Content: Owners of rights to video productions received approximately 25 percent of revenues for movie channels. Would that remain constant or change in the future? With more and more of America's entertainment companies becoming owned by Japanese investors, could access to the critical resource of cable TV content ever become a bargaining chip in some future international negotiation over standards or in an important equipment supply contract? Could content also be used to drive customer choice, and if so, how would the CATV company assess the risks of new, unproven television shows?

Market: The market for many new services was only hypothesized or at best substantiated based on a few small market trials. Consequently, Dixon wondered about customer behavior in the future. Would the new services now on the drawing board persuade customers to spend more time in front of their televisions than they did in early 1994?

Video on Demand: Most people who watched the industry thought that VOD could supplant video rental companies as the preferred distribution channel to satisfy American demand for movie entertainment. That, thought Dixon, would certainly depend on the CATV operators'

Exhibit 5.5   Selected Cable Analysts' Comments, March, 1994

". . . Trophy cable properties will sell at 12x cash flow multiples, or $2,800–3,000 per subscriber, but systems tied to regulated revenues will only get 8x–10x if they're lucky."

". . . The multiple isn't 12x cash flow and it isn't likely to be 12x for a while."

"I anticipate that smaller systems will sell for 7x–8x cash flows . . . but sooner or later reregulation will only be a bad memory."

". . . Telephony is now what will drive system values."

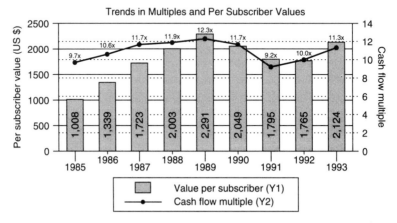

". . . Look at the trends, the numbers are coming back up and there won't be much on sale for some time."

"While the cable companies' low and non-investment-grade ratings will improve if they merge with the telephone companies, remember that the telcos' ratings will be hurt by any kind of merger activity. And the new rating for the merged companies won't necessarily be the average of the two partners."

"Competition will be a bigger driver in helping determine values and creditworthiness. The government seems to be moving toward deploying two broadband communications networks into the home. This means there'll be lots of opportunities to offer high-growth, high-margin services. Both cable and telephone companies will have to learn to compete hard."

"Cash flow multiples are used to compare cable companies because they make it possible to perform a consistent comparison between companies, regardless of where they operate. Since cable companies are so capital intensive, using cash flow multiples makes some sense, and it's consistent with the way that utilities are measured everywhere. But this industry is becoming more competitive, and it's getting that way because of technology. When I look at a company in the future, yes, I'm going to worry about net free cash flow,[4] but I'm also going to look at cash flow adequacy,[5] debt-to-earnings before interest, taxes, depreciation, and cash flow coverage of cash interest obligations."

"Earnings before interest, taxes, and depreciation. And cash flow, of course."

"Government will change this industry, and I'm not sure it'll be for the better. Competition between telcos and cable companies could be a big departure from the way things have been done in the past, where the telcos and cable companies ran their businesses behind a lot of shelter from the market."

"Cable companies have always been evaluated using cash flow measures, and I don't see any reason to change. What's most important for me will be net free cash flow and the right cash flow adequacy ratio."

Exhibit 5.5 Selected Cable Analysts' Comments, March, 1994 *(continued)*

"To me, it's unlikely that the cable industry will generate any kind of significant revenues from telephony for the next three years. Even then, does anybody seriously expect the RBOCs to sit back and watch their market being nibbled away?"

"Where's the value? In content, of course. Think about it: who'd you rather own – Disney or CBS? Carriers will become commodities within ten years, just wait for technology to level the playing field."

Reprinted from *Cable TV Investor*, March 31, 1994, with the permission of Paul Kagan Associates, Inc., Carmel, CA.
[4]Defined as cash flow after interest, taxes, and capital expenditures.
[5]Annual net free cash flow relative to the average scheduled debt maturity over the next five years.

Exhibit 5.6 Carol Dixon's Tentative Conclusions

Cable TV distribution architecture is evolving into digitally-switched regional hubs, just like those that exist in the telephone network.

This regional hub strategy is making it possible for cable operators to consider whether they should connect headends in various cities. This could lead to territory swaps with other operators, but also produce scale economies. As low-cost providers, the realigned cable companies could become effective competitors for local telephone access.

To become full-service networks for both residential and commercial customers, cable TV operators must consider strategies that include long distance carriers. They may be able to bypass local loop telephone service altogether.

The demand for more programming will lead to an expansion in the number of channels that an MSO must offer. If 150 channels becomes the norm, MSOs must shift to either fiber or higher bandwidth-capable coaxial cable. This observation is supported by the current construction/rebuild plans of most MSOs. A hybrid fiber-coax network is the low cost solution for broadcast-dominated video services.

Re-regulation of cable rates will ultimately harm the consumer as well as make it difficult for firms to raise money on Wall Street to expand their networks and services.

Competition from alternative providers (e.g., RBOCs, DBS, etc.) will change the monopolistic nature of the cable industry. The big question then becomes: is the existing management capable of handling the transition to a competitive environment?

ability to offer VOD at prices which were competitive to those charged by video rental stores. Moreover, would the owners of the movies be content to let control of their secondary distribution channel (i.e., after in-theatre screening) become concentrated in the hands of the cable companies? She also wondered what effect the initial limited movie selection would have on customer acceptance of the technology, and hence, on VOD revenues.

The FCC: The long-term intentions of this agency were not clear. While re-regulation of cable rates seemed to Dixon to be bad economics, but perhaps good politics, she knew that FCC intervention in price-setting would introduce a random, uncertain element into investors' thinking. That would lower the share price since future revenue streams would become less reliable, and, therefore, the cost of capital for cable system expansion or rebuilding would be raised.

Dixon also thought that two key questions of strategy had to enter into a proper determination of a price for the Maclean Hunter assets.

Alliances with Local and Long Distance Telephone Companies: A cable company should consider forging an alliance with a long distance carrier such as AT&T, MCI, or Sprint. The cable carrier could provide a way to bypass the RBOC that delivered local loop telephone service and in so doing, create a possibility for making a small profit on long distance calling. Alternatively, the cable company could explore an alliance or joint venture with the RBOC in their service area, which could lead to scale and scope efficiencies as far as billing, repair, and customer service were concerned. As well, an integrated company would have a wealth of information about the buying habits of customers, meaning that micro-marketing or mass customization initiatives could become viable.

Bundling: Could a cable carrier find a way to offer a bundle of high-value services at low cost? An example that had been discussed for the West Coast involved bundling cable, Home Box Office (a specialty movie channel), and a new home energy management service from Pacific Gas & Electric.

The vendor's situation would also influence the selling price to a great extent. Rogers had shouldered a huge debt load in order to buy Maclean Hunter Ltd. While Dixon knew that Rogers would not dispose of Maclean Hunter's U.S. cable assets without seeking to maximize proceeds from the sale, she also understood that Rogers was under pressure to play down their borrowings. As well, it was widely known in the industry that Rogers had no real interest in operating Maclean Hunter's cable franchises, and as a result, it was believed that Rogers was anxious to find a suitable buyer. Dixon wondered whether these twin pressures could work for her client in any subsequent negotiations over price.

But the most important question in Carol Dixon's view was identifying the new value chain for the cable industry produced by rapid technological change and steady deregulation. Once that was clear, then she could make a price and cash flow multiple recommendation for the Maclean Hunter assets.

NOTES

1. Cable systems passed by many homes that chose not to subscribe to cable. The "passed by" figure is thus a measure of a CATV carrier's potential market, since only homes passed by cable service could ever subscribe to it.
2. All amounts are in U.S. dollars, unless indicated otherwise. At the time of the case, US$1 = C$1.3643.
3. The bandwidth of a system is measured in the range of frequencies that it can carry. One megahertz (MHz) represents a bandwidth of 1,000 hertz. One gigahertz (GHz) equals 1,000 MHz. The wider the bandwidth, the greater the number of signals (amount of information) that can be transmitted simultaneously.

The Diaper War: Kimberly-Clark versus Procter & Gamble

On November 1, 1989, the management of Kimberly-Clark (K-C) watched with great interest and concern as Procter & Gamble (P&G) announced the appointment of a new CEO, Edwin Artzt. Artzt had considerable international experience in the disposable diapers industry, and K-C's management wondered if his appointment would signal a new phase of competition within the industry. Six months prior to Artzt's appointment, P&G had introduced gender-specific disposables with designer colors. While a significant product improvement, gender-specific disposables were not in the tradition of prior technological competitive breakthroughs. K-C had responded with test marketing of a similar product, but a national rollout would still be several months away.

The decision to proceed with a national rollout was tempered by concern that such a move would acknowledge P&G's market leadership. K-C's managers also questioned whether a move into gender-specific disposables would distract the company from important research and development efforts aimed at the environmental concerns now confronting the industry. In considering options, K-C managers were faced with significant financial constraints and wondered whether greater opportunities would be available outside the increasingly competitive North American industry. International opportunities in Europe and Japan merited greater attention, particularly given recent moves by overseas competitors to enter the North American diaper industry. Also of interest to K-C management were the company's ongoing efforts to build a market position for its adult incontinence products. As K-C faced the 1990s, managers braced for heightened competition and wondered how and when to respond.

THE NORTH AMERICAN DIAPER INDUSTRY

The disposable diaper, invented in postwar Sweden, was introduced to America by Johnson & Johnson in the late 1940s. Kendall and Parke Davis entered the market a decade later. Marketing efforts were focused on traveling parents with infants. These early diapers were used with fastening pins and plastic pants and were generally perceived as ineffective in keeping both babies and parents dry. With slow sales, prices remained high ($.10 ea. for disposables versus $.03–$.05 for cloth diaper services and $.01–$.02 for home-laundered diapers), and most firms remained uninterested in making significant investments in the disposable diaper segment.

In 1961, P&G entered the disposable diapers industry with the introduction of Pampers; test marketing began in 1962. The move to disposable diapers followed progress P&G had made in cellulose fiber research through its 1957 purchase of the Charmin Paper Company. Pampers provided a clear technological breakthrough from previous products, as it was the first disposable diaper to use a plastic back-sheet coupled with absorbent wadding and a porous rayon sheet facing the baby's skin.

Despite these advantages, national rollout was hindered by Pamper's high price of $.10 per diaper. This price, similar to that charged by other firms, reflected P&G's approach of purchasing partially completed components to be assembled later. In 1964, P&G engineers developed a continuous process technology that was many times faster than prior processes and allowed the use of minimally processed raw materials, thus significantly cutting costs. Pampers was successfully reintroduced into a second test market site at a price of $.055 per diaper. Full national distribution was achieved by 1969.

Diaper research at K-C also began in earnest in the mid-1960s, focusing primarily on new product technology. K-C used its experience with feminine napkins to develop a product that used fluff pulp in place of tissue. The pulp provided both better absorbency and competitive cost savings. These advantages, coupled with the introduction of adhesive tabs and an improved shape, were incorporated into a new product, called Kimbies, introduced by K-C in 1968. Kimbies was parity priced with Pampers and competitive cost savings were not passed through to consumers. Rather, K-C reinvested the excess profits into further product improvements. This strategy fit with industry market research that showed a strong relationship between improved product features and market and sales growth. The cost of product improvements could be passed on, as many consumers seemed to show a high degree of price indifference.

Other companies active during the late 1960s included Scott Paper, Borden, and International Paper, each of which was experimenting with a two-piece disposable diaper system. The system relied on technology developed in Europe and involved a disposable inner liner and a reusable plastic outer shell. Using snaps instead of pins gave these products a distinct advantage over Pampers.

By 1970, industry rivalry was increasingly focused on product innovation. However, these improvements were not always translated into market share gains for reasons that appeared to be two-fold: poor marketing communication of product benefits and the inability of some firms to reduce manufacturing costs to P&G's level. Although regarded by some as an inferior product, Pampers appeared unstoppable, peaking at an estimated market share of 92 percent in 1970.

Industry Shakeout

There was a rapid shakeout of the disposable diaper industry in the early 1970s, hastened by a constant series of modifications undertaken by P&G to further strengthen its Pampers line. For example, P&G converted from tissue to pulp fluff in 1972 and to adhesive tabs in 1973. As a result of the heightened competition and the continuous costly improvements upping the ante in the U.S. market, Borden exited the industry in 1970, Scott in 1971, and both International Paper and Johnson & Johnson in 1972.

In 1971, K-C undertook efforts to reduce its reliance on core newsprint and paper operations, and to strengthen its position in consumer products. Kimbies was an early benefactor of this strategic change. Buoyed by increased marketing expenditures, Kimbies' market share peaked in 1974 at 20 percent. However, as the decade progressed, K-C management became preoccupied with other activities and sales began to decline.

In spite of the industry's transformation, disposable diapers were only used regularly on about 35 percent of U.S. babies in 1976. Total market growth remained flat. To most parents, the benefits of disposables were not large enough to support their added cost.

P&G and K-C Introduce Premium Products

In 1976, P&G announced the test marketing and selected regional introduction of a new diaper product, Luvs. This diaper offered several improvements over Pampers, including a fitted shape and a flexible snap closing system. In an effort to create a new premium market segment, Luvs were priced at 25 to 30 percent above Pampers, moving the latter into a middle segment. P&G continued regional market testing for over two years, but seemed indecisive on a national decision. Many observers believed that this hesitation was related to test market results indicating a large negative impact on Pampers.

By 1978, K-C's corporate transformation was nearly complete and attention was refocused on the diaper sector. K-C introduced Huggies to replace Kimbies. Compared to both Pampers and Luvs, Huggies was better fitting, more absorbent, and offered an improved tape-fastening system. To support the new product, K-C hired top marketing talent and backed the introduction with large promotional and advertising investments.

At the time of Huggies' introduction, Luvs was still available only on a limited regional basis. With the introduction of Huggies, P&G was forced to complete Luvs' national rollout. Luvs suffered from inferior performance relative to Huggies, and was unable to gain control of the premium segment. K-C continued to produce Kimbies for the market's middle segment, but concentrated resources on Huggies, allowing Kimbies to die a slow death. Production of Kimbies was discontinued in 1986.

Huggies' sales grew rapidly as consumers discovered the diaper's superior characteristics. Sales growth came not only through market share growth, but also as a result of the increased use of disposable diapers. With Huggies, consumers could more clearly see the benefit of switching from traditional cloth diapers to disposable products. Market penetration of disposables increased rapidly.

Procter & Gamble Responds

P&G initially did little to respond to K-C's new market entry, partly because K-C introduced Huggies after upgrading its manufacturing processes, and P&G had large investments in older diaper machines. P&G was hesitant to make the huge investments necessary to match K-C production processes. This older technology limited P&G's ability to match K-C's product modifications and put P&G at a cost disadvantage. P&G responded by aggressively promoting Pampers, but sales continued to slump. Brand market share fluctuated widely during the 1981–1989 period; the early 1980s being the most difficult period for P&G (Exhibit 6.1). By 1983, market research began to convince P&G management that the middle sector was disappearing. Consumers either wanted the best products despite their

Exhibit 6.1   Market Share Data (% of U.S. Retail Shipments)

BRAND	1980	1981	1982	1983	1984	1985	1986	1987	1988	1989
K-C HUGGIES	7.1	11.7	12.3	18.1	24.0	31.3	35.0	31.3	31.7	32.0
P&G PAMPERS	55.7	48.0	44.7	40.0	35.0	30.5	32.0	42.2	35.6	31.6
P&G LUVS	9.8	17.2	18.0	17.7	17.5	19.0	21.0	15.2	16.1	17.4
OTHER	27.4	23.1	25.0	24.2	23.5	19.2	12.0	11.3	17.6	19.0

Source: Various publicly available documents on product shipments.

high prices, or they wanted low priced – typically private label – products, regardless of performance. Pampers was stuck in the middle.

Not until late 1984, when Huggies had 30 percent market share, did P&G upgrade its products with comparable features and fight to regain share. First, P&G repositioned Pampers as a premium product, comparable to Luvs, through improvements in Pamper's shape and fastening system. Second, to improve cost structure and offer improved features, P&G invested an estimated $500 million in upgrading its production system, and $225 million in additional advertising and promotion was used to re-launch their slumping brands.

Super-Thin Diapers

During 1986, competition between P&G and K-C entered a new stage of intense technological rivalry with both companies introducing super-thin, super-absorbent disposables. The new diapers contained polyacrylate, a powder crystal that absorbed 50 times its weight in liquid. By using polyacrylate, diapers could be made 30 percent thinner. The two firms had to re-educate consumers into not associating absorbency with thickness. The campaign was a success, and parents seemed to like the new diaper's sleek profile and improved performance. P&G and K-C achieved a 33 percent reduction in transportation costs, as well as improved shelf utilization for retailers.

P&G introduced the new technology early in 1986. K-C's introduction followed nine months later. P&G's competitive leadership in North America came not from R&D work in the U.S., but rather from access to technology developed in Japan, where P&G had considerable operations. Lacking a significant presence in Japan, K-C was forced to follow P&G's introduction in North America. Initially, P&G and K-C were dependent on Japanese suppliers for this key material. In 1988, Cellanese, a U.S. chemical firm, was finally able to obtain a license to manufacture in North America.

Market Segments

The introduction of super-thin technology hastened the demise of the mid-market segment. Super-thin technology was regarded as so unique that its use automatically positioned a product at the high end of the market. The re-positioning of Pampers in 1984 and the withdrawal of Kimbies in 1986 represented an effective abandonment of the mid-price segment by the major industry players. More traditional, lower technology diapers were positioned in the low-price segment.

During the early 1980s, P&G and K-C had unsuccessfully tested products aimed at the low-priced segment. Their inability to place products in the low-priced segment was primarily due to mass merchandisers' reluctance to give adequate shelf space to their low-priced entries. Retailers were able to earn much higher margins from private label brands, targeted at the same segment.

HEAD-TO-HEAD COMPETITION

By the fall of 1989, the industry had essentially become a duopoly dominated by K-C, with a 32 percent market share, and P&G with a 48 percent share. Both companies sold super-thin diapers exclusively. In 1989, total retail sales of disposable diapers exceeded $4.5 billion in the U.S. and $400 million in Canada.

Competition between P&G and K-C was intense. Given the huge fixed costs involved in the production of disposable diapers, it was estimated that each 1 percent increase in market share resulted in $6–10 million in additional annual profit. As the disposable diaper market appeared saturated, with little growth in the total market expected, it was becoming increasingly apparent that market-share competition would intensify. Historically, market-share positions had been volatile, but market growth had helped reduce the risk of low capacity utilization. In a stable market, market-share fluctuations could lead to reduced capacity utilization and profitability pressures for the losing firm.

As the rivalry between P&G and K-C heated up, it was uncertain whether the principal focus of the competitive battle would remain fixed on technological innovation and strong promotional support. The stakes were clearly high, and both companies were intent on winning the battle. It was estimated that K-C and P&G both enjoyed net profit margins of 15 percent on diapers, as compared to less than 10 percent on most of their other consumer paper products. In determining the future basis of competition, both P&G and K-C had different resource bases and corporate interests, as described in the following two sections.

Procter & Gamble Company

In 1989, P&G was a leading competitor in the U.S. household and personal care products industries with $13.3 billion in U.S. sales (Exhibit 6.2). P&G's products held dominant positions in North America in a variety of sectors, including detergents (Tide, Cheer), bar soap (Ivory), toothpaste (Crest), shampoos (Head and Shoulders), coffee (Folgers), bakery mixes (Duncan Hines), shortening (Crisco), and peanut butter (Jiff). Disposable diapers were an important product group, comprising approximately 17 percent of P&G's total North American sales.

Historically, most of P&G's annual growth had come from the expansion of existing brands where the company's marketing expertise was well known. In building these brands, P&G typically followed a strategy based on developing a superior consumer product, branding it, positioning it as a premium product, and then developing the brand through advertising and promotion. The strategy was consistent with P&G's objectives of having top brands and highest market shares in its class.

P&G's marketing strengths were supported by core competencies in R&D. With shorter product lifecycles for many non-food consumer products, R&D was becoming more important to P&G. Much of P&G's R&D efforts were focused on upgrading existing products. However, in the late 1980s, P&G devoted extensive R&D resources toward several new products, such as Olestra, a fat substitute. In 1989, total P&G R&D expenditures were $628 million, including approximately $100 million for diapers. Some analysts sug-

Exhibit 6.2   Procter & Gamble Consolidated Statement of Earnings

Years Ended June 30
(Millions of Dollars Except Per Share Amounts)

	1989	1988	1987
Income			
Net sales	$21,398	$19,336	$17,000
Interest and other income	291	155	163
	21,689	19,491	17,163
Costs and expenses			
Cost of products sold	13,371	11,880	10,411
Marketing, administrative, and other expenses	5,988	5,660	4,977
Interest expense	391	321	353
Provision for restructuring	–	–805	
	19,750	17,861	16,546
Earnings before income taxes	1,939	1,630	617
Income taxes	733	610	290
Net earnings	1,206	1,020	327

Consolidated Balance Sheet
June 30 (Millions of Dollars)

	1989	1988
Assets		
Current assets	6,578	5,593
Property, plant, and equipment	6,793	6,778
Goodwill and other intangible assets	2,305	1,944
Other assets	675	505
Total	$16,351	$14,820
Liabilities and shareholders' equity		
Current liabilities	4,656	4,224
Long term debt	3,698	2,462
Other liabilities	447	475
Deferred income taxes	1,335	1,322
Shareholders' equity	6,215	6,337
Total	$16,351	$14,820

Segment Information

Geographic areas Millions of dollars		United States	Inter- national	Corporate	Total
Net sales	1987	$11,805	$5,524	$(329)	$17,000
	1988	12,423	7,294	(381)	19,336
	1989	13,312	8,529	(443)	21,398
Net Earnings	1987	329	120	(122)	327
	1988	864	305	(149)	1,020
	1989	927	417	(138)	1,206

*Net earnings have been reduced by $357 million in the United States, and $102 million in International by the provision for restructuring.
Source: Procter & Gamble, 1989 Annual Report.

gested that the slowdown of innovations in the diaper wars may have been partially a result of P&G channelling R&D resources to new product areas.

While P&G had generally been successful with its internal development efforts, gross margins had not been as high as those of its competitors. During the late 1980s, P&G also showed signs of wavering in its approach to market development. Attracted by opportunities in other markets, P&G had circumvented the development process and proceeded with several highly publicized acquisitions, including Richardson-Vicks (Vicks cough/cold remedies, Oil of Olay, Clearasil, Vidal Sassoon hair care products), G.D. Searle (Metamucil, Dramamine, Icy Hot), Bain de Soleil (sun care products), and Sundor Group (fruit drinks). The results of these acquisitions were not yet clear in 1989.

In addition to being a dominant competitor in the U.S. household and personal care products industries, P&G also had a strong position in several key international markets. In 1989, international sales surpassed $8.5 billion and income from international operations soared to $417 million, up almost 37 percent from the previous year. Sales growth in Europe and Japan were particularly impressive, with European sales up almost 15 percent and Japanese sales up more than 40 percent over 1988 figures. Performance in international markets was led by strong showings in diapers and detergents.

Kimberly-Clark

In 1989, K-C was a leading manufacturer and marketer of personal, health care, and industrial products made primarily from natural and synthetic fibers. In 1989, K-C had revenues of $5.7 billion and net income of $424 million (Exhibits 6.3 and 6.4). Well known K-C products included Kleenex facial tissues, Kotex and New Freedom feminine care products, Hi-Dri household towels, and Depend incontinence products (Exhibit 6.5). Huggies disposable diapers were K-C's largest single product, contributing $1.4 billion to 1989 sales and an estimated 37 percent of net income.

K-C was organized into three divisions. The largest division was personal, health care, and industrial products, contributing 77 percent of K-C's 1989 sales and 78 percent of net income. Personal products included disposable diapers, feminine care products, disposable hand towels, and various incontinence products. Health care products included surgical gowns, packs, and wraps. Industrial products included cleaning wipes made of unwoven materials.

K-C's second division manufactured newsprint and groundwood printing papers, premium business and correspondence papers, cigarette papers, tobacco products, and specialty papers. This division represented 19 percent of K-C's sales and net income. The importance of woodlands-related products had diminished throughout much of the 1970s and 1980s as K-C shifted resources into consumer products. The two divisions were, however, closely linked to the degree that many of the consumer products relied on cellulose fibers supplied by K-C's woodlands operations. It was estimated that 65 percent of the wood pulp needs for consumer products were supplied in-house, a level considered high in the industry. It was thought that vertical control provided the advantage of flexibility and security under rapidly changing competitive conditions. However, it also significantly complicated strategic planning and potentially magnified swings in performance that accompanied shifting competitive conditions. Prices for newsprint and paper products had been highly cyclical during the 1980s. In 1989, there was an indication that prices were softening and would remain

Exhibit 6.3   Kimberly-Clark Corporation and Subsidiaries Consolidated Income Statement

Year Ended December 31
(Millions of dollars, except per share amount)

	1989	1988	1987
Net sales	$5,733.6	$5,393.5	$4,884.7
Cost of products sold	3,654.1	3,404.2	3,065.9
Distribution expenses	195.8	185.2	181.2
Gross profit	1,883.7	1,804.1	1,637.6
Advertising, promotion, and selling expense	813.4	784.1	674.9
Research expense	118.0	110.9	110.5
General expense	278.9	268.5	266.1
Operating profit	673.4	640.6	586.1
Interest income	19.3	11.2	7.2
Other income	24.2	24.2	26.2
Interest expense	(68.2)	(80.6)	(65.6)
Other expense	(17.9)	(11.5)	(19.8)
Income before income taxes	630.8	583.9	534.1
Provision for income taxes	242.4	229.8	230.5
Income before equity interests	368.4	354.1	303.6
Share of net income of equity companies	49.3	46.0	35.3
Minority owner's share of subsidiaries' net income	(13.9)	(21.5)	(13.7)
Net Income	$ 423.8	$ 378.6	$ 325.2

Consolidated Balance Sheet
(Millions of dollars)

	1989	1988
ASSETS		
Total current assets	1,443.2	1,278.3
Net fixed assets	3,040.9	2,575.3
Investments in equity companies	296.6	291.7
Deferred charges and other assets	142.3	121.8
TOTAL ASSETS	$4,923.0	$4,267.6
LIABILITIES		
Total current liabilities	$1,263.2	$ 925.7
Long-term debt	745.1	743.3
Other noncurrent liabilities	79.9	53.7
Deferred income taxes	643.5	585.0
Minority owners' interests in subsidiaries	105.5	94.3
Total stockholders' equity	2,085.8	1,865.5
Total liabilities and equity	$4,923.0	$4,267.6

Source: Kimberly-Clark, 1989 Annual Report.

depressed, as large amounts of capacity were expected to be added to the industry in the early 1990s.

K-C's smallest division (4 percent of revenues and 3 percent of net income) operated a commercial airline based in Wisconsin (Midwest Express Airlines), and a business aircraft maintenance and refurbishing subsidiary.

Exhibit 6.4 Kimberly-Clark Corporation and Subsidiaries Analysis of 1989 Consolidated Operating Results

	($ Millions) By Geography % Change 1989	% of 1988 vs. 1988	% of 1989 Consolidated
Sales			
North America	$4,664.0	+ 6.4%	81.3%
Outside North America	1,087.1	+ 6.0	19.0
Adjustments	(17.5)		(.3)
Consolidated	$5,733.6	+ 6.3%	100.0%
Net Income			
North America	$ 316.7	+ 12.1%	74.8%
Outside North America	107.1	+ 11.3	25.2
Consolidated	$ 423.8	+ 11.9%	100.0%

Source: Kimberly-Clark, 1989 Annual Report.

Segment Breakdown, 1981–1989
($ Millions)

Net sales	1981	1982	1983	1984	1985	1986	1987	1988	1989
Consumer Products									
Division	$2,103	$2,205	$2,464	$2,734	$3,172	$3,370	$3,809	$4,165	$4,481
Forestry Division	781	742	795	845	856	876	1,001	1,121	1,096
Aviation Division	44	61	75	97	118	99	125	166	211
Subtotal	$2,928	$3,008	$3,334	$3,676	$4,146	$4,345	$4,935	$5,452	$5,788
(Interclass)	(42)	(62)	(60)	(60)	(73)	(42)	(50)	(59)	(54)
TOTAL	$2,886	$2,946	$3,274	$3,616	$4,073	$4,303	$4,885	$5,394	$5,734
Operating income									
Consumer Products									
Division	$ 171	$ 173	$ 221	$ 263	$ 361	$ 363	$ 434	$ 435	$ 535
Forestry Division	120	109	118	139	162	145	177	204	129
Aviation Division	3	7	8	11	2	9	13	23	26
Subtotal	$ 294	$ 289	$ 347	$ 413	$ 525	$ 516	$ 624	$ 662	$ 690
Corporate	(16)	(19)	(31)	(38)	(39)	(32)	(38)	(21)	(17)
TOTAL	$ 278	$ 270	$ 316	$ 375	$ 486	$ 485	$ 586	$ 641	$ 673
Return on average assets									
Consumer Products									
Division	1.4%	10.5%	12.0%	12.7%	15.3%	14.0%	15.9%	14.2%	15.0%
Forestry Division	22.5	19.6	20.4	23.9	27.1	22.8	26.0	27.7	15.7
Aviation Division	5.0	10.8	12.3	15.0	2.8	12.3	17.0	17.4	16.5
Subtotal	14.%	2.7%	13.9%	13.1%	17.4%	15.7%	17.9%	12.0%	11.9%
Unallocated/Interclass	N.M.	N.M.	N.M.	N.M.	N.M.	N.M.	N.M.	N.M.	N.M.
TOTAL	11.7%	10.6%	11.3%	12.3%	14.6%	13.5%	15.5%	11.9%	11.7%

Source: Duff & Phelps Research Report, November 1988. Kimberly-Clark Annual Report.

Exhibit 6.5 Kimberly-Clark Consumer, Health Care and Industrial Products ($ in millions)

Domestic Categories	1987 Est. Sales	1987 Est. Oper. Profit	1988 Est. Mkt. Share	Est. Rank of Brands	Major Competitors/ Mkt. Share
Disposable diapers	1,220	220	32%	2	Pampers 31%, Luvs 17% (PG); Private Label 20%
Facial tissue	450	52	45%	1	Puffs 17% (PG); Scotties 10% (Scott Paper)
Feminine pads	270	21	26%	2	J&J 37%; Always 20% (PG); Maxithins 5%; Priv. Lab. 12%
Tampons	30	2	6%	4	Tambrands 58%; Playtex 26%; J&J 8%
Paper household towels	170	10	10%	4	Scott Paper 23%; PG 20%; James River 11%
Bathroom tissue	35	0	N.M.	N.M.	PG 30%; Scott Paper 19%; James River 13%
Table napkins	30	2	N.M.	N.M.	Scott Paper 23%; James River 8%
Consumer incont. products	60	3	49%	1	Attends 28% (PG); Serenity 8% (J&J); Private label 15%
Inst./ind. tissue products	170	5			
Inst. healthcare	180	4			
Other nonwovens	176	4			
Medical	30	2			
Total domestic	2,821	325			
Canada	250	20			
Sub-total North America	3,071	345			
Outside North America	738	89			
Total consumer division	3,809	434			

Source: Duff & Phelps Research Report, November 1988.

K-C's international operations provided 29 percent of sales and 30 percent of operating income in 1989. K-C's major markets, on a consolidated basis, were Canada, the United Kingdom, France, the Philippines, and Brazil. K-C had several international equity investments; the largest, in Mexico, provided $36 million in net income. In 1989, K-C manufactured disposable diapers in nine countries and had sales in more than 100 countries. Outside North America and Europe, however, sales of disposable diapers were very low, largely because of undeveloped markets. Also, K-C had abandoned the Japanese market and weakened the potential for expansion into growing Asian markets.

Battling for Market Share

The search for a superior product had historically driven rivalry in the disposable diaper industry. However, product features were only translated into market share by the more visible aspects of marketing implementation. The battle for market share began in maternity wards, where both P&G and K-C paid hospitals to distribute disposable diapers free of charge to new mothers. Hospital usage suggested a medical endorsement and was believed to influence mothers to continue using a particular brand once she and the baby left for home. After the free samples and coupons had been used, mothers realized just how expensive disposables would be. In 1989, at a price of $0.18–.36 each, depending on size, it would cost $1,400–1,700 to diaper one child for two and one-half years in brand name disposables. It was estimated that the cost of cloth diapers supplied by diaper services was comparable, but could be up to 20 percent lower, depending on the type of service provided. Generic or private label disposables were about 30 percent cheaper than national brands, but most suffered from distressing performance problems. Cloth diapers washed at home would cost $600 or less. Increasingly, price was being discounted as a purchasing criterion. With up to 75 percent of new mothers working outside the home, many families valued time more than money. Similarly, as family size diminished, parents showed an increased willingness to spend money on outfitting babies. This meant that more families were prepared to pay for quality disposable diapers.

In North America, P&G and K-C spent a total of more than $100 million annually on diaper promotion, primarily via commercials and coupons. Retailers often used diapers as loss leaders and the companies supported these activities through volume rebates based upon the number of tons of diapers sold. Couponing potentially saved a consumer 10–15 percent, but the unwritten rule was that neither firm would undercut the other on price.

Manufacturing

The production of disposable diapers was capital intensive, involving a continuous flow of assembly utilizing large, complex, high speed machines. The machines were several hundred feet long and cost $2–$4 million apiece, depending on speed and features. Usually, several machines were grouped at each plant location. Despite technological improvements, diapers were still a bulky product and transportation costs were estimated to compose at least 7 percent of the retail value. To minimize transportation costs, both K-C and P&G had traditionally built regional plants. Due to high capital costs, capacity planning and utilization were essential to profitability. Firms attempted to operate their diaper machines twenty-four hours a day, seven days a week.

Additions to manufacturing capacity required a lead time of twelve to eighteen months. In addition, most facilities needed several months to de-bug new equipment. In the past, uncertain market share forecasts and fluctuations had led, at different times, to capacity surpluses and product shortages for both firms. The competition between P&G and K-C had resulted in a history of wide swings in market share. Ironically, both firms would have had lower manufacturing costs with reasonable industry stability.

INTERNATIONAL OPPORTUNITIES AND THREATS

With the introduction of super-thin technology from Japan, it was apparent that competitive conditions in North America could not be viewed in isolation. By the late 1980s, competitive conditions in Europe and Japan were having a significant influence on opportunities and threats facing North American competitors.

Japan

Historically, Japanese consumers had enjoyed better-quality cloth diapers than consumers in other countries, thus slowing the acceptance of disposables. Following World War II, national standards were introduced for cloth diapers as a means of improving overall hygiene. The standards resulted in the development of a highly effective two-layer cloth diapering system. The use of cloth diapers was encouraged by a Japanese tradition – when a woman became pregnant, her mother-in-law would present her with approximately 1,000 cloth diapers. As a result, cloth diapers became a common gift at baby showers, and the use of disposable diapers was strongly resisted by Japanese women. In recent years, benefits provided by disposables became more apparent, and changing roles of women in Japanese society led to a rapid growth in the demand for disposable diapers.

P&G's competitive experiences in Japan's diaper industry were remarkably similar to its experiences in North America. In the early 1970s, P&G had over 90 percent of the Japanese disposable market. However, the product had performance problems and total market penetration was weak. In 1982, P&G was making its diapers with old fashioned wood pulp. In the same year, Japan's Uni-Charm Corp. (1989 sales: $600 million) introduced a highly absorbent, granulated polymer to soak up wetness and hold it in the form of a gel, keeping babies dry longer. In 1984, KAO Corporation, a Japanese soapmaker (1989 sales: $4 billion), launched a similar brand of super-thin diapers, named Merries. P&G did not begin selling its polymer-packed Pampers in Japan until January, 1985. By that time, P&G's share of the Japanese market had fallen below 7 percent. Uni-Charm controlled almost half the market and KAO about 30 percent. After its initial setback, P&G recommitted itself to the battle and enjoyed several important gains. The reintroduction of Pampers and a premium Luvs helped P&G's market share recover to a level of 15–20 percent.

In recommitting to the Japanese market, P&G recognized that Japanese product technology was years ahead of U.S. levels. Being well positioned in Japan meant that P&G would have greater access to Japanese technology, which could be exported to the U.S. to use in its battle with K-C. Having sold its interest in a Japanese equity company in 1987, K-C was not a major competitor in Japan.

By 1989, the Japanese market had not yet reached the same level of maturity demonstrated in the U.S. While the market was worth over $1 billion, market penetration for disposables remained under 50 percent. These penetration figures included parents that used disposable diapers "on occasion." Many families used a combination of disposables and traditional cloth diapers. Japanese parents changed their babies more frequently (twice as often) as North American parents and thus used many more diapers. Despite a population less than half the size, industry estimates indicated that the Japanese market would be almost as large as the U.S., if developed to the same degree (85–90 percent penetration, most of which was exclusively disposable).

Faced with intense domestic competition, Japanese firms historically showed little interest in moving internationally. However, there was growing concern in North America that Japanese preoccupation with domestic competition was beginning to change. In 1988, KAO acquired Jergens Ltd., a U.S. producer of personal care products, and several analysts speculated this was the beachhead for a major thrust into the North American market for personal products, including disposable diapers. There was also speculation that Uni-Charm had begun negotiations with Weyerhauser to set up joint production/distribution operations in the U.S. Weyerhauser was a large, integrated U.S. forest products company that held a 50 percent share of the low-priced, private label market for disposable diapers. It was known that Weyerhauser had been considering a major move into the mid-priced segment for disposables.

Europe

The development of the disposable diapers industry in Europe was different than in North America. Europeans began producing disposable diapers using a two-piece system in the early 1960s. Europe did not experience the high degree of rationalization of the North American industry for two main reasons. First, Europe was composed of very different, often protected national markets, thus limiting production, marketing, and distribution economies. Second, no large European industry leaders emerged, and foreign competitors from North America and Japan were preoccupied with domestic competitive battles. As a result, several strong country-specific firms emerged.

Penetration of disposable diapers varied widely across Europe. In Northern Europe, the market had long been saturated. In France, for example, 98 percent of diaper changes were done using disposables. Consumers seemed increasingly preoccupied with environmental concerns, and many were experimenting with alternatives to disposables. In Southern Europe, penetration levels remained much lower and the market less sophisticated. Here, the percentage of women employed outside the home was lower. Many observers felt that these markets offered significant growth opportunities. European disposable diaper sales were growing faster than sales of most other household products. Development of a unified European market suggested industry rationalization opportunities.

Since the mid-1980s, both P&G and K-C had re-focused attention on Europe, achieving some success. However, by 1989, the market was still fragmented, with neither firm enjoying the dominant position experienced in their domestic market. In weighing opportunities in Europe, both P&G and K-C had to determine whether limited investment capital for expensive market development would be better spent at home or overseas; and, if overseas, in which market? Also of concern was the potential reaction of European firms, both overseas and in North America, to the perceived aggressiveness of U.S. firms in their home markets.

CURRENT ISSUES

In 1989, almost 19 billion disposable diapers were sold in North America. This produced an estimated four billion to five and one-half billion pounds of discarded diapers. Some tests of residential landfills showed that disposable diapers constituted as much as 20 percent of the total volume (industry studies showed less than 2 percent), leading to widespread criticism of the industry for the non-biodegradable nature of the plastics in the product. (It took an estimated 250 years for a plastic disposable diaper to biodegrade.) Environmental groups had highlighted concerns about potential health risks for sanitation workers and the threat to groundwater. By 1989, legislation taxing, regulating, or banning the sale of disposable diapers had been introduced in eleven U.S. states. Most punitive measures were scheduled to come into effect in 1992–1994, giving competitors some time to react.

There were signs that the seriousness of the environmental problem had not fully reached either P&G or K-C. In public statements, both companies cited studies showing that the laundering of cloth diapers used six times the amount of water as was used in the manufacture of disposables, and the laundering created ten times as much water pollution. P&G went even further, arguing that its disposable diapers were 60 percent to 70 percent biodegradable. Richard Nicolosi, vice-president in charge of P&G's worldwide diaper operations, commented: "We don't think mothers are willing to give up one of the greatest new products of the postwar era." Although they had a note in their 1989 annual report citing the potential seriousness of the threat, K-C had been reticent about specific plans for dealing with the issue. According to Tina Barry, VP-Corporate Communications at K-C, "We're working with our suppliers to find a reliable plastic that is biodegradable. But we haven't come across any plastic material that breaks down and maintains product performance and reliability."

Many analysts believed that, unless environmentally friendly disposables were introduced, cloth diapers would continue to gain in popularity. By 1989, cloth diapers comprised 10–15 percent of the North American diaper market. In the late 1980s, both Fisher-Price and Gerber had introduced form fitting, two piece diaper systems, reflecting an appreciation that cloth diapers could be sold either directly to consumers or to diaper services.

The industry had a clear R&D challenge, but by 1989, no promising technologies had been introduced to address rising environmental concerns. This was in contrast to the Japanese market, where the market leaders had avoided or minimized the use of non-biodegradable plastics. It was also recognized that Japanese firms had considerable technological experience with biodegradable external retaining fabrics. Both P&G and K-C had yet to adopt such technology and were skeptical of biodegradability claims.

As the North American disposable diaper market became saturated, both P&G and K-C sought other market opportunities that might utilize the technological expertise gained from diapers. One avenue that seemed particularly attractive was increased development of incontinence products (similar to diapers) for adults. Incontinence products appeared to be an ideal product extension for the super-thin technology utilized in disposable diapers. With the improvement in incontinence product performance, sales and market penetration had exploded. It was estimated that sales would reach $1 billion in the U.S. market by 1990, and that the potential size of this market could eventually exceed that of diapers. Of the thirty-one million North Americans over sixty-five, it was estimated that about 10 percent had a problem with incontinence. An aging population would allow total market growth opportunities as well as growth through increased penetration. The fight for market share was shaping up to be a replay of the disposable diaper war, with the same players. A difference was the contrasting strengths possessed by each firm in the distribution network. P&G dominated the institutional distribution channel, while K-C was the leader in the commercial/retail channel. K-C had broken important new ground in this market and strengthened their distribution position by successfully developing a television advertising program that tastefully promoted the benefits of their incontinence products.

RECENT EVENTS

On November 1, 1989, Edwin Artzt was appointed as P&G's new CEO. Chosen over an heir apparent, Artzt had directed P&G's international operations since 1984. In that capacity, he had been responsible for P&G's spectacular recovery in Japan, particularly in diapers, and its double digit growth in Asia and Europe.

Managers at K-C wondered whether Artzt's appointment signalled a shift in P&G's emphasis away from the U.S. market. They also speculated whether his appointment was designed to strengthen P&G's access to new Japanese technology that could produce more environmentally friendly diapers. In response to these concerns, managers at K-C wondered what sort of action to take, either internationally or in North America.

With external pressures mounting, the nature of the competition in the North American disposable diaper industry showed signs of change in 1989. For the first time, neither of the competitors had introduced major product improvements, rather, they made style changes. In the summer of 1989, P&G introduced His and Hers diapers with designer-color patterns and special absorbent pads strategically placed for boy and girl babies. P&G backed the introduction with a huge advertising and promotional campaign, which made it difficult to gauge the true market share impacts of the new products. In response, K-C developed a similar product and was in the test marketing phase. It was estimated that a similar national product introduction for K-C would cost $50–75 million. In responding to mounting competitive pressures, both K-C and P&G recognized that balance between short term and long term perspectives was essential. The focus of this balance was, however, the basis of considerable uncertainty.

7

First Fidelity Bancorporation

This case was prepared by Barbara L. Marcolin and Kerry McLellan with the assistance of Professor Paul W. Beamish of the Western Business School. Copyright © 1992, The University of Western Ontario.

In April 1990, Don Parcells, recently appointed Head of Corporate Operations and Systems at First Fidelity Bancorporation (FFB), New Jersey, was considering ways to improve the productivity of the bank's Operations and Systems departments. As he sat down to ponder his organizational restructuring and operational consolidation he wondered which of the three main options he should use to effect the change. FFB could use the internal systems department resources, an information systems consulting company, or a new method for operating Information Systems departments – outsourcing. He knew how important cost effective, innovative information technology was to the bank's competitive position. Whichever path FFB were to proceed down, he knew he had better identify the risks and the benefits expected. Considering the faltering economy and the FFB president's desire for a lean organization within eighteen months, Parcells realized that a decision would have to be made quickly.

UNITED STATES BANKING INDUSTRY

The structure of the United States (U.S.) banking industry was characterized by small, local and regional banks serving local customers. Except for a few of the larger, money-center banks, services varied widely by bank and by branch. A customer could not receive the same set of services in multiple locations, and electronic interconnection was cumbersome. This industry structure had developed in response to historically restrictive legislation that had limited inter-state banking and the products that banks were able to offer. These restrictions, as well as anti-trust legislation, had limited the growth potential of individual firms in the industry.

During the past twenty years there had been a gradual easing of banking regulations. Many of the restrictions confining banking activities had been removed, enabling banks to expand their product offerings and geographic scope. The standard growth pattern that emerged involved friendly acquisitions with the acquired banks being organized under a holding company structure. In general, these acquired banks continued to operate autonomously with little consolidation of bank operations or systems. This led to incompatibility between the banks' systems and limited efficiencies within the holding company structure. Despite these problems, banks within the industry continued to amalgamate at a fairly fast pace.

Recently, there were pressures which prompted a shift from this historical pattern. Pressure was growing within the U.S. Congress to develop a global banking strategy and to allow greater financial sector consolidation. Further, there was a growing market demand for transparent banking; both commercial and personal customers wanted consolidated bank access for interstate transactions. Although the legislative barriers to consolidation were decreasing, the recent failure of the savings & loan institutions had introduced a countervailing pressure for more regulation. In response to this financial disaster, the government had tightened banking regulations, particularly those concerning the reporting of financial information. The government also developed more stringent guidelines for reviewing the asset quality and operating procedures of all financial institutions. It appeared that all bank functions would soon be subjected to more careful scrutiny with assets being more thoroughly reviewed, new products more closely examined, and acquisitions and financial performance more attentively monitored.

HISTORY OF FFB

First Fidelity was established in 1812 as the State Bank of Newark, and grew gradually during its first 150 years. However, the last thirty years had witnessed many changes caused by reorganization, acquisitions, and mergers. The introduction of new statewide bank holding laws in the late 1960s was a major force for change. In 1969, the bank was reorganized under a holding company structure. This enabled First Fidelity to become increasingly involved in business beyond its historical boundaries of Newark, New Jersey.

Capitalizing on the new bank holding laws, major expansion occurred in the 1980s when several banks were brought under the holding company's control. During this expansion period, the company's name was changed to reflect its increased dimensions; it became the First Fidelity Bancorporation. The acquisition of a healthy savings bank in 1986 had reinforced the innovative, aggressive posture of FFB. It was the first time a financially strong savings bank had been acquired by a commercial bank holding company. Although the holding company was expanding rapidly, each acquired bank continued to operate as an independent unit with FFB reporting the consolidated financial statements.

In 1988, FFB continued its strategy of expanding into contiguous geographic regions when it merged with another holding company, Fidelcor Inc., which had a similar history of growth and acquisition in the Philadelphia area. Bringing these banks under the FFB umbrella gave the bank access to new business products such as Trust and International Banking, and also enabled FFB to serve New Jersey customers in the neighboring state with these acquisitions. FFB was poised to respond to the call for standardized products in a larger geographic region for commercial and retail customers. In the late 1980s, FFB experienced a period of lackluster performance. The stock price had dropped well below its book value, making it an attractive takeover target. The bank's operating efficiency was ranked forty-fourth of the top 50 U.S. banks. The asset quality of the Philadelphia and Newark banks surfaced as a problem after the 1988 merger, and the company was forced to write off a large portion of these assets in 1989. In an attempt to strengthen FFB's position in the industry, the old management team was replaced in February 1990.

The new Chairman and Chief Executive Officer, Tony Terracciano, immediately announced three new executive vice president positions. Don Parcells, one of the new executive vice presidents, was given responsibility for operations and systems.

Parcells' past experience in both the international and domestic operations of several larger banks made him particularly well-qualified for this position. His association with Terracciano began in the mid-1970s when Terracciano, then Chief of Staff for international affairs at Chase Manhattan Bank, asked him to assume responsibility for the bank's European operations area. This job was challenging as the situation was chaotic and costs were out of control. Parcells successfully turned around the Operations department and within two years had the area functioning at top efficiency. This experience had allowed him to develop the skills needed to successfully implement major operational restructuring.

Following his European success, Parcells accepted a position with another major U.S. bank. Eventually, as head of international operations, he integrated the U.S. branch operations with their international counterparts. These experiences in consolidation and integration prepared Parcells for his current challenge at FFB.

FFB Today

In April 1990, FFB was the holding company for eight independent banks representing 500 branches and $28 billion in assets. FFB was ranked as one of the top twenty-five super regional banks in the U.S. The holding company acted as the corporate integrating level, while the operating banks were autonomous, decentralized units. Each operating bank had a president and vice presidents responsible for the major business units (Exhibit 7.1).

Little progress had been made in consolidating services or banking activities. However, by April 1990, several initiatives had begun. Treasury operations for two banks were now the responsibility of one person. Furthermore, the physical processing sites for check activities were being consolidated into fewer operational units which provided services to numerous branches. In addition, all Trust operations were now under the control of central management. Plans were also being developed to consolidate additional functions such as installment loan and customer services, and mortgage processing under one structure with services provided to other banks. Some progress was being made in the consolidation of physical systems. However, each bank was still processed as a stand-alone entity with its own software application set.

These pockets of centralized management were integrated into the decentralized holding company structure through the cumbersome decision-making process that existed. Committees had been used to coordinate activities, because direct-line authority only existed at the FFB CEO level. This coordinating mechanism consumed significant management time and resources that could be better spent on more fundamental operational problems. However, consolidation efforts were hampered because no corporate-wide plan for operational activities or computer architecture existed to guide future development and restructuring efforts.

Overview of Operations and Systems

The operations and systems within the banks included all the major activities required to support the daily banking transactions. Each was critical to the functioning and performance

Exhibit 7.1 FFB Current Operational Structure

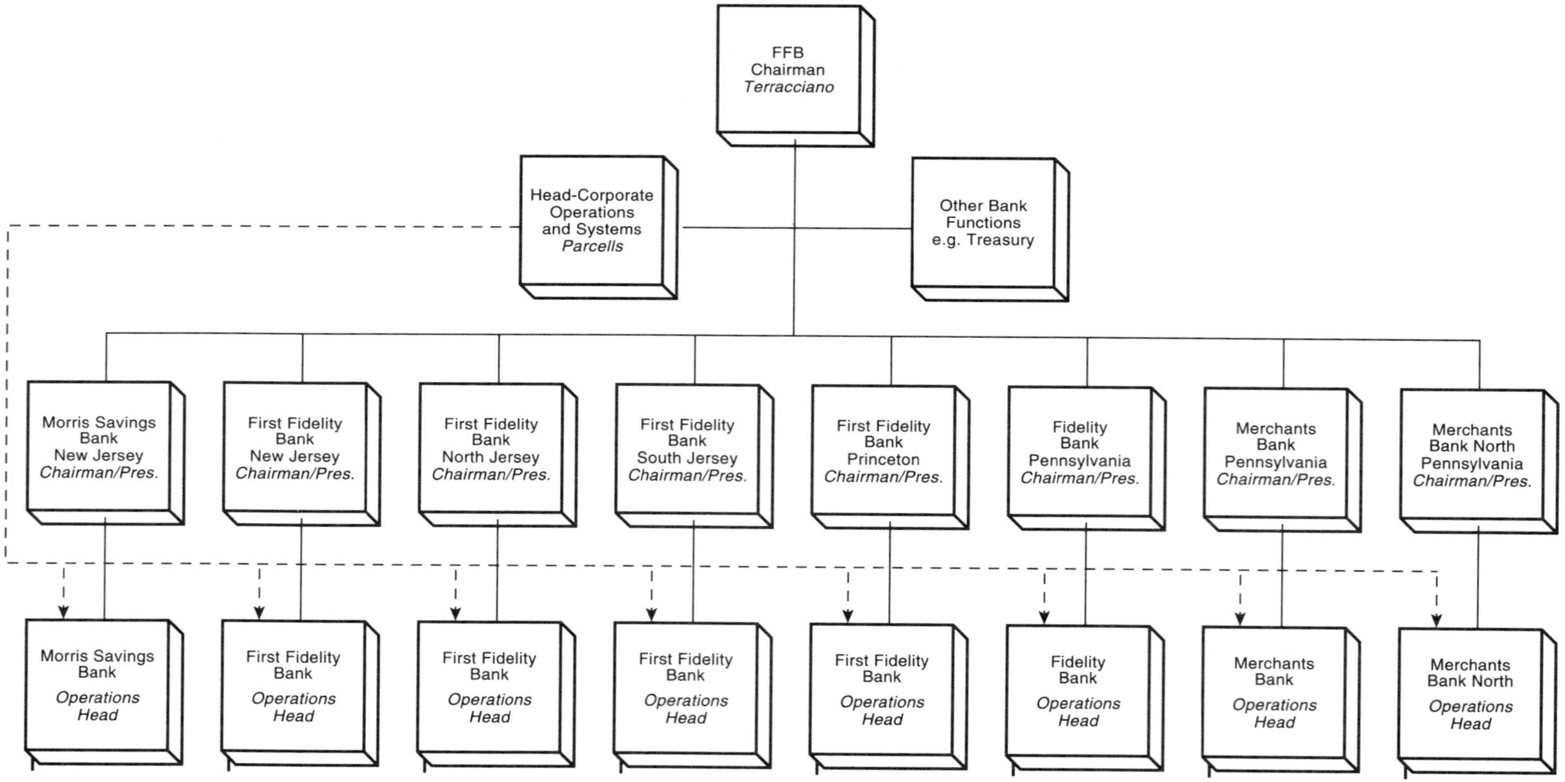

FFB
Chairman
Terracciano

Other Bank Functions
e.g. Treasury

Head-Corporate Operations and Systems
Parcells

Merchants Bank North Pennsylvania
Chairman/Pres.

Merchants Bank Pennsylvania
Chairman/Pres.

Fidelity Bank Pennsylvania
Chairman/Pres.

First Fidelity Bank Princeton
Chairman/Pres.

First Fidelity Bank South Jersey
Chairman/Pres.

First Fidelity Bank North Jersey
Chairman/Pres.

First Fidelity Bank New Jersey
Chairman/Pres.

Morris Savings Bank New Jersey
Chairman/Pres.

Merchants Bank North
Operations Head

Merchants Bank
Operations Head

Fidelity Bank
Operations Head

First Fidelity Bank
Operations Head

First Fidelity Bank
Operations Head

First Fidelity Bank
Operations Head

First Fidelity Bank
Operations Head

Morris Savings Bank
Operations Head

Reporting to *each* Operations Head were divisions for: Retail Operations, Wholesale Operations, Information Services, Staff Services, and Securities Operations.

of that bank, and both were intricately linked to each other in a complex network of activities. Operations involved a number of back office activities that supported the processing of transactions and services. Typically, these functions were labor-intensive and included activities such as encoding, exception processing, proofing, clearing, mortgage servicing, lock box services, and trust activities.

Management Information Systems (MIS) within the bank involved three major activities: system development, relationship management, and data processing. The latter activity was most closely tied to the bank operations. Commonly referred to as "the systems" data processing involved the data center activities where application systems processed the daily transactions including mortgage, loan, deposit, and commercial services.

Whether an activity was defined as an operation or a system varied from function to function and, for some business procedures, was best defined as a combination of both. Check processing, for example, involved many steps from capturing the check data to processing it and finally to clearing the funds between banks. The line between operational and systems activities was often blurred. In general, systems were used to support major business functions or product offerings and were critical to these operations.

Banking services could be separated into two distinct groups: commodity-type functions and stand-alone products (Exhibit 7.2). Commodity-type functions were those activities that were transparent to the customer. Changes to these functions would not affect customer perceptions, as long as the services were presented in a similar manner. This limited the strategic and marketing risks associated with consolidating these functions. Stand-alone products were those activities that were used directly by the customer, and thus changes to these activities would be seen by the marketplace. Given the high visibility of these products, proposal changes would have to be given careful consideration. Since the strategic fit of these products was not yet determined, the firm's strategic positioning would dictate how these products were handled.

Making changes to custom stand-alone products was a difficult process. The major functional and business unit groups usually defended their territory with aggressive actions, resulting in many compromises across banks so that customers could maintain their individualized services. Though two banks might be using the same operating procedures or computer systems, they might have tailored them in specific ways to meet local demands. These

Exhibit 7.2 Banking Services

Commodity-Type Functions	Stand-Alone Products
• Courier and Messenger Services	• Lock Box
• Mail Processing	• Credit Card
• Printing and Reproduction	• Corporate Trust
• Physical Security	• Estate Banking Trust and Personal Trust
• Automated Teller Machine Switching	• Stock Transfer
• Network Management	• Custody Services
• Coin and Currency	• Check Processing
• Facilities Services	
• Data Processing Operations	
• Mortgage Servicing	

differences caused several difficulties across the banks. Each branch scheduled statement printouts based on their own demands and produced statement printouts with individualized messages. Systems efficiencies were impossible to achieve within the present structure. It was not uncommon to have bank branches offering different interest rates at the same time! Corporate customers who dealt with a few branches were not pleased with these discrepancies. If this situation persisted, there could be negative ramifications for marketing and customer services. Although FFB looked like a larger bank, it had realized few of the potential efficiencies or benefits.

Senior management was aware of the problems inherent in FFB's holding company structure and recognized the need for systems integration and operational consolidation. Although rapid and drastic modifications were needed, there were built-in cultural impediments to change. Many of the bank presidents and employees had developed within one bank and strongly identified with its local area. If operating procedures or systems were to be changed, these employees would have to expand the scope of their loyalty to encompass the institution as a whole. FFB had initiated a lengthy process of education and negotiation to accomplish this goal.

Pressure for Rapid Change

FFB was under pressure to develop standardized products, global banking capability, and improved efficiency. Consolidation appeared to be the only way FFB could respond to these pressures, as well as the need to improve the reporting and management control information required to run a firm as large as FFB. Better controls were also needed to respond to governmental regulatory bodies who were becoming more stringent regarding asset quality and capital requirements. The government was vigorously enforcing these requirements against other banks, and management figured it would be eighteen months at the most before the focus shifted to FFB.

From the beginning, it was clear that drastic consolidation action was needed within this firmly set eighteen-month time frame. The time pressure led to the realization that only two options were available: make the bank as efficient as possible and sell it; or consolidate and grow. The general feeling was that the business had the capacity to support growth. As Parcells recalls:

"With all the problems, there were some interesting aspects. We had over 500 branches in the most densely populated state in the country, with the second highest per capita income. We had one of the lowest funding costs of almost any bank in the U.S. and, if run efficiently, it could make a lot of money. If you make money, you can get your share price up and then make acquisitions in a market which was fairly depressed. We felt that if we could get better faster than some of the others, then we would have a window of opportunity to grow."

With the determination to fix up the business, management set forth to review the situation. Three problems emerged in the early analysis. First, the economy was heading into a recession. Second, the asset quality was beginning to deteriorate as the economy worsened. The commercial real estate market, which was beginning to soften, would need increased reserve requirements and would put a strain on working capital. Although working capital was not an immediate problem, steps would have to be taken to improve credit policies and to reduce potential drains. This could not be done quickly, and, in fact, might not have an effect for several years. Third, productivity had to be improved and expenses had to be cut. The unconsolidated operational structure represented significantly higher costs than comparable banks in the industry. In March 1990, a 10 percent arbitrary cut of operating expenses and staff was made across the organization. This action was intended to save $95 million that year and an estimated $125 million in subsequent years (see financial statements in Exhibit 7.3). Management recognized that significant further cuts would be more difficult to make, and any subsequent cost savings would only come through the difficult task of organizational rationalization and consolidation. There was little the bank could do to reverse the recession, but it could address the other two problems. Management immediately began reviewing asset quality and taking appropriate actions. Parcells' responsibility was to address the productivity and expense issue.

Information Gathering to Reach a Decision

Parcells undertook an immediate review of the back office operations and systems to determine what potential savings could be realized. An experienced consultant was hired to help identify a new structure for operations and systems, to calculate the estimated savings, and to itemize the rationalization steps.

Senior management considered every possible option for a new corporate structure. Each of these alternatives was evaluated against an explicit set of criteria.

- Cost effectiveness
- Responsiveness to business needs
- Responsiveness to individual bank needs
- Ability to standardize product and service offerings
- Ability to support outsourcing options
- Ability to support acquisitions
- Service/quality orientation/incentives

The structural options that were considered ranged from keeping the current structure to realigning operations management centralized by bank, centralized by function, centralized by business, centralized by a hybrid of function and business, or organized as a service company. The consultant discussed the key features of each of these options in his report to Parcells, as shown in Exhibit 7.4. Each of these options could be compared against the strategic objectives. Clearly, the latter two options supported more of the proposed criteria, and of these, the centralized hybrid structure seemed the most logical at the time. This structure would allow FFB to gain the benefits from the functions and businesses of the lowest cost operating structure, the greatest standardization of products and services, the greatest flexibility, and the future support for assimilating acquisitions. While FFB would still be poised to move into a service corporation structure if desired, it seemed the centralized hybrid structure would be an intermediary step in any case. Accordingly, the proposed high-level operations structure divided this organization into five major functions and businesses: retail operations, wholesale operations, information services, staff services, and securities operations (Exhibit 7.5). These new departments would replace the independent bank operations.

Exhibit 7.3   FFB Financial Statements

Consolidated Income Statement 1989 ($000)

Total interest income	2,677,777		
Total interest expense	1,693,312		
Net interest income		984,465	
Provision for possible credit losses		200,254	
Net income after loss provision		784,211	
Trust income	77,624		
Other income (e.g., service charges, security transactions)	272,626		
Total non-interest income		350,250	
Total income			1,134,461
Total non-interest expenses (e.g., salaries & benefits, equipment)			945,797
Income before taxes			188,664
Income taxes			28,616
Net income			160,048

Consolidated Balance Sheet
as of Dec. 31, 1989 ($000)

Assets			
Cash		1,685,068	
Interest bearing time deposits		80,801	
Investment securities		7,937,379[1]	
Total loans and leases			19,243,024
Other assets			1,781,543
Total assets			30,727,815
Liabilities			
Total deposits		22,872,460	
Short-term borrowing		4,509,198	
Other liabilities		1,000,753	
Long-term deposits		780,438	
Total liabilities			29,162,849
Preferred Stock		157,271	
Common Stock	58,492		
Surplus	663,398		
Retained earnings	685,805		
Total Common stakeholders' equity		1,407,695	
Total stakeholders' equity			1,564,966
Total liabilities and stakeholder equity			30,727,815

[1]Market value 1990, $6,707,209.

Exhibit 7.4 Evaluation of Possible Structures

	Dedicated Bank Operations	Centralized by Bank	Centralized by Function	Centralized by Business	Centralized Hybrid	Services Company
Cost Effectiveness	○	◕	●	◑	●	●
Responsiveness to Business Needs	◒	◒	○	●	◕	◔
Responsiveness to Bank Needs	●	◔	○	◒	◒	◒
Standardized Product and Service	○	○	●	●	●	●
Flexibility for Outsourcing	◒	◒	●	○	●	●
Ability to Support Acquisitions	○	○	●	●	●	●
Service and Quality Orientation	●	●	○	◒	◒	●

● - Full support   ○ - Does not support

Source: Consultant's report and FFB Board of Director's presentation.

Together, Parcells and the consultant determined that a consolidated organization would offer significant savings over the current organizational structure. The annual savings from an operational consolidation were determined to be more than $65 million, which would be incremental to the 10 percent arbitrary cut already made. Together, the cuts represented a 20 percent reduction of the $1 billion expense base, and would contribute directly to the bottom line. The problem was determining how to get these incremental savings within the time frame available.

The rationalization of operations meant that all commodity-type functions would be reviewed against market opportunities. Since the functions were transparent to the customer, they presented few obstacles if changed. It appeared that most functions could be purchased at a lower cost than they could be done within FFB, and thus should be contracted out.

The rationalization of systems meant that a common set of applications had to be found, and one data center had to be assembled. This would require the consolidation of the physical data centers including renovating and expanding an existing site, moving all hardware, restructuring the communications network, and phasing out other sites. A few capture and encoding sites (possibly 2 and 5, respectively) for check processing and commercial loan operations would be used as logistics dictated. Currently, there were data processing operations in each bank, and eight capture and eighteen encoding stations. The software applications would have to be standardized to establish a common application platform upon which marketing could build new products. This would involve the rationalization of 260+

Exhibit 7.5   Proposed Operations and Systems Structure

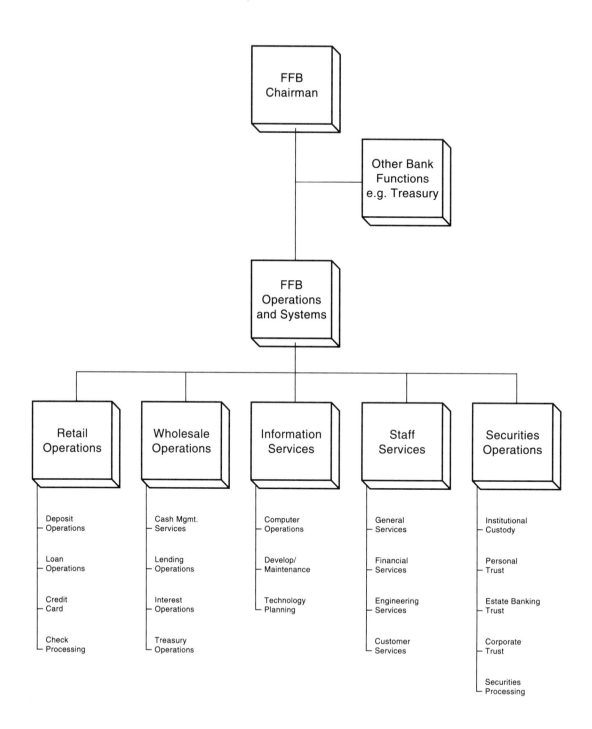

applications down to approximately sixty. Though most application packages processed similar functions within the banks, they had been acquired from different vendors. Few banks used the same commercial package and, unfortunately, when common applications did exist, they were tailored to the local bank and were, therefore, not compatible with other sites. The final task would be to convert all banks to this common application platform. The banks would have to standardize all products and services, convert existing data and files, and train staff in the new procedures.

The consolidation plans did not include all of the MIS department. Systems development and, to a lesser extent, the IS-user relationship management activities would continue to operate as an independent, decentralized department. Since systems development activities were so critical to bank products and marketing services, FFB would be able to control this department, yet keep it focused on individual bank needs and market forces. The combination of consolidating data processing while retaining the old systems development process promised to give FFB better strategic control in the future and lower costs now.

RATIONALIZATION OPTIONS

Since systems were vitally important to the bank's operations, Parcells knew the rationalization and consolidation had to be done well and fit with the bank's new strategic direction. He saw three options available: the rationalization could be done in-house, by consultants, or through an outsourcing agreement. Each of these options had to be considered in terms of its fit with the organizational objectives.

Criteria

It was important to management that the employees be treated well. Any solutions had to include comparable pay and benefits for existing staff. In terms of time frame, the job had to be done in eighteen months. No other time frame was acceptable. The group had to have the capacity to do the job in terms of staff numbers and appropriate skill levels. Also, the applications had to be taken from the existing software packages currently used by the eight banks. Many packages were the best commercial products available, and were already designed to fit FFB's banking environment.

If an outside vendor were to become involved, additional criteria would have to be met. First, the contract would have to be for a fixed price over a ten-year period. Second, the vendor's experience and track record would play an important role in determining the best candidate. Third, both resources and their quality would be considered. Finally, the vendor's commitment to the business would be of the utmost importance.

Any savings to be realized by involving a third party would have to be compared to the projected $65 million savings made possible by rationalizing the Operations and Systems departments in-house. "Comparing to any other standard," Parcells observed, "would be absurd!" The discussions would also include identifying additional savings beyond the internal review.

Options

Internal The first option was to achieve the operations and systems consolidation with the internal staff and resources. Some efforts were already being made to centralize operations and systems (e.g., Trust and Check Processing), however, these were relatively superficial reporting changes or simple sharing of physical hardware. Such minor changes were not of the magnitude being considered by upper management. Were the job to be done in-house, current staff would have to undergo a fundamental change in their thinking about consolidation. While upper management foresaw the need for fundamental change to operations and systems, the banks and department heads were more inwardly focused on their respective domain. For instance, the current IS head did not understand the magnitude of upper management's consolidation plans. He had spent $102 million in 1989, and, while "consolidating," had proposed to spend $112 million on systems in 1990. This conflicted with Parcells' evaluation of an $80 million consolidation budget with savings from reduced staff, software and hardware maintenance, professional fees, telecommunications expenses, and hardware leases.

In addition to reorienting the current staff, FFB would have to hire up to 100 temporary people with the requisite skills to complete the job. Perhaps three to five months would be required to hire and educate these people about the FFB environment and where it was going. While this introduced another layer of complexity to the project management task, this would be temporary.

After reviewing the Information Systems department consolidation estimates, Parcells was concerned that the internal resources required to complete the project in-house could not be mustered within the preferred eighteen-month time frame. The shortest estimate for completing the consolidation project was about three years. This estimate, of course, was only tentative as the IS staff had never attempted a conversion of this magnitude before, and could not be sure how quickly things would progress.

Parcells also considered whether a third party vendor could ensure that the rationalization was completed on time. There were many third party vendors who were willing to provide assistance in consolidating the bank's operations and systems. These vendors ranged from consultants who would offer advice on the process to outsourcing companies who would take over the data center operations and system development.

Consultants   The consultants were large firms which specialized in information systems applications and generally had developed expertise in outsourcing activities. For a fee, these firms would come into an organization and offer advice on the planning and implementation of the systems solutions. These consultants brought both a broad perspective of the information technology (IT) options and many narrowly-focused, specialized skills to the client's organization. This broad IT perspective enabled the consultant to consider all configuration alternatives and to apply more creative solutions in design and implementation. The narrowly-focused, specialized skills provided efficiency in the systems development activities and provided technical sophistication.

As an example, Arthur Andersen, one of the top firms in this business, would be a suitable candidate to review FFB's consolidation efforts. Andersen had considerable experience with applications in the financial services industry, and had conducted outsourcing activities in the United Kingdom, and to a lesser extent in the North American market. Arthur Andersen was anxious to build upon their existing track record. Arguably such an interest might be used as a lever to get them to moderate their costs, which were viewed as quite expensive by FFB at the time. Most other consultant organizations had similar benefits and risks.

Outsourcing   Outsourcing involved the provision of services to an organization by a third party vendor. From a quick review of the marketplace, FFB had identified several outsourcing vendors who offered the range of outsourcing approaches from service bureau to private label. See Exhibit 7.6 for further background on outsourcing. Of these vendors (Exhibit

Exhibit 7.6   Background on Outsourcing

In the late 1980s, outsourcing was applied to information processing activities, but had existed for many years in various forms. Service bureau support had been around since the 1960s and represented one of the earliest forms of outsourcing activities. A service bureau was a vendor who processed data transactions from a remote site on a prearranged schedule. The computer processing time would be allocated to clients depending on their demands. In the 1980s, facilities management became another popular form of outsourcing. A vendor would run systems and provide operational support on the client's premises. The next type of outsourcing became known as private label. The vendor would provide all computer services in support of a function or business from a facility which it managed. It usually involved the vendor taking over the client's physical data center facilities and operating them as part of the vendor's business. In addition, vendors offered both proprietary and non-proprietary applications for the operation of these data processing facilities. Proprietary private label vendors would convert all applications to their software and run the business from this basis. Non-proprietary private label vendors would take over and manage the client's application architecture in the data center.

By 1990, the scope of outsourcing had expanded and become a complex and varied activity. The companies which engaged in this activity used words like strategic rationale, strategic partnership, vision, and commitment. This approach went beyond the off-loading of an inefficiently run operation. It reflected a perspective which sought a strategic partnership with the outsourcing vendor. First, the employees were transferred to the vendor's organization and became employees of that firm. The partnership, if successful, was characterized by cooperation on both sides and a striving toward discovering business opportunities. This was different from the supplier/buyer relationship of other "outsourcing" options. As a buyer the client would only get a specific service within well-defined bounds which, when completed, would terminate the relationship. Outsourcing relied upon a shared vision and a long-term commitment to the partnership which guided the relationship through day-to-day conflicts. Ideally, both parties focused on the same goals, and if the company succeeded, the outsourcing vendor succeeded.

Many financial sector firms were taking a renewed interest in outsourcing for several reasons. There had been a dramatic increase in mergers and acquisitions, straining internal management resources when integrating these new entities. This strain could sometimes be alleviated by purchasing the required resources. The outsourcing vendor offered leverage through technical resources, infrastructure, software investment, and technology. The client usually gained access to a technology platform and experienced personnel which were unavailable to them before. Since additional resources would accelerate conversion and consolidation, firms would sometimes realize any savings sooner. Further, outsourcing could provide significant cost savings, notwithstanding the vendor's need for profitability! It introduced economies of scale and overcame inefficiencies that would not have been realized without the vendor's participation. Also, outsourcing could facilitate operational consolidation by acting as a catalyst for change. Not only could outsourcing propel change, but it sometimes did so at a guaranteed price, reducing some of the company's financial risk during the rationalization. This commitment would increase the probability of success. Outsourcing sometimes generated revenue improvements. The banks could increase revenue by offering integrated state-of-the-art services demanded by commercial and retail customers. Finally, outsourcing was more available within the marketplace from a wider range of vendors who were flexible in their approach. This created a willingness on behalf of the vendors to bundle or unbundle the services as required and, consequently, produced more opportunities to fit this service to the company's needs. Against these potential benefits, however, were some definite costs to the bank, not least of which was potential loss of control over a piece of its operation.

7.7), the ones that offered a wide range of services were the most likely candidates. These included Systematics, M&I Data Services (M&I), Electronic Data Services (EDS), International Business Machines (IBM), Mellon Financial Services Corp. (Mellon), and Perot Syscorp. As Parcells reviewed the consultant's report, he focused on the general characteristics of these firms.

First, the firms seemed to be focused on different outsourcing market segments. Two firms, Mellon and M&I, predominately pursued service bureau activities and used proprietary software applications. In contrast, EDS, Perot, and IBM pursued private-label activities and offered non-proprietary software applications. Systematics appeared to be strongly entrenched in the private-label/proprietary software application outsourcing business. Although companies might offer other services, these market positions represented the main outsourcing strategy for each vendor.

Second, these vendors had different track records in the private-label outsourcing business. Systematics and EDS were industry leaders with vast experience serving financial institutions. Respectively, these two firms generated $230 and $700 million in revenue during 1989. As a relative newcomer to this business, IBM was serving five financial institutions with outsourcing-related services. However, this experience represented a limited range of activities. Likewise, Perot Syscorp had gained very little experience in the two years it had been in business even though its corporate staff had been recruited from EDS. M&I and Mellon had not participated in the private-label outsourcing business.

Exhibit 7.7   Vendor Market Positioning

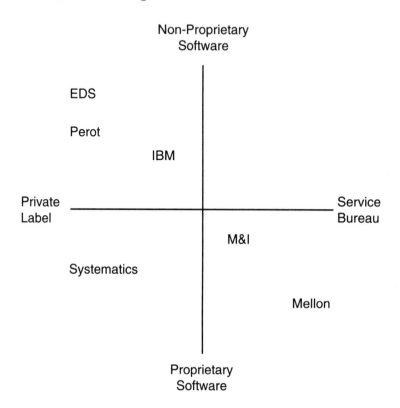

A fundamental concern was how outsourcing could help in the Operations and Systems department's restructuring and consolidation. If the bank were to proceed with the outsourcing option, many factors would have to be considered: Which activities should be outsourced? What services were available in the market? How would the bank maintain control over its information technology resources? What would be the nature of the relationship with the outsourcing vendor: partner or supplier?

CONCLUSION

As Don Parcells reviewed the three main options, he realized that he needed to be very clear on the advantages and disadvantages of each. While some of the costs and benefits were certain to occur, others were "promised" or potential. Whichever option was chosen would represent a very significant allocation of resources.

Kao Corporation

This case was written by Charlotte Butler, Research Assistant, under the supervision of Sumantra Ghoshal, Associate Professors at INSEAD. It is intended to be used as a basis for class discussion rather than to illustrate either effective or ineffective handling of an administrative situation. Reprinted with the permission of INSEAD-EAC.

Copyright © 1992 INSEAD-EAC, Fontainebleau, France.

Dr. Yoshio Maruta introduced himself as a Buddhist scholar first, and as President of the Kao Corporation second. The order was significant, for it revealed the philosophy behind Kao and its success in Japan. Kao was a company that not only learned, but "learned how to learn." It was, in Dr. Maruta's words, "an educational institution in which everyone is a potential teacher."

Under Dr. Maruta's direction, the scholar's dedication to learning had metamorphosed into a competitive weapon which, in 1990, had led to Kao being ranked ninth by Nikkei Business in its list of excellent companies in Japan, and third in terms of corporate originality (Exhibit 8.1). As described by Fumio Kuroyanagi, Director of Kao's overseas planning department, the company's success was due not merely to its mastery of technologies nor its efficient marketing and information systems, but to its ability to integrate and enhance these capabilities through learning. As a result, Kao had come up with a stream of new products ahead of its Japanese and foreign competitors and, by 1990, had emerged as the largest branded and packaged goods company in Japan and the country's second largest cosmetics company.

Since the mid 1960s, Kao had also successfully used its formidable array of technological, manufacturing, and marketing assets to expand into the neighboring markets of SE Asia. Pitting herself against long established multinationals like Procter & Gamble and Unilever, Kao had made inroads into the detergent, soap, and shampoo markets in the region. However, success in these small markets would not make Kao a global player, and since the mid-1980s, Kao had been giving its attention to the problem of how to break into the international markets beyond the region. There, Kao's innovations were being copied and sold by her competitors, not by Kao itself, a situation the company was keen to remedy. But would Kao be able to repeat its domestic success in the U.S. and Europe? As Dr. Maruta knew, the company's ability to compete on a world-wide basis would be measured by its progress in these markets. This, then, was the new challenge to which Kao was dedicated: how to transfer its learning capability, so all-conquering in Japan, to the rest of the world.

THE LEARNING ORGANIZATION

Kao was founded in 1890 as Kao Soap Company with the prescient motto, "Cleanliness is the foundation of a prosperous society." Its objective then was to produce a high quality soap that was as good as any imported brand, but at a more affordable price for the Japanese

Exhibit 8.1 The Ranking of Japanese Excellent Companies (1990)

1.	Honda Motors	79.8
2.	IBM-Japan	79.4
3.	SONY	78.4
4.	Matsushita Electrics	74.5
5.	Toshiba	69.9
6.	NEC	69.8
7.	Nissan Motors	69.8
8.	Asahi Beer	67.4
9.	KAO	66.6
10.	Yamato Transportation	66.4
11.	Fuji-Xerox	66.3
12.	Seibu Department Store	66.2
13.	Suntory	65.8
14.	Nomura Security	65.4
15.	NTT (Nippon Telegraph & Telephone)	65.3
16.	Omron	65.1
17.	Ajinomoto	64.3
18.	Canon	64.3
19.	Toyota Motors	63.9
20.	Ohtsuka Medicines	63.8

Note: Points are calculated on the basis of the following criteria:
1. the assessment by Nikkei Business Committee's member corporate originality, corporate vision, flexibility, goodness;
2. the result of the researches among consumers;
Source: Nikkei Business 9.4.1990.

consumer, and this principle had guided the development of all Kao's products ever since. In the 1940s, Kao had launched the first Japanese laundry detergent, followed in the 1950s by the launch of dishwashing and household detergents. The 1960s had seen an expansion into industrial products to which Kao could apply its technologies in fat and oil science, surface and polymer science. The '70s and '80s, coinciding with the presidency of Dr. Maruta, had seen the company grow more rapidly than ever in terms of size, sales, and profit, with the launching of innovative products and the start of new businesses. Between 1982 and 1985 it had successfully diversified into cosmetics, hygiene, and floppy disks.

A vertically-integrated company, Kao owned many of its raw material sources and had, since the 1960s, built its own sales organization of wholesalers who had exclusive distribution of its products throughout Japan. The 1980s had seen a consistent rise in profits, with sales increasing at roughly 10 percent a year throughout the decade, even in its mature markets (Exhibit 8.2). In 1990, sales of Kao products had reached ¥620.4 billion ($3,926.8 million), an 8.4 percent increase on 1989. This total consisted of laundry and cleansing products (40 percent), personal care products (34 percent), hygiene products (13 percent), specialty chemicals and floppy disks (9 percent), and fatty chemicals (4 percent) (Exhibit 3). Net income had increased by 1.7 percent, from ¥17.5 billion ($110 million) in 1989 to ¥17.8 billion ($112.7 million) in 1990.

Kao dominated most of its markets in Japan. It was the market leader in detergents and shampoo, and was vying for first place in disposable diapers and cosmetics. It had decisively

Exhibit 8.2 The Trend of Kao's Performance

Years ended March 31	1985	1986	1987	1988	1989	1990	Millions of US$ 1990
	Billions of Yen						
Net Sales	398.1	433.7	464.1	514.4	572.2	620.4	3,926.8
(Increase)		+8.9%	+7.0%	+10.9%	+11.2%	+8.4%	
Operating Income	16.5*	19.853*	31.7	36.5	41.4	43.5	275.5
(Increase)				+15.2%	+13.5%	+5.1%	
Net Income	9.4	10.5	12.9	13.4	17.5	17.8	112.7
(Increase)		+12.3%	+22.5%	+4.2%	+30.4%	+1.7	
Total assets	328.3	374.4	381.0	450.4	532.3	572.8	3,625.5
Total shareholders' equity	114.4	150.9	180.2	210.7	233.8	256.6	1,624.1

*non-consolidated

Note: The U.S. dollar amounts are translated, for convenience only, at the rate of ¥156 = $1, the approximate exchange rate prevailing on March 30, 1990.

Source: Kao Corporation.

beaten off both foreign and domestic competitors, most famously in two particular instances: the 1983 launch of its disposable diaper brand Merries which, within twelve months, had overtaken the leading brand, Procter & Gamble's Pampers, and the 1987 launch of its innovative condensed laundry detergent, the aptly named Attack; as a result, of which the market share of Kao's rival, Lion, had declined from 30.9 percent (1986) to 22.8 percent (1988), while in the same period Kao's share had gone from 33.4 percent to 47.5 percent.

The remarkable success of these two products had been largely responsible for Kao's reputation as a creative company. However, while the ability to introduce a continuous stream of innovative, high quality products clearly rested on Kao's repertoire of core competences, the wellspring behind these was less obvious: Kao's integrated learning capability.

This learning motif had been evident from the beginning. The Nagase family, founders of Kao, had modelled some of Kao's operations, management, and production facilities on those of U.S. corporations and in the 1940s, following his inspection of U.S. and European soap and chemical plants, Tomiro Nagase II had reorganized Kao's production facilities, advertising, and planning departments on the basis of what he had learned. As the company built up its capabilities, this process of imitation and adaptation had evolved into one of innovation until, under Dr. Maruta, a research chemist who joined Kao in the 1930s and became President in 1971, "Distinct creativity became a policy objective in all our areas of research, production and sales, supporting our determination to explore and develop our own fields of activity."

THE PAPERWEIGHT ORGANIZATION

The organizational structure within which Kao managers and personnel worked embodied the philosophy of Dr. Maruta's mentor, the seventh century statesman Prince Shotoku, whose constitution was designed to foster the spirit of harmony, based on the principle of absolute equality: "Human beings can live only by the Universal Truth, and in their dignity of living, all are absolutely equal." Article 1 of his constitution stated that "If everyone discusses on an equal footing, there is nothing that cannot be resolved."

Exhibit 8.3   Review of Operations

HOUSEHOLD PRODUCTS

Personal Care
Cosmetics

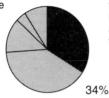

34%

toilet soap, body cleansers, shampoo, hair rinse, hair care products, cosmetics and skin care products, toothpaste and toothbrushes

Net Sales *(Yen in billions)*

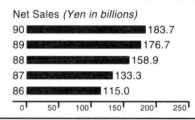

90 183.7
89 176.7
88 158.9
87 133.3
86 115.0

0   50   100   150   200   250

Laundry and
Cleansing

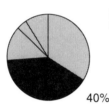

40%

laundry, kitchen and other household detergents, laundry finishing agents

Net Sales *(Yen in billions)*

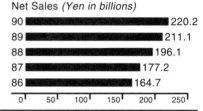

90 220.2
89 211.1
88 196.1
87 177.2
86 164.7

0   50   100   150   200   250

Hygiene

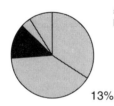

13%

sanitary products, disposable diapers, bath agents

Net Sales *(Yen in billions)*

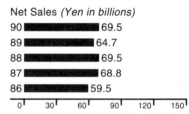

90 69.5
89 64.7
88 69.5
87 68.8
86 59.5

0   30   60   90   120   150

CHEMICAL PRODUCTS

Fatty Chemicals

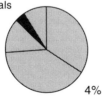

4%

edible fats and oils, fatty acids, fatty alcohols, glycerine, fatty amines

Net Sales *(Yen in billions)*

90 22.9
89 22.6
88 22.1
87 21.2
86 26.2

0   30   60   90   120   150

Specialty
Chemicals and
Floppy Disks

9%

surface active agents, polyurethane systems and additives, plasticizers for synthetic resins, polyester resins, floppy disks

Net Sales *(Yen in billions)*

90 49.0
89 46.3
88 43.4
87 40.6
86 40.3

0   30   60   90   120   150

Source: Kao Corporation annual report 1990, p. 5.

Accordingly, Kao was committed to the principles of equality, individual initiative, and the rejection of authoritarianism. Work was viewed as "something fluid and flexible like the functions of the human body," therefore the organization was designed to "run as a flowing system" which would stimulate interaction and the spread of ideas in every direction and at every level (Exhibit 8.4). To allow creativity and initiative full rein, and to demonstrate that hierarchy was merely an expedient that should not become a constraint, organizational boundaries and titles were abolished.

Dr. Maruta likened this flat structure to an old-fashioned brass paperweight, in contrast to the pyramid structure of Western organizations: "In the pyramid, only the person at the top has all the information. Only he can see the full picture, others cannot . . . The Kao organization is like the paperweight on my desk. It is flat. There is a small handle in the middle, just as we have a few senior people. But all information is shared horizontally, not filtered vertically. Only then can you have equality. And equality is the basis for trust and commitment."

This organization practiced what Kao referred to as "biological self control." As the body reacted to pain by sending help from all quarters, "If anything goes wrong in one department,

Exhibit 8.4   Organizational Structure

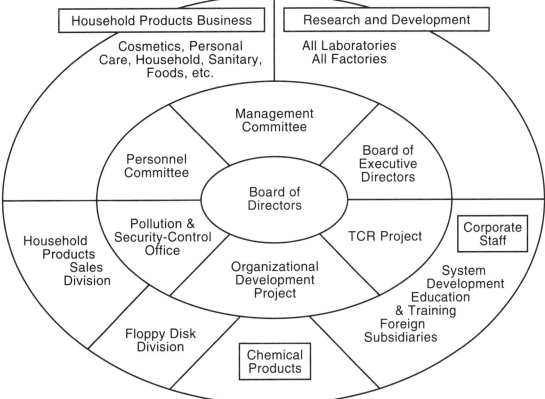

Source: Company Profile Brochure.

the other departments should know automatically and help without having to be asked." Small group activities were encouraged in order to link ideas or discuss issues of immediate concern. In 1987, for example, to resolve the problem of why Kao's Toyohashi factory could achieve only 50 percent of the projected production of Nivea cream, workers there voluntarily formed a small team consisting of the people in charge of production, quality, electricity, process, and machinery. By the following year, production had been raised to 95 percent of the target.

In pursuit of greater efficiency and creativity, Kao's organization has continued to evolve. A 1987 program introduced a system of working from home for sales people, while another will eventually reduce everyone's working time to 1800 hours a year from the traditional level of 2100 hours. Other programs have aimed at either introducing information technology or revitalizing certain areas. 1971 saw the "CCR movement," aimed at reducing the workforce through computerization. "Total Quality Control" came in 1974, followed in 1981 by "Office Automation." The 1986 "Total Cost Reduction" program to restructure management resources evolved into the "Total Creative Revolution," designed to encourage a more innovative approach. For example, five people who were made redundant following the installation of new equipment, formed, on their own initiative, a special task force team, and visited a U.S. factory which had imported machinery from Japan. They stayed there for three months until local engineers felt confident enough to take charge. Over time, this group became a flying squad of specialists, available to help foreign production plants get over their teething troubles.

MANAGING INFORMATION

Just as Dr. Maruta's Buddha was the enlightened teacher, so Kao employees were the "Priests" who learned and practiced the truth. Learning was "a frame of mind, a daily matter," and truth was sought through discussions, by testing and investigating concrete business ideas until something was learned, often without the manager realizing it. This was "the quintessence of information . . . something we actually see with our own eyes and feel with our bodies." This internalized intuition, which coincides with the Zen Buddhist phrase *kangyo ichijo*, was the goal Dr. Maruta set for all Kao managers. In reaching it, every individual was expected to be a coach; both to himself and to everyone else, whether above or below him in the organization.

Their training material was information. Information was regarded not as something lifeless to be stored, but as knowledge to be shared and exploited to the utmost. Every manager repeated Dr. Maruta's fundamental assumption: "in today's business world, information is the only source of competitive advantage. The company that develops a monopoly on information, and has the ability to learn from it continuously, is the company that will win, irrespective of its business." Every piece of information from the environment was treated as a potential key to a new positioning, a new product. What can we learn from it? How can we use it? These were the questions all managers were expected to ask themselves at all times.

Access to information was another facet of Kao's commitment to egalitarianism: as described by Kuroyanagi, "In Kao, the 'classified' stamp does not exist." Through the development of computer communication technologies, the same level of information was available to all: "In order to make it effective to discuss subjects freely, it is necessary to share all information. If someone has special and crucial information that the others don't have, that is against human equality, and will deprive us and the organization of real creativity."

Every director and most salesmen had a fax in their homes to receive results and news, and a bi-weekly Kao newspaper kept the entire company informed about competitors' moves, new product launches, overseas development, or key meetings. Terminals installed throughout the company ensured that employees could, if they wished, retrieve data on sales records of any product for any of Kao's numerous outlets, or product development at their own or other branches. The latest findings from each of Kao's research laboratories were available for all to see, as were the details of the previous day's production and inventory at every Kao plant. "They can even," said Dr. Maruta, "check up on the president's expense account." He believed that the increase in creativity resulting from this pooling of data outweighed the risk of leaks. In any case, the prevailing environment of omnes flux meant that things moved so quickly "leaked information instantly becomes obsolete."

The task of Kao managers, therefore, was to take information directly from the competitive environment, process it, and, by adding value, transform it into knowledge or wisdom. Digesting information from the marketplace in this way enabled the organization to maintain empathy with this fast moving environment. The emphasis was always on learning and on the future, not on following an advance plan based on previous experience. "Past wisdom must not be a constraint, but something to be challenged," Dr. Maruta constantly urged. Kao managers were discouraged from making any historical comparisons. "We cannot talk about history," said Mr. Takayama, Overseas Planning Director. "If we talk about the past, they (the top management) immediately become unpleasant." The emphasis was rather, what had they learned today that would be useful tomorrow? "Yesterday's success formula is often today's obsolete dogma. We must continuously challenge the past so that we can renew ourselves each day," said Dr. Maruta.

"Learning through cooperation" was the slogan of Kao's R&D; the emphasis was on information exchange, both within and outside the department, and sharing "to motivate and activate." Glycerine Ether, for example, an emulsifier important for the production of Sofina's screening cream, was the product of joint work among three Kao laboratories. Research results were communicated to everyone in the company through the IT system, in order to build a close networking organization. Top management and researchers met at regular R&D conferences, where presentations were made by the researchers themselves, not their section managers. "Open Space" meetings were offered every week by the R&D division, and people from any part of the organization could participate in discussions on current research projects.

A number of formal and informal systems were created to promote communication among the research scientists working in different laboratories. For example, results from Paris were fed daily into the computer in Tokyo. The most important of these communication mechanisms, however, were the monthly R&D working conferences for junior researchers which took place at each laboratory in turn. When it was their own laboratory's turn to act as host, researchers could nominate anyone they wished to meet, from any laboratory in the company, to attend that meeting. In addition, researchers could nominate themselves to attend meetings if they felt that the discussions could help their own work, or if they wanted to talk separately with someone from the host laboratory. At the meetings, which Dr. Maruta often attended to argue and discuss issues in detail, researchers reported on studies in progress, and those present offered advice from commercial and academic perspectives.

THE DECISION PROCESS

"In Kao, we try collectively to direct the accumulation of individual wisdom at serving the customer." This was how Dr. Maruta explained the company's approach to the decision process. At Kao, no-one owned an idea. Ideas were to be shared in order to enhance their value and achieve enlightenment in order to make the right decision. The prevailing principle was tataki-dai; present your ideas to others at 80 percent completion so that they could criticize or contribute before the idea became a proposal. Takayama likened this approach to heating an iron and testing it on one's arm to see if it was hot enough. "By inviting all the relevant actors to join in with forging the task," he said, "we achieve zo-awase; a common perspective or view." The individual was thus a strategic factor, to be linked with others in a union of individual wisdom and group strategy.

Fumio Kuroyanagi provided an illustration. Here is the process by which a problem involving a joint venture partner, in which he was the key person, was resolved: "I put up a preliminary note summarizing the key issues, but not making any proposals. I wanted to share the data and obtain other views before developing a proposal fully. This note was distributed to legal, international controllers to read . . . then in the meeting we talked about the facts and came up with some ideas on how to proceed. Then members of this meeting requested some top management time. All the key people attended this meeting, together with one member of the top management. No written document was circulated in advance. Instead, we described the situation, our analysis and action plans. He gave us his comments. We came to a revised plan. I then wrote up this revised plan and circulated it to all the people, and we had a second meeting at which everyone agreed with the plan. Then the two of us attended the actual meeting with the partner. After the meeting I debriefed other members, discussed and circulated a draft of the letter to the partner which, after everyone else had seen it and given their comments, was signed by my boss."

The cross fertilization of ideas to aid the decision process was encouraged by the physical layout of the Kao building. On the tenth floor, known as the top management floor, sat the Chairman, the President, four Executive Vice Presidents and a pool of secretaries (Exhibit 8.5). A large part of the floor was open space, with one large conference table and two smaller ones, and chairs, blackboards, and overhead projectors strewn around. This was known as the Decision Space, where all discussions with and among the top management took place. Anyone passing, including the President, could sit down and join in any discussion on any topic, however briefly. This layout was duplicated on the other floors, in the laboratories, and in the workshop. Workplaces looked like large rooms; there were no partitions, but again tables and chairs for spontaneous or planned discussions at which everyone contributed as equals. Access was free to all, and any manager could thus find himself sitting round the table next to the President, who was often seen waiting in line in Kao's Tokyo cafeteria.

The management process, thus, was transparent and open, and leadership was practiced in daily behavior rather than by memos and formal meetings. According to Takayama, top

Exhibit 8.5 Layout of Kao Offices

Top Management Floor

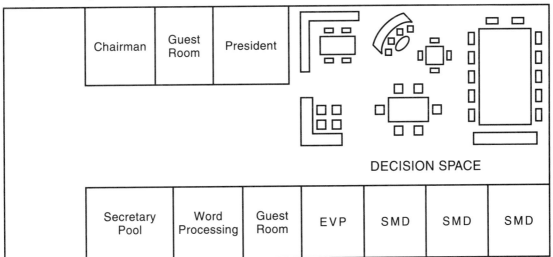

Other Floors

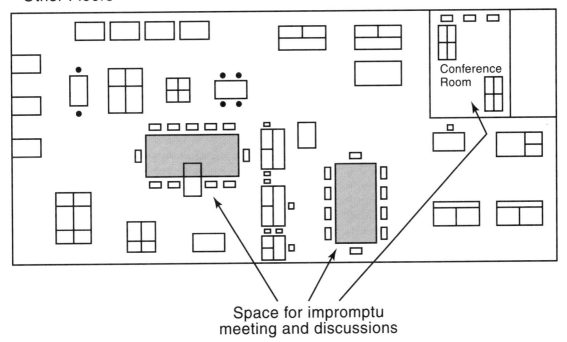

Space for impromptu
meeting and discussions

Source: Kao Corporation.

management "emphasizes that 80 percent of its time must be spent on communication, and the remaining 20 percent on decision making." While top management regularly visited other floors to join in discussions, anyone attending a meeting on the tenth floor then had to pass on what had happened to the rest of his colleagues.

INFORMATION TECHNONOGY

Information Technology (IT) was one of Kao's most effective competitive weapons, and an integral part of its organizational systems and management processes. In 1982, Kao made an agreement to use Japan Information Service Co.'s VAN (Value Added Networks) for communication between Kao's head office, its sales companies, and its large wholesalers. Over time, Kao built its own VAN, through which it connected upstream and downstream via information linkages. In 1986, the company added DRESS, a new network linking Kao and the retail stores receiving its support.

The objective of this networking capability was to achieve the complete fusion and interaction of Kao's marketing, production, and R&D departments. Fully integrated information systems controlled the flow of materials and products, from the production planning of raw materials to the distribution of the final products to local stores – no small task in a company dealing with over 1,500 types of raw materials from 500 different suppliers, and producing over 550 types of final products for up to 300,000 retail stores.

Kao's networks enabled it to maintain a symbiotic relationship with its distributors, the hansha. Developed since 1966, the Kao hansha (numbering thirty by 1990) were independent wholesalers who handled only Kao products. They dealt directly with 100,000 retail stores out of 300,000, and about 60 percent of Kao's products passed through them. The data terminals installed in the hansha offices provided Kao with up-to-date product movement and market information, which was easily accessible for analysis.

Kao's Logistics Information System (LIS) consisted of a sales planning system, an inventory control system, and an on-line supply system. It linked Kao headquarters, factories, the hansha and Logistics centers by networks, and dealt with ordering, inventory, production, and sales data (Exhibit 8.6). Using the LIS, each hansha salesperson projected sales plans on the basis of a head office campaign plan, an advertising plan, and past market trends. These were corrected and adjusted at corporate level, and a final sales plan was produced each month. From this plan, daily production schedules were then drawn up for each factory and product. The system would also calculate the optimal machine load and the number of people required. An on-line supply system calculated the appropriate amount of factory stocks and checked the hansha inventory. The next day's supply was then computed and automatically ordered from the factory.

A computerized ordering system enabled stores to receive and deliver products within 24 hours of placing an order. Through a POS (point of sale) terminal, installed in the retail store as a cash register and connected to the Kao VAN, information on sales and orders was transmitted to the hansha's computer. Via this, orders from local stores, adjusted according to the amount of their inventory, were transmitted to Kao's Logistics center, which then supplied the product.

Two other major support systems, KAP and RSS, respectively, helped the wholesale houses in ordering, stocking, and accounting, and worked with Kao's nine distribution information

Exhibit 8.6   Kao's Information Network

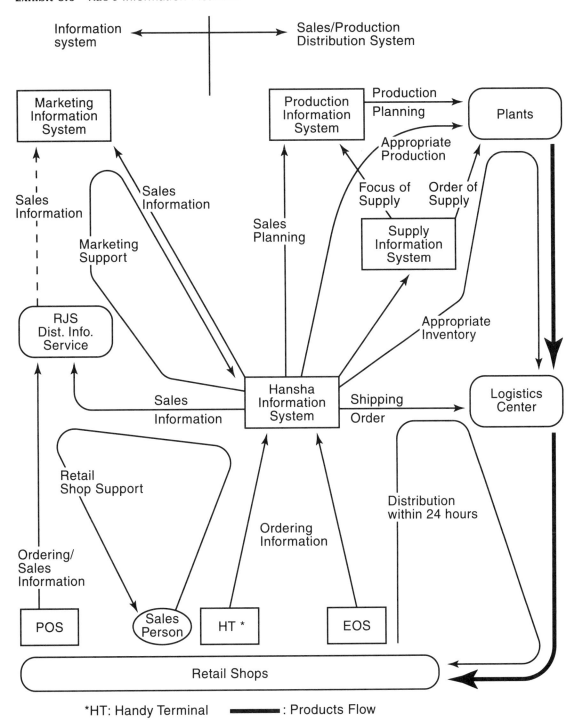

Source: Nikkei Computer Oct. 9, 1989 (Nippon Keizai shinbunsha).

service companies, the Ryutsu Joho Service Companies (RJSs). Each RJS had about 500 customers, mainly small and medium-sized supermarkets who were too small to access real-time information by themselves. The RJSs were essentially consulting outfits, whose mandate was to bring the benefits of information available in Kao VAN to those stores that could not access the information directly. They guided store owners by offering analysis of customer buying trends, shelf space planning, and ways of improving the store's sales, profitability, and customer service. The owner of one such store commented: "A Kao salesperson comes to see us two or three times a week, and we chat about many topics. To me, he is both a good friend and a good consultant. I can see Kao's philosophy, the market trend, and the progress of R&D holistically through this person." According to Dr. Maruta, the RJSs embodied Kao's principle of the information advantage: their purpose was to provide this advantage to store owners, and the success of the RJSs in building up the volume and profitability of the stores was ample evidence of the correctness of the principle.

Kao's Marketing Intelligence System (MIS) tracked sales by product, region, and market segment, and provided raw market research data. All this information was first sifted for clues to customer needs, then linked with R&D "seeds" to create new products. New approaches to marketing were sought by applying artificial intelligence to various topics, including advertising and media planning, sales promotion, new product development, market research, and statistical analysis.

Additional information was provided by the Consumer Life Research Laboratory which operated ECHO, a sophisticated system for responding to telephone queries about Kao products. In order to understand and respond immediately to a customer's question, each phone operator could instantly access a video display of each of Kao's 500 plus products. Enquiries were also coded and entered into the computer system on-line, and the resulting data base provided one of the richest sources for product development or enhancement ideas. By providing Kao with "a direct window on the consumer's mind," ECHO enabled the company to "predict the performance of new products and fine tune formulations, labelling, and packaging." Kao also used a panel of monitor households to track how products fitted into consumers' lives.

In 1989, Kao separated its information systems organization and established a distinct entity called Kao Software Development. The aim was to penetrate the information service industry, which, according to Japan Information, was projected to reach a business volume of ¥12,000 billion ($80 billion) by the year 2000. In 1989, the market was ¥3,000 billion ($20 billion). One IBM sales engineer forecast, "by 2000, Kao will have become one of our major competitors, because they know how to develop information technology, and how to combine it with real organization systems."

In 1989, Kao's competitors including Lion and Procter & Gamble, united to set up Planet Logistics, a system comparable to Kao's VAN. Through it, they aimed to achieve the same information richness as Kao. But Dr. Maruta was not worried by this development. Irrespective of whatever information they collected, he believed that the competitors would not be able to add the value and use it in the same way as Kao did. "As a company we do not spend our time chasing after what our rivals do. Rather, by mustering our knowledge, wisdom, and ingenuity to study how to supply the consumer with superior products, we free ourselves of the need to care about the moves of our competitors. Imitation is the sincerest form of flattery, but unless they can add value to all that information, it will be of little use."

SOFINA

The development of Sofina was a microcosm of Kao's modus operandi. It illustrated the learning organization in action since it sought to create a product that satisfied the five principles guiding the development of any new offering. "Each product must be useful to society. It must use innovative technology. It must offer consumers value. We must be confident we really understand the market and the consumers. And, finally, each new product must be compatible with the trade." Until a new product satisfied all these criteria, it would not be launched on the market. At every stage during Sofina's creation, ideas were developed, criticized, discussed, and refined or altered in the light of new information and learning by everyone involved, from Dr. Maruta down.

The Sofina story began in 1965 with a "vision." The high quality, innovative product that finally emerged in 1982 allowed Kao to enter a new market and overtake well-established competitors. By 1990, Sofina had become the highest selling brand of cosmetics in Japan for most items except lipsticks.

The Vision

The vision, according to Mr. Daimaru (the first director of Sofina marketing), was simple: to help customers avoid the appearance of wrinkles on their skin for as long as possible. From this vision an equally simple question arose: "What makes wrinkles appear?" Finding the answer was the spring that set the Kao organization into motion.

Kao's competence until then had been in household and toiletry personal care products. However, Kao had long supplied raw materials for the leading cosmetics manufacturers in Japan, and had a technological competence in fats and soap that could, by cross pollination, be adapted to research on the human skin. Accordingly, the efforts of Kao's R&D laboratories were directed toward skin research, and the results used in the company's existing businesses such as Nivea or Azea, then sold in joint venture with Beiersdorf. From these successes came the idea for growth that steered the development of Sofina.

The Growth Idea

The idea was to produce a new, high quality cosmetic that gave real value at a reasonable price. During the 1960s, there was a strong perception in the Japanese cosmetics industry that the more expensive the product, the better it was. This view was challenged by Dr. Maruta, whose travels had taught him that good skin care products sold in the U.S. or Europe were not as outrageously expensive. Yet in Japan, even with companies like Kao supplying high quality raw materials at a low price, the end product was still beyond the reach of ordinary women at ¥10–20,000.

As a supplier of raw materials, Dr. Maruta was aware of how well these products performed. He also knew that though cosmetics' prices were rising sharply, little was being spent on improving the products themselves, and that customers were paying for an expensive image. Was this fair, or good for the customer? Kao, he knew, had the capacity to supply high quality raw materials at low cost, and a basic research capability. Intensive research to develop new toiletry goods had led to the discovery of a technology for modifying the surface of powders, which could be applied to the development of cosmetics. Why not use these assets to develop a new, high quality, reasonably priced product, in keeping with Kao's principles?

To enter the new market would mean a heavy investment in research and marketing, with no guarantee that their product would be accepted. However, it was decided to go ahead; the product would be innovative and, against the emotional appeal of the existing competition in terms of packaging and image, its positioning would embody Kao's scientific approach.

This concept guided the learning process as Sofina was developed. It was found that the integration of Kao's unique liquid crystal emulsification technology and other newly developed materials proved effective in maintaining a "healthy and beautiful skin." This led Kao to emphasize skin care, as opposed to the industry's previous focus on make-up only. All the research results from Kao's skin diagnosis and dermatological testing were poured into the new product and, as Dr. Tsutsumi of the Tokyo Research Laboratory recalled, in pursuing problems connected with the product, new solutions emerged. For example, skin irritation caused by the new chemical was solved by developing MAP, a low irritant, and PSL, a moisturizer. By 1980, most of the basic research work had been done. Six cosmetics suitable for the six basic skin types had been developed, though all under the Sofina name.

During this stage, Kao's intelligence collectors were sent out to explore and map the new market environment. Information on products, pricing, positioning, the competition and above all, the customers, was analyzed and digested by the Sofina marketing and R&D teams, and by Kao's top management. Again and again Dr. Maruta asked the same two questions: How would the new product be received? Was it what customers wanted?

The Growth Process

Test marketing began in September 1980, in the Shizuoka prefecture, and was scheduled to last for a year. Shizuoka was chosen because it represented 30 percent of the national market and an average social mix, neither too rich or too poor, too rural or too urban. Its media isolation meant that television advertisements could be targeted to the local population, and no one outside would question why the product was not available elsewhere. The local paper also gave good coverage. In keeping with Kao's rule that "the concept of a new product is that of its advertising," the Sofina advertisements were reasoned and scientific, selling a function rather than an image.

Sofina was distributed directly to the retail stores through the Sofina Cosmetics Company, established to distinguish Sofina from Kao's conventional detergent business and avoid image blurring. No mention was made of Kao. Sofina's managers found, however, that retailers did not accept Sofina immediately, but put it on the waiting list for display along with other new cosmetics. The result was that by October 1980, Kao had only succeeded in finding 200 points of sale, against an objective of 600. Then, as the real parentage of Sofina leaked out, the attitude among retailers changed, and the Sofina stand was given the best position in the store. This evidence of Kao's credibility, together with the company's growing confidence in the quality and price of the product, led to a change of strategy. The thirty-strong sales force was instructed to put the Kao name first and, by November, 600 outlets had been found.

Sofina's subsequent development was guided by feedback from the market. Direct distribution enabled Kao to retain control of the business and catch customer responses to the product at first hand. To Mr. Masashi Kuga, director of Kao's Marketing Research Department, such information "has clear added value, and helps in critical decision making." During the repeated test marketing of Sofina, Kao's own market research service, formed in 1973 to ensure a high quality response from the market with the least possible distortion, measured the efficacy of sampling and helped decide on the final marketing mix. This activity was usually supported by "concept testing, focus group discussions, plus product acceptance research." Mr. Daimaru visited the test market twice or three times each month and talked to consumers directly. Dr. Maruta did the same.

Every piece of information and all results were shared by the Sofina team, R&D, Kao's top management, corporate marketing and sales managers. Discussions on Sofina's progress were attended by all of these managers, everyone contributing ideas about headline copy or other issues on an equal basis. Wives and friends were given samples and their reactions were fed back to the team.

From the reactions of customers and stores, Kao learned that carrying real information in the advertisements about the quality of the product had been well received, despite differing from the normal emphasis on fancy packaging. This they could never have known from their detergent business. Another finding was the importance of giving a full explanation of the product with samples, and of a skin analysis before recommending the most suitable product rather than trying to push the brand indiscriminately. They also learned the value of listening to the opinion of the store manager's wife who, they discovered, often had the real managing power, particularly for cosmetics products.

Decisions were implemented immediately. For example, the decision to improve the design for the sample package was taken at 3:30 p.m., and by 6:30 p.m. the same day the engineer in the factory had begun redesigning the shape of the bottle.

The results of this test marketing, available to the whole company, confirmed the decision to go ahead with Sofina. Kao was satisfied that the product would be accepted nationally, though it might take some time. A national launch was planned for the next year. Even at this stage, however, Dr. Maruta was still asking whether consumers and retail store owners really liked Sofina.

The Learning Extended

Sofina finally went on nationwide sale in October 1982. However, the flow of learning and intelligence gathering continued via the hansha and MIS. Kao, the hansha, the retailers, and Sofina's customers formed a chain, along which was a free, two-way flow of information. The learning was then extended to develop other products, resulting in production of the complete Sofina range of beauty care. In 1990, the range covered the whole market, from basic skin care to make-up cosmetics and perfumes.

In fact, the product did not achieve real success until after 1983. Dr. Tsutsumi dated it from the introduction of the foundation cream which, he recalled, also faced teething problems. The test result from the panel was not good; it was too different from existing products and was sticky on application. Kao, however, knowing it was a superior product that lasted longer, persevered and used their previous experience to convert the stickiness into a strength: the product was repositioned as the longest lasting foundation that does not disappear with sweat.

In the early 1980s, while market growth was only 2–3 percent, sales of Sofina products increased at the rate of 30 percent every year. In 1990, sales amounted to ¥55 billion, and

Kao held 15.6 percent of the cosmetics market behind Shiseido and Kanebo, though taken individually, Sofina brands topped every product category except lipsticks.

Within Japan, Sofina was sold through 12,700 outlets. According to Mr. Nakanishi, director of the Cosmetics Division, the marketing emphasis was by that time being redirected from heavy advertising of the product to counselling at the point of sale. Kao was building up a force of beauty counsellors to educate the public on the benefits of Sofina products. A Sofina store in Tokyo was also helping to develop hair care and cosmetics products. A Sofina newspaper had been created which salesmen received by fax, along with the previous month's sales and inventory figures.

Knowledge gathered by the beauty advisers working in the Sofina shops was exploited for the development of the next set of products. Thus, Sofina "ultra-violet" care, which incorporated skin lotion, UV care, and foundation in one, was positioned to appeal to busy women and advertised as "one step less." The Sofina cosmetics beauty care consultation system offered advice by phone, at retail shops, or by other means to consumers who made enquiries. From their questions, clues were sought to guide new product development.

A staff of Field Companions visited the retail stores to get direct feedback on sales. Every outlet was visited once a month, when the monitors discussed Kao products with store staff, advised on design displays, and even helped clean up. Dr. Maruta himself maintained an active interest. Mr. Kuroyanagi described how Dr. Maruta recently "came down to our floor" to report that while visiting a certain town, he had "found a store selling Sofina products, and a certain shade sample was missing from the stand." He asked that the store be checked and the missing samples supplied as soon as possible.

Despite Sofina's success, Kao was still not satisfied. "To be really successful, developing the right image is important. We've lagged behind on this, and we must improve."

As the Sofina example showed, in its domestic base Kao was an effective and confident company, renowned for its ability to produce high quality, technologically advanced products at relatively low cost. Not surprising then, that since the 1960s it had turned its thoughts to becoming an important player on the larger world stage. But could the learning organization operate effectively outside Japan? Could Kao transfer its learning capability into a very different environment such as the U.S. or Europe, where it would lack the twin foundations of infrastructure and human resource? Or would internationalization demand major adjustments to its way of operating?

KAO INTERNATIONAL

When the first cake of soap was produced in 1890, the name "Kao" was stamped in both Chinese characters and Roman letters in preparation for the international market. A century later, the company was active in fifty countries but, except for the small neighboring markets of Southeast Asia, had not achieved a real breakthrough. Despite all its investments, commitment, and efforts over twenty-five years, Kao remained only "potentially" a significant global competitor. In 1988, only 10 percent of its total sales was derived from overseas business, and 70 percent of this international volume was earned in Southeast Asia. As a result, internationalization was viewed by the company as its next key strategic challenge. Dr. Maruta made his ambitions clear; "Procter and Gamble, Unilever and L'Oreal are our competitors. We cannot avoid fighting in the 1990s." The challenge was to make those words a reality.

The Strategic Infrastructure

Kao's globalization was based not on a company-wide strategy, but on the product division system. Each product division developed its own strategy for international expansion and remained responsible for its worldwide results. Consequently, the company's business portfolio and strategic infrastructure varied widely from market to market.

Southeast Asia   As Exhibit 8.7 illustrates, Kao had been building a platform for production and marketing throughout Southeast Asia since 1964, when it created its first overseas subsidiary in Thailand. By 1990, this small initial base had been expanded, mainly through joint ventures, and the company had made steady progress in these markets. The joint ventures in Hong Kong and Singapore sold only Kao's consumer products, while the others both manufactured and marketed them.

One of Kao's biggest international battles was for control of the Asian detergent, soap, and shampoo markets, against rivals like P&G and Unilever. In the Taiwanese detergent market, where Unilever was the long established leader with 50 percent market share, Kao's vanguard product was the biological detergent, Attack. Launched in 1988, Attack increased Kao's market share from 17 percent to 22 percent. Subsequently, Kao decided on local production, both to continue serving the local market and for export to Hong Kong and Singapore. Its domestic rival, Lion (stationary at 17 percent) shortly followed suit. In Hong Kong, Kao was the market leader with 30 percent share and in Singapore, where Colgate-Palmolive led with 30 percent, had increased its share from 5 percent to 10 percent. Unilever, P&G, and Colgate-Palmolive had responded to Kao's moves by putting in more human resources, and consolidating their local bases.

In Indonesia, where Unilever's historic links again made it strong, Kao, Colgate-Palmolive, and P&G competed for the second position. In the Philippines, Kao had started local production of shampoo and liquid soap in 1989, while in Thailand it had doubled its local facilities in order to meet increasing demand. To demonstrate its commitment to the Asian market where it was becoming a major player, Kao had established its Asian headquarters in Singapore. In that market, Kao's disposable diaper Merrys had a 20 percent share, while its Merit shampoo was the market leader.

North America   Step 1 – Joint venture In 1976, Kao had embarked on two joint ventures with Colgate-Palmolive Company, first to market hair care products in the U.S., and later to develop new oral hygiene products for Japan. The potential for synergy seemed enormous; Colgate-Palmolive was to provide the marketing expertise and distribution infrastructure; Kao would contribute the technical expertise to produce a high quality product for the top end of the U.S. market.

1977 saw a considerable exchange of personnel and technology, and a new shampoo was specially developed by Kao for the U.S. consumer. Despite the fact that tests in three major U.S. cities, using Colgate-Palmolive's state of the art market research methods, showed poor market share potential, the product launch went ahead. The forecasts turned out to be correct, and the product was dropped after ten months due to Colgate-Palmolive's reluctance to continue. A Kao manager explained the failure thus; "First, the product was not targeted to the proper consumer group. High price, high end products were not appropriate for a novice and as yet unsophisticated producer like us. Second, the U.S. side believed in the

Exhibit 8.7   The History of Kao's Internationalization

Area	Company	Year	Capital	Main Products
ASIA				
Taiwan	Taiwan Kao Co. Ltd.	1964	90	detergent, soap
Thailand	Kao Industrila Co. Ltd.	1964	70	hair care products
Singapore	Kao Private Ltd.	1965	100	sales of soap, shampoo, detergents
Hong Kong	Kao Ltd.	1970	100	sales of soap, shampoo, detergents
Malaysia	Kao Ptc. Ltd.	1973	45	hair care products
Philippines	Pilippinas Kao Inc.	1977	70	fats and oils
Indonesia	P. T. PoleKao	1977	74	surfactants
Philippines	Kao Inc.	1979	70	hair care products
Indonesia	P. T. Dino Indonesia Industrial Ltd.	1985	50	hair care products
Malaysia	Fatty Chemical Sdn. Bdn.	1988	70	alcohol
Singapore	Kao South-East Asia Headquarters	1988		
Philippines	Kao Co. Philippines Laboratory			
NORTH AMERICA				
Mexico	Qumi-Kao S. A. de C. V.	1975	20	fatty amines
	Bitumex	1979	49	asphalt
Canada	Kao-Didak Ltd.	1983	89	floppy disk
U.S.A.	Kao Corporation of American (KCOA)	1986	100	sales of household goods
	High Point Chemical	1987	100 (KCOA)	ingredients
	Kao Infosystems Company	1988	100 (KCOA)	duplication of software
	The Andrew Jergens	1988	100 (KCOA)	hair care products
U.S.A.	KCOA Los Angeles Laboratories			
EUROPE				
W. Germany	Kao Corporation GmbH	1986	100 (KCG)	sales of household goods
	Kao Perfekta GmbH	1986	80 (KCG)	toners for copiers
	Guhl Ikebana GmbH	1986	50 (KCG)	hair care products
Spain	Kao Corporation S. A.	1987	100	surfactants
W. Germany	Goldwell AG	1989	100	cosmetics
France	Kao Co. S. A. Paris Laboratories			
Spain	Kao Co. S. A. Barcelona Laboratories			
W. Germany	Kao Co. GmbH Berlin Laboratories			

Source: Kao Corporation.

result of the market research too seriously and did not attempt a second try. Third, it is essentially very difficult to penetrate a market like the shampoo market. Our partner expected too much short term success. Fourth, the way the two firms decided on strategy was totally different. We constantly adjust our strategy flexibly. They never start without a concrete and fixed strategy. We could not wait for them."

The alliance was dissolved in 1985. However, Kao had learned some valuable lessons: about U.S. marketing methods, about Western lifestyles, and, most of all, about the limitations of using joint ventures as a means of breaking into the U.S. market.

Step 2 – Acquisition In 1988, Kao had made three acquisitions. In May, it bought the Andrew Jergens Company, a Cincinnati soap, body lotion, and shampoo maker, for $350 million. To acquire Jergens's extensive marketing know-how and established distribution channels, Kao beat off seventy other bidders, including Beiersdorf and Colgate-Palmolive, and paid 40 percent more than the expected price. Since then, Kao has invested heavily in the company, building a new multimillion dollar research center and doubling Jergens's research team to over fifty. Cincinnati was the hometown of P&G, who have since seen Jergens market Kao's bath preparations in the U.S.

High Point Chemical Corporation of America, an industrial goods producer, was also acquired in 1988. As Kao's U.S. chemical manufacturing arm, it had since begun "an aggressive expansion of its manufacturing facilities and increased its market position." The third acquisition, Info Systems (Sentinel) produced application products in the field of information technology.

In Canada, Kao owned 87 percent of Kao-Didak, a floppy disk manufacturer it bought out in 1986. A new plant, built in 1987, started producing 3.5 inch and 5.25 inch diskettes, resulting in record sales of $10 million that same year. Kao viewed floppy disks as the spearhead of its thrust into the U.S. market. As Mr. Kyroyanagi explained: "This product penetrates the U.S. market easily. Our superior technology makes it possible to meet strict requirements for both quantity and quality. Our experience in producing specific chemicals for the floppy disk gives us a great competitive edge." In what represented a dramatic move for a Japanese company, Kao relocated its worldwide head office for the floppy disk business to the U.S., partly because of Kao's comparatively strong position there (second behind Sony) but also because it was by far the biggest market in the world. The U.S. headquarters was given complete strategic freedom to develop the business globally. Under the direction of this office a plant was built in Spain.

Europe Within Europe, Kao had built a limited presence in Germany, Spain, and France. In Germany, it had established a research laboratory, and, through its 1979 joint venture with Beiersdorf to develop and market hair care products, gained a good knowledge of the German market. The strategic position of this business was strengthened in 1989 by the acquisition of a controlling interest in Goldwell AC, one of Germany's leading suppliers of hair and skin care products to beauty salons. From studying Goldwell's network of beauty salons across Europe, Kao expected to expand its knowledge in order to be able to develop and market new products in Europe.

Kao's French subsidiary, created in January 1990, marketed floppy disks, skin toner, and the Sofina range of cosmetics. The research laboratory established in Paris that same year was given the leading role in developing perfumes to meet Kao's worldwide requirements.

Kao's vanguard product in Europe was Sofina, which was positioned as a high quality, medium priced product. Any Japanese connection had been removed to avoid giving the brand a cheap image. While Sofina was produced and packaged in Japan, extreme care was taken to ensure that it shared a uniform global positioning and image in all the national markets in Europe. It was only advertised in magazines like Vogue, and sales points were carefully selected; for example, in France, Sofina was sold only in the prestigious Paris department store, Galeries Lafayette.

Organizational Capability

Organizationally, Kao's international operations were driven primarily along the product division axis. Each subsidiary had a staff in charge of each product who reported to the product's head office, either directly or through a regional product manager. For example, the manager in charge of Sofina in Spain reported to the French office where the regional manager responsible for Sofina was located, and he in turn reported to the director of the Divisional HQ in Japan. Each subsidiary was managed by Japanese expatriate managers, since Kao's only foreign resource was provided by its acquired companies. Thus, the German companies remained under the management of its original directors. However, some progress was made toward localization; in Kao Spain (250 employees) there were "only six to ten Japanese, not necessarily in management." Kao's nine overseas R&D laboratories were each strongly connected to both the product headquarters and laboratories in Japan through frequent meetings and information exchange.

Mr. Takayama saw several areas that needed to be strengthened before Kao could become an effective global competitor. Kao, he believed "was a medium-sized company grown large." It lacked international experience, had fewer human resource assets, especially in top management and, compared with competitors like P&G and Unilever, had far less accumulated international knowledge and experience of Western markets and consumers. "These two companies know how to run a business in the West and have well established market research techniques, whereas the Westernization of the Japanese lifestyle has only occurred in the last twenty years," he explained. "There are wide differences between East and West in, for example, bathing habits, that the company has been slow to comprehend."

Kao attempted to redress these problems through stronger involvement by headquarters managers in supporting the company's foreign operations. Mr. Kuroyanagi provided an insight into Kao's approach to managing its overseas units. He described how, after visiting a foreign subsidiary where he felt change was necessary, he asked a senior colleague in Japan to carry out a specific review. The two summarized their findings, and then met with other top management members for further consultation. As a result, his colleague was temporarily located in the foreign company to lead certain projects. A team was formed in Japan to harmonize with locals, and sent to work in the subsidiary. Similarly, when investigating the reason for the company's slow penetration of the shampoo market in Thailand, despite offering a technologically superior product, headquarters' managers found that the product positioning, pricing, and packaging policies developed for the Japanese market were unsuitable for Thailand. Since the subsidiary could not adapt these policies to meet local requirements, a headquarters' marketing specialist was brought in, together with a representative from Dentsu – Kao's advertising agent in Japan – to identify the source of the problem and make the necessary changes in the marketing mix.

Part of Mr. Kuroyanagi's role was to act as a "liaison officer" between Kao and its subsidiaries. Kao appointed such managers at headquarters to liaise with all the newly acquired companies in Europe and Asia. Their task was to interpret corporate strategies to other companies outside Japan and ensure that "We never make the same mistake twice." He described himself as "the eyes and ears of top management, looking round overseas moves, competitors' activities and behaviors and summarizing them." He was also there to "help the local management abroad understand correctly Kao as a corporation, and give hints about how to overcome the cultural gap and linguistic difficulties, how to become open, aggressive, and innovative."

Kao's 1990 global strategy was to develop "local operations sensitive to each region's characteristics and needs." As Mr. Takayama explained, these would be able "to provide each country with goods tailored to its local climate and customs, products which perfectly meet the needs of its consumers." To this end, the goals of the company's research centers in Los Angeles, Berlin, Paris, and Santiago de Compostela in Spain, had been redefined as: "to analyze local market needs and characteristics and integrate them into the product development process," and a small market research unit had been created in Thailand to support local marketing of Sofina. Over time, Kao hoped, headquarters' functions would be dispersed to Southeast Asia, the U.S., and Europe, leaving to the Tokyo headquarters the role of supporting regionally based, locally managed operations by giving "strategic assistance." There were no plans to turn Jergens or other acquired companies into duplicate Kaos; as described by Dr. Maruta, "We will work alongside them rather than tell them which way to go."

The lack of overseas experience among Kao's managers was tackled via a new ¥9 billion training facility built at Kasumigaura. The sixteen hectare campus, offering golf, tennis, and other entertainment opportunities, was expected to enjoy a constant population of 200, with ten days training becoming the norm for all managers. To help Kao managers develop a broader and more international outlook, training sessions devoted considerable attention to the cultural and historical heritages of different countries. A number of younger managers were sent to Europe and the United States, spending the first year learning languages and the second either at a business school, or at Kao's local company offices.

"If you look at our recent international activity," said Mr. Kuroyanagi, we have prepared our stage. We have made our acquisitions . . . the basis for globalization in Europe, North America, and Southeast Asia has been facilitated. . . . We now need some play on that stage." Kao's top management was confident that the company's R&D power, "vitality and open, innovative, and aggressive culture" would ultimately prevail. The key constraints, inevitably, were people. "We do not have enough talented people to direct these plays on the stage." Kao could not and did not wish to staff its overseas operations with Japanese nationals, but finding, training, and keeping suitable local personnel was a major challenge.

Kao expected the industry to develop like many others until "there were only three or four companies operating on a global scale. We would like to be one of these." Getting there looked like taking some time, but Kao was in no rush. The perspective, Dr. Maruta continually stressed, was very long term, and the company would move at its own pace. "We should not," he said, "think about the quick and easy way, for that can lead to bad handling of our products. We must take the long term view . . . and spiral our activity towards the goal. . . . We will not, and need not hurry our penetration of foreign markets. We need to avoid having unbalanced growth. The harmony among people, products, and world wide operations is the most important philosophy to keep in mind . . . only in fifteen years will it be clear how we have succeeded."

9

Labatt Ice

"Labatt Ice Beer is Here," blared the car radio. "It definitely is," grinned Hugo Powell, president of Labatt Breweries of Canada. As his car whisked along the highway toward his office in downtown Toronto, Mr. Powell looked out over Lake Ontario, but his mind wasn't on the early morning rowers. Rather, he was thinking of the opportunities for Labatt Ice Beer that lay beyond the southern shores of the lake in the potentially lucrative United States (U.S.) beer market. Ice Beer started out as an idea only a short time ago in early 1992. Since then it had been developed, introduced, and gained rapid consumer acceptance in Canada's $11.1 billion[1,2] Canadian beer industry. Now, in August 1993, five months after the Canadian launch, Mr. Powell wrestled with the idea of how best to introduce Labatt Ice Beer into the U.S. beer market.

JOHN LABATT LIMITED

Founded in 1847, in London, Ontario, by John Kinder Labatt, John Labatt Limited was one of Canada's oldest companies. John Labatt Limited was organized into two divisions, brewing and entertainment. The brewing division was organized into three divisions: Labatt Breweries of Canada, Labatt's USA, and Labatt Breweries of Europe. The entertainment group was also organized into three divisions: JLL Broadcast Group, the Toronto Blue Jays Baseball Club, and the John Labatt Entertainment Group.

Consolidated net sales from continuing operations for John Labatt Limited were $2.135 billion in 1993, of which the brewing segment contributed $1.672 billion; earnings from continuing operations were $133 million. In early 1993, John Labatt Limited had completed the spin-off of a third segment, its dairy operations.[3] The spin-off was part of the company's strategy to focus on its strengths.

Labatt Breweries of Canada

In 1847, when it was founded, the company had the capacity to produce 500 hectolitres (hL)[4] of beer a year. By 1992, Labatt Breweries of Canada operated ten breweries across Canada (Exhibit 9.1) and produced thirty-six brands of beer. The company also had opera-

Exhibit 9.1   Labatt and Molson Brewery Locations and Capacities

Labatt Breweries	
Halifax, Nova Scotia	680,000 hL
Saint John, New Brunswick	381,800 hL
La Salle, Quebec	2,550,000 hL
Etobicoke, Ontario	1,785,000 hL
London, Ontario	1,620,000 hL
Winnipeg, Manitoba	585,000 hL
Saskatoon, Saskatchewan**	285,000 hL
Edmonton, Alberta	750,000 hL
Creston, British Columbia	620,000 hL
New Westminster, British Columbia	875,000 hL
Molson Breweries	
St. John's, Newfoundland	300,000 hL
Montreal, Quebec	4,000,000 hL
Barrie, Ontario	2,500,000 hL
Etobicoke, Ontario	3,500,000 hL
Winnipeg, Manitoba	400,000 hL
Regina, Saskatchewan	300,000 hL
Calgary, Alberta++	800,000 hL
Edmonton, Alberta	400,000 hL
Vancouver, British Columbia	1,200,000 hL

FROM: The Beer Book 1993, ScotiaMcLeod Equity Research.
**At the time of the case, Labatt was in the process of closing its Saskatoon facility.
++Industry rumors suggested that Molson was planning on closing its Calgary brewery, which had been acquired in the merger with Carling O'Keefe.

tions in Britain, Italy, and the United States. It produced 11,700,000 hL of beer, 8,300,000 hL domestically and the remainder at its international locations. This volume translated into the equivalent of over three billion bottles of beer in 1992. In Canada, seven of the company's brands were marketed nationally while the rest were sold regionally. In 1992, the company's average national market share stood at 42.3 percent; this compared to a 51 percent average market share for its main rival, Molson Breweries (formed by the merger in 1989 of Molson Breweries and Carling O'Keefe Breweries).

In 1992, Labatt embarked on a strategy which focused on innovative new products and cost management. Recently, the company reduced the number of breweries in operation to ten from twelve (with additional closures planned in 1993) in order to help lower Labatt Canada's per-hectolitre cost of beer production, thereby improving the company's competitive position in the increasingly open and competitive marketplace for beer in Canada. Conversion to a new standard bottle was also expected to produce significant cost savings that would translate into improved results.

In its attempt to offer consumers a balanced portfolio of leading brands, Labatt had recently launched three new brand families: Labatt Genuine Draft (March 1992), Wildcat (1993), and Labatt Ice Beer (March 1993). All three had made a significant contribution to the divisions' continued success and followed in the tradition of excellence of Labatt

Blue, Canada's most popular beer.[5] Exhibit 9.2 contains estimated market share data for Canada's top selling brands of beer.

Labatt's USA

Labatt's USA operated in the high-quality segment of the U.S. beer business. The division brewed and marketed the Rolling Rock brands of its Latrobe (Pennsylvania) Brewing Company, predominantly in the Northeastern United States. Through Labatt Importers, the division also imported and marketed Labatt's Blue, Labatt's Blue Light, and other Labatt Canada brands. The Specialty Import Division marketed and distributed niche malt beverage products such as Clausthaler non-alcoholic beer from Germany, Red Stripe and Dragon Stout from Jamaica, and Moretti from Labatt's own Italian breweries. In 1992, Labatt's USA sold approximately 707,000 hL of beer in the United States, an increase of 9 percent over the previous year's volume. This volume represented 7.26 percent of the U.S. import beer market and 0.33 percent of the total U.S. beer market. This performance was particularly strong in light of an 8 percent decline in imports and a flat total beer consumption in the United States in 1992.

THE BREWING INDUSTRY IN CANADA

The brewing and marketing of beer contributed $11.1 billion to the Canadian economy in 1992, representing 1.6 percent of Canada's Gross National Product. Nationally, 21.57 million hL of beer were produced, of which 19.05 million hL were consumed domestically and 2.52 million hL were exported (approximately 55 percent to the United States). During the same period, 604,623 hL of beer were imported into Canada. The industry employed, directly and indirectly, 173,800 people or 1.3 percent of Canada's labor force. The brewing industry was a major source of government revenue, contributing $3.125 billion in the form of commodity taxes (federal excise, duty, and sales taxes, and provincial liquor authority

Exhibit 9.2   Market Share of Major Beer Brands in Canada

Brand	Brewer	Share (%) 1992	Share (%) 1993
Blue/Blue Light	Labatt	16.0	15.0
Canadian/Cdn Light	Molson	12.0	7.0
Export	Molson	7.0	6.0
Budweiser	Labatt	5.0	6.0
Labatt Ice	Labatt	–	6.0
Coors/Coors Light	Molson	5.0	4.0
Molson Special Dry	Molson	5.0	4.0
Labatt Genuine Draft	Labatt	5.0	3.5
Canadian Ice	Molson	–	3.0
Labatt 50	Labatt	4.0	3.0
Wildcat/Wildcat Strong	Labatt	–	3.0
O'Keefe Ale	Molson	4.0	2.5
Other Brands	Various	45.0	37.0

FROM: Equity Research Associates (Globe and Mail, June 9, 1994); Labatt Breweries Annual Report; Molson Companies Annual Report.

profits and sales taxes). Another $1.673 billion was paid to all levels of government in the form of employee and corporate income taxes. The sales volume of the Canadian brewing industry had decreased in 1992 by 3.2 percent; per capita consumption of beer decreased from 75.40 liters per person in 1991 to 71.07 liters per person in 1992.

In recent years, many new trends had emerged in the industry. Consumers were looking for different and distinctive tasting beers, a trend which had helped the growth of regional and microbreweries. Customers were also looking for a greater pricing mix: some wanted a cheaper priced product, while others were willing to pay more for a differentiated beer. In the early 1990s, Canada's recession, coupled with high taxation on beer (53 percent of the retail price), rendered the retail price of beer prohibitively expensive for many consumers. As a result, many consumers either decreased their consumption, or sought alternative sources of domestic beer, including: cross-border shopping, U-Brew, and home brew.

Two major brewers dominated the Canadian industry, Labatt Breweries and Molson Breweries. Together, these two companies accounted for more than 95 percent of all beer sales in Canada. Three other sectors existed in the brewing industry: regional brewers with annual production over 50,000 hL but considerably less than 1.0 million hL; microbrewers with annual production under 50,000 hL; and licensed establishments, called brewpubs, that brewed their own products for on-premises sale and consumption.

Regional breweries and microbreweries were active in many provinces, and had developed market niches for their products by targeting their own communities. While the entry of these brewers had encouraged greater interest in beer, their volume had come at the expense of the major brewers. Regional brewers included Sleeman Breweries (Ont.), Lakeport Brewing (Ont.), Moosehead (NS/NB), Pacific Western Brewing (BC), and Drummond Breweries (Alta). Microbrewers included Brick Brewing, Upper Canada, and Connors (all in Ont.).

Competition for market share in the Canadian brewing industry was fierce, with brewers annually directing, at consumers, millions of dollars in advertising. Labatt and Molson both maintained a broad line of products, each appealing to a different segment in the market.

When compared to large plants found in the United States, Canadian brewing facilities operated at a cost disadvantage. Canadian input costs were often higher than in the U.S. For example, the price of malting barley was set by the Canadian Wheat Board at prices that were often double the price in the U.S.; packaging costs were also higher due to tariffs of 10 to 12 percent on packaging materials, although these were dropping under provisions of the Canada-U.S. Free Trade Agreement.

The Canadian distribution system also added to costs. Eighty-one percent of Canadian packaged beer was sold in returnable reusable glass bottles (the exceptions were in Alberta and British Columbia in which cans predominated). The use of glass bottles increased packaging costs because of the heavier shipping weight of glass as well as the need to run a bottle return system.

A 1987 study of the brewing industry in Canada and the United States, written by Woods Gordon to assess the potential impact of a free trade agreement between the two countries, noted that wage costs in Canada on a per-hectoliter basis were twice that of the U.S. Canadian brewers felt that this commonly quoted statistic was significantly out of date, that recent changes in the Canadian industry had significantly narrowed the per-hectoliter wage costs between the two countries.

Finally, provincial governments required brewers to build facilities within each province in order to obtain the right to sell beer within provincial boundaries. The result was a large number of small brewing facilities located across the country. In contrast, U.S. brewers did not have to meet this requirement in order to sell beer in Canada. In recent years, these location restrictions had been loosened up somewhat, allowing some rationalization to take place in the Canadian industry.

An industry analyst[6] reported that the minimum capacity of a brewery for cost minimization was in the range of four to five million hL of production per year. Breweries were essentially built to a brewer's specifications, and estimates for new construction or the reconstruction of existing facilities ranged from $100 to $200 per hectoliter of capacity.[7]

MOLSON BREWERIES OF CANADA

Molson Breweries had an even longer history in the Canadian brewing business than Labatt, having been founded in Montreal by John Molson in 1786. During the 1950s and 1960s, Molson turned itself into a national brewer through the construction or acquisition of plants across Canada. Molson also moved into the British market, and during the 1970s became one of the largest imported beers in the United States.

In 1989, Molson Breweries and number three brewer Carling-O'Keefe Breweries (then owned by Australia's Elders IXL) merged their operations. The product of this merger, Molson Breweries, was the largest brewer in Canada, with annual net sales of $2.35 billion in 1992, representing 11,600,000 hL (of which 10.1 million hL was domestic sales). One of Molson's first actions was to rationalize its brewing capacity, closing seven smaller plants (out of a total of sixteen) and shifting production to other underutilized facilities. Analysts predicted that once the rationalization was complete, further improvements in cost competitiveness would be modest as Molson's remaining facilities were still of suboptimal size and location.

In April of 1993, The Molson Companies and Foster's Brewing (which owned the Elders IXL stake in the Molson Breweries partnership) each sold 10 percent of Molson Breweries to Miller Brewing Company in the United States, giving Miller a 20 percent stake in Molson. Molson stated that it was following what it called a "North American brewing strategy."

GOVERNMENT REGULATION IN CANADA

The Canadian beer industry evolved not only in response to geographic and demographic forces, but also in response to federal and provincial government regulation and intervention.

The provincial governments restricted the shipment of beer from one province to another. Some provinces (Prince Edward Island, Nova Scotia, and New Brunswick) allowed beer that had been produced in other provinces to be sold in their province, but imposed higher markups and taxes on "nondomestic" beer. Other provinces had, at various times, banned the sale of out-of-province beer. These restrictions contributed to the development of small to medium-sized production plants in each province.

In all Canadian provinces, beer was distributed through both government owned stores (e.g. LCBO Stores in Ontario) or regulated retail outlets (e.g. Brewers' Retail Stores in Ontario, which were owned by Labatt, Molson, and Northern Breweries). The exceptions were Quebec, in which grocery stores were allowed to sell beer, and Newfoundland, which allowed beer sales in corner stores and also allowed the establishment of privately owned liquor stores. Alberta was in the process of planning the privatization of its liquor retailing system. In contrast, in the United States, beer was sold through grocery stores, private liquor stores, and, in some states, through state owned retailers.

In all provinces except Alberta and British Columbia, beer prices were established by the brewer who made an application to the provincial liquor board, which had the authority to set the retail and wholesale prices. Alberta and British Columbia used a system that they called "free pricing." Under "free pricing," brewers set the province-wide retail price of each product without having to seek the approval of the provincial liquor board. Each brewer was allowed to change prices once each month. The final consumer price in these two provinces was still affected by government taxation policies and other relevant regulations. Exhibit 9.3 provides pricing data for Canadian provinces.

Government regulations often imposed other constraints on pricing. Many provinces had minimum price mark-ups, set minimum allowable prices, and required uniform pricing throughout the province. Canadian beer consumers paid among the highest taxes in the world for their beer (Exhibit 9.4), with an average "tax bite" of 53 percent of the retail price of a bottle of beer.

CANADA/U.S. TRADE

Foreign brands of beer had had a presence in the Canadian marketplace for a number of years. Labatt was the first Canadian brewer to introduce a major U.S. brand to Canadian consumers through a 1980 licensing arrangement with the world's largest brewer, Anheuser-Busch, brewers of Budweiser beer. Other brewers had followed suit, leading to licensing agreements between Molson and Coors, and Carling-O'Keefe and Miller (the Miller licenses were transferred to Molson after the merger with Carling). Foreign brands, under license, currently held approximately 15 percent of the Canadian market.

While brands produced under license were available through regular beer outlets, beers imported from other countries were generally sold only at government owned liquor outlets. In Ontario, for example, in order to buy beer brewed outside Canada, consumers had to

Exhibit 9.3   Average Prices and Taxes on a Six Pack of Cans (1992)

Province	Federal Taxes	Provincial Taxes & Markups	Average Net Retail Price	Taxes & Markups as % of Price
Newfoundland	1.10	3.14	8.55	49.6%
P.E.I.	n/a	n/a	n/a	n/a
Nova Scotia	1.07	3.57	7.95	58.4%
New Brunswick	1.18	3.85	8.35	60.2%
Quebec	1.15	2.68	8.80	43.5%
Ontario	1.03	2.72	7.40	50.7%
Manitoba	1.04	3.34	7.31	59.9%
Saskatchewan	1.02	3.76	7.10	67.3%
Alberta	1.08	2.92	7.40	54.1%
British Columbia	1.00	3.02	6.75	59.6%

FROM: The Beer Book 1993, ScotiaMcLeod Equity Research.
n/a: not available.
The overall average tax on beer in Canada is 53 percent of the retail price.

Exhibit 9.4 Total Taxes on Beer as a Percentage of Retail Price

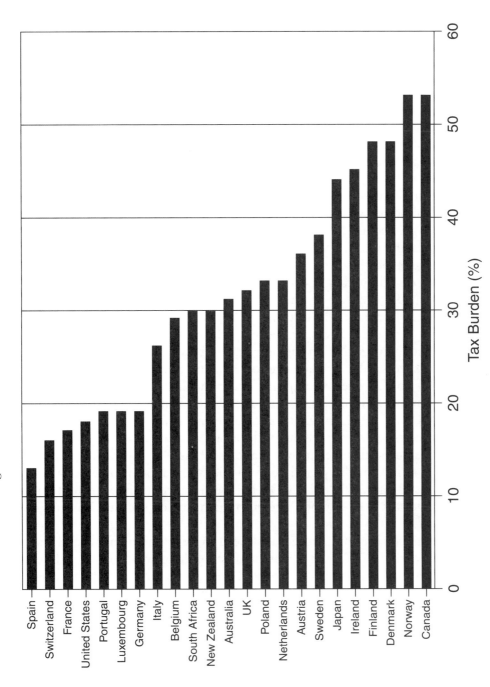

Tax Burden (%)

Brewing Industry in Canada 1992,
Brewers Association of Canada

visit the local Liquor Control Board of Ontario (LCBO) outlet. Ontario's Brewers' Retail was prohibited from selling imported beer. Brewers' Retail, however, was willing to provide access to imported beer if foreign brewers paid a "fair" share of the retail system's costs.[8]

Overall, imports accounted for 3 percent of beer sales in Canada. The import share was small because of the low penetration of U.S. brands in Ontario and Quebec. The largest U.S. exports to Canada were to the provinces of Alberta and British Columbia, in which U.S. brands held market shares of 12 percent and 4.6 percent, respectively. In Alberta, "free pricing" had allowed Rainier and Olympia to generate substantial sales in the low-price segment of the market. In response to the penetration of imports into Alberta and British Columbia, Canadian brewers introduced or repositioned brands to serve as low-priced import fighters.[9] In British Columbia, Canadian brewers had been able to prove a dumping[10] case against U.S. brewers, with the result that duties were levied against imports from the U.S.

Following extensive lobbying by the brewing industry, the Canadian and U.S. governments agreed that beer would be specifically exempted from almost all provisions of the Canada – U.S. Free Trade Agreement. The only aspect covered in the agreement was that, over a ten-year period, Canada and the U.S. would remove their respective tariffs on beer[11]; Canadian governments retained their right to regulate with floor prices, restrictions on imports' access to shelf space, and discriminatory taxes on imports.

In late 1992, Canada reached a tentative agreement with the United States and Mexico for a North American Free Trade Agreement (NAFTA). As per the Canada – U.S. Free Trade Agreement, the beer industry was exempt from the provisions of the agreement, except for the reduction of tariffs on the beer traded between the three countries.

In response to a successful U.S. challenge to Canadian beer regulations, and a successful Canadian challenge to U.S. beer regulations (under the General Agreement on Trade and Tariffs, also known as GATT), Canada and the United States signed a Memorandum of Understanding (MOU) in 1992. In Ontario, the agreement, when implemented, would give U.S. brewed beer access to Brewers' Retail outlets; similar changes would take place in other provinces. For consumers, this meant that brands such as Old Milwaukee and Busch, not brewed under license in Canada, would be available where most people bought their beer (e.g., at the Brewers' Retail). While the MOU had been signed, its implementation was held up as negotiators worked to overcome some outstanding issues, such as Ontario's minimum floor price for beer.

Canada and its major trading partners had been in negotiation for several years under the Uruguay round of the GATT, with the intent of establishing broad-based tariff reductions. Tentative agreement had been reached in several areas, with tariff reductions averaging 40 percent or more on a wide range of industrial and resource products. In brewing, duty-free entry into Canada for beer would be achieved over an eight-year period to allow for industry adjustment. However, the final outcome of the GATT negotiations was still unclear, as the final agreement was held up by disputes over the issue of agricultural subsidies.

THE BREWING INDUSTRY IN THE UNITED STATES

The United States produced (and consumed) 25 percent of all of the beer brewed in the world. In 1992, the U.S. brewing industry consisted of 392 licensed or authorized breweries.

Total sales were 212,079,490 hL, with a retail value in excess of $51 billion (U.S.). The industry directly employed almost 49,000 people in all facets of the production process.

Sales

Packaged beer (cans, bottles) accounted for 88 percent of sales volume in the U.S., while draft beer accounted for 12 percent of the sales volume; of the packaged beer, 70 percent was sold in cans. The brewing industry generated over $5 billion (U.S.) per year in sales and excise taxes for local, state, and the federal government.

From 1970 to 1980, the volume of beer produced in the United States grew at a rate of 3 percent per annum. Since the mid-1980s, however, total volume had grown at a rate of 0.5 percent per annum, and, in 1992, it declined by 0.4 percent. Consumption per capita was 86.1 liters per person, a drop of about two liters per person since the mid-1980s.

Industry Leaders

The U.S. brewing industry was dominated by three brewers: Anheuser-Busch (46 percent market share), Miller Brewing Company (23 percent), and Coors (11 percent). Heileman, Stroh, Pabst, and Genesee formed the next industry tier, each being a large regional player. The top five firms accounted for approximately 90 percent of U.S. beer sales.

The top three U.S. brewers each sold more beer than the entire Canadian market of 19.05 million hL. In the period 1982 to 1992, Anheuser-Busch increased its sales volume from 63 to 100 million hL. This 37 million hL increase was accomplished by taking market share from other brewers, not by acquisition. Anheuser-Busch's top brand, Budweiser, held approximately 25 percent of the entire U.S. market. Miller sold over 52 million hL per year, and Coors, 26.9 million hL annually. Miller and Coors also increased their market shares at the expense of other firms in the industry.

Exports/Imports

Annual U.S. beer exports were 3,065,000 hL, representing 1.45 percent of annual production. Of these exports, 13 percent, approximately 398,500 hL, was shipped into Canada. The largest single market for U.S. beer exports was Japan, with approximately 30 percent of exports; total exports to Asian countries accounted for 42 percent of total shipments.

The U.S. imported approximately 9,742,000 hL of beer each year, representing 4.6 percent of the U.S. market in 1992. Of this total, 25 percent came from Canada, representing 2,435,500 hL of Canadian beer each year, or approximately 1.15 percent of the total U.S. beer market. Only the Netherlands shipped more beer into the U.S. market, with 29 percent of U.S. imports, or 2,825,000 hL of beer.

Capacity

In the U.S., the brewing infrastructure of plant locations and distribution systems was a function of market size, geography, and transportation costs, not state legislation. Breweries could ship product across state lines. As a result, breweries were located in twenty-six of the forty-nine mainland states. The average new brewery built in the United States was in the eight to ten million hL size; the average size of a U.S. brewery was three million hL.[12] A 1988 profile of the brewing industry published by Industry, Science, and Technology Canada[13] predicted that in order to be a national player in the United States (that is, market through out the U.S.), a brewer would need to have a minimum annual capacity of twenty-six million hL.

The excess capacity of the U.S. brewing industry in 1991 was forty-eight million hL, more than twice the size of the Canadian market of 19.05 million hL. The excess capacity existed for two reasons. The first was that facilities were built to meet peak consumption demand for beer, which varied with the seasons and within regions of the country.[14] The second reason was due to market share swings between brewers. For example, Stroh lost significant market share,[15] but retained its production capacity.

Costs

U.S. brewers enjoyed some cost advantages over their Canadian counterparts. In place of a proliferation of regional brands, the leading U.S. brewers sold only a few national brands; this allowed for longer, more efficient production runs on each product. Supplies such as malting barley were purchased on the open market, whereas Canadian brewers had to purchase at a (premium) price set by the Canadian Wheat Board. U.S. brewers also held a cost advantage in distribution over their Canadian counterparts. Most U.S. beer was shipped in "one-way" containers, primarily aluminum cans. A U.S. brewer could ship a load of cans a distance of 1450 kilometers for the same price that a Canadian brewer would pay to ship and return a load of bottles a distance of 480 kilometers.[16]

Distribution

In the United States, legislation required beer producers to ship their products (intended for domestic consumption) to a wholesaler who had the exclusive right to distribute product to retailers licensed to sell alcoholic beverages. Beer was sold to consumers through a wide variety of stores, from grocery and convenience stores to dedicated liquor stores. The result was a three-tier system for the distribution of beer.

A situation of very close-knit relationships between brewers and distributors had evolved in the U.S.; major breweries often had unwritten "understandings" with distributors. The major breweries dominated the wholesaler network because of the volume of product that they could sell through a distributor. These brewers exercised considerable economic suasion over their wholesale networks, discouraging wholesalers from taking on competitors' labels. Consequently, smaller U.S. brewers and importers of foreign beer had had a difficult time gaining access to the distribution system. In addition, several of the breweries were buying out their largest distributors, in the process ensuring that competing brands, including imports, could not access the market through these distributors.

GOVERNMENT INVOLVEMENT IN THE U.S. INDUSTRY

Unlike Canada, in the U.S., the government only influenced prices to the extent that excise and sales taxes were levied on the beer. Wholesale and retail prices were set by the members of the distribution and retail network in response to market conditions and supply. While beer could be shipped across state lines, twenty-seven states had packaging and labelling requirements that favored U.S. producers and discriminated against imported products.

At the Federal level, brewers had to be licensed under the Federal Alcohol Administration Act. Under the Twenty-First Amendment to the U.S. Constitution, state governments were granted the authority to regulate the methods of sale and distribution of beer. To sell beer, retailers had to obtain state and often local licenses. Thirty-two states were considered "open" states in which the wholesale and retail sale of beer was managed by private enterprise, subject to applicable state regulations. In the remaining 18 states, a system similar to that in Ontario existed: some type of alcohol beverage control agency managed the wholesale distribution and retail sale of beer.

In the U.S., beer advertising was largely self-regulated, although there was a general code administered by the Bureau of Alcohol, Tobacco and Firearms. In contrast, the Canadian industry had its advertising regulated at the federal level by the Canadian Radio Telecommunications Commission and at the provincial level by provincial liquor authorities. The result was that while U.S. brewers could mount national advertising campaigns, Canadian brewers often had to produce separate commercials for each province.

LABATT ICE BEER

In 1982, in an attempt to develop a method for exporting beer more cheaply, researchers at Labatt's facility in London, Ontario, experimented with a number of different processes. One involved the freeze concentrating of liquids, similar to the process used for concentrated orange juice. Researchers hoped that this method would enable brewers to remove the water from the beer, to transport the concentrate, and then to rehydrate the concentrate upon arrival at its final destination.

While the process worked, the company was not able to develop a viable business plan for it. The use of "partner brewers," in Europe (under which a European brewer produced the product to Labatt standards under Labatt supervision), was found to be a more efficient method of placing the product in Europe than exporting beer concentrate and reconstituting it in Europe. As well, there were concerns that consumers would reject a "reconstituted" beer. The testing was discontinued and the elaborate notes on the technology were stored away in the research laboratory in London.

In 1992, Labatt Breweries of Canada embarked on a new product development strategy. While consumer preferences had shifted toward a lighter beer, and many products had been introduced to respond to this segment, another segment had been all but neglected. Market research showed that this segment was looking for a "full bodied" beer with more "taste." The product development group experimented with a number of different concepts. Two that were particularly well received by consumer focus groups were the idea of ice and the idea of a more flavorful, slightly higher alcohol, but drinkable beer. More importantly, the consumer research showed that beer drinkers wanted a real product, not just another label on what they perceived as the "same old stuff."

At one of the product development group meetings, someone from the research and development team mentioned the fact that ten years earlier a process had been examined for concentrating beer without destroying the flavor. The group concluded that the process might form the basis for the development of a new product.

With equipment from NIRO, a Dutch company, Labatt set to work to develop Labatt Ice Beer, refining its ice brewing process, using in part the work done in 1982. The marketing and product development groups had a product which responded to consumer preferences, and consumers had a product which filled a gap in the existing market.

THE ICE BREWING PROCESS

According to the Brewers' Association of Canada:

> Brewing is fundamentally a natural process. The art and science of brewing is in using and controlling the process to convert natural food materials into a pure, pleasing beverage. Although great strides have been made in the techniques for achieving high-quality production, beer today is still a beverage brewed from natural products in the traditional way.[17]

The regular brewing process involves several steps: malting, mashing, lautering, boiling, cooling, fermentation, aging, and packaging. Appendix 1 contains an explanation of the steps in the brewing process.

Labatt's Ice Brewing process inserted an extra step between the fermenting and aging processes. From the fermentation vessels, the beer was moved to a special heat exchanger in which the beer was continuously chilled until all of the liquid in the heat exchanger reached 40°C. This temperature was well below that of normal brewing temperatures. The beer was then moved into a recrystallizer, in which the ice crystals grew larger. The beer was treated at that lower temperature and then removed from the ice for aging. The resulting beer was a darker, richer, smoother, less bitter beer with a higher alcohol content.

With regular equipment and technology, the formation of ice would normally stop the beer's flow, bringing production to a halt. The ability of the deep-chilled beer to be moved from the chiller to the recrystallizer and treated in continuous process was the revolutionary key to Labatt's Ice Brewing technology.

ICE BEER IN CANADA

In early 1993, Molson Breweries believed that Labatt was in the process of developing a new product that joined the name "ice" and packaged draft beer. In an attempt to beat Labatt to the market, Molson issued press releases and ran television commercials that introduced Molson Canadian Ice Draft in late March 1993; the Molson product was targeted at Labatt Genuine Draft. On March 25, 1993, Labatt launched its Labatt Ice Beer into Quebec and Ontario, produced with Ice Brewing technology that had been installed in the Montreal brewery. Whereas Molson had run advertisements about its product, Labatt was able to serve its product to the press on launch day, and had arranged for its London beer store to sell the first cases to the public.

Molson had expected Labatt to introduce a draft beer product in new packaging, and was surprised that Labatt's product was the result of an entirely new process. Labatt advertised that its ice brewing process was what allowed it to produce its new Ice Beer. In comparison, when asked what production technology differentiated its ice beer from its regular beer, Molson was unable to give a consistent answer.

Realizing that it had guessed incorrectly, Molson tried to combat the potential success of Labatt Ice Beer by launching a variety of beers labelled "Ice." For example, a week after it launched its product,[18] Molson launched a second product into Quebec called Black Ice (an attempt to capture some of the success enjoyed by its previously successful Black Label brand), and later launched Carling Ice. In contrast to Molson's product proliferation under an ice label, Labatt had a process that required capital investment in production equipment, thus slowing Labatt Ice's launch rate.

While initial consumer trial rates for Molson's product were similar to those for the Labatt Ice products, the retrial rate for Canadian Ice, Molson's ice product, was very low. To encourage retrial, Molson reduced the price of Canadian Ice nationally. In contrast, by avoiding discounting, Labatt was able to sell its Ice Beer at full margin.

ICE BEER IN THE UNITED STATES

Initial interest by brewers in the U.S. indicated that Ice Beer could be received as warmly as it had been in Canada. The potential in this market was enormous, and there was not much time to decide what approach, if any, would best position Labatt Ice Beer for its entry into the United States. Rumors in the industry reported that Molson Ice was going to be launched into the United States in September 1993, and that Miller Brewing would be using its Molson U.S. division to manage the launch.

Immediately before the product launch of Labatt Ice Beer, Labatt began discussions with Anheuser-Busch about licensing the ice brewing process to Anheuser-Busch for the U.S. market. Labatt knew that Anheuser-Busch was paying close attention to the events in Canada and would be pursuing the U.S. market if the Canadian situation showed signs of permanence. By August, Anheuser-Busch had indicated that it was not interested in a licensing agreement. If it went ahead with an ice product, it would go it alone.

Labatt also knew that Coors was doing its own market research to assess the marketing phenomenon in Canada. Coors ran several focus groups in Canada to assess the potential for ice beer.

THE DECISION

In the first four months after it was launched in Canada, Labatt Ice Beer achieved an estimated 6 percent share of the Canadian beer market, unprecedented in the history of new beer introductions. Although it was clear that an opportunity existed in the U.S., Mr. Powell was unsure about how to best exploit that opportunity.

He wondered if Labatt should produce the product in Canada and export it to the United States. In addition, Labatt could produce Ice Beer in the United States by investing directly in an existing U.S. operation (such as increased capacity at its Latrobe Breweries or by buying another firm's excess plant capacity). Its U.S. division could also build a new facility to supply the U.S. market. Perhaps, the alternative was to license the ice brewing process to a U.S. brewer, much as Labatt licensed Budweiser from Anheuser-Busch. Given the limited resources of Labatt's operation, maybe the United States was not the right market at all. Japan's per capita beer consumption rivalled that of the United States. Was Labatt missing an opportunity by focusing on the U.S.[19] rather than considering other global opportunities such as Japan?

NOTES

1. This number, supplied by the Canadian Brewers Association, includes direct and indirect benefits of the brewing industry: wages, inputs, taxation, etc. Sales by Canada's brewing companies comprise a portion of this number.
2. All dollar amounts are in Canadian funds unless noted otherwise.

3. The dairy segment had operated under the name of Ault Dairies. Its results are not included in the figures noted above.

4. The brewing industry reported its statistics in hectoliters. One hectoliter was equal to 700 liters and was the equivalent of 253 bottles of beer.

5. In 1992, the combined market share of Labatt Blue and Blue Light was 16% (see Exhibit 2).

6. "The Canadian Brewing Industry," ScotiaMcLeod Equity Research, 1990.

7. Estimates of the cost of construction are taken from "Note on the Canadian Brewing Industry (Condensed)," Western Business School case # 9-89-MOO7.

8. Brewers' Retail costs were allocated on the basis of the market share held by its owners.

9. Labatt introduced "Wildcat" as a discount beer and captured a 3% share of the market with little or no advertising support. Molson was positioning "Carling" as its discount beer.

10. Dumping is the process of selling a product for less in a foreign market than it is sold for in its home market.

11. The Canadian Tariff was $3.30 per hectoliter, and the U.S. tariff was $1.10 per hectoliter. These tariffs were to be eliminated in equal steps over a ten year period ending January 1, 1998. Current tariff levels were $1.32 per hectoliter levied by Canada, and $0.44 per hectoliter levied by the United States.

12. In comparison, the average size of a Canadian brewery was approximately 1.24 million hL. New brewery construction in Canada had been limited to regionals and microbreweries; neither major brewer had built a new brewery in years.

13. The department is now known as Industry Canada. The 1988 profile was the last one the department published on the brewing industry.

14. Beer consumption increased during the summer months, as well as exhibiting a "spike" in December, attributable to the holiday season.

15. In the ten year period 1981 to 1991, Stroh's annual shipments of beer declined from 27,431,000 hL to 17,316,000 hL.

16. "Challenge of the 90's: An Overview of the Canadian Brewing industry," The Brewers' Association of Canada, June 1991.

17. "The Brewing Process," Brewers' Association of Canada.

18. Molson's official product launch came April 1, 1953; however, Molson had run television advertisements during the Juno Awards program on March 21/93, and had issued a press release announcing the April 1/94 launch date on March 22.

Appendix 1 The Brewing Process

Malt and Water

The basic ingredients used in brewing beer were malt barley and water. Malt barley was harvested and kiln-dried to control growth. In the brewery it was screened and crushed, separating flour, husks, and other undesirable materials. The water used in brewing was purified to rigidly set standards and adjusted for calcium and acidic content to ensure maximum enzyme activity in the mash.

Mashing and Lautering

In mashing, enzymes break down starches into sugars, and complex proteins into simpler nitrogen compounds. Mashing takes place in a large round tank called a "mash mixer," and requires careful temperature control. After mashing, the mash was transferred to a straining or "lautering" vessel. The liquid extract was drained through a false bottom and piped to the brew kettle.

Boiling and Hopping

The brew kettle was a large copper or stainless steel cauldron holding 700 to 900 hL designed to boil its contents, called "wort," under carefully controlled conditions. Boiling served to concentrate and to sterilize the wort. During the boil (usually about two hours) hops were added to the wort. The hop resins contributed flavor, aroma, and bitterness to the brew.

Hop Separation and Cooling

After boiling, the hops were removed and the wort proceeded to the "hot wort tank" where it was cooled. Cooling was done by a plate cooler in which the wort and a coolant flowed past each other, dropping the wort's temperature from boiling to about 4°C.

Fermentation

The wort was moved to the fermenting vessels in which yeast was added. The yeast was used to break down the sugars in the wort into carbon dioxide and alcohol, as well as to add several vital beer-flavoring components. When fermentation was over, the yeast was removed.

Brewers used one of two types of yeast. The first, which rose to the top of the liquid at the completion of fermentation, was used in brewing ale and stout. The other, which dropped to the bottom of the fermentation tank, was used in brewing lager. Through the use of pure yeast cultures, a particular beer flavor could be produced year after year.

Aging and Packaging

Following fermentation, the beer was cooled and placed in primary storage at 0°C for one to three weeks. The beer was then filtered, and moved to finishing storage for further aging. After aging from one to several weeks, the beer was "polished" by filtration, and transferred to tanks for bottling/canning or "racking" into kegs.

FROM: "The Brewing Process," Brewers' Association of Canada

10

Roaring Back: Harley-Davidson Inc. in 1988

". . . you've shown us how to be the best. You've been leaders in new technology. You've stuck by the basic American values of hard work and fair play . . . Most of all, you've worked smarter, you've worked better, and you've worked together . . . as you've shown again, America is someplace special. We're on the road to unprecedented prosperity . . . and we'll get there on a Harley."
  President Ronald Reagan, speech at Harley-Davidson plant, York, Pennsylvania, May 6, 1987.

It was with pride and satisfaction that Vaughn Beals, Chairman and Chief Executive of Harley-Davidson, reviewed his company's provisional financial statements for 1987. With the inclusion of Holiday Rambler recreational vehicle company, acquired in 1986, total sales more than doubled over the previous year, and net income had soared from under $5 million to $21 million. Even more satisfying to Beals was Harley's gains in market share at the expense of its Japanese competitors. In 1987, Harley boosted its share of the "super-heavyweight" segment of the market to 40 percent, leaving Honda a poor second. These solid performance gains reflected a tumultuous 1987. Harley's turnaround strategy had received an unexpected boost by the rapid depreciation of the U.S. dollar against the Japanese yen, greatly improving Harley's competitive position against its Japanese rivals. In March, Harley requested that the tariff on Japanese heavyweight bikes (for which it had lobbied in 1982 to give the company temporary protection) be lifted. In response, President Reagan had visited a Harley plant to salute the company's return to world competitiveness. Despite the October 1987 stock market crash, Harley's shares were trading at a substantial premium above their 1986 issue price. After teetering on the edge of bankruptcy for most of 1981 and 1982, Harley was roaring back.

Beals' satisfaction was tempered by recognition that the management team's success in turning Harley-Davidson around during the 1981–87 period was simply the first stage of a continuing struggle to reestablish Harley as a world class motorcycle manufacturer. Harley-Davidson, the sole survivor of a once-dominant U.S. motorcycle industry, remained a minnow among the ranks of the world's leading motorcycle manufacturers – all Japanese, and all supported by a diversified range of businesses. Despite the improvements made in the quality and design of Harley's bikes, its product technology lagged years behind that of the Japanese. Closing the technological gap between Harley-Davidson and the industry leaders called for considerable investment both in product and process innovation. Given the company's small size, such investment risked stretching Harley's still-precarious financial position. The recent installation of eight Japanese-built, computer-controlled machining centers had cost Harley over $1.5 million.

Most serious was the eagerness of the Japanese companies to invade Harley's own market niche. The cornerstone of Harley's market appeal was the distinctiveness of its traditionally-styled, throaty V-twins, which contrasted with the multi-cylinder, sleek, technologically-advanced Japanese entries in the heavyweight motorcycle division. But since 1986, all four leading Japanese manufacturers – Honda, Yamaha, Suzuki, and Kawasaki – had introduced Harley-lookalikes. While Beals and other Harley enthusiasts were publicly dismissive of the Japanese imitators, claiming that "imitation is the sincerest form of flattery," privately Beals was less sanguine. It was not that the Japanese were able and willing to build motorcycles that, to all intents and purposes, looked, sounded, and performed just like Harleys. It was the fact that they were able to do so at recommended retail prices which undercut those of Harley-Davidson by some 30 to 40 percent. Exhibits 10.1 to 10.4 give details of Harley's market and financial performance.

THE U.S. MOTORCYCLE INDUSTRY AND MARKET

Harley-Davidson is the sole U.S.-owned survivor of a once-thriving U.S. motorcycle industry. At the close of the First World War, Harley-Davidson was one of about 150 U.S. manufacturers of motorcycles. During the interwar period the domestic market expanded rapidly, but amalgamations and failures resulted in rapid concentration. After a temporary boost provided by the Second World War, the U.S. industry went into rapid decline, as the motorcycle lost its appeal as a basic form of transportation. The problems of declining demand were compounded by increased import competition. The first wave of imports was from the British, whose 500cc and 650cc motorcycles were lighter, more maneuverable, and faster than comparable American bikes. By the early 1960s, Harley-Davidson's sales were down to around 15,000 bikes a year.

Then came the Japanese. Honda's invasion of the U.S. motorcycle market was a pointer to similar Japanese incursions into automobiles, consumer electronics, and a wide range of

Exhibit 10.1   Shares of the U.S. Market for Heavyweight Motorcycles

	1982	1983	1984	1985	1986	1987
Over 650cc						
New registrations (,000s)						
Total	2134	2170	1940	1853	1611	1417
Harley	32.4	27.0	30.2	29.8	31.3	34.7
Market shares (%)						
Harley	15.2	12.5	15.6	16.1	19.4	24.5
Honda	40.2	50.4	43.2	45.9	36.9	31.8
Yamaha	17.0	15.2	17.1	14.7	16.1	17.5
Kawasaki	14.4	11.4	13.2	12.5	11.9	12.4
Suzuki	11.7	8.5	8.6	7.9	12.0	11.2
Other	1.5	2.0	2.3	2.9	3.7	2.6
Over 850cc						
Market shares (%)						
Harley	28.8	23.0	26.9	27.8	33.3	40.0
Honda	35.9	44.3	38.1	38.8	31.1	29.4
Kawasaki	12.5	9.4	11.7	10.7	12.7	11.2
Yamaha	10.1	13.1	13.8	13.8	12.6	7.1
Suzuki	10.5	8.1	7.1	5.6	6.9	10.5
BMW	1.9	1.8	2.3	3.3	3.4	1.8

Source: R. L. Polk & Co.

Exhibit 10.2   Harley-Davidson: Consolidated Balance Sheet

(Dollar Amount in Thousands)				
Year Ended December 31	1984	1985	1986	1987
Assets				
Current assets:				
Cash	$ 2,056	$ 9,070	$ 7,345	$ 68,226
Temporary investments	–	4,400	20,500	
Accounts receivable net of allowance for doubtful accounts	27,767	27,313	36,462	34,419
Inventories	32,736	28,868	78,630	83,748
Prepaid expenses	2,613	3,241	5,812	3,763
Total current assets	65,172	72,892	148,758	197,904
Property, plant, and equipment, at cost, less accumulated depreciation and amortization	33,512	38,727	90,932	100,426
Deferred financing costs	–	2,392	3,340	7,194
Intangible assets	–	–	82,114	74,162
Other assets	523	81	2,052	1,186
	$ 99,207	$114,092	$327,196	380,872
Liabilities and Stockholders' Equity				
Current liabilities:				
Notes payable	$ –	$ –	$ 14,067	$ 19,958
Current maturities of long-term debt	2,305	2,875	4,023	8,377
Accounts payable	21,880	27,521	29,587	35,855
Accrued expenses and other liabilities	24,231	26,2S1	61,144	69,492
Total current liabilities	48,416	56,647	108,821	133,682
Long-term debt, less current maturities	56,258	51,504	191,594	178,762
Long-term pension liability	856	1,319	622	642
Stockholders' equity				
Common stock 6,200,000 issued in 1986 and 4,200,000 in 1985, + 7.43m in 1987	42	42	62	74
Class B common stock, no shares issued	–	–	–	–
Additional paid-in capital	9,308	10,258	26,657	41,714
(Deficit)/Surplus	(15,543)	(5,588)	(717)	20,498
Cumulative foreign currency translation adjustment	–	40	287	730
	(6,193)	4,752	26,289	63,043
Less treasury stock (520,000 shares) at cost	(130)	(130)	(130)	(130)
Total stockholders' equity	(6,323)	4,622	26,159	52,913
	$99,207	$114,092	$327,196	380,872

other U.S. manufacturing industries. Paradoxically, however, the major impact of the Japanese success was to give Harley-Davidson a new lease of life. The success, first of the Honda 50cc Supercub, then of a wide range of lightweight on-road and off-road motorcycles sold by Honda, Suzuki, and Yamaha, was to trigger a whole new life cycle for the motorcycle. Although the motorcycle was in decline as a means of primary transport, the new demand was for recreational use. From initial sales of 1,315 bikes in 1960, Honda's U.S. sales rose to a peak of 707,800 bikes in 1972.

Exhibit 10.3 Harley-Davidson: Consolidated Statement of Income

	($,000s)					
Year Ended December 31	1982	1983	1984	1985	1986	1987
Income statement data:						
Net sales	$210,055	$253,505	$293,825	$287,476	$295,322	$685,358
Cost of goods sold	174,967	194,271	220,040	217,222	219,167	518,670
Gross profit	35,088	59,234	73,785	70,254	76,153	166,688
Operating expenses:						
Selling and administrative	37,510	36,441	47,662	47,162	51,060	110,841
Engineering, research and development	13,072	9,320	10,591	10,179	8,999	
Total operating expenses	50,582	45,761	58,253	57,341	60,059	110,841
Income (loss) from operations	(15,494)	13,473	15,532	12,913	16,096	55,847
Other income (expenses):						
Interest expense	(15,778)	(11,782)	(11,256)	(9,412)	(8,373)	(25,508)
Other	(1,272)	188	(311)	(388)	(388)	(2,143)
	(17,050)	(11,594)	(11,567)	(9,750)	(8,761)	(27,651)
Income (loss) before provision (credit) for income taxes, extraordinary items, and cumulative effect of change in accounting principle	(32,544)	1,879	3,965	3,163	7,335	30,854
Provision (credit) for income taxes	(7,467)	906	1,077	526	3,028	13,181
Income (loss) before extraordinary items and cumulative effect of change in accounting principle	(25,077)	973	2,888	2,637	4,307	17,673
Extraordinary items and cumulative effect of change in accounting principle	–	7,795	3,578	7,318	564	3,542
Net income (loss)	$ (25,077)	$ 8,768	$ 6,466	$ 9,955	$ 4,871	$ 21,215
Average number of common shares outstanding	4,016,664	3,720,000	3,680,000	3,680,000	5,235,230	
Per common share:						
Income (loss) before extraordinary items and cumulative effect of change in accounting principle	$(6.61)	$ .26	$ .79	$ .72	$ .82	$2.72
Extraordinary items and cumulative effect of change in accounting principle	–	2.10	.97	1.99	.11	.55
Net income (loss)	$(6.61)	$2.36	$1.76	$2.71	$.93	$3.27

Exhibit 10.4 Harley-Davidson: Sales and Income by Business Segment

	$ milllons				
	1983	1984	1985	1986	1987
Sales					
Motorcycles & related products	229	261	241	261	325
Transportation vehicles	–	–	–	–	343
Defense and other business	24	33	47	34	18
Operating income					
Motorcycles & related products	16.5	15.5	10.0	16.7	29.9
Transportation vehicles	–	–	–	–	28.8
Defense and other business	3.6	7.0	9.4	4.6	0.8
Assets, depreciation, and investment, 1987					
Motorcycles Transportation Vehicles Defense & Other Identifiable assets			181	216	1.0
Depreciation			8.6	6.6	0.04
Capital expenditures			13.6	3.4	0.04

Initially, Japanese producers concentrated their attention on the lightweight and off-road segments of the market. As the new surge in demand benefited all segments of the market, the U.S. and European producers of bikes displayed remarkable complacency.

> The success of Honda, Suzuki, and Yamaha has been jolly good for us. People start out by buying one of the low-priced Japanese jobs. They get to enjoy the fun and exhilaration of the open road and they frequently end up buying one of our more powerful and expensive machines.
> (Eric Turner, Chairman, BSA Limited, in *Advertising Age*, December 27, 1965)

> Basically, we do not believe in the lightweight market. We believe that motorcycles are sports vehicles, not transportation vehicles. Even if a man says he bought a motorcycle for transportation, it is generally for leisure-time use. The lightweight market is only supplemental. Back around World War I, a number of companies came out with lightweight bikes. We came out with one ourselves. We came out with another in 1947, and it just didn't go anywhere. We have seen what happens to these small sizes.
> (William Davidson, President, Harley-Davidson, *Forbes*, September 16, 1966)

The complacency of the American and European producers even survived the entry of the Japanese into the heavyweight segment at the end of the 1960s. Honda's introduction, in 1968, of a 450cc, mediumweight, twin-cylinder cycle, was followed by a 750cc, four-cylinder in 1970. In 1975, Honda introduced its 1,000cc "Gold Wing" which set a new standard in comfort and sophistication among heavyweight, touring motorcycles. In the meantime, BMW was also challenging hard in the heavyweight segment, basing its appeal on its unsurpassed reputation for smoothness, reliability, and quality engineering. The rush of new large-displacement motorcycles created an unprecedented expansion in the heavyweight segment. In 1970, new registrations of motorcycles exceeding 650cc totaled 53,300. In 1973 the total was 222,200, of which Honda held 39 percent; Harley-Davidson, 17 percent; Yamaha, 13 percent; and Triumph, Norton, and BSA together accounted for 14 percent.

The rapid increase in sales of heavyweight motorcycles during the 1970s was reflected in increasing demand for Harley-Davidsons. However, the intensity of Japanese competition and its substantial cost advantage resulted in constant pressure on margins. Throughout the 1970s, Harley-Davidson was barely profitable, while the financial performance of the British producers was disastrous. In an effort to save the industry, the British government merged BSA, Norton, and Triumph into a single company, Norton-Villiers-Triumph, but even generous financial support from government could not stave off bankruptcy. By 1980, the Japanese were dominant in every segment of the U.S. motorcycle market.

Rapid expansion of heavyweight motorcycles sales caused increasing complexity in the heavyweight segment of the motorcycle market. During the 1980s, two main types of heavyweight bike could be identified: touring bikes and sports bikes. The heavyweight touring bikes were built for endurance and comfort. They featured broad, well-padded seats; upright riding positions; protective fairings; and, most recently, accessories such as radio/cassette players and plentiful instrumentation. This segment was represented by the Honda Gold Wing, the BMW twins and four-cylinders, and the Harley "Glide" models. The heavyweight sports bikes traced their pedigree to the racetrack. Their main features were high-performance engines in a range of cylinder numbers and configurations, aerodynamic styling, with only limited concessions to rider comfort. The Japanese manufacturers' dominance of motorcycle racing since the early 1960s was reflected in their dominance of this segment of the market. Exhibits 10.5 and 10.6 compare a number of different heavyweight motorcycles.

COMPANY HISTORY

Harley-Davidson's long and proud history has been summarized in an earlier case.[1]

The Harley-Davidson story began in 1903 when William Harley, aged 21, a draftsman at a Milwaukee manufacturing firm, designed and built a motorcycle with the help of three Davidson brothers: Arthur, a pattern maker employed by the same company as Harley; Walter, a railroad mechanic; and William, a toolmaker. At first, they tinkered with ideas, motors, and old bicycle frames. Legend has it that their first carburetor was fashioned from a tin can. Still, they were able to make a three-horsepower, twenty-five-cubic-inch engine and successfully road test their first motorcycle.

Exhibit 10.5   Harley-Davidson and the Harley Lookalikes

Model	Harley FXRS Sport	Harley, Electra-Glide Classic	Suzuki Intruder	Yamaha Virago	Honda Shadow
Price	$8799	$11,450	$5899	$5499	$5198
Engine	1338cc, V-twin 2 valves/cylinder push-rod operated air cooled 51 b.h.p.	1338cc, V-twin 2 valves/cylinder push-rod operated air cooled	1360cc, V-twin 3 valves/cylinder o.h.c water cooled	1098cc, V-twin 3 valves/cylinder o.h.c air cooled	1099cc, V-twin 2 valves/cylinder o.h.c water cooled 54 b.h.p
1/4 mile	14.1 sec., 91 mph	15.1 sec, 84 mph	13.5 sec., 95 mph	11.4 sec., 114 mph	13.3 sec., 98 mph
0–60 mph	4.5 sec.	–	–	3.9 sec.	4.4 sec.
Braking distance (60–0 mph)	127 ft.	134 ft.	135 ft	125 ft	120 ft

Exhibit 10.6   Heavyweight Sports Motorcycles: Comparisons Between Some 1988 Models

Model	Suzuki GSX-R1100	Honda CBR1000F Hurricane	Yamaha FZR1000	Kawasaki ZH750 Ninja
Price	$6599	$5698	$7200	$5299
Engine	1127cc, transverse four, o.h.c, 4 valves/ cylinder water cooled 108.4 b.h.p.	998cc, transverse four, o.h.c., 4 valves/cylinder water cooled 108 b.h.p.	1003cc, transverse four, o.h.c, 5 valves/cylinder water cooled 115 b.h.p.	748cc, transverse four, o.h.c. 4 valves/ cylinder water cooled 84.7 b.h.p.
1/4 mile	10.8 sec., 125 mph	11.0 sec., 122 mph	10.8 sec., 129 mph	11A sec., 114 mph
0–60 mph	2.9 sec.	2.95 sec.	2.85 sec.	2.95 sec.
Braking (60–0 mph)	119 ft	125 ft	117 ft	119 ft.

Operating out of a shed in the Davidson family's backyard, the men built and sold three motorcycles. Production was expanded to eight in 1904. In 1906, the company's first building was erected on the current Juneau Avenue site of the main Milwaukee offices. On September 17, 1907, Harley-Davidson Motor Company was incorporated.

Arthur Davidson set off to recruit dealers in New England and in the South. William Harley completed a degree in engineering, specializing in internal combustion engines, and quickly applied his expertise in the company. He developed the first V-twin engine in 1919. He followed this with a major breakthrough in 1912 – the first commercially successful motorcycle clutch. This made possible the use of a roller chain to power the motorcycle. The first three-speed transmission was offered in 1915.

During the early 1900s, the U.S. experienced rapid growth in the motorcycle industry, with firms such as Excelsior, Indian, Merkel, Thor, and Yale growing and competing. Most of the early U.S. motorcycle companies turned out shoddy, unreliable products. But this was not considered to be true for Harley-Davidson and Indian cycles. Continued early success in racing and endurance made Harleys favorites among motorcyclists. The company's V-twin engines became known for power and reliability.

During World War I, Harley-Davidson supplied the military with many motorcycles. By virtue of very strong military and domestic sales, Harley-Davidson became the largest motorcycle company in the world in 1918. The company built a 300,000-square-foot plant in Milwaukee, Wisconsin in 1922, making it one of the largest motorcycle factories in the world.[2] In the late 1930s, Harley-Davidson dealt a strong competitive blow to the Indian motorcycle company – it introduced the first overhead-valve engine. The large, sixty-one-cubic-inch engine became very popular and was thereafter referred to as the "Knucklehead." Indian could not make a motorcycle to compete with these Harleys.

Harley introduced major innovations in the suspensions of its cycles in the 1940s. However, in 1949, Harley's first international competition came from Great Britain. The British motorcycles, such as Nortons and Triumphs, were cheaper, lighter, better handling, and just as fast, even though they had smaller engines.

To counter the British threat, Harley-Davidson further improved the design of the engines, and thereby increased the horsepower of their heavier cycles. The result, in 1957, was what some consider to be the first of the modern superbikes, the Harley Sportster. It was also during the 1950s that Harley developed the styling that made it famous.

As the 1950s drew to a close, new contenders from Japan entered the lightweight (250cc and below) motorcycle market. Harley welcomed the little bikes because it believed that small-bike customers would quickly move to larger bikes as the riders became more experienced. The Japanese cycles proved to have some staying power, however, and Japanese products began to successfully penetrate the off-road and street cycle markets. In the 1960s, Japan entered the middleweight (250–500cc) market.

As Harley entered the 1960s, it made an attempt to build smaller, lightweight bikes in the United States, but the company found it difficult to build small machines and still be profitable. As a result, Harley acquired 50 percent of Aermacchi, an Italian cycle producer, and built small motorcycles for both street and off-road use. The first Aermacchi Harleys were sold in 1961.[3] The Italian venture endured until 1978, but was never highly successful. Few took Harley's small cycles seriously, and some Harley dealers refused to handle them. In the meantime, Japanese cycles dominated the small and middleweight markets. Harley seemed trapped in the heavyweight segment.

In an attempt to expand its production capacity and raise capital, Harley went public in 1965. The company merged with the conglomerate AMF, Inc. in 1969. AMF, a company known for its leisure and industrial products expanded Harley's production capacity from 15,000 units in 1969 to 40,000 units in 1974.[4] With the expanded capacity, AMF pursued a milking strategy favoring short-term profits rather than investment in research and development, and retooling. The Japanese continued to improve while Harley began to turn out heavy, noisy, vibrating, laboriously handling, poorly finished machines.

Under AMF's ownership, Harley-Davidson appeared doomed to the same fate that had overtaken Norton, Triumph, and most of the world's other non-Japanese motorcycle manufacturers. Although the worldwide market for motorcycles, and particularly for large motorcycles, was booming during the 1970s, the tradition-constrained, financially-weak North American and European producers were no match for the internationally-orientated, technologically-progressive Japanese manufacturers with their huge scale economies. (Exhibit 10.7 provides details of Honda's motorcycle operations.) While AMF was willing to fund capacity expansion at Harley, investment in upgrading Harley's older production facilities and developing new products could not be justified under AMF's capital investment criteria. The pressure to expand production caused a stream of quality problems which did much to soil Harley's reputation for reliability. Equally damaging to Harley's reputation was the requirement that the AMF name be emblazoned on the motorcycles' fuel tanks. Michael J. Lombardi, a Staten Island Harley dealer commented: "AMF was almost the ruination of Harley-Davidson. They had no quality control. They forced Harley to overproduce bikes, and they forced us to take them. It was a dictatorship . . . I used to feel bad taking customers' money, the quality was so bad.[5]

THE BUY-OUT

Vaughn L. Beals joined AMF in 1975 as chief executive of its Harley-Davidson subsidiary. He had a degree in engineering from MIT and had held management positions in firms manufacturing logging machines and diesel engines. In 1979, sales hit a record 50,000 bikes, but quality problems continued to dog the company. Beals asked AMF for $80 million to develop a new series of engines. AMF refused and Beals became convinced that independence was essential for the company's survival.

Exhibit 10.7   Honda: Giant of the Motorcycle Industry

	1983	1984	1985	1986	1987
Motorcycles sold worldwide	3.66m	3.18m	2.95m	3.08m	62m
Motorcycle revenue (Yen)	535b	500b	423b	413b	302b
Motorcycles as % of total revenue	24%	21%	16%	14%	10%
U.S. motorcycle dealerships			1,500		
U.S. sales revenue (all products) (Yen)			1516 b		
Expenditure on R&D and engineering (Yen)			145b		
Number of patents held			2,300		
Number of patent applications pending			11,900		

m = million
b = billion
Motorcycle production facilities:

Location	Capacity (no. of motorcycles)	Size (square feet)
Suzuki, Japan	2.009 million	4.4 million
Hamanatsu, Japan	0.422 million	1.6 million
Kumanoto, Japan	0.478 million	1.3 million
Marysville, Ohio	60,000	3.2 million
Aalst, Belgium	47,000	0.22 million

Source: Honda Motor Company Ltd. 10K Report

In 1981, Beals, together with twelve other Harley-Davidson managers (including chief designer Willie G. Davidson, the grandson of co-founder Arthur Davidson) negotiated a buyout variously estimated to be worth between $65 million and $80 million. Finance was provided by banks and by the former parent, AMF, but as Beals emphasized, "All the officers are shareholders, and all the shareholders are officers." The new owner-managers celebrated their purchase with a cross-country motorcycle trek from the York, Pennsylvania, assembly plant to the company's Milwaukee headquarters.

A DIFFICULT REBIRTH

Despite the early enthusiasm of managers, employees, and dealers for the "new Harley-Davidson," together with the continuity provided by a group of long-established, highly experienced managers, the early years saw Harley-Davidson struggling for survival. The buy-out coincided with one of the severest economic recessions in the U.S. during the post-war period and, especially troublesome for a highly-leveraged business, soaring interest rates under the Fed's tight-money policies. Registrations of heavyweight motorcycles fell during 1981 and 1982, and Harley's own sales plummeted – by 1982 its sales of bikes were down by more than a third from 1979. During 1981 and 1982, Harley-Davidson lost a total of $60 million. Redundancies came thick and fast – 30 percent of office staff was dismissed, with similar cutbacks among hourly workers. I can remember when we used to have 2700 people working here," recalled Ken Beaudry, vice-president of AIW local 209 adjacent to Harley's Milwaukee engine and transmission plant. "Now we've got 535 members left."[6]

Part of the problem was aggressive price discounting by Japanese manufacturers as they sought to lower inventories in the face of weak demand. In 1982, Beals petitioned the

International Trade Commission (ITC) complaining of dumping by Japanese manufacturers and requesting temporary protection. The ITC, despite a previous inquiry which found no evidence that the competitive practices of Japanese manufacturers had caused injury to Harley-Davidson, reported in favor of a temporary tariff on large motorcycles. President Reagan confirmed the ITC recommendations and in April 1983 imposed a declining five-year tariff on imports of Japanese motorcycles exceeding 700cc. The tariff rates were to be as follows:

1983	45%	1986	15%
1984	35%	1987	10%
1985	20%	1988	eliminated.

The purpose of the tariff protection, in Beals' mind, was to provide a period of breathing space so that Harley could continue its process of internal transformation while not having to contend simultaneously with unfair price competition from its Japanese rivals, but the effectiveness of the tariff protection was less clear. Both Honda and Kawasaki had U.S. manufacturing plants which produced large-capacity bikes for the American market. All the Japanese companies had large stocks of imported bikes which would delay the impact of the tariff, and all four Japanese producers introduced new high-performance models with displacements of 650 or 698cc.

Production

Central to Beals' turnaround strategy were improvements to Harley's manufacturing operations. The process of upgrading manufacturing was begun when Beals joined Harley-Davidson in 1975 and teamed up with Thomas Gelb, who had worked for Harley between 1960 and 1966, then returned in 1974 to head up operations. In 1977, Harley introduced quality circles, but their effectiveness was limited by the strains caused by doubling Harley's production capacity and shifting final assembly to the plant at York, Pennsylvania.

In upgrading Harley's manufacturing, Beals and Gelb sought to learn from their Japanese competitors. Visits to Japanese motorcycle factories and learning about the manufacturing practices of exemplars such as Toyota and Komatsu, convinced Beals and Gelb of the value of innovations such as just-in-time scheduling, statistical process control, and total quality control. But the key to Japanese productivity and quality, Gelb learned, lay not in robotics or advanced manufacturing systems, but in the organization of the production systems and the company's employees.

> I came away, as many others did, thinking "There's no magic." The plants weren't filled with robots, and the three I saw were surrounded by people watching them. There's no super-duper machinery that's different from ours. I did notice that the labor pace was greater than ours by 20 to 30 percent, but the real difference between U.S. and Japanese management is in the staff – the manufacturing engineers, the accountants, the salaried workers."

Hence, the most important changes in improving manufacturing performance were in organization and specific working practices which included greater employee involvement, a just-in-time inventory system, and statistical process control training for all employees.

The goal, Beals stated, was "to achieve cost and quality parity with foreign competition." Rod Willis of *Management Review* outlined the changes made.

Armed with the latest in Japanese manufacturing concepts – or as much as they could pry from their often tight-lipped competitors – Beals and his cadre of top managers returned to Milwaukee to reorganize Harley-Davidson. The first big change was in plant management structure. The traditional American hierarchy of responsibilities was replaced with a system in which each employee from the line up has "ownership" in running an efficient operation. Each plant is assigned four to seven area managers, each responsible for everything that takes place in his or her area. Staff jobs were cut throughout the company and divided among area managers and line workers. There are no corporate or plant heads of quality control. The area managers can't blame problems on staff failures, and line workers can't blame faulty equipment for productivity problems unless there are serious malfunctions. The chickens come home to roost.

By eliminating staff functions, Beals reports, the company obtained a "shallower" organizational chart – and huge savings. "Our biggest savings came from decreasing the number of salaried staff," he says. "That is, I think, where the greatest improvements in productivity have occurred . . . The presence of those service functions tends to emasculate the basic line with regard to authority, and that's what we are trying to avoid."

All, the line workers are responsible for inspecting and making basic adjustments to the machinery they use and managers "should run their parts of the plant fully," Beals says. "It's a long-term transition to making each plant a profit center." He considers this plant reorganization the most vital part of Harley's comeback effort: "It's like taxis. When you get in, you can tell if the driver owns it or not. If it's all beat up, it belongs to the cab company. If it's kept up, he owns it." Similarly he explains, line workers formerly were given quotas from above and told to meet them. Now all line workers have a voice in setting realistic quotas based on actual production capacity and needs, and thus feel a sense of ownership in meeting those goals. In the past, line workers had to wait for a repairman to come and fix broken or malfunctioning machinery; now they can make most repairs themselves.

The introduction of a just-in-time system of scheduling and inventory management was responsible for a substantial reduction in inventory costs as well as increased quality and productivity. The system devised by Thomas Gelb is called "Material As Needed" or simply, "MAN." Achieving savings in inventories and work-in-progress required a shift from Harley-Davidson's traditional batch method of production in which a single model was produced on any one day to more flexible system involving the production of a mix of models each day. The key requirement for such a system to work efficiently was a drastic reduction in the set-up time required for changing models.

In Pennsylvania, the program started with the final assembly line, which was turning out one of 13 to 14 different models of motorcycle on any given day. By working with the marketing department to improve forecasts of demand for each model, Gelb and others were able to establish a two-hour repeating cycle of models for a better-coordinated production process. All inventory and stockrooms have been eliminated from the plants; everything is delivered at point of use, from raw material to finished components.

The MAN system initially ran into resistance from vendors, Gelb reports, because to deliver at the exact time and place of use Harley's suppliers had to change their own manufacturing methods. They also had to meet Harley's new, more stringent quality standards. At special courses for vendors' employees, hundreds have learned how to stop doing batch processing, use statistical process control, reduce set-up time, and create employee participation programs.

Transfer of authority and responsibility to the shop floor was further encouraged by replacing assembly lines with a series of connected "work cells." A work cell comprised a number of workers and machines engaged in a particular production activity. The work cells were often arranged in a U-shape, which encouraged close interaction within the group, and reduced the movement of product within the cell. Work cells were well-suited to the establishment of self-managing employee work groups.

By 1986, emphasis was shifting toward improving the design process and integrating design with manufacture. Investments in CAD/CAM equipment and software were accompanied by efforts to reduce manufacturing costs and speed the introduction of design changes through close collaboration between design and manufacturing. Cost consciousness was built into the design process through value analysis, while "simultaneous engineering" was introduced to overcome the traditional sequential approach to design and manufacturing engineering.

The essence of Harley-Davidson's approach to manufacturing was its philosophy of continuous improvement. James Paterson, President of the Motorcycle Division, explained commitment to continuous improvement as meaning, ". . . never being satisfied with the status quo. It means working every day to improve upon the prior day's performance. By paying attention to both the minor things we do, and by using fully the talents and energy of our employees, we have made significant improvements in the way we run the Motorcycle Division."[7]

The performance consequences of the manufacturing strategy were apparent in several areas. In the 1987 Annual Report, Paterson reported, "Manufacturing lead times have been dramatically reduced. For example, it now takes only three days instead of thirty to transform new tubing to a finished motorcycle frame. Bar stock is converted into finished gears and shafts in five days instead of twenty weeks. Some of our other improvements include a 150 percent increase in inventory turns, a 68 percent reduction in scrap, and a 50 percent improvement in productivity." Emphasis on quality was reflected in the percentage of ready-to-ride bikes coming off the production rising from 50 percent of total production in 1981 to 99 percent by the end of 1987. Meanwhile, the continuing war on costs resulted in Harley's breakeven level being reduced from 53,000 to 35,000 bikes.

Products

Harley-Davidson's primary business is the design, manufacture, and selling of heavyweight motorcycles. While heavyweight motorcycles are conventionally defined as motorcycles with engine displacements exceeding 650 cubic centimeters, Harley's models all fall into the "super-heavyweight" class – bikes exceeding 850ccs. In 1988, Harley sold twenty-four models of custom and touring bikes ranging in price from $3,995 to $11,000. These twenty-four models are built on four basic chassis designs and include one of three basic engine types: 883cc, 1200cc, and 1340cc. However, these engines differ primarily in their displacement. All are air cooled, V-twins with overhead valves and many common components. The models feature two types of transmission: a four-speed, constant mesh gearbox with a single-row chain driving the rear wheel, and a five speed constant-mesh gearbox with a Gates Kelvar reinforced poly chain belt driving the rear wheel. Apart from some basic differences in frames and rear suspension, most of the differences between the models are in styling and accessories. The different models feature two types of tank, different instrument location, differences in handlebars, seats, mudguards, and front-fork design, together with different accessories (such as fairings, windshields, saddlebags, and radio/tape player).

Although the V-twin heavyweight had been Harley's staple model almost since 1909, Harley had made several attempts at broadening its product range in order to capture a larger share of the market. The most recent was the Aermacchi-Harleys introduced during the 1960s which were intended to compete with the Japanese lightweights. However, because of low volume and inferior product and process technology, Harley could not compete effectively with the Japanese producers in this segment of the market, while the presence of such undersized Harleys was viewed by many dealers and owners as undermining the Harley-Davidson reputation.

After 1978, Harley gave up any aspirations of being a broad-line player in the world motorcycle industry and defined its market as in heavyweight motorcycles. Within this segment, however, the company made efforts to broaden the market appeal of its product range. In order to encourage new buyers of Harleys, the company introduced its 883cc Sportster model in mid-1985. At $3,995, this model was some $800 cheaper than the previous lowest-price Harley. Since its introduction, sales of all Harley's Sportster range more than doubled, with over 80 percent of the purchasers of Sportsters being first-time motorcycle buyers or switching from competitor brands. Moreover, Harley's market research shows that 90 percent of Harley owners who purchase another motorcycle, purchase another Harley. Harley's expectation is that a large proportion of buyers of the 883cc Sportster will ultimately move up to one of Harley's higher-priced models.

While Honda, Yamaha, and Kawasaki have embraced constant product innovation, annual restyling, and the introduction of a three to -four year cycle of entirely new models, the Harley model range is characterized by continuity. Indeed, Cycle magazine argues that it is the style which Harley created with its original Super-Glide in 1970, which has established an enduring "signature" for Harley bikes which is the equivalent of the product signature which Mercedes-Benz has established through its hood insignia, its radiator grille, and its profile. It is the clarity of Harley's product identity which sets it apart from the products of Honda, Yamaha, and Suzuki.

While Harley-Davidson developed an identity around a couple of key motorcycles, the Japanese makers took quite a different tack. Competing with one another in every part of motorcycling, the Japanese brought out new models one after another, because new, updated, technologically-advanced motorcycles sold. This system created a frenzied product torrent . . . Very few Japanese motorcycle models lasted long enough to develop their own enduring signature . . . In such confusion, clear product signatures stand out. As with Mercedes-Benz, so with Harley-Davidson. By 1980, the Harley-Davidson cruise was the clearest single image in American motorcycling.[8]

The Harley product signature was not simply one of design, and it had little to do with performance, which compared to Japanese machines was decidedly sluggish. It was much more to do with overall image:

But Harley – well, the Harley Hog, that was a motorcycle. There was nothing delicate about it. It had big grips, big levers, big foot rests, a big engine. It made a throaty, rumbling, threatening sound . . . "You pull up next to a guy in a station wagon and you're riding a Harley, that guy gives you respect," said Mr. Dean of *Cycle World*. "If you were riding a Honda, he'd smile at you.

However, even with its traditional appeal, it was essential for Harley to upgrade its product to meet the standards of performance, comfort, reliability, and ease of maintenance expected by the market in the 1980s. In 1984, Harley introduced its improved "Evolution" range of V-twin engines. However, its much-heralded four-cylinder, water-cooled "Nova" engine was halted in the development stage because of the high cost of development and tooling, and doubts over the market's acceptance of so big a departure from Harley's traditional V-twin. The Gates Poly Chain belt drive first appeared in 1980, and by 1988 had been extended to most of Harley's larger models. Offering quietness and reliability, it was considered that the belt drive system combined the best features of chain and shaft-drive systems. Other improvements have included redesigned engine mounts to reduce vibration, a new carburetor offering a smoother power delivery, an improved starter, and redesigned gear case which helped Harley meet the 1986 Federal noise limit for motorcycles.

However, the most significant feature of design changes at Harley had been the way in which classic design features have not only been retained and accentuated, but have also been reintroduced. Such reintroductions include the addition of kickstarts to several models, the reincarnation of the Harley "Springer" front suspension, and the introduction of models such as the Heritage Softail Classic which replicate the features of earlier Harley models.

Marketing

Critical to the success of Harley has been maintaining Harley's traditional image, while broadening Harley's market appeal. Proliferation of models within the constraints of three engine types and four basic frames has been one element of this approach. The other has been a repositioning of the Harley image to improve its commercial viability. "The individual who buys a Harley-Davidson has a spirit of adventure, a kind of rugged individualism that is part of their personality," observed Mike Craig, owner of Alabama Harley-Davidson, Huntsville. "I think for the most part they try to suppress it, but a Harley is too strong a temptation. It lets them live out a part of themselves they've been trying to suppress at cocktail parties and tea parties."[9]

A critical task for Beals was to build upon Harley's identification with American values of independence, ruggedness, and dependability, while undermining Harley's association with rebellious, law-flouting motorcycle gangs. To build and reposition its image, Harley has sought to gain the maximum benefit from active public relations, community and charitable projects, and media exposure. The Chicago office of the advertising agency, Bozell, Jacobs, Kenyon, and Eckhardt, played a major role in this process. The agency began by increasing awareness of Harley's strides in improving quality. Articles in technical magazines such as *American Machinist, Quality,* and *Industrial Engineering* had the effect of portraying Vaughn Beals as a Lee Iacocca on two wheels and created a spillover of interest into more general newspapers. This turned into a torrent of publicity following President Reagan's visit to Harley. The agency also generated maximum exposure for publicity events such as the Harley-sponsored rides to raise money for the Muscular Dystrophy Association, and its organization of a Los Angeles to Washington D.C. "Ride for

Liberty" to raise donations for the restoration of the Statue of Liberty. A notable publicity coup for Harley was a widely-syndicated column by Bob Greene which reflected on the new spirit of Harley-Davidson.

> It's Saturday morning and you're out on the highway. In your rearview mirror you spot a group of black leather-clad bikers approaching on Harley-Davidsons. At a stoplight, they pull up next to you. You're nervous; you're scared. You roll your windows up to try to ignore them.
>
> Suddenly one of the bikers points a finger, lifts the visor on his helmet and calls out something to you. Full of fear, you look over at him. And he's your dentist!

By the beginning of 1988, it was apparent that Harley's attempts to extend its appeal to a whole new group of more affluent customers was making steady progress. Market research data showed that the median age of Harley customers was a little over thirty-four – much higher than the average for motorcycle customers as a whole. The median household income for Harley customers was almost $40,000 and over half were married.

Basic to Harley's brand strength was the loyalty of Harley owners. Harley-Davidson's brand identity extended beyond the reputation and status value associated with other powerful brand franchises. To own a Harley was not only a personal statement of values, it also conferred membership to a society of Harley owners. Harley-Davidson goes to considerable lengths to nurture these close relations with customers. By the beginning of 1988, the Harley Owners Group (HOG) numbered 94,000 members in 450 chapters throughout the U.S. Managers and employees were encouraged to play an active part in HOG, including riding with members.

On the back of Harley's solid gains in quality and reliability, the company also sought to win back sales to public authorities, most of which had been lost to its Japanese rivals. In 1987, Harley made sales of some 4,000 bikes to police departments and had chalked up some notable successes, including a switch by the California Highway Patrol from Honda to Harley.

The international market represented a particular challenge for Harley. Exports represented 13.6, 15.7, and 17.2 percent of Harley's sales of motorcycles and related products in 1985, 1986, and 1987, respectively. The International Division located at Danbury, Connecticut managed overseas sales. The biggest single export market was Canada, which was viewed as a natural extension of the U.S. market. The other main export markets were, in order of importance, Japan, Australia, and West Germany, though in none of these countries had Harley been successful in wresting a substantial share of the heavyweight market from the grip of the Japanese and BMW. It appeared that outside North America the Harley image and mystique failed to justify its price premium over more technologically-advanced Japanese bikes.

It was not only in the motorcycle market that Harley-Davidson was able to exploit the strength of the Harley brand image. The Harley-Davidson name was licensed to suppliers of tee-shirts, jackets, underwear, jewelry, and toys. Although licensing income accounted for less than 1 percent of Harley's revenue from motorcycles and related products, it was almost all profit. In 1982, Harley began vigorously enforcing protection of its trademarks. From its own dealerships to tattoo parlors (where the Harley-Davidson logo was the most popular single tattoo design), Harley prohibited unauthorized use of its trademarks, and drove out bootleg products. The starting point was the major motorcycle trade shows. Initially Harley found that bootleg merchandise was so prevalent, that legitimate Harley-licensed products were hard to find. The result was a rise in licensing income to Harley, plus tighter controls against the Harley name being used in connection with poor quality or pornographic products.

Distribution

Establishing Harley as a quality motorcycle with appeal to middle-class, respectable Americans required special efforts from Harley's dealers. Harley's bikes were distributed through 620 independently-owned, full-service dealerships in the U.S. The dealers were obliged to carry a full line of Harley replacement parts and accessories, and perform service on Harley bikes. About 70 percent of dealers were exclusive to Harley. The number of dealers had declined by 19 percent between 1979 and 1988, but dealer turnover was low – less than 5 percent annually between 1982 and 1987. Harley's dealer development program involved imposing higher standards of pre- and after-sales service on dealers, and better dealer facilities. Harley-Davidson placed a strong emphasis on training dealers to help them meet the higher service requirements, and encouraging dealers to cater their services to meet the needs of professionals and yuppies as well as the more traditional Harley enthusiasts.

Finance

The 1981 buyout had left Harley-Davidson debt-heavy. The buyout was financed with a $30 million loan, $35 million in revolving credit from institutional lenders, and $9 million in preferred stock held by AMF. The losses of 1982–83 further strained Harley's finances and made it difficult for Harley to undertake sorely-needed investments in capital equipment and new products. In 1984, AMF agreed to cancel its holdings of Harley preferred stock in exchange for direct payments from Harley's future profits.

On July 8, 1986 Harley-Davidson went public with an offering through Dean Witter Reynolds Inc. Two million shares were offered at a price of $11 per share, and $70 million in subordinated notes were issued. The proceeds were used to repay a portion of the debt to AMF, refinance some of Harley's other debt to provide working capital and to provide finance for diversification. On July 3, 1987 a further two million shares were issued at a price of $16.50 a share.

To help compete with the attractive financial terms offered by its Japanese competitors, Harley has entered arrangements to provide both dealer and customer financing. Most of Harley's sales to dealers are financed by ITT Commercial Financing Corporation. Under the scheme Harley indemnifies ITT for losses incurred by ITT in the sale or disposition of motorcycles repossessed by ITT. In December 1983 an agreement was made with Ford Motor Credit Company to provide dealer and customer financing. About 7 percent of Harley's motorcycle sales were financed by FMCC consumer credit during 1985–87.

Diversification

Despite a near doubling of market share between 1983 and 1987, volume increase was modest, and Harley sought new areas of profitable expansion. Harley's prior record of diversification was not encouraging. In 1971, it had introduced its own line of snowmobiles, but problems arising from the seasonal nature of the business and intense Japanese competition caused Harley to abandon the venture in 1975. In 1984, Harley acquired Trihawk, a small manufacturer of three-wheelers, but after estimating the start-up costs involved in marketing the product, terminated the project.

A more successful diversification was defense contracting using Harley's existing production capacity. By 1985, contracting was generating $47 million worth of business and was earning almost as much profit as the motorcycle business. The major products were bomb and shell casings and rocket engines for military target drones. Successes in this area convinced management that Harley-Davidson's manufacturing skills, the flexibility of its plants and workers, and its excellent labor relations conferred considerable advantages in competing in closely related businesses. During 1987 the company entered the following contracts:

- A five-year contract to supply $5 million of machined components to the Marine and Industrial Division of Acustar Inc., a subsidiary of Chrysler Corporation.
- An agreement to supply 50,000 small engines worth $2 million to Briggs and Stratton Corporation over a two-year period.
- The acquisition from Armstrong Equipment plc. of the rights to the British MT5OO military motorcycle which was followed by a contract with the British Ministry of Defense to supply spare parts.

Despite the profitability of Harley's contracting business, it did not represent a secure basis on which to support Harley's long-term development. By 1986, Vaughn Beals was looking for a large-scale diversification which would reduce Harley's dependence upon the motorcycle market.

He felt Harley needed to diversify in order to be a truly stable performer, that is why Harley acquired the Holiday Rambler Company in December of 1986. Beals saw the fit as a good one because Holiday was a recreational vehicle producer and was what he called "manufacturing intensive" just as Harley was.

Holiday Rambler manufactured premium motorhomes, specialized commercial vehicles, and travel trailers. Holiday employed 2,300 people and was headquartered in Wakarusa, Indiana. Holiday was the largest privately-owned maker of recreational vehicles at the time of the acquisition. The company was recognized as one of the leaders in the premium-class motorhome and towable-trailer markets. It ranked fourth, in 1986, in market share in the motorhome market

Exhibit 10.8 Harley-Davidson's Facilities (excluding those of Holiday Rambler)

Type of Facility	Location	Area (sq. feet)	Status
Executive offices, engineering, and warehouse	Milwaukee, Wisconsin	502,720	Owned
Manufacturing	Wauwatosa, Wisconsin	342,430	Owned
Manufacturing	Tomahawk, Wisconsin	50,600	Owned
Manufacturing	York, Pennsylvania	869,580	Owned
Engineering test laboratory	Milwaukee, Wisconsin	6,500	Lease expiring 1991
Motorcycle testing	Talladega, Alabama	9,326	Lease expiring 1988
International offices	Danbury, Connecticut	2,850	Lease expiring 1988
Office and workshop	Raunheim, West Germany	4,300	Lease expiring 1989

and fifth in towable recreational vehicles. Its products were gaining share in the industry as a whole.

A Holiday subsidiary, Utilimaster, built truck trailers and bodies for commercial uses. The company had contracts with companies such as Purolator-Courier and Ryder Truck Rentals. Other Holiday subsidiaries produced office furniture, custom wood products, custom tools, van conversions, and park trailers.

Acquisition was followed by a restructuring of Rambler's product line. During 1987 and 1988, design improvements were made to Rambler's towable products, a small walk-in van using a chassis made by Harley-Davidson was introduced, and several unprofitable models were deleted from the product line.

The acquisition of Holiday Rambler for $156.7 million in cash almost doubled the size of Harley-Davidson. Such expansion necessitated an overhaul of Harley-Davidson's organizational structure. In 1987, Harley moved to a divisional structure. Richard Teerlink, the chief financial officer, was appointed president and CEO of the Motorcycle Division, while H. Wayne Dahl was promoted to president and CEO of the Holiday Rambler Corporation. To undertake strategic planning, an Executive Committee for each of the two divisions was established under the chairmanship of the division president. In addition, a seven-person corporate Policy Committee was established to guide overall corporate strategy.

NOTES

1. S.C. Hinrich, C.B. Shrader, and A.N. Hoffman, "Harley-Davidson Inc.: The Eagle Soars Alone" in Wheelan and Hunger, Strategic Management
2. "Now Harley-Davidson is all over the road." *New York Times,* Sunday, April 17, 1988, p. F12.
3. "Made in America." Cycle, February, 1985, p. 18
4. Harley-Davidson Inc. Annual report, 1987, p. 4
5. "Why Milwaukee Won't Die." Cycle, June, 1987, p. 37
6. See note 3 above.
7. See note 4 above.
8. "Why Milwaukee Won't Die." Cycle, June 1987, p. 37
9. "Harley on the high wire." Cycle, October 1986, p. 38

11

SCOTCH-BRITE (3M)

In June 1990, the 3M operating committee met in world headquarters in St. Paul, Minnesota, to consider a proposal to rationalize the North American production and distribution of SCOTCH-BRITE hand scouring pads. Due to increased consumer demand, the decision had been made to upgrade the equipment which converted the jumbo-sized rolls into consumer and industrial-sized packages and quantities. At issue was where this upgraded processing equipment would be located.

Currently, most of the conversion took place in Alexandria, Minnesota from jumbo rolls supplied from Perth, Ontario. The Alexandria facility then shipped finished goods to eight distribution centers around the United States. (See Exhibit 11.1.)

The Canadian division of 3M was now proposing that all production and distribution for SCOTCH-BRITE hand pads take place from Perth. This would mean $4 million in new equipment would go to Perth, the current SCOTCH-BRITE workforce in Alexandria would be shifted to different responsibilities, and Perth would now ship directly to the various distribution centers. (See Exhibit 11.2.) This proposal to grant a regional product mandate to Perth had not gone unopposed. The Alexandria plant felt it would be preferable to place the new converting equipment in their facility, and to maintain the existing relationship with Perth.

3M BACKGROUND

3M was a multinational enterprise with 80,000 employees, subsidiaries and operations in 50 countries, and worldwide annual sales in excess of U.S.$10 billion. During the past decade, 3M's outside-the-US (OUS) sales had climbed from about one-third to nearly one-half of total sales. This growth was a result of a conscious strategy of global expansion. The company was organized into four divisions: Industrial and Consumer, Electronic and Information Technologies, Life Sciences, and Graphic Technologies.

Among the more familiar products were SCOTCH brand transparent tapes, magnetic tapes, cassettes, and cartridges. Abrasives and adhesives were early products of the company and still formed a very important portion of the business.

Exhibit 11.1   Present SCOTCH-BRITE Product Flowchart

PRESENT SCOTCH-BRITE PRODUCT FLOWCHART

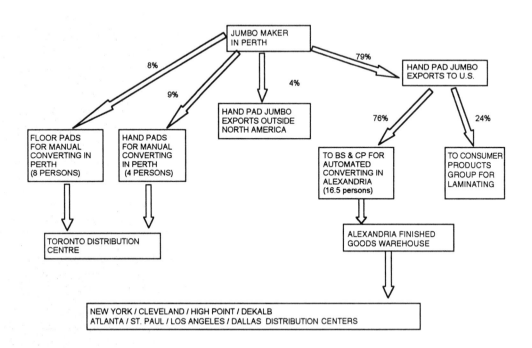

Developing other technologies and applying them to make problem-solving products was the basis on which 3M had been able to grow. So many new products were produced on an on-going basis that 25 percent of any year's sales were of products that did not exist five years before.

Like its parent company, 3M Canada Inc. was a highly diversified company which manufactured thousands of different products for industry, business, the professions, and the consumer. The head office and main plant were located in London, Ontario with sales and service centers across the country. 3M Canada was established as part of the newly founded International Division in 1951. Additional subsidiaries were set up at that time in Australia, Brazil, France, West Germany, Mexico, and the United Kingdom. 3M Canada employed about 2,000 people. In addition to operations in London and Perth, the company had manufacturing plants in Toronto, Havelock, and Simcoe, Ontario and Morden, Manitoba. Canada was the sixth largest of 3M's subsidiaries.

With the exception of two or three people from the worldwide organization, everyone working for 3M Canada was Canadian. The Canadian subsidiary annually lost ten to fifteen people to the worldwide organization. Although a high proportion of the professional management group in Canada had a career goal to work in the worldwide organization at some stage, this was not a requirement. For example, several managers at the plant manager level and above had indicated a preference to stay in Canada despite offers within the worldwide organization.

Exhibit 11.2 Proposed SCOTCH-BRITE Product Flowchart

PROPOSED SCOTCH-BRITE PRODUCT FLOWCHART

(ALL HAND PAD)

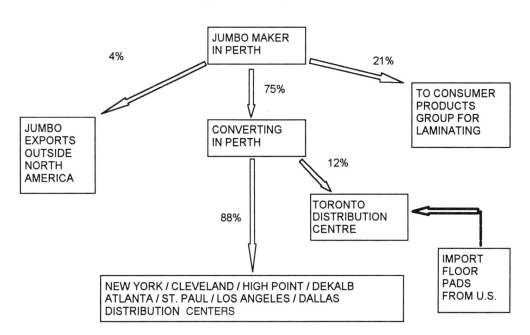

The Canadian subsidiary, under the direction of its president, Jeffery McCormick, was expected to generate sales growth and to produce an operating income on Canadian sales. Increasingly, emphasis was being placed on achieving certain target market share levels.

Within Canada, the twenty-five individual business units were split among eight groups, each of which operated as a profit center. Variability existed in each with respect to the amount of divisional input from the United States.

The headquarters perception of the competencies of the Canadian subsidiary varied according to the business and functional area. For example, Canadian manufacturing and engineering had a solid reputation for getting things done.

In terms of research, Canada specialized in three somewhat narrow areas. These dealt with polymer chemistry, materials science, and electro-mechanical telecommunications. Several dozen scientists pursued research in these areas within Canadian laboratories.

The Canadian subsidiary did not have a critical mass in R & D for all the technologies necessary to support SCOTCH-BRITE. In addition it was not deemed feasible to move (or build) a pilot plant to Canada for SCOTCH-BRITE testing purposes since pilot plants tended to serve a multitude of products.

Partly as a consequence of the 1988 Canada–U.S. Free Trade Agreement, the overall level of company harmonization between the two countries had risen. Some U.S. divisions were asking for more direct control over their businesses in Canada. The Canadian president needed to deal with these issues and to develop the necessary organizational response.

The Canadian subsidiary had placed a lot of importance on building intercompany sales. Over 20 percent of its sales were of this type, and further increases were intended.

3M Canada sales in 1990 were over $500 million while after-tax earnings were in the range of 10 percent. (See Exhibits 11.3 and 11.4 for financial statements.)

THE PERTH SCOTCH-BRITE PLANT

The $5 million Perth plant went into operation in 1981, employing twenty-two people. The plant covered 36,000 square feet on a seventy-eight-acre site and was the first Canadian production facility for this product line. It was built to supplement the jumbo output of Alexandria, which was nearing capacity. The plant was designed with sufficient capacity to produce enough hand pads and floor pads to eliminate imports, but with exports in mind. In 1981, the Canadian duty on shipments from the U.S. to Canada was 13.5 percent, while shipments from Canada could enter the U.S. duty free.

Over the next decade, the plant was expanded several times, and employment grew to eighty people. Throughout this period, the plant exclusively produced SCOTCH-BRITE. SCOTCH-BRITE was a profitable, growing product line in a core business area. The total scouring pad market in which SCOTCH-BRITE competed was estimated to be $60 million in the United States and nearly $5 million in Canada.

Exhibit 11.3   3M Canada Inc. Consolidated Statement of Earnings and Retained Earnings for the Year Ended October 31, 1989

(Dollars in Thousands)	1989	1988
Revenue		
Net sales*	561,406	516,663
Other income	8,823	3,536
	570,229	520,199
Costs and expenses		
Cost of goods sold and other expenses	451,298	412,826
Depreciation and amortization	16,908	15,921
Interest	312	239
Research and development	1,876	2,010
	470,394	430,996
	99,835	89,203
Provision for income taxes	41,636	38,339
Net earnings for the year	58,199	50,864
Retained earnings – beginning of year	215,960	185,496
	274,159	236,360
Dividends	28,046	20,400
Retained earnings – end of year	246,113	215,960

*Includes net sales to parent and affiliated Companies 106,773   89,709

Exhibit 11.4 3M Canada Inc. Consolidated Balance Sheet as of October 31, 1989

(Dollars in Thousands)	1989	1988
Assets		
Current assets		
Interest bearing term deposits	66,998	52,896
Accounts receivable	73,524	69,631
Amounts due from affiliated companies	18,050	13,670
Other receivables and prepaid expenses	5,472	4,592
Inventories –		
Finished goods and work in process	67,833	63,745
Raw materials and supplies	9,321	10,601
	241,198	215,135
Fixed Assets		
Property, plant, and equipment – at cost	180,848	164,313
Less accumulated depreciation	85,764	75,676
Other Assets	9,590	8,856
	345,872	312,628
Liabilities		
Current liabilities		
Accounts payable – trade	21,600	18,388
Amounts due to affiliated companies	18,427	17,985
Income taxes payable	9,394	12,437
Deferred payments	1,437	1,422
Other liabilities	20,832	18,367
	71,690	68,599
Deferred income taxes	14,669	14,669
	86,359	83,268
Shareholder's equity		
Capital stock		
Authorized – unlimited shares		
Issued and fully paid – 14,600 shares	13,400	13,400
Retained earnings	246,113	215,960
	259,513	229,360
	345,872	312,628

SCOTCH-BRITE material was a web of non-woven nylon or polyester fibers impregnated throughout with abrasive particles. The result was a pad, disk, or wheel used to scour, clean, polish, or finish materials such as wood, metal, plastic, and many other surfaces.

As SCOTCH-BRITE material wears down it exposes more abrasives, so that it continues to be effective all through its life. Because it is made of a synthetic fiber it does not rust or stain. Some types of SCOTCH-BRITE have a sponge backing so that both scouring and washing can be done with the one product. Other versions of this material have integral backing pads and handles made of strong plastic to enable the user to scour and clean flat surfaces and corners with ease.

SCOTCH-BRITE products were made in sheet, roll, and wheel shapes, and used in a wide variety of applications in the metal-working, woodworking, and plastics industries, as well as in the hotel and restaurant trade, and the home.

Floor and carpet cleaning companies, schools, hospitals, and building maintenance personnel used a wide variety of SCOTCH-BRITE disks and pads for floor maintenance. Other smaller hand-held pads were used for cleaning painted surfaces such as door frames, stairs, walls, sinks, and tile surfaces. SCOTCH-BRITE products were used in hotels and restaurants for griddle and grill cleaning, deep fat fryer scouring, as well as for carpet and floor maintenance. Several types of SCOTCH-BRITE products were available for home use. These ranged from a gentle version designed for cleaning tubs, sinks, tile, and even fine china, to a rugged scouring pad with a built-in handle for scouring barbecue grills.

THE PERTH PROPOSAL

During the 1980s, as the Perth plant grew in size and experience, its reputation as a workforce with a demonstrated ability to work effectively began to develop. With increased confidence came a desire to assume new challenges. An obvious area for potential development would be to take on more of the SCOTCH-BRITE value-added function in Perth, rather than to ship semi-finished goods to the United States.

In the mid '80s, the Perth managers advocated that they should now supply finished goods to the U.S. for certain mandated products. The SCOTCH-BRITE Manufacturing Director during this period opposed this approach. He claimed that nothing would be saved as all the finished goods would have to be sent to Alexandria anyway, for consolidation and distribution to the customer.

The U.S.-based manufacturing director also argued that mandating products could reduce the utilization of the larger, more expensive maker at Alexandria which would increase the unit burden costs on other products there. During this period, the Perth maker operated as the swing maker with utilization cycling in order to keep the Alexandria maker fully loaded.

With a change in management came a willingness to take a fresh look at the situation. The new manager, Andy Burns, insisted that a more complete analysis of all the delivered costs be provided. To that end, a study was initiated in December 1989 to determine the cost of converting and packaging SCOTCH-BRITE hand pads in Perth, rather than shipping jumbo to Alexandria for converting and packaging.

The task force struck in Canada was led by Len Weston, the Perth Plant Manager. Procedurally, any proposal would first go to Gary Boles, Manufacturing Director for Canada, and Gord Prentice, Executive Vice President of Manufacturing for Canada. Once their agreement had been obtained, the Perth plant manager would continue to champion the project through the 3M hierarchy, although people such as Prentice would facilitate the process.

The proposal would next go to the Building Service and Cleaning Products (BS + CP) division for review and agreement. If successful, the proposal would then be sent back to Canadian engineering to develop an Authority for (capital) Expenditure, or AFE. It would then be routed through senior Canadian management and U.S. division and group levels.

The final stage was for the AFE to go to the Operating committee at the sector level for assessment. See Exhibits 11.5 and 11.6 for partial organization charts for 3M Worldwide and International.

The Perth proposal acknowledged that Alexandria was a competently managed plant and that putting the new equipment in either location would reduce costs from their current levels. At issue was where the greater cost savings would be generated. The Perth proposal argued that these would occur in Perth (see Exhibit 11.7) through a combination of reduced freight and storage costs, and faster and more efficient manufacturing. The Perth proposal's overall approach was to emphasize what was best for shareholders on the basis of total delivered costs.

Overall employment needs were expected to increase by eight in Canada yet decline by at least double that in Alexandria. (See Table 11.1.)

Some of the modest employment increases in Canada could be traced to the fact that the small amount of manual converting in Perth would now be automated. It had been viable to convert a small quantity of hand pads in Canada, even manually, when shipping costs and duties were factored in.

The biggest reason for the small number of proposed new hires in Canada was the plan to discontinue floor pad manual converting in Perth and to shift those operators to the

Exhibit 11.5 3M International – Partial Organization Chart

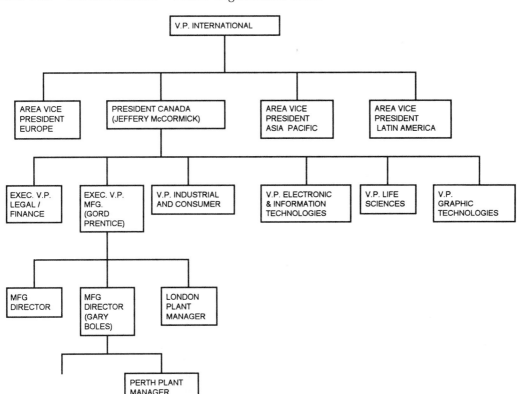

Exhibit 11.6   3M Worldwide – Partial Organization Chart

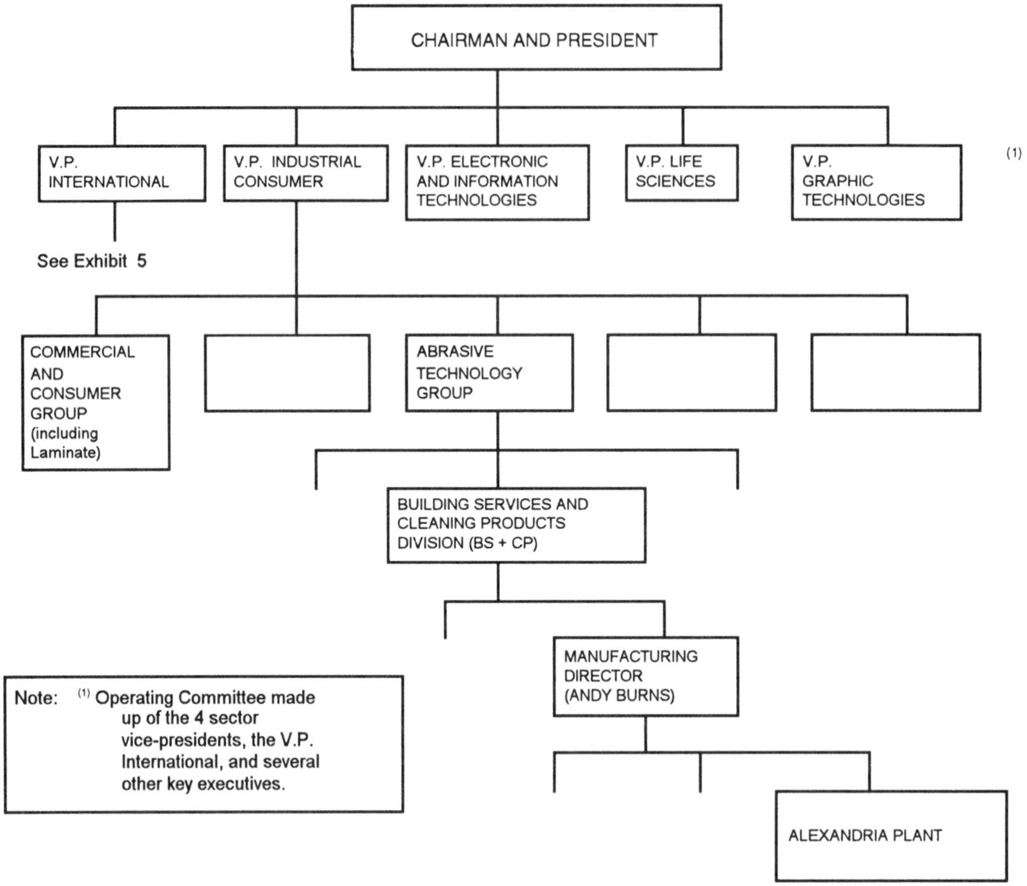

automated hand pad area. The initial response to this in Canada, in several quarters, had been less-than-enthusiastic.

The Canadian floor pad business manager felt that he might now have to pay a premium if purchasing from the United States. As well, he was concerned that some of his customers might notice a difference in performance. He felt the manually converted floor pads from Perth were of a slightly higher quality than the automatically converted ones from Hutchison, Minnesota. The Canadian business manager had built a higher market share for 3M floor pads in Canada than his U.S. counterparts, and he did not wish to see this jeopardized.

A shift from floor pad manual converting to hand pad automated converting would also have immediate implications for the operators. Currently, most of the manual floor pad (and hand pad) jobs were on a one shift (day) basis. A second, evening shift was sometimes required, but no one worked the midnight-to-morning shift. With automation, all operators would now need to work a three shift rotation in order to maximize machine utilization. In a non-union plant, with a ten year tradition of day jobs in converting, and with a no lay-off policy, this could be an emotional issue. The task of selling it to the operators would fall to Weston.

Exhibit 11.7 Sample Unit Cost Comparison (U.S. Dollars per Case)

	Current Alexandria Operation	Upgraded Cutter Alexandria	Upgraded Cutter Perth
Jumbo cost ex Perth	$6.20	$6.20	$6.20
Jumbo freight to Alexandria	$0.70	$0.70	–
Jumbo storage	$0.70	$0.70	$0.05
Jumbo burden absorption	–	–	($0.20)[1]
Input cost to converting	$7.60	$7.60	$6.05
Converting waste	$0.95	$0.65	$0.45
Converting labor	$1.35	$0.30	$0.15[2]
Variable converting overhead	$0.60	$0.45	$0.30
Fixed converting overhead	$1.00	$0.55	$0.85[3]
Packaging supplies	$1.20	$1.20	$1.20
Fin goods whse/mat hand	$0.45	$0.45	$0.25
Fin goods direct charges	$1.15	$1.15	$0.90
Cost including converting	$14.30	$12.35	$10.10
Freight to branch	$0.90	$0.90	$1.05
Cost delivered to branch	$15.20	$13.25	$11.15

[1]Volume savings through equipment usage.
[2]Lower than Alexandria due to faster equipment speed and smaller production teams.
[3]Higher than Alexandria due to larger investment in equipment.
Source: Perth Proposal

Table 11.1 Changes in Staffing for Each Proposal

Perth Proposal	
Add in Perth	– 1 Maintenance
	– 3 Shippers
	– 4 Production Operators*
Total	– 8 Persons @ Labor Rate U.S. $13.18/hr
Delete in Alexandria	– Maintenance ?
	– Shipping / Receiving ?
	– 16.5 Production Operators
Alexandria Proposal	
Add in Alexandria	– 6 Operators @ $15.43

* In addition, eight persons in floor pad manual conversion, and four persons in hand pad manual conversion would now be shifted to hand pad automated conversion in Perth.

THE ALEXANDRIA RESPONSE

The Alexandria response was less a proposal, and more a reaction to the Perth initiative. A variety of concerns, some old and some new, were raised.

- First: the increased production volume in Canada and the resultant re-exports to the United States would cause an increased vulnerability to currency fluctuations.
- Second: lengthening the supply distance would make it more difficult to guarantee delivery to U.S. customers.

- Third: the Perth plant would now need to be interfaced with the 3M-USA computer-based materials management system in order to have effective transportation. This would require the Canadian information technology group to work with the logistics people in order to develop a program which would allow for cross-border integration of information.
- Fourth: cost of shipping finished goods to the branches would increase in both Perth and Alexandria. In Perth it would be due to the smaller volumes, and increased distances associated with shipping a single product line. In Alexandria it would now take longer to make up a truckload without the hand pads.
- Fifth: since SCOTCH-BRITE converting was already well established in Alexandria, and there would be savings wherever the new equipment was located, it was safer to keep it where the manufacturing experience already existed rather than to rely on optimistic projections from Perth.

CONCLUSION

In part, due to the distances involved, regional production mandates on various products had been granted as early as the 1970s by 3M in Europe. SCOTCH-BRITE, in fact, was already also being produced in Europe, Asia, and Mexico. However, unlike these other production mandates, the Perth proposal was to supply the core U.S. market. For the operating committee, the decision would come down to how much confidence they had in the Perth proposal.

12
Logitech

Early in the spring of 1990, Pierluigi Zappacosta, CEO of Logitech, reflected on the changing market conditions in North America and Europe and wondered what would be required to maintain and expand Logitech's position in the computer peripherals marketplace. Logitech had become one of three companies that dominated the global market for pointing devices for computers. While Logitech had captured a large unit share of the OEM (Original Equipment Manufacturer) mouse market, Microsoft was the clear leader in terms of industry standards and dollar share of the retail market, and KYE (Genius), having a strong retail presence in Europe, was poised to compete aggressively in North America.

Zappacosta recognized that Logitech had been slow to react to changes in market conditions, such as the 1987 introduction of Microsoft's "white mouse," a shapely design that had developed considerable consumer appeal. This, combined with eroding margins on the OEM mouse business, had left Zappacosta wondering whether Logitech could maintain a leadership position in the pointing device market. Logitech had been successful in developing leadership positions in other niches, such as scanners, and other opportunities existed. Committed to their mission of "connecting the computer to the world" by giving it "senses," Zappacosta wondered what direction(s) the company should take and what the priorities should be.

COMPANY BACKGROUND

Logitech SA was founded in October 1981 by Mr. Zappacosta and Daniel Borel in Switzerland after Bobst Graphics, the company with which the two had been developing a European word-processing/DTP package, was sold and the new owners did not want to continue the project. Zappacosta had met Borel at Stanford University, while they were completing their MS (Computer Science) degrees. After an initial attempt to bring U.S. technology to Europe with their own software company, Borel, and then Zappacosta, had joined Bobst to gain industry contacts. They had then formed their own software company with Bobst as the major client. Giacomo Marini, a software manager at Olivetti and a friend of Zappacosta's from the time when they had both worked in Pisa, Italy, joined in founding Logitech together with a group of young engineers.

Two contracts set the stage for the initial growth and development of the organization. First, they won a $1 million contract with Ricoh to develop hardware and software for use with Ricoh printers and scanners. Shortly thereafter, Logitech won a contract with Swiss Timing to develop hardware and software for use at the Olympic Games. Wanting to be close to Ricoh and developments in Silicon Valley, Zappacosta, and later Borel, and then Marini, moved to Palo Alto, California and created Logitech Inc. In March 1982, Logitech Inc. learned of a Swiss watch company, Depraz, that had developed a mouse. Recognizing the advantages of the mouse relative to other pointing devices such as cursor keys, light pens, and touch screens, Logitech secured the rights to market the Depraz mouse in the U.S. and packaged it with software for the operation of text and graphics programs.

A major turning point in the strategic direction of the organization came after Logitech secured a contract with Hewlett-Packard to supply 25,000 mice under an OEM contract. It quickly became evident that Hewlett-Packard's price and quality requirements could not be met by Logitech's initial strategy of contracting out manufacturing to Depraz. Adhering to a philosophy of having direct control of the critical elements of the business, Logitech bought the rights to manufacture and market a mouse designed by CC Corp. With help from Hewlett-Packard, Logitech redesigned the mouse for mass production and set up a manufacturing operation in Redwood City, California in 1984. Production was moved to Fremont, California in 1987 to a facility across the street from Logitech's U.S. headquarters.

Control over manufacturing and a commitment to quality led to rapid growth in the OEM mouse market with contracts from Apollo, Olivetti, AT&T, and other key computer manufacturers. However, Apple and IBM were wary of Logitech's manufacturing expertise and continued to buy most of their mice from Alps, a Japanese company operating in California, which had purchased Apple's keyboard and mouse facility and was the exclusive supplier to Microsoft.

In 1986 two events took place that would help solidify Logitech's future in the mouse market. First, due to slow growth in OEM sales, Logitech entered the retail market with the Series 7 mouse, a product that had been successful in the OEM market. Then, to win a piece of the Apple business and to satisfy the demands of OEM customers for Logitech to lower the cost of mice, Logitech set up a manufacturing base in Hsinchu, Taiwan, with an initial production capacity of one million mice per year, but potentially expandable to ten times that volume. In retrospect, Zappacosta thought they had been a bit lucky. For a $300,000 investment, they had secured a high volume, state-of-the-art, manufacturing plant in Taiwan's "Silicon Valley" just before Taiwan became a leader in manufacturing technology and a hot-bed of design creativity, and just as the mouse industry took off under the combined forces of Apple's Macintosh, desktop publishing, Microsoft's Windows, and other applications using graphical user interfaces.

In 1988, anticipating a unified Europe in 1992, and wanting to be close to Apple and potential customers such as IBM and Compaq in Europe, Logitech opened another manufacturing facility in Cork, Ireland, which had a capacity, similar to that of the Fremont plant, of about 1.5 million mice per year. At the same time, they broadened their product line with the introduction of a hand-held scanner, a product that shared some technological features with the mouse, that capitalized on Logitech's experience in software development, and that could be marketed through established retail channels.

By the end of 1989, Logitech had reached sales of over $100 million, employed about 1,000 people, had manufacturing facilities on three continents, and had sales offices in England, Germany, Italy, France, Japan, Sweden, Switzerland, the United States, and Taiwan.

CULTURE

The culture at Logitech reflected the global nature and operations of the organization. Because employees had varied life and educational experiences from around the globe, they were appreciative and accepting of differences in backgrounds, perspectives, and styles. As Fabio Righi, Vice President Sales and Marketing, put it, "our greatest strength as well as our biggest challenge is that Logitech is an international company. It is difficult to be international and local at the same time. Local flavor affects/impacts everything."

Deeply rooted in the Logitech culture was a strong product/technical orientation. Employees gained considerable job satisfaction from being on the leading edge and working on bold, exciting projects. Fabio Righi, for example, talked of the elusive "atomic mouse" like a grail that helps define the common purpose of the employees. As senior executives admitted, employees tended to be quite internally focused and did not make a great effort to have their beliefs validated before launching a new product into the marketplace. As Ron McClure, Vice President Strategic Marketing, put it, "We are the most critical users of our products. Customer need recognition is limited by their understanding of technology – they don't know what is possible!"

Related to this technical orientation was a strong design and production orientation. According to Chip Smith, Production Manager in Fremont, "Everything evolves around production. The floor, receiving and shipping, traffic, and order processing are key processes by which we satisfy consumers." Therefore, manufacturing was seen as a key marketing success factor.

There was also a strong spiritual component to the culture at Logitech. This was supported in part by the personal philosophies of the founders, but also by the shared vision that employees had for shaping the future. For example, aesthetics were a high priority, not only in the products, but also in the workplace itself. One might infer that if there was a Logitech company handbook, it would probably be *Zen and the Art of Motorcycle Maintenance.*

Working relationships at Logitech tended to be very informal, flexible, open, and close. Employees were genuinely excited to be on the leading edge and found their jobs and the "family" atmosphere fun. This "family" atmosphere was reinforced by Logitech's policy of hiring talented young professionals from around the world and relocating them to enrich their own and other's perspectives. Dislocated from their own families and culture, employees often relied on each other for social, emotional, and cultural support.

Consistent with the informal, close working relationships, there were few formal procedures and structures within Logitech. Executive decisions were generally made by consensus after seeking employee input. Worldwide interaction of management and staff was maintained on a daily basis by an electronic mail system.

BUSINESS STRATEGY

Pierluigi Zappacosta explained the long-term Logitech vision by saying, "Only if the computer becomes a little more human will it become an effective tool for the mind. And evolution of our own brain through computers is our long-term vision. Our more immediate mission is to connect the computer with the world by giving it 'senses,' humanize the interface to the computer, and help people turn data into meaningful information. Our goals are to maintain/attain the number one position in whatever markets we play in by redefining and continually changing the products and markets we compete in. We want to have a Logitech product on every computer desk."

To achieve their mission and objectives, Logitech's business strategy was to recognize major trends and technologies early, move fast in bringing quality products to market (forming alliances if necessary), develop in-house expertise for product extensions, become effective and efficient manufacturers, have the best sales force and channels to sell the products, and keep ahead of the competition by an accelerated pace of innovation.

Logitech competed aggressively in both the OEM and retail sides of the personal computer accessory business. On the OEM side of the business, they competed using innovation and skill in manufacturing and design that allowed them to bring new technology to market at very competitive prices. (See estimated manufacturing costs in Table 12.1.) Toward this end, Logitech had achieved an experience curve in mouse manufacturing of about 70 percent. On the retail side of the business, Logitech focused on image management. They wanted to be perceived in the marketplace as innovators that develop neat products that were fun to use and were easy to sell.

About 60 percent of Logitech's unit sales were in the OEM segment but more than 60 percent of their revenue came from the retail segment. In both the OEM and retail markets, Logitech's financial success (see Exhibit 12.1) had been, and would continue to be, tied to the development and growth of the PC marketplace and recognition of the need to "humanize" the computer.

PRODUCT DEVELOPMENT

Product development at Logitech involved finding or developing technologies that required Logitech's skills in design, mass manufacturing, and distribution to bring them to market. Logitech had three basic development strategies: start from scratch, evolve current in-house technology, or buy required technology at an advanced development stage from others. Starting from scratch added about a year to the product development process since employees had to learn about a technology, decide what to develop, and test product concepts. Building on current expertise to extend or develop new generations of products was the most common approach taken. If required technology was not available internally, then Logitech would

Table 12.1 Estimated Manufacturing Costs and Selling Prices

Mouse	Estimated Manufacturing Costs (Jan. 1990)	Estimated Average Selling Price to Channel
Logitech S9	$25.00	$60.00
Microsoft Mouse	27.00	75.00
Pilot Mouse	17.40	33.00
Dexxa	16.30	19.50
Logitech OEM	15.20	22.00
Taiwanese OEM	13.10	16.50
Ergonomic (corded)	19.60	Not on the market
Ergonomic (cordless)	64.30	Not on the market

Source: Company records

Exhibit 12.1   Selected Financial Data

Logitech International SA, Apples
(In Swiss Francs)
Projected

Full year ending	3/31/87	3/31/88	3/31/89	3/31/90
Consolidated revenue	33,543,351	62,806,740	124,110,684	180,000,000
Net income after tax	1,459,888	7,032,066	11,206,922	14,000,000
Percent of revenues	4.35%	11.20%	9.03%	7.78%
Cash flow	2,136,959	9,413,623	14,290,273	17,500,000
Percent of revenues	6.37%	14.99%	11.51%	9.72%
Earnings per bearer share		54	76	96
Dividend per bearer share		–	12	16
Engineering, research & development expenses	2,579,023	4,663,430	8,396,799	13,700,000
Percent of revenues	7.69%	7.43%	6.77%	7.61%
Number of personnel	240	442	731	1,000
Current assets	12,117,422	27,026,936	75,526,814	108,000,000
Property, plant & equipment gross	6,212,338	8,843,297	22,421,727	30,600,000
Less accumulated depreciation	(1,412,316)	(2,139,330)	(5,222,681)	(8,500,000)
Property, plant & equipment net	4,800,022	6,703,967	17,199,046	22,100,000
Other non-current assets	328,775	2,273,945	1,184,542	3,900,000
Goodwill	0	14,214,241	13,093,605	11,200,000
Total assets	17,246,219	50,219,089	107,004,007	145,200,000
Current liabilities	8,945,618	18,701,970	36,775,490	37,200,000
Long-term debt & deferred taxes	3,858,044	5,517,119	10,541,326	43,500,000
Stockholders' equity	4,442,557	26,000,000	59,687,191	69,500,000
Total liabilities & stockholders' equity	17,246,219	50,219,089	107,004,007	145,200,000

Logitech International SA, Apples
(In Swiss Francs)

	1988	1989
Net sales	62,806,740	124,110,684
Cost of goods sold	30,921,004	71,493,833
Gross profit	31,885,736	52,616,851
Operating expenses		
Marketing, sales and support	10,070,523	21,081,432
General and administration	5,553,719	10,276,622
Research, development and engineering	4,663,430	8,396,799
	20,287,672	39,754,853
Income from operations	11,598,064	12,861,998
Other expenses, net	191,569	59,656
Income before income taxes	11,406,495	12,802,342
Provision for taxes on income	4,374,429	1,595,420
Net income	7,032,066	11,206,922

buy it, make minor adjustments to bring it to market, then develop internally the skills required for product evolution.

Decisions on product development were usually based on consensus among senior managers and tended to be emotional and based on "gut feel" rather than extensive analysis and research. Some of the decision criteria that were considered, however, included licensing or development costs, manufacturing cost, margins, a six-month payback, whether it was going to be fun to work on, and whether the product could gain a 40 percent share of its market. Focus groups were sometimes used late in the process to validate the "gut feelings." However, Pierluigi Zappacosta recognized that more effort was needed to get qualitative feedback at earlier stages of the product development cycle.

At any given time there were twenty to thirty official projects in various stages of development, as well as others that were "unofficial." The major projects were managed by multifunctional new product teams. Currently, there was no central authority on any particular project, but Zappacosta recognized the need to have someone who knew how the whole picture was coming together. Logitech was spending over 7 percent of sales on R&D and money could be found for important projects. Zappacosta thought the biggest problem that Logitech faced in new product development was not getting caught up in "the fun of it."

PERSONAL COMPUTER INDUSTRY

After five years of rapid growth, the PC industry was in turmoil in early 1990. The initial standards established by IBM and Apple had given way to a confusing array of technologies, including IBM's Micro-Channel, EISA (the Micro-Channel alternative offered by Compaq and six other major vendors), RISC (various versions of reduced instruction set computing used primarily by engineering/scientific work-stations running under the Unix operating system), and Apple's Macintosh. Confusing matters even more were competing operating systems such as DOS, OS/2, and Unix and competing graphical user interfaces such as Microsoft's Windows (version 2), IBM's Presentation Manager, the Open Systems Foundation's "X," AT&T's Unix System 5, and Next's "NextStep." All of these competing operating system and user interfaces, however, used mice or another pointing device to control the operating environment. While it was expected that graphical user interfaces would be adopted on most, if not all, systems, the rate of adoption would depend heavily on the success of Microsoft's newly announced Windows 3.0 for DOS and IBM's OS/2.

The industry itself exhibited characteristics of the maturity phase of the product life cycle. Competition was intense and a shakeout of the market was underway, which affected even some relatively large companies. Consumers were becoming more sophisticated and knowledgeable and did not require the same level of support and sales assistance that they had a few years earlier. Consequently, manufacturers were beginning to make inroads through alternative channels such as mail order, price clubs, and superstores, while traditional full-service retailers such as ComputerLand and Business Land were refocusing their efforts on organizations using outbound direct sales forces. Personal computers themselves were quickly becoming commodity items as limited product differentiation, short technology lifecycles, and steep experience curves combined to put substantial downward pressure on prices. With the early mystique of computers wearing off, users, and in particular corporations, were beginning to question and evaluate the impact of computer technology on employee productivity, health, and other aspects of organizational life. Stress injuries, for example, were gaining prominence and were being linked to workplace computer operation. One of these was carpal tunnel syndrome, which involved painful damage to the nerve that runs through the arm as a result of repetitive strain from the use of typewriters, computers, and other arm- or hand-operated equipment. Carpal tunnel syndrome had received considerable media attention (see Exhibit 12.2) and a recent ordinance in California required corporations to take measures to reduce this type of workplace injury. Other concerns were also being raised about cathode ray tubes in terms of possible harmful emissions from computer screens and in terms of eye strain. Thus, while unit growth in the PC industry was expected to be in the 10 to 15 percent range, profits were eroding and consumers were becoming more critical and discerning.

THE MOUSE MARKETPLACE

In the computer sense, "mice" were handheld mobile devices that used a combination of hardware and software to translate physical movement into digital signals that controlled

Exhibit 12.2   Carpal Tunnel Syndrome

"Repetitive Strain Repetitive Pain: Carpal Tunnel Becomes Major Workplace Hazard" Himanee Gupta, The Seattle Times, Vol. 112, Iss: 223, September 18, 1989, Section F, Page 1.

. . . Throughout the country and in Puget Sound, companies are realizing the painful, often crippling condition (carpal tunnel syndrome) has grown into a major workplace hazard. No one's sure just when and how hard it will hit, but any worker who types at computers, works with electronic scanners or regularly performs other repetitive tasks on automated equipment is at risk.

Carpal tunnel syndrome, one of several ailments known as repetitive strain injuries, occurs when constant bending of the hands, wrists and arms inflames tendons that squeeze the main nerve that runs through the arm . . . The problems start with swelling, tingling and discomfort, and can wind up causing numbness, severe pain and paralysis. Treatment often means slow, painful therapy or surgery followed by therapy. And in terms of treatment, therapy and disability claims, the costs for employers can be enormous . . .

In 1988, the state Department of Labor and Industries paid $6.5 million for 1,910 workers' compensation claims filed for carpal tunnel syndrome. That compares with 1,228 claims in 1986 and 123 in 1979.

"Pressing for New Ways to Type," Ronald Roel, Newsday, Vol. 50, #50, October 22, 1989, Section 1, Page 71.

. . . Hodges is one of a handful of iconoclasts promoting radical alternatives to today's conventional keyboard designs. Their devices, which so far have been roundly rejected by the big U.S. keyboard makers, range from variations on Hodges' split keyboard to keys that are moved much like a computer mouse. Like Hodges, most keyboard inventors say their passion for change has been spurred, in part, by an interest in reducing hand and wrist injuries, known as repetitive strain injuries, or RSI, experienced by thousands of computer users each year. Some medical experts believe that conventional flat keyboard designs may contribute to RSI. . . .

IBM and other major manufacturers say they have no plans to radically change the keyboards used by 25 million office workers. If big changes are made within the next decade, it will probably be to eliminate the keyboard altogether, substituting them with other inputting devices that convert handwriting or human speech directly to computer print, says Maryann Karinch, a spokeswoman for the Computer and Business Equipment Manufacturers' Association, a Washington, D.C.-based trade group.

---

cursor movement on a computer screen and executed commands. Named for their basic shape, mice (and trackballs) were more precise and flexible than other pointing devices such as light pens, touch screens, and cursor keys and were generally more intuitive and easier to use. While the first mice developed in the 1960s were mechanical in design and were used predominantly by engineers, mice were now mostly opto-mechanical in technology and were used by a wide variety of users, including children, for a variety of applications ranging from drawing to interacting with most business software.

Market Development

In December 1985, Logitech entered the retail mouse market, first in North America and then in Europe with the Logitech mouse, a retail version of their successful Series 7 OEM mouse. Adopting a penetration strategy for the more knowledgeable and price-sensitive North American market, Logitech priced the Logitech mouse at $99 U.S., about half the suggested price of both the Microsoft mouse and the mouse offered by Mouse Systems Corporation (the first into the U.S. market). Targeting the computer "techies," Logitech initially sold the Logitech mouse directly to consumers by soliciting phone and mail orders in trade publications. Initial success generated sufficient market pull to enable Logitech to establish a dealer network and increase the price of their mouse by 10 to 20 percent. In the less sophisticated European market, Logitech followed Microsoft's lead and used a skimming price strategy, charging about 30 percent more than it did in the U.S. Instead of using mail-order for distribution, Logitech developed relationships with a strong dealer network in Europe, who were able to support higher prices and margins by meeting the full-service needs of customers with high quality and prestige image products. In 1987, Microsoft launched its new ergonomic "white mouse," for $200 in the U.S., but $350 in Europe. Logitech was slow to react and did not bring out their Microsoft-compatible Series 9 mouse until 1988. This new mouse was priced about 20 percent below Microsoft in North America and Europe. At this time, Logitech also introduced a "low-end" mouse under the Dexxa brand name to compete against the more than twenty Taiwanese manufacturers, who were pricing their mice in the $20 to $35 range. These Taiwanese manufacturers had captured about 40 percent unit market share, compared to the 30 percent unit shares of both Logitech and Microsoft in the U.S. and Europe.

Supporting their R&D efforts from their high margins in Europe, both Logitech and Microsoft were slow to react to changes in the increasingly sophisticated and price-conscious European market. KYE (Genius), the largest of the Taiwanese manufacturers, had introduced a high quality mouse at $50 in mid-1988 and had captured a major share of the European market. In response, Microsoft and Logitech lowered their prices to $200 and $180, respectively, and Logitech began developing a new mouse at a price of $50 to $60. This new "Pilot Mouse" was introduced in Europe at the end of 1989. Microsoft had unbundled their "paint" software from their mouse in the U.S., and had lowered the price to within 20 percent of Logitech's. KYE (Genius) had just bought Mouse Systems Corporation and were poised to bring their "Genius" product into the U.S. under the Mouse Systems brand name, which had a strong user recognition despite its decreasing market share.

The positioning of the major mouse vendors in Europe and North America in early 1990 is shown in Exhibit 12.3. Worldwide dollar market shares were approximately 40 to 45 percent for Microsoft, 30 percent for Logitech, and 20 percent for KYE/Mouse Systems.

Exhibit 12.3 Positioning of Products in the Retail Market in January 1990

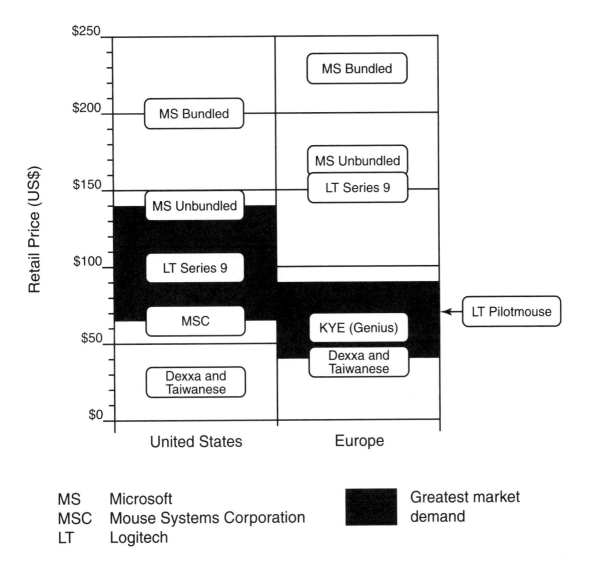

Demand for mice was expected to grow about 50 percent in 1990 and only slightly less in the foreseeable future due to trends toward graphical user interfaces. Sales of portables and laptops were expected to grow 22 percent in 1990 to 1.2 million units (14 percent of the PC market) and were expected to account for almost half of PC sales within a few years. Manufacturers of these computers would have to offer a built-in pointing device. Mice or trackballs seemed to be the logical choice for these pointing devices, but other technologies involving track pens and pen-based computing would likely play an increased role. Moreover, there would be increasing retail demand for replacement products and upgrades. Industry observers expected KYE/Mouse Systems to experience unit sales growth of 60 percent in 1990. Microsoft was expected to experience 50 percent growth and Logitech was expected to experience slightly lower growth. Logitech's retail sales were expected to remain at 40 percent of total unit sales in 1990. Previous years' unit sales are presented in Table 12.2.

Buyer Behavior

The mouse marketplace could be segmented into home/personal users, home/business users, corporate and educational users. Home/personal buyers, who accounted for about 48 percent of Logitech retail sales, were thought to be more price-sensitive than other segments and were less concerned about compatibility with software that they did not yet own. These consumers tended to buy from discount houses or no frills dealers and would choose among the alternative mice available at the most convenient location. Home/business buyers, representing about 26 percent of Logitech's retail sales, were thought to be value- and brand-conscious, but less concerned about compatibility than corporate users. These consumers were thought to be influenced by articles in *PC World, Byte,* and other trade magazines, and to a lesser extent, advertisements in those magazines. Word-of-mouth and sales representative recommendations were thought to have the most influence of all. Finally, corporate buyers, representing 25 percent of Logitech's retail sales, but 50 percent of Microsoft's, were thought to be more concerned with the brand name of a mouse and its likely compatibility with future hardware and software products. If use of the mouse was "mission critical" in the sense of being tied to productivity or used extensively, corporate buyers tended to play it safe and bought Microsoft.

While the profile of the Logitech mouse buyer was not completely understood, Logitech did keep track of who their retail customers were. Some 82 percent were desktop users and 48 percent of buyers were also the users. For 60 percent, the Logitech mouse was the second mouse they had purchased and 27 percent bought the mouse "bundled" with a paint program. Some 50 percent purchased the product at a retail store, 26 percent at a superstore, and 13 percent through mail order. Forty percent made the brand decision at the store. In terms of demographics, 80 percent were male, 55 percent were aged thirty to forty-five, and over 60 percent had five or more years of computer experience.

Competition

On the retail end of the business, the major competitors were Microsoft, Logitech, and KYE/Mouse Systems. Microsoft was positioned as the compatibility leader for both hardware and software and marketed its product to the premium, brand-conscious segment. It used its software reputation to help sell mice, and often bundled its mouse with Microsoft programs that required one. The second major competitor, Mouse Systems, was a bit of an enigma. It traditionally competed aggressively on price and promotions, but had limited resources and product quality was not believed to be as high as Logitech's or Microsoft's.

Table 12.2 Estimated World Retail Sales (in thousands of units)

Calendar year	Logitech	Microsoft	Mouse Systems	Other	Total Retail	Percentage of total market
1988	577	803	630	361	2371	35
1989	883	1321	334	400	3138	40

Source: Company records

However, with KYE's purchase of Mouse Systems, KYE was now claiming to be the largest mouse producer in the world (in terms of units) and was expected to become a force in North America.

On the OEM end of the business, Logitech's main competitors were Alps and Mitsumi, (the two Japanese companies that supplied Microsoft), KYE/Mouse Systems, Z-nix, Truedox, Primax and Silitec Taiwanese manufacturers). Primax and Silitec were suppliers to Packard Bell, the fourth largest PC vendor. All these competitors competed aggressively on price, resulting in low margins and profits. While Logitech felt it had a superior product both technically and in terms of quality, new users often could not tell the difference and most products met their basic needs.

LOGITECH'S POSITIONING AND MARKETING STRATEGY

Logitech's overall mouse strategy was to compress technology life cycles and give consumers more options for increasing productivity. They competed by developing innovative designs and technologies, producing high quality products, and pricing the products to deliver good customer value. They aggressively managed their costs and tried to maintain strong relationships with their distributors. Traditionally, their products had been positioned to attract the serious and technically oriented user, but were now also attracting creative and aesthetically oriented users looking for fun, form, and function. This overall strategy had led to an increase in unit sales of over 74 percent in 1989, but because the average selling price had decreased 22 percent, revenues increased at only about half the rate of unit sales.

Product Strategy

Logitech's product strategy was to develop products that were consistent with, but not obvious extensions of, current offerings. The image they were attempting to develop was that Logitech offered neat products which were fun to use. Marketed under the theme "tools for the imagination," Logitech's current retail product offering included: the Logitech (Series 9) Mouse, the Pilot (Series 15) Mouse (in Europe only), the Dexxa brand mouse, Trackman (a trackball pointing device), ScanMan (a hand-held scanner); and utility software (desktop publishing, a DOS management shell, a paint program, and character recognition). The mice were sold unbundled or bundled with popular software such as Microsoft's Windows. On the OEM side, they offered the Series 9 Mouse (a three-button Microsoft-compatible mouse), the Series 14 Mouse (a uniquely shaped two-button, Microsoft-compatible mouse that was expected to be very popular), and the new Series 15 mouse.

Pricing Strategy

Logitech's pricing strategy was to support a street price $10 to $20 below Microsoft by differential channel pricing. This involved starting with a target street price and working back to the manufacturer's selling price using the margins expected by different channels. This was particularly tricky since different channels had very different expectations. Electronic superstores and price clubs worked with 8 to 25 percent margins, while traditional dealers and department stores worked with 30 to 40 percent margins and stores would carry the Logitech product only if they could get their margin. Pricing was further complicated by grey marketing and cross-channel ownership. The former would arise if differential pricing in different countries created opportunities for the product to be bought by distributors in one market to be sold at a profit in another. The latter arose if a holding company owned more than one type of Logitech distributor and was able to supply a superstore, for example, with a product bought for a full-service dealer. Estimated average wholesale prices for Logitech's and Microsoft's mice products are presented in Table 12.1.

Distribution and Sales Strategy

Logitech used a mix of direct sales, telemarketing, and distributors to achieve their objective of intensive distribution. Six OEM sales reps backed by eleven support staff managed ongoing relationships with key customers. On the retail side, Logitech had four retail channel groups: major retail and corporate accounts, education/government, international corporate accounts, and other retail chains or independents. While traditionally Logitech's sales force had focused on developing channel relationships, management had increasing concerns about the lack of inroads made into corporate markets. Where Microsoft marketed directly to major corporations, Logitech had tried to reach the corporations through dealers.

Logitech's distribution goals were to be everywhere they could be, to have as many stock-keeping units (skus) as possible in each store to maximize their shelf space, and to maintain strong distributor relationships. This required utilizing a mix of wholesaling intermediaries and retailers ranging from small independent computer stores to major international chains. Logitech believed they had successfully covered 98 percent of the market with their distribution strategy and led the industry with 50 percent coverage in the rapidly growing channel of consumer electronic superstores. However, they actively sought alternative channels of distribution, such as mail-order and telemarketing, as the industry matured and evolved toward commodity products.

Communication Strategy

Logitech's communication strategy had traditionally been a no-nonsense cognitive feature-function-benefit approach designed to present solutions to customer needs. Wanting to develop an upscale image and develop greater affective appeal, Logitech created a new avant-garde visual identity and logo in January 1989. Although Logitech wanted to create an image of being a market leader in design and quality, and to communicate core product benefits of fun, creative freedom, and solution uniqueness, change was not achieved overnight. By the spring of 1990, some Logitech executives were concerned that they had not yet achieved a consistent feeling with their communication strategy. They had used a wide variety of communication media to spread their messages, but relied heavily on print advertising in trade magazines as well as point of purchase materials and packaging. Logitech also paid particular attention to cooperative advertising and special channel programs to motivate and support distributors.

THE SITUATION IN EARLY 1990

While Pierluigi Zappacosta was happy with the performance of Logitech, he was concerned with Logitech's ability to maintain margins in the mouse marketplace and wondered how he could maintain the current rate of growth and profitability into the 1990s. The Series 9 mouse had been a success, but it had been a quick response to Microsoft's sleek redesign and was not perceived internally as leading edge. As most mice now provided the same level of productivity, Zappacosta felt that a move toward ergonomic differentiation might be appropriate. Shortly after the launch of the Series 9 mouse, Logitech had begun developing two versions of a new ergonomic mouse based on the technology of the Series 9. One of these was designed specifically for right-handed users and the other for left-handed users. These new designs were shaped to fit the curve of the hand at rest and would help reduce repetitive stress problems, such as carpal tunnel syndrome. Prototypes of the ergonomic mouse had been completed and had been received well in focus groups. In a second mouse development, Logitech engineers had developed a radio "cordless" mouse that could be used to control a computer without the impediment of a cord and without the line-of-sight requirement of an infrared mouse. This technology could be packaged in the Series 9 mouse shape or the new ergonomic mouse shape at a price about $100 higher than a corded mouse. Finally, Logitech had developed technology for a three-dimensional mouse that showed promise for high-end CAD/CAM and design applications.

Zappacosta had to decide whether to launch one, two, or all of these new products, and if so, how. The cordless mouse and the 3-D mouse were "neat" from a technological perspective and had generated some excitement among the engineers. The ergonomic mouse was not particularly exciting from a technological perspective, but it might help differentiate the Logitech product in the marketplace. In addition, it might provide a "foot in the door" for attracting corporate business. However, from a strategic perspective, not everyone was comfortable with the right- and left-handed approach. Ron McClure, Vice President Strategic Marketing, had expressed concerns about the potential reception for the product among corporate customers and resellers. Corporate buyers would probably not know whether the user would be left-handed or right-handed and many mice would be shared by multiple users. It was not clear, for example, how a purchaser for a school lab would decide how many right-handed versions and how many left-handed versions to buy. Corporate users also might not have much input into the purchase decision to specify brand preference. The "safe" corporate strategy would be to buy a generic "one size fits all" mouse.

Ron had a similar concern about OEM customers. An OEM usually bundled the Logitech mouse with the OEM's software or hardware and would probably not want to package left-handed and right-handed versions. Resistance to the new ergonomic mouse was also based on three other factors. Distributor representatives said it could be a sku nightmare for resellers if they had to carry left- and right-handed, corded and cordless mice as well as the current bus, serial port, mouseport, serial and mouseport, IBM and Apple versions, bundled or unbundled. Many employees were concerned that it would be the first Logitech product launched that was not based purely on a technological innovation/advantage. Finally, for many of the reasons outlined above, Logitech SA did not think they would want to launch the product in Europe.

While Logitech had been built on mouse technology, there were other directions that seemed to have great long-term potential. Scanner technology was similar to mouse technology and Logitech's hand-held Scanman had been a great success in terms of market share, margins, and product image. Driven by increased demand for desktop publishing and multimedia solutions, the scanner market was expected to grow 25 to 30 percent per year and opportunities existed to produce better grey-scale or even color scanners. Another opportunity related to scanners would be to develop a digital camera that captured black and white images and downloaded them to a computer. Finally, the interactive gloves developed for computer games might be improved upon to use with computers.

There were lots of neat products to develop, but Zappacosta knew he needed to act strategically. Personally, he was a strong champion of the new ergonomic mouse, but he recognized that it might be risky. The product was ready to launch and he could not put off the decision much longer. He wondered, if they did launch, how it should be done. Would this be an addition to the line or a replacement? How could Europe be convinced to carry the product? Should the cordless mouse be launched as part of the new ergonomic product line, or separately, or not at all? How should the products be priced? How would Microsoft react? Would pursuit of other opportunities be a better use of resources? Zappacosta thought the best place to start looking for answers and directions was in their mission statement and long-term vision. He wondered whether "humanizing the computer" by giving senses to the computer adequately reflected their current and potential operation.

13

Rosenbluth International Mexico

On May 11, 1994, Enrique Felgueres, Jr., General Manager of Rosenbluth International's Mexican operations, contemplated the multi-national company's future in Mexico. Rosenbluth International (RI) had recently finalized the acquisition of Servicios de Viaje Bancomer (Bancomer Travel Services) from Bancomer, S.A., a sub-entity of Valores Industriales, S.A., more commonly known as Grupo[1] VISA. Hal Rosenbluth, the President and CEO of RI, had departed that morning after a two day visit to familiarize himself with the new operation. Hal had given Enrique the task of transforming Bancomer Travel Services, a small Mexican owned agency, into a branch office of his company, which was known worldwide for its exceptional customer service and expertise in corporate travel management. Hal's instructions to Enrique had been very specific:

> While concentrating on corporate travel in Mexico, Rosenbluth International Mexico must be able to provide RI clients from around the world who are travelling in Mexico with the same level of service that is available to them from any other RI agency.

Enrique understood that the level of service which Hal had referred to was far superior to that which was available from the former agents of Bancomer Travel Services. He also knew that the success of RI's agencies was linked to the company's unique set of service philosophies and values. Enrique wondered if and how he could instill these philosophies and values in the former Bancomer agents so that they would be able to provide clients with a level of service that was consistent with that of RI agencies worldwide.

ROSENBLUTH INTERNATIONAL (RI) – THE CORPORATE TRAVEL INDUSTRY

Rosenbluth International was the third largest travel management company in the United States, with revenues in 1993 in excess of U.S.$1.6 billion and more than 3,100 associates located throughout the world. Started in 1892 as a steamship ticket office by Marcus

Rosenbluth, the company had always been owned and managed by the Rosenbluth family. Hal Rosenbluth, the current president and CEO, had played a pivotal role in the company's rapid growth from a one office agency in Philadelphia, Pennsylvania, to an international diversified services company with offices in thirty-six states, Canada, Europe, and East Asia.

RI had been extremely successful in taking advantage of the opportunity presented by the deregulation of the airline industry in 1978. Deregulation had caused extreme volatility in fares and schedules, making budgeting and tracking corporate travel information and expenses very difficult for large corporate travel customers. Hal, who quickly recognized the impact that this information explosion would have on corporate travel, developed a strategy for RI to become an expert in corporate travel management, based on providing value-added services to corporate clients.

Information technology (IT) played a key role in the success of this strategy. In a time when most travel agencies relied completely on an airline computerized reservation system (CRS) for their information infrastructure, RI developed proprietary systems allowing it to offer complete corporate travel reporting services on a real time basis. RI built information systems that pulled data from all of the available CRSs, thus liberating the agency from reliance on a single airline's system. Software was developed internally to ensure that reservations were made accurately and client and traveller needs were met consistently.

Hal Rosenbluth's vision of the future of corporate travel proved to be correct. In 1990, U.S. corporations spent over U.S.$115 billion on corporate travel, a good portion of which flowed through travel agents. The travel agency industry, which had become much more consolidated, was dominated by the mega-agencies that possessed the economies of scale to service large corporate clients effectively. Purchasing relationships also became much more important in dealing with suppliers, since the ability to direct share toward preferred suppliers led to discounts that could in turn be offered to large corporate clients.

RI captured a significant share of this market by pursuing a differentiation strategy based on service excellence, client driven IT, product development, and significant reinvestment in the company to support growth without sacrificing service levels. This investment took the form of systems development, employee training, and facilities expansion. RI grew from a company with U.S.$40 million in sales and eight offices in 1980 to a mega-agency with sales of over U.S.$1.5 billion and 450 offices in 41 countries in 1993.

Corporate culture and leadership also had a large impact on RI's success. Early on in his career, Hal was able to visualize the type of service level that he wanted the company to offer and began formulating values and instituting programs that could create the kind of culture which could support this type of service. RI's values incorporated ideas such as focus on its people, trust, sharing, and social responsibility. The programs included extensive training in service and quality principles, as well as technical courses and a multitude of communications vehicles to gauge employee happiness and gather suggestions for improving the company's operations. (*Live the Spirit* was created in a three-day conference.) Attended by all RI associates, the conference was designed to celebrate success and to introduce new programs. *Live the Spirit* electronic messages were sent out daily to all Rosenbluth offices. The messages gave up-to-the moment information on suppliers, clients, and company successes. Hal had also set up a voice mailbox accessible to all associates so that they could communicate directly with him. He was committed to addressing all problems that were raised, as soon as possible, and his message was directed to each associate,

"We celebrate what everyone has done . . . we will ask more of you than anyone else in the travel industry . . . we will give more also, but we will stretch you . . . you are our competitive advantage and you should demand from the company the absolute best."

RI's organizational structure also supported communication and delegated authority to those on the front lines. Set up as an inverted pyramid, each business unit was limited to three levels: Travel Services Associate, Account Leader, and General Manager. [Hal] firmly believed that, "If associates are given information, they cannot help but do something with it." RI's confidence in its service levels was demonstrated by the Rosenbluth Performance Promise, implemented in 1988, which was a service guarantee that committed the company to reimburse its commission to customers for any segment of their travel experience with which they had not been completely satisfied. As Hal explained:

Our pride in our people's ability, attitude, and performance record give[s] us the confidence to issue the Performance Promise to our corporate clients. If we should not fulfil a component of our Promise with every business trip, we will refund that portion of our commission to your corporation. In other words, we will not accept payment for basic services not rendered to your satisfaction or to ours.

Hal also believed very strongly that putting employee happiness first would automatically result in exceptional service to customers. His commitment to such ideals was so strong that in 1992 he co-authored a book, called *The Customer Comes Second and Secrets of Exceptional Service,* that outlined his philosophy and described how it had been so successful at Rosenbluth. Exhibit 13.1 provides a book review.

TRENDS IN CORPORATE TRAVEL

In the late 1980s, many corporations consolidated their corporate travel accounts because they could achieve greater control over expenditures by using a single travel agency, and they could also exploit their purchasing relationships with travel agencies, bargaining both for special services and for reduced prices. RI took advantage of this trend by offering customized information services driven by customer needs. The customized services that were offered by travel agencies resulted in increased switching costs, thereby reinforcing long-term, cooperative relationships with clients. Exhibit 13.2 shows business travel by U.S. residents for some of the years between 1985 and 1991.

The travel management industry was influenced by trends in business as a whole. Advances in telecommunications, ongoing technological innovation, trade liberalization, and rapid growth in emerging markets had combined to force corporations to compete globally. This trend resulted in a shift in corporate travel needs toward increasing international travel, which in turn put pressure on large travel agencies to have a global presence. Global presence was important in providing service for global corporate clients for two reasons, local travel support and global travel management. International business travellers demanded local travel support throughout the world. This service ranged from adjustments in travel plans to handling medical or legal emergency services. Global travel management required the ability to aggregate information worldwide via a global information system infrastructure. Firms had to be able to pinpoint high-volume routes and adjust policies to control travel

Exhibit 13.1   The Customer Comes Second

by Hal Rosenbluth with Diane McFerrin Peters

WHO SHOULD READ IT

Anyone in business.

THE BOOK

How does a travel agency grow to $1.5 billion in sales? Not by merely selling a lot of tickets and not, surprisingly, by putting customers first.

Philadelphia's Rosenbluth, Inc., is not just any agency. It manages travel plans for a few Fortune 50 firms, so an account worth $50 million a year is not uncommon.

Why do they stick with a company that puts them second? Because employees are, in the words of author Hal Rosenbluth, "valued, empowered, and motivated to care for their clients. When a company puts its people first, the results are spectacular." That, to Rosenbluth, is simply a matter of putting the horse before the cart.

But the firm also has a few other tricks up its sleeves. Valuing employees starts, for instance, the first day of work when recruits gather at headquarters for training designed to imbue them with the firm's culture and high standards.

Then, back in the workplace, the agency does all in its power (besides paying well) to keep workers happy. That includes free "familiarization trips" to the vacation spots Rosenbluth sends clients, focus sessions in which they can "voice frustration and make suggestions" directly to Rosenbluth himself, and anything else that makes work a more vibrant environment that fosters friendship and camaraderie.

No company, however, grows 7,500 percent in fifteen years on warm fuzzies. Rosenbluth trains relentlessly in any area that helps serve clients better. Training runs the gamut from relaxation techniques that reduce stress to professional development seminars to technical topics. Each of the firm's 2,600 employees participate – as do some of the firm's clients.

Other important chapters cover recruiting the best people, showing how service is an art as well as a process, creating a corporate culture that endures and thrives in any economic climate, and creating an atmosphere that encourages forward thinking and creativity.

OUR OPINION

Rosenbluth knows how to put it all together, which means this book is exceptionally instructive. Besides superb people skills, for instance, Rosenbluth's jaw-dropping technical systems help the firm achieve a rarity – regular increases in white-collar productivity. It's worth describing them, for they show how deep the concepts of quality and service are rooted here.

Rosenbluth's proprietary systems begin with READOUT, a computer program that tracks fares and timetables for all air carriers. Fares show up in ascending order to make it easy to see the lowest. The PRECISION system factors in a client company's travel policies as well as individual preferences. ULTRAVISION automates quality assurance; it double-checks reservation information and makes sure the airline's schedule hasn't changed and that the client gets the lowest fare.

VISION, finally, collects data from all of Rosenbluth's locations electronically. That helps it negotiate with suppliers, and it permits clients to download their travel information (like expenditures) directly into their own computers.

Sound intriguing? No matter what business you're in, Rosenbluth's methods will stimulate you. You'll rediscover that success is not whimsical – it's the result of service, sweat, and new ideas.

Exhibit 13.1 The Customer Comes Second *(continued)*

FYI

The author: Hal Rosenbluth is the chief executive of Rosenbluth, Inc.
Publisher: William Morrow, © 1992.
Area: Management.
Pages: 288.
Price/ISBN: $20.00; 0-688-11466-0.
To buy: Call Soundview, 1-800-521-1227 (outside the USA and Canada, 1-802-453-4062) or fax 1-802-453-5062 and charge to your credit card. Send mail orders, in U.S. funds drawn on a U.S. bank, to Soundview, 5 Main St., Bristol, VT 05443-1398, USA. Please include the book price plus $2.50 shipping and handling for the first book and $1 for each additional book; in Canada and Mexico, $3.50 for the first book and $1.50 for each additional book; all other countries, $8.00 for each book. Canadians: Add 7 percent GST.

Exhibit 13.2 Historical Volumes of U.S. Business Travel

Purpose of Travel	Trips					Person Trips[4]				
	1985	1988	1989	1990	1991	1985	1988	1989	1990	1991
Pleasure[5]	177.6	241.5	225.9	214.5	239.3	376.0	502.1	469.3	447.5	496.5
Business or convention	133.3	155.6	169.7	155.6	152.8	185.2	211.7	232.0	209.5	209.1

Characteristic	Unit		Business Trips			
		1980	1985	1990	1991	
Total trips	Millions	97.1	133.3	155.6	152.8	
Used a travel agent	Percent	21	28	21	16	
Also a vacation trip	Percent	10	13	17	26	

Year	Air[6]
1980	10,301
1981	23,405
1982	25,598
1983	27,519
1984	31,437
1985	33,343
1986	33,846
1987	37,555
1988	41,963
1989	45,320
1990	45,324

Source: U.S. Travel Data Center, Washington, DC, *National Travel Survey*
[4]A count of times each person (child or adult) goes on a trip.
[5]Excludes visits to see friends and relatives.
[6]U.S. certified carriers in domestic service.

costs and to negotiate for discounts with suppliers, in the same way that RI had been successfully operating in the United States. The travel manager of a European multi-national chemical manufacturer explained the importance of global travel services:

> It is important that we know we can reach everywhere we need to go, with comparable levels of service, and that we can assure our people are making the best use of available service providers. We want a global agency with buying power for negotiation and with technology to make certain we take best advantage of these deals.

THE ROSENBLUTH INTERNATIONAL ALLIANCE (RIA)

Hal recognized the potential for significant opportunities in global travel management. A global service network would offer new sources of business, increased purchasing power, and a larger business base to support capital expenditures. Successful handling of a company's travel needs could lead to additional business in servicing the client's overseas subsidiaries and affiliates. A global network could also dramatically increase the bargaining power of the firm when dealing with suppliers, and the capital outlays required for technology infrastructure could be shared by all participants, lowering the cost to any individual participant.

The company's initial response to the global challenge was to establish the Rosenbluth International Alliance (RIA) in 1987. By 1993, it encompassed thirty-four agencies in forty-one countries, had over U.S.$5 billion in sales, and essentially functioned as a global strategic business alliance. RI adopted the alliance structure after carefully considering several other options, such as establishing or acquiring operations in selected key markets worldwide or participating in a worldwide travel management consortium. And although several competitors, such as American Express and the Carlson Group, chose to establish new, wholly owned subsidiaries overseas, historically this ownership strategy was not feasible or desirable to RI. According to Carl Nurick, then VP, International Development:

> Global business requires omnipresence, and trying to establish owned entities throughout the world would have been prohibitively expensive for RI. As a privately held company, it had no desire to lose autonomy through either massive equity or debt financing. The capital requirements for such a strategy are proving burdensome even for giants such as the Carlson Group. Besides, the nature of the travel business varies tremendously from country to country. We thought that attempting to manage that diversity within a single firm would have been close to impossible. RIA is structured as an alliance of independent organizations bound by common interest. Each member has the freedom to adjust to local conditions as it sees fit and the areas of cooperation within the alliance are determined by mutual business needs. We call this approach *globalization*.

Maintaining RI's culture and service level was another concern for the company. David Miller, Chief Information Officer, also expressed an initial reluctance to support the contention that buy-outs could work on a global scale:

> You can't necessarily provide high quality service and entrepreneurial zeal by owning people. As soon as you own them they no longer feel excited. We would have cut our own throat. We recognize that we don't understand other cultures. Even if you have deep pockets you have to get the local market right or you will not succeed. We are very careful about how we do this.

RI had spurned the notion of participating in a worldwide travel consortium, such as Woodside or the Business Travel International. According to Carl:

> Previous cooperative approaches have not worked, because of either burdensome administrative structures or lack of adequate integration. The RIA has attempted to avoid these problems through an innovative organizational structure and an extensive technology infrastructure to ensure integration. Consortia have traditionally found it very difficult to get their members to standardize front office systems so that communication could be done efficiently.

In addition, independent foreign nationals had significant marketing advantages over owned subsidiaries when selling to foreign multi-national corporations. As Carl said,

> "It is difficult to sell a foreign company a U.S. system. The RIA has the advantage that it looks like a global American company to an American client and a global Austrian company to an Austrian client."

Therefore the global alliance could strengthen each player locally, rather than forcing it to serve as a satellite for a single national strategy. According to Hal,

> "In a few select markets we have elected to open our own offices, make an acquisition, or establish joint ventures. The beauty of the program is that it is entirely flexible, and with the global changes that are taking place day to day, that's essential."

Exhibit 13.3 presents the structure of the RIA in December 1993.

Organization

To ensure the success of global cooperation, the RIA was based on two principles, the selection of compatible players and cooperation among equal partners. Rosenbluth researched potential partners through local Chambers of Commerce, industry associations, subsidiaries of U.S. clients and suppliers. As part of its research in each country, RI interviewed clients, airlines, and car rental associates, along with the owners and managers of the travel agencies.

RI developed selection criteria based on finding partners that would fit with its corporate vision. According to Carl:

> Whatever we did, it had to be legal and ethical from U.S. business standards and ethics, and we both had to be profitable. You want to find partners who understand their market, have a good relationship with their customers, have a strong financial background, can communicate in English, have well-trained and respected leadership and staff, and in whom you can place your trust.

Trust was particularly important. "Of course all of the criteria went out the window if, after meeting with the owners, I did not feel I could trust them," said Carl. Potential members had to possess a compatible service orientation and culture. The RIA looked for service innovators and leaders in each national market. Variables such as image, reputation of the agency, training programs, treatment of associates, financial strength, and years in business

Exhibit 13.3

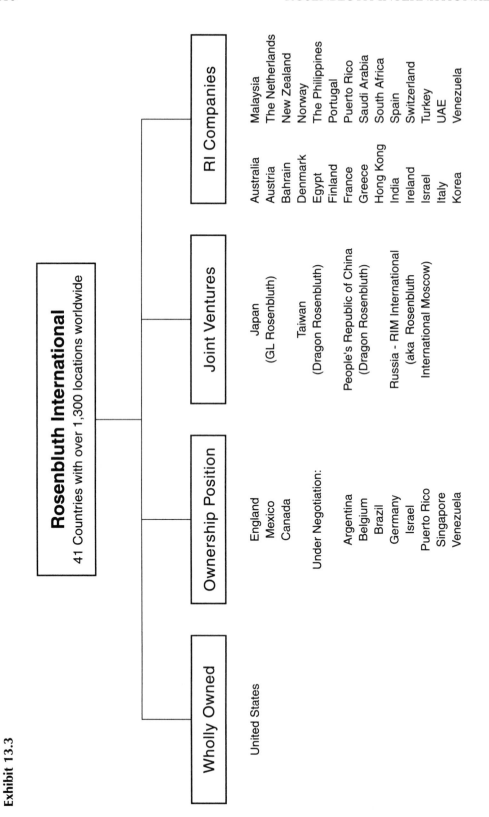

| Rosenbluth International |
| 41 Countries with over 1,300 locations worldwide |

Wholly Owned

United States

Ownership Position

England
Mexico
Canada

Under Negotiation:

Argentina
Belgium
Brazil
Germany
Israel
Puerto Rico
Singapore
Venezuela

Joint Ventures

Japan
(GL Rosenbluth)

Taiwan
(Dragon Rosenbluth)

People's Republic of China
(Dragon Rosenbluth)

Russia - RIM International
(aka Rosenbluth
International Moscow)

RI Companies

Australia
Austria
Bahrain
Denmark
Egypt
Finland
France
Greece
Hong Kong
India
Ireland
Israel
Italy
Korea
Malaysia
The Netherlands
New Zealand
Norway
The Philippines
Portugal
Puerto Rico
Saudi Arabia
South Africa
Spain
Switzerland
Turkey
UAE
Venezuela

Source: Rosenbluth International
July 1993

were all examined. Potential members also had to demonstrate a technological responsiveness that would support RI's view of the role of IT in global travel management.

Once a short list had been developed, each of the companies on the list was approached and was invited to investigate RI in the same manner. Finally, RI entered into an arrangement with one company from each country.

By all accounts, careful selection of partners paid off. According to David Whittaker, Managing Director of The Travel Company (the RIA partner in the U.K.) and Chairman of the British Guild of Business Travel Agents, "There is an uncanny synergy among RIA members. I've never seen this before. It must come from the selection process." Sometimes the partnerships were not successful. According to David Miller: "Our first company in the U.K. shirked its responsibilities. It talked a good game but did not walk the talk, so we had to get rid of it. Our next partner was AT Mays; it was good, but it was bought by Carlson. For our current partner in the U.K., we bought 10 percent of the company and secured a seat on the board."

The RIA was instituted according to several key business principles. RIA strategy and plans were established by the entire membership. Decision-making was by consensus whenever possible, with one vote per member regardless of size. The RIA budget was funded by members, with each contribution based upon the size of the member. The strategy of the RIA was to pursue aggressive cross selling of services and products on a multilateral basis. However, the local RIA member reserved the right to first refusal on a multi-national proposal sponsored by another member. According to Paul Howard, Director of Austravco, the RIA member in Australia:

> The RIA can serve international clients through independently-owned local organizations of similar types of business mix with a philosophy of providing excellent service and professionalism. We have a distinct advantage over global organizations such as Thomas Cook and American Express who become distracted by bureaucracy and corporate politics.

Management and liaison offices were set up in Philadelphia, London, and Singapore to oversee the RIA, and standing committees for Hotels, Industry Relations, Global Access, and Global Management Information Systems (MIS) were established, staffed by participants. The key to providing seamless global service to RIA customers was the technology infrastructure already put in place by RI, called the Global Distribution Network (GDN). The backbone of the network was the APOLLO CRS offered by Covia, to which the RIA added an expanded front end that provided for e-mail, an RIA member reference system, and a proprietary international hotel system. The GDN allowed RIA members to access any RIA client's itinerary and profile information in an on-line reference system, message each other instantaneously, and take advantage of hotel rates negotiated by all the partners in their respective countries, anywhere in the world. The GDN made the RIA the first travel management organization to have global access to traveller information. According to Hal, "The key to the Alliance is our ability to globally collect travel information for our multi-national clients while delivering the best service on a local basis."

Other services offered by the RIA included global travel management reporting and local assistance worldwide in English via access to the local RIA agency. Global travel management reporting allowed global clients to harness their total volumes in negotiating better rates and fares with travel suppliers. As well, it allowed global clients to ensure that travellers adhered to established travel policies and that any negotiated agreements were being followed.

In providing this service, the RIA encountered the problem that the APOLLO system was not available as a truly global MIS infrastructure. APOLLO was not the primary CRS of many RIA members, since markets tended to be dominated by national CRS systems, typically run by the state-owned airline. For example, in Canada, the GEMINI reservation system was co-owned by Air Canada and Canadian Airlines and listed flights in Canada exclusively on that system.

Information recorded on one CRS was not available on another CRS, a major problem that was compounded in the international environment because of the many different national systems. In these cases the RIA member was compelled to use the closed national system to gain access to necessary local travel providers for making reservations; the APOLLO system was used only for communication among RIA members and for access to RIA applications. The variety in CRSs around the world was matched in the travel agents' back offices, as each market had its own mechanism for processing, paying for, and accounting for tickets. These islands of technology greatly complicated the global coordination needed in the RIA. However, RI still viewed its ability to integrate the RIA as much as possible as a significant advantage. As Hal said, "Ultimately, global infrastructure will be a commodity, but by then our global advantage should be entrenched."

David Miller summarized the progress of the RIA as follows:

> What surprised a lot of people is that even though we reacted out of necessity, the model we adopted minimized our risk. We also need to tie it a lot tighter. Relationships seem to mean a great deal in other countries. We play to these relationships both formally and informally. We recognized that by concentrating on developing mutually beneficial relationships, we would benefit in the long run. The stereotypical American being superficially more friendly would not have worked. The next step is to move further. The idea is to move from this mutually beneficial situation into a more tightly coupled relationship using other mechanisms, such as financing.

Global Expansion

Notwithstanding the success of the RIA in helping it to develop a worldwide network and gain international expertise, by 1994, RI revealed its global expansion plans based on securing ownership positions in strategic markets worldwide. RI intended to serve multinational companies in a superior fashion by providing uniform service standards: a single, worldwide electronic computer reservation and ticket distribution system; globally negotiated discounts; fully integrated global MIS systems; consistent global corporate branding; centralized point-of-decision-making for pricing and supplier negotiations; and, greatly fortified global strength. The organization would operate only under the name Rosenbluth International and the RIA name was eliminated. Those companies that did not share the U.S. company's vision for the future did not become part of the new structure.

In addition to the Bancomer Travel Services acquisition in Mexico, RI owned and operated offices in Canada, Russia, Japan, Singapore, and Israel. The company had announced intentions to expand its equity interest in travel firms in the United Kingdom, Australia, Germany, Belgium, the Netherlands, and South Africa. Additional acquisitions were being prioritized based on the travel demands of the company's clients.

FELGUERES TRAVEL

In 1987, Carl Nurick was searching for a Mexican travel agency to become a member of the RIA. Through the International Association of Travel Agencies (IATA), as well as the Mexican Chamber of Commerce, he located several candidates. The largest agencies operating in Mexico were owned by Rosenbluth's U.S. competitors, American Express and Carlson-Avali, with annual sales in Mexico of approximately U.S.$120 million and U.S.$80 million, respectively. Carl turned to the three or four next largest, Mexican-owned, agencies and interviewed each. Felgueres Travel in Mexico City was one of the firms that he interviewed.

Felgueres Travel, the third largest travel agency in Mexico, was founded in 1965 by Enrique Felgueres, Sr. and Ricardo Felgueres, and had 1992 sales in excess of U.S.$28 million. The company which focused primarily on specialized leisure travel, had carved itself a strong niche in the Mexican travel market by catering to the Mexican elite. Its success depended on high quality, customized travel services, based on long-term personal relationships. Felgueres Travel was not strong in corporate travel, but was relatively advanced in its use of technology to serve its clients. Enrique Felgueres, Sr. maintained a strong leadership role in the company, and his two sons, Enrique, Jr. and Gerardo, were actively involved in the daily operations of the business.

Carl liked the feel of Felgueres Travel and was impressed by the firm's solid financial position. For these and several other reasons, in 1988, he invited Felgueres Travel to join the RIA. The RIA appeared to represent a no-lose proposition for Felgueres Travel. The minor service fees that were required of all members of the RIA represented a small cost when compared to the increased international business and expanded client base the company stood to gain as a result of its membership in the alliance.

By 1992, four years after joining the RIA, Enrique Jr. began to question the benefits of his father's company's participation in the alliance. Although Felgueres Travel had referred business to Rosenbluth in the U.S. and had used the RIA to refer group travel proposals to other alliance members, the RIA had not brought much business to the company. According to Enrique, Jr.,

"The RIA only brought two new accounts to Felgueres . . . The only good thing they brought was the APOLLO system in 1991. We did not have to pay for APOLLO or even the supporting computers or telephone lines; we only had to pay for the connections.

NORTH AMERICAN FREE TRADE AGREEMENT (NAFTA)

It was around this same time that NAFTA became a very realistic possibility. Mexico was the United States' third-largest trading partner behind Canada and Japan. Bilateral trade between the two countries had grown from U.S.$21 billion in 1937 to U.S.$62 billion in 1991. About 70 percent of Mexico's trade was with the United States. Foreign direct investment into Mexico was also growing, and reached a high of U.S.$24 billion in September of 1992, two thirds of which was in the manufacturing sector. As the Mexican economy grew and developed, the volume of Mexican corporate travel both inside and outside Mexico was expected to increase dramatically. Exhibit 13.4 presents data on past volumes of travel between the United States and Mexico, 1985–1992, and Exhibit 13.5 presents forecasts to 2004.

Exhibit 13.4 U.S. Travel to Mexico and Other Countries

(travellers in thousands, expenditures in millions of U.S. dollars)								
Total travellers	1985	1986	1987	1988	1989	1990	1991	1992
Mexico	10,461	11,512	13,074	13,463	14,163	16,380	15,417	17,130
Total overseas	12,696	12,038	13,616	14,443	14,791	15,990	14,521	15,840
Expenditures abroad								
Mexico	2,548	2,568	3,058	3,622	4,276	4,879	5,149	5,300
Total overseas	19,504	20,311	23,313	25,260	25,746	28,929	28,104	35,400

Source: U.S. Travel Data Center, Washington, D.C., *National Travel Survey*

Exhibit 13.5 Aviation Forecasts

	FAA Aviation Activity Forecasts Fiscal 1993–2004							
	Forecast			Percent Average Annual Growth				
Aviation Activity	1993	1994	2004	85–92	91–92	92–93	93–94	92–04
Air Carrier								
Enplanements (millions)								
Domestic	436.7	458.6	646.7	2.9	3.8	1.8	5.0	3.5
Latin America	15.3	16.5	30.5	8.1	(7.7)	12.8	7.8	7.0
RPMs[7] (billions)								
Domestic	355.5	375.1	548.4	3.9	3.8	2.6	5.5	3.9
Latin America	19.5	21.1	39.9	8.4	(6.5)	13.9	8.2	7.3

	ICAO Scheduled Passenger Traffic Forecast for 1993–1995							
	(Passenger-kilometers performed)							
	Actual	Estimated				Forecast		
Region of Airline	1991	1992	Growth	1993	Growth	1994	Growth	1995	Growth
Registration	(billions)	(billions)	(%)	(billions)	(%)	(billions)	(%)	(billions)	(%)
Latin America/ Caribbean	87.5	90.7	3.6	96.0	5.9	102.8	7.1	110.9	7.9

[7]RPMs = Revenue Passenger Miles.

Prior to 1988, Mexican business was highly regulated. Many industries such as oil and gas were government run. Upon assuming office on December 1, 1988, President Carlos Salinas de Gortari introduced a number of reforms that led to significant deregulation and a reduction in import tariffs. The government relinquished much of its control over the banks, as well as the trucking industry, electricity, mining, and tourism. However, the private sector continued to be dominated by a tight oligarchy where connections often mattered more than merit. Wealth was concentrated, and a significant disparity existed between rich and poor. Wages remained very low for workers, but per capita GDP was growing at a healthy rate (see Exhibit 13.6).

With the advent of NAFTA in January of 1993, Mexico became a more strategic destination for U.S. and Canadian businesses. Although the RIA was in place, the alliance structure was not entrenched to the extent that Felgueres Travel could offer the same service levels that Rosenbluth's corporate clients had grown to expect north of the border. Felgueres did not have the same information system capability as RIA nor were its travel associates focused

Exhibit 13.6 Mexico – Nominal GDP Per Person, 1981–1991

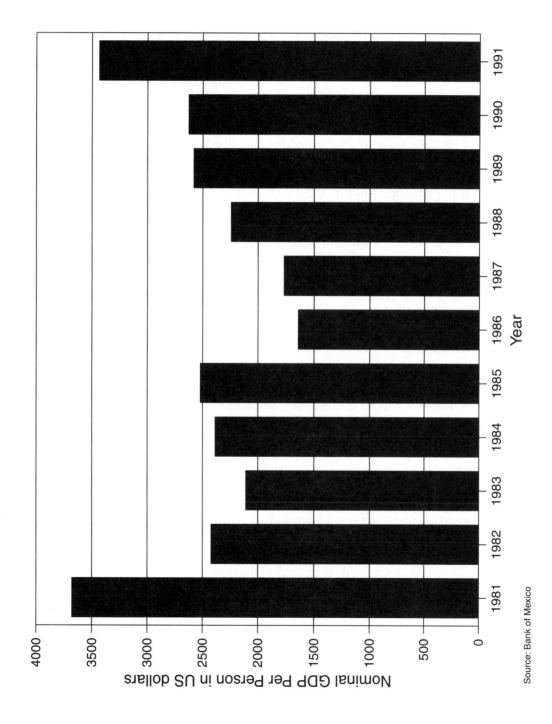

Source: Bank of Mexico

on extremely high quality customer service. Because of its focus on leisure travel, Felgueres also lacked the extensive base of corporate accounts that were a critical element of the success of all other members of the RIA.

RI in the U.S. recognized the changes that were taking place in the Mexican business environment and in 1992 expressed a desire to expand its presence in Mexico. In November of 1992, Carl Nurick approached Enrique, Jr. with a proposal to open a Rosenbluth International subsidiary in Mexico that would be associated with Felgueres Travel, but would be focused exclusively on corporate travel. Enrique, Jr. recognized the potential for the success of such a venture, and accepted the offer to become General Manager of Rosenbluth International Mexico. He hired his brother Gerardo to assist in setting up the operation with the intention that Gerardo would eventually become an account leader. Initially, it was RI's intention that Enrique, Jr. and Gerardo would open a small RI office that would be operated by the two brothers and an assistant. It was expected that the company would generate sales of U.S.$4 million per year.

RI Mexico's strategy was to build a corporate travel management company to serve the needs of Mexican corporations and the subsidiaries of RI's American clients. By concentrating on corporate travel only, RI would avoid having to compete directly with Felgueres Travel but could also benefit from the affiliation with an established Mexican company. The goal was to provide the same technology and standards of customer service to its new Mexican clients as it did to its American ones. It would be considered a branch office of RI and receive exactly the same support in terms of training, information systems, and supplier relations as any other Rosenbluth office. According to Enrique Felgueres, Jr., General Manager, RI Mexico:

> We will introduce products and services that will allow us to provide our clients with service levels never before seen in Mexico. These products will enable our clients to manage their travel budgets more efficiently. In this way, RI Mexico will become the leader in the corporate travel industry in Mexico. We want to be the best. We now have the tools.

Bancomer Travel Services

RI's initial growth strategy for its Mexico operation was to target the Mexican subsidiaries of its U.S. clients. However, in December of 1993, during a chance encounter with an American Airlines marketing representative, Enrique, Jr. learned that Bancomer Financial Services (Bancomer) was selling its travel services division: Bancomer Travel Services. Bancomer was Mexico's largest and strongest financial services organization. When the Mexican banks were privatized in 1992, Grupo VISA, one of Mexico's largest private companies, purchased Bancomer, and began spinning off its non-financial divisions. Grupo VISA had been in business for more than 100 years and employed over 90,000 Mexican and foreign nationals, was a diversified conglomerate that owned Mexico's largest brewery, Cerveceria Cuauhtemoc Moctezuma, and also held interests in the processed foods, packaging, soft drink bottling, hotel, and auto parts industries. The company was controlled by the Garza family. Its consolidated revenues and market capitalization exceeded U.S.$6 billion and U.S.$10 billion, respectively. Mark Harris, Director, New Business Development, RI, commented on the acquisition,

"This acquisition demonstrates RI's ongoing commitment to providing seamless travel management services for our clients within NAFTA and throughout the Americas. Our presence in Mexico City and Monterrey is a highly strategic move which will provide a host of long-term benefits for all of our clients doing business in and with Mexico."

Bancomer Travel Services handled a portion of Bancomer's corporate travel arrangements and had a small client base of other Mexican businesses, including Mercedes Benz Mexico. It had total sales of approximately U.S.$14 million and net profits of U.S.$280,000 in 1992. Bancomer also used dozens of agencies besides its own. In addition to selling the travel services division, Bancomer planned to consolidate its corporate travel account and award all of its travel management business to a single agency. In 1993, Bancomer spent approximately N$²32 million (U.S.$9.7 million) on corporate travel. This figure included expenditures on airline tickets for 32,959 domestic and 3,825 international trips. Enrique, Jr. realized that the opportunity also existed to obtain the corporate travel business for all Grupo VISA companies in Mexico. This business represented approximately U.S.$45 million of annual travel revenues.

When Enrique Jr. first learned of the opportunity to buy Bancomer Travel Services, Bancomer Financial was ready to close a deal with Thomas Cook, one of RI's largest competitors. He was forced to act quickly. He convinced Bancomer to entertain a bid for the travel division and then immediately called Hal Rosenbluth to ask for RI's support. The company quickly prepared a package outlining the services it could offer to Bancomer, including a wide range of travel management reports, customized information services, and a guarantee of exceptional service worldwide. The bid also emphasized RI's long-standing affiliation with Felgueres Travel. As part of the process, RI invited Bancomer executives to Philadelphia to tour the company's global headquarters. The level of service, IT support, and professionalism of RI was unparalleled by anything in the Mexican travel business, and significantly impressed the Bancomer group. Although Bancomer had been on the verge of selling its travel division to Thomas Cook, RI's bid succeeded in swaying its decision and the travel division was sold to RI.

Not only did RI receive Bancomer Travel Services' assets and its 33 employees in the sale, but also a five-year contract to handle all of Bancomer's corporate travel.

THE CHALLENGES

One of the first decisions RI had faced was how to physically organize its new operation. At the time of the sale, Bancomer Travel Services operated three offices in Monterrey, one in the Polanco district in Mexico City, another at the Bancomer Financial headquarters in Mexico City, and two small in-plant offices at Mercedes Benz Mexico and at the VISA-owned brewery in Monterrey.

A second decision with which the Felgueres brothers had been confronted was how to communicate the sale to the former Bancomer Travel Services employees. Although the sale of the company was finalized in February of 1994, the acquisition was not made public until April 26, 1994. Prior to that date the Bancomer employees had been unaware of RI's bid, and had expected that Thomas Cook would acquire the business.

A third issue that still plagued the Felgueres brothers was how to educate their new employees about the RI service philosophies and values and how to train their employees to provide clients with the level of service consistent with RI agencies worldwide. Rosenbluth International Mexico's goal was to be able to live up to the company's Performance Promise by June 26, 1994. Enrique, Jr. and Gerardo had less than two months to transform Bancomer Travel Services into RI Mexico. The Performance Promise appears in Exhibit 13.7.

Providing the Technology

The Felgueres brothers' key challenge lay in overcoming major cultural, technological, and service/product differences between the Mexican travel industry and the U.S. travel industry. Mexican travel agencies were primarily "Mom and Pop" operations that handled both corporate and leisure travel arrangements. The idea of a corporate travel "management" business simply did not exist in Mexico. Travel agents fulfilled both sales[3] and reservation roles. In contrast, RI's Travel Services Associates acted solely as dedicated reservation agents. Mexican customers were accustomed to always dealing with the same person for all of their needs. As Gerardo explained:

> We plan to build a modern reservation center to become our main headquarters in Mexico City. All calls will be routed and reservations will be queued via APOLLO to the appropriate office for ticketing. We plan to have a group of people designated to deal with particular clients, so that the clients will become comfortable dealing with more than one familiar voice.

This system would be identical to RI Reservations Centers in the United States, where the agents were sometimes located hundreds of miles away from the ticketing office.

Because modern technology and access to a CRS were non-existent in most Mexican travel agencies, employees used the telephone to inquire about flight schedules or to make flight or hotel reservations. However, the unreliability of the telephone system further exacerbated the process. It was uncommon for a business traveller to complete travel

Exhibit 13.7 Rosenbluth International's Philosophy and Values

PEOPLE FOCUS	We develop and enrich our associates by providing the proper resources and information to guide their development and achieve their goals.
CLIENT FOCUS	Our clients are our associates' first priority. We will understand their needs and dedicate ourselves to satisfying them.
TRUST	We value each others' integrity, creativity, ability, judgment, and opinions.
TEAMWORK	We are interdependent and will continue to cooperate for the good of the "team." We will work together so the total effect is greater than the sum of the individual efforts.
GROWTH	Our expansion is client driven. As we grow so does our company. The information provided to our clients as well as our dedication to service will ensure the continued growth of our client base.
EXCELLENCE	We strive to exceed our clients' expectations and continue to be the very best in the interest of our company and ourselves.
SHARING	We share responsibilities for our company's success. Therefore, we believe in sharing information, recognition, and financial rewards.
SOCIAL RESPONSIBILITY	We demonstrate the highest ethical standards. We have an aggressive affirmative action and equal opportunity commitment. We strongly support and endorse our social responsibilities.

arrangements with one telephone call to an agent. Organizing travel plans was an activity that often took several days to complete. Because Felgueres Travel was one of the few travel agencies to have access to the APOLLO CRS, it was one of the most technologically sophisticated travel agencies in Mexico. The former Bancomer Travel Services had used a different CRS called WORLDSPAN that was not compatible with APOLLO, operated much differently from APOLLO, and was less sophisticated than APOLLO. In order to be able to interact with other RI agencies, RI Mexico would have to adopt the APOLLO system. From a systems perspective the conversion from WORLDSPAN to APOLLO would be painless. In some cases interface software would need to be developed in order, for example, to link Mexican accounting software to APOLLO, but the software development and implementation would not be difficult. The more difficult, and by far the more important, task would be to train the former Bancomer Travel Services employees how to perform their jobs using APOLLO. The Felgueres brothers wondered how they would train the employees and how they could best manage the changeover. It was clear that the employees would be forced to learn quickly because the APOLLO system would be up and running a few weeks after the new management took over the travel agency.

Services such as travel management reporting were not available from Mexican travel agencies. Mexican corporate clients had very low expectations of service from travel agencies, considering them simply ticket delivery services. If the agency failed to deliver services as required, Mexican companies would take their business elsewhere. Even RI's traditional competitors such as American Express had decided not to offer its Mexican clients the same services that were available to its U.S. clients. Although the corporate travel management reports had been a great selling point in winning the five-year contract to handle Bancomer's corporate travel account, Enrique, Jr. and Gerardo wondered how many other Mexican companies would perceive this service as valuable. This problem was further complicated by the fact that, because most Mexican corporations did not pay attention to their travel costs, responsibility for managing these costs often was delegated to the administrative assistants or secretaries, who made travel arrangements. Communicating the value of some of RI's specialized services to these people could be difficult, both because of their relatively low level of education and their lack of power to make decisions such as switching travel agencies. Enrique, Jr. and Gerardo also realized that choice of a travel agency was often made based on personal connections.

Support for the introduction of these services would be provided by RI in the U.S. Plans were made for the office in San Diego to handle international reservations and corporate reporting. Spanish-speaking agents would be dedicated to handle calls from Mexico via a toll-free number. Because of the difficulty in transmitting the information electronically from RI's data-processing headquarters in Philadelphia to Rosenbluth International Mexico's office in Mexico City, the corporate management reports for Mexican clients would be printed in San Diego and mailed monthly to Mexico City.

Dealing with the Mexican Business Traveller

In general, the Mexican business traveller's expectations were different than those of an American. Unfamiliar with being differentiated as a "business traveller," a Mexican business person had less sophisticated expectations of the types of service that a travel agency should provide to its corporate clients. Services such as emergency support phone numbers, travel reporting, and even clear-cut travel policies were unusual. As Enrique Jr. and Gerardo explained:

> The U.S. business traveller is much more "picky" than the Mexican business traveller. The U.S. business traveller will generally specify the airline, hotel, and car agency that he or she wishes to use. The U.S. traveller is also concerned about travel miles and non-smoking facilities. The Mexican business traveller thinks that anything is possible, but is accustomed to receiving poor service, and therefore has very low expectations.

Mexicans rarely complained about poor service and were often unaware of amenities such as non-smoking facilities or vegetarian or low salt meals, although Gerardo believed that they would begin to request them as they become more knowledgeable about differences in service levels.

Although there was little information that characterized the habits of the Mexican business traveller, the Felgueres brothers agreed that Mexican business travellers could be divided into two groups: traditional and "new."

The traditional Mexican business traveller was not concerned about cost, but instead insisted on comfort and image. Since the hotel was often used as a criterion for measuring the success and stability of the company, staying at the "wrong" hotel could have a negative impact on business relations. As Gerardo explained:

> The traditional Mexican business traveller is accustomed to staying in five-star hotels and paying upwards of U.S.$300 per night for a hotel room. They are generally not concerned about cost, and they do not like to wait. They are used to good quality and good service. Mexicans with money have had money for years, and they are used to the best but they recognize that such service is only available for a price. They often prefer European air carriers, which they perceive to be more prestigious.

The "new" Mexican business traveller was far more conscious of price, valued comfort and convenience, and was much less concerned about image. Where the traditional traveller would travel the extra distance to stay in a particular hotel, the new traveller looked for a comfortable hotel that was centrally located and offered easy access to clients and the airport. This traveller often represented a newer Mexican company or the subsidiary of a U.S. or European company, both of which recognized the potential savings that were possible through the management of travel costs.

Providing RI Service

Providing the RI guarantee of service was a big challenge for the fledgling Mexican agency. According to Gerardo:

> Felgueres Travel has distinctive service, but probably not even 10 percent of the level of service provided by RI. Mexican airlines are also a problem. They are often oversold and then a reservation will simply get cancelled. They always blame the travel agency. I have even seen a situation where the airline forged a fax that I had supposedly sent to cancel a client's reservation. We will have to try to build a more cooperative relationship. We need to devise a way to negotiate for better service.

RI's people-focused, team-based culture was completely atypical of the Mexican business environment. However, Enrique, Jr. believed in it strongly,

"I am not God. I do make mistakes. I need my people to help me to act in the best interests of the company. Forget about the boss-staff relationship – every position is equally important. We all must do our jobs well for everything to work."

This philosophy was a shock for the former Bancomer employees. They had never even met their former managers from Bancomer Financial and now they would be required to work next to their new managers. On April 27, Enrique, Jr. held a cocktail party at the Polanco office to introduce RI to each of the Bancomer employees, and to present everyone with a new contract from RI. As Guillermo Cordoba, Manager of the Bancomer Headquarters explained,

"The base salary offered was above average, vacation allowance was fourteen days more than the industry average, and the bonus was much higher than in the past. All of the seniority was preserved as well as the benefits we had as Bancomer employees. Everyone signed immediately."

On May 9, 1994, employees (now called associates) were further exposed to the RI approach with the visit of Hal, who made a point of introducing himself to everyone in the company. According to Guillermo Cordoba,

"At first we were suspicious of what we had heard about the Rosenbluth methods. But it is unheard of in Mexico to actually meet the Chief Executive Officer of your company. And when Mr. Rosenbluth actually made his own cup of coffee, we could not believe it. It was then that we started to buy into RI."

Training remained a critical issue. According to Enrique, Jr.,

Travel agents in Mexico do not appreciate their jobs as much as agents in the rest of North America. U.S. and Canadian agents must perform well because it is very competitive. Mexicans take everything for granted. They don't understand the fact that we depend on clients for our jobs. We have to make them understand that their priority is serving the clients' needs. My first job is to get to know everyone. The people feel abandoned, as they have had no support in the past. But because they are used to working without support they are good people who can perform independently. We also plan to hire someone who will be sent to the United States to learn to train people. This person will return to be our full-time trainer.

Any training would have to be sensitive to the cultural differences between the United States and Mexico. "We have to put a Mexican twist on it," said Enrique, Jr. Things like High Tea and games won't go over very well in Mexico. We plan to create a mini-Mexican version of RI's *Live the Spirit* orientation program. This will be a two-hour seminar to simulate the ideals and philosophies of Rosenbluth." Technical training on APOLLO and other RI systems was also necessary. Since WORLDSPAN and APOLLO were the two CRSs that had the least in common, the new associates were unfamiliar with how to use APOLLO. Therefore RI trainers from Philadelphia were scheduled to come and conduct week-long seminars in APOLLO for all associates. On June 6, 1994, all offices were scheduled to cut over to the new system permanently.

The next three months would be critical to the success of RI Mexico. Enrique, Jr. knew what a challenge it was going to be to attain the requisite service levels. The concept of service, the expectations of the customer, and the level of technological familiarity were all vastly different in Mexico than in the United States. But he was very excited about the possibilities, and was confident that RI Mexico would be running smoothly by the end of June.

> "We have a huge opportunity to do great things in Mexico. Then we can jump to South America. I truly believe in every aspect of RI. I couldn't admire a company more. I think I am very lucky. I was the only guy in Mexico who got a chance to work with these people."

NOTES

1. A Grupo is a family of companies that are controlled by a common parent. Grupo VISA was the fiftieth-largest publicly traded company in Mexico.
2. N$ = New Peso. To help simplify foreign exchange transactions the Mexican government introduced a new peso on January 1, 1993. The new peso was worth 1,000 of the old pesos.
3. In the case of travel agents, the sales role involves arranging for payment, printing and delivering the client's tickets, as well as all other financial and administrative activities associated with these processes.

14

Cast North America
Managing a Telecommunications Infrastructure

This case was prepared by Kathleen Ryan, under the supervision of Professor Sid L. Huff of the Western Business School. Copyright © 1991, The University of Western Ontario.

This material is not covered under authorization from CanCopy or any reproduction rights organization. Any form of reproduction, storage or transmittal of this material is prohibited without written permission from Western Business School, The University of Western Ontario, London, Canada N6A, 3K7. Reprinted with permission, Western Business School.

"Communications have become the backbone of our system. There is a great deal of interaction between our sales personnel in North America and Europe coordinating the movement of containers, handling cargo bookings, and confirmations. Using electronic data interchange facilities between Antwerp and Montreal, we exchange bills of lading and container status nightly. We both have online access to each other's computers to produce up-to-the-minute reports," explained Dade Dudgeon, Manager of Information Systems at CAST North America. Mr. Dudgeon was speaking with a representative from Teleglobe Canada, Canada's overseas telecommunications carrier, about CAST's private international telecommunications network which supported the CAST container shipping system. The CAST network had evolved significantly over the past few years. In June 1990, it included a satellite link between the firm's central offices in Montreal, Canada, and Antwerp, Belgium, and an undersea cable link between the Montreal and Hamilton, Bermuda offices. The Montreal and Antwerp hubs served CAST's eleven North American and twenty European district offices. Mr. Dudgeon viewed the network as a strategic resource which gave CAST a competitive advantage in the global container shipping industry. He knew that the network was operating near its capacity, though, and would need to be expanded soon to ensure that it kept pace with CAST's growing business. Decisions had to be made concerning upgrading the existing Montreal/Antwerp satellite and Montreal/Bermuda cable links, adding an Antwerp/Bermuda link and expanding the intra-North American and European networks.

THE CAST GROUP OF COMPANIES

The CAST Group of Companies was acknowledged as a leader and innovator in the transport of containerized, conventional, and bulk cargoes, and operated the world's largest fleet of container/bulk carrier ("Conbulker") vessels on a scheduled trade route between Montreal and Antwerp. The group included CAST North America, headquartered in Montreal; CAST

Europe, headquartered in Antwerp; and a Bermuda corporate office. The Montreal headquarters coordinated all North American operations in Canada and the United States, and container movement worldwide. The Antwerp headquarters coordinated European operations and the CAST Short Sea Relay Service, which provided a secondary water link in the shipment of CAST containers between Belgium and the U.K., northern Europe and Scandinavia. The Bermuda corporate office oversaw CAST's worldwide shipping operations. Other CAST operations included Pan Bulk Shipping Ltd., which provided service to shippers of bulk cargo, and St. Lawrence Stevedoring, which provided bulk cargo terminal services in Montreal and Quebec.

CAST operated in an industry strapped by an overtonnage of container capacity, and faced heavy competition from other world shipping companies operating on the North Atlantic trade route: Hapag-Lloyd, Atlantic Container Lines, Orient Overseas Container Line (OOCL), and Canada Maritime, a joint company of Canadian Pacific in Canada and CMB SA in Belgium. Despite the competition, CAST provided the highest frequency of North Atlantic sailings. To handle its increasing traffic, CAST was constructing one of the world's most advanced container port facilities in Zeebrugge, Belgium, due for completion in the early 1990s. Mr. Dudgeon explained that CAST was known as "the rebel in the industry"; CAST "set the trend" because of innovative initiatives pursued by the company. Their strategy had proven successful, and had allowed CAST to retain 40 percent market share of traffic passing through the Port of Montreal, and 10 percent market share of all North Atlantic container traffic.[1]

THE CONTAINERIZATION INDUSTRY AND CAST HISTORY

The evolution of the container shipping industry began in the 1950s with the rapid increase in international demand for dry bulk commodities, and the introduction of bulk carrier vessels. Bulk carriers were created to transport large volume commodities efficiently, and took over more and more deep-sea transport of dry bulk commodities from old multi-deck freighters. Traditional bulk carrier transportation, however, entailed a high degree of manual handling during the entire journey over land and sea, with a resulting high labor component of total shipping costs. Labor costs were on the rise in the 1950s and 1960s, pushing overall operating costs up sharply. Industry developments to reduce shipping costs focused on increasing cargo space utilization and reducing cargo loading/unloading times, and led to the introduction of an efficient land and sea worldwide general cargo intermodal transportation system – containerization.

Containers made it possible to ship a combination of various pieces of general cargo in a large standardized "parcel" which could be handled efficiently by mechanical means. The twenty-foot container, known as one teu (twenty-foot equivalent units), became the universally accepted standard size and dominated the cargo market. The forty-foot container, known as one feu (forty-foot equivalent units, or two teus), also was widely used on large container ships from the early 1980s onward. The containers could be efficiently handled by cranes and other such equipment, decreasing loading and discharging time, handling costs, and port turnaround time. Many port cities, seeking a share of world container traffic, built specialized container handling terminals to attract shipping traffic to their ports.

Different types of container-carrying vessels emerged, including fully cellular container ships, container/bulk vessels and semi-container ships. The container/bulk vessel ("Conbulker"), which CAST operated, combined the operation of containerized cargo with the shipping of bulk commodities, offering a more flexible approach on routes where neither fully containerized nor dedicated dry bulk carrier vessels were wholly appropriate.

CAST began operations in Canada in 1969 with a strategy of providing efficient and economical transportation of goods between Canada, the United States, and Europe. Service centered around a transatlantic intermodal container transportation system known as The Blue Box System. "Intermodal" meant that containers could be easily transferred from trucks or railcars to ships and back again. The Blue Box System allowed CAST to provide customers with door-to-door transportation of a container over land and sea. The Blue Box System was the first intermodal container service operating on the North Atlantic.

CAST's service strategy was to retain total control of the shipment of a container along the transport chain, to offer customers a comprehensive door-to-door "one-stop shopping" service. CAST invested heavily in intermodal facilities. It owned and operated trucking operations on both sides of the Atlantic, fully equipped ocean terminals in Canada, Belgium, and the United Kingdom which incorporated the latest container management and handling technology, and a fleet of new, fuel-efficient conbulker vessels. CAST oversaw the movement of containers from the customer to the final destination, including the transfer of containers into the hands of non-CAST owned rail transport where necessary. Its strategy of maintaining end-to-end control of container shipment allowed CAST to differentiate itself from the competition and to control overall operating transport costs. Customers were charged on a simple, door-to-door flat rate per container box basis, rather than the competition's more complex commodity-oriented pricing.

CAST'S USE OF INFORMATION TECHNOLOGY – BACKGROUND

CAST's world-wide operations were linked by advanced telecommunications, data processing, and EDI[2] technology. The Blue Box system was supported by an information system designed to track, and allow rapid tracing of, the location of a specific container among the 20,000 containers in service at any given time. The system also provided vital shipping and billing details. The information system ran on CAST's central computers in Montreal and in Antwerp. It was divided into a transportation logistics sub-system which had been developed in Canada and duplicated in Europe, and an accounting sub-system developed in Europe and duplicated in Canada. The information system also incorporated an internal messaging facility (electronic mail) used to oversee and control world-wide operations. Eighty percent of the employees at CAST's North American, European, and Bermuda locations accessed the information system.

The information system began with the installation of a Univac 9030 central computer and an online booking and container tracking system in Montreal in 1979. Customer bookings made at the branch offices were previously telexed to the Montreal head office. There, along with container status and bills of lading information, they were entered into a batch file for nightly transmittal to a Montreal service bureau. The service bureau produced reports which were manually distributed to CAST's North American operations. Service did not prove reliable, however, and the Univac computer was installed. A similar set-up was installed in Antwerp one year later. Bills of lading information exchanged between Montreal and Antwerp was keyed onto tape and airfreighted.

In 1980 and 1981, data entry terminals and dedicated analog 9600 bps data lines and 75 baud telex lines were installed at the North American and European branches to allow branch personnel online access to the information system.[3] The lines ran between the North American branch offices and the Montreal central computer, and between the European branch offices and the Antwerp central computer. The lines were leased from Unitel (formerly CNCP Telecommunications) in Canada, from Western Union in the U.S., and from the local European telephone companies (generally known as PTTs) in Europe.[4] Branch personnel could now access the Montreal and Antwerp central computers to input and retrieve up-to-date rate information, container status, customer data, and customer billing details. Local branch access to the information system improved CAST's responsiveness to client enquiries and allowed the branches to initiate local customer billing which reduced CAST's customer revenue collection period by three days.

In 1981, a second UNIVAC 9030 was added in both Europe and Canada to support the increased volume of online transactions. The telecommunications network was also expanded internationally with the installation of a private 75 baud telex line between Montreal and Antwerp. The line was leased from Teleglobe Canada, Canada's overseas telecommunications carrier, and Regie des Telegraphes et Telephones (RTT) Belgique, the Belgian PTT. Later that year, a 1200 baud dial-up data line was added to handle CAST's increasing transatlantic data traffic. Bill of lading information, previously delivered by airfreight courier, was now transmitted electronically, reducing information delivery time by two days, and lowering operating costs. The long distance public telephone network continued to be used for voice communications.

CAST experienced problems with several of the North American leased analog data lines in 1981. The lines were sometimes out of service for as much as three days at a time. When this happened, work which would normally be entered at the affected branch had to be telexed to the closest unaffected branch for input and transmittal to the Montreal central computer. Mr. Dudgeon noted that such downtime often caused "an extra day to close a vessel before sailing" and a loss of one day's revenue (about $400,000 U.S.).

The problems were alleviated in 1982 when CAST North America's network was switched to digital lines leased through Bell Canada's Dataroute data service.[5] The digital lines increased reliability by "one thousand percent," and also decreased CAST's telecommunication costs. While CAST North America's network was switched to digital facilities, CAST Europe's network remained analog.

Corporate offices were moved from Montreal to Bermuda in 1983, though world-wide container movement was still controlled out of Montreal. The move required the creation of an internal messaging system which would allow senior management in Bermuda to monitor and control world-wide day-to-day operations. In particular, a copy of all messages sent from the North American and European offices had to be transmitted to Bermuda. Two dedicated telex lines were leased in 1983 and 1984 from Teleglobe Canada and from Cable & Wireless (Bermuda) to handle the internal message communication.[6] These facilities, however, were quickly taxed by the increasing flow of messages, which averaged 1000 per day. Computer processing power was also upgraded at this time, with a Unisys System 80 Model 8 installed in Montreal and in Antwerp.

Mr. Dudgeon began to consider installing a private international telecommunications network in 1987. The volume of online transactions was increasing dramatically, fuelled by a sharp rise in the annual volume of transported teu's (see Exhibit 14.1 for selected CAST computer and communications activity level statistics) and a high degree of computer literacy among CAST employees. CAST telex facilities could no longer handle the data and message traffic and international telephone charges were on the rise. A private international network could improve CAST's inter-site communications and reduce overall telecommunications costs.

PRIVATE INTERNATIONAL NETWORKS

A private international network consisted of point-to-point communications lines (or "circuits") between different countries, which were leased by organizations from the telecommunications carriers for a flat, monthly fee and provided unlimited dedicated, private use. Providing the leased circuits required a cooperative effort among the world's telecommunications carriers. These international networks made extensive use of two types of facilities, submarine cables and satellite links. Each submarine cable was owned and operated by a consortium of two or more telecommunications carriers, who leased out cable capacity to other carriers. The satellites were owned and operated by INTELSAT (International Telecommunications Satellite Organization) based in Washington, D.C.

The submarine cables and communications satellites carried voice, data, and other electronic communications around the world. The world's telecommunications carriers maintained close relations with one another through memberships in international organizations such as INTELSAT, INMARSAT (the International Maritime Satellite Organization), and the International Telecommunications Union (lTU), a specialized U.N. agency based in Geneva. Global telecommunications services were the result of negotiations and bi- and multi-lateral agreements between the carriers. (Exhibit 14.2 lists the top twenty world telecommunications carriers.)

A private international network consisted of two parts, a domestic ("local loop") portion and an international portion. The local loop ran from the organization's place of business to the telecommunications carrier's "international gateway center," a switching center which

Exhibit 14.1   CAST N.A. Computer and Communications Volume and Usage Statistics

Year	Employees	Offices	Annual TEUs	Online Transaction Volume Per Day	Storage And Processing Capacity
1981	289	12	55,000	11,000	0.6 Gigabytes 39K instr./sec
1986	246	9	118,000	31,000	3.0 GB. 600K instr./sec
1988	246	9	140,000	41,000	4.0 GB. 600K instr./sec
1990	250	11	180,000**	70,000***	8.0 GB. 1.3M instr./sec

**Estimated number. It is also estimated that CAST will transport 250,000 TEUs through the Port of Antwerp in 1990.
***European online transactions are estimated at 100,000 per day.
Source: CAST North America

Exhibit 14.2 Listing of the Top 20 Public Telecommunications Carriers Worldwide

Rank	Carrier	Country	Outgoing Minutes (millions)	Market Share (%)
1	BellSouth	USA	316428	7.1
2	Bell Atlantic	USA	284835	6.3
3	Ameritech	USA	283098	6.3
4	Nynex	USA	252528	5.6
5	Southwestern Bell	USA	214962	4.8
6	GTE	USA	201615	4.5
7	Pacific Telesis	USA	201444	4.5
8	NTT	Japan	191467	4.3
9	AT&T	USA	144637	3.2
10	US West	USA	133714	3.0
11	France Telecom	France	86506	1.9
12	Bell Canada	Canada	83548	1.9
13	British Telecom	UK	79930	1.8
14	Deutsche Bundesport	W Germany	74236	1.7
15	Soviet PTT	USSR	62872	1.4
16	Telebras	Brazil	58974	1.3
17	SIP/ASST	Italy	49285	1.1
18	DG Telecoms Taiwan	Taiwan	41267	0.9
19	Telefonica	Spain	30500	0.7
20	Telecom Australia	Australia	27089	0.6
	TOTAL OF TOP 20 PUBLIC CARRIERS		2818936	62.8
	WORLD TOTAL		4488159	100.00

Source: International Institute of Communications, 1989
*Carrier rankings are based on total domestic (exchange and interexchange) plus outgoing international minutes of telecom traffic carried by public voice circuits in 1986.

provided interconnectivity between the domestic and international networks. The cost of the local loop could account for a significant component of network costs in some countries. The international circuit was provided by the international telecommunications carriers in the home and foreign country. Each carrier provided one-half of the international circuit, up to the "mid-point." An organization would require leasing agreements with each carrier concerned. The leased service arrangements, pricing schemes, and telecommunications facilities varied considerably from country to country.

In most countries, both domestic and international telecommunications services were provided by a single carrier. This was the case in most European countries and in Bermuda, where CAST dealt with RTT Belgique, the European PTTs, and Cable & Wireless (Bermuda) for domestic and international telecommunications services. In Canada, however, there was a separate company which handled overseas transmission. CAST dealt with Bell Canada, a member company of the Telecom Canada association, for domestic services, and with Teleglobe Canada for overseas services.

THE CAST INTERNATIONAL NETWORK DECISION

Mr. Dudgeon and his European counterpart, Mr. Marc Vermeir, looked at various alternatives for the Montreal/Antwerp link which would serve as the backbone of CAST's private international network. The possibilities included installing a second telex line, a dedicated 9600 bps line, or a new INTELSAT Business Satellite (IBS) circuit offered by Teleglobe Canada and other major world-wide telecommunications carriers in conjunction with INTELSAT. The first two alternatives provided analog data transmission over copper transoceanic cables and were considered "traditional" leased line services, while the third alternative provided integrated digital voice and data communications and incorporated newer technology. Mr. Dudgeon noticed that "there would be a significant cost reduction and improvement in message throughput if we consolidated those different communications modes into a 64 Kbps[7] satellite link." In March 1988, a recommendation was made to lease a satellite circuit; the idea was sold to CAST Bermuda senior management in "less than an hour." Exhibit 14.3 outlines the costs of each alternative.

GLOBESAT/INTELSAT BUSINESS SERVICE

Teleglobe marketed its INTELSAT Business Service under the trade name Globesat. The Globesat Service was a digital satellite service based on the INTELSAT V series of satellites. It utilized "small antenna" community (customer shared) earth stations (3.7 to 8.0 meters) located in urban centers. The use of smaller earth stations provided operating economies because they were significantly less expensive for the telecommunications carriers to deploy than the traditional large earth stations located at the carriers' international gateway centers. A user's local loop terrestrial communications costs were also reduced because the distance between the user's premises and the satellite dish (earth station) would normally be shorter. For example, CAST's downtown Montreal location was approximately two kilometers away from the Globesat Montreal earth station, whereas it was over fifty kilometers away from the Teleglobe international gateway in Weir, Quebec. There were also Globesat earth stations located in downtown Toronto and Vancouver. The Globesat service was available between Canada and the United Kingdom, France, Germany, Switzerland, Belgium, Chile, the Dominican Republic, Holland, Sweden, Hong Kong, and Japan.

The Globesat Service allowed users to integrate voice and data in one private high-speed digital stream at less cost than was involved with separate voice and data streams using traditional leased services. Globesat operated on the 14/11 Ku-band frequency, and provided communication circuits at international standard data rates of 64 Kbps, incrementally up to a digitally-compressed full-motion videoconferencing rate at 2.048 Mbps. A user could integrate a number of voice, data, and facsimile channels on a single high-speed link through the use of time division multiplexing.[8]

CAST leased a 64 Kbps Globesat satellite circuit from Teleglobe Canada and RTT Belgique in March 1988; the circuit was installed in July 1988. Before installation, Mr. Dudgeon met with North American and European equipment suppliers to exchange network specifications to ensure that the necessary multiplexing equipment was installed on CAST's premises. North American and European equipment standards differed, and it was critical that compatible equipment be installed on both sides of the Atlantic. CAST chose General Datacom as their world-wide supplier of multiplexing equipment.

Exhibit 14.3 Communication Line Costs (U.S.$)

CNA – CEUR Line	Present	Add CEUR to EDA TLX (2x75 Baud)	9600 Baud	64 KB (3 Voice Lines)
CNA				
TELEX	16,154	33,698		
TAL LINE	17,308	17,308		
L/D PHONE	27,692	27,692	27,692	
DIRECT			41,843	
MUX			3,018	37,555
AUTOCON PORT			2,878	12,267
SUB TOTAL	61,154	78,698	75,431	49,822
ONE TIME INSTALLATION		385	385	4,192
PBX UPGRADE (TELEPHONE)		–	–	7,115
SUB TOTAL INSTALLATION		385	385	11,307
CEUR				
TELEX	17,363	34,955		
TAL LINE	17,308	17,308		
L/D PHONE	30,368	30,368	30,368	
DIRECT			58,311	85,917
MUX			3,895	12,267
SUB TOTAL	65,039	62,631	92,574	98,184
ONE TIME INSTALLATION				
LINE (ESTIMATED)		2,385	5,759	5,893 (EST)
PBX UPGRADE (TELEPHONE)				7,692 (EST)
SUB TOTAL INSTALLATION		2,385	5,769	13,585
CNA–CEUR TOTALS – ANNUAL				
CNA	61,154	78,698	75,431	49,822
CEUR	65,039	82,531	92,574	98,184
	126,193	161,229	168,005	148,006
ONE TIME INSTALLATION				
CNA	385	385	11,308	
CEUR	2,385	5,769	13,585	
	2,770	6,154	24,893	

Note: "CNA" = "CAST North America." "CEUR" = "CAST Europe"
Source: CAST North America

The 64 Kbps satellite circuit was multiplexed at CAST's Montreal and Antwerp premises into three 16.8 Kbps voice channels and one 9.6 Kbps data channel. Exhibit 14.4 provides an overview diagram of CAST's world-wide telecommunications network. Using one of the voice channels, a CAST manager in Montreal could talk with a counterpart in Antwerp without having to place a dial-up toll call. Furthermore, on the Canadian end, the voice channels were able to be connected (or "off-ended") into the Canadian telephone network.

Exhibit 14.4 CAST's Computer and Telecommunications Facilities

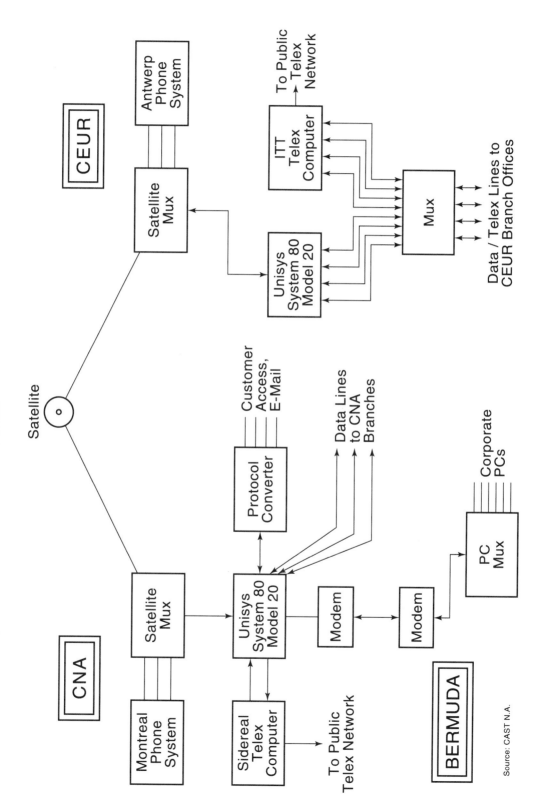

Source: CAST N.A.

Thus a CAST manager in Toronto, say, could call a counterpart in Antwerp by placing a regular dial-up toll call to the CAST Montreal office, then accessing one of the leased international voice channels. The voice channels, however, could not be interconnected to the Belgian public telephone network at the European end for onward call extension to the CAST Europe branch offices or other European locations; Belgian PTT policy did not allow "off-ending." This meant that voice calls placed between Montreal and the European branches (other than Antwerp) had to be over the public telephone network. Personnel in the Bermuda head office could call long distance over the public telephone system to the CAST Montreal office, then connect to one of the Montreal/Antwerp voice channels to reach the Antwerp office, a less expensive route than phoning long distance directly from Bermuda to Antwerp. The satellite data channel could be interconnected with CAST's other leased data lines to provide a Bermuda-North America-Europe data communications path. This allowed Mr. Dudgeon to implement a company-wide electronic mail system which provided more rapid transmittal of internal messages. The data channel also allowed CAST to initiate, in 1990, customer access to CAST's online information system, which allowed customers to easily and quickly answer their own container status enquiries.

To support the increased message throughput, the Montreal/Bermuda telex lines were upgraded in 1988 to a 9.6 Kbps analog leased data line. The line was leased from Teleglobe Canada and Cable & Wireless (Bermuda) and carried both data and telex traffic over the CANBER submarine cable which ran between Canada and Bermuda. In 1990, CAST transmitted an average of 1,500 internal messages a day between their North American, European, and Bermuda offices. Computer processing power was also upgraded with the installation of an Unisys System 80 Model 20S in Antwerp in January 1990, and in Montreal four months later.

Their international private telecommunications network gave CAST an advantage over competitors by improving customer service and allowing CAST management to better monitor world-wide operations. Up-to-date information was exchanged and transferred more rapidly among Montreal, Antwerp, and Bermuda. Customer container status enquiries could be answered in a few seconds, a factor which impressed customers and helped CAST to maintain a competitive edge. The network also provided computer processing protection if one of CAST's central computers went down. Since the Montreal and Antwerp computers ran duplicate systems, CAST could re-link its terminals to the other computer via distributed communications processors and carry on its business.

THE EUROPEAN SITUATION

Management of the European network and coordination of all European computer processing activities were handled out of Antwerp by Mr. Marc Vermeir, General Manager Information Systems and Telecommunications. The European network had grown with the rapid expansion of CAST's European operations throughout the 1980s. By mid-1990, it included a hybrid network of analog leased lines, new digital leased lines which replaced older analog facilities, and public packet switched[9] data links between the European branch offices and Antwerp. It also included an electronic link to a large U.K. customer through the Geisco world-wide packet switched data network for electronic transmittal of shipping documents.

In mid-1990, the European network transmitted 100,000 online transactions per day. The main leased facilities ran between the Antwerp and Birmingham, U.K. offices, the Antwerp and Dusseldorf offices, and the Antwerp office and the Brussels community INTEL-SAT Business Service earth station. The public telephone was used for voice communication between the European offices and Antwerp, the Antwerp and Bermuda offices, and for backup to the leased lines in the event of network failure.

Mr. Vermeir faced a complex situation because telecommunications service offerings, pricing schedules, and policies differed from country to country. Telecommunications service had to be arranged with the regional PTT office which serviced each CAST Europe branch office. This presented several obstacles for Mr. Vermeir. First, there were language barriers. For example, in Italy regional PTT personnel servicing CAST Europe's Milan office spoke only Italian. Mr. Vermeir noted that it took his office a full year to translate the PTT manuals from Italian. Second, pricing differed from one PTT to another, and was not consistent. A leased line could cost the same between the Milan and Fribourg, Switzerland offices, a distance of approximately 225 km, as between the Milan and Antwerp offices, a distance of approximately 800 km. Third, PTT telecommunications policies differed and could change without notice. "All the PTTs have different rules. You don't know what the differences are until you stumble on them," stated Mr. Vermeir. For example, the Frankfurt and Munich offices were connected to Antwerp via the public packet switched data network because the Deutsche Bundespost (the German PTT) charged very high rates for leased line services in order to force users onto the public data networks. Other offices, however, were connected via leased lines because other PTTs charged substantially lower rates for leased line services. Fourth, PTT telecommunications policies and service offerings were changing rapidly because of competitive pressures and European-wide deregulation stemming from Europe 1992, the purported economic union of Europe that was to occur in 1992, and the 1987 European Community Green Paper, which called for the end of monopoly services. The PTTs, which once had a strong monopoly on telecommunications services and could dictate services and policies within their country, were being forced to compete with other PTTs to provide the European hub for corporate international networks and to attract voice and data traffic to their networks. The competition was leading to decreased tariffs and new service options which could affect how a telecommunications network was configured. Though Mr. Vermeir found that the PTTs were becoming more commercially aware and more service oriented, he noted that Europe was "not yet one single market," and it was necessary to build good local relations to help deal with the PTT idiosyncrasies. "It's a very frustrating business because you can't explain to management why you're not making any progress. Europe is a more complicated place," he added.

EXPANSION ISSUES

The network served CAST's communications needs throughout 1988 and 1989, but business was growing rapidly with the advent of free trade in North America and the 1992 economic union in Europe. The number of sailings between Montreal and Antwerp had increased from one per week to one every five to six days, and the CAST Short Sea Relay Service had been expanded to include northern England and Scandinavia. The CAST Short Sea Relay Service, because of short distance sailings and multi-port routes, contributed to the significant increases in world-wide online transaction levels, which were expected to reach 170,000 transactions per day by the end of 1990. CAST depended heavily on effective communications and fast access to container status information to keep their business responsive to the marketplace. Mr. Dudgeon and Mr. Vermeir both knew the network would need to be expanded to keep pace with CAST's changing communications needs.

European network expansion planned throughout 1990 and 1991 was aimed at providing "faster communications" and improving network service, reliability, and dependability. "Time is critical," stated Mr. Vermeir, explaining that a CAST container could be in ports in Belgium, Germany, and the Netherlands all in the same day; therefore, fast transfer of logistics information was critical to the success of the CAST Short Sea Relay Service and European operations. The Antwerp/Birmingham analog leased line was to be upgraded to handle more data traffic. The old line would be replaced with a 64 Kbps digital fiber optic circuit, leased from British Telecom or Mercury Communications[10] and RTT Belgique within the next year, to improve response time in the communications between the Antwerp and U.K./Irish offices. The Antwerp/Dusseldorf leased analog line would also be replaced with digital facilities, and a Milan/Antwerp leased line installed to support the fast-growing Milan office.

North American network expansion over the next couple of years involved the potential upgrade to the leased digital data lines to 56 Kbps circuits, the North American standard for high-speed digital data. These new lines would be multiplexed to provide increased voice and data channels. The multiplexed voice channels would reduce long distance public telephone charges between Montreal and the U.S. branch offices. If 56 Kbps North American circuits were leased, the international private network would also need to be expanded to support the increased throughput of North American voice and data traffic.

International network decisions focused on expansion of the existing links, installation of an Antwerp/Bermuda private link, and diversification issues. The telecommunications carriers had introduced new transmission facilities, notably transoceanic fiber optic cables (which were marketed by Teleglobe Canada under the trade name Globestream, and by other major telecommunications carriers under different trade names) and offered an alternative routing and different economics relative to satellite circuits.

SATELLITE VERSUS FIBER OPTIC TRANSMISSION

There were advantages and disadvantages to both satellite and fiber optic transmission which needed to be considered when expanding the CAST international network. CAST had the option of staying with the Globesat satellite service, or switching to a fiber optic link which was marketed by Teleglobe under the Globestream trade name. Globesat was a mature service which, according to Mr. Neil Bronson, Globesat Product Manager at Teleglobe Canada, provided "greater long-term reliability" than the new transoceanic fiber optic cable services.[11] The transoceanic fiber optic cables were still experiencing "teething problems" and were subject to long restoration times if a cable went down. Mr. Bronson noted that the TAT-8 transatlantic fiber optic cable had been accidentally severed in the fall of 1989, and was down for one and one-half months, adding that Globesat satellite restoration time was typically "a matter of hours." Second, Globesat service tariffs were less than Globestream service tariffs for the Canadian half of the circuit. A Globesat circuit was approximately $800 (Cdn) less per month than a corresponding Globestream circuit.[12] While Teleglobe Canada placed a pricing premium on Globestream circuits for the Canadian half, telecommunications carriers providing the foreign half followed different pricing policies. Third, Globesat was not as geographically limited as Globestream. The transatlantic fiber optic cables had limited landing points and required interconnectivity with another cable to reach Belgium. Fourth, INTELSAT was planning to introduce a new VSAT[13] Service in the early 1990s, which would allow international satellite communications with small antenna dishes located right on customer premises. It was expected that the VSAT Service would become widely accepted by multinationals in the years to come.

In spite of all this, many multinational corporations were jumping on the fiber-optic bandwagon and switching their facilities to fiber-optic cables because of the purity of transmission and the high speed digital capability they provided. Also, land-based cable transmission was preferred to satellite transmission because there was no discernible propagation delay. This delay, which was a function of the length of the transmission path, was a frustration for both telephone callers and users of interactive information systems when the signals were transmitted via satellite. The fiber optic cables also offered users diversification within their international private networks.

INTERNATIONAL NETWORK DECISIONS

The first decision that had to be made involved upgrading the 64 Kbps satellite circuit between Montreal and Antwerp. Mr. Vermeir noted, "our applications are increasing so much that we will have to upgrade from 64 Kbps to 128 Kbps." There were several alternatives to choose from: adding a second 64 Kbps Globesat satellite circuit, adding a 64 Kbps transatlantic fiber optic cable circuit, or switching completely to a 128 Kbps Globestream fiber optic circuit. Mr. Dudgeon knew that the Globesat circuit had performed very well in the past couple of years, with the exception of a period from March to June 1990, when equipment and Belgian local loop problems caused the Globesat circuit to shut down. Mr. Dudgeon had experienced difficulty coordinating service response between Teleglobe Canada, RTT Belgique, Unisys, and General DataCom. The restoration times had ranged from one-half hour to five hours during which the CAST internal messaging system came to a standstill. Mr. Vermeir also pointed out that RTT Belgique had reduced the Belgian half of IBS satellite tariffs from 220,000 BF/month in December 1989 to 170,000 BF/month in June 1990. On the other hand, adding a fiber optic link would provide diversification on the transatlantic route, but at a premium cost. CAST would also need to enter into a separate contract with yet another telecommunications carrier (British Telecom or Mercury Communications) for the transatlantic fiber optic link.

The second decision involved upgrading the leased analog line running between Montreal and Bermuda. A second analog data line could be added, but there was also the possibility of leasing a circuit on the Bermuda spur of the PTAT-1 fiber optic cable. The fiber optic link to Bermuda would be multiplexed to provide voice and data channels, which would avoid long distance public telephone charges between Bermuda and Montreal.

The third decision involved adding a link between Antwerp and Bermuda to form a triangular network. Long distance telephone charges placed from Antwerp to Bermuda were costing the company approximately $2,000 (U.S.) per month, Mr. Vermeir estimated. There were also long distance telephone charges for calls placed from Bermuda to Antwerp (even though Mr. Dudgeon noted that Bermuda personnel were instructed to place voice calls to Antwerp via the Montreal PBX which provided interconnection to the Globesat satellite circuit). Most importantly, disaster recovery was a major concern, and the fiber optic link would provide a lifeline between CAST Bermuda senior management and the European operations in the advent of failure along the Bermuda/Montreal Antwerp network. Mr. Dudgeon stated that CAST had "very common systems and redundant applications" on their central computers and North America served as a back-up to Europe and vice versa.

NOTES

1. The majority of CAST's traffic (75 percent to 80 percent) passing through the Port of Montreal originated from or was destined to the United States.
2. EDI (electronic data interchange) refers to the direct linking of the information systems of a business with those of its customers or suppliers, thereby reducing the need for multiple key-boarding, a potential source of errors, delays, and added financial costs. EDI may be viewed as a kind of "electronic mail" – mail between computer systems, as opposed to mail between individuals.
3. BPS or bits per second is a common measure of data communications speed. Baud is another such measure, and for low-speed devices is normally equivalent to BPS.
4. PTT; or Postal Telephone and Telegraph, is the common name for a government organization in foreign countries responsible for telecommunications services. Most PTTs are state owned monopolies, though there has been a trend toward privatization which began in the 1980s and continued in the 1990s.
5. With digital transmission, the information signal – speech, text, data, facsimile, video – is converted into and transmitted as a stream of bits, then reconverted back into its original form at the receiving end.
6. Cable & Wireless (Bermuda) is the Bermuda telecommunications carrier, and is a member of the Cable & Wireless Group headquartered in the United Kingdom. The Cable & Wireless Group consists of regional operating subsidiaries, associates, and alliances whose networks are linked by satellite and submarine cable facilities. Teleglobe Canada is Canada's international telecommunications carrier.
7. Kbps = kilo-bits per second.
8. Time-division multiplexing is a technique for combining several streams of data onto one transmission channel. Each data stream is allotted a specific position in the signal based on time. At the receiving end, the combined data streams are separated to reconstruct the individual components. The electronic device which performs the multiplexing is often called a "mux."
9. Packet switched data services were offered by the world's telecommunications carriers for data communications by the public. A user subscribed to a packet switched network, and then paid a variable usage fee normally based on volume, not distance. Packet switched networks were used when a user did not have sufficient data volumes to warrant a leased line.
10. Mercury Communications, a member of the Cable & Wireless Group of Companies, was authorized by the British Government in 1981 to compete with British Telecom, which until then had enjoyed a monopoly position in Britain. Mercury was established to operate a new public voice end data network based entirely on digital technology.
11. Reliability, as applied to Globesat, means that satellite transmission will normally continue to function reliably, albeit at a reduced performance level, in the face of disruptions (such as poor weather conditions). In contrast, with fiber optic cable, disruptions tend to put the cable completely out of service until the problem is fixed.

12. A Globesat 64 Kbps circuit between Montreal and Brussels was tariffed at Cdn $3,800/month. This was for the Canadian half of the international portion only.
13. Very Small Aperture Terminal
14. At the time of writing, one Belgian Franc = Cdn $ 0.03. The reduction of 50,000 BF/month therefore amounted to about Cdn$1,500.00 per month.

15

Quadra Logic Technologies, Inc.

In late June 1987, Ron MacKenzie, Executive Vice-President of Quadra Logic Technologies Inc. (QLT) located in Vancouver, was thinking over the firm's latest opportunity to commercialize a product. The small company's research group had come up with a drug which, when combined with laser technology, could be used in the treatment of cancer. "Killing malignant tumors with beams of light . . . it's right out of science fiction," he muttered to himself. "We've got to market this product. But how? Can we do it ourselves or should we sell it to someone else? Maybe we should wait until we're in a better position to support it."

Ron knew that QLT's product presented a major opportunity for his firm because it was potentially superior to alternative treatments for several forms of cancer. Their decision on which direction to take with this product could not be delayed. Ron wanted to have a well-developed marketing strategy worked through before entering into serious negotiations on any of the alternatives. He decided to have the strategy worked out in time to present it at the next board meeting, slated for July 10.

THE COMPANY

Quadra Logic Technologies Inc. (QLT) was considered a rising star in the biotechnology industry in Canada. In five years, it had gone from existing only on paper to being the only publicly traded biotechnology firm in Canada and the twelfth largest publicly-traded biotechnology firm in North America.

The company was formed in February 1981 by five individuals who believed that considerable improvements could be made in the existing links between academic research and commercialization of discoveries. Four were university professors with specialties in biology and medicine. The fifth, Ron MacKenzie, was a business executive who held chemical engineering and MBA degrees, and who had experience as a health care management consultant.

The firm's primary goal was to be a leader in the field of medical diagnostics and therapeutics. This would be achieved through developing products that featured unique biological materials and product formats. QLT specialized in the development, production, and marketing of human and veterinary health products, mainly through the application of monoclonal antibody and genetic engineering technology. Essentially, these technologies consisted of the manipulation of cells and/or the DNA purified from the cells. From the beginning, the partners' objective had been to identify and to exploit those areas of their research that represented the greatest commercial potential. They aggressively pursued opportunities by acquiring technologies or the right to further develop products which had demonstrated feasibility in the lab and had apparent market potential for the end product.

"The fact that we're totally market-driven is not so unusual. Scratch almost any academic and you'll find a latent entrepreneur," Julia Levy, VP and Director of Research, was heard to comment. A colleague in the financial area of QLT had described the concept slightly differently in an interview with *B.C. Business* magazine: "Rather than pure researchers, our people could more accurately be called developmental scientists."

During the first five years, QLT had focused on research, funded predominantly by government grants with some income resulting from royalties generated from licensing of early products. The major change occurred late in 1986 when the firm went public. It raised $4.7 million and three of the five principals became employees of the company in anticipation of the commercialization of their own products. In addition to three of the founding members, the company had sixty employees, fifteen of whom were Ph.D.s or medical doctors (see Exhibit 15.1).

QLT PRODUCT LINES

The company handled three main product areas: diagnostics, pharmaceuticals, and therapeutics. The products were directed at three market segments:

- the over-the-counter (OTC) segment, consisting of end users treating themselves,
- the professional segment, in which sales were made to the medical practitioner treating patients in his or her office,
- the clinical segment, in which sales were made to hospitals or clinics for treatment, testing, and diagnostic services.

QLT's diagnostic products included pregnancy and ovulation test kits, infectious disease testing (e.g., AIDS), and microbiological testing (to determine the antibiotic profile of bacteria). They were particularly popular in less developed countries because of their fast application, accuracy, and inexpensive prices.

Through its pharmaceutical area, QLT also functioned as a bulk commodity distributor of pharmaceutical products, predominantly for the North American market. QLT was in a 50 percent partnership with Guangdong Enterprises in China where the drugs were manufactured, and it aimed to become a key supplier of pharmaceuticals to the generic drug industry in North America. At first, easily-imported commodity products such as aspirin, vitamin C, and acetaminophen had been produced, but QLT planned rapid expansion to higher-risk/higher-return products such as tetracycline and lincomycin.

Exhibit 15.1   Quadra Logic Technologies, Inc. (A)

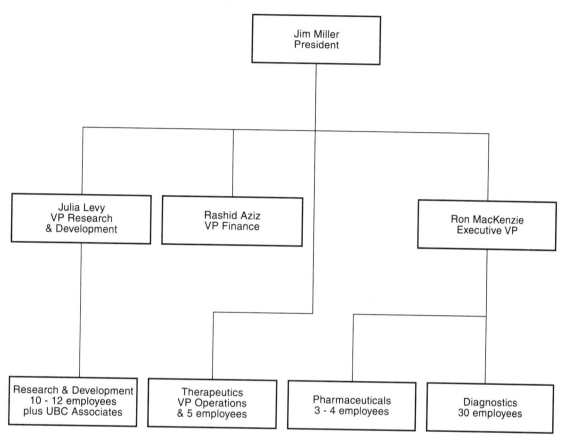

By 1986, diagnostics and pharmaceuticals had begun to provide a source of income which QLT regarded as financing to be used to develop its therapeutic product line. While most companies concentrated on either diagnostics or therapeutics, QLT worked on both to provide a more diverse product portfolio and to give greater insulation from competitive advances that could threaten the future of individual QLT products. However, developing therapeutic products was a high priority for QLT as they were perceived as the long-term moneymakers. They were considered key to long-term growth, because a higher sales volume was likely and profit margins were more favorable. (See Exhibit 15.2 for financial statements and forecasts.) Within therapeutics, QLT concentrated on three major areas:

- photodynamic therapy for the treatment of cancer tumors;
- growth promoters to stimulate animal growth rates;
- immune modulation to regulate the body's immune system in humans and in animals and to provide greater protection against infections and diseases.

QLT was considered to have several potential "blockbuster" products in developmental stages. In the world of pharmaceuticals, a blockbuster product is one whose annual sales volume is expected to exceed $100 million (U.S.). Margins for these products are very comfortable, generally in the neighborhood of 95 percent. Production is economic at rela-

Exhibit 15.2 Quadra Logic Technologies, Inc. (A)

Consolidated Statement of Loss and Deficit
Year Ended January 31

	1987	1986	1985
Research and development costs	$1,190,062	$ 422,872	$ 209,830
Less:			
Government grants and contracts	350,463	249,872	253,467
Interest income	95,758	3,242	5,846
Gross margin on sales	4,411	9,677	11,745
	450,632	262,191	271,058
(Loss) Income before taxes and extraordinary items	(739,430)	(160,081)	61,228
Income tax recovery and extraordinary items	30,330	49,939	(80,269)
Net loss for the year	(709,100)	(110,142)	(19,041)

Consolidated Balance Sheets
Year Ended January 31

	1987	1986
Assets		
Current assets		
Cash and term deposits	$3,603,688	$ 18,101
Receivables and prepaid expenses	134,543	120,716
Investment tax credits recoverable + loans receivable	261,562	170,300
	3,999,792	309,117
Fixed assets	201,030	94,126
	$4,200,823	$403,243
Liabilities		
Current liabilities	140,265	174,605
Debenture payable, government grants & deferred income taxes	31,128	235,120
	171,393	409,725
Shareholders' equity		
Share capital	5,042,488*	332,476
Contributed surplus	47,743	12,743
Deficit	(1,060,801)	(351,701)
	4,029,430	(6,482)
	$4,200,823	$403,243

*Share issue – in November 1986, $4.7 million in shares was issued in a public offering.

tively low volumes. Research and development, as well as marketing costs, are the major expenses related to these products. It is not uncommon for the total costs of $80 million to be expended in developing a new drug and bringing it through the clinical trial process.

THE INDUSTRY

Through the 1980s, the biotechnology industry experienced unprecedented growth, and it played a major role in many other industries, from agriculture to mining. The health care industry especially felt the impact of biotechnology. In North America alone, there were over 200 small firms which operated on the basis of research only. They licensed or sold the results of their work to a handful of firms who had the resources to produce and market the product, and they subsequently retained approximately 90 percent of the profits. Very few small firms combined research and commercialization like QLT.

DRUG DEVELOPMENT AND TESTING

Therapeutic products, developed for treating diseases, were administered to induce certain biological changes in a patient. Developing any therapeutic drug was a five- to ten-year process requiring substantial investment of both human and financial resources with no assurance that the end result would be approved for marketing by government agencies. Competitive risk was also high. The product development efforts of one company might reach the final stages only to find that an equivalent or superior competitive product had beaten it to the market.

After developing a product, a firm had to subject it to three phases of clinical trials which were monitored by a government agency, the FDA (Food and Drug Administration) in the United States, and the HPB (Health Protection Branch) in Canada. The trials alone generally spanned a five-year period: six to twelve months in Phase 1, in which the safety of the drug was established; eight to twelve months in Phase 2, in which a pilot study determined the drug's effectiveness; and twenty-four to thirty-six months in Phase 3, in which it was determined whether the proposed treatment was superior to existing ones. The drug had to complete all three phases successfully before the agency would allow its release on the market. Conventional wisdom was that of 100 products which began the process of FDA approval, only twenty-five would reach Phase 3. Of those 25, 92 percent would receive final approval.

Photodynamic Therapy (PDT)

PDT involved the use of light-sensitive drugs, in combination with light, to treat a range of conditions including cancer in both humans and animals. It differed from other light therapies in that cancerous tissue destruction resulted from changes induced by the photosensitizing drug, not from thermal effects of the light source or laser. Consequently, treatment left the surrounding normal tissues intact.

QLT's version of PDT, Benzoporphyrin Derivative or BPD, was the second one developed in the world. The original PDT product was being developed by Photomedica, a division of Ortho Pharmaceuticals (a subsidiary of Johnson and Johnson), and had been in Phase 3 of clinical trials for almost two years. Photomedica's product, Photofrin II, had been demonstrated effective in the treatment of cancers of the lung, skin, esophagus, bladder, breast, colon, and rectum, and was expected to receive FDA approval by early 1989. QLT's BPD product was known to be superior to Photofrin II, as it could access tumors up to 5 cm deep, rather than the 1 to 2 cm achieved by Photofrin II. BPD had a greatly reduced affinity for skin tissue, causing minimal discomfort and damage due to light sensitivity. In addition, it was a singular synthesized molecule, so distinct that its actual form was promising from a patenting perspective. This was an advantage relative to Photofrin II, which was more of a "soup" of many different molecules.

"Imagine the body as a doughnut," said Ron MacKenzie. "The sterile envelope is contained on the outside by the skin and the inside by the walls of the digestive and respiratory systems. The respiratory and digestive systems are themselves 'exterior' to the body as they allow foreign substances such as food and air in. We can access many forms of cancer by entering the 'hole' from either end." The implication was that BPD could treat any cancer within 5 cm of the internal or external surface, anywhere but in the brain.

PDT involved development of a porphyrin compound, a light-sensitive chemical derived from red blood cells. The solution, containing modified porphyrins and sterile water, was injected into the cancer patient. Then it circulated in the patient's bloodstream and, over the course of two to three days, accumulated in greater concentration in the cancerous tissue. A specific wavelength of light was introduced to the area through the use of fiber optics and laser technology. The light caused the porphyrins to be activated, which resulted in cell necrosis or death, effectively "killing" the tumor.

It was expected that Quadra Logic's BPD drug would successfully complete the Phase 2 clinical trials within six months, and Phase 3 trials would begin immediately thereafter, early in 1988. In addition to synthesizing and developing the light-activated chemical BPD, Dr. Levy and Dr. David Dolphin, her colleague from UBC, inserted radioisotopes in the porphyrins so that tumors could be detected through radio-imagery (scanning). A procedure was also developed to link the compound to monoclonal antibodies, which could ultimately be designed to improve the efficiency of delivery by seeking out specific types of cancer cells, for example, squamous lung cancer. As a result, the compound could be used simultaneously for the localization and treatment of cancers. Thus, significantly improved delivery efficiency by this manner signalled the birth of a third generation of this PDT drug. The third generation was only in the early stages of research and not yet ready to begin clinical trials.

The "product" itself consisted of three parts: the laser and fiber optic linking equipment (capital investment), fiber optics which delivered the laser beams to the cancer site, and the drug which was injected into the patient's bloodstream.

An example of the use of BPD or second generation compound was in the case of lung cancer. After the drug had circulated for two to three days and accumulated in the area of the tumor, the patient was prepared for the procedure through the use of a local anesthetic. A bronchoscope was then inserted down the throat to the lungs so as to accurately locate the tumor(s) visually. A six-foot, flexible pipe/channel (fiber optic) was then inserted. It has a specially designed head which diffused light through radial distribution. That head was pushed into the tumor so the doctor could be sure it would impact the tumor to the maximum extent before turning the laser on. Light was applied for eight to twelve minutes to kill the tumor. The procedure was repeated with any other tumors that still existed. Visual confirmation of efficacy and removal of dead tumor tissue was made one to two days later and, if necessary, the procedure was repeated for any remaining tumor tissue.

THE MARKET

Cancer therapy piqued the public's interest more than any of QLT's other therapeutic product areas, not just because it promised to replace chemotherapy and other procedures, but because it brought the prospect of actual cure within the realm of possibility. In that context, potential market demand was conceivably as great as the number of new cancer cases in a given year. Estimates based on cancer data indicated that there were one million new cases of cancer per year in the United States alone. The rest of the world had twice that number. These figures did not include skin cancer, which was readily treatable through existing means. This initial data suggested a market large enough to support any activity QLT could generate.

The direct customer for the product, however, was not the patient, but large hospitals or specialized cancer facilities. QLT estimated that there were three potential customer sites in British Columbia, approximately thirty in the rest of Canada, and a few hundred in the U.S. A purchase decision involved a number of individuals in the facility. There needed to be at least one doctor who indicated a strong interest in performing the new procedure, either as a result of treating many cancer patients or because of a strong interest in lasers. Unless both the administrative and the medical staff supported the purchase, the sale was unlikely to be successful. Although the company would be selling to the hospital, it would influence the doctors through pharmaceutical retailers. These were company representatives who would describe the product and its features without actually selling it.

A sale would be complicated by the fact that a purchase decision would not only entail purchasing the drug, but would also require a capital investment in the laser and related equipment. Exhibit 15.3 contains QLT's estimates of those costs.

Because of the high cost and lengthy decision making process, it was estimated that sales efforts would involve six to twelve visits to each potential customer per year to initiate the relationship and then half as many to maintain it. A salesperson could only be expected to make one to two calls per day because in most regions of North America, medical centers are not located close enough to permit three visits during business hours. QLT felt that there were so many variables involved in making the initial sale that the buyer/seller relationship would be complex, rather than superficial; thus, the first firm marketing a PDT drug had a competitive advantage. Most customers were expected to continue purchasing the drug from the same company that coordinated the total package and trained their staff rather than switch to a "new, improved version" – unless it had major advantages. It was expected that a specialist operating with a trained staff at a medical facility would draw large numbers of referrals from the general practitioners in the local system.

Exhibit 15.3   Quadra Logic Technologies, Inc. Cost of Cancer Treatment with PDT

QLT estimates were:	
Capital costs	
$100,000	laser
10,000	instrumentation to link laser & fiber optics
$110,000	total capital costs
Annual costs	
$40,000–50,000	technician
15,000–20,000	service contract/year
5,000	training (repeated annually as refresher)
$60,000–75,000	total annual costs
Drug costs per treatment	
$150	fiber optics
to be priced	PDT compound (drug itself)

Segmentation

QLT management segmented the global health care market along geographical lines. The segments, in order of priority, were: Canada/US, Western Europe, Japan, and developing countries, with China singled out because of its unique relationship with QLT through the pharmaceutical division.

QLT management knew very little about most of these segments, and in some cases, did not know who to approach to find out more. As they already had contacts in North America and some knowledge of the market there, they hired a New York market research firm to assemble market data. As of late June 1987, many of the tentative results were already available. A complete report was expected by the end of the summer.

After deciding to focus on the North American market, QLT estimated that it would cost $3 to $12 million to put PDT through the clinical trial process. Further, it was thought that it would take up to five years before they could reasonably expect to put PDT on the market.

Competition

The health care industry was dominated by firms with financial, technical, and marketing resources greater than QLT's. Its competitors were thus better equipped than QLT to develop diagnostic and therapeutic products. For example, within the field of cancer treatment alone, researchers in twenty-five countries were developing products and processes which could eventually compete with those QLT was developing. This competition would extend well beyond Johnson & Johnson's expected rivalry in the photodynamic therapy market. Although QLT management had not invested time or resources in evaluating competition other than that expected from Photomedica in PDT therapy, they expected strong competition from other forms of cancer treatment such as surgery, radiation, and chemotherapy.

QLT felt that its major advantage in such a highly competitive race was the product itself. In addition, however, QLT was developing leading edge products in a number of major areas so as not to be "caught out" if another firm experienced early success in PDT therapy.

Alternative Strategies

By June, 1987 Ron MacKenzie felt QLT knew enough to make a decision on what they should do with their new PDT compound. The management group perceived several alternatives:

Go-it-alone   Escalate development of the PDT compound with the objective of getting it to the market as soon as possible, relying exclusively on the company's resources to do so. This would involve spending $3 to $12 million over three to five years in clinical trials, hiring someone well-versed in running trials and in dealing with the FDA ($100,000–150,000 per year), developing a sales force to handle the Canadian and U.S. markets, and pursuing arrangements with laser and fiber optic companies to ensure that the other parts of the product would also be ready once the compound was approved for market. This alternative would likely include further government research grants in bringing the product to a marketable stage. Grants had been consistently available and were not expected to dry up at this stage.

QLT had strong production capability in place. They considered the sales/marketing function to be their weakest area; they had a number of strong individuals, but no sales force of any consequence. Products had only recently begun to reach the commercialization stage. In pursuing this go-it-alone alternative, QLT would need a sales force on board in approximately four years, when they would expect to have received FDA approval. At that stage, they would expect to raise money on the public market in addition to using revenues from diagnostic kits and pharmaceuticals to fund the marketing of PDT.

Ron felt that this alternative could best meet some important company objectives as it would preserve QLT's autonomy and realize the original goal of linking discovery and commercialization. By pursuing this alternative, QLT would develop a marketing capability and receive full public recognition for the result of their work. However, Ron was concerned about the following:

1. developing and supporting an international sales force on a single compound.
2. the requirement for additional capital funding:
    (a) QLT did not want to raise large amounts of money on public markets at the current price (just under $5 a share) as it could significantly dilute the current shareholders' equity.
    (b) QLT was reluctant to rely on future capital markets because of the uncertainty of these markets to deliver capital when required due to the U.S. trade deficit, interest rate uncertainty, etc.
    (c) the consequence of program success but financing failure would be a great opportunity for another company, not QLT.

License   Cease research and development and license the PDT product out as it was. QLT had proceeded this way with a number of previous discoveries and inventions. Every deal was slightly different but, under this arrangement, over the life of the product QLT expected to receive about 5 to 10 percent of revenues stemming from its sale. Some audit costs to monitor the purchaser would be involved.

There were a number of firms interested in taking on a license from QLT. Pursuing this alternative would simplify things considerably for QLT as they would effectively drop any further market development of the product. There would be no need to develop marketing capability. They would remain focused on research and development. Furthermore, licensing out PDT would provide financing for further R&D in other areas of research.

Do nothing   Continue to develop the drug, wait and see how things unfolded in this market. Then, cash in on a "new improved version" once Photofrin II, the first PDT drug, was on the market (expected approval date of early 1989).

Joint Venture   Continue to develop the product, but in a joint venture with another firm with stronger marketing and distribution resources. QLT would retain ownership, continue R&D, and do the manufacturing. The partner would market and distribute the product. Criteria which would be used in considering a joint venture include:

(a) a firm truly interested in the technology;
(b) a reputable company that QLT could work with;
(c) the prospects for QLT to retain control of the program and the manufacturing.

QLT management were reluctant to return to the equity market as they had just raised $4.7 million in November, 1986. Returning so soon with so much unresolved would not be a strong signal.

To be certain that these were all viable alternatives, QLT management had done some legwork. They felt that getting PDT to the market, regardless of the alternative chosen, required the following:

- development of all three product components: the drug, the laser, and the fiber optics. Only the drug had been developed. Without the right kind of equipment in place, the drug could not be put to use.
- access to expertise and financial resources to get through the FDA process.
- development of a sales force and distribution system that could handle sales. (Whereas Johnson & Johnson could take advantage of its existing sales force, QLT would have to develop its own from scratch, unless it were to benefit from another company's infrastructure.)

Preliminary discussions had taken place with various laser and fiber optic companies to determine whether they could work together on a product package. It appeared that the time frame necessary to complete clinical trials for the drug allowed plenty of scope to modify laser equipment and to develop fiber optics to meet the needs of QLT. QLT was entirely satisfied with the way arrangements were shaping up with regards to the equipment. It could, therefore, concentrate on the further development and marketing of the drug itself.

The market research was almost completed. Preliminary results gave QLT a much better sense of what they could expect from the North American market. The study identified their initial market as being 15 percent or 150,000 cases per year in the U.S. This was calculated on the basis of selecting eight forms of cancer, comparing alternative treatments available, cost of treatments, and success rates. They assumed that there was no particular reason for using their new treatment for cancers which were already being effectively treated with another method (see Exhibit 15.4).

In arriving at these market estimates, the research firm had assumed a per patient treatment price of $600 to $1000 for the QLT product. By way of comparison, drug costs for chemotherapy treatments were in the range of $2500 to $5000 per person. However, QLT needed to consider the pricing issue much more closely. To what should they relate this

Exhibit 15.4 Quadra Logic Technologies, Inc. (A) Market Research Results

Summary – Realistic Market Potential for Photodynamic Therapy
Estimated treatments/year

Market	Most likely case	Best case
Lung cancer	42,800	100,000
Bladder cancer	20,400	47,600
Esophageal cancer	18,000	18,000
Head/neck	7,400	7,400
Basal cell carcinoma	25,000	25,000
Melanoma	–	–
Breast cancer	2,600	2,600
Cervical cancer	33,800	33,800
Total	150,000	234,400

product when there were no equivalent products on the market? There was no standard margin in the industry. Production costs were expected to run at $25 to $75 per treatment. The most recent drug to be marketed in the biotechnology field was one reducing tissue damage after heart attacks. It was being sold for $2200 U.S. per treatment and it was causing some controversy about unethical pricing practices. Other firms were pricing new therapeutic biotech products in the range of $1000 to $2000.

Although cost was not a primary decision-making criteria when compared with effectiveness, Ron MacKenzie noted that the "retail" cost of PDT treatment was less than $10,000, which compared well with the cost of surgery ($20–25,000). The breakdown is as follows (assuming Canadian rates that hospitals use to bill the health insurance plans):

- 5 inpatient days @$500–600 per day   2500–3000
- 5 to 6 hours doctor's time @$300–400 per hour   1500–2400
- tests, etc. @$50–75 per day × 5 days   250–375
- laser amortization (machine obsolete in 3 years)   250–300
- technician salary + overhead ($80,000/year, with 800 treatments/year at capacity)   100
- service contract   100
- PDT compound   600–2200
- fiber optics   150
  Total: $5450–8625

From February through June, 1987, QLT had approached three pharmaceutical firms in turn to explore their interest in the possibility of a joint venture to market the product. All three were initially interested. However, two were obliged to terminate the discussions, one because it had been acquired by another company and the second because of poor communications between the American parent and Canadian subsidiary. The third, American Cyanamid (AC), was of particular interest to Ron as AC had already established a working relationship with QLT in assessing other product offerings. AC had particularly strong industry expertise and was generally recognized in the industry as a major distributor of oncology products. In addition, QLT had gained an understanding of Cyanamid's R&D interests and capabilities during technical discussions held several months earlier. There were several other similar potential venture partners which QLT could pursue if AC turned out not to be a favorable choice.

An agreement with American Cyanamid would likely give them all marketing rights for QLT's PDT products for cancer only, current and future, in exchange for a percentage of revenues. Unlike licensing out fully, this option would allow QLT to retain product ownership. Under a joint venture, QLT would receive 30 to 40 percent of sales revenue from the PDT compound, with responsibilities to include: research for clinical trials and regulatory approvals, manufacturing scale-up, and manufacturing. In comparison, under a licensing agreement, QLT revenues would equal 5 to 10 percent of PDT sales revenue with no accompanying responsibilities other than sharing ongoing R&D support and financial administration. Ron believed that American Cyanamid would prefer to have control of the clinical trials and research that they would receive under the licensing alternative, but that they were still interested in the joint venture possibility as well.

With the knowledge that any of the alternatives could be pursued, Ron felt it was time to make a decision and to develop a comprehensive strategic plan for the product in line with the decision. His intention was to present it at the next board meeting, slated for July 10, 1987.

16

Sharp Corporation: Technology Strategy

This case was prepared by Tomo Noda under the direction of David J. Collis as the basis for class discussion rather than to illustrate either effective or ineffective handling of an administrative situation.
Copyright © 1993 by the President and Fellows of Harvard College. Harvard Business School case 793-064. Reprinted by permission of the Harvard Business School.

Established in 1912, Sharp Corporation owed its name and beginning to the invention of the "Ever-Sharp" mechanical pencil by founder Tokuji Hayakawa. By 1992, with sales of ¥1,518 billion (U.S.$11,497 million) and net income of ¥39 billion (U.S.$296 million),[1] Sharp had grown to include businesses ranging from consumer electronics and information systems to electronic components employing 41,000 people, of whom about 20,000 worked overseas (Exhibit 16.1).

Rooted in the creed "Sincerity and Creativity," entrepreneurship and technological innovation had always been mainstays of the company. However, Sharp had originally been seen as a second-tier assembler of television sets and home appliances which competed mainly on price, because any new products were quickly imitated by larger competitors, including Matsushita, Hitachi, and Toshiba. A critical turning point came in the early 1970s, when Sharp developed expertise in certain electronic devices, such as specialized integrated circuits (ICs) and liquid crystal displays (LCDs), and used them to develop innovative end products. As a result, the company consistently improved its performance so that, by 1992, it was regarded as a world leader in opto-electronics and a premier comprehensive electronics company.

COMPANY HISTORY

The Era of Tokuji Hayakawa (1912–1970)

Tokuji Hayakawa opened his own small workshop with two employees in 1912, making the snap belt buckle which he had designed himself (Exhibit 16.2). After three years, Hayakawa invented a mechanical pencil, consisting of a retractable graphite lead in a metal rod, and named it the Ever-Sharp pencil. He introduced assembly line processes, uncommon in Japan at that time, and the business grew rapidly. Unfortunately, the Great Kanto Earthquake of 1923 took everything away from Hayakawa: he lost his wife, two infant sons, many employees, and his workshop.

In 1924, Hayakawa reestablished his company in Osaka with three employees. With radio broadcasting scheduled to begin in Japan the following year, he bought one of the first crystal radio sets imported from the U.S. and gradually mastered the technology by disassembling this model. The company began to assemble Japan's first domestically-produced crystal radio sets in 1925. When, in 1929, several competitors entered the crystal

Exhibit 16.1 Sharp Corporation – Financial Summary

	Dollar Millions	Japanese Yen Millions												
	1992	1992	1991	1990	1989	1988	1987	1986	1985	1980	1975*	1970*	1965*	1960*
Consolidated														
Sales	11,497	1,517,538	1,496,111	1,344,799	1,238,401	1,225,186	1,148,881	1,216,048	1,166,651	514,884	190,185	120,822	30,210	19,922
Gross profit	3,309	436,794	437,232	388,389	315,835	247,253	235,602	283,373	285,511	129,712	27,429	24,130	5,995	5,273
Selling, general, administration	2,777	366,597	351,185	307,457	262,093	228,584	219,156	239,956	220,067	100,243	22,662	12,501	4,502	2,493
Operating income	531	70,197	86,047	88,932	53,742	20,669	16,446	43,417	65,444	29,469	4,767	11,628	1,493	2,780
Income before tax	629	83,103	99,648	93,511	68,586	43,196	42,831	70,875	78,326	29,596	4,112	8,226	1,070	2,701
Net income	295	39,057	46,918	41,720	29,103	20,341	20,775	35,935	39,903	16,747	2,617	5,271	805	1,429
Total assets	16,270	2,147,690	2,077,030	2,032,598	1,764,662	1,618,625	1,400,352	1,232,747	1,110,153	450,205	168,347	99,673	32,506	14,039
Long-term debt	1,558	205,652	261,639	247,515	196,075	145,787	125,865	128,446	130,394	27,195	13,512	6,420	1,947	0
Shareholders' equity	5,724	755,561	726,763	685,351	534,758	477,925	390,107	379,471	357,891	128,263	38,664	30,540	11,669	5,225
Acquisition of plant and equipment	995	131,373	122,670	116,675	80,722	55,264	59,328	82,042	91,794	39,192	6,881	12,355	N/A	1,751
Depreciation and amortization	758	100,107	89,625	75,032	68,449	61,268	58,864	55,541	45,645	15,549	5,936	3,839	805	226
Return on sales (%)		2.57%	3.14%	3.10%	2.35%	1.66%	1.81%	2.96%	3.42%	3.25%	1.38%	4.36%	2.66%	7.17%
Return on assets (%)		1.82%	2.26%	2.05%	1.65%	1.26%	1.48%	2.92%	3.59%	3.72%	1.55%	5.29%	2.48%	10.18%
Return on equity (%)		5.17%	6.46%	6.09%	5.44%	4.26%	5.33%	9.47%	11.15%	13.06%	6.77%	17.26%	6.90%	27.35%
Income per share (yen)		36.61	44.13	39.57	30.65	22.40	28.19	49.01	54.57	31.28	11.08	25.10	6.71	35.73
Dividend per share (yen)		11.00	11.00	11.00	11.00	11.00	11.00	11.00	11.00	7.50	8.25	9.00	6.00	10.70
Number of employees		41,029	36,539	34,017	32,298	29,351	29,346	28,873	28,221	18,743	9,804	15,442	5,591	4,457
Non-consolidated														
Sales	9,106	1,202,014	1,152,678	1,057,282	992,665	872,707	868,587	955,252	909,581	395,246	190,185	120,822	30,210	19,922
Net income	273	36,063	44,340	37,536	26,232	18,857	20,104	34,735	33,863	12,526	2,617	5,271	805	1,429

*Non-consolidated (consolidated data for these years are not available).
Source: Sharp Corporation.

Exhibit 16.2   Sharp Corporation – Corporate History

1912	Founded by Tokuji Hayakawa in Tokyo. Invented the *snap buckle*.
1915	Invented a *mechanical pencil*[a] named the Ever-Sharp Pencil.
1925	Relocated to Osaka after the 1922 Great Kanto Earthquake. Established as Hayakawa Metal Works. Began production of *crystal radio sets*[b] and components.
1930	Started export of crystal radios.
1935	Incorporated as Hayakawa Metal Works Institute Co.
1942	Renamed Hayakawa Electric Industry Co.
1953	Developed *black & white TV sets.*[b]
1962	Developed *microwave ovens.*[b] Established a marketing subsidiary in the United States.
1963	Introduced a multidivisional organization structure.
1964	Developed and began mass-production of *all transistor-diode desktop calculator – Compet.*[a]
1968	Established a marketing subsidiary in Germany.
1970	Established Advanced Development Planning Center (Central Research Laboratories, ELSI Plant and training center) in Tenri, Nara. Renamed Sharp Corporation.
1971	Established Sharp Digital Information Products Inc. Established production companies in Taiwan and Brazil.
1973	Developed *COS electronic calculator incorporating LCD.*[a] Established a company in Korea.
1976	Organized New Life Committee.
1979	Established Sharp Manufacturing Company of America. Started local production of color TVs in Memphis.
1985	Established Sharp Manufacturing Company of Europe. Established Creative Lifestyle Focus Center in Osaka.
1988	Developed *14″ TFT color liquid crystal.*[a]
1990	Established Sharp Laboratories of Europe, Ltd.
1992	Established the Multimedia Systems Research and Development Center.

[a]World's first.
[b]Japan's first.

radio market, Hayakawa developed a radio using vacuum tubes that could amplify and receive signals from a wider range. The mass production of this radio, called the Sharp Dyne, and the commencement of its export to South Asia established the company as a leading manufacturer of radios. In 1935, the Hayakawa Metal Works Institute Co. was incorporated with ¥300,000 in capital. The company was renamed Hayakawa Electric Industry Co. (Hayakawa Electric) in 1941.

In 1953, in anticipation of the TV era, Hayakawa Electric got a license from RCA to manufacture Japan's first black-and-white TV sets under the Sharp brand name. By 1955, the company was a leading Japanese TV manufacturer with nearly a quarter of the market.[2] This positioned Sharp to grow with the domestic electrical goods market at more than 30 percent each year, as first black-and-white and then color TV sets, refrigerators, washing machines, and air conditioners became household status symbols in Japan. In addition to increasing production capacity and developing market channels for these consumer electronic goods and appliances, Hayakawa Electric also introduced Japan's first microwave ovens in 1962 using technology learned while working with Litton, the U.S. innovator in microwave ovens. By 1965, TVs and radios accounted for 53 percent of the company's sales, down from 84 percent in 1960.

Throughout this period, although founder Hayakawa advocated making innovative products that competitors would want to imitate, the company remained primarily an assembler. Its limited size and capital restricted its ability to vertically integrate, and competitors rapidly copied its products. These problems were exacerbated in the mid-1960s when the Japanese economy experienced a severe recession; independent "mom and pop" stores, which had been the dominant distribution channel, coped with the recession by becoming exclusive retailers for large electrical goods producers, such as Matsushita, Toshiba, and Hitachi. Despite its best efforts, Hayakawa Electric was only able to build a distribution network one-seventh the size of Matsushita's and one-third that of Hitachi's and Toshiba's. Because of its smaller distribution network and the continuing imitation of its products, Hayakawa Electric's market share in radios and TVs began to decline.

At the same time, Hayakawa, like many other large electrical products manufacturers, invested in the emerging computer technology. In 1961, it established a corporate research laboratory to begin research on computers, solar cells, and microwaves. However, the Ministry of International Trade and Industry (MITI) soon restricted the benefits of its industrial policy for the computer industry to six companies, in effect shutting Hayakawa Electric out of the development of mainframe computers. In order to continue their work, Hayakawa Electric's researchers chose desktop electronic calculators as an alternative target because calculators matched the company's orientation toward the mass consumer market.

The company's refocusing of its computer research led to its introducing the world's first all transistor-diode electronic desktop calculator, called Compet, in 1964. The Compet weighed 25 kilograms (55 pounds), was 25 centimeters (8.7 inches) thick, and sold for ¥535,000 (about $1,500 at that time), almost – as much as a 1300 cc passenger car. The so-called electronic calculator wars soon followed when Sony, Canon, and then Casio, a leading producer of mechanical calculators, all introduced their own electronic calculators within a few months of one another.

In response, under the direction of Dr. Sasaki, a recently hired outsider who had been a researcher at Bell Laboratories and RCA, Hayakawa Electric introduced the world's first electronic calculators incorporating integrated circuits (ICs) in 1966. These calculators initially used Bipolar ICs which processed commands quickly but consumed much electricity. Dr. Sasaki judged that energy efficiency, not speed, would be critical for consumer electronics and he convinced Hayakawa Electric to switch to a new technology, MOS ICs, because they consumed less electricity and their chip density could easily be increased.[3] By employing MOS ICs supplied by the North American Rockwell Company to make progressively smaller calculators, Sharp quickly assumed a leading position in electronic calculators.

The Era of Akira Saeki (1970–1986)

On a visit to Rockwell in 1969, Mr. Saeki, then senior executive vice president of Hayakawa Electric, was impressed by Rockwell's semiconductor technology that had made the Apollo space mission possible. Although he had spent most of his career in finance and accounting and did not have a technology background, he was convinced of the semiconductor's potential. Worried about his company's position as an assembler, Saeki also recognized the importance of in-house manufacturing of key components in developing unique products.[4] He repeatedly said, "We can hardly contribute to society if we only make the same products that other manufacturers do . . . [we need to develop] products which others cannot imitate even if they want to do so."[5]

With the support of President Hayakawa, Saeki proposed canceling the company's participation in the international exhibition scheduled for the following year in Senri, so that the company could build a semiconductor factory in nearby Tenri, instead. Despite the concern of many executives, the company built a C-MOS LSI (Large Scale Integration) plant and a central research laboratory. Investing ¥7,500 million (U.S.$21 million) in the projects (one quarter of the company's equity), the catch-phrase of "Tenri rather than Senri" appeared almost spontaneously in the company as Hayakawa Electric became the thirteenth semiconductor manufacturer in Japan. Unfortunately, due to a lack of technological expertise, manufacturing yields in the new semiconductor factory were low, and the operation incurred annual losses of ¥400–¥600 (approximately $1.3 to $2 million) in its first five years.[6] Only in the mid-1970s did the company's production of C-MOS semiconductors turn profitable.

In January 1970, Hayakawa Electric was renamed Sharp Corporation to reflect the company's brand name and herald its transition from an electrical appliance manufacturer to an electronics company. Mr. Saeki formally assumed the presidency when Tokuji Hayakawa retired from day-to-day operations to become chairman later that year. Competition in electronic desktop calculators then intensified in August 1972, when Casio introduced the revolutionary Casio Mini, a six-digit calculator costing only ¥12,800 (about $40 at that time). Challenged by Casio's low-cost strategy, most firms, including Sony, exited the market.

Stunned by the "Casio Shock" and trying to avoid a price war, a project team sought to develop, by April of 1973, a thinner calculator which would consume less electricity and therefore be truly portable. The team's efforts resulted in the world's thinnest calculator, the LC Mate, which cost ¥26,800, but weighed only 200 grams (0.44 pounds) and was only 2.1 centimeters (0.7 inch) thick. This palm-sized model consumed less than 1/100 of the electricity of conventional fluorescent tube models by incorporating an LCD into a calculator for the first time ever.

LCDs consume little electricity because the liquid crystals themselves do not emit light; rather, their molecules are arranged along an electric field, allowing external rays to pass through when voltage is applied. A Sharp engineer had learned about the application of liquid crystals to displays, which had been pioneered by RCA in the late 1960s, while watching a television program about the United States. RCA had since stopped LCD research and exited the business because, Sharp management believed, RCA senior management had seen only a small market for the product at that time.

Sharp soon improved upon the LC Mate, developing a seven-mm-thick electronic calculator using in-house CMOS LSIs in 1976, and a 1.6-mm version in 1979. The incorporation of photovoltaic cells eliminated the need for an external electricity source, and the introduction of a fully-automated chip-on-sheet (COS) manufacturing process contributed to a drastic reduction in product price. As a result of these efforts, Sharp won the Japanese calculator wars and held nearly half of the domestic market share by the end of the 1970s.

Using the same distribution channels and technology developed for calculators, Sharp quickly diversified within the information equipment business in the 1970s. It developed a broad range of office automation products, including microcomputers (1971), electronic cash registers (1971), liquid toner copiers (1972), personal computers (1979), Japanese word processors (1979), and facsimiles (1980).

During the same period, the domestic market for TVs and other appliances was approaching saturation. In response, Sharp abandoned its previous goal of catching up with its rivals in sales volume and concentrated on "distinguishing between where [it could] win and where [it could not], and winning completely in the former."[7] In 1973, a task force proposed introducing "New Life Products" to meet the demands of more diversified and sophisticated customers and to actively propose new life styles to those consumers. The New Life Committee, composed of directors, general managers of business groups, and top managers of sales subsidiaries, was organized to achieve this in 1976. One of the first New Life Products was a three-door refrigerator with a freezer at the bottom. This was introduced because customer research had shown that the frequency of use was 80 percent for coolers and 20 percent for freezers. With the cooler at the top, users had to bend less frequently. In addition to functionality, the New Life committee emphasized color and design, which most manufacturers considered to be of secondary importance at that time, and it carefully coordinated these elements across several business groups. With the successful promotion of a series of New Life products, Sharp's appliance business attained annual growth of more than 10 percent in the late 1970s and early 1980s, despite the sluggish 3 percent annual growth of the industry as a whole during the period.[8]

Sharp's other achievements during the 1970s, which later led to a strategic thrust to redefine the company as an optoelectronics company, centered on opto-semiconductors, which act as converters between light and electricity. Sharp had developed the world's largest solar cells for a lighthouse in 1963, and further research led to the development of solar cells for satellites in 1976. The central R&D laboratory also developed electro-luminescent (EL) displays and laser diodes. While the potential of electro-luminescence for displays had been known for a long time, most firms had discontinued research in this area because of technological difficulties. Sharp, however, persevered and developed an EL panel in 1978, which was used in space shuttle displays. A few years later, it mass-produced ultra-thin, high definition EL displays. As for laser diodes, the "optical needle" for compact disks and video disks, Sharp's development of a durable diode in 1981 gained it the leading position in the world market.

The Era of Haruo Tsuji (1986–present)

Sharp's steady growth was interrupted in 1985 by the drastic appreciation of the Japanese yen against the U.S. dollar because of the Plaza Accord. The company's fiscal 1987 nonconsolidated sales dropped by about 10 percent and operating profits by more than 60 percent. In this difficult environment, Haruo Tsuji, a company veteran with extensive experience in the appliance business, assumed the post of president.

Under Tsuji, Sharp continued its New Life Strategy to design products that appealed to different individual tastes. The company introduced new products, such as electronic organizers (i.e., the Wizard in the United States), dual-swing door refrigerators, home-use facsimile machines, and the first combination cordless telephone/answering machines, and furthered its reputation among retailers and customers for user-friendliness.

In addition to experiencing continued success in consumer electronics, Sharp made advances in electronic devices, particularly in LCDs, which it chose to develop in preference to the cathode ray tubes it had always purchased from outside vendors, even for TV sets. Since its first use of LCDs in calculators, Sharp had maintained its leadership in the technology by continuing to develop larger, higher quality displays. It introduced an alphabetical LCD for calculators in 1979 and a large monochrome LCD for personal computers and word processors in 1983. Using a new thin-film-transistor (TFT) active matrix technology, it then developed a three-inch color LCD with faster response and a higher picture quality in 1986, and a fourteen-inch color TFT LCD in 1988. Based on these LCDs, the company continuously introduced a number of first-in-the-world products, such as a 110-inch color LCD video projector, a 8.6-inch wall-mount LCD monitor (1991), and the "ViewCam" camcorder with a four-inch color LCD monitor (1992), even though some of these products were initially unprofitable because they only met a small market need.

As Sharp recorded five years of consecutive growth in sales and operating profits to fiscal 1991, its reputation in Japan grew stronger. One corporate image survey showed Sharp climbing from sixty-third to twenty-first in the three years to 1992. Another survey ranked Sharp in ninth position in 1992. In the United States, Sharp was ranked twenty-fifth among all companies, U.S. and foreign, in patents filed behind such technological giants as IBM, GM, GE, AT&T, Du Pont, and 3M.[9]

Globalization

Sharp's overseas activities began in 1930, with the export of radios to South Asia. After World War II, Hayakawa Electric rapidly expanded its exports to the United States under the Sharp brand name, starting with transistor radios and then adding black-and-white TV sets in the 1960s (Exhibit 16.3). It established a wholly-owned sales subsidiary in the United States in 1962, and gradually developed a global sales network.

Also, in the early 1970s, in response to cost pressure because of the yen's appreciation, Sharp transferred labor-intensive activities overseas, establishing production companies in Taiwan, Brazil, Korea, and Malaysia. These overseas production facilities were established

Exhibit 16.3   Sharp Corporation: Exports and Exchange Rates

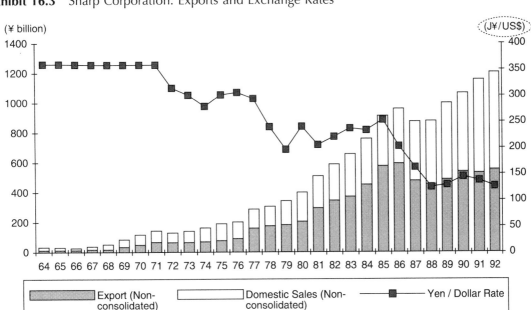

as joint ventures based on technology licensing rather than as wholly-owned subsidiaries. This structure reflected Tokuji Hayakawa's philosophy that his company would not exploit developing countries, but rather prosper with them.

To mitigate U.S. trade frictions, particularly concerning TV sets, Sharp established the Sharp Manufacturing Company of America (SMCA) to produce color TVs in 1979. SMCA steadily expanded its operations, adding LCD production by 1992. Similarly, Sharp Manufacturing Company of U.K., established in 1985, further localized Sharp's overseas operations. Finally, in order to better exploit rapid changes in technology, the company established its first overseas development center in the United States in 1972. In 1990, the company added a research laboratory in the U.K. to conduct basic research in opto-electronics and information processing technologies (e.g., Pan-European translation technology).

SHARP'S BUSINESSES IN 1992

Sharp products fell into three broad areas: consumer electronics and appliances, information and office automation equipment, and electronic devices (Exhibits 16.4, 16.5, and 16.6).

Consumer Electronics and Appliances

The TV and Video Systems Group was the largest single manufacturing group in the company with sales of about ¥400 billion (25.9 percent of the company's total) in fiscal 1992. The company strove to develop a new market niche by applying state-of-the-art LCD technologies to this relatively mature business segment. For example, it introduced 5.6-inch, portable, flat screen, LCD color TVs, only two inches deep, which were increasingly installed in cars and used as second or third sets in homes, and LCD projectors, which offered television set picture quality with a 100-inch screen. In preparation for the coming of HDTV, Sharp also developed HDTV projection systems using LCDs and broke a new price point when it introduced a vacuum tube HDTV set in 1992 for ¥1,000,000, a price one-third that of competitors.

Exhibit 16.4   Sharp Corporation – Transition of Business Portfolio (on a nonconsolidated basis)

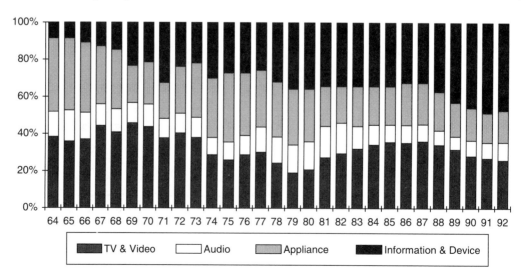

Exhibit 16.5 Sharp Corporation – Current Businesses (Overview)

Area	Manufacturing Groups	Consolidated Sales (FY 1992)	Manufacturing Divisions	Major Products	Major Competitors
Consumer Electronics	TV & Video System Group	¥393.4 billion (US$2,981 million) 25.9%	• TV Systems Division • LCD Visual Systems Division • Video Systems Division	Color TVs, TVs with built-in VCRs, video cameras, video camera recorders, LCD color TVs, LCD projectors, personal workstations, video printers, HDTV converters and decoders, etc.	1. Hitachi, Toshiba, Mitsubishi Electric, Fuji Electric (started as heavy electric machinery manufacturers)
	Audio System Group	¥171.6 billion (US$1,300 million) 11.3%	• Audio Equipment Division • Personal Communications Systems Division • Business Communication Systems Division	Radio cassette tape recorders, headphone stereos, stereo component systems, CD players, laser disc players, DAT tape decks, car stereo systems, cordless telephones, facsimiles, DAT memory storage systems, optical disc storage systems, etc.	2. Sony, JVC, Pioneer, Aiwa, Kenwood, Akai Electric (specialized in audio-visual products)
Home Appliances	Appliance System Group	¥265.7 billion (US$1,850 million) 17.5%	• Refrigeration Systems Division • Kitchen Appliances Systems Division • Air-Conditioning Systems Division • Laundry Systems Division	Central heating and air conditioning systems, kerosene heaters, electric blankets, refrigerators, microwave ovens, dishwashers, washing machines, vacuum cleaners, tele-control systems, electric kitchen tools, etc.	3. Matsushita Electric, Sanyo Electric, NEC Home Electronics, Fujitsu General (started as appliance manufacturers)
Information Systems & Office Automation Equipment	Information Systems Group	about ¥350 billion* (US$2,640 million) about 23%	• Computer Division • OA Equipment Division • Personal Equipment Division • Calculator Division • Nara Plant	Calculators, electronic organizers, office computers, personal computers, integrated communication systems, word processors, etc.	Casio, Canon, NEC, Fujitsu, Toshiba, Hitachi, Mitsubishi Electric, Matsushita
	Printing & Reprographic Systems Group		• Reprography Division • Printer and Scanner Division	Copiers, scanners, POS systems, electronic medical devices, FA systems, CAD systems, OA peripherals, etc.	NEC, Toshiba, Canon, Ricoh, Matsushita Electric, Fuji Xerox, Seiko-Epson, Konica

Exhibit 16.5   Sharp Corporation – Current Businesses (Overview) (*continued*)

Area	Manufacturing Groups	Consolidated Sales (FY 1992)	Manufacturing Divisions	Major Products	Major Competitors
Electronics Components/ Devices	Integrated Circuits Group	about ¥350 billion* (US$2,640 million) about 23%	• Tenri Plant • Fukuyama Plant 1 • Fukuyama Plant 2	LSIs, ICs, gate arrays, LCD drivers, etc., flash memory, masked ROM	NEC, Hitachi, Toshiba, Fujitsu, Matsushita Electric, Sanyo, Mitsubishi Electric, Oki Electric
	Electronic Components Group		• Electronic Components Division • Opto-Electronic Devices Division • Photovoltaics Division	LEDs, semiconductor laser diode units, satellite transmission components, electronic tuners, printed circuit boards, solar batteries, optomagnetic disks, optoelectric terminals, etc.	Hitachi, Toshiba, Sanyo, Matsushita Electric, Mitsubishi Electric
	Liquid Crystal Display Group		• Nara Plant • Tenri Plant	Passive matrix LCDs, TFT active matrix LCDs, etc.	Seiko-Epson, Optrex (Asahi Glass & Mitsubishi Electric), Hitachi, Hoshiden, Toshiba, Sanyo, Citizen Watch

*Estimates of the case writer. (A breakdown of sales and share between information systems and electronic devices was not publicly available.)

Exhibit 16.6   Sharp Corporation – Market Shares for Major Products

Consumer Electronics and Home Appliances

Color TVs (a)		VCRs (a)		Mini Stereo Sets (a)	
1 Matsushita	22.5%	1 Matsushita	25.0%	1 Sony	24.0%
2 Toshiba	14.5%	2 Toshiba	13.0%	2 Pioneer	18.0%
3 Sharp	14.5%	3 JVC	13.0%	3 Kenwood	16.0%
4 Hitachi	10.5%	4 Mitsubishi	12.5%	4 Matsushita	13.0%
5 Sony	10.5%	5 Sharp	12.0%	5 JVC	11.0%

Home Phones (d)		Refrigerators (a)		Microwave Ovens (a)	
1 Sharp	22.5%	1 Matsushita	22.5%	1 Matsushita	27.8%
2 Sanyo	18.9%	2 Toshiba	18.0%	2 Sharp	20.4%
3 NTT	16.0%	3 Hitachi	16.0%	3 Hitachi	12.4%
4 Matsushita	11.0%	4 Sanyo	13.0%	4 Toshiba	9.2%
5 Pioneer Comm.	8.2%	5 Sharp	11.0%	5 Mitsubishi	9.1%

Camcorders (a)		Air Conditioners (a)	
1 Sony	43.0%	1 Matsushita	23.0%
2 Matsushita	32.0%	2 Toshiba	18.0%
3 JVC	10.0%	3 Hitachi	15.0%
4 Hitachi	3.0%	4 Mitsubishi	13.0%
5 Canon	2.0%	5 Sanyo	11.0%

Information & Office Systems and ICs

Facsimiles (e)		Plain Paper Copiers (a)		Japanese Wordprocessors (b)	
1 Matsushita	16.2%	1 Ricoh	30.2%	1 Sharp	19.8%
2 Ricoh	16.0%	2 Canon	30.1%	2 Toshiba	15.0%
3 Canon	16.0%	3 Fuji Xerox	22.1%	3 NEC	12.4%
4 Sharp	11.0%	4 Sharp	6.8%	4 Fujitsu	12.3%
5 NEC	10.0%	5 Konica	4.8%	5 Matsushita	10.2%

Personal Computers (c)		Office Computers (c)		Integrated Circuits (f)	
1 NEC	53.1%	1 NEC	27.3%	1 NEC	21.1%
2 Fujitsu	12.7%	2 Fujitsu	27.1%	2 Toshiba	17.1%
3 Toshiba	10.8%	3 Toshiba	9.5%	3 Hitachi	13.4%
4 Seiko-Epson	8.2%	4 Japan IBM	9.0%	4 Fujitsu	12.5%
5 Japan IBM	7.0%	5 Mitsubishi	8.5%	5 Mitsubishi	9.5%

Electronic Calculators (b)		Mainframe Computers (e)	
1 Casio	53.5%	1 Fujitsu	25.0%
2 Sharp	39.0%	2 Japan IBM	23.8%
3 Canon	2.8%	3 Hitachi	18.0%
4 Sanyo	2.3%	4 NEC	17.3%
5 Toshiba	2.2%	5 Japan Unisys	10.1%

Source: "Nikkei Sangyo Shimbun," June 11, 1992.

• The data is based on the survey by "Nihon Keizai Shimbun (The Japan Economic Journal)."

• The product's market share is calculated based on (a) its domestic unit production, (b) its domestic unit shipment, (c) its total unit shipment including exports, (d) its domestic sales amount, (e) its domestic production amount, and (f) its total production amount including exports.

• Sharp holds the sixth position or below for those products where its name is not listed.

The Communication and Audio Systems Group recorded a 40 percent increase in sales between 1989 and 1991 because of its market leadership in combination cordless phone/ answering machines, pioneered by Sharp. In 1992, the ¥40 billion facsimile business held the leading share in the U.S. market, having pioneered the move to mass distribution channels. That year, the business was transferred from the Information Equipment Group to this group because top management anticipated the spread of facsimiles to homes and their integration with telephones.

Sales of the Appliance Systems Group amounted to ¥266 billion, or 17.5 percent of the company's total in fiscal 1992. Sharp's New People Products, such as a refrigerator with bi-directional doors and a microwave oven with a fuzzy-logic control system, were particularly popular with young people because of their unique functions and appealing designs and colors. However, their share of company sales was declining as the industry matured.

Sharp's major competitors in consumer electronics and appliances fell into three groups based on their original business foci (Exhibit 16.7). The first group, comprising Hitachi, Toshiba, and Mitsubishi Electric, had started as heavy electric machinery manufacturers and diversified into appliances early in their histories, capitalizing on their strength in electric motors. The second group of competitors, including Matsushita Electric and Sanyo, had been established as appliance manufacturers. Matsushita was the world leader in consumer electronics, well-known for its National brand in Japan and its Panasonic brand overseas. Founded in 1917, it had long dominated the industry because of its unparalleled nationwide retail network (National Shops). Sharp was often compared with Sanyo because it was the same size and was located in the same district, but the two firms differed significantly in their corporate cultures and strategies, with Sanyo regarded primarily as a low-cost player. The third group of competitors, comprising Sony, JVC, Pioneer, Aiwa, and Kenwood, did not produce white goods and concentrated instead on audio-visual products. Sony was particularly well-known for its innovative products and technologies, such as the world's first transistor radios, portable cassette recorders, CD players, and 8-mm camcorders.

Information Systems and Office Automation Equipment

In fiscal 1992, the area of Information Systems and Office Automation Equipment generated about 23 percent of Sharp's sales. Major products of the Information Systems Group were calculators, electronic organizers, office and personal computers, and Japanese word processors, all of which used displays of one type or the other. The Printing and Reprographic Systems Group produced copiers, scanners, OA peripherals, and associated products. For these products, Sharp concentrated on its color capability, stressing, for example, four-color copiers rather than monochrome ones.

As technology evolved, several firms in such areas as computers, communications equipment, cameras, and appliances entered the information equipment business. Sharp's competitors and market share therefore differed by product market. In electronic calculators and organizers, Sharp had a leading market share and its main competitors were Casio and Canon. In Japanese word processors, where it also had a leading market share, and in personal computers, where it had only a foothold, its main competitors were NEC, Toshiba, Fujitsu, Japan IBM, and Seiko-Epson. Sharp had a strong market position in facsimiles against Matsushita, Ricoh, and Canon, but a smaller share of the plain paper copier market against Ricoh, Canon, Fuji Xerox, and Konica.

Exhibit 16.7 Sharp Corporation – Major Competitors in Consumer Electronics and Appliances (Fiscal 1992)

	Sharp	Hitachi	Toshiba	Mitsubishi	Sony	JVC	Pioneer	Matsushita	Sanyo (FY1991)*
(Million Yens)									
Revenue	1,554,920	7,765,545	4,722,383	3,343,271	3,915,396	838,669	613,009	7,449,933	1,615,887
(previous year)	(1,532,571)	(7,736,961)	(4,695,394)	(3,316,243)	(3,690,776)	(926,256)	(599,693)	(6,599,306)	(1,496,085)
Operating profit	61,640	352,027	118,460	146,702	166,278	–18,331	57,649	388,957	49,511
	(76,041)	(506,419)	(262,103)	(208,757)	(297,449)	(13,396)	(72,323)	(472,590)	(48,611)
Net income	39,057	127,611	39,487	36,074	120,121	1,990	28,469	132,873	16,837
	(46,918)	(230,185)	(120,852)	(79,760)	(116,925)	(16,010)	(34,315)	(225,000)	(17,499)
Total assets	2,147,690	8,857,910	5,724,439	3,448,673	4,911,129	664,830	519,294	9,019,707	2,062,575
	(2,077,030)	(8,526,121)	(5,530,370)	(3,318,058)	(4,602,495)	(670,698)	(488,152)	(8,761,143)	(1,998,354)
Shareholders' equity	755,561	2,917,951	1,182,050	810,204	1,536,795	309,121	329,670	3,495,867	742,412
	(726,763)	(2,811,141)	(1,178,753)	(792,213)	(1,476,414)	(308,937)	(310,508)	(3,434,747)	(738,212)
R&D expenditures**	98,129	411,614	279,200	183,000	240,591	41,000	23,600	418,100	77,237
	(89,351)	(391,898)	(265,300)	(183,000)	(205,787)	(39,288)	(8,080)	(383,912)	(69,531)
(%)									
Return on sales	2.5%	1.6%	0.8%	1.1%	3.1%	0.2%	4.6%	1.8%	1.0%
	(3.1%)	(3.0%)	(2.6%)	(2.4%)	(3.2%)	(1.7%)	(5.7%)	(3.4%)	(1.2%)
Return on assets	1.8%	1.4%	0.7%	1.0%	2.4%	0.3%	5.5%	1.5%	0.8%
	(2.3%)	(2.7%)	(2.2%)	(2.4%)	(2.5%)	(2.4%)	(7.0%)	(2.6%)	(0.9%)
Return on equity	5.2%	4.4%	3.3%	4.5%	7.8%	0.6%	8.6%	3.8%	2.3%
	(6.5%)	(8.2%)	(10.3%)	(10.1%)	(7.9%)	(5.2%)	(11.1%)	(6.6%)	(2.4%)
Equity ratio	35.2%	32.9%	20.6%	23.5%	31.3%	46.5%	63.5%	38.8%	36.0%
(Yen)									
Earning per share	36.60	36.90	12.00	15.90	293.10	63.00	158.50	60.60	8.60
Dividend per share	11.00	11.00	10.00	10.00	50.00	7.50	25.00	12.50	7.50
Employees**	21,521	82,221	73,714	49,566	18,130	13,561	8,707	47,634	29,638
(Number of exclusive retailers)									
Retailer network	3,800	11,00	12,000	5,500	1,500	N/A	N/A	27,000	4,500

Source: "Japan Company Handbook" (Tokyo: Toyo Keizai Inc., 1991 & 1992), and "Kaden Gyokai (Appliance Industry)" (Tokyo: Kyoikusha 1987, p. 88) (for retailer network).
*Sanyo's fiscal year ends on November 30. Fiscal years for other companies end on March 31.
**Non-consolidated.

Electronic Components/Devices

In the late 1980s and early 1990s, Electronic Components were the driving force behind Sharp's growth. As a result of aggressive investment, this sector had grown to about 23 percent of total sales in fiscal 1992, as compared with only about 8.0 percent in 1975.

The Integrated Circuits Group was in the semiconductor business. In contrast to larger companies, such as NEC, Toshiba, Hitachi, and Fujitsu, which manufactured commodity chips and aggressively competed on price and processing performance by exploiting scale economies and accumulated learning, Sharp generated 80 percent of its semiconductor sales from customized and semi-customized products. It had applied the CMOS technology first used for electronic calculators to gate-arrays and microprocessors, and held a 35 percent global market share in masked ROMs (manufacturer-programmed memory chips) used in VCRs, video games such as Nintendo game cassettes, and microwaves.

The Electronics Component Group developed products such as high-frequency satellite transmission components, printed circuit boards, opto-magnetic discs, and solar cells. Among these, opto-electronic devices were the most unique to Sharp. Sharp had been the world leader in this segment for eight consecutive years up to 1992,[10] holding dominant global market shares for a number of products, such as 60 percent for electro-luminescent displays, 40 percent for laser diodes, and 65 percent for remote control beam receiver units for VCRs, TVs, and other audio visual products.[11]

The Liquid Crystal Display Group was spun off from the Electronic Components Group in 1990. The company's LCD business had grown so remarkably that Sharp was increasingly associated with LCDs. Considered the most promising flat panel display technology in the early 1990s, LCDs were used for a wide range of end products and were expected to replace cathode ray tubes in most applications, including TVs, by the beginning of the twenty-first century. Worldwide production for LCDs reached ¥299 billion in fiscal 1992, and were predicted to exceed ¥1 trillion (U.S.$7.1 billion) by fiscal 1995 and ¥2 trillion by the turn of the century. Sharp was the largest supplier of LCDs in the world, and its sales of passive-matrix and TFT active-matrix LCDs represented a dominant 40 percent world share. The company was particularly well represented in the most advanced TFT color LCDs. Sharp's major competitors in LCDs included Seiko-Epson, OPTREX (a joint-venture between Asahi Glass and Mitsubishi Electric), Hitachi, Hoshiden, and Toshiba. Despite the huge initial investment and accumulated manufacturing experience required to start an LCD business, several other Japanese companies, such as NEC, Matsushita, and Canon were also entering the industry. To further strengthen its leading position and obtain a 50 percent world market share in active matrix LCDs by fiscal 1996, Sharp planned to make a capital investment of ¥80 billion (U.S.$640 million) in LCD plants between fiscal 1993 and 1995.

International Business

In 1992, Sharp had nineteen sales subsidiaries and twenty-seven manufacturing bases in eighteen countries and four R&D laboratories in three countries. Exports represented 45 percent of company sales in 1992, although their importance was decreasing with the increase in local manufacturing (about 25 percent of total overseas sales in 1992) as Sharp strove to integrate design and manufacturing capabilities in local markets. The geographical composition of exports was 40 percent for North America, 30 percent for Europe, and 30 percent for the rest of the world. Eighty-five percent of exports were final products (92 percent of which were sold under the Sharp brand name), and the rest were components/devices.

ORGANIZATION STRUCTURE

In 1992, Sharp's organization structure shared responsibilities among eight manufacturing groups, five sales and marketing groups, an international business group, a corporate research and development group, and a number of central service groups (Exhibit 16.8). All of these groups, except the International Business Group, reported directly to the five top manager's – the president and the four senior executive vice presidents. The manufacturing groups, the International Business Group, and the sales and marketing groups were profit centers, while the corporate R&D group and central service groups were cost centers. Reconfiguration of this organization structure occurred frequently in response to market and technological changes. Examples were the consolidation of the phone equipment business, which had previously been handled both by the Appliance System Group and by the Audio System Group, and the transfer of the facsimile business to the Audio System Group. Also, as the company had grown in size and product scope, it had expanded from three to eight manufacturing groups since the early 1980s.

The manufacturing groups were at the core of Sharp's organization structure. The name "manufacturing group" reflected the company's traditional orientation toward production. Each group controlled its domestic production facilities and was responsible for the technical performance of overseas production facilities. It was also in charge of new product development on a worldwide basis. A manufacturing group did not, however, have authority for sales and marketing. Instead, it negotiated sales targets and price levels with domestic sales and marketing groups and overseas sales subsidiaries while assuming overall responsibility for product profitability. Typically, a manufacturing group consisted of its own laboratory, a staff of up to 100 for accounting, purchasing, and other administrative functions, and several product divisions. Each of these in turn comprised several departments, including product planning, engineering, and production. Central to each division was the product planning department which coordinated R&D, manufacturing, and marketing for its products. Located in the manufacturing group, managers in this department met weekly to discuss projects and problems, but spent substantial amounts of time with the marketing groups. The head of the product planning department for the Wizard, for example, spent about two and a half months each year in the U.S. sales subsidiary.

Of the five sales and marketing groups, four were in charge of domestic sales and one was in charge of the international sales of electronic components. The four domestic sales and marketing groups were organized by distribution channel. One sold consumer electronics products through an exclusive network of independent retailers, called Sharp Friend Shops. The second group was responsible for marketing consumer electronic and information equipment to special outlets, such as independent large-volume retailers. The third domestic sales and marketing group distributed communication and information equipment to specialized retailers, such as stationery stores and office equipment retailers. The fourth domestic sales and marketing group marketed electronic devices directly to other manufacturers.

The International Business Group coordinated the company's exports and international activities, acting, for example, as a liaison between sales subsidiaries in the various countries

Exhibit 16.8   Sharp Corporation – Organization Structure

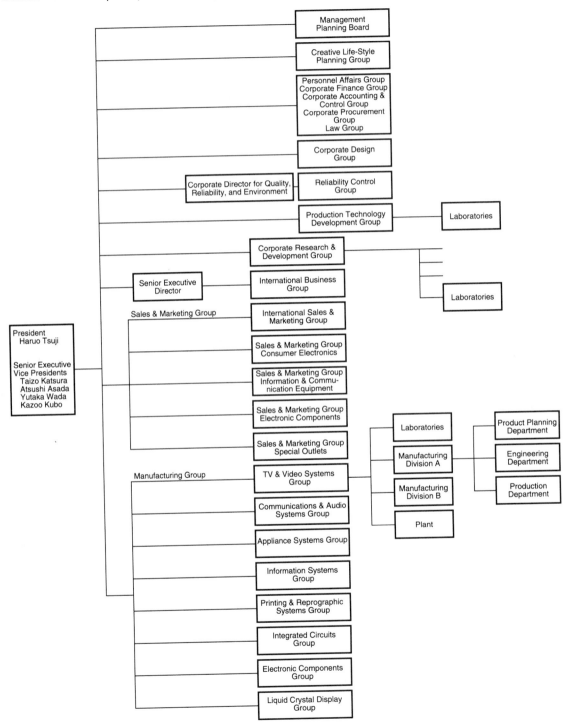

Source: Sharp Corporation.

and the manufacturing groups in their twice-yearly transfer price negotiations. Each country's sales subsidiary negotiated independently with the manufacturing groups in order to foster internal competition and resolve the allocation of scarce products. The International Business Group also supervised the overseas sales subsidiaries, which were each independent profit centers, and was responsible for overseas manufacturing, deciding on the location of new manufacturing sites and coordinating production across the company's international TV and VCR factories.

The corporate Research and Development Group was established in 1976 to more effectively coordinate the activities of the manufacturing group laboratories with those of the central research laboratories. It was restructured with the establishment of the Multimedia Systems Research and Development Center in 1992, which prepared the company for computerized fusion of visual and audio information.

In 1992, about 1,500 people worked at the central service groups, engaged in strategic planning, administrative support, and coordinating activities across business groups and subsidiaries.

THE ROLE OF THE CORPORATE OFFICE

Top Management

In 1922, Sharp had about twenty senior directors who, in addition to their individual assignments, coordinated functions across groups. These executives met formally twice a month, attending an executive committee meeting in the morning and a management meeting (called "Keiei Kaigi") in the afternoon to ratify critical decisions and to discuss the company's future.

In contrast to other large Japanese companies with bottom-up, consensus-building decision-making styles, Sharp had a tradition of top-down decision-making with most critical decisions being made by a team of top decision-makers who complemented one another in personalities and skills. The technological creativity and entrepreneurship of founder Hayakawa was complemented by the administrative skills of Akira Saeki. During his presidency, Saeki benefitted from the marketing expertise of Masaki Seki and the technological insights of Dr. Tadashi Sasaki. Haruo Tsuji, well-known for his cosmopolitan marketing sense, was initially assisted by two senior executive vice presidents, Taizo Katsura, who had a background in international, and Dr. Atsushi Asada, who had a background in technology. Tsuji was well-known for frequently walking around business groups and divisions to gather information, and he sometimes provided specific business ideas for new products.

Culture and Business Philosophy

Sharp emphasized its business philosophy and creed (Exhibit 16.9) and believed its acceptance by employees worldwide was critical to the company's long-term prosperity. The creed was displayed in each office, and employees were asked to commit themselves to its ideals.

Sharp's culture of innovativeness was also enhanced by a feeling of crisis. Hiroshi Nakanishi, the senior manager of the Information Systems Group, who had headed the electronic organizer development project, explained:

Exhibit 16.9   Sharp Corporation – Business Philosophy and Creed

Business Philosophy

We do not seek merely to expand our business volume. Rather, we are dedicated to the use of our unique, innovative technology to contribute to the culture, benefits, and welfare of people throughout the world.

It is the intention of our corporation to grow hand-in-hand with our employees, encouraging and aiding them to reach their full potential and improve their standing of living.

Our future prosperity is directly linked to the prosperity of our customers, dealers, and shareholders . . . indeed, the entire Sharp family.

Business Creed

Sharp Corporation is dedicated to two principal ideals: "Sincerity and Creativity."

By committing ourselves to these ideals, we can derive genuine satisfaction from our work, while making a meaningful contribution to society.

Sincerity is a virtue fundamental to humanity . . . always be sincere.

Harmony brings . . . trust in each other and working together.

Politeness is a merit . . . always be courteous and respectful.

Creativity promotes progress . . . remain constantly aware of the need to innovate and improve. Courage is the basis of a rewarding life . . . accept every challenge with a positive attitude.

Source: Sharp Corporation.

A strong pressure prevails in our manufacturing divisions. We are always afraid that we might be behind other consumer electronics companies. We also feel threatened by low-cost Asian countries. These pressures continuously force us to expand the range of functions of existing products and think about what will come next.

Human Resources Management

Like most Japanese companies, Sharp had a paternalistic relationship with its employees, and top management reinforced the view that the company was a family, or community, whose members should cooperate. Employee turnover was very low in accordance with the practice of life-time employment. If a research project or a manufacturing plant closed, researchers and workers were not laid off but transferred elsewhere inside the company. Sharp extended these human resource policies outside Japan: for example, Sharp Manufacturing Company of America celebrated its ten-year anniversary in 1988 with nearly half of its original 230-person workforce.

In the early 1990s, Sharp's performance measurement and reward system was undergoing a gradual transition from an egalitarian seniority system to a merit system in an attempt to motivate employees, particularly young ones who were becoming more individualistic and less loyal to the organization. There were three parts to an employee's reward – salary, bonus, and promotion. Salary was based on three equal criteria – seniority, job type, and performance – although the performance variation was not significant from one individual to the next. The semi-annual bonuses, which constituted about one third of compensation, varied on a forced curve within a range of plus or minus 10 percent among the workers within a job category. Because of the importance of rank in Japanese society, promotion was the most critical element of reward. Most career-track employees were promoted mainly on the basis of seniority and subtle skills, such as teamwork and communication, until they reached a middle management position.

General managers of profit centers were evaluated on their units' performance, although specific criteria varied by group and by division. For example, in 1992, performance criteria for the general manager of the LCD Group included financials, market share, and product availability. For the general manager of the International Business Group, the criteria were primarily financial, but included balanced product sales, employee training, and the cultivation of new distribution channels.

Career-track employees were regularly transferred across manufacturing groups and between functions (e.g., between R&D and marketing and between domestic and overseas operation). In addition, Sharp employed several other personnel schemes to exploit employees' diversity and creativity. The top 3 percent of each rank of researchers were compulsorily transferred between laboratories every three years in a process called "chemicalization." As Tadashi Saaki said, "It is only hydrochloric acid that is produced when hydrochloric acid is added to hydrochloric acid: while, a new material will come out when hydrochloric acid and something else are blended."[12] Chemicalization was further promoted by the company's aggressive head-hunting and mid-career hiring. Out of thirty board members in 1992, ten had been scouted or joined the company after extensive experience at another company. Similarly, four of the seven general managers of the Corporate Research and Development Group's laboratories and centers had been recruited from outside Sharp.

The company's system of in-house job application was also designed to exploit the full potential of its employees (the "right person for the right job") and to promote their creativity and ambition. Every year, the company announced available managerial or staff positions and invited applications from all employees. Those who were interested could apply confidentially – an important condition in Japan where applying for another job could be interpreted by a supervisor as a sign of disloyalty. Once an application was accepted, divisions could not oppose the transfer. Roughly 100 employees, most of them engineers, moved in this way each year.

Strategic Planning

The Management Planning Board prepared Sharp's overall strategic plans. The planning process consisted of a ten-year vision, a three-year medium-term plan revised every year, and six-month operating plans, which, in the words of Executive Director Yutaka Iuchi, "existed to be altered." Plan targets for each business group were established mainly in terms of sales, overall profit, and market share. The planning staff then disaggregated the targets and allocated them to individual divisions and products. Financial budgets were made twice a year in parallel with operating plans. The basic rule for capital expenditures was that each profit center could spend its depreciation plus half of its profit after tax. However, each project exceeding ¥5 million had to be authorized by corporate management. In addition to basic financial criteria, such as profit and growth, strategic criteria were considered in approving these capital expenditures.

After plans were set up, they were extensively communicated to all the levels of the organization. The president presented the company's basic management policy in his New Year's address via satellite to middle managers, explaining the company's long-term goals and its annual slogan and strategic objectives. Group general managers then explained the annual goals to their members and outlined detailed strategies for their groups.

In 1992, Sharp's long-term vision was called STAR 21 – (**S**trategic and creative minds, **T**otal customer satisfaction, **A**dvanced technology, and **R**apid action for the 21st century). Its strategic target was to attain ¥5 trillion consolidated sales by the year 2000, one third from each of the three areas, Consumer Electronics and Appliances, Information Systems, and Electronic Components.

Technology Strategy

Sharp's R&D expenditures had increased steadily, reaching ¥98 billion or 8.2 percent of nonconsolidated sales in fiscal 1992. The company's overall research and development activities were supervised by the Corporate Research and Development Group, which specified research themes and coordinated basic research and product development. The Corporate R&D Group's five laboratories and two R&D centers were engaged in fundamental research looking more than four to five years ahead. They accounted for 10 percent to 15 percent of total R&D expenditures, and employed 800 out of 7,600 total engineers. The manufacturing groups' six laboratories handled product development that would pay off in two to three years and accounted for about 30 percent of corporate R&D. The remaining R&D expenditures were concentrated on more immediate product development in the manufacturing divisions. Careful attention was paid to coordinating activities across the three levels and to promoting the effective transfer of technology between R&D and product development. Once a technology or a product was developed in a laboratory, there was a formal program to transfer that learning to manufacturing groups. Indeed, personnel often followed from the R&D laboratory to the manufacturing group as a technology was commercialized.

The company's overall technology strategy was extensively discussed in a monthly Corporate Technical Strategy Meeting at which one division would also present its research plans for approval (Exhibit 16.10). This meeting was chaired by the general manager of Corporate Research and Development Group and attended by the president, the senior executive vice presidents, the general managers of the manufacturing groups, and the directors of the research laboratories. Prior to this meeting, the laboratory directors met monthly to examine technical matters in detail.

After reviewing the technological capabilities of the company ("technological seeds") and the needs of potential customers ("market needs"), technologies for development were identified where needs existed but seeds did not (Exhibit 16.11). Decision criteria that determined whether a technology was to be developed in-house included the extent of competition around that technology, the availability of the technology on the outside, the technology's potential to be a source of differentiation to end products, its minimum efficient scale of production, its potential to make Sharp a world leader in an area, the future market size, and its potential to promote valuable learning.

Dr. Asada's view was that, "We invest in the technologies which will be the 'nucleus' of the company in the future. Like a nucleus, such technologies should have an explosive power to self-multiply across many products." He continued, "Our guiding principle for investment should be quality not quantity." For example, Sharp's ¥100 billion investment in LCD factories from 1990 to 1992 was based on top management's faith that LCD technology

Exhibit 16.10 *Sharp Corporation – Technology Development*

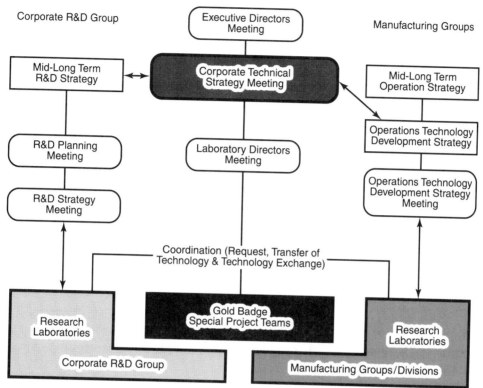

Source: Sharp Corporation.

could be leveraged into several end products in the future. Conversely, Sharp had avoided DRAMs, capacitors, and resistors as commodities readily available from competitive suppliers and instead focused on specialties like masked ROMs.

Once it chose to develop a technology, Sharp committed to it for the long term. For example, it pursued LCD research throughout the 1970s, although the market for LCDs did not take off until the 1980s. Similarly, it continued research in gallium arsenide laser diodes long after most competitors had abandoned their research in this area until the first big market for CD players developed in the mid-1980s. Even if a technology seemed to be going nowhere, Sharp continued researching it, though on a very slim budget. For example, it continued its research in solar cells, using the amorphous silica technology it had learned in active-matrix LCDs, although the market for this technology remained tiny. As Dr. Asada noted:

Unlike the purchaser of real estate who decides which land to buy and which not to buy, technology decisions can hardly set a clear boundary for areas to invest. They are essentially the judgment of possibilities. If the potential of one technology is certain, we are going to assign a large number of researchers. However, even though the other technology has a lot of uncertainties, we cannot stay away from it. In such a case, we let, for example, one researcher study it. If it turns out to have more potential, we will allocate more researchers. If not, and the uncertainties have been resolved, we will stop at that time.

Exhibit 16.11   Sharp Corporation – Seeds & Needs Coupling

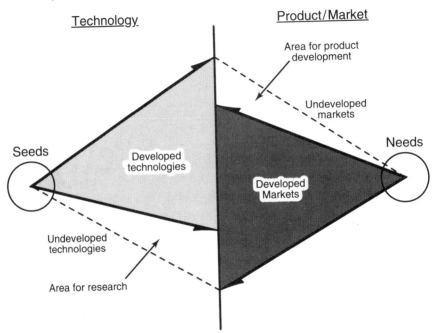

Source: JMA Management Center ed. *Sharp no Gijutsu Senryaku (Technology Strategy of Sharp)* (Tokyo: JMA, 1986) p. 47.

Because of such technological uncertainty, Sharp often maintained small R&D projects on alternative technologies. It was currently researching all possible alternatives to the TFT active-matrix LCD technology, including Ferro LCDs, light-emitting diodes (LED), and plasma and electro-luminescent (EL) displays.

Dr. Hiro Kawamoto, general manager of Corporate Staff Planning and Development at the Tokyo Research Laboratories, also mentioned:

> We do not spend much on basic research. LCDs, MOS ICs, solar cells, semiconductor laser diodes were originally developed elsewhere. But we are prepared to make bets on what we judge will be key technologies for the future and commit ourselves to make them work. Our approach is incremental, yet consistent. We make a small start on a technology in response to tiny existing market needs. Engineers work to generate a new product. We earn some money, invest it on R&D, gradually expand activities, thus approaching, over time, a long term vision. We do not exit from a technology as RCA did from VCRs. . . . We do not follow the behavior of our rivals, rather purposefully avoiding the "herd behavior." We invest in niches, which might grow up to become grand niches.

New Product Development

After the success of the electronic calculators project, Sharp formalized its task-force-based product development process in order to increase development speed and to enhance the effective transfer and integration of technologies among manufacturing groups. To do so, it established a system of Gold Badge projects in 1977. Nearly one-third of the total corporate

R&D budget was spent on the ten to fifteen Gold Badge projects in progress at any time. These were selected at the Corporate Technical Strategy Meeting according to whether the product was differentiated and based on original technologies, whether it involved many cross-group linkages, and whether it would be a core of the company's competitiveness. Projects often focused on areas where technological seeds existed but where Sharp did not offer products that met existing market needs (Exhibit 16.11).

Once selected, Gold Badge projects were financed by corporate because it was believed that since projects cut across manufacturing groups, no one group would be willing to finance a project alone. Manufacturing groups ultimately paid back half of a project's expenditures when they began to market a product that resulted from the project.

A senior manager at the rank of general manager or higher was chosen to be a project's champion, and a middle level researcher was chosen to be its leader. The leader freely chose his or her twenty to forty member staff from the company as a whole. During the one-and-a-half or two-year project period, all project members reported directly to the company president, wore the same gold-color badge as did the president, and were vested with his authority. As such they received top priority for the time of specialists in other divisions that they would not normally have access to. Project members were given wide discretion regarding the way they conducted their project, although the project champion and leader were held accountable for the initial schedule set up at the monthly Corporate Technical Strategy Meeting. Once completed, a Gold Badge project was turned over to the relevant manufacturing group.

One successful Gold Badge project was the Wizard electronic organizer. This project was proposed by the Information Systems Group in response to the slowing growth of its core calculator business. Observing that customer needs for data storage and organization, which had been satisfied by stationery such as the Filofax, could be better met electronically, the project aimed to develop a combined calculator and information processing product by integrating several Sharp technologies, such as CMOS chips, LCD displays, solar cells, and software. Other Gold Badge projects had included a Color LCD TV, an HDTV Projector with an LCD screen, a magnet-optical disc memory, and an EL display.

Sharp's regular product development activities were coordinated through several committees that cut across manufacturing groups. The New People Strategy Meeting attended by the president, vice presidents, and the general managers of manufacturing groups and sales and marketing groups discussed both the basic goals of the New People strategy and the details of specific new products using input from the Creative Life-Style Planning Group. This group conducted market research and surveys with extensive input from the manufacturing groups and overseas sales subsidiaries. Additionally, the Corporate Design Group coordinated design and colors across manufacturing group products.

The components groups were also involved in intense discussions with end product groups to understand their needs. The group general manager of the LCD Group, for example, attended a monthly product development meeting with end product groups.

Operations Strategy

Sharp's domestic manufacturing plants were clustered in seven geographical locations. The LCD plant, for example, was on site with the semiconductor facility in part because they shared similar production processes. Sharp manufactured a product in Japan until its life cycle had matured and innovations no longer occurred. The manufacturing of nearly all calculators, for example, had been transferred outside of Japan. The company also outsourced components and products, such as CRTs and black and white TVs, whenever it saw poor profitability in their production and no potential for technological breakthroughs.

At the corporate level, the Production Technology Development Group developed and integrated the company's process technology. Its group general manager chaired a monthly meeting – attended by the president, senior executive vice presidents, group managers of manufacturing groups, and laboratory directors – to enhance information sharing and technology transfer across plants and laboratories. A similar Quality Group monitored the manufacturing group's product quality and coordinated company-wide quality circle activities.

Internal Coordination

Despite its strategic emphasis on components/devices in the late 1980s and early 1990s, Sharp viewed it as necessary to compete in both end products and devices because improvement in device technologies required continuous feedback on final customer needs. Indeed, Taizo Katsura suggested, "Real value added comes from the link." However, Sharp's involvement in the components business brought about conflicts between component and end product groups. For components also available from outside suppliers, the company took an internal-market approach to resolve such conflicts. The components groups could choose what and to whom they could sell – to the outside customers or the inside end product groups. Similarly, the end product groups had no obligation to purchase from the components groups. They could freely purchase from outside suppliers if the quality or price were better.

All component sales to end product groups took place at an agreed upon transfer price that was normally close to the market price. These transfer prices were determined through intensive discussions at the same time as the six month operating plans and budgets were set. Prices were, however, renegotiated in response to unexpected changes in the market. According to Yutaka Iuchi, former head of the LCD Group:

> We never sell our LCDs below cost to the other groups. We need profits to fund our vast capital investment expenditures. Even when one of our end products groups and one of our outside customers compete in the same market, for example, in notebook computers, the supply price of our LCDs should be the same for both. If we sell LCDs cheaper and give a cost advantage to our notebook computer division, the division will be spoiled and its long-term competitiveness in the market will decline.

When components were in short supply, as had occurred in LCDs, about 80 percent of which were sold to outside customers, the components groups faced the difficult decision of allocating its output between inside and outside customers. In general, this was resolved by giving priority to all customers with whom Sharp expected to have a long term relationship. Yutaka Iuchi commented:

> There were several instances in the past where we had to give some priority to satisfying the demand of our internal groups at the time of supply-demand imbalance. Our group, however, has to maintain a reliable relationship with outside customers. My biggest task is therefore to

carefully predict the future demand of LCDs, expand production capacity based on those predictions, and avoid a shortage of our supply capacity.

The timing of the introduction of new components could also be a source of tension because the company's end product groups preferred delaying the availability of new components to competitors if those components enabled them to differentiate their products. Such dilemmas were solved on a case-by-case basis through intensive discussions. In most situations, new components were introduced to both inside and outside customers at the same time. However, the external launch of a few components of substantial strategic importance were deferred after the involvement of the president and senior executive vice presidents.

Transfer prices were also a major issue between the manufacturing groups and sales and marketing groups. Again, Sharp employed an internal market approach. Although it had never happened, the sales and marketing groups could, in principle, refuse to sell a manufacturing group's product if it was of unsatisfactory quality or price. For new products, transfer prices took into account the strategic objective of establishing a competitive position in the market, and both sides were expected to make concessions to reach an agreement.

Transfer prices for exports were determined by direct negotiation between manufacturing groups and overseas sales subsidiaries. Yutaka Wada, Senior Executive Vice President for International Business, commented:

> Competition is our principle. [The International Business Group] sets up basic rules, but in general, lets sales subsidiaries negotiate directly with manufacturing groups. We do not employ a set transfer pricing approach, such as marginal cost plus a certain mark-up. Such a rule is easy to apply and can be energy-saving. We believe, however, that it would weaken management muscles in the long run.

MAJOR ISSUES FACING SHARP IN 1992

In 1992, Sharp was facing several new challenges. The Japanese economy, which had been over-inflated during the late 1980s, entered into recession as the "bubble" burst and stock and land prices declined. As domestic demand for consumer electronics products and information systems fell, Sharp's operating profits declined, though less so than other companies, after five years of growth.

More fundamentally, as Sharp grew in size and scope, it faced increasing technological opportunities and uncertainties. President Tsuji commented:

> Technological innovation is more and more accelerated all over the world. Also, its structure is changing drastically, and keeping up with developments in hardware and software is getting increasingly important. In such an environment, it is difficult for one firm to do everything itself. Companies with similar goals need to cooperate to develop new businesses by complementing each other.

In 1992, Sharp was considering two major strategic alliances – one with Intel for flash memories and the other with Apple for pocket-sized portable computers. Flash memory was a high-density, nonvolatile technology which retained stored information even when the power was turned off. As its name suggested, it could be rapidly erased and reprogrammed. As a storage alternative to hard and floppy disks, flash memory was better suited to the consumer marketplace due to its cost-effectiveness, reliability, and performance. In 1992, the market for flash memories was approximately $130 million, 85 percent of which was supplied by Intel, and it was projected to grow to nearly $1.5 billion by 1995. Sharp and Intel planned to jointly design and manufacture flash memories in the future. The partnership would allow Sharp to buy flash memories from Intel for use in its own products or for resale under the Sharp name and to develop new applications for flash memory in its own consumer-oriented markets. In return, Sharp would build a new $500 million plant in Japan that would be the main production base for flash memories for Intel and Sharp in the future.

The Apple and Sharp partnership aimed to jointly develop, manufacture, and market the next generation personal digital assistant (PDA), the Newton, by combining Apple's computer and system software know-how with Sharp's display technologies and expertise in consumer electronics. This alliance was expected to allow Sharp to prepare for the approaching multi-media era.

As Sharp set a goal of becoming a premier "creative-intensive" company in the twenty-first century, while for the first time relying on external partners for innovation, it faced the challenge of meeting Tsuji's belief that, "As a manufacturing company, Sharp has to contribute to society by developing innovative products that create market demand and fulfill new customer needs."

NOTES

1. Sharp's fiscal year ends March 31.
2. Hideo Hirayama, *Waga Kaisoroku: Sharp (My Memories on Sharp)* (Tokyo: Denpa Shimbunsha, 1991), p. 52.
3. Masahiko Tonedachi, *Denatku-to-Shinkansen (Electronic Calculators and Super Express Trains: The Arts of the Japanese Advanced Technologies)* (Tokyo: Shinchosa, 1983), p. 75.
4. Sharp Corporation, *Seii-to-Soi: Hachijunen no Ayumi (Sincerity and Creativity: The 80-year History of Sharp Corporation)* (Tokyo: Sharp Corp, 1992), p. 42.
5. Hirayama, H., p. 79.
6. Hirayama, H., p. 85.
7. Comment of Masaki Seki originally cited by Hirayama, H., p. 93.
8. Takeuchi, H., Sakakibara, K., Kagono, T., Okumura, A. and Nonaka, I. *Kigyo no Jiko Kakushin (Self-Renewal of the Japanese Firms)* (Tokyo: Chuokoronsha, 1986), p. 85.
9. *Business Week,* August 3, 1992, pp. 68–69.
10. A survey by Data Quest.
11. *Business Week,* April 29, 1991, pp. 84–85.
12. Takeuchi, H., et al., p. 87.

17

IKEA (Canada) Ltd. 1986 (condensed)

This case was prepared by Professor Paul W. Beamish and condensed by Peter Killing of the Western Business School. Copyright © 1988, The University of Western Ontario.

Founded as a mail order business in rural Sweden in 1943, IKEA had grown to more than $1 billion (U.S.) in sales and 70 retail outlets by 1985, and was considered by many to be one of the best-run furniture operations in the world. Although only 14 percent of IKEA's sales were outside Europe, the company's fastest growth was occurring in North America.

Success, however, brought imitators. In mid-1986, Bjorn Bayley and Anders Berglund, the senior managers of IKEA's North American operations, were examining a just-published Sears Canada catalogue, which contained a new twenty-page section called "Elements." This section bore a striking resemblance to the format of an IKEA Canada catalog, and the furniture being offered was similar to IKEA's knocked-down, self-assembled line in which different "elements" could be ordered by the customer to create particular designs. Bayley and Berglund wondered how serious Sears was about its new initiative, and what, if anything, IKEA should do in response.

The Canadian Furniture Market

Canadian consumption of furniture totalled more than $2 billion in 1985, an average of well over $600 per household. Imports accounted for approximately 18 percent of this total, half of which originated in the United States. The duties on furniture imported into Canada were approximately 15 percent.

Furniture was sold to Canadian consumers through three types of stores: independents, specialty chains, and department stores. Although the independents held a 70 percent market share, this figure was declining due to their inability to compete with the chains in terms of advertising, purchasing power, management sophistication, and sales support. The average sales per square meter in 1985 for furniture stores of all three types was $1,666 (the figure was $2,606 for stores which also sold appliances) and the average cost of goods sold was 64.5 percent.

While the major department stores such as Eaton's and Sears tended to carry traditional furniture lines close to the middle of the price/quality range, chains and independents operated from one end of the spectrum to the other. At the upper end of the market, specialty stores attempted to differentiate themselves by offering unique product lines, superior service, and a specialized shopping atmosphere. The lower end of the market, on the other hand, was dominated by furniture warehouses which spent heavily on advertising, and offered lower price, less service, and less emphasis on a fancy image. The warehouses usually kept a larger inventory of furniture on hand than the department stores, but expected customers to pick up their purchases. Over half the warehouse sales involved promotional financing arrangements, including delayed payments, extended terms, and so on.

The major firms in this group – both of whom sold furniture and appliances – were The Brick and Leon's. The Brick had annual sales of $240 million from fifteen Canadian stores, and was rapidly expanding from its western Canada base. With thirty additional stores in California under the Furnishings 2000 name, The Brick intended to become the largest furniture retailing company in the world. Leon's had annual sales of $160 million from fourteen stores, and was growing rapidly from its Ontario base. These fourteen stores were operated under a variety of names. Leon's also franchised its name in smaller cities in Canada. For part of their merchandise requirements, The Brick and Leon's often negotiated with manufacturers for exclusive products, styles, and fabrics and imported from the U.S., Europe, and the Far East. Although both firms had had problems earlier with entry to the U.S. market, each intended to expand there.

Most furniture retailers in Canada purchased their products from Canadian manufacturers after examining new designs and models at trade shows. There were approximately 1,400 Canadian furniture manufacturers, most of whom were located in Ontario and Quebec. Typically, these firms were small (78 percent of Canadian furniture plants employed fewer than fifty people), undercapitalized, and minimally automated. One industry executive quipped that one of the most significant technological developments for the industry had been the advent of the staple gun.

Canadian-produced furniture typically followed American and European styling and was generally of adequate to excellent quality but was often more costly to produce. The reason for high Canadian costs was attributed to a combination of short manufacturing runs and high raw material, labor, and distribution costs. In an attempt to reduce costs, a few of the larger manufacturers such as Kroehler had vertically integrated – purchasing sawmills, fabric warehouses, fiberboard and wood frame plants – but such practices were very much the exception in the industry.

THE IKEA FORMULA

IKEA's approach to business was fundamentally different from that of the traditional Canadian retailers. The company focused exclusively on what it called "quick assembly" furniture, which consumers carried from the store in flat packages and assembled at home. This furniture was primarily pine, had a clean European-designed look to it, and was priced at 15 percent below the lowest prices for traditional furniture. Its major appeal appeared to be to young families, singles, and frequent movers, who were looking for well-designed items that were economically priced and created instant impact.

According to company executives, IKEA was successful because of its revolutionary approach to the most important aspects of the business: product design, procurement, store operations, marketing, and management philosophy, which stressed flexibility and market orientation rather than long-range strategy. Each of these items is discussed in turn.

Product Design

IKEA's European designers, not the company's suppliers, were responsible for the design of most of the furniture and accessories in IKEA's product line, which totalled 15,000 items.

The heart of the company's design capability was a fifty-person Swedish workshop which produced prototypes of new items of furniture and smaller components such as "an ingenious little snap lock for table legs which makes a table stronger and cheaper at the same time" and a "clever little screw attachment which allows for the assembly of a pin back chair in five minutes." IKEA's designers were very cost conscious, and were constantly working to lower costs in ways that were not critical to the consumer. The quality of a work top, for example, would be superior to that of the back of a bookshelf which would never be seen. "Low price with a meaning" was the theme.

Although it was not impossible to copyright a particular design or process, IKEA's philosophy was "if somebody steals a model from us we do not bring a lawsuit, because a lawsuit is always negative. We solve the problem by making a new model that is even better."

Procurement

IKEA's early success in Sweden had so threatened traditional European furniture retailers that they had promised to boycott any major supplier that shipped products to the upstart firm. As a result, IKEA had no choice but to go to the smaller suppliers. Since these suppliers had limited resources, IKEA began assuming responsibility for the purchase of raw materials, packaging materials, storage, specialized equipment and machinery, and engineering. What began as a necessity soon became a cornerstone of IKEA's competitive strategy, and by 1986 the firm had nearly one hundred production engineers working as purchasers. Together with IKEA's designers, these engineers assisted suppliers in every way they could to help them lower costs, dealing with everything from the introduction of new technology to the alteration of the dimensions of a shipping carton.

Although IKEA sometimes leased equipment and made loans to its suppliers, the firm was adamant that it would not enter the furniture manufacturing business itself. In fact, to avoid control over – and responsibility for – its suppliers, the company had a policy of limiting its purchases to 50 percent of a supplier's capacity. Many products were obtained from multiple suppliers, and frequently suppliers produced only a single standardized component or input to the final product. Unfinished pine shelves, for example, were obtained directly from saw mills, cabinet doors were purchased from door factories, and cushions came from textile mills.

In total, IKEA purchased goods from 1,500 suppliers located in forty countries. About 52 percent of the company's purchases were from Scandinavia, 21 percent from other countries of western Europe, 20 percent from eastern Europe, and 7 percent elsewhere.

Store Operations

IKEA stores were usually large one or two-story buildings situated in relatively inexpensive stand-alone locations, neither in prime downtown sites nor as part of a shopping mall. Most stores were surrounded by a large parking lot, adorned with billboards explaining IKEA's delivery policy, product guarantee, and the existence of a coffee shop and/or restaurant.

On entering a store, the customer was immediately aware of the children's play area (a room filled with hollow multi-colored balls), a video room for older children, and a receptionist with copies of IKEA catalogs, a metric conversion guide, index cards for detailing purchases, and a store guide. The latter, supplemented by prominent signs, indicated that the store contained lockers and benches for shoppers, a first-aid area, rest rooms, strollers, and a baby-care area, an "As-Is" department (no returns permitted), numerous check-outs, suggestion boxes, and, in many cases, a restaurant. All major credit cards were accepted.

Traffic flow in most IKEA stores was guided in order to pass by almost all of the merchandise in the store, which was displayed as it would look in the home, complete with all accessories. Throughout the store, employees could be identified by their bright red IKEA shirts. Part-time employees wore yellow shirts which read "Temporary Help – Please Don't Ask Me Any Hard Questions." The use of sales floor staff was minimal. The IKEA view was that "salesmen are expensive, and can also be irritating. IKEA leaves you to shop in peace."

While IKEA stores were all characterized by their self-serve, self-wrapping, self-transport, and self-assembly operations, the company's philosophy was that each new store would incorporate the latest ideas in use in any of its existing stores. The most recent trend in some countries was an IKEA Contract Sales section, which provided a delivery, invoicing, and assembly service for commercial customers.

Marketing

IKEA's promotional activities were intended to educate the consumer public on the benefits of the IKEA concept and to build traffic by attracting new buyers and encouraging repeat visits from existing customers. The primary promotional vehicle was the annual IKEA catalog which was selectively mailed out to prime target customers who, in the Toronto area for instance, had the following characteristics:

Income $35,000+	Primary Age Group 35–44
Owner Condominium or Townhouse	Secondary Age Group 25–34
University Degree	Husband/Wife both Work
White Collar	2 Children
	Movers

With minor variations, this "upscale" profile was typical of IKEA's target customers in Europe and North America. In Canada, IKEA management acknowledged the target market, but felt that, in fact, the IKEA concept appealed to a much wider group of consumers.

IKEA also spent heavily on magazine advertisements, which were noted for their humorous, slightly off-beat approach. In Canada, IKEA spent $2.5 million to print 3.6 million catalogs, $2 million on magazine advertising, and $1.5 million on other forms of promotion in 1984.

Management Philosophy

The philosophy of Ingvar Kamprad, the founder of IKEA, was "to create a better everyday life for the majority of people." In practice, this creed meant that IKEA was dedicated to offering, and continuing to offer, the lowest prices possible on good quality furniture, so that IKEA products were available to as many people as possible. Fred Andersson, the head of IKEA's product range for the world, stated: "Unlike other companies, we are not fascinated with what we produce – we make what our customers want." Generally, IKEA management felt that no other company could match IKEA's combination of quality and price across the full width of the product line.

IKEA also made a concerted effort to stay "close to its customers," and it was not unusual for the General Manager of IKEA Canada, for instance, to personally telephone customers who had made complaints or suggestions. Each week an employee newsletter detailed all customer comments, and indicated how management felt they should be dealt with.

Another guiding philosophy of the firm was that growth would be in "small bites." The growth objective in Canada, for instance, had been to increase sales and profits by 20 percent per year, but care was given to sequence store openings so that managerial and financial resources would not be strained.

Internally, the company's philosophy was stated as "freedom, with responsibility," which meant that IKEA's managers typically operated with a good deal of autonomy. The Canadian operation, for instance, received little in the way of explicit suggestions from head office, even in the one year when the budget was not met. The Canadian management team travelled to head office as a group only once every several years. As Bjorn Bayley explained, "We are a very informal management team, and try to have everyone who works for us believe that they have the freedom to do their job in the best way possible. It's almost impossible to push the philosophy down to the cashier level, but we try."

IKEA in Canada

IKEA's formula had worked well in Canada. Under the direction of a four-man management team, which included two Swedes, the company had grown from a single store in 1976 to nine stores totalling 800,000 square feet and, as shown in Exhibit 17.1, predicted 1986 sales of more than $140 million. The sales of IKEA Canada had exceeded budget in all but one of the past five years, and usually by a wide margin. Net profits were approximately 5 percent of sales. Profit and loss statements for 1983 and 1984, the only financial statements available, are presented in Exhibit 17.2.

IKEA Canada carried just less than half of the company's total product line. Individual items were chosen on the basis of what management thought would sell in Canada, and if IKEA could not beat a competitor's price by 10 to 15 percent on a particular item, it was

Exhibit 17.1   IKEA Canada Sales by Store (including mail-order %)**

	1981	1982	1983	1984	1985	1986 Forecast	Mail Order %
Vancouver	12122	11824	12885	19636	19240	25500	6.8
Calgary	7379	8550	7420	7848	9220	11500	8.6
Ottawa	5730	6914	8352	9015	10119	12500	1.8
Montreal			8617	12623	15109	22000*	2.2
Halifax	3634	4257	4474	6504	7351	9000	22.9
Toronto	11231	13191	16249	18318	22673	30500	1.8
Edmonton	6506	7474	8075	8743	9986	16000	15.4
Quebec City		5057	8284	9027	10037	12000	6.1
Victoria					2808	3500	–
TOTAL	46611	57267	74176	91714	106543	142500	6.7

*Projected growth due to store size expansion.
**1984 most recent data available.

Exhibit 17.2   Statement of Earnings and Retained Earnings

Year ended August 31, 1984
(With comparative figures for 1983)

	1984	1983
Sales	$92,185,188	74,185,691
Cost of merchandise sold	49,836,889	38,085,173
Gross profit	42,348,299	36,100,518
General, administrative, and selling expenses	28,016,473	23,626,727
Operating profit before the undernoted	14,331,826	12,473,791
Depreciation and amortization	1,113,879	1,066,286
Franchise amortization	257,490	257,490
Franchise fee	2,765,558	2,225,571
	4,136,927	3,549,347
Earnings from operations	10,194,899	8,924,444
Rental income	769,719	815,683
Less rental expense	245,803	258,296
	523,916	557,387
Interest expense	2,453,116	3,042,471
Less other income	438,683	65,757
	2,014,433	2,976,714
Earnings before income taxes	8,704,382	6,505,117
Income taxes:		
Current	3,789,773	2,716,645
Deferred	(70,400)	175,500
	3,719,373	2,892,145
Net earnings for the year	4,985,009	3,612,972
Retained earnings, beginning of year	5,501,612	1,888,640
Retained earnings, end of year	$10,486,621	5,501,612

Source: Consumer and Corporate Affairs, Canada.

dropped. Most of the goods sold in the Canadian stores were supplied from central ware-houses in Sweden. To coordinate this process a five-person stock supply department in Vancouver provided Sweden with a three-year forecast of Canada's needs, and placed major orders twice a year. Actual volumes were expected to be within 10 percent of the forecast level. As Bayley noted, "you needed a gambler in the stock supply job."

Individual stores were expected to maintain 13.5 weeks of inventory on hand (10.5 weeks in the store and three weeks in transit), and could order from the central warehouse in Montreal, or, if a product was not in stock in Montreal, direct from Sweden. Shipments from Sweden took six to eight weeks to arrive, shipments from Montreal two to three weeks. In practice, about 50 percent of the product arriving at a store came via each route.

IKEA's success in Canada meant that the firm was often hard pressed to keep the best selling items in stock. (Twenty percent of the firm's present line constituted 80 percent of sales volume.) At any given time Canada IKEA stores might have 300 items out of stock, either because actual sales deviated significantly from forecasts or because suppliers could not meet their delivery promises. While management estimated that 75 percent of customers were willing to wait for IKEA products in a stockout situation, the company nevertheless began a deliberate policy of developing Canadian suppliers for high demand items, even if this meant paying a slight premium. In 1984, the stock control group purchased $57 million worth of goods on IKEA's behalf, $12 million of which was from thirty Canadian suppliers, up from $7 million the previous year.

As indicated in Exhibit 17.1, IKEA Canada sold products, rather reluctantly, by mail order to customers who preferred not to visit the stores. A senior manager explained: "To date we have engaged in defensive mail order – only when the customer really wants it and the order is large enough. The separate handling, breaking down of orders, and repackaging required for mail orders would be too expensive and go against the economies-through-volume approach of IKEA. Profit margins of mail order business tend to be half that of a store operation. There are more sales returns, particularly because of damages – maybe 4 percent – incurred in shipping. It is difficult to know where to draw the market boundaries for a mail order business. We don't want to be substituting mail order customers for store visitors."

In 1986, the management team which had brought success to IKEA's Canadian operations was breaking up. Bjorn Bayley, who had come to Canada in 1978, was slotted to move to Philadelphia to spearhead IKEA's entry into the U.S. market, which had begun in June 1985 with a single store. With early sales running at a level twice as high as the company had predicted, Bayley expected to be busy, and was taking Mike McDonald, the controller, and Mike McMullen, the personnel director, with him. Anders Berglund who, like Bayley, was a long-time IKEA employee and had been in Canada since 1979, was scheduled to take over the Canadian operation. Berglund would report through Bayley to IKEA's North American Sales Director, who was located in Europe.

NEW COMPETITION

IKEA's success in Canada had not gone unnoticed. IDOMO was a well-established Toronto-based competitor, and Sears Canada was a new entrant.

IDOMO

Like IKEA, IDOMO sold knocked down furniture which customers were required to assemble at home. IDOMO offered a somewhat narrower selection than IKEA but emphasized teak furniture to a much greater extent. With stores in Hamilton, Mississauga (across from IKEA), Toronto, and Montreal, IDOMO appeared to have capitalized on the excess demand that IKEA had developed but was not able to service.

The products and prices offered in both the 96-page IDOMO and 144-page IKEA catalogs were similar, with IKEA's prices slightly lower. Prices in the IKEA catalog were in effect for a year. IDOMO reserved the right to make adjustments to prices and specifications. A mail order telephone number in Toronto was provided in the IDOMO catalog. Of late, IDOMO had begun to employ an increased amount of television advertising. IDOMO purchased goods from around the world and operated a number of their own Canadian factories. Their primary source of goods was Denmark.

SEARS

The newest entrant in the Canadian knocked-down furniture segment was Sears Canada, a wholly owned subsidiary of Sears Roebuck of Chicago and, with $3.8 billion in annual revenues, one of Canada's largest merchandising operations. Sears operated seventy-five department stores in Canada, selling a wide range (700 merchandise lines comprising 100,000 stock keeping units) of medium price and quality goods. Sears Canada also ran a major catalog operation which distributed twelve annual catalogs to approximately 4 million Canadian families. Customers could place catalog orders by mail, by telephone, or in person through one of the company's 1,500 catalog sales units, which were spread throughout the country.

A quick check by Bayley and Berglund revealed that Sears' Elements line was being sold only in Canada and only through the major Sears catalogs. Elements products were not for sale, nor could they be viewed, in Sears' stores. In the fall–winter catalog that they examined, which was over 700 pages in length, the Elements line was given twenty pages. Although Sears appeared to offer the same "type" of products as IKEA, there was a narrower selection within each category. Prices for Elements' products seemed almost identical to IKEA prices. One distinct difference between the catalogs was the much greater emphasis that IKEA placed on presenting a large number of coordinated settings and room designs.

Further checking indicated that at least some of the suppliers of the Elements line were Swedish, although it did not appear that IKEA and Sears had any suppliers in common.

The IKEA executives knew that Sears was generally able to exert a great deal of influence over its suppliers, usually obtaining prices at least equal to and often below those of its competitors, because of the huge volumes purchased. Sears also worked closely with its suppliers in marketing, research, design and development, production standards, and production planning. Many lines of merchandise were manufactured with features exclusive to Sears and were sold under its private brand names. There was a 75 percent buying overlap for the catalog and store and about a 90 percent overlap between regions on store purchases.

Like any Sears' product, Elements furniture could be charged to a Sears charge card. Delivery of catalog items generally took about two weeks, and for a small extra charge catalog orders would be delivered right to the consumer's home in a Sears truck. If a catalog item were out of stock, Sears policy was either to tell the customer if and when the product would be available, or to substitute an item of equal or greater value. If goods proved defective (10 percent of Sears Roebuck mail-order furniture purchasers had received damaged or broken furniture), Sears provided home pick-up and replacement and was willing, for a fee, to install goods, provide parts, and do repairs as products aged. Sears emphasized that it serviced what it sold, and guaranteed everything that it sold – "satisfaction guaranteed or money refunded." In its advertising, which included all forms of media, Sears stressed its "hassle-free returns" and asked customers to "take a look at the services we offer . . . they'll bring you peace of mind, long after the bill is paid."

In their assessment of Sears Canada, Bayley and Berglund recognized that the company seemed to be going through something of a revival. Using the rallying cry that a "new" Sears was being created, Sears executives (the Canadian firm had ten vice presidents) had experimented with new store layouts, pruned the product line, and improved customer service for catalog orders. Richard Sharpe, the Chairman of Sears Canada, personally addressed as many as 12,000 employees per year, and the company received 3,000 suggestions from employees annually. Perhaps as a result of these initiatives, and a cut in workforce from 65,000 to 50,000 over several years, Sears Canada posted its best ever results in 1985.

CONCLUSION

With the limited data they had on Sears, IKEA management recognized that their comparison of the two companies would be incomplete. Nonetheless, a decision regarding the Sears competitive threat was required. Any solution would have to reflect Kamprad's philosophy: "Expensive solutions to problems are often signs of mediocrity. We have no interest in a solution until we know what it costs."

18

British Airways plc.

This case was prepared by D. B. Lanning under the supervision of Professors J. N. Fry and R. E. White of the Western Business School. Copyright © 1994, The University of Western Ontario.

In the summer of 1994, executives at British Airways (BA) were reviewing their investment in faltering USAir and its implications for BA's global-leadership strategy. Following many setbacks, BA had purchased 25 percent of USAir's equity for U.S.$400 million in early 1993 to secure a marketing partner and access to a route structure in the United States. Now, sixteen months later with USAir still not profitable, BA's options varied from severing the marketing relationship and writing-off the investment to injecting further cash.

In prospect, BA's investment in USAir and an accompanying code-sharing authority were viewed as a tremendous coup – so much so that the combination prompted accusations of unfair competition by several major U.S. carriers.[1] Code sharing with USAir allowed BA to expand its presence in the U.S. market from seventeen airports to fifty-nine by May 1994. In addition, twenty-three more USAir markets were scheduled to begin code sharing with BA later in 1994.

It had taken BA almost two years to acquire its partial share in USAir. The U.S. Departments of Transport (DOT) and Justice (DOJ) had scrutinized the proposed equity alliance/code share pact, causing delays and imposing conditions. DOT/DOJ were concerned by the possibility of BA exercising tacit control over USAir following completion of the equity alliance/code share pact. Explicitly, DOT/DOJ were concerned by the potential for price fixing. Frustrated by the delays, BA had terminated negotiations, only to reopen them six months later with a revised offer. This second offer was amended over a five month period before it was finally acceptable to U.S. DOT and DOJ.

In hindsight, the competitive damage feared by the U.S. majors had not materialized. The passenger traffic on BA's North Atlantic route exceeded 4 million one-way trips before code sharing. After one year of phasing in code sharing on the North Atlantic route, BA's cumulative incremental traffic totalled 6,700 passengers.[2] Alternately, daily incremental traffic arising from code sharing had only reached sixty passengers in each direction by May 1994. Current annualized incremental revenue equalled approximately U.S.$2 million, less than three one-hundredths of a percent of BA's 1994 revenue. Finally, BA's decision to invest in USAir was clouded by the continuing poor performance of USAir: loss of U.S.$1,229 million in 1992 was followed by loss of U.S.$393 million in 1993 and U.S.$197 million in the first quarter of 1994.

BA was among a number of participants in the airline industry that believed the industry was trending toward a few globe-spanning confederations or partnerships which would dominate international air travel. Under this scenario, those airlines that failed to make the leap to a global carrier were expected to serve as regional carriers and suffer lower profitability.

Accordingly, BA had invested U.S.$1.5 billion in the period 1992–93 to acquire partial ownership of strategically located airlines world-wide. A global network was created using equity alliances – 25 percent of Qantas covering the Asia-Pacific region, 49 percent of Deutsche BA in Germany, 49.9 percent of TAT in France, and 25 percent of USAir – to feed traffic from strategic markets to BA's inter-continental routes. Because the U.S. market represented 29 percent of global passenger traffic and the North Atlantic routes 28 percent of international passenger traffic, an alliance with a U.S. airline was critical to BA's strategy. The alliance with USAir completed a major portion of BA's global network, and would supposedly capture additional U.S. passenger "feed" between the U.S.A and Europe.

TRENDS IN GLOBAL DEMAND

The globe could be segmented into six key air travel markets: three intra-regional markets (North America, Europe, and the Asia-Pacific region) and three inter-regional markets (the North Atlantic, trans-Pacific, and Asia-Europe). North America was the largest of these markets in terms of revenue passenger-kilometers (the number of passengers multiplied by the distance flown – RPK).

High GDP growth in the Asia-Pacific countries was spurring high air travel growth in the Asia-Pacific, trans-Pacific, and Asia-Europe markets. As a result, over the next twenty years the North America-Europe-Japan proportion of total global demand would decrease while the Asia-Pacific region proportion increased. Air traffic within and to/from the Asia-Pacific region was expected to experience 41 percent of world-wide RPK growth and increase from 25 percent to 31 percent of world-wide demand by 2013. International carriers were scrambling to position themselves in these fast growing markets. North America was expected to maintain high proportions of world-wide RPK growth (20 percent) despite lower annual growth rates due to its large base of RPK traffic. Table 18.1 details predicted changes in travel consumption.[3]

Other trends of particular note concerned customer mix and expectations. By 1994, business travelers were voluntarily moving (or being pushed by their company comptroller) to economy-class fares. Compounding this trend were proportionately fewer business travelers in the airlines' customer profile – 55 percent of all travel was business-related in 1984; 52 percent in 1991; but only 37 percent in 1994. Facsimile machines, tele- and video-conferencing, return to one person sales presentations in place of team presentations, and flatter organizational structures were changing business-related demand.

The shift in customer profile toward the leisure traveler created significant revenue yield and cost management implications for airlines. Business travelers had traditionally returned a higher yield to the airlines per passenger because of premiums paid for upper-class seats, short-notice bookings, and flights during the premium mid-week period. Increasing proportions of leisure travelers meant all fares should rise to correct reduced yields, but leisure

Table 18.1   1993 Regional Traffic Data and 20 Year Regional Forecast: 1994–2013

Geographic Region	1993 Passenger Traffic (1)	1993 Revenue Passenger-Km (RPK) Traffic (1)	Forecast Average Annual Incremental RPK Traffic (2)	Forecast Average Annual % Change 1994–2013 (2)
Intra Asia-Pacific	130,338	173,028	37,800	6.8
North America	390,259	546,027	36,500	4.0
Trans-Pacific	24,066	165,153	21,400	6.8
Intra Europe	158,754	121,425	18,000	4.4
North Atlantic	33,846	217,665	15,800	4.4
Asia-Europe	16,292	130,337	14,200	7.2
Between the Americas	20,737	48,604	6,100	5.5
Europe-Latin America	5,038	32,433	4,000	4.8
Intra Latin America	28,426	20,324	3,000	5.6
Europe-Africa	10,289	41,690	3,100	4.3
TOTAL	818,045	1,496,686	160,300	5.2
	thousands	*millions*	*millions*	*percent*

Sources: (1) IATA, *World Air Transport Statistics, 1994*; (2) Boeing, *1994 World Market Outlook.*

travel was sensitive to pricing. If fares rose, load factors would plummet and excess capacity rise.

Furthermore, balancing operations was made more complicated by the nature of leisure travelers. They were cyclical, following the health of the economy and generating seasonal peaks [50 to 70 percent extra travelers] in November and August.

Finally, as business and leisure travel became increasingly international, airlines were forced to respond to customers' changing expectations. The physical reality of "hopping" from one continent to another was incredibly tiring. Low fares were important, but so were convenient connections, elapsed travel time, in-bond transit of people and baggage through international hubs, and prompt delivery to the final destination. Combinations of real and perceived customer expectations regarding "seamless air travel" created a need for global networks of airlines.

ECONOMICS OF THE AIRLINE INDUSTRY

Airline industry profitability was very volatile. The six year period 1984–89 witnessed record industry operating profits of U.S.$39 billion; 1989 posted an industry net profit of U.S.$3.5 billion. In stark contrast, the industry reported cumulative net losses of U.S.$20 billion for the period 1990 to 1993. The Gulf War and 1990–91 recession had stalled traffic growth and resulted in airlines discounting fares to stimulate demand. Meanwhile, fuel prices spiked upwards. The airlines cost structure prevented them from shedding costs as quickly as yields fell.

BA was consistently profitable during this four year drought, an exception among major carriers. Superior performance was attributed to BA's route structure centered on the Heathrow hub giving it a strong market position, and 1988 Thatcher-*ite* privatization which had forced BA to rationalize operations in the late 1980s.

Table 18.2 compares key inter-regional data reflecting yield and cost differences. The Pacific Rim carriers had the lowest labor costs in the industry. Singapore Airlines had a very different revenue-ton-kilometer composition from the others which, with its lower labor costs, gave it radically lower revenue/RTK and cost/ATK.[4] U.S. carriers experienced relatively high labor as a percentage of their operating costs, but rationalized higher costs over much larger system networks. The result was that even the highest cost U.S. carriers were cost competitive internationally.

The conditions necessary to improve an airline's profitability can be presented very simply. It was necessary to achieve either (1) a greater load factor for a constant revenue yield, (2) higher fares and hence greater revenue yield for a constant load factor, (3) lower operating costs, or preferably, (4) higher load factor and revenue yield combined with lower operating costs. [See Glossary at end for definitions.]

Actually achieving profitability was much more complicated. Load factors could be stimulated in the short term by effective promotion and pricing but cutting fares eroded revenue yield. Skillful balancing of the trade-off between load factors and yield was vital to airline competitive advantage and profitability. On the other hand, cost reductions were dependent upon increasing productivity of labor and equipment without diminishing passenger service and safety. Underlying the factors above was a second level driving cost and yield management performance. These were (1) a non-variable cost structure, (2) cost management hobbled by dependence on several key inputs, (3) incremental advantages between airlines on their yield management, and (4) limited route structure economies available to reduce unit costs.

BA must understand these underlying issues if it were to make an accurate analysis of the U.S. airline industry and USAir's future prospects. There were a limited number of avenues available to reverse USAir's plight. BA's understanding of U.S. industry cost structure

Table 18.2 Comparison of 1993 Revenue and Cost Data for Selected Major Carriers

Measure	Canadian Industry	USA Industry	British Airways	USAir	Japan Airlines	Singapore Airlines
Passenger revenue yield/RPK	8.0¢	8.1¢	9.4¢	10.7¢	11.5¢	10.1¢
Passenger load factor	67.0%	67.7%	70.0%	59.2%	65.2%	71.4%
Salaries & benefits/ operating cost	29.8%	34.9%	27.9%	39.7%	–	21.7%
Revenue yield/RTK	79.1¢	82.7¢	75.5¢	est. 105¢	107.0¢	48.4¢
Operating expense/ ATK	45.0¢	44.7¢	46.3¢	est. 66¢	71.9¢	31.7¢
Achieved weight load factor	55.8%	54.5%	66.5%	59.2%	64.1%	69.5%
Breakeven weight load factor	56.8%	54.1%	61.3%	61.7%	67.2%	65.5%
Operating margin (%)	–1.0%	1.7%	7.9%	–1.1%	–2.7%	9.6%
Net profit margin (%)	–9.4%	–2.6%	4.5%	–5.6%	–2.6%	13.0%

Currency values in U.S. Funds, 1.324 CDN$ = 1U.S.$; 1£ = 1.48U.S.$; 1.57SI$ = 1U.S.
Source: Carriers' 1993 Annual Reports & IATA *World Air Transport Statistics, 1994.*

and yield management opportunities would determine how it decided its future involvement with USAir.

Cost Structure

A large proportion, 82 percent, of airline operating costs were fixed or semi-variable; only 18 percent of operating costs were truly variable – travel agency commissions, ticketing fees, and meals. Semi-variable costs could be varied only by large and expensive "steps" over the medium- and long-term. The implications were that once an airline determined its route structure – the combination of destinations, frequencies, and aircraft – fuel, crew, and ground staff costs were fixed. Almost the same amount of fuel was used whether a plane flew empty or full; crew and ground staff size were determined by the type of aircraft, not the passenger load. Of the 82 percent fixed and semi-variable operating costs, approximately 38 points related to provision of airborne transportation; the balance, 44 points, related to ground service – maintenance, provision of hubs, and administration.

Yield Management

The industry's cost structure pressured carriers to sell more seats on each flight at higher yields – contribution to profit was increased by improving load factors and/or revenue yield per RPK. By 1993, the airline industry was increasing load factors and total revenue with millions of new passengers annually, most of whom were vacationers. The industry set a new record in 1993 with 2,000 billion RPKs travelled. Increased volumes of travelers reduced aircraft over-capacity and increased load factors, however, leisure travelers paid lower fares through advance bookings and group rates which reduced yields per RPK and in turn required further increases to load factors.

"Yield management," optimally balancing load factor and yield to maximize operating profit, was entrusted to sophisticated computer software embedded in the computer reservation system (CRS) operated by each major airline. Yield management software constantly reviewed bookings data for each flight to forecast demand and attempt to optimize final load factor and yield. Sophisticated algorithms calculated the opportunity on individual flights to charge selectively discounted fares within a class of service, to offer different classes of service (e.g., first, business, economy, excursion), and to vary fares with advance purchase conditions and with restrictions such as limited return or exchange privileges. By varying fares and classes of service, yield management attempted to optimize load factor and yield combinations on every flight, and in turn, maximize system-wide net revenue.

Industry conditions had resulted in steady declines in revenue yield per RPK of approximately 2 percent per year. This trend was expected to continue downwards unabated. Recent attempts by American Airlines (AA) to increase yields with simplified fares had been fruitless – the industry lacked pricing discipline; it would not limit the availability of discounted fares; individual airlines simply scrambled for market share.

Cost Management

Given the downward pressure on fares and intense competition for patronage, airline management placed priority on reducing operating costs. Unfortunately, two principal operating costs, fuel and labor (13 percent and 39 percent of costs, respectively, for U.S. carriers) offered limited opportunity for reduction. Both were non-variable costs dictated by route structure and fleet configuration. Fuel efficiency was closely monitored and modifications such as "hush-kitting" to improve efficiency were introduced, but oil price spikes could not be fully hedged. Accordingly, fuel costs occasionally increased to a much greater degree than fares could be supplemented with fuel surcharges.

Furthermore, as a service industry, and because of the critical nature of flying safety, labor was a large part of costs and good labor relations were vital. High frequencies of employee/customer interaction and error-free mechanical records required highly trained staff to preserve customer patronage and confidence. Moreover, the older, larger carriers could not easily introduce more flexible and efficient work rules due to restrictive collective agreements. These carriers consequently struggled to compete with the younger airlines' higher labor productivity and efficiency ratios, and subsequently lower unit costs.

The age of active fleets of aircraft was closely watched. Newer aircraft offered significant efficiency and productivity savings due to reduced fuel and flight crew costs. So, not only must an airline match the capability of its fleet to its route structure to be efficient, it must replace aircraft to take advantage of efficiency improvements offered by newer aircraft. However, delivery queues, previous lease commitments, and limited cash flow made whole-sale fleet changes impossible. A Boeing 747-400 cost U.S.$150 million. Revamping fleets could be accomplished only as cash flow allowed.

Looking forward, significant reductions in labor costs would remain elusive: favorable fuel prices, not increased labor productivity, accounted for reduced 1993 operating costs. Furthermore, employee stock ownership initiatives with associated wage and benefit concessions at UAL, TWA, and Northwest were not expected to add lasting value to operations. Finally, increasing interest rates and fuel prices and the increasing need to replace ageing aircraft foretold of greater airline indebtedness. Only those airlines able to increase productivity quickly – more quickly than nose-diving fares – could look forward to profitable operations.

Route Structure Economies

North American airlines generally had structured their operations around so-called "hub and spoke" networks since the hub structure was introduced by AA in 1982. Spokes fed passengers from outlying points into a central airport (hub) where passengers connected with other flights to other hubs, often travelling another spoke to their final destination. For passengers, hubs created the inconvenience of a transfer but offset the inconvenience with greater frequency of flights and lower fares.

Hubs were the most cost efficient method of distributing services over a large network – 20 percent less costly system-wide than point-to-point service – and dramatically reduced the number of flights and aircraft necessary to serve the U.S. market versus a continent-wide system offering point-to-point service with equivalent frequency.

Airlines had been able to generate extra cost efficiencies in the mid-1980s by expanding their operations. By increasing the number of flights offered within a fixed route structure or alternately, by expanding the route structure with new destinations, airlines had stimulated passenger traffic faster than they increased costs. Additional flights from existing hubs were inexpensive to add because 55 to 70 percent of usual costs did not apply – the costs were already "sunk" into a previously established hub and trained ground crew. The allure of low break-even load factors and additional passenger "feed" was a powerful incentive to expand operations.

However, by the early-1990s, route structure economies were no longer valid options to "grow out of" the industry recession. Instead, the airlines were left to stimulate traffic on specific routes through marketing promotions – an expensive proposition. Stimulation amounted to discounting fares, offering frequent flyer plans, and increasing service.

AERO-POLITICAL CONSIDERATIONS AND MARKET INTERFERENCE

Every nation has a history of using its airline(s) to achieve social and technological objectives, and undeniably, the motives influencing government engagement in an airline overlap into an expression of national pride. This mix of purpose and emotion required delicate negotiation between the airlines and their respective governments, and then between governments. The major influences – government subsidization, the social needs of developing nations, restrictive bilateral agreements, congestion, and government policy – are outlined below.

Government Subsidization

Subsidization of state-owned *flag carriers* was a major component of the continuing international over-capacity problem. The prestige associated with a flag carrier prevented serious debate regarding termination of unprofitable national airlines in many countries. As an example of government subsidization and market interference, Air France received U.S.$3.7 billion in 1994 from the French and European Community governments for capital re-financing after 1993 losses of U.S.$1.9 billion on revenues of U.S.$12.9 billion.

Developing Nations with Social Needs

In developing countries, governments weighed the social role of aviation against the interests of private capital. Pressing internal development requirements would not be met by external, private airlines; governments were forced to operate and subsidize airlines. Naturally, these airlines attempted to expand internationally to equalize balance of payments and underwrite internal operations, adding to global over-capacity.

Bilateral Agreements, Cabotage, and Fifth Freedom Rights

Bilateral negotiations between two countries determined what airline rights would be traded to balance economic and material benefits. Negotiations centered upon *cabotage* and six negotiable rights, the so-called six *freedoms of the air*. Negotiations received great emphasis because export of air service to foreign passengers typically repatriated 60 to 70 percent of fares, subsequently improving a country's balance of payments, GDP, and overall transportation system. As a result, governments jealously protected their airline(s) during negotiation of reciprocal agreements.

Cabotage was the right of an airline to carry "local traffic in a foreign market." As a general rule, cabotage was strictly prohibited. For example, Lufthansa was unable to board passengers originating in Atlanta for Dallas on its Frankfurt-Atlanta-Dallas service. Similarly, UAL could not board and deliver traffic between Munich and Frankfurt.

The *fifth freedom of the air* allowed carriers the privilege of boarding passengers in one foreign country for transport to another foreign country. Fifth freedom privileges acquired by the U.S. government following World War II were extremely important to U.S. carriers in Europe. Compact European geography allowed those with fifth freedoms to serve several major European cities on a single flight, for example New York-London-Frankfurt. Conversely, European carriers making a trip of similar distance and configuration, say Frankfurt-Atlanta-Dallas, were unable to board passengers on the Atlanta-Dallas leg. European carriers required, but could not obtain, cabotage privileges to carry "local traffic within a foreign (U.S.) market." This aberration in commercial access between carriers of different nations was created using the prevailing fifth freedom and cabotage privileges contained in the bilateral agreements. As an aside, there was a consensus that the U.S. government's position on multilateral agreements and *open skies* (relaxation of the *six freedoms*) would eventually force free trade on air service.

A related issue was limits to foreign ownership of airlines. With foreign ownership of airlines currently capped in many countries at 25 percent of voting stock and 50 percent of total equity, national legislatures were being pressured by airlines to relax restrictions and allow ingress of foreign equity. Existing equity restrictions would eventually be relaxed and foreign direct investment would be possible.

Congestion

Airport facility capacity constraints and landing rights became a contentious issue in the 1990s. It was practically impossible to gain access to major airports. New competitors were often denied access to important airports and routes while the incumbents further monopolized those airports. London Heathrow, New York JFK, Tokyo Narita, Chicago O'Hare, Paris Orly, Hong Kong, Singapore: all were operating beyond design capacity and would grow more congested in the foreseeable future. Furthermore, access to airport gates as they became available was controlled either by local governments and airport authorities (in the USA) or by the airport's incumbent airlines.

The Walking Wounded

United States bankruptcy law allows insolvent firms to shelter themselves from creditors under a section titled Chapter 11. This provides the firm's management a moratorium period under the supervision of the bankruptcy court while financial reorganization is attempted. Theoretically, Chapter 11 preserves creditors' wealth more effectively by allowing restructuring rather than simply "shutting the doors."

Use of Chapter 11 provisions had become an exit strategy in the U.S. airline industry. Exit was very difficult as excess aircraft suitable for most routes were readily available – on-going airlines could demand unreasonably low prices for used aircraft. Also, routes were over-crowded and therefore less valuable than several years earlier. Facing a hostile environment, several airlines had slipped into Chapter 11, and by using the moratorium on their outstanding liabilities, had conducted a managed withdrawal over several years. The largest U.S. carriers claimed that Chapter 11, by delaying final bankruptcy decisions, promoted persistence of endemic over-capacity.

Furthermore, Chapter 11, by freezing creditors' claims, could drastically lower a firm's breakeven point. As a result, those airlines sheltering in Chapter 11 could survive on "artificially" low fares while they attempted to boost their load factors to self-sufficient levels. Other airlines were forced to match fares, disrupting industry pricing and further weakening those not yet in bankruptcy. Continental, TWA, Eastern, and Pan Am operated domestic and international routes under bankruptcy court protection in the 1989 to 1992 period. Only Continental and TWA reorganized successfully, but all four had aggressively discounted their fares while under court protection.

Competitive Developments

In light of eroding yields, constant effort was made to increase load factors through better service – more attentive personnel, greater frequency of flights, more convenient connections, and larger networks. This became an increasingly costly endeavor as service improvements had limited sustainable advantage. Airlines routinely matched each other's offerings on fares, frequent flyer plans, and service enhancements with the result that aircraft seats were reduced to a commodity. Industry competition in the 1990s centered on:

(1) a variety of alliances forming expansive global networks,
(2) the relative capabilities of computer reservation systems, and
(3) the relative attractiveness of frequent flyer plans.

MARKETING AND EQUITY ALLIANCES AND CODE SHARING

By 1994, international route expansion was being accomplished by marketing alliances and code sharing, outright purchase of routes having become relatively expensive or not possible. Alliances were less capital intensive and quicker to assemble, and therefore, more effective avenues to international route expansion. For instance, marketing alliances allowed both UAL and Delta to complete world-wide route structures connecting all key markets during 1992. This would have been a drawn-out process if route acquisition alone had been pursued.

Alliance arrangements ranged from arm's length marketing partnerships to minority equity purchases and swaps, resulting in varying degrees of mutual commitment, complexity, stability, and reversibility. The most common alliance (with the least mutual commitment) was a marketing agreement between carriers involving preferential exchange of traffic. For example, Canadian Airlines International (CAI) had a marketing agreement with Lufthansa under which CAI traffic to a variety of European destinations was booked onward from Frankfurt on Lufthansa. In return, Lufthansa traffic to Canada was booked to its final destination on CAI. Marketing alliances were volatile with partners and terms changing often. At one time, Air Canada had marketing alliances with Qantas, Air New Zealand, and Lufthansa; these airlines were now allied with CAI.

Intermediate levels of commitment involved code sharing while the greatest mutual commitment with significant penalties for withdrawal was an equity alliance. Lufthansa and UAL had extensive code share arrangements without equity encumbrances while BA used equity alliances to secure "permanent" code share partnerships. Delta, Swissair, and Singapore Airlines had one of the most complex equity alliances, requiring mutual exchange of 5 percent of each airline's equity and coordinated purchase of common aircraft and specialized maintenance. Their ultimate aim was creation of an integrated global operation. Table 18.3, Alliances of Selected Carriers, illustrates typical carrier alliance networks.

BA/USAIR CODE SHARING ARRANGEMENTS

Code sharing by European carriers with U.S. carriers circumvented U.S. cabotage barriers by linking two carriers' intra-regional flights using one of the carrier's international flights.

Table 18.3 Alliances of Selected Carriers

	AA	UAL	Delta	NWA	CO	BA	USAir
Equity	Canadian	–	Singapore Airlines Comair Skywest Swissair	KLM	Air Canada	Deutsche BA GB Airways Qantas TAT USAir	British Airways
Marketing only	British Midland Gulf Air LOT Polish Qantas South African	ALM Antillean Air Canada Aloha Ansett British Midland China Southern Emirates Iberia Cyprus Airways Thai International Lufthansa	Aeromexico Aeroflot Austrian Korean Air Air New Zealand Malev Sabena Varig Vietnam Airlines Virgin Atlantic	Alaska Airlines USAir America West	Air France Alitalia SAS America West Malaysia Airlines	Aeromexico Aer Lingus Korean Air Maersk Air Cathay Pacific Malaysia Airlines	All Nippon Airways Alitalia Northwest Qantas

Source: Air Transport World

Code sharing did not require an equity partnership, but BA deliberately withheld code sharing from USAir until the equity purchase was completed. Code sharing between USAir and BA in conjunction with an equity position was intended to create a stable platform for BA to build passenger traffic to and from the U.S. market to points around the world. BA clearly preferred more permanent marketing partners as it established a global network. USAir's flights would integrate into BA's route structure, and conversely, BA's flights into USAir's route structure.

For fiscal 1995, BA was estimating U.S.$105 million incremental revenue from its global marketing/equity alliances detailed as follows: U.S.$30-35 million was attributed to incremental code-sharing traffic; another U.S.$30-35 million to cross-linked FFPs attracting incremental traffic; and U.S.$40 million to cost reductions through shared marketing and purchasing. A large proportion of these savings was anticipated originating in the USAir alliance, a dubious prospect given the results of the first twelve months of code sharing.

Moreover, dependence upon code sharing to build and channel passenger volume was risky as code sharing authorities were temporary. The U.S. Department of Transport (DOT) issued or renewed orders authorizing code sharing for one year periods. The existing BA/USAir authorities on sixty-five airports expired March 17, 1995. In addition, approval of outstanding BA/USAir applications for code sharing authorities in another sixty-five U.S. and seven foreign destinations was being delayed by U.S. DOT.

COMPUTER RESERVATION SYSTEMS

American Airlines' Sabre division originated computer reservation systems (CRSs) as an intentional competitive hurdle. Over time, all of the largest airlines developed proprietary CRSs to administer co-ordination of booking and ticket distribution activity, yield and cost management, and internal operations such as accounting. Smaller airlines co-operated in joint systems, or licensed another airline's CRS.

By 1994, CRSs were no longer effective in differentiating performance and distribution activities. Systems differences were insignificant when compared to disruptions caused by market rivalry and airlines operating under Chapter 11 protection.

FREQUENT FLYER PROGRAMS

Frequent flyer programs (FFPs) rewarded passengers with free trips and other benefits based on kilometers flown. First introduced by American Airlines, this marketing innovation favored large carriers with extensive route systems on which customers could more readily accumulate mileage and select desirable reward destinations. As the power of FFPs became apparent, all major North American airlines quickly followed AA's lead. By 1994, most large European and Asian carriers had initiated their own FFPs or allied with North American carriers' FFPs. Like CRSs, FFPs were a mature innovation offering little or no advantage.

THE U.S. MARKET SITUATION – POINT-TO-POINT CARRIERS ATTACK

AA, Delta, and UAL – the "Big Three" – competed with increasing difficulty in the USA due to their unadaptable cost structures, full-service philosophy, and hub orientation. Attacks by lower cost, higher productivity point-to-point carriers, particularly Southwest Airlines of Dallas, created intense competition in the short-haul market.

Over time, each of the Big Three had focused its operations on a unique hub and spoke network resulting in limited competition at many airports. For example, at Dallas/Fort Worth International Airport, AA had a market share of over 60 percent and Delta accounted for a large part of the remainder; at Chicago-O'Hare, UAL and AA dominated. The result of unique networks and hub dominance was restriction of competition which enabled the airlines to charge fares as much as 20 percent higher than fares in openly contested markets.

THE "SOUTHWEST EFFECT"

The only continuously profitable major North American airline, Southwest Airlines, avoided operating an expensive hub and spoke system. Instead, Southwest offered high frequency "no frills" point-to-point service in high volume short-haul corridors, not unlike a bus route. It was the antithesis of the Big Three.

Southwest fundamentally changed the U.S. short-haul air travel industry – its demand characteristics, cost structure, and industry barriers. By not offering expensive service options like food and CRS listings and by reducing payment of expensive travel agency commissions with toll-free in-house reservation desks, Southwest kept costs low. Meanwhile, it boosted load factors by attracting customers from other forms of transportation – bus, auto, train – with fares 50 to 70 percent below full-service competitors. The diseconomies of point-to-point flying were overcome by focusing on high volume corridors and maintaining the lowest costs of the U.S. major airlines.

By 1993, the Southwest and its imitators had stolen a significant share of the U.S. domestic market from the Big Three. Full-service hub-oriented carriers like AA, Delta, and UAL could not compete profitably at the prevailing short-haul fares. As a result, they reduced flights and gates serving short-haul markets and re-emphasized long-haul and international routes. Market share of the Big Three slipped to 57 percent in 1993, down from 70 percent three years earlier.

The major airlines' hub and spoke operations could not compete effectively on short haul-high volume routes with high frequency, no frills point-to-point service. The majors' route and cost structures were poorly suited to frequent, short flights with many take-off and landing cycles. Hubs were interdependent and must mesh connecting flights flawlessly. A congestion delay at one airport could cause passengers inconvenience and airlines/hubs disruption for the balance of the day. Time delays must be built into hub schedules, reducing productivity of personnel and equipment. Increasing productivity on short-haul flights required greater utilization of aircraft and crew which required de-linking flights from hubs and interdependent schedules and instead flying point-to-point.

This presented the full service airlines with a dilemma: their extensive networks required hub systems to achieve economies; corrupting the hub system with hybrid point-to-point and hub route structures could dangerously increase costs, diminish service frequency, disrupt on-time connections, and de-stabilize connector systems feeding into long-haul and overseas routes.

The Big Three had yet to respond to attacks on the short-haul market. Instead, they dealt with their non-competitive unit costs on short-haul operations with layoffs, wage rollbacks and concessions, allying with regional carriers, and retreating to long-haul and international routes – a route structure better suited to full-service, high cost operations. By mid-1994, Continental and USAir had responded directly to the Southwest challenge with fundamental route structure changes. In addition, UAL had announced introduction of *Shuttle by UAL* with point-to-point service beginning in the fall of 1994. It was yet to be determined if hub-oriented airlines could change to point-to-point service and achieve Southwest's industry-low cost structure. To date, airlines had found imitating Southwest's point-to-point route structure very expensive.

USAIR: PERFORMANCE AND PROSPECTS

USAir was the weakest of the eight major U.S. airlines: its cost structure was non-competitive with low cost and financially restructured airlines; its equity was severely depleted from losses estimated to reach U.S.$2.4 billion by the end of the three years, 1991 to 1993; its operations focused on business travel in the short-haul Eastern U.S. market; its fleet was older than most; and its labor unions were not yet convinced of a pressing need to give concessions to improve productivity.

USAir was also different than its U.S. competitors from an operations perspective. Its history as a conglomeration of smaller commuter airlines – Allegheny, Piedmont, PSA, Suburban, and Pennsylvania – made it unique and gave it a different competitive focus. USAir operations were isolated in the Eastern U.S. commuter market, allowing it to offset higher operating costs associated with flying short-haul routes through congested airports with higher traffic volumes and the ability to extract premium net yields per RPK.

Following 1991, USAir lost control of its unit costs in comparison to other major U.S. carriers. Costs per ASK had risen more than 9 percent in the past two years while its competitors had held or reduced their costs. Furthermore, USAir's fares were subjected to constant promotions, eroding their once industry high net yields.

Until 1993, the other U.S. airlines had been content to focus in other markets, not challenging USAir on the Eastern U.S. short-haul routes. However, in Fall 1993, Southwest Airlines (LUV) inaugurated high frequency service to Chicago and Cleveland from Baltimore/Washington International Airport with fares 75 to 80 percent below those offered by USAir. USAir responded by matching most fares and increasing the frequency of its service.

Then, in October 1993, Continental Airlines (CAL) announced route changes centered on the high volume Eastern USA corridors, primarily adopting the low-cost, no-frills point-to-point system. By early-1994, Continental Lite (CALite) accounted for 15 percent of CAL's domestic route structure with its "Peanuts Fares." CAL planned to convert 50 percent of its domestic route to point-to-point service by mid-1994.

USAir responded by introducing "Project High Ground" and "Quick Turns" in the first quarter of 1994 to introduce point-to-point service and enhance productivity. It immediately started conversion of 25 percent of its daily flights to point-to-point service. By late April, USAir reported 20 percent more ASKs flown without adding assets due to point-to-point conversions, and that it was on target for a breakeven operating profit in the second quarter.

With competition escalating in its traditional market, it was probable that USAir would continue to suffer losses. Whereas LUV and CAL had low cost structures and could subsidize low and below-cost fares from operations elsewhere, USAir's high cost structure, limited cash reserves, and base in the Eastern U.S. business travel market left it vulnerable. USAir was forecasting pre-tax losses of U.S.$350 million for 1994.

Exhibit 18.1 contains comparative performance data on the U.S. majors and BA. BA ranked first in international RPK and passenger counts, whereas USAir ranked fiftieth with minimal international traffic or route structure, principally Frankfurt, Paris, and Mexico City. The section Foreign Revenue presents 1993 regional revenues where available, or otherwise, notes regions in which the airlines have active international operations. Foreign Revenue Growth indicates year-over-year international revenue by company, where available.

Following release of USAir's 1993 losses in March, BA announced it would not invest further in USAir until the outcome of USAir's efforts to reduce operating costs was known. However, with U.S.$400 million already invested in USAir, and U.S.$1.5 billion invested in equity alliances globally, BA could ill afford to ignore the situation.

Glossary of Common Measurements of Performance and Activity

1. *Revenue Passenger Kilometers (RPK)*
   The number of revenue passengers carried multiplied by the distance flown.
2. *Available Seat Kilometers (ASK)*
   The number of seats available for sale multiplied by the distance flown.
3. *Passenger Load Factor*
   RPK expressed as a percentage of ASK.
4. *Revenue Yield*
   Passenger revenue from scheduled operations divided by scheduled RPKs.

Exhibit 18.1   1993 Performance Data: U.S. Carriers and British Airways

	AA	UAL	Delta	NWA	CAL	BA	USAir	South-west
RPK TRAFFIC (millions)								
International	46,419	62,647	36,532	40,977	17,465	75,044	3,960	–
Rank	4	2	9	7	16	1	50	–
Domestic	109,883	99,879	96,813	52,572	50,649	5,042	52,720	30,481
Total	156,302	162,526	133,345	93,549	68,113	80,086	56,681	30,481
Rank	1	2	3	4	6	5	7	(16)
PASSENGER TRAFFIC (thousands)								
International	14,305	10,942	8,202	7,481	5,076	22,367	–	–
Rank	3	5	10	13	20	1	–	–
Domestic	68,240	58,730	76,829	36,640	33,551	5,766	52,774	36,955
Total	82,545	69,672	85,032	44,121	38,627	30,595	53,678	36,955
Rank	2	3	1	5	6	9	4	(7)
PASSENGER LOAD FACTOR %								
International	63.3	70.7	64.5	71.1	67.4	70.0	69.1	–
Domestic	59.2	65.1	61.6	63.6	61.8	68.9	58.6	68.4
Total load factor %	60.4	67.1	62.3	66.7	63.2	69.9	59.2	68.4
Breakeven load factor	~58.	65.6	65.5		65.2	61.3	61.7	
COST STRUCTURE (U.S. ¢)								
Revenue Yield/RPK	8.3	7.8	8.4		7.1	9.4	10.7	7.3
Unit Cost/ASK	5.1	5.8	5.9	5.2	4.9	7.3	6.9	5.2
FOREIGN REVENUE (U.S.$ millions)								
Asia-Pacific	362	✓	✓	✓	✓			
Europe	1,659	✓	✓	✓	✓	3,603		
Latin America	1,888	✓	✓		✓			
Middle-East				✓				
Africa						1,332		
The Americas						3,003		
Mid-East, India, Asia-Pacific						1,390		
FOREIGN REVENUE GROWTH (U.S.$ billions)								
1991	2.67	3.87	1.18		1.1	5.50	n/a	n/a
1992	3.68	4.86	1.95		1.2	5.03	n/a	n/a
1993	3.91	5.56	2.58		1.1	5.74	n/a	n/a

5. *Unit Costs*
   Operating costs from scheduled operations divided by scheduled ASKs.
6. *Available Tonne-Kilometers (ATK)*
   The number of tonnes (2,204 lb.) of capacity available for carriage of revenue load (passenger and cargo) multiplied by the distance flown.
7. *Revenue Tonne-Kilometers (RTK)*
   The revenue load in tonnes multiplied by the distance flown.
8. *Breakeven Weight Load Factor*
   The load factor required to equate total traffic revenue with operating costs.

Exhibit 18.1 1993 Performance Data: U.S. Carriers and British Airways *(continued)*

	AA	UAL	Delta	NWA	CAL	BA	USAir	South-west
FINANCIAL DATA (U.S.$ millions)								
Operating revenue	14,737	14,511	11,997	8,650	3,284	9,328	7,083	2,296
Operating profit (loss)	374	263	−575	272	112	734	−75	291
Operating profit margin	2.5%	1.8%			3.4%	7.8%		12.7%
Net expense and interest	−688	−310	−76		−122	−289	−274	32
Income before taxes and accounting changes	−314	−47	−651		−11	445	−350	259
Net income	*−110	−50	−1,002	−115	−39	423	−393	169
Less preferred dividend	*60	33	110		−	157	74	5
Net income to stockholders	*−170	−83	−1,112		−39	266	−467	164
Total assets less current liabilities	13,509	7,944	8,898		2,797	8,365	4,641	2,097
Long-term debt; redeemable preferred stock	(7,290)	(3,529)	(3,799)		(1,579)	(5,563)	(3,203)	(639)
Deferred credits & other liabilities	(3,051)	(3,212)	(3,186)		(497)	(98)	(1,651)	(404)
Total stockholders' equity	3,168	1,203	1,913		721	2,350	(213)	1,054

Reported in U.S. funds.
CAL emerged from Chapter 11 4.28.94.
*Net income, dividend and net income apply to AMR Corp 1993 Consolidated Statement, AA's parent.

NOTES

1. A code sharing authority allowed two carriers to "link" their connecting flights using the same flight number, thus giving the impression of a through flight. Consequently, code share flights were listed earlier on travel agents' computer reservation systems (CRSs), received more exposure, and had greater probability of being booked. In reality, passengers transferred airline and aircraft where the two airlines' flights connected.
2. Air Transport World, 6/94: 174.
3. Columns one and two include passenger and RPK data for 147 carriers, excluding Aeroflot, as compiled by the International Air Travel Association (IATA), the airline industry trade association. The RPK data from IATA accounts for 83 percent of 1993 world-wide traffic. The third and fourth columns of Table 1 relate to average annual change in RPK traffic and average annual percent change in RPK traffic, as predicted by Boeing Commercial Airplane Group. Differences in reporting methods make data in columns one and two not directly comparable with columns three and four.
4. Note introduction of Revenue Tonne-Kilometers (RTK) and Available Tonne-Kilometers (ATK) reflect combined passenger and cargo tonnage multiplied by the distance flown. These measures are used similarly to RPK and ASK introduced earlier.

19

Perdue Farms, Inc. 1994

This case was prepared by George C. Rubenson, Frank M. Shipper, and Jane M. Hanebury solely to provide material for class discussion. The case is not intended to illustrate either effective or ineffective handling of a managerial situation.

COMPANY HISTORY

"I have a theory that you can tell the difference between those who have inherited a fortune and those who have made a fortune. Those who have made their own fortune forget not where they came from and are less likely to lose touch with the common man." (Bill Sterling, 'Just Browsin' column in Eastern Shore News, March 2, 1988)

In 1917, Arthur W. Perdue, a Railway Express agent and descendent of a French Huguenot family named Perdeaux, bought fifty leghorn chickens for a total of $5 and began selling table eggs near the small town of Salisbury, Maryland. A region immortalized in James Michener's *Chesapeake,* it is alternately known as "the Eastern Shore" or the "Delmarva Peninsula" and includes parts of DELaware, MARyland and VirginiA.

Initially, the business amounted to little more than a farm wife's chore for "pin money," raising a few "biddies" in a cardboard box behind the wood stove in the kitchen until they were old enough to fend for themselves in the barnyard. But in 1920, when he was thirty-six, Railway Express asked "Mr. Arthur" to move to a station away from the Eastern Shore, he quit his job as Salisbury's Railway Express agent and entered the egg business full-time. His only child, Franklin Parsons Perdue, was born that same year.

Mr. Arthur soon expanded his egg market and began shipments to New York. Practicing small economies such as mixing his own chicken feed and using leather from his old shoes to make hinges for his chicken coops, he stayed out of debt and prospered. He tried to add a new chicken coop every year. By the time young Frank was ten, he had fifty chickens or so of his own to look after, earning money from their eggs. He worked along with his parents, not always enthusiastically, to feed the chickens, clean the coops, dig the cesspools, and gather and grade eggs. A shy introverted country boy, he went for five years to a one room school, eventually graduated from Wicomico High School, and attended the State Teachers College in Salisbury for two years before returning to the farm in 1939 to work full-time with his father.

By 1940, it was obvious to father and son that the future lay in selling chickens, not eggs. But the Perdues made the shift to selling broilers only after careful attention to every detail – a standard Perdue procedure in the years to come. In 1944, Mr. Arthur made his son Frank a full partner in what was then A. W. Perdue and Son, Inc., a firm already known for quality products and fair dealing in a toughly competitive business. In 1950, Frank took over leadership of Perdue Farms, a company with forty employees. By 1952, revenues were $6,000,000 from the sale of 2,600,000 broilers.

By 1967, annual sales had increased to about $35,000,000 but it was becoming increasingly clear that additional profits lay in processing chickens. Frank recalled in an interview for *Business Week* (September 15, 1972) ". . . processors were paying us ten cents a live pound for what cost us fourteen cents to produce. Suddenly, processors were making as much as seven cents a pound."

A cautious, conservative planner, Arthur Perdue had not been eager for expansion and Frank Perdue himself was reluctant to enter poultry processing. But, economic forces dictated the move and, in 1968, Perdue Farms became a vertically integrated operation, hatching eggs, delivering the chicks to contract growers, buying grain, supplying the feed and litter, and, finally, processing the broilers and shipping them to market.

The company bought its first plant in 1968 – a Swift and Company operation in Salisbury – renovated it, and equipped it with machines capable of processing 14,000 broilers per hour. Computers were soon employed to devise feeding formulas for each stage of growth so birds reached their growth potential sooner. Geneticists were hired to breed larger-breasted chickens and veterinarians were put on staff to keep the flocks healthy, while nutritionists handled the feed formulations to achieve the best feed conversion.

From the beginning, Frank Perdue refused to permit his broilers to be frozen for shipping, a process that resulted in unappetizing black bones and loss of flavor and moistness when cooked. Instead, Perdue chickens were (and some still are) shipped to market packed in ice, justifying the company's advertisements at that time that it sold only "fresh, young broilers." However, this policy also limited the company's market to those locations that could be serviced overnight from the Eastern Shore of Maryland. Thus, Perdue chose for its primary markets the densely populated towns and cities of the East Coast, particularly New York City, which consumes more Perdue chicken than all other brands combined.

During the 1970s, the firm entered the Baltimore, Philadelphia, Boston, and Providence markets. Facilities were expanded rapidly to include a new broiler processing plant and protein conversion plant in Accomac, Virginia; a processing plant in Lewiston, North Carolina; a hatchery in Murfreesboro, North Carolina; and several Swift and Company facilities including a processing plant in Georgetown, Delaware; a feedmill in Bridgeville, Delaware; and a feedmill in Elkin, North Carolina.

In 1977, Mr. Arthur died at the age of ninety-one, leaving behind a company with annual sales of nearly $200,000,000, an average annual growth rate of 17 percent compared to an industry average of 1 percent a year, the potential for processing 78,000 broilers per hour, and annual production of nearly 350,000,000 pounds of poultry per year. Frank Perdue, who says without a hint of self-deprecation that "I am a B-minus student. I know how smart I am. I know a B-minus is not as good as an A," said of his father simply, "I learned everything from him."

Stew Leonard, owner of a huge supermarket in Norwalk, Connecticut, and one of Perdue's top customers, describes Frank Perdue as "What you see is what you get. If you ask him a question you will get an answer." Perdue disapproves the presence of a union between himself and his associates and adds, "The absence of unions makes for a better relationship with our associates. If we treat our associates right, I don't think we will have a union." On conglomerates, he states, "Diversification is the most dangerous word in the English language." His business philosophy is, "I'm interested in being the best rather than the biggest. Expansion is OK if it has a positive effect on product quality. I'll do nothing that detracts from product quality."

Frank Perdue is known for having a temper. He is as hard on himself, however, as he is on others, readily admitting his shortcomings and even his mistakes. For example, in the '70s, he apparently briefly discussed using the influence of some unsavory characters to help alleviate union pressure. When an investigative reporter in the late 1980s asked him about this instance, he admitted that it was a mistake, saying, ". . . it was probably the dumbest thing I ever did."

In 1981, Frank Perdue was in Massachusetts for his induction into the Babson College Academy of Distinguished Entrepreneurs, an award established in 1978 to recognize the spirit of free enterprise and business leadership. Babson College President Ralph Z. Sorenson inducted Perdue into the academy which, at that time, numbered eighteen men and women from four continents. Perdue had the following to say to the college students:

> There are none, nor will there ever be, easy steps for the entrepreneur. Nothing, absolutely nothing, replaces the willingness to work earnestly, intelligently towards a goal. You have to be willing to pay the price. You have to have an insatiable appetite for detail, have to be willing to accept constructive criticism, to ask questions, to be fiscally responsible, to surround yourself with good people and most of all, to listen. (Frank Perdue, speech at Babson College, April 28, 1981)

The early 1980s proved to be a period of further growth as Perdue diversified and broadened its market. New marketing areas included Washington, D.C.; Richmond, Virginia; and Norfolk, Virginia. Additional facilities were opened in Cofield, Kenly, Halifax, Robbins, and Robersonville, North Carolina. The firm broadened its line to include value added products such as Oven Stuffer roasters and Perdue Done It!, a new brand of fresh, prepared chicken products featuring cooked chicken breast nuggets, cutlets, and tenders. James A. (Jim) Perdue, Frank's only son, joined the company as a management trainee in 1983.

The latter 1980s tested the mettle of the firm. Following a period of considerable expansion and concentric diversification, a consulting firm was brought in to recommend ways to cope with the new complexity. Believing that the span of control was too broad, the consulting firm recommended that strategic business units, responsible for their own operations, be formed. In other words, the firm should decentralize.

Soon after, the chicken market leveled off and eventually began to decline. At one point the firm was losing as much as one million dollars a week and, in 1988, Perdue Farms experienced its first year in the red. Unfortunately, the decentralization had created duplication of duties and enormous administrative costs. MIS costs, for example, had tripled. The firm's rapid plunge into turkeys and other food processing, where it had little experience, contributed to the losses. Waste and inefficiency had permeated the company. Characteristically, Frank Perdue took the firm back to basics, concentrating on efficiency of operations, improving communications throughout the company, and paying close attention to detail.

On June 2, 1989, Frank celebrated fifty years with Perdue Farms, Inc. At a morning reception in downtown Salisbury, the Governor of Maryland proclaimed it "Frank Perdue Day." The Governors of Delaware and Virginia did the same.

The 1990s have been dominated by market expansion to North Carolina; Atlanta, Georgia; Pittsburgh, Pennsylvania; Cleveland, Ohio; Chicago, Illinois; and Florida. New product lines have included fresh ground chicken, fresh ground turkey, sweet Italian turkey sausage, turkey breakfast sausage, fun-shaped chicken breast nuggets in star and drumstick shapes, and BBQ and oven roasted chicken parts in the Perdue Done It! line. A new Fit 'n Easy label was introduced as part of a nutrition campaign using skinless, boneless chicken and turkey products.

In 1991, 12,500 associates and 3,000 producers generated an estimated $1.2 billion in revenue. Frank was named Chairman of the Executive Committee and Jim Perdue became Chairman of the Board. Sitting in the small unpretentious office that had been his dad's for forty years, Jim looked out the window at the house where he had grown up, the broiler houses Frank built in the 1940s, his grandfather's homestead across the road where Frank was born, and a modern hatchery. "Dad would come home for dinner, then come back here and work into the early hours of the morning. There's a fold-out cot behind that credenza. He got by on three or four hours of sleep a night."

MISSION STATEMENT AND STATEMENT OF VALUES

From the beginning, Mr. Arthur's motto had been to ". . . create a quality product, be aware of your customers, deal fairly with people, and work hard, work hard, work hard . . ."

In a speech in September 1991 to the firm's lenders, accountants, and Perdue associates, Frank reiterated these values, saying:

> If you were to ask me what was the biggest factor in whatever success we have enjoyed, I would answer that it was not technology, or economic resources, or organizational structure. It . . . has been our conscious decision that, in order to be successful, we must have a sound set of beliefs on which we premise all our policies and actions. . . . Central to these beliefs is our emphasis on quality. . . . Quality is no accident. It is the one absolutely necessary ingredient of all the most successful companies in the world.

The centrality of quality to the firm is featured in its mission statement and its statement of values. To ensure that all associates know what the company's mission, quality policy, values, and annual goals are, managers receive a fold-up, wallet-sized card imprinted with them. (See Exhibit 19.1.)

SOCIAL RESPONSIBILITY

To realize its corporate statement of values, Perdue Farms works hard to be a good corporate citizen. Two areas in which this is especially clear are its code of ethics and its efforts to minimize the environmental damage it causes.

Code of Ethics

Perdue Farms has taken the somewhat unusual step of setting forth explicitly the ethical standards it expects all associates to follow. Specifically, the Code of Ethics calls upon associates to conduct every aspect of business in the full spirit of honest and lawful behavior. Further, all salaried associates and certain hourly associates are required to sign a statement

Exhibit 19.1 Perdue Fiscal Year 1994

MISSION STATEMENT

Our mission is to provide the highest quality poultry and poultry-related products to retail and food service customers.

We want to be the recognized industry leader in quality and service, providing more than expected for our customers, associates, and owners.

We will accomplish this by maintaining a tradition of pride in our products, growth through innovation, integrity in the management of our business, and commitment to Team Management and the Quality Improvement Process.

QUALITY POLICY

We shall produce products and provide services at all times which meet or exceed the expectations of our customers.

We shall not be content to be of equal quality to our competitors.

Our commitment is to be increasingly superior.

Contribution to quality is a responsibility shared by everyone in the Perdue organization.

STATEMENT OF VALUES

Our success as a company, and as individuals working at Perdue, depends upon:

- Meeting customer needs with the best quality, innovative food and food-related products and services.
- Associates being team members in the business and having opportunities to influence, make contributions, and reach their full potential.
- Working together as business partners by implementing the principles of the QIP so that mutual respect, trust, and a commitment to being the best are shared among associates, customers, producers, and suppliers.
- Achieving the long-term goals of the company and providing economic stability and a rewarding future for all associates through well-planned, market-driven growth.

- Being the best in our industry in profitability as a low-cost producer, realizing that our customers won't pay for our inefficiencies.
- Staying ahead of the competition by investing our profits to provide a safe work environment; to pay competitive wages; to maintain up-to-date facilities, equipment, and processes; and to create challenging opportunities for associates.
- Serving the communities in which we do business with resources, time, and the creative energies of our associates.

FY 1994 COMPANY GOALS

1) PEOPLE – Provide a safe, secure, and productive work environment
   - Reduce OSHA recordable incidents by 12%
   - Reduce per capita workers' compensation by 28%
   - Implement an associates satisfaction survey process
   - Provide an annual performance evaluation for all associates

2) PRODUCTS – Provide the highest quality products and services at competitive costs.
   - Develop an improved measurement of consumer satisfaction
   - Improve the "Customer Service Satisfaction Index"
   - Improve our quality spread over competition
   - Consistently achieve a plant weighted ranking score for product quality of 212 points
   - Increase sales from new products

3) PROFITABILITY – Lead the industry in profitability.
   - Achieve a 10% ROE
   - Broiler Agrimetrics Index to be equal to the Southeast Best Eight Average
   - Turkey Agrimetrics Index to be equal to the Best Eight National Average
   - Increase market share by growing at a rate which exceeds the industry

acknowledging that they understand the code and are prepared to comply with it. Associates are expected to report to their supervisor any dishonest or illegal activities as well as possible violations of the code. If the supervisor does not provide a satisfactory response, the employee is expected to contact either the Vice President for Human Resources or the Vice President of their division. The code notes that any Perdue manager who initiates or encourages reprisal against any person who reports a violation commits a serious violation of the code.

Minimizing Environmental Damage

Historically, chicken processing has been the focus of special interest groups whose interests range from animal rights to repetitive-motion disorders to environmental causes. Perdue Farms has accepted the challenge of striving to maintain an environmentally friendly work place and feels that goal requires the commitment of all of its associates, from Frank Perdue down. Frank Perdue states it best, "We know that we must be good neighbors environmentally. We have an obligation not to pollute, to police ourselves, and to be better than EPA requires us to be."

For example, over the years, the industry had explored many alternative ways of disposing of dead birds. Perdue research provided the solution – small composters on each farm. Using this approach, dead birds are reduced to an end product that resembles soil in a matter of a few days. This has become a major environmental activity.

Another environmental challenge is the disposal of hatchery wastes. Historically, manure, and unhatched eggs that make up these wastes were shipped to a landfill. Perdue produces about ten tons of this waste per day! However, Perdue has reduced the waste by 50 percent by selling the liquid fraction to a pet food processor who cooks it for protein. The other 50 percent is recycled through a rendering process. In 1990, Perdue spent $4.2 million to construct a state-of-the-art waste water treatment facility at its Accomac, Virginia plant. This facility uses forced hot air heated to 120 degrees to cause the microbes to digest all traces of ammonia, even during the cold winter months. In April 1993, the company took a major step with the creation of the Environmental Steering Committee. Its mission is "...to provide all Perdue Farms work sites with vision, direction, and leadership so that they can be good corporate citizens from an environmental perspective today and in the future." The committee oversees how the company is doing in such environmentally sensitive areas as waste water, storm water, hazardous waste, solid waste, recycling, biosolids, and human health and safety.

Jim Perdue sums it up as follows: "...we must not only comply with environmental laws as they exist today, but look to the future to make sure we don't have any surprises. We must make sure our policy statement is real, and that there's something behind it, and that we do what we say we're going to do."

MARKETING

In the early days, chicken was sold to groceries as a commodity, i.e., producers sold it in bulk and butchers cut and wrapped it. The consumer had no idea what company grew the chicken. Frank Perdue was convinced that higher profits could be made if Perdue's products were premium quality so they could be sold at a premium price. But the only way the premium quality concept would work was if consumers asked for it by name – and that meant the product must be differentiated and "branded" to identify what the premium qualities are. Hence, the emphasis over the years on superior quality, a higher meat-to-bone ratio, and a yellow skin (the result of mixing marigold petals in the feed), which is an indicator of bird health.

In 1968, Perdue spent $40,000 on radio advertising. In 1969, the company spent $80,000 on radio, and in 1970 spent $160,000, split fifty-fifty between radio and television. The advertising agency had recommended against television advertising, but the combination worked. TV ads increased sales and Frank Perdue decided the old agency he was dealing with did not match one of the basic Perdue tenets: "The people you deal with should be as good at what they do as you are at what you do."

That decision set off a storm of activity on Frank's part. In order to select a new ad agency, Frank studied intensively and personally learned more about advertising than any poultry man before him. He began a ten-week immersion on the theory and practice of advertising. He read books and papers on advertising. He talked to sales managers of every newspaper, radio, and television station in the New York City area, consulted experts, and interviewed forty-eight ad agencies.

On April 2, 1971, Perdue Farms selected Scali, McCabe, Sloves as their new advertising agency. As the agency tried to figure out how to successfully "brand" a chicken – something that had never been done – they realized that Frank Perdue was their greatest ally. "He looked a little like a chicken himself, and he sounded a little like one, and he squawked a lot!" Ed McCabe, partner and chief copywriter of the firm, decided that Frank Perdue should be the firm's spokesperson. Initially Frank resisted. But in the end, he accepted the role and the campaign based on "It takes a tough man to make a tender chicken" was born. Frank set Perdue Farms apart by educating consumers about chicken quality. The process catapulted Perdue Farms into the ranks of the top poultry producers in the country.

The firm's very first television commercial showed Frank on a picnic in the Salisbury City Park saying:

A chicken is what it eats . . . and my chickens eat better than people do . . . I store my own grain and mix my own feed . . . and give my Perdue chickens nothing but pure well water to drink . . . That's why my chickens always have that healthy golden yellow color . . . If you want to eat as good as my chickens, you'll just have to eat my chickens . . . Mmmm, that's really good!

Additional ads, touting superior quality and more breast meat read as follows:

Government standards would allow me to call this a grade A chicken . . . but my standards wouldn't. This chicken is skinny . . . It has scrapes and hairs . . . The fact is, my graders reject 30 percent of the chickens government inspectors accept as grade A . . . That's why it pays to insist on a chicken with my name on it . . . If you're not completely satisfied, write me and I'll give you your money back . . . Who do you write in Washington? . . . What do they know about chickens? Never go into a store and just ask for a pound of chicken breasts . . . Because you could be cheating yourself out of some meat . . . Here's an ordinary one-pound chicken breast, and here's a one-pound breast of mine . . . They weigh the same. But as you can see, mine has more meat, and theirs have more bone. I breed the broadest-breasted, meatiest chicken you can buy . . . So don't buy a chicken breast by the pound . . . Buy them by the name . . . and get an extra bite in every breast.

The ads paid off. In 1968, Perdue Farms held about three percent of the New York market. By 1972, one out of every six chickens eaten in New York was a Perdue chicken. Fifty-one percent of New Yorkers recognized the label. Scali, McCabe, Sloves credited Frank Perdue's "believability" for the success of the program. "This was advertising in which Perdue had a personality that lent credibility to the product." Today, 50 percent of the chickens consumed in New York are Perdue.

Frank had his own view. As he told a Rotary audience in Charlotte, North Carolina, in March 1989, ". . . the product met the promise of the advertising and was far superior to the competition. Two great sayings tell it all: 'nothing will destroy a poor product as quickly as good advertising' and 'a gifted product is mightier than a gifted pen!' "

Today, the Perdue marketing function is unusually sophisticated. Its responsibilities include deciding (1) how many chickens and turkeys to grow, (2) what the advertising and promotion pieces should look like, where they should run, and how much the company can afford, and (3) which new products the company will pursue. The marketing plan is derived from the company's five-year business plan and includes goals concerning volume, return on sales, market share, and profitability. The internal Marketing Department is helped by various service agencies including: Lowe & Partners/SMS – advertising campaigns, media buys; R. C. Auletta & Co. — public relations, company image; Gertsman & Meyers – packaging design; Group Williams – consumer promotional programs; and various research companies for focus groups, telephone surveys, and in-home use tests.

OPERATIONS

Two words sum up the Perdue approach to operations – quality and efficiency – with emphasis on the first over the latter. Perdue, more than most companies, represents the Total Quality Management (TQM) slogan, "Quality, a journey without end." Some of the key events are listed in Exhibit 19.2. The pursuit of quality began in 1924 when Arthur Perdue purchased breeding roosters from Texas for the princely sum of $25 each. For comparison, typical wages in 1925 were $1.00 for a ten-hour workday.

Frank Perdue's own pursuit of quality is legendary. One story was told in 1968 by Ellis Wainwright, the State-of-Maryland grading inspector, during start-up operations at Perdue's first processing plant. Frank had told Ellis that the standards he wanted were higher than the Government Grade A standard. The first two days had been pretty much disastrous. On the third day, as Wainwright recalls,

We graded all morning, and I found only five boxes that passed what I took to be Frank's standards. The rest had the yellow skin color knocked off by the picking machines. I was afraid Frank was going to raise cain that I had accepted so few. Then Frank came through and rejected half of those.

To ensure that Perdue continues to lead the industry in quality, it buys about 2000 pounds of competitors' products a week. Inspection associates grade these products and the information is shared with the highest levels of management. In addition, the company's Quality Policy is displayed at all locations and taught to all associates in quality training (Exhibit 19.1).

Exhibit 19.2   Milestones in the Quality Improvement Process at Perdue Farms

1924	Arthur Perdue buys leghorn roosters for $25
1950s	Adopts the company logo of a chick under a magnifying glass
1984	Frank Perdue attends Philip Crosby's Quality College
1985	Perdue recognized for its pursuit of quality in *A Passion for Excellence*
	200 Perdue Managers attend Quality College
	Adopted the Quality Improvement Process (QIP)
1986	Established Corrective Action Teams (CAT's)
1987	Established Quality Training for all associates
	Implemented Error Cause Removal Process (ECR)
1988	Steering Committee formed
1989	First Annual Quality Conference held
	Implemented Team Management
1990	Second Annual Quality Conference held
	Codified Values and Corporate Mission
1991	Third Annual Quality Conference held
	Customer Satisfaction defined
1992	Fourth Annual Quality Conference held
	"How to" implement Customer Satisfaction explained for team leaders and QIT's

Perdue insists that nothing artificial be fed or injected into its birds. The company will not take any shortcuts in pursuit of the perfect chicken. A chemical- and steroid-free diet is fed to the chickens. Young chickens are vaccinated against disease. Selective breeding is used to improve the quality of the chickens sold. Chickens are bred to yield more breast meat because that is what the consumer wants.

Efficiency is improved through management of details. As a vertically integrated producer of chickens, Perdue manages every detail including breeding and hatching its own eggs, selecting growers, building Perdue-engineered chicken houses, formulating and manufacturing its own feed, overseeing the care and feeding, operating its own processing plants, distributing via its own trucking fleet, and marketing. Improvements are measured in fractional cents per pound. Nothing goes to waste. The feet that used to be thrown away are now processed and sold in the Orient as a barroom delicacy.

Frank's knowledge of details is also legendary. He not only impresses people in the poultry industry, but those in other industries as well. At the end of one day the managers and engineers of a new Grumman plant in Salisbury, Maryland, were reviewing their progress. Through the door unannounced came Frank Perdue. The Grumman managers proceeded to give Frank a tour of the plant. One machine was an ink-jet printer that labeled parts as they passed. Frank said he believed he had some of those in his plants. He paused for a minute and then he asked them if it clogged often. They responded yes. Frank exclaimed excitedly, "I am sure that I got some of those!" To ensure that this attention to detail pays off, eight measurable items are tracked: hatchability, turnover, feed conversion, livability, yield, birds per man-hour, utilization, and grade.

Frank Perdue credits much of his success to listening to others. He agrees with Tom Peters that "Nobody knows a person's twenty square feet better than the person who works there." To facilitate the transmission of ideas through it, the organization is undergoing a cultural transformation beginning with Frank (Exhibit 19.3). He describes the transition from the old to the new culture and himself as follows:

". . . we also learned that *loud and noisy* were worth a lot more than mugs and pens. What I mean by this is, we used to spend a lot of time calling companies to get trinkets as gifts. Gradually, we learned that money and trinkets weren't what really motivated people. We learned that when a man or woman on the line is going all out to do a good job, that he or she doesn't care that much about a trinket of some sort; what they really want is for the manager to get up from behind his desk, walk over to them, and, in front of their peers, give them a hearty and sincere 'thank you.'

When we give recognition now, we do it when there's an audience and lots of peers can see. This is, I can tell you, a lot more motivating than the 'kick in the butt,' that was part of the old culture – *and I was the most guilty!*"

Changing the behavioral pattern from writing-up people who have done something wrong to recognizing people for doing their job well has not been without some setbacks. For example, the company started what it calls the *Good Egg Award* which is good for a free lunch. Managers in the Salisbury plant were all trained and asked to distribute the awards by "catching" someone doing a good job. When the program manager checked with the cafeteria the following week to see how many had been claimed, the answer was none. A meeting of the managers was called to see how many had been handed out. The answer was none. When the managers were asked what they had done with their award certificates, the majority replied they were in their shirt pocket. A goal was set for all managers to hand out five a week.

The following week, the program manager still found that very few were being turned in for a free lunch. When employees were asked what they had done with their awards, they replied that they had framed them and hung them up on walls at home or put them in trophy cases. The program was changed again. Now the *Good Egg Award* consists of both a certificate and a ticket for a free lunch.

Perdue also has a beneficial suggestion program that it calls *Error Cause Removal*. It averages better than one submission per year per three employees. Although that is much less than the twenty-two per employee per year in Japan, it is significantly better than the

Exhibit 19.3 Perdue Farms, Inc. Cultural Transformation

Old Culture	New Culture
1. Top-down management	1. Team management
2. Poor communications	2. Focused message from senior management
3. Short-term planning	3. Long-range planning
4. Commitment to quality	4. Expanded commitment to quality
5. Profitability focus	5. Focus on people, products, and profitability
6. Limited associate recognition	6. Recognition is a way of life
7. Limited associate training	7. Commitment to training
8. Short-term cost reduction	8. Long-term productivity improvements
9. Annual goals as end target	9. Continuous improvement
10. Satisfied customers	10. Delighted customers

national average in the United States of one per year per five employees. As Frank has said, "We're 'one up'. . . because with the help of the Quality Improvement Process and the help of our associates, we have *thousands* of 'better minds' helping us."

MANAGEMENT INFORMATION SYSTEMS (MIS)

In 1989, Perdue Farms employed 118 IS people who spent 146 hours per week on IS maintenance – "fix it" jobs. Today, the entire department has been reduced to fifty associates who spend only fifty-two hours per week in "fix it," and 94 percent of their time building new systems or reengineering old ones. Even better, a six-year backlog of projects has been eliminated and the average "build-it" cost for a project has dropped from $1,950 to $568 – an overall 300 percent increase in efficiency.

According to Don Taylor, Director of MIS, this is the payoff from a significant management reorientation. A key philosophy is that a "fix-it" mentality is counterproductive. The goal is to determine the root cause of the problem and reengineer the program to eliminate future problems.

Developer-user partnerships – including a monthly payback system – were developed with five functional groups: sales and marketing, finance and human resources, logistics, quality assurance, and fresh-poultry and plant systems. Each has an assigned number of IS hours per month and defines its own priorities, permitting it to function as a customer.

In addition, a set of critical success factors (CSFs) were developed. These include:

1. Automation is never the first step in a project; it occurs only after superfluous business processes are eliminated and necessary ones simplified,
2. Senior management sponsorship – the vice-president for the business unit – must sponsor major projects in their area,
3. Limit the size, duration and scope. IS has found that small projects have more success and a cumulative bigger payoff than big ones. All major projects are broken into three to six month segments with separate deliverables and benefits,
4. Ascertain a precise definition of requirements. The team must determine up front exactly what the project will accomplish, and
5. Commitment of both the IS staff and the customer to work as a team is necessary.

Perdue considers IS key to the operation of its business. For example, IS developed a customer ordering system for the centralized sales office (CSO). This system automated key business processes that link Perdue with its customers. The CSO includes thirteen applications including order entry, product transfers, sales allocations, production scheduling, and credit management.

When ordering, the Perdue salesperson negotiates the specifics of the sale directly with the buyer in the grocery chain. Next, the salesperson sends the request to a dispatcher who determines where the various products are located and designates a specific truck to make the required pickups and delivery, all within the designated one-hour delivery window that has been granted by the grocery chain. Each truck is even equipped with a small satellite dish that is connected to the LAN so that a trucker on the New Jersey Turnpike headed for New York can call for a replacement tractor if his rig breaks down.

Obviously, a computer malfunction is a possible disaster. Four hours of downtime is equivalent to $6.2 million in lost sales. Thus, Perdue has separate systems and processes in place to avoid such problems. In addition to maximizing on-time delivery, this system gives the salespeople more time to discuss wants and needs with customers, handle customer relations, and observe key marketing issues such as Perdue shelf space and location.

On the other hand, Perdue does not believe that automation solves all problems. For example, it was decided that electronic monitoring in the poultry houses is counterproductive and not cost effective. While it would be possible to develop systems to monitor and control almost every facet of the chicken house environment, Perdue is concerned that doing so would weaken the invaluable link between the farmer and the livestock, i.e., Perdue believes that poultry producers need to be personally involved with conditions in the chicken house in order to maximize quality and spot problems or health challenges as soon as possible.

RESEARCH AND DEVELOPMENT

Perdue is an acknowledged industry leader in the use of technology to provide quality products and service to its customers. A list of some of its technological accomplishments is given in Exhibit 19.4. As with everything else he does, Frank Perdue tries to leave nothing to chance. Perdue employs twenty-five people full-time in the industry's largest research and development effort, including five with graduate degrees. It has specialists in avian science, microbiology, genetics, nutrition, and veterinary science. Because of its research and development capabilities, Perdue is often involved in U.S.D.A. field tests with pharmaceutical suppliers.

Knowledge and experience gained from these tests can lead to a competitive advantage. For example, Perdue has the most extensive and expensive vaccination program among its breeders in the industry. As a result, Perdue growers have more disease-resistant chickens and one of the lowest mortality rates in the industry.

Perdue is not complacent. According to Dr. Mac Terzich, Doctor of Veterinary Medicine and Laboratory manager, Perdue really pushes for creativity and innovation. Currently, they are working with and studying some European producers who use a completely different process.

HUMAN RESOURCE MANAGEMENT

When entering the Human Resource Department at Perdue Farms, the first thing one sees is a prominently displayed set of human resource corporate strategic goals (see Exhibit 19.5). Besides these human resource corporate strategic goals, Perdue sets annual company goals that deal with people. FY 1995's strategic "people" goals center on providing a safe, secure, and productive work environment. The specific goals are included on the wallet-size, fold-up card mentioned earlier (Exhibit 19.1).

Exhibit 19.4 Perdue Farms, Inc. Technological Accomplishments

- Breed chickens with 20 percent more breast meat
- First to use digital scales to guarantee weights to customers
- First to package fully-cooked chicken products on microwaveable trays
- First to have a box lab to define quality of boxes from different suppliers
- First to test both its chickens and competitors' chickens on fifty-two quality factors every week
- Improved on time deliveries 20 percent between 1987 and 1993

Exhibit 19.5   Human Resource Corporate Strategic Goals

- Provide leadership to the corporation in all aspects of human resources including safety, recruitment and retention of associates, training and development, employee relations, compensation, benefits, communication, security, medical, housekeeping, and food services.
- Provide leadership and assistance to management at all levels in communicating and implementing company policy to ensure consistency and compliance with federal, state, and local regulations.
- Provide leadership and assistance to management in maintaining a socially responsible community image in all our Perdue communities by maintaining positive community relations and encouraging Perdue associates to be active in their community.
- Provide leadership and assistance to management in creating an environment wherein all associates can contribute to the overall success of the company.
- Be innovative and cost efficient in developing, implementing, and providing to all associates systems which will reward performance, encourage individual growth, and recognize contribution to the corporation.

Strategic Human Resource planning is still developing at Perdue Farms. According to Tom Moyers, Vice President for Human Resource Management,

"Every department in the company has a mission statement or policy which has been developed within the past eighteen months . . . Department heads are free to update their goals as they see fit. . . . Initial strategic human resource plans are developed by teams of three or four associates. . . . These teams meet once or twice a year company-wide to review where we stand in terms of meeting our objectives."

To keep associates informed about company plans, Perdue Farms holds "state of the business meetings" for all interested associates twice a year. For example, during May 1994, five separate meetings were held near various plants in Delmarva, the Carolinas, Virginia, and Indiana. Typically, a local auditorium is rented, overhead slides are prepared, and the company's progress toward its goals and its financial status is shared with its associates. Discussion revolves around what is wrong and what is right about the company. New product lines are introduced to those attending and opportunities for improvement are discussed.

Upon joining Perdue Farms, each new associate attends an extensive orientation that begins with a thorough review of the *Perdue Associate Handbook*. The handbook details Perdue's philosophy on quality, employee relations, drugs and alcohol, and its code of ethics. The orientation also includes a thorough discussion of the Perdue benefit plans. Fully paid benefits for all associates include (1) paid vacation; (2) eight official paid holidays; (3) health, accident, disability, and life insurance; (4) savings and pension plans; (5) funeral leave, and (6) jury duty leave. The company also offers a scholarship program for children of Perdue associates.

Special arrangements can be made with the individual's immediate supervisor for a leave of absence of up to twelve months in case of extended non-job related illness or injury, birth or adoption of a child, care of a spouse or other close relative, or other personal situations. Regarding the Family and Medical Leave Act of 1993, although opposed by many companies because its requirements are far more than their current policies, the Act will have little impact on Perdue Farms since existing leave of absence policies are already broader than the new Federal law.

Perdue Farms is a non-union employer. The firm has had a long standing open door policy and managers are expected to be easily accessible to other associates, whatever the person's concern. The open door has been supplemented by a formal peer review process. While associates are expected to discuss problems with their supervisors first, they are urged to use peer review if they are still dissatisfied.

Wages and salaries, which are reviewed at least once a year, are determined by patterns in the poultry industry and the particular geographic location of the plant. Changes in the general economy and the state of the business are also considered.

Informal comparisons of turnover statistics with others in the poultry industry suggest that Perdue's turnover numbers are among the lowest in the industry. Perdue also shares workers' compensation claims data with their competitors, and incidence rates (for accidents) are also among the lowest in the industry. Supervisors initially train and coach all new associates about the proper way to do their jobs. Once trained, the philosophy is that all associates are professionals and, as such, should make suggestions about how to make their jobs even more efficient and effective. After a sixty-day introductory period, the associate has seniority based on the starting date of employment. Seniority is the determining factor in promotions where qualifications (skill, proficiency, dependability, work record) are equal. Also, should the work force need to be reduced, this date is used as the determining factor in layoffs.

A form of Management by Objectives (MBO) is used for annual performance appraisal and planning review. The format includes a four-step process:

1. Establish accountability, goals, standards of performance, and their relative weights for the review period.
2. Conduct coaching sessions throughout the review period and document these discussions.
3. Evaluate performance at the end of the review period and conduct appraisal interview, and
4. Undertake next review period planning.

The foundation of human resources development includes extensive training and management development plus intensive succession planning and career pathing. The essence of the company's approach to human resource management is captured in Frank Perdue's statement:

We have gotten where we are because we have believed in hiring our own people and training them in our own way. We believe in promotion from within, going outside only when we feel it is absolutely necessary – for expertise and sometimes because our company was simply growing faster than our people development program. The number one item in our success has been the quality of our people.

FINANCE

Perdue Farms, Inc., is a privately held firm and considers financial information to be proprietary. Hence, available data is limited. Stock is primarily held by the family and a limited amount by Perdue management. Common numbers used by the media and the poultry industry peg Perdue Farm's revenues for 1994 at about $1.5 billion and the number of associates at 13,800.

The firm's compound sales growth rate has been slowly decreasing during the past twenty years, mirroring the industry which has been experiencing market saturation and overproduction. However, Perdue has compensated by wringing more efficiency from its associates, e.g. twenty years ago, a 1 percent increase in associates resulted in a 1.3 percent increase in revenue. Today, a 1 percent increase in associates results in a 2.5 percent increase in revenues (see Table 19.1).

Perdue Farms has three operating divisions: Retail Chicken (62 percent of sales – growth rate 5 percent), Foodservice Chicken and Turkey (20 percent of sales – growth rate 12 percent), and Grain and Oilseed (18 percent of sales – growth rate 10 percent). Thus, the bulk of sales comes from the sector – retail chicken – with the slowest growth rate. Part of the reason for the slow sales growth in retail chicken may stem from Perdue Farm's policy of selling only fresh – never frozen – chicken.

This has limited their traditional markets to cities that can be serviced overnight by truck from production facility locations, i.e., New York, Boston, Philadelphia, Baltimore, and Washington – which are pretty well saturated (developing markets include Chicago, Cleveland, Atlanta, Pittsburgh, and Miami). On the other hand, foodservice and grain and oilseed customers are nationwide and include export customers in eastern Europe, China, Japan, and South America.

Perdue Farms has been profitable every year since its founding with the exception of 1988. Company officials believe the loss in 1988 was caused by a decentralization effort begun during the early eighties. At that time, there was a concerted effort to push decisions down through the corporate ranks to provide more autonomy. When the new strategy resulted in higher costs, Frank Perdue responded quickly by returning to the basics, reconsolidating and downsizing. Now the goal is to constantly streamline in order to provide cost-effective business solutions.

Perdue Farms uses a conservative approach to financial management, using retained earnings and cash flow to finance asset replacement projects and normal growth. When planning expansion projects or acquisitions, long-term debt is used. The target debt limit is 55 percent of equity. Such debt is normally provided by domestic and international bank and insurance companies. The debt strategy is to match asset lives with liability maturities, and have a mix of fixed rate and variable rate debt. Growth plans require about two dollars in projected incremental sales growth for each one dollar in invested capital.

THE U.S. POULTRY INDUSTRY

U.S. annual per capita consumption of poultry has risen dramatically during the past forty years from 26.3 pounds to almost eighty pounds in 1990. Consumption continued to grow through 1993 according to a broiler industry survey of the largest integrated broiler

Table 19.1 Perdue Farms, Inc. Annual Compound Growth Rate: Revenues and Associates

	Revenue Growth	Associate Growth
past 20 years	13%	10%
past 15 years	11%	8%
past 10 years	9%	5%
past 5 years	5%	2%

companies. Output of ready-to-cook product increased 5.8 percent in 1991, 5.3 percent in 1992, and 6.0 percent in 1993 to 476 million pounds per week.

Recent growth is largely the result of consumers moving away from red meat due to health concerns and the industry's continued development of increased value products such as pre-cooked or roasted chicken and chicken parts. Unfortunately, this growth has not been very profitable due to chronic overcapacity throughout the industry which has pushed down wholesale prices. The industry has experienced cyclical troughs before and experts expect future improvement in both sales and profits. Still, razor-thin margins demand absolute efficiency.

Fifty-four integrated broiler companies account for approximately 99 percent of ready-to-cook production in the United States. While slow consolidation of the industry appears to be taking place, it is still necessary to include 22 companies to get to 80 percent of production. Concentration has been fastest among the top four producers. For example, since 1986 market share of the top four has grown from 35 percent to 40.5 percent (see Table 19.2).

Although the Delmarva Peninsula (home to Perdue Farms, Inc.) has long been considered the birthplace of the commercial broiler industry, recent production gains have been most rapid in the southeast. Arkansas, Georgia, and Alabama are now the largest poultry producing states – a result of abundant space and inexpensive labor. The southeast accounts for approximately 50 percent of the $20 billion U.S. chicken industry, employing 125,000 across the region. Still, Delmarva chicken producers provide about 10 percent of all broilers grown in the United States. This is due largely to the region's proximity to Washington, Baltimore, Philadelphia, New York, and Boston. Each weekday, more than 200 tractor-trailers loaded with fresh dressed poultry leave Delmarva headed for these metropolitan markets.

Eight integrated companies operate ten feed mills, fifteen hatcheries, and thirteen processing plants on Delmarva, employing approximately 22,000 people and producing approximately 10 million broilers each week (see Table 19.3).

THE FUTURE

Considering Americans' average annual consumption of chicken (almost eighty pounds per person in 1990), many in the industry wonder how much growth is left. For example, after wholesale prices climbed from fourteen cents per pound in 1960 to about thirty-four cents per pound in 1990, the recession and a general glut in the market have caused prices to fall back. In real terms, the price of chicken is at an all time low. A pound of chicken is

Table 19.2 Nation's Top Four Broiler Companies, 1993*

	Million Head	Million lbs.
1. Tyson Foods, Inc.	26.50	84.15
2. ConAgra, Inc.	11.25	40.53
3. Gold Kist, Inc.	12.60	39.70
4. Perdue Farms, Inc.	7.51	28.28

*Based on average weekly slaughter; Broiler Industry Survey, 1993

Table 19.3   Integrated Broiler Producers Operating on Delmarva Peninsula*

	National Rank
Tyson Foods, Inc.	1
ConAgra, Inc.	2
Perdue Farms, Inc. (Hq in Salisbury, Md)	4
Hudson Foods, Inc.	7
Townsend, Inc. (Hq in Millsboro, De)	9
Showell Farms, Inc. (Hq in Showell, Md)	10
Allen Family Foods, Inc. (Hq in Seaford, De)	17
Mountaire Farms of Delmarva, Inc. (Hq in Selbyville, De)	28

*Delmarva Poultry Industry, Inc.; 1993 fact sheets

down from thirty minutes of an average worker's 1940 wage to only four and one half minutes of a 1990 wage.

While much of this reduction can be justified by improved production efficiencies, prices are clearly depressed due to what some consider overcapacity in the industry. For example, in 1992, ConAgra, Inc. temporarily stopped sending chicks to thirty Delmarva growers to prevent an oversupply of chickens and several chicken companies have started to experiment with producing other kinds of meats – from pork to striped bass – to soften the impact. (Kim Clark, *The Sun*, July 4, 1993).

The trend is away from whole chickens to skinless, boneless parts. Perdue has responded with its line of *Fit 'n Easy* products with detailed nutrition labeling. It is also developing exports of dark meat to Puerto Rico and chicken feet to China. Fresh young turkey and turkey parts have become an important product and the *Perdue Done it!* line has been expanded to include fully cooked roasted broilers, Cornish hens, and parts. Recently the company has expanded its lines to include ground chicken and turkey sausage.

Frank Perdue reflected recently that "... we have a very high share of the available supermarket business in the Middle Atlantic and Northeastern United States, and if we were to follow that course which we know best – selling to the consumer through the retailer – we'd have to consider the Upper Midwest – Pittsburgh, Chicago, Detroit, with 25 to 30 million people."

PUBLIC SOURCES OF INFORMATION

Barmash, Isadore. "Handing Off to the Next Generation." *The New York Times,* July 26, 1992, Business, p 1.

Bates, Eric and Bob Hall. "Ruling the Roost." *Southern Exposure,* Summer 1989, p. 11.

Clark, Kim. "Tender Times: Is Sky Falling on the Chicken Boom?" *The Sun,* July 4, 1993, p. 4F/Business.

"Facts About the DelMarVa Broiler Industry – 1973." Industry Bulletin, Feb. 25, 1974.

"Facts About the DelMarVa Poultry Industry," DelMarVa Poultry Industry, Inc., July 28, 1994.

Fahy, Joe. "All Pain, No Gain." *Southern Exposure,* Summer 1989, pp. 35–39.

Flynn, Ramsey. "Strange Bird." *The Washingtonian,* December 1989, p. 165.

Gale, Bradley T. "Quality Comes First When Hatching Power Brands." *Planning Review,* July/August 1992, pp. 4–48.

"Golden Jubilee! Company Honors Frank Perdue for His 50 Years of Service." *Perdue Courier (Special Edition),* July 1989.

Goldoftas, Barbara. "Inside the Slaughterhouse." *Southern Exposure,* Summer 1989, pp. 25–29.

Hall, Bob. "Chicken Empires." *Southern Exposure,* Summer 1989, pp. 12–19.

"In the Money: Downhome Retailer Is Nation's Richest, Forbes says." *The Washington Post,* Oct. 14, 1986.

MacPherson, Myra. "Chicken Big." *The Washington Post, Potomac Magazine,* May 11, 1975, p. 15.

"Perdue Chicken Spreads its Wings." *Business Week,* Sept. 16, 1972, p. 113.

Perdue Farms Incorporated – Historical Highlights. Perdue Farms publication, September 1992.

Perdue, Frank. Speech at Babson College, April 28, 1981.

Perdue, Frank. Speech to firm's lenders, accountants, and Perdue Associates, September 1991.

Poultry Industry file – miscellaneous newspaper clippings from 1950 to 1994. The Maryland Room, Blackwell Library, Salisbury State University.

Santosus, Megan. "Perdue's New Pecking Orders." *CIO,* March 1993, pp 60–68.

Scarupa, Henry. "When is a Chicken Not a Football?" *The (Baltimore) Sun Magazine,* March 4, 1973, pp. 5–12.

"Silent Millionaires in America." *Economist,* V270, #7072, March 17, 1979.

Sterling, Bill. "Just Browsin'" *Eastern Shore News,* March 2, 1988.

"The Perdue Story. And the Five Reasons Why Our Consumers Tell It Best." Perdue Farms, Inc. publication, October 1991.

Thornton, Gary. "Data from BROILER INDUSTRY." Elanco Poultry Team, Partner with the Poultry Industry, December 1993.

Yeoman, Barry. "Don't Count Your Chickens." *Southern Exposure,* Summer 1989, pp. 21–24.

20

Neilson International in Mexico

In January 1993, Howard Bateman, Vice President of International Operations for Neilson International, a division of William Neilson Limited, was assessing a recent proposal from Sabritas, a division of Pepsico Foods in Mexico, to launch Neilson's brands in the Mexican market. Neilson, a leading producer of high quality confectionery products, had grown to achieve a leadership position in the Canadian market and was currently producing Canada's top selling chocolate bar, *Crispy Crunch*. In the world chocolate bar market, however, Neilson was dwarfed by major players such as M&M/Mars, Hershey/Lowney and Nestlé-Rowntree. Recognizing their position as a smaller player with fewer resources in a stagnant domestic market, Neilson, in 1990, formed its International Division to develop competitive strategies for their exporting efforts.

Recent attempts to expand into several foreign markets, including the United States, had taught them some valuable lessons. Although it was now evident that they had world class products to offer to global markets, their competitive performance was being constrained by limited resources. Pepsico's joint branding proposal would allow greater market penetration than Neilson could afford. But, at what cost?

Given the decision to pursue international opportunities more aggressively, Bateman's biggest challenge was to determine the distributor relationships Neilson should pursue in order to become a global competitor.

THE CHOCOLATE CONFECTIONERY INDUSTRY[1]

The "confectionery" industry consisted of the "sugar" segment, including all types of sugar confectionery, chewing gum, and the "chocolate" segment which included chocolates and other cocoa based products. Most large chocolate operations were dedicated to two major products: boxed chocolates and bar chocolates which represented nearly 50 percent of the confectionery industry by volume.

Competition from imports was significant with the majority of products coming from the United States (39 percent). European countries such as Switzerland, Germany, the United

Kingdom, and Belgium were also major sources of confectionery, especially for premium products such as boxed chocolates. (See Exhibit 20.1 for a profile of chocolate exporting countries.) In order to maintain production volumes and to relieve the burden of fixed costs on operations, Canadian manufacturers used excess capacity to produce goods for exporting. Although nearly all of these products were traditionally exported to the United States, in the early nineties, the world market had become increasingly more attractive.

Firms in the confectionery industry competed on the basis of brand name products, product quality, and cost of production. Although Canadian producers had the advantage of being able to purchase sugar at the usually lower world price, savings were offset by the higher prices for dairy ingredients used in products manufactured for domestic consumption. Other commodity ingredients, often experiencing widely fluctuating prices, caused significant variations in manufacturing costs. Producers were reluctant to raise their prices due to the highly elastic demand for chocolate. Consequently, they sometimes reformatted or reformulated their products through size or ingredient changes to sustain margins. Three major product types were manufactured for domestic and export sales:

- *Blocks:* These products are molded blocks of chocolate that are sold by weight and manufactured in a variety of flavors, with or without additional ingredients such as fruit or nuts. Block chocolate was sold primarily in grocery outlets or directly to confectionery manufacturers. (Examples: baking chocolate, Hershey's Chocolate Bar, Suchard's Toblerone.)
- *Boxed Chocolates:* These products included a variety of bite-sized sweets and were generally regarded as "gift" or "occasion" purchases. Sales in grocery outlets tended to be more seasonal than for other chocolate products, with 80 percent sold at Christmas and Easter. Sales in other outlets remained steady year round. (Examples: Cadbury's Milk Tray, Rowntree's Black Magic and After Eights.)
- *Countlines:* These were chocolate covered products sold by count rather than by weight, and were generally referred to by consumers as "chocolate bars." The products varied widely in

Exhibit 20.1   World Chocolate Exports (Value as Percent of Total) – 1990

	1987	1988	1989	1990
Africa	x1.5	x1.0	x1.1	x0.7
Americas	8.1	9.1	9.2	x9.1
LAIC[1]	2.1	1.9	1.4	x1.4
CACM[2]	0.1	x0.1	x0.1	x0.1
Asia	2.5	3.2	3.4	2.9
Middle East	x0.5	x0.5	x0.7	x0.4
Europe	86.4	85.0	84.2	85.4
EEC (12)[3]	73.3	71.8	71.3	73.5
EFTA[4]	12.5	12.7	12.1	11.5
Oceania	x1.5	1.8	x2.1	x1.8

Figures denoted with an "x" are provisional or estimated.
Adapted from: The United Nations' "International Trade Statistics Yearbook," Vol. II, 1990.
[1]LAIC = Latin American Industrialists Association.
[2]CACM = Central American Common Market.
[3]EEC (12) = The twelve nations of the European Economic Community.
[4]EFTA = European Free Trade Association.

size, shape, weight, and composition, and had a wider distribution than the other two product types. Most countlines were sold through non-grocery outlets such as convenience and drug stores. (Examples: Neilson's Crispy Crunch, Nestlé-Rowntree's Coffee Crisp, M&M/Mars' Snickers, and Hershey/Lowney's Oh Henry!)

Sweet chocolate was the basic semi-finished product used in the manufacture of block, countline, and boxed chocolate products. Average costs of sweet chocolate for a representative portfolio of all three product types could be broken down as follows:

Raw material	35%
Packaging	10
Production	20
Distribution	5
Marketing/sales	20
Trading profit	10
Total	100% (of manufacturer's selling price)

For countline products, raw material costs were proportionately lower because a smaller amount of cocoa was used.

In value terms, more chocolate was consumed than any other manufactured food product in the world. In the late eighties, the world's eight major markets (representing over 60 percent of the total world chocolate market) consumed nearly three million tonnes with a retail value close to $20 billion. During the 1980s countline was the fastest growing segment with close to 50 percent of the world chocolate market by volume and an average annual rate of growth of 7 percent. An increasing trend toward indulgence in snack and "comfort" foods strongly suggested that future growth would remain strong.

COMPETITIVE ENVIRONMENT

In 1993, chocolate producers in the world included: M&M/Mars, Hershey Foods, Cadbury-Schweppes, Jacobs Suchard, Nestlé-Rowntree, United Biscuits, Ferrero, Nabisco, and George Weston Ltd. (Neilson). Chocolate represented varying proportions of these manufacturers' total sales.

For the most part, it was difficult to sustain competitive advantages in manufacturing or product features due to a lack of proprietary technology. There was also limited potential for new product development since the basic ingredients in countline product manufacturing could only be blended in a limited variety of combinations. This forced an emphasis on competition through distribution and advertising.

Product promotion played a critical role in establishing brand-name recognition. Demand was typified by high-impulse and discretionary purchasing behavior. Since consumers, generally, had a selection of at least three or four favorite brands from which to choose, the biggest challenge facing producers was to create the brand awareness necessary to break into these menus. In recognition of the wide selection of competing brands and the broad range of snack food substitutes available, expenditures for media and trade promotions were considerable. For example, Canadian chocolate bar makers spent more than $30 million for advertising in Canada in 1992, mostly on television. This was often a barrier to entry for smaller producers.

MAJOR COMPETITORS

M&M/Mars

As the world leader in chocolate confectionery M&M/Mars dominated the countline sector, particularly in North America and Europe, with such famous global brands as Snickers, M&Ms, and Milky Way. However, in Canada, in 1992, M&M/Mars held fourth place with an 18.7 percent market share of single bars. Exhibits 20.2 and 20.3 compare Canadian market positions for major competitors.

M&M/Mars' strategy was to produce high quality products which were simple to manufacture and which allowed for high volume and automated production processes. They supported their products with heavy advertising and aggressive sales, focusing marketing efforts on strengthening their global brands.

Hershey/Lowney

Hershey's strength in North America was in the block chocolate category in which it held the leading market position. Hershey also supplied export markets in Asia, Australia, Sweden,

Exhibit 20.2 Single Bars Canadian Market Share: 1991–1992

Manufacturer	1992	1991
Neilson	28.1%	29.4%
Nestlé/Rowntree	26.9%	26.2%
Hershey/Lowney	21.6%	21.9%
M&M/Mars	18.7%	19.0%
Others	4.7%	3.5%

Source: Neilson News – Issue #1, 1993

Exhibit 20.3 Top Single Bars in Canada: 1991–1992

Top Single Bars	Manufacturer	1992	1991
Crispy Crunch	Neilson	1	1
Coffee Crisp	Nestlé/Rowntree	2	3
Kit Kat	Nestlé/Rowntree	3	2
Mars Bar	M&M/Mars	4	4
Caramilk	Cadbury Schweppes	5	6
Oh Henry!	Hershey/Lowney	6	5
Smarties	Nestlé/Rowntree	7	7
Peanut Butter Cups	Hershey/Lowney	8	8
Mr. Big	Neilson	9	11
Aero	Hershey/Lowney	10	10
Snickers	M&M/Mars	11	9
Crunchie	Cadbury Schweppes	12	12

Source: Neilson News – Issue #1, 1993

and Mexico from their chocolate production facilities in Pennsylvania. In Canada, in 1992, Hershey held third place in the countline segment with a 21.6 percent share of the market.

Hershey's strategy was to reduce exposure to volatile cocoa prices by diversifying within the confectionery and snack businesses. By 1987, only 45 percent of Hershey's sales came from products with 70 percent or more chocolate content. This was down from 80 percent in 1963.

Cadbury Schweppes

Cadbury was a major world name in chocolate, with a portfolio of brands such as Dairy Milk, Creme Eggs, and Crunchie. Although its main business was in the United Kingdom, it was also a strong competitor in major markets such as Australia and South Africa.

Cadbury Schweppes diversified its product line and expanded into new geographic markets throughout the 1980s. In 1987, Cadbury International sold the Canadian distribution rights for their chocolate products to William Neilson Ltd. Only in Canada were the Cadbury brands incorporated into the Neilson confectionery division under the name Neilson/Cadbury. In 1988, Cadbury sold its U.S. operations to Hershey.

Nestlé-Rowntree

In 1991, chocolate and confectionery comprised 16 percent of Nestlé's SFr 50.5 billion revenue, up sharply from only 8 percent in 1987. (In January 1993, SFr1 = CDN$.88 = US$.69.) This was largely a result of their move into the countline sector through the acquisition in 1988 of Rowntree PLC, a leading British manufacturer with strong global brands such as Kit Kat, After Eights, and Smarties. In 1990, they also added Baby Ruth and Butterfinger to their portfolio, both "Top 20" brands in the U.S. Considering these recent heavy investments to acquire global brands and expertise, it was clear that Nestlé-Rowntree intended to remain a significant player in growing global markets.

NEILSON

Company History

William Neilson Ltd. was founded in 1893, when the Neilson family began selling milk and homemade ice cream to the Toronto market. By 1905 they had erected a house and factory at 277 Gladstone Ave., from which they shipped ice cream as far west as Winnipeg and as far east as Quebec City. Chocolate bar production was initiated to offset the decreased demand for ice cream during the colder winter months and as a way of retaining the skilled labor pool. By 1914, the company was producing one million pounds of ice cream and 500,000 pounds of chocolate per year.

William Neilson died in 1915, and the business was handed down to his son Morden, who had been involved since its inception. Between 1924 and 1934, the Jersey Milk, Crispy Crunch, and Malted Milk bars were introduced. Upon the death of Morden Neilson in 1947, the company was sold to George Weston Foods for $4.5 million.

By 1974, Crispy Crunch was the number one selling bar in Canada. In 1977, Mr. Big was introduced and became the number one teen bar by 1986. By 1991, the Neilson dairy operations had been moved to a separate location and the ice cream division had been sold to Ault Foods. The Gladstone location continued to be used to manufacture Neilson chocolate and confectionery.

Bateman explained that Neilson's efforts under the direction of the new president, Arthur Soler, had become more competitive in the domestic market over the past three years, through improved customer service and retail merchandising. Significant improvements had already been made in Administration and Operations. All of these initiatives had assisted in reversing decades of consumer share erosion. As a result, Neilson was now in a position to defend its share of the domestic market and to develop an international business that would enhance shareholder value. Exhibit 20.4 outlines the Canadian chocolate confectionery market.

Neilson's Exporting Efforts

Initial export efforts prior to 1990 were contracted to a local export broker – Grenadier International. The original company objective was to determine "what could be done in foreign markets" using only working capital resources and avoiding capital investments in equipment or new markets.

Through careful selection of markets on the basis of distributor interest, Grenadier's export manager, Scott Begg, had begun the slow process of introducing Neilson brands into the Far East. The results were impressive. Orders were secured for containers of Mr. Big and Crispy Crunch countlines from local distributors in Korea, Taiwan, and Japan. Canadian Classics boxed chocolates were developed for the vast Japanese gift (Omiyagi) market. Total 1993 sales to these markets were projected to be $1.6 million.

For each of these markets, Neilson retained the responsibility for packaging design and product formulation. While distributors offered suggestions as to how products could be improved to suit local tastes, they were not formally obliged to do so. To secure distribution in Taiwan, Neilson had agreed to launch the Mr. Big bar under the distributor's private brand name, Bang Bang, which was expected to generate a favorable impression with consumers. Although sales were strong, Bateman realized that since consumer loyalty was linked to brand names, the brand equity being generated for Bang Bang, ultimately, would

Exhibit 20.4   Canadian Confectionery Market – 1993

	Dollars (millions)	%
Total Confectionery Category	$1,301.4	100.0
Gum	296.5	22.8
Boxed Chocolates	159.7	12.3
Cough Drops	77.0	5.9
Rolled Candy	61.3	4.7
Bagged Chocolates	30.3	2.3
Easter Eggs	22.0	1.7
Valentines	9.4	0.7
Lunch Pack	3.6	0.3
Countline Chocolate Bars	641.6	49.3
Total Chocolate Bar Market Growth	+ 8%	

Source: Neilson Marketing Department Estimates

belong to the distributor. This put the distributor in a powerful position from which they were able to place significant downward pressure on operating margins.

Market Evaluation Study

In response to these successful early exporting efforts Bateman began exploring the possible launch of Neilson brands into the United States (discussed later). With limited working capital and numerous export opportunities, it became obvious to the International Division that some kind of formal strategy was required to evaluate and to compare these new markets.

Accordingly, a set of weighted criteria was developed during the summer of 1992 to evaluate countries that were being considered by the International Division. See Exhibit 20.5 for a profile of the world's major chocolate importers. The study was intended to provide a standard means of evaluating potential markets. Resources could then be allocated among those markets that promised long term incremental growth and those which were strictly opportunistic. While the revenues from opportunistic markets would contribute to the fixed costs of domestic production, the long term efforts could be pursued for more strategic reasons. By the end of the summer, the study had been applied to thirteen international markets, including the United States. See Exhibit 20.6 for a summary of this study.

Meanwhile, Grenadier had added Hong Kong/China, Singapore, and New Zealand to Neilson's portfolio of export markets, and Bateman had contracted a second local broker, CANCON Corp. Ltd, to initiate sales to the Middle East. By the end of 1992, the International Division comprised nine people who had achieved penetration of eleven countries for export sales. See Exhibit 20.7 for a description of these markets.

THE U.S. EXPERIENCE

In 1991, the American chocolate confectionery market was worth U.S.$5.1 billion wholesale. Neilson had wanted to sneak into this vast market with the intention of quietly selling off

Exhibit 20.5 World Chocolate Imports (Value as % of Total) – 1990

	1987	1988	1989	1990
Africa	x0.7	x0.7	x0.7	x0.7
Americas	x15.6	x15.0	x13.9	x13.2
LAIC[1]	0.2	0.4	1.1	x1.3
CACM[2]	x0.1	x0.1	x0.1	x0.1
Asia	11.7	x13.9	x15.6	x12.9
Middle East	x3.5	x3.3	x3.9	x2.8
Europe	70.8	68.9	67.7	71.4
EEC (12)[3]	61.1	59.5	57.7	59.3
EFTA[4]	9.3	9.0	8.9	8.4
Oceania	x1.3	x1.7	x2.1	x1.8

Figures denoted with an "x" are provisional or estimated.
Adapted from: The United Nations' "International Trade Statistics Yearbook," Vol. II, 1990.
[1]LAIC = Latin American Industrialists Association.
[2]CACM = Central American Common Market.
[3]EEC (12) = The twelve nations of the European Economic Community.
[4]EFTA = European Free Trade Association.

Exhibit 20.6   Summary of Criteria for Market Study (1992)

Criteria	Weight	Australia	China	Hong Kong	Indo-nesia	Japan	Korea	Malay-sia	New Zealand	Singa-pore	Taiwan	Mexico	EEC	USA
* U.S. Countline	–	4	4	4	4	4	4	4	4	4	4	4	4	4
1 Candybar Economics	30	20	20	30	20	20	28	20	15	25	15	20	10	10
2 Target Market	22	12.5	14	13	15.5	19	15	10	7	9.5	12.5	21	22	22
3 Competitor Dynamics	20	12	15	8	7.5	11	13.5	10	12	14.5	12	11	20	6.5
4 Distribution Access	10	9	4	4	3.5	5	6	6.5	9	3.5	7.5	9.5	9	9
5 Industry Economics	9	2.5	3.5	6	5.5	2	5	2.5	7	4.5	3	3.5	3.5	4.5
6 Product Fit	8	7	6	6	6	3	7.5	7.5	7.5	8	4	8	5	8
7 Payback	5	4	4	1	2.5	4	5	2.5	4	2	2	5	2	1
8 Country Dynamics	5	5	1	4	3	5	3.5	4.5	4.5	5	4	3	2	4
Total	109	72	67.5	72	63.5	69	83.5	63.5	66	72	60	81	73.5	65

Due to Neilson/Cadbury's limited resources, it was not feasible to launch the first western-style brands into new markets. The basic minimum criteria for a given market, therefore, was the presence of major western industry players (ie: Mars or Hershey). Countries were then measured on the basis of 8 criteria which were weighted by the International Group according to their perceived importance as determinants of a successful market entry. (See above table.) Each criterion was then subdivided into several elements as defined by the International Group, which allocated the total weighted score accordingly. (See table, right.)

This illustration depicts a single criteria, subdivided and scored for Mexico.

Competitor Dynamics	Score	Mexico
Financial Success of Other Exporters	0–8	5
Nature (Passivity) of Competition	0–6	2.5
Brand Image (vs Price) Positioning	0–6	3.5
SCORE /20	/20	11

Source: Company Records

excess capacity. However, as Bateman explained, the quiet U.S. launch became a Canadian celebration

> Next thing we knew, there were bands in the streets, Neilson t-shirts and baseball caps, and newspaper articles and T.V. specials describing our big U.S. launch!

The publicity greatly increased the pressure to succeed. After careful consideration, Pro Set, a collectible trading card manufacturer and marketer, was selected as a distributor. This relationship developed into a joint venture by which the Neilson Import Division was later appointed distributor of the Pro Set cards in Canada. With an internal sales management team, full distribution and invoicing infrastructures, and a forty-five-broker national sales network, Pro Set seemed ideally suited to diversify into confectionery products.

Unfortunately, Pro Set quickly proved to be an inadequate partner in this venture. Although they had access to the right outlets, the confectionery selling task differed significantly from

Exhibit 20.7   Neilson Export Markets – 1993

Agent (Commission)	Country	Brands
Grenadier International	Taiwan	Bang Bang
	Japan	Mr. Big, Crispy Crunch, Canadian Classics
	Korea	Mr. Big, Crispy Crunch
	Hong Kong/China	Mr. Big, Crispy Crunch, Canadian Classics
	Singapore	Mr. Big, Crispy Crunch
CANCON Corp. Ltd.	Saudi Arabia	Mr. Big, Crispy Crunch, Malted Milk
	Bahrain	Mr. Big, Crispy Crunch, Malted Milk
	U.A.E.	Mr. Big, Crispy Crunch, Malted Milk
	Kuwait	Mr. Big, Crispy Crunch, Malted Milk
Neilson International	Mexico	Mr. Big, Crispy Crunch, Malted Milk
	U.S.A.	Mr. Big, Crispy Crunch, Malted Milk

Source: Company Records

card sales. Confectionery items demanded more sensitive product handling and a greater amount of sales effort by the Pro Set representatives who were used to carrying a self-promoting line.

To compound these difficulties, Pro Set sales plummeted as the trading-card market became oversaturated. Trapped by intense cashflow problems and increasing fixed costs, Pro Set filed for Chapter 11 bankruptcy, leaving Neilson with huge inventory losses and a customer base that associated them with their defunct distributor. Although it was tempting to attribute the U.S. failure to inappropriate partner selection, the U.S. had also ranked poorly relative to other markets in the criteria study that had just been completed that summer. In addition to their distribution problems, Neilson was at a serious disadvantage due to intense competition from the major industry players in the form of advertising expenditures, trade promotions, and brand proliferation. Faced with duties and a higher cost of production, Neilson was unable to maintain price competitiveness.

The International Division was now faced with the task of internalizing distribution in the U.S., including sales management, broker contact, warehousing, shipping, and collections. Neilson managed to reestablish a limited presence in the American market using several local brokers to target profitable niches. For example, they placed strong emphasis on vending-machine sales to increase product trial with minimal advertising. Since consumer purchasing patterns demanded product variety in vending machines, Neilson's presence in this segment was not considered threatening by major competitors.

In the autumn of 1992, as the International Division made the changes necessary to salvage past efforts in the U.S., several options for entering the Mexican confectionery market were also being considered.

MEXICO

Neilson made the decision to enter the Mexican market late in 1992, prompted by its parent company's, Weston Foods Ltd., own investigations into possible market opportunities which would emerge as a result of the North American Free Trade Agreement (NAFTA). Mexico was an attractive market which scored very highly in the market evaluation study. Due to their favorable demographics (50 percent of the population was within the target age group), Mexico offered huge potential for countline sales. The rapid adoption of American tastes resulted in an increasing demand for U.S. snack foods. With only a limited number of competitors, the untapped demand afforded a window of opportunity for smaller players to enter the market.

Working through the Ontario Ministry of Agriculture and Food (OMAF), Neilson found two potential independent distributors:

- *Grupo Corvi*: a Mexican food manufacturer, operated seven plants and had an extensive sales force reaching local wholesalers. They also had access to a convoluted infrastructure which indirectly supplied an estimated 100,000 street vendor stands or kiosks (known as "tiendas") representing nearly 70 percent of the Mexican confectionery market. (This informal segment was usually overlooked by marketing research services and competitors alike.) Grupo Corvi currently had no American or European style countline products.
- *Grupo Hajj*: a Mexican distributor with some experience in confectionery, offered access to only a small number of retail stores. This limited network made Grupo Hajj relatively unattractive when compared to other distributors. Like Grupo Corvi, this local firm dealt exclusively in Mexican pesos, historically, a volatile currency. (In January 1993, 1 peso = $0.41 Cdn.)

While considering these distributors, Neilson was approached by Sabritas, the snack food division of Pepsico Foods in Mexico, who felt that there was a strategic fit between their organizations. Although Sabritas had no previous experience handling chocolate confectionery, they had for six years been seeking a product line to round out their portfolio. They were currently each week supplying Frito-Lay type snacks directly to 450,000 retail stores and tiendas. (The trade referred to such extensive customer networks as "numeric distribution.") After listening to the initial proposal, Neilson agreed to give Sabritas three months to conduct research into the Mexican market.

Although the research revealed strong market potential for the Neilson products, Bateman felt that pricing at 2 pesos (at parity with other American style brands) would not provide any competitive advantage. Sabritas agreed that a one-peso product, downsized to forty grams (from a Canadian-U.S. standard of forty-three to sixty-five grams), would provide an attractive strategy to offer "imported chocolate at Mexican prices."

Proposing a deal significantly different from the relationships offered by the two Mexican distributors, Sabritas intended to market the Mr. Big, Crispy Crunch, and Malted Milk bars as the first brands in the Milch product line. Milch was a fictitious word in Spanish, created and owned by Sabritas, and thought to denote goodness and health due to its similarity to the word "milk." Sabritas would offer Neilson 50 percent ownership of the Milch name, in exchange for 50 percent of Neilson's brand names, both of which would appear on each bar. As part of the joint branding agreement, Sabritas would assume all responsibility for advertising, promotion, distribution, and merchandising.

The joint ownership of the brand names would provide Sabritas with brand equity in exchange for building brand awareness through heavy investments in marketing. By delegating responsibility for all marketing efforts to Sabritas, Neilson would be able to compete on a scale not affordable by Canadian standards.

Under the proposal, all Milch chocolate bars would be produced in Canada by Neilson. Neilson would be the exclusive supplier. Ownership of the bars would pass to Sabritas once the finished goods had been shipped. Sabritas in turn would be responsible for all sales to final consumers. Sabritas would be the exclusive distributor. Consumer prices could not be changed without the mutual agreement of Neilson and Sabritas.

ISSUES

Bateman reflected upon the decision he now faced for the Mexican market. The speed with which Sabritas could help them gain market penetration, their competitive advertising budget, and their "store door access" to nearly a half million retailers were attractive advantages offered by this joint venture proposal. But what were the implications of omitting the Neilson name from their popular chocolate bars? Would they be exposed to problems like those encountered in Taiwan with the Bang Bang launch, especially considering the strength and size of Pepsico Foods?

The alternative was to keep the Neilson name and to launch their brands independently, using one of the national distributors. Unfortunately, limited resources meant that Neilson would develop its presence much more slowly. With countline demand in Mexico growing at 30 percent per year, could they afford to delay? Scott Begg had indicated that early entry was critical in burgeoning markets, since establishing market presence and gaining share were less difficult when undertaken before the major players had dominated the market and "defined the rules of play."

Bateman also questioned their traditional means of evaluating potential markets. Were the criteria considered in the market evaluation study really the key success factors, or were the competitive advantages offered through ventures with distributors more important? If partnerships were necessary, should Neilson continue to rely on independent, national distributors who were interested in adding Neilson brands to their portfolio, or should they pursue strategic partnerships similar to the Sabritas opportunity instead? No matter which distributor was chosen, product quality and handling were of paramount importance. Every chocolate bar reaching consumers, especially first time buyers, must be of the same freshness and quality as those distributed to Canadian consumers. How could this type of control best be achieved?

NOTES

1. Some information in this section was derived from: J. C. Ellert, J. Peter Killing, and Dana Hyde, "Nestlé-Rowntree (A)," in *Business Policy, A Canadian Casebook*, Joseph N. Fry, et al. (Eds.), Prentice Hall Canada Inc., 1992, pp. 655–667.

21

Imasco Limited: The Roy Rogers Acquisition

This case was prepared by Kent E. Neupert under the supervision of Professor Joseph N. Fry of the Western Business School. Copyright © 1992, The University of Western Ontario.

This material is not covered under authorization from CanCopy or any reproduction rights organization. Any form of reproduction, storage or transmittal of this material is prohibited without written permission from Western Business School, The University of Western Ontario, London, Canada N6A, 3K7. Reprinted with permission, Western Business School.

In January 1990, Purdy Crawford, the chairman, president, and CEO of Imasco Limited, was reviewing an acquisition proposal from one of Imasco's operating companies, Hardee's Food Systems, Inc. (Hardee's) to purchase the Roy Rogers restaurant chain. Bill Prather, Hardee's CEO, was coming to Montreal the following day to present the proposal to the Imasco board. Prather thought the acquisition would permit Hardee's to expand rapidly into markets where they had very little presence. While Crawford was inclined to support Prather's proposal, he wanted to carefully weigh its broader impact for Imasco as a whole. The probable price of more than $390 million represented a substantial commitment of funds, at a time when growth in the U.S. fast food business was slowing.

IMASCO BACKGROUND

Imasco was a diversified Canadian public corporation with consolidated revenues of $5.7 billion in 1989 and net profits of $366 million. Imasco's founding and largest shareholder was B.A.T Industries (B.A.T), which had maintained a relatively constant 40 percent equity ownership over the years. B.A.T was a very large diversified British company with roots, like Imasco, in the tobacco business. The balance of Imasco shares was widely held.

In 1990, Imasco's operations were focused on four major operating companies, "the four legs of the table," as Crawford referred to them. The companies were: Imperial Tobacco, Canada's largest manufacturer and distributor of cigarettes; CT Financial, the holding company for Canada Trust, a major Canadian retail financial services business; Imasco Drug Retailing Group, made up of Shoppers Drug Mart in Canada and Peoples Drug Stores in the U.S.; and Hardee's Food Systems, Inc. in the U.S. A fifth, smaller company was The UCS Group, Canada's leading small space specialty retailer. Highlights of Imasco's operations for the years 1985–89 are shown in Table 21.1.

IMASCO DIVERSIFICATION ACTIVITIES

Imasco Limited was created in 1969 as a corporate entity to encompass and oversee the tobacco, food, and distribution businesses of Imperial Tobacco Limited, and to manage a program of further diversification. The aim was to build a broadly based corporation that would rely less on the tobacco business and be better received in the stock market.

Table 21.1   Imasco Operating Highlights

	($ million unless otherwise noted)				
	1989	1988	1987	1986	1985
System-wide sales	14715.6	13836.5	12951.5	11132.2	8371.8
Revenues	5724.7	6000.6	5924.4	5596.6	5110.2
Operating earnings	692.0	636.7	578.4	455.6	464.1
Total assets	5378.0	5310.2	5656.6	5505.5	2905.7
Earnings before extraordinary items	366.1	314.3	282.7	226.4	261.6
EPS before extraordinary items	2.87	2.51	2.24	1.92	2.40
DVDS/Share	1.12	1.04	0.96	0.84	0.72

Paul Paré was the first president, chairman, and CEO of Imasco, and the person with prime responsibility for its diversification program up to his retirement from the chairmanship in 1987. Paré's 38-year career began in the legal department of Imperial Tobacco and led to senior positions in the marketing areas. He became President and CEO in 1969 and Chairman in 1979. Except for a two-year stint with the Department of National Defence, his career was always in the tobacco industry. Paré's approach to diversification in the early years had been a conservative one. He preferred to make a number of relatively small investments, and build or divest the positions as experience dictated.

Crawford, Paré's successor, pictured the first ten years of diversification as a process of experimentation and learning. He described the evolution of thought and action. "Imperial's first attempt at diversification had been through vertical integration." Crawford explained, "Although it appeared logical that if Imperial bought a tinfoil company and made foil wrap themselves there were economies to be realized, we quickly learned that making cigarettes and making tinfoil are two different things." Imperial knew little about the highly specialized tinfoil business, and also discovered that "the competition didn't like the idea of buying tinfoil from us."

Upon reflection, management determined that they were "in the business of converting and marketing agricultural products." Crawford recounted: "It made sense then that the next acquisition was a winery. Unfortunately, we failed to take into consideration provincial liquor regulations which made it impossible to operate at a sufficient scale to be profitable."

Management then broadened its perspective and decided that they were best at marketing. This led to acquisitions that "embodied exciting new marketing concepts," such as two sporting goods companies, Collegiate and Arlington, and a discount bottler and retailer of soft drinks called PoP Shoppes. These investments were held for several years, but they failed to live up to their promise and were subsequently sold off. Other acquisitions, in food processing and distribution, for example, were quite successful, but not on a scale of importance to Imasco. These were later divested when Imasco refocused its efforts.

For the most part, these early diversification moves involved the acquisition of several small companies, and subsequent restructuring of them into a larger enterprise. Most of these acquisitions were then later divested. For example, Imasco's three food companies, which were sold in the late 1970s and early 1980s, were originally ten different companies. Amco Vending, sold in 1977, was built up from eight separate vending companies across Canada. Other businesses which were grown and later sold included wines, drycleaning, and video tape services.

With time, Paré's team built an understanding of its capabilities, sharpened its sense of mission, and focused its acquisition criteria. The mission was to "create shareholder value as a leading North American consumer products and services company." Based on their learning, the criteria for acquisitions were formalized. Imasco would acquire companies that (1) were well positioned in the consumer goods and services sector of the economy; (2) had a capable management team in place, or were able to be smoothly integrated into an existing operating division; (3) had above average growth potential, and were capable of making a meaningful and immediate contribution to profits; and (4) were North American based, preferably in Canada. Crawford noted that "perhaps the most important end result of approximately ten years of experimentation was that we developed a clear vision of what the company was and was not."

As Imasco became more focused and confident of its skills, the acquisitions became less frequent and larger in size, and the diversification from tobacco more significant. Imasco's acquisitions and net investments are given in Exhibit 21.1. The most significant events of the 1980s are described below in the review of the present-day Imasco operating companies. The net result of twenty years of diversification was that Imasco increased its revenues tenfold and its earnings twentyfold. Moreover, its reliance on tobacco for corporate earnings went from 100 percent in 1970 to 48 percent in 1989. A twenty-year review of Imasco performance is given in Exhibit 21.2.

Exhibit 21.1 Imasco Acquisitions: Distinguishable Eras in Acquisition Size

1963–77
  Canada Foils
  Growers Wine
  Simtel and Editel
  S&W Foods: $18.4 million (Canadian)
  Uddo & Taormina (Progresso): $32.5 million (Canadian)
  Pasquale Brothers (Unico): $4 million (Canadian)
  Grissol: $12.2 million (Canadian)
  Collegiate: $1.4 million (Canadian)
  Arlington Sports
  Top Drug Mart and Top Value Discount
  Tinderbox: $1.4 million (U.S.)
  PoP Shoppes investment: $10.5 million (Canadian)
  Canada Northwest Land Ltd. investment
  Hardee's Food Systems investment: $15 million (U.S.)
  – Includes Imperial Tobacco Limited acquisitions
1978–86
  Shoppers Drug Mart (Koffler's): $66.6 million (Canadian)
  Further Hardee's investment: $15 million (Canadian)
  Hardee's totally acquired: $76 million (U.S.)
  Burger Chef: $44 million (U.S.)
  Peoples Drug Stores: $398 million (Canadian)
  Rea & Derick Drug Stores: $114 million (Canadian)
  Genstar: $2.4 billion (Canadian)

Exhibit 21.2 Twenty-Year Financials: Imasco Ltd. and Tobacco Business

($ million unless noted)

Year	Imasco Ltd.				Tobacco Business			Imasco Ltd.		
	Total Revenues	Operating Earnings	Net Earnings Before Extraordinary Items	Earnings Per Common Share[4,5]	Tobacco Operating Earnings/Total Operating Earnings (%)	Tobacco Revenue	Tobacco Operating Earnings	Stock Price High[6]	Stock Price Low[6]	Annual Dividend[5] Per Common Share
1970[1]	582.2	37.3	15.7	.20	.88	435.2	32.7	16.13	12.00	0.10
1971[1]	569.6	40.6	17.7	.22	.88	418.0	35.9	20.50	15.25	0.125
1972[1]	625.6	48.1	22.2	.28	.84	430.4	40.4	28.38	19.00	0.1375
1973[1]	717.1	56.0	28.0	.36	.81	446.9	45.4	34.75	25.75	0.15
1975[3]	1030.3	78.5	36.8	.47	.79	610.5	62.0	33.25	18.75	0.19375
1976[2]	941.2	74.9	36.5	.47	.81	560.1	60.7	32.00	26.00	0.1625
1977[2]	1031.6	74.7	34.9	.45	.81	605.4	60.9	27.25	20.63	0.169
1978[2]	1049.4	84.2	43.1	.55	.81	655.0	68.3	31.63	24.00	0.18
1979[2]	1161.5	114.8	56.4	.70	.69	741.4	78.8	40.75	29.75	0.205
1980[2]	1150.5	132.1	68.2	.83	.75	826.7	99.1	47.25	38.25	0.25
1981[2]	1423.7	168.8	89.6	1.07	.73	952.9	123.2	38.25	21.25	0.30
1982[2]	2190.7	247.0	124.2	1.39	.63	1120.2	156.0	44.50	29.50	0.35
1983[2]	2713.9	300.3	156.8	1.73	.61	1242.9	182.3	37.50	18.00	0.40
1984[2]	2873.2	339.6	194.2	2.03	.60	1358.9	205.2	36.25	29.88	0.50
1985[2]	4353.2	432.0	234.1	2.25	.52	1451.1	224.0	28.25	17.38	0.645
1986[2]	5325.1	465.9	261.7	2.40	.53	1769.8	246.0	35.00	22.63	0.75
1987[1]	5924.4	578.4	282.7	2.24	.48	1926.0	279.1	46.00	24.25	0.96
1988[1]	6000.6	636.7	314.3	2.51	.48	2018.1	308.0	29.50	23.75	1.04
1989[1]	5724.7	692.0	366.1	2.87	.48	2385.6	334.0	40.50	27.63	1.12

[1]January–December Fiscal Year.
[2]April–March Fiscal Year.
[3]Reflects 15-month period from January 1974 to March 1975.
[4]Before extraordinary items.
[5]Prior to 1980, adjusted to reflect three stock splits; after 1980, 2 for 1 stock splits July 1980, November 1982, and March 1985.
[6]Not adjusted for stock splits.
Source: Imasco Limited.

CORPORATE MANAGEMENT

While Imasco's diversification policy was directed from the central office, its operations were not centralized. The corporate management structure was decentralized and rather flat. Only fifty people staffed the head office in Montreal. The various companies, with operations across Canada and most of the U.S., were encouraged to aggressively pursue the development of their businesses and related trademarks. Management believed that "combining the experience and expertise that flow from the individual operating companies creates a unique opportunity to add value to all of its (Imasco's) operations and assets." Accordingly, Imasco saw its greatest strengths as the high degree of autonomy, and clear lines of authority and responsibility, which existed between Imasco's head office (the Imasco Center) and the operating companies. While each company's CEO operated with the widest possible autonomy, they also contributed to the development of the annual and five-year plans, and "to furthering Imasco's overall growth objectives." The role of the Imasco Center was to guide Imasco's overall growth without interfering with the operating companies. The 1988 business plan stipulated that "the role of the Imasco Center is to be a source of excellence in management dedicated to achieving overall corporate objectives, and supporting Imasco's operating companies in the fulfillment of their respective missions and objectives."

It was very important to Imasco that any acquisition be friendly. While it was not formally stipulated in the acquisition criteria, it was evident in Imasco's actions, such as the aborted acquisition of Canadian Tire in 1983.

In June of that year, Imasco initiated an acquisition attempt of Canadian Tire, but later withdrew the offer. Imasco had outlined a proposal to the members of the Billes family, majority shareholders in Canadian Tire, and the management of Canadian Tire in which Imasco would purchase as many of Canadian Tire's outstanding common and Class "A" shares as would be tendered. Imasco stipulated the offer was conditional on family and management support. Imasco expected the cost of the acquisition to be about $1.13 billion.

Several days later, Paré issued a press release in which he stated:

We at Imasco are obviously disappointed with the reaction of the senior management group at Canadian Tire to purchase all of the outstanding shares of the company. We stated at the outset that we were seeking both the support of the major voting shareholders and the endorsement of management. It now appears that such support and endorsement are not forthcoming. In light of this and in view of the announcement made . . . by the trustees of the John W. Billes estate, we have concluded that one or more of the conditions to our offer will not be satisfied. Therefore, we do not propose to proceed with our previously announced offer.

In explaining Imasco's rationale for withdrawing the offer, Paré continued:

Throughout the negotiations, we have been keenly aware of the essential ingredients that have made Canadian Tire one of the retail success stories in Canada. These ingredients include the able leadership of the management group, the unique relationship between management and the associate-dealers, and the employee profit-sharing and share-ownership plans. As we have mentioned on several occasions, it was our intention to preserve these relationships and the formulas that have so obviously contributed to the success of the Canadian Tire organization.

OPERATING COMPANIES

Imperial Tobacco

Imperial Tobacco was the largest tobacco enterprise in Canada, with operations ranging from leaf tobacco buying and processing, to the manufacture and distribution of a broad range of tobacco products. The manufacture and sale of cigarettes constituted the largest segment of its business, representing 89.4 percent of Imperial Tobacco's revenues in 1989. Highlights of Imperial Tobacco's operations for the years 1985–89 are shown in Table 21.2.

Over the years, Imperial had concentrated on building its market share in Canada from a low of 36 percent in 1970 to 57.9 percent in 1989. Revenues in 1989 reached an all time high of almost $2.4 billion, in spite of a 4 percent decline in unit sales to 27.5 billion cigarettes. The market share gains had been achieved by focusing on the strength of Imperial Tobacco's trademarks, particularly the continued growth of its two leading Canadian brands, Player's and du Maurier. Together these two brands held 47.4 percent of the market in 1989.

Imperial Tobacco had production and packaging facilities in Montreal and Joliette, Quebec, and Guelph, Ontario, and leaf processing facilities in Joliette and LaSalle, Quebec, and Aylmer, Ontario. Imperial continually modernized its production facilities to the point that management claimed them to be "the most technologically advanced in the tobacco industry in Canada." The distribution and promotion of Imperial Tobacco's products to wholesalers and retailers were carried out through a nationwide sales staff operating out of the sales offices and distribution centers in St. Johns, Moncton, Montreal, Toronto, Winnipeg, Calgary, and Vancouver.

Imasco Enterprises (Including Canada Trust)

Imasco Enterprises Inc. (IEI) was wholly owned through Imasco Limited and three of its other companies, making it an indirect wholly owned subsidiary. In 1986, Imasco announced its intention to acquire all of the outstanding common shares of Genstar Corporation (Genstar) through IEI. At the time, Imasco's primary objective was to gain entry into the financial services sector by assuming Genstar's 98 percent ownership position in Canada

Table 21.2 Imperial Tobacco Operating Summary

	($ million unless otherwise noted)				
	1989	1988	1987	1986	1985
Revenues	2385.6	2018.1	1926.0	1754.6	1701.8
Revenues, net of sales and excise taxes	896.2	862.0	816.2	712.0	757.5
Operating earnings	334.0	308.0	279.1	208.1	243.7
Operating margins (%)	37.3	35.7	34.2	29.2	32.2
Market share–domestic	57.9	56.2	54.4	51.5	52.6
Capital employed*	558.1	496.4	513.9	594.6†	587.0†

*Capital employed of each consolidated segment consists of directly identifiable assets at net book value, less current liabilities, excluding income taxes payable and bank and other debt. Corporate assets and corporate current liabilities are also excluded.
†Reflects fiscal year ending March 31.

Trust. Genstar had purchased Canada Trust in 1985 for $1.2 billion dollars and merged it with Canada Permanent Mortgage Corporation, which Genstar had purchased in 1981. This merger created Canada's seventh largest financial institution with $50 billion in assets under administration.

Once acquired, Imasco intended to sell off all of Genstar's non-financial assets. Within the year, all of the shares were acquired at a cost of approximately $2.6 billion. This was the first acquisition orchestrated by Crawford.

In addition to Canada Trust, Genstar had holdings in an assortment of other businesses. Most of these, such as the cement and related operations, Genstar Container Corporation, and Seaspan International, were sold off. The cost of those assets retained, including Canada Trust, was about $2.4 billion, of which all but $150 million was attributed to the Canada Trust holding. The balance of the amount was accounted for by a variety of assets which included Genstar Development Company, Genstar Mortgage Corporation, a one-third limited partnership in Sutter Hill Ventures, a portfolio of other venture capital investments, and certain other assets and liabilities. Genstar Development Company was involved in land development in primary Canadian metropolitan areas, such as Vancouver, Calgary, Edmonton, Winnipeg, Toronto, and Ottawa. U.S.-based Sutter Hill Ventures had capital investments in over forty-three different companies. Most of these investments were in the areas of medical research, biotechnology, communications, and computer hardware and software. Highlights of investments in IEI are shown in Table 21.3.

CT Financial was the holding company for the Canada Trust group of companies. In 1989, Canada Trust was Canada's second largest trust and loan company and a major residential real estate broker. The principal businesses of Canada Trust were financial intermediary services, such as deposit services, credit card services, mortgage lending, consumer lending, corporate and commercial lending, and investments. It also offered trust services, real estate services, and real estate development. Canada Trust operated 331 financial services branches, 22 personal and pension trust services offices, and 275 company operated and franchised real estate offices. Total assets under the administration of Canada Trust at the end of 1989 were $74.1 billion, comprised of $32.7 billion in corporate assets, and $41.4 billion in assets administered for estate, trust, and agency accounts. Total personal deposits were estimated to be the fourth largest among Canadian financial institutions. The return of common shareholders' average equity was 17.3 percent compared with an average of 7.7 percent for Canada's six largest banks. Highlights of CT Financial operations are shown in Table 21.4.

Table 21.3   Investments in Imasco Enterprises, Inc.

($ million)	1989	1988	1987*
Equity in net earnings of Imasco enterprises	152.5	142.1	126.5
Investment in Imasco enterprises	2,700.2	2,655.4	2,613.5

*Financial information is shown beginning with 1987 to reflect the acquisition of Canada Trust in 1986.

Table 21.4   Operating Performance Data for CT Financial

($ million unless otherwise noted)	1989	1988	1987*
Assets under administration	74096.0	67401.0	60626.0
Corporate assets	32666.0	29219.2	25514.8
Deposits	30403.0	27319.5	23859.0
Loans	24201.1	22661.7	19679.3
Net earnings attributed to common shares	240.2	232.0	201.0
Return on common shareholders average equity (%)	17.3	19.0	19.4

*Financial information is shown beginning with 1987 to reflect the acquisition of Canada Trust in 1986.

IMASCO DRUG RETAILING

Shoppers Drug Mart

Shoppers Drug Mart provided a wide range of marketing and management services to a group of 633 associated retail drug stores located throughout Canada, operating under the trademarks Shoppers Drug Mart (585 stores), and Pharmaprix in Quebec (48 stores). The Shoppers Drug Mart stores also included the extended concepts of Shoppers Drug Mart Food Baskets and Shoppers Drug Mart Home Health Care Centers.

In 1989, Shoppers Drug Mart was the largest drug store group in Canada with about 33 percent of the retail drug store market. In system-wide sales, it ranked first and fifth among all drug store groups in Canada and North America, respectively. In the past, competition had come primarily from regional chains and independent drug stores, but food stores with drug departments represented a growing challenge. During 1989, management had emphasized strengthening the productivity and profitability of existing stores, particularly the former Super X Drugs and Howie's stores, recently converted to Shoppers Drug Mart stores.

The Shoppers Drug Mart operating division utilized licensing and franchise agreements. Under the licensing arrangement, each Shoppers Drug Mart was owned and operated by a licensed pharmacist, called an Associate. In Quebec, Pharmaprix stores used a franchise system. In return for an annual fee, each associate of a Shoppers Drug Mart store and franchisee of a Pharmaprix store had access to a variety of services, such as store design, merchandising techniques, financial analysis, training, advertising, and marketing. Highlights of Shoppers Drug Mart operations are shown in Table 21.5.

Peoples Drug Stores

Peoples Drug Stores, Incorporated (Peoples) operated 490 company-owned drug stores in the U.S. during 1989. The stores were primarily operated from leased premises under the trade names Peoples Drug Stores, Health Mart, and Rea and Derick..Imasco had built the Peoples operating division from several acquired drug store chains in six eastern U.S. states and the District of Columbia.

After a disappointing performance in 1986, Peoples began a comprehensive plan to revitalize the chain and focus on areas of market strength. Earnings steadily improved, with operating earnings of $8.0 million in 1989, compared with operating losses of $8.3 million

Table 21.5 Shoppers Drug Mart Operating Summary

	($ million unless otherwise noted)				
	1989	1988	1987	1986	1985
System-wide sales	2597.7	2355.6	2073.4	1775.0	1522.3
Revenues	136.2	114.9	95.7	86.6	73.4
Operating earnings	70.6	57.1	51.3	48.9	42.5
Operating margins (%)	51.8	49.7	53.6	56.5	57.9
Average sales per store	4.1	4.2	4.1	3.9	3.6
Number of stores	633	613	586	543	431
Capital expenditures	24.0	28.0	27.6	23.3	16.4
Capital employed*	204.1	209.8	194.2	117.9	106.8†
Depreciation	26.6	20.6	17.9	13.0	11.8

*Capital employed of each consolidated segment consists of directly identifiable assets at net book value, less current liabilities, excluding income taxes payable and bank and other debt. Corporate assets and corporate current liabilities are also excluded.
†Reflects fiscal year ending March 31.

in 1988 and $22.5 million in 1987. The turnaround involved restructuring and included the divestment of Peoples' Reed, Lane, Midwest, Bud's Deep Discount, and other smaller divisions. During 1989, a total of 326 drug stores were sold, twenty-one were closed, and thirteen opened for a net decrease of 334 stores. At the beginning of 1990, only five Bud's stores remained to be sold. The result was a concentration on Peoples strongest markets, primarily, the District of Columbia, Maryland, Virginia, West Virginia, and Pennsylvania. The highlights of Peoples operations are shown in Table 21.6.

The UCS Group

In 1989, The UCS Group operated 531 stores in Canada from leased premises. The stores carried a wide variety of everyday convenience items, including newspapers and magazines, cigarettes and smokers' accessories, confectionery, snack foods, gifts, and souvenir selections. The retail outlets were all company-operated, and included UCS newsstands in shopping centers, commercial office towers, airports, hotels, and other high consumer traffic locations.

Table 21.6 Peoples Drug Stores Operation Summary

	($ million unless otherwise noted)				
	1989	1988	1987	1986	1985
Revenues	1207.2	1841.6	1850.2	1922.5	1737.3
Operating earnings	8.0	(8.3)	(22.5)	0.1	52.5
Operating margins (%)	0.7	(0.5)	(1.2)	–	3.0
Average sales per store (U.S. $)	2.1	1.8	1.7	1.7	1.5
Number of stores	490	829	819	830	824
Capital expenditures	12.4	41.9	29.1	32.7	58.5
Capital employed*	369.4	523.5	703.6	819.5†	653.5†

*Capital employed of each consolidated segment consists of directly identifiable assets at net book value, less current liabilities, excluding income taxes payable and bank and other debt. Corporate assets and corporate current liabilities are also excluded.
†Reflects fiscal year ending March 31.

The UCS group operated 531 stores in five divisions: Woolco/Woolworth, Specialty Stores, Hotel/Airport, Den for Men/AuMasculin, and Tax and Duty Free. Highlights of The UCS Group operations are shown in Table 21.7.

Hardee's Food Systems

Imasco's move to make a major investment in a U.S.-based company arose in part from the greater opportunity offered by the U.S. economy for potential acquisitions of an interesting nature and scale, and in part from the constraints on Canadian acquisitions posed by the Foreign Investment Review Act (FIRA). The purpose of FIRA was to review certain forms of foreign investment in Canada, particularly controlling acquisitions of Canadian business enterprises, and diversifications of existing foreign controlled firms into unrelated businesses. For several years, Imasco came under the control of FIRA due to B.A.T's 40 percent ownership of Imasco. In later years, however, Imasco was re-classified as a Canadian owned enterprise.

Imasco's involvement with Hardee's and the U.S. restaurant business developed slowly. Imasco first became acquainted with Hardee's in 1969 when its pension fund manager was on holiday in South Carolina. The manager and his family were so fond of the Hardee's hamburgers that upon returning to Montreal, he investigated Hardee's as a possible pension fund investment. The following year, Imasco made a relatively small investment in Hardee's.

Later, when Hardee's was looking for expansion capital, it approached Imasco. In March 1977, Imasco invested $18.2 million in convertible preferred shares which, if converted, would give Imasco a 25 percent position in Hardee's. Between March 1980 and January 1981, Imasco converted their preferred shares and purchased the outstanding common shares at a cost of $114.1 million. At this time, Hardee's was the seventh largest hamburger restaurant chain in the U.S. Later, Imasco made additional investments in Hardee's to facilitate growth and acquisition.

By 1989, Hardee's Food Systems, Inc. (Hardee's) was the third largest hamburger restaurant chain in the U.S., as measured by system-wide sales and average unit sales volume. In number of outlets, it ranked fourth. With its head office in Rocky Mount, North Carolina, Hardee's restaurant operations consisted of 3,298 restaurants, of which 1,086 were

Table 21.7   The UCS Group Operating Summary

($ million unless otherwise noted)					
	1989	1988	1987	1986	1985
Revenues	286.1	256.6	235.3	206.0	187.8
Operating earnings	8.3	7.5	6.7	6.6	5.5
Operating margins (%)	2.9	2.9	2.9	3.2	2.9
Average sales per store ($000)	543	489	461	432	410
Average sales per sq.ft. ($)	790	718	675	651	629
Number of stores	531	525	524	494	460
Capital employed (Est.)*	41.4	45.6	40.7	37.6†	57.2†

*Capital employed of each consolidated segment consists of directly identifiable assets at net book value, less current liabilities, excluding income taxes payable and bank and other debt. Corporate assets and corporate current liabilities are also excluded.
†Reflects fiscal year ending March 31.

company-operated and 2,212 were licensed. Of these restaurants, 3,257 were located in thirty-nine states and the District of Columbia in the U.S., and forty-one were located in nine other countries in the Middle East, Central America, and Southeast Asia. Average annual unit sales for 1989 were $1,060,300, compared with $1,058,000 in 1988. Highlights of Hardee's operations are shown in Table 21.8.

Hardee's had encouraged multi-unit development by licensees. In some cases, Hardee's granted exclusive territorial development rights to licensees on the condition that minimum numbers of new licensed restaurants in the area be opened within specific periods of time. As of December 31, 1989, Hardee's had license agreements with 234 licensee groups operating 2,205 restaurants. The ten largest of these licensees operated 1,213 restaurants, representing 55 percent of the licensed restaurants in the chain, and the two largest operated 738 licensed restaurants, or approximately 33 percent of the licensed restaurants.

Hardee's restaurants were limited-menu, quick-service family restaurants, and featured moderately priced items for all meals. These products were principally hamburgers, roast beef, chicken, turkey club, ham and cheese and fish sandwiches, breakfast biscuits, frankfurters, french fries, salads, turnovers, cookies, ice cream, and assorted beverages for both take-out and on-premise consumption. Recent additions to the Hardee's menu included a grilled chicken sandwich, Crispy Curl fries, and pancakes. These new products followed a series of initiatives taken in 1988, which included being the first hamburger chain to switch to all vegetable cooking oil in order to lower fat and cholesterol levels in fried products. Hardee's also introduced more salads and more desserts to the menu.

Fast Food Merchandisers, Inc. (FFM) was an operating division of Hardee's that furnished restaurants with food and paper products through its food processing and distribution operations. All company-operated Hardee's restaurants purchased their food and paper products from FFM. Although licensees were not obligated to purchase from FFM, approximately 75 percent of Hardee's licensees purchased some or all of their requirements from

Table 21.8 Hardee's Operating Summary

($ million unless otherwise noted)					
	1989	1988	1987	1986	1985
System-wide sales	4146.7	4058.9*	4059.1	3721.6	3248.4
Revenues	1786.5	1756.9	1801.7	1642.0	1457.0
Operating earnings	118.6	130.3	137.3	129.0	117.1
Operating margins (%)	6.6	7.4	7.6	7.9	8.0
Average sales per restaurant (U.S. $)	922	920	877	837	801
Capital expenditures	155.3	209.9	217.0	135.6	99.9
Depreciation	78.9	78.0	75.5	63.0	53.4
Restaurants company-owned	1086	1070	995	893	876
Restaurants franchised	2212	2081	1962	1818	1662
Total restaurants	3298	3151	2957	2711	2538
Capital employed**	618.3	587.7*	777.5	668.1†	555.4†

*Includes sale and leaseback of properties.
**Capital employed of each consolidated segment consists of directly identifiable assets at net book value, less current liabilities, excluding income taxes payable and bank and other debt. Corporate assets and corporate current liabilities are also excluded.
†Reflects fiscal year ending March 31.

FFM. FFM operated three food processing plants and eleven distribution centers. FFM also sold products to other food service and supermarket accounts.

THE PROPOSED ROY ROGERS ACQUISITION

The U.S. Food Service Industry[1]

Over the past twenty years, Americans spent a rising portion of their food dollars at restaurants. More two-income families, fewer women as full-time homemakers, and a decline in the number of children to feed made dining out increasingly popular. In 1989, U.S. consumers spent $167 billion at 400,000 restaurants. This excluded an estimated $61 billion spent at other food and beverage outlets, such as employee cafeterias, hospitals, ice-cream stands, and taverns. Although sales growth for the restaurant industry outpaced the economy in recent years, industry analysts noted indications of outlet saturation. In 1989, franchise restaurant chains expected to have U.S. sales of $70.4 billion, up 7.4 percent from the year before. However, on a per unit basis, 1989 sales for franchise chain units averaged $737,000, up only 4.3 percent from the previous year. Analysts pointed out that this rise corresponded to increases in menu prices.

Quick service or "fast food" restaurants had led industry growth for several decades, and were expected to do so over the near term. However, industry analysts cautioned that, as the average age of the American consumer increased, a shift away from fast food restaurants toward mid-scale restaurants might occur. Increased emphasis on take-out service and home delivery would help to maintain momentum, but analysts expected that fast food sales and new unit growth would not be up to the 6.6 percent compound annual rate from 1985 to 1989. McDonald's 8,000 U.S. outlets had sales of $12 billion, or about 7 percent of total U.S. restaurant spending. Chains that emphasized hamburgers, hot dogs, or roast beef were the largest part of the U.S. franchise restaurant industry, with 1989 sales of $33.8 billion from 36,206 outlets. McDonald's U.S. market share in the segment was about 36.1 percent, followed by Burger King (19.2 percent), Hardee's (9.9 percent), and Wendy's (8.5 percent).

Nature of Operations

The large hamburger chains generated revenues from three sources: (1) the operation of company-owned restaurants; (2) franchising, which encompassed royalties and initial fees from licensees operating under the trade name; and (3) commissary, consisting of food processing and the distribution of food, restaurant supplies, and equipment essential to the operation of the company and franchised outlets. Profitable operation of company-owned restaurant operations called for high unit sales volume and tight control of operating margins.

Franchising had been the major chains' initial growth strategy. This enabled them to increase revenues, establish a competitive position, and achieve the scale necessary for efficient commissary and marketing operations. In 1989, there were 90,000 franchise operations accounting for 40 percent of U.S. restaurant operations. In 1989, McDonald's operating profit from franchising ($1.2 billion) substantially exceeded its profit from company operated restaurants ($822 million).

It was often the case that in a franchising relationship, the cost of the land, building, and equipment were the responsibility of the franchisee. The franchisee also paid a royalty, typically 3 to 6 percent of sales, and were charged 1 to 5 percent of sales for common advertising expenses. In return, the franchisee got brand name recognition, training, and marketing support. However, some of the larger chains had taken an alternate approach by owning the land and the building. Not only did such an approach provide lease revenue but it also allowed the company to maintain some control over the franchisee's facilities.

Competition

Fast food restaurants competed with at-home eating, other restaurant types, and each other. To build and maintain unit volumes, top chains developed strategies to differentiate themselves by target market, style of operation, menu, and promotional approach, among other methods.

McDonald's

McDonald's was the leader of the fast food restaurant business. The chain began in the early 1950s in California. The McDonald brothers discovered that a combination of assembly line procedures, product standardization, and high volume made it possible to offer exceptional value, providing consistent quality food at a reasonable price. The potential of their concept was recognized by Ray Kroc, a paper cup and milkshake mixer salesman. He acquired the operations, and provided the leadership for the formation and subsequent growth of the McDonald's corporation.

McDonald's had traditionally targeted children, teens, and young families, and focused its menu of products around hamburgers and french fries. Scale, experience, and simplified operating procedures permitted McDonald's to operate at significantly lower costs than its competitors. In the late 1970s, the company broadened its target market to follow demographic shifts and increase unit volumes. The menu was expanded to include breakfast line and chicken items, and the hours of operation were increased. The emphasis on simplicity and efficiency was maintained, and the company continued its rigorous dedication to quality, service, and cleanliness. This strategy was supported by the largest promotional budget in the industry. McDonald's typical arrangement with franchisees was that it owned the property, which the franchisee then leased. Highlights of McDonald's operations are shown in Table 21.9.

Burger King

Burger King had been a subsidiary of Pillsbury until December 1988, when Grand Metropolitan PLC acquired Pillsbury and its holdings, which included Burger King. Burger King's traditional target market had been the twenty-five to thirty-nine age group, but it was trying to improve its appeal to the family trade. The key element of Burger King's competitive strategy had been to offer more product choice than McDonald's. Burger King's food preparation system was centered around a hamburger that could be dressed to customer specifications, with onions, lettuce, tomato, etc. Burger King had been the first hamburger chain to diversify significantly into additional hot sandwich items, but this had resulted in somewhat longer service times and higher food preparation costs.

In 1989, Burger King's profits were $48.2 million, down 49 percent from the previous two years. Its market share was 19.2 percent, down from 19.9 percent in 1987. Average unit sales in 1989 were $1.05 million. Burger King had four different CEOs during the past

Table 21.9   McDonald's Operating Summary

(US $ million unless otherwise noted)	1989	1988	1987
Revenues	6142.0	5566.3	4893.5
Depreciation	364.0	324.0	278.9
Operating income	1459.0	1283.7	1161.9
Operating profit margin (%)	23.7	23.1	23.7
Interest expense	332.0	266.8	224.8
Pretax income	1157.0	1046.5	958.8
Net income	727.0	645.9	596.5
Net income margin (%)	11.8	11.6	12.2
Earnings per share	1.95	1.72	1.45
Dividend per share	.30	.27	.24
Market price year end	34.50	24.06	22.00
Price/earnings ratio	17.7	14.0	15.2
Shareholders' equity	3549.0	3412.8	2916.7
Total common shares outstanding (million)	362	375	378

Source: Worldscope 1990.

ten years, and was having problems with its marketing program, changing advertising campaigns five times in two years. Additionally, Burger King had experienced problems with their franchisees prior to the acquisition by Grand Metropolitan, but these were beginning to subside with the ownership change.

Wendy's

Wendy's also targeted the young adult market. Like Burger King, it provided food prepared to specification, and had broadened its initial emphasis on hamburgers to cover a variety of items, including chili and a self-service buffet and salad bar. In 1989, Wendy's 3,490 restaurants had average unit sales of $.79 million. This was an increase from $.76 million and $.74 million in 1988 and 1987, respectively. Highlights of Wendy's operations are shown in Table 21.10.

Hardee's

Hardee's was the third largest hamburger-based fast food chain in the U.S., in terms of total sales and unit sales volume; and fourth in outlets. Approximately 30 percent of Hardee's sales were at breakfast, and it was a leader in the breakfast trade. The other major sales category was hamburgers, with 34 percent of sales.

The demographic profile of Hardee's customers was skewed slightly to males. Children and twenty-five- to thirty-four-year-olds were two groups that had been targeted for higher penetration. The introduction of ice cream in 1987 had spurred a 98 percent increase in visits by children under thirteen. Packaged salads and the broadening of menu selections were expected to help attract twenty-five- to thirty-four-year-olds.

Hardee's management was highly regarded in the food service industry for taking a very shaky firm in 1972–73 and turning it into a good performer. In 1979, Hardee's was cited by Restaurant Business magazine as a prime example of a corporate turnaround. In 1981,

Table 21.10 Wendy's Operating Summary

($ US million unless otherwise noted)	1989	1988	1987
Revenues	1069.7	1045.9	1051.1
Depreciation	56.4	57.3	55.4
Operating income	51.3	44.0	0.1
Operating profit margin (%)	4.8	4.2	NIL
Interest expense	22.3	16.9	24.2
Pretax income	36.9	43.8	(12.8)
Net income	30.4	28.5	4.5
Net income margin %	2.8	2.7	0.4
Earnings per share ($)	.25	.30	.04
Dividend per share ($)	.24	.24	.24
Market price year end ($)	4.63	5.75	5.63
Price/earnings ratio	18.5	19.2	140.6
Shareholder's equity	428.9	419.6	412.2
Total common shares outstanding (million)	96	96	96

Source: Worldscope 1990.

Jack Laughery, Hardee's CEO through the turnaround period, was awarded the Food Manufacturer's Association gold plate award for exemplary involvement in the food service industry. In 1990, Laughery was Hardee's Chairman, and Bill Prather was the President and CEO.

HARDEE'S ACQUISITION OF BURGER CHEF

In 1981, Hardee's was relatively small in the industry, and decided it had to expand quickly just to keep pace with its larger competitors. Competition had intensified, and the ability to support heavy fixed promotional costs became increasingly critical. Hardee's viewed an acquisition as a way to build a stronger market share base to support an increased television campaign.

Burger Chef, acquired by General Foods in 1968, had 1981 sales of $391 million. General Foods had nurtured it into a profitable regional chain. However, due to management changes at General Foods and the acquisition of the Oscar Meyer company, Burger Chef was no longer important to General Foods' future plans.

Imasco and Hardee's saw this as an opportunity. The Burger Chef chain was made up of about 250 company units and 450 franchised units, located primarily in the states of Michigan, Ohio, Indiana, Iowa, and Kentucky. Most of the locations complemented Hardee's markets. Imasco purchased Burger Chef in 1981 for $51.8 million. During the next three years, they converted the sites to Hardee's at a cost of about $80,000 per unit. The acquisition of Burger Chef created two more market areas for Hardee's overnight. By 1986, the stores in these areas were, and still are, the most profitable in the entire Hardee's system. Similarly, in 1972, Hardee's had expanded their market base by acquiring Sandy's Systems, a fast food chain of about 200 restaurants for $5.7 million.

THE ROY ROGERS OPPORTUNITY

The Roy Rogers restaurant chain was owned by the Marriott Corporation (Marriott), and was located in the northeastern U.S. In Baltimore, Washington, D.C., Philadelphia, and New York, it was second only to McDonald's in number of locations. Roy Rogers restaurants were well-known for fresh fried chicken and roast beef sandwiches. In 1989, Roy Rogers system-wide sales[2] were $713 million, up from the previous year's $661 million. In 1988, revenues were $431 million, up from $399 million in 1987. Operating earnings in 1988 were $43.7 million, up from $38 million the year before. The chain had 660 units, up from 610 the previous year, with average annual unit sales of $1,081,000.

Marriott was a leader in the hotel lodging industry and had extensive restaurant holdings. In 1988, Marriott began to refocus on lodging. As a result, it had reevaluated its other holdings, among these the Roy Rogers chain. In 1988, Marriott had talked to Hardee's about the possible sale of Roy Rogers. However, Marriott was not yet committed to selling the chain and the two companies were unable to agree on a sale price. In late 1989, Marriott announced it was again interested in selling Roy Rogers.

Prather contacted Marriott about the details. Marriott was offering to sell 648 of its Roy Rogers units, of which 363 were company owned and 285 were franchised. These units were in attractive market locations that would not otherwise be available. However, Marriott wanted to retain several sites located on various turnpikes and interstate highways. Additionally, Marriott had a fourteen-point contract to which any purchaser had to agree. The contract addressed such things as Marriott's concern for Roy Rogers franchisees and indemnification against future litigation.

Prather saw this as the opportunity he had been waiting for and began putting together an acquisition proposal. Before he could make a serious offer to Marriott, he had to first get the approval of Crawford and the Imasco board. While preparing the proposal, Prather had reflected on what it was like to work in the Imasco organization. He had built his career in the food service industry, coming up through the ranks, starting as an assistant store manager. Until 1986, he had been the Number Three man at Burger King, Vice President in charge of World Operations. Prather had spent fourteen years with the company when it was owned by Pillsbury. Pillsbury, a highly-centralized company, had required that any expenditures over $1 million had to be authorized by the head office. He thought how much this contrasted with Imasco. For him, Imasco was "like a breath of fresh air," a decentralized organization in the best sense. He had a great working relationship with Crawford and the others at the Center, in contact by phone every couple weeks or as required. There was easy and open access with no surprises.

Prather had received preliminary approval from Crawford to proceed with the negotiations. Marriott had structured the Roy Rogers sale in two rounds. In the first round, all those parties who were interested in the chain were interviewed, "much like a job interview," Prather recalled. It was during this first round that Marriott expressed their concerns for their franchisees, and assessed the capabilities and sincerity of those interested in buying the chain. To Prather, "the first round was a screening process just to get into the game."

Prather made it through the first round, but there were three or four other interested groups still in the running. During the next round, the terms of the sale would be negotiated. Although the rumored price had initially been $390 million, Prather thought that it might be more. Prather felt he could convince Marriott that Hardee's offered the best means of exit, given Marriott's concern for the franchisees, and that a solid offer of $420 million would convince them to sell Roy Rogers to Hardee's.

Prather figured conversion to Hardee's outlets would cost $80,000 to $115,000 per unit, depending on local conditions. He weighed this against the average "from scratch" start-up cost of $1.2 million per site. Additionally, Roy Rogers' menu, which included their popular fresh fried chicken, would complement Hardee's current menu. However, he was not sure it would be an "easy sell" in Montreal. Imasco's 40 percent shareholder, B.A.T, was in the midst of fighting off a takeover bid from Sir James Goldsmith (see Appendix). Prather knew that Crawford and the board would be concerned about Goldsmith's run at B.A.T, but the Roy Rogers deal was just what he needed to solidify Hardee's number three industry position.

Appendix
IMASCO Limited, 1990

In the summer of 1989, Sir James Goldsmith formed a syndicate of investors under the name of Hoylake Investments Limited to mount a takeover attempt on B.A.T, Imasco's largest shareholder. Goldsmith's argument was that B.A.T was being valued by the market at less than the sum of its parts, and that the true value would only be realized by the "unbundling" of B.A.T. The stakes in the bid were enormous – it was estimated that Hoylake and its partners would have to put up over $25 billion to carry through on the transaction. Hoylake's intentions with respect to the block of Imasco's shares that B.A.T owned were unknown. Imasco's position was that, while it was an "interested observer," it was not directly involved in the proceedings and would only monitor developments related to the offer. While the specifics of Goldsmith's case are not pertinent here, the general arguments are. These are given below as excerpts from Goldsmith's letter to B.A.T shareholders dated August 8, 1989.

The Key Questions

The case for this bid must rest on the answer to simple questions. Has the existing management placed B.A.T in a position to compete successfully? Are the subsidiaries growing healthily, or are they failing relative to their competitors? Have shareholders' funds been invested in a wise and progressive way which adds value to the shares of the company? Is the conglomerate structure able to provide strength and innovation over the longer term to its diversified subsidiaries? In short, is B.A.T in a state to compete in the modern world and to face the future with confidence? Or has it been managed in a way which could lead to progressive senescence and decay? That is the crux of the argument.

Conglomeration – B.A.T's Failure

It is our case that B.A.T's management has sought size rather than quality or value; it has used shareholders' funds to acquire totally unconnected businesses, about which it knew little, and which are being damaged by having been brought under the control of B.A.T's bureaucratic yoke.

The Cause of Failure

Before presenting the case in factual detail, I would like to explain why such a state of affairs can occur. It is not that the men in charge are malevolent. Not at all. No doubt they are serious administrators. The problem originates from their belief that tobacco was a declining business, and that the company should diversify into other industries. This logic sounded compelling. The flaw was that B.A.T's management knew something about tobacco, but little about the businesses of the companies that it was acquiring. Also there exists a very natural conflict of interest between management and shareholders. Management wishes its company to be big. The bigger it is, the greater the respect, power, and honors that flow to management. Shareholders, on the other hand, want value. They do not seek size for the sake of size. They want growth to be the result of excellence, and thereby to improve the short- and long-term value of their investment. Some conglomerates have performed well under the leadership of their founders. But that ceases when the flame of the founder is replaced by the dead hand of the corporate bureaucrat. That is why great conglomerates often have been well advised to de-conglomerate before they retire.

Purpose of the Offer

1. We intend to reverse B.A.T's strategy. Instead of accumulating miscellaneous companies within B.A.T, we intend to release them and, as described below, return the proceeds to you.
2. We would concentrate B.A.T's attention on running its core business, tobacco. That is the process which we have described as "unbundling."

Consequences

Of course, you will be concerned to know the consequences for the companies being released, and for those who work within them. Will those companies suffer? Will jobs be sacrificed? Would their future be jeopardized, for example, by a reduction in the level of investment in research, development, and capital equipment? That is what you may have been led to believe. The reality is the opposite. Instead of vegetating within B.A.T, those companies would either return to independence, or they would join more homogeneous companies. Such companies have the skills which would contribute to future development, and a true mutuality of interest would result. This would lead to increased opportunity for employees, greater long-term investment, productivity, and growth. The real danger to employees is that they should remain trapped within B.A.T, and condemned to slow but progressive relative decline. Ultimately that would lead to employee hardship, despite the benevolent intentions of existing management.

Conclusion

To summarize, the flawed architecture of the tobacco-based conglomerates was exposed, first with the acquisition of Imperial Group by Hanson in 1986, and late last year when the management and directors of RJR/Nabisco recognized that shareholder values could only be properly realized by a sale of the company.

Size is often a protection against change, but these same basic structural defects have now been revealed, and the logic of unbundling B.A.T has become inescapable.

NOTES

1. Industry figures in U.S. dollars.
2. System-wide sales reflect retail sales figures of both company-owned and franchisee stores. Revenues reflect retail sales of only company-owned stores, in addition to royalties received from franchisees.

22

Grupo Industrial Saltillo, S.A.

This case was prepared by Ronald J. Salazar of Idaho State University and Kenneth J. Rediker of the University of Houston.

INTRODUCTION

Grupo Industrial Saltillo, S.A. de C.V. (GISSA), is a Mexican conglomerate which was started and remains a family-owned company. It is now managed by a second generation of the del Bosque family that owns a majority of the stock of the various companies forming GISSA. Almost all voting shares of GISSA are held by the Lopez del Bosque family with a few shares traded on the Mexican stock exchange. Because of its family-owned status, access to some details of GISSA's operations remains closely guarded.

This case describes the challenging domestic and macro-economic environment confronting GISSA, a major family-controlled, diversified, Mexican firm through the end of 1991. The next section of the case provides a brief history of GISSA. Following this are descriptions of GISSA's major businesses: CIFUNSA, VITROMEX, and CINSA. Then, GISSA's financial history and current performance are reviewed along with comparisons of other relevant Mexican conglomerates and American firms. The case concludes with an overview of the Mexican economic and political situation including information on capital markets, the automotive market, and the U.S.-Mexico-Canada Free Trade Agreement (NAFTA).

OVERVIEW AND HISTORY OF GISSA

GISSA was established by the del Bosques in 1928 as a manufacturer (called El Alumina S.A.) of small household items. In 1932, the company set up CINSA and its smelting department. Since 1932, CINSA has produced kitchenware, Melamine (heavy plastic) dishes, and porcelain sinks. Table 22.1 outlines the two primary producing divisions of GISSA

Table 22.1 GISSA's Current Corporate Structure

Division	Affiliate Name (Year of Creation)	Products
Metal-Mecanica	CIFUNSA (1967)	engine blocks, auto parts, pipe fittings
	DITEMSA (1980)	pattern molds
Construccion y Hogar	CINSA (1932)	kitchenware, stainless steel sinks
	EXITO (1942)	paint brushes, paint rollers
	ESVIMEX (1942)	enamel
	VITROMEX (1967)	bathroom fixtures, ceramic tiles, water heaters
	CERAMICA (1990)	ceramic dishes

along with the respective manufacturing subsidiaries, the dates of their formation, and primary products produced by each.

EXITO was formed in 1942, and produces paint brushes and rollers for the construction market. Also founded in 1942 was ESVIMEX; this subdivision manufactures alloys for sheet metal and ceramics used as materials for enamel paints. Another foundry established in 1967, CIFUNSA, produces blocks and heads for motors and connections of malleable iron for the construction market. Another major subdivision, VITROMEX, was established in 1967 and produces ceramics, tiles, and accessories. GISSA formed DITEMSA in 1980 to produce pattern molds and automotive tools used by its sister company CIFUNSA. At the end of May 1990, GISSA created yet another subsidiary, CERAMICA, for the production of ceramic dishes for the home.

The del Bosque family has always been the major shareholder of GISSA. No foreign investors own shares in the company. Isidro Lopez del Bosque, the eldest of eight children, is Chairman of the Board and conducts administrative roles. Javier Lopez del Bosque, the second oldest son, is Vice President, with responsibility for day-to-day operations. The board of directors of GISSA consists of members of the del Bosque family and other Mexican businessmen, some of whom also serve on the boards of other publicly-held Mexican industrial conglomerates. GISSA's top management faces a problem in dealing with the different viewpoints expressed by members of the board as to either reinvest in the company or to "cash in." This situation is exacerbated by the upcoming retirement of the second generation of del Bosques, as there is no determined line of succession within the company.

The company concentrates its efforts primarily on the manufacture of auto parts, home products, and construction materials. During 1989, GISSA restructured its organization to better address the needs of its markets. This reorganization produced the current three main divisions: Metal-Mecanica (Metals and Metal Fabrication); Construccion y Hogar (Construction and Housewares); and Division Corporativa (Corporate Division). GISSA is the seventh largest industrial conglomerate in Mexico. To place GISSA within the context of the Mexican economy, Exhibit 22.1 compares the net sales volume and net worth of GISSA to those of the ten largest Mexican conglomerates. As of 1990, GISSA employed over 10,000 people and approached $262 million in annual sales (Exhibit 22.2).

Seven operating plants are located close to the company's headquarters in Saltillo, Coahuila, about 100 miles from the U.S. border. The main manufacturing operations are:

- Empaques y Maquilas de Saltillo (Packages and Maquilas [assembly operations] of Saltillo): providing export packing and import/export brokerage services to GISSA companies and others.
- Corporation Internacional de Negocios (International Business Corporation): sales, purchasing, and marketing activities for international GISSA manufacturers.
- Compania General de Bienes Raices y Construcciones (General Real Estate and Construction Company): builds, leases, and designs the facilities and plants used by GISSA manufacturers along with the private residences and investments of board members.
- Asesoria y Servicios GISSA (GISSA Consulting and Services): provides management consultation, training, and programs.
- Servicios de Production Saltillo (Saltillo Production Services): maintains and modifies manufacturing equipment of subsidiaries.

CINSA, VITROMEX, and CIFUNSA, the three major GISSA subsidiaries, contributed 96 percent of the company's total sales in 1990. The contribution of these operations as a percentage of total sales is shown in Figure 22.1.

The stated Corporate Mission of GISSA is:

GISSA is a group of companies dedicated to the manufacturing and commercialization of a variety of products for the automobile parts market, for construction, and for the home.

GISSA strives for leadership in industries where it can offer world class quality and service to its clients.

The company strives for permanent growth of its business while achieving attractive returns for the shareholders.

GISSA is dedicated to the growth of Mexico, the development of free enterprise, the creation of opportunities for employment, and to investment in the community.

GISSA'S MAIN DIVISIONS

CIFUNSA – Operations

The largest of GISSA's operating divisions, CIFUNSA, employed 3,491 union employees in 1990, 46 percent of GISSA's union workers. Operating revenues at the time were $102 million, 39 percent of total GISSA revenues (Figure 22.2). Its primary business is the production of automotive parts, engine blocks, heads, and camshafts.

CIFUNSA's products have won several quality awards from Ford, Chrysler, and GM. CIFUNSA's plants are currently operating at 72 percent of installed capacity. Investments of almost $8 million have been made to expand capacity and implement technological improvements.

Other related activities which GISSA subsidiaries provide for CIFUNSA are:

- HIERRO MALEABLE DE MEXICO is a wholly owned subsidiary which supplies and transports iron ore to CIFUNSA along with foundry sands and the trace elements required in casting processes. HIERRO could easily be expanded to include other foundries due to its low consolidated delivery costs and excessive capacity.

Figure 22.1 Grupo Industrial Saltillo: Sales by Market Segment

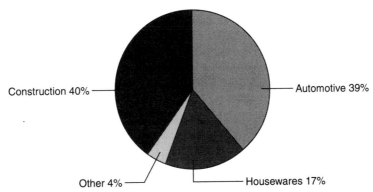

Construction 40% — Automotive 39% — Other 4% — Housewares 17%

Source: GISSA

Figure 22.2   CIFUNSA, S.A. de C.V.: Product/Market Analysis

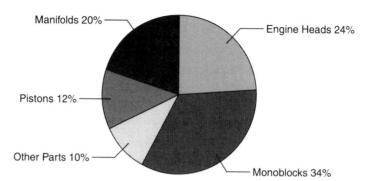

Source: GISSA

- DITEMSA produces industrial molds, tools, and patterns for manufacturing industries. Primary customers are other GISSA companies: patterns for CIFUNSA; molds for VITROMEX; and set-up forms for all GISSA companies. DITEMSA's plant (capacity of 238,900 tons) operates at 90 percent capacity. Current forecasts are for a modest growth rate of 1–2 percent.
- COMPANIA IMPULSORA MECANICA with sales approximating $3.3 million, employs 400 workers as of 1990. The company is an Original Equipment Manufacturer (OEM), supplying various automotive parts such as brand-label hydraulic jacks, filters, and brake pads for companies including Fram, Bendix, GM, and Ford.
- PISTONES INDUSTRIALES (one of the original GISSA companies) manufactures aluminum pistons for compressors, motorcycles, and other light products. The company supplies OEM components for motorcycles and small components to COMPANIA IMPULSORA MECANICA.

CIFUNSA – Markets

In general, CIFUNSA's markets are characterized by the slowing growth and demand typical of markets in maturity. The company is currently experiencing consolidation demand from its U.S. clients (its largest indirect market) and markets in America. Its major customers are GM, Chrysler, Renault, Ford, and Volkswagen. Each client has configured its Mexican operations to comply with a Mexican law dictating that 60 percent of the content of cars be sourced from within the country; the primary function of their plants is to assemble vehicles made from largely local parts for sale in Mexico.

In 1990, 90 percent of CIFUNSA's products were eventually exported. Almost all of the company's products are sold in Mexico and later exported as part of a finished motor or vehicle by such buyers as General Motors, Chrysler, etc. The typical GISSA-produced component represents a large-value-added item or assembly that eventually finds its way into the U.S. market under the brand name of a well-known American firm.

CIFUNSA's domestic market share is about 33 percent. The market share of exported automobiles using CIFUNSA's parts is similar (the sum of GM's, VW's, and Chrysler's market share, using CIFUNSA's parts, is about 50 percent). The domestic car market is highly dependent on real GDP growth. Since the early 1980s, the demand for cars in Mexico has been stagnant, experiencing only a slight increase. Unlike the domestic market, Mexico's automobile export sales have grown explosively since 1980 from $340 million to $3,297 million in 1989.

CIFUNSA – Competition

Domestic rivalry for CIFUNSA is not intense because of government sanctioned market segmentation. Major Mexican competitors for automobile parts production have specialized in slightly different products. Because of the historically protected economy Mexican businesses have enjoyed, competitors have experienced the luxury of high returns within market segments with little or no direct competition. Through a system analogous to "a gentlemen's agreement," the economic sectors of the Mexican economy have been divided by preexisting tacit understandings. Specifically, the following list of competitors illustrates how slightly different marketing mixes currently exist.

- VITRO produces mainly laminated glass.
- MORESA specializes in pistons, pins, valves, and tappets.
- SPICER produces spark plugs, castings, piston rings, axles, transmission gearing, wheel rims, etc.
- TREMAC manufactures transmission gearing, spare parts, castings, hoists, and winches.

Ford Mexico may also be considered a domestic competitor because of its capability to produce its own components. Unlike domestic producers, U.S. suppliers to automakers are more competitive. About sixty companies in the U.S., ranging in size from small firms to large diversified firms, produce engine castings. These companies include Textron, Dana Corporation, Brillion Iron Works, and Emerson Electric. It would be difficult for CIFUNSA to compete with the American firms in the U.S. because of the high costs of shipping heavy items such as engine blocks from Mexico.

CIFUNSA – Outlook

The growth of CIFUNSA depends on increased car sales, especially exports. In general, U.S. car markets have experienced slow growth in the last decade. Growth forecasts predict a further slowdown. Because of the possible free trade agreement with the United States and Canada, American competitors could become an increasing threat as sales growth slows and the Mexican market becomes more accessible to them.

VITROMEX – Operations

With 1,629 employees and sales of $105 million, VITROMEX was the largest contributor of GISSA's total revenues (40 percent) in 1989 [Figure 22.1]. VITROMEX manufactures a range of construction products including bathroom and kitchen fixtures, floor coverings, water heaters, and ceramic tiles. Like CIFUNSA, VITROMEX has expanded its production capacity and has constructed facilities for production of a new type of wall tile. Both plants of VITROMEX operate at almost 100 percent of capacity.

Subdivisions related to VITROMEX are:

- ISLO, a subdivision of VITROMEX, builds gas water heaters for the residential and light commercial marketplace.

- ESVIMEX is a producer of high quality enamels for ceramics and metals. The company has a virtual monopoly over the Mexican market with no domestic competition. ESVIMEX supplies products to VITROMEX and CINSA for the colorization of household appliances and cookware (it also supplies the paint used by Compania Impulsora Mecanica and other Maquila plants for the automotive industry). Furthermore, it distributes the EXITO line of paint brushes.
- EXITO is a manufacturer of brooms, brushes, and wire wheels used in the construction industry for buffing. EXITO's products are used in the construction industry and will grow in step with the increase in housing construction in Mexico. Brushes are distributed through VITROMEX and ESVIMEX as additions to their product lines.
- CERAMICA SANTA ANITA (CERAMICA) is a new venture for GISSA representing an investment of 130 billion pesos (current approximate exchange rate is 3,120 pesos = $1.00) and further diversification. Currently, CERAMICA is starting to manufacture tiles and high quality ceramic pottery type stoneware using Japanese technology The product line will use enamels from ESVIMEX and will be distributed by VITROMEX vendors. The quality of the products is expected to allow exportation to the North American market.

VITROMEX – Competition

Competition within this segment of the Mexican market is fierce, the closest competitors being: Ceramic, Lamosa, Porcela, and American Standard. Among these competitors, Ceramic appears to be the most aggressive. Although smaller than VITROMEX, Ceramic expanded its production capacity at a 100 percent rate in 1989 and intends to expand at the same rate again by 1992. In particular, the alliance between Ceramic and Armstrong, a large U.S. construction materials company, seems to be a substantial threat for GISSA's future domestic market share. Lamosa and Porcela are smaller than VITROMEX in terms of total sales. Both companies compete mainly in the domestic market. American Standard, which produces sinks, bathtubs, and toilets in its Mexican manufacturing facility, is an active competitor for VITROMEX for the top of the product line.

VITROMEX – Markets and Outlook

The current markets of VITROMEX are 80 percent domestic and 20 percent exports equally distributed between Canada and the U.S. [Figure 22.3]. The demand for construction products is closely linked to growth in population and real GDP as are CIFUNSA's car parts markets. The growth rate of VITROMEX is expected to approximate the growth rate of the Mexican economy of around 3 percent. Because of the limited growth rate in the Mexican market and the cost advantage of VITROMEX (labor) compared to competitors in the U.S. and Canada, the export opportunities to North American markets seem important for VITROMEX if substantial growth is to be realized over the next several years.

CINSA – Operations

Employing almost 2,000 union workers CINSA yielded $45 million in sales in 1990 (17 percent of GISSA's total revenues) [Figure 22.1]. CINSA produces pots, pans, and other utensils using baked enamel on steel. The products are of relatively low price with an average unit price of $1.70. Like VITROMEX, CINSA's sales are primarily domestic with 80 percent of production sold in Mexico and 20 percent exported to Central America, the U.S.A., and Canada [Figure 22.4].

Figure 22.3VITROMEX, S.A. de C.V.: Product/Market Analysis

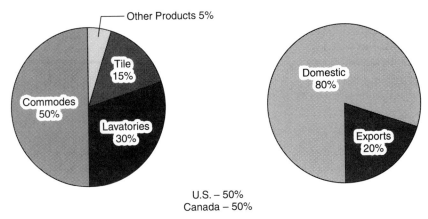

U.S. – 50%
Canada – 50%

Source: GISSA

Figure 22.4CINSA, S.A. de C.V.: Product/Market Analysis

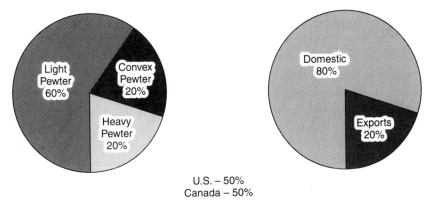

U.S. – 50%
Canada – 50%

Source: GISSA

CINSA – Markets and Outlook

CINSA controls 55 percent of the Mexican market for kitchen products. Growth for CINSA is also closely related to the GDP in Mexico. The standard of living and population growth are the major sources of demand for kitchenware. Sales growth has been about 3 percent per annum in the last ten years. Although there exist many private and public companies producing kitchen articles, the vast array and variety of substitute products (aluminum, plastic, steel) do not allow for meaningful comparison among competitors.

Major expansion opportunities lie in the export market, but there is a problem. The U.S. consumer has shown low confidence in Mexican kitchenware because of well-publicized problems of lead leaching from ceramic products (late '70s and early '80s) and current concerns over certain other Mexican products.

GISSA CORPORATE OPERATIONS

GISSA plans to invest $150 million in the next three years. Funds for these investments are provided by joint venture partners and the GISSA corporation. The largest investments will be to CIFUNSA, with projects of $77 million approved for improvement and expansion of production facilities. One joint venture partner is Teksid S.P.A. (a Spanish producer of foundry molds, and a subsidiary of FIAT/Italy). Twenty-one million dollars will be invested in projects to upgrade and expand the production plants of VITROMEX. Another joint venture partner is the German pharmaceutical producer Bayer which will invest $52 million in CINSA's plants EXITO, ESVIMEX, and CERAMICA. Yet another joint venture partner is Yamaka, a Japanese producer of household articles and kitchenware.

Finally, general corporate investments of $1.8 million will be devoted to education, upgrading of plant facilities, and environmental controls. The purpose of these investments is to enable GISSA to double its size by the year 2000 and to develop and maintain technological leadership.

GISSA'S FINANCIAL ANALYSIS

Historical Performance and Growth

Between 1988 and 1990 GISSA's sales grew 3 percent, slightly better than the Mexican economy, which grew only 2.5 percent. During 1989–90, adjusting to economic reforms launched by the Mexican Government and better addressing the markets in which it participates, GISSA restructured its organization, creating the three aforementioned divisions.

In 1990, costs of operations were 108,216 million pesos, 13 percent less than 1989. The decrease was due to measures established by the Pact for Stability and Economic Growth (PSEC), better known in Mexico as El Pacto. The PSEC was, as its name describes it, a pact or agreement among the government, industry, retailers, and the Mexican population in general to stabilize prices, tariffs, and salaries in order to fight inflation. Net consolidated profits for 1990 were 90,776 million pesos, 19 percent less than 1989, as a result of operations, payment of interest on capital, and prepayments of foreign debt obligations. The company maintained excellent liquidity ending 1989–90 with a very solid financial reserve of 293,862 million pesos. During 1989–90, total assets for GISSA declined about 6 percent in real terms. This decrease was due to the sale of one of GISSA's companies, Enseres Electroindustriales, S.A. de C.V.

In October 1989 with the authorization of the National Commission of Shares, a Fideicomiso (trust) was established to make the GISSA stock more attractive. This trust was made up of 2,708,571 stock shares, representing 9.4 percent of the total existing shares. The objective of the trust was to strengthen GISSA stock. A 67 percent increase in the price of the stock (from January to June of 1990) signaled the accomplishment of this objective.

GISSA's demand for capital over the next one to two years is expected to be $105 million. GISSA has a large proportion of its funds in cash and marketable securities. GISSA self-finances most of its operations. This strategy is encouraged by the Mexican tax structure, which penalizes excessive borrowing. Most anticipated projects are to be internally funded. The company may choose to source new debt over the period, but the amount of new borrowing is likely to be small. If GISSA continues to grow and expand, capital sourcing will become increasingly important.

Financial Ratios

GISSA's financial ratios presented in Table 22.2 show GISSA with an excellent cash reserve. The collection period improvement and the strong showing with the turnover ratios are indicative of the company's concentration on its core businesses and conservative fiscal policy. The improvement in leverage ratios was due primarily to the repayment of debt and GISSA's commitment to maintain a low debt burden. In spite of a declining trend in profitability ratios, GISSA still reflects positive and strong profitability.

Comparison with Other Mexican Conglomerates

Because of the diversified nature of GISSA, no other corporation in Mexico can be considered a direct competitor. The following profiles of three Mexican conglomerates, however, provide some basis for comparison in terms of asset and debt utilization and financial performance. Each of the three conglomerates for which financial ratios are shown in Table 22.3 is, to some degree, involved in automobile manufacturing. San Luis and Sidek are comparable in size to GISSA while Vitro, with annual revenues of nearly $2 billion, is considerably larger than the other three.

Table 22.2 Grupo Industrial Saltillo Financial Analysis

Leverage Ratios	F.Y. 1990	F.Y. 1989	F.Y. 1988	F.Y. 1987	F.Y. 1986	F.Y. 1985	Avg. 1989	Avg. 1986
Debt ratio	0.1245	0.1520	0.2065	0.4321	0.4880	0.5292	0.22	0.41
Debt to equity	0.1422	0.1793	0.2602	0.7609	0.9530	1.1242	0.29	0.69
Times interest earned	12.6200	12.1306	3.2014	2.4536	1.9589	1.7947	6.45	2.95
Liquidity ratios								
Net working capital to total assets	0.3417	0.3998	0.2432	0.3241	0.2083	0.1421	0.38	0.15
Current ratio	3.0724	3.8851	1.7472	3.4888	2.4941	1.7434	2.3	1.75
Cash ratio	1.8342	1.7211	0.6096	0.2246	0.2139	0.1920	0.3	0.18
Interval measure	216.0284	172.1566	306.8158	208.4694	301.4556	302.5647	245	268
Profitability ratios								
Sales to total assets	0.8688	0.7059	0.9786	0.8788	0.8396	0.6454	1.81	0.89
Sales to net working capital	2.3618	2.2424	3.6560	3.0569	4.5535	4.5410	3.9	4.33
Net profit margin	0.0731	0.1283	0.1766	0.0853	0.0639	0.0418	0.035	0.05
Inventory turnover	6.8269	6.2659	5.7073	5.9865	5.8576	7.9489	7.25	8.1
Average collection period	47.7033	101.8819	149.1823	160.8674	148.9684	58.0000	96	90
Return on total assets	0.0804	0.1292	0.1729	0.0750	0.0537	0.0270	0.06	0.05
Payout ratio	1.1200							
Year to Year Comparisons (% change)								
Net sales	25.0%	−7.3%	151.9%	111.5%	80.0%	20.0%		
Net income	−19.2%	−3.9%	421.4%	182.2%	175.2%	30.0%		
Total assets	22.1%	−15.7%	130.7%	116.4%	76.8%	60.0%		
Stockholders' equity	22.2%	15.0%	150.0%	142.5%	104.6%	70.0%		
Labor cost	37.9%	49.8%	93.6%	89.6%	102.8%	18.0%		
Cost of goods sold	34.5%	51.2%	140.3%	102.4%	69.5%	29.0%		

Source: GISSA Annual Report 1989–1990

Table 22.3   GISSA vs. Mexican Firms

	EPS	ROA%	ROE%
SAN LUIS	0.28	7.58	15.58
SIDEK	0.14	5.24	11.72
VITRO	2.19	8.02	12.58
GISSA	1.56	14.10	19.50

Source: Global Consultants, "Grupo Industrial Saltillo Strategic Analysis," December 1990.

Corporacion Industrial San Luis S.A. De C.V was established in Mexico in 1890. In 1960 Mexican Candelarin Co. and San Luis Mining Co. were consolidated into Minas San Luis S.A. In 1984 the company was organized as the holding company for Grupo San Luis. San Luis is engaged in a diversified range of activities such as mining, retailing, tourism, manufacturing and exports. In 1990 the company's net sales were $S65 million.

Vitro Corporation was established in Mexico in 1936 as Fomento de Industria y Comercio, S.A. The present name was adopted in 1980. Vitro is a manufacturer of glass and plastic containers, thermoformed articles, luggage, flat glass for architectural and automotive use, crystal products, fiberglass, related industrial chemical products, enamelware articles, and capital goods. The company also performs research and development of technology related to the above-mentioned products. During 1990, Vitro's net sales were $1.128 billion.

GISSA compares favorably with these competitors in terms of its most important financial ratios. GISSA's historical resistance to a debt-laden balance sheet is reflected in its liquidity and leverage ratios. The current ratio for GISSA was 3.9, twice that of Vitro. GISSA has a higher ratio of cash and overall current assets to current liabilities than the other firms.

In 1989, GISSA enjoyed an operating margin of 17.7 percent, significantly higher than either San Luis or Sidek and somewhat less than Vitro. Although GISSA has compiled better return on equity averages than the other three companies, its stock trades at the lowest multiple to earnings. This disparity is indicative of a lack of liquidity in GISSA stock due to the large percentage held by the family, rather than to market discontent with the issue.

Comparison with U.S. Corporations

GISSA's performance also compares favorably with several U.S. firms in both the ceramic tile and automobile sectors. However, American competitors have substantially more capitalization and access to capital to pursue growth strategies. They also enjoy the advantage of dealing in a more stable economic environment. All of the U.S. competitors have significantly higher earnings per share than GISSA, even though the company's return on assets is much higher. Table 22.4 shows financial ratio comparisons with the following corporations: Armstrong World Industries, Inc., Dana Corporation, and Textron Inc.

Armstrong World Industries, Inc. was incorporated in Pennsylvania on January 14, 1895 as Armstrong Cork Company. The present name was adopted in April 1980. The company is a manufacturer and marketer of interior furnishings. Its products include floor coverings (resilient flooring and all ceramic tile and carpets), building products, and furniture. It also markets a variety of specialty products for the building, automotive, textile, and other industries. Armstrong is a major competitor in the ceramic tile industry. In 1989, Armstrong had $2 billion in assets and only $181 million in long-term debt. Foreign sales accounted

Table 22.4 GISSA vs. U.S Firms

	EPS	ROA%	ROE%
ARMSTRONG	3.17	7.8	17.7
DANA	3.24	2.6	13.3
TEXTRON	3.02	2.0	10.7
GISSA	1.56	14.1	19.5

Source: Global Consultants, "Grupo Industrial Saltillo Strategic Analysis," December 1990.

for 22 percent of Armstrong's total sales and 23 percent of profits in 1989. The company's activities extend worldwide. As of January 1990, the company has sixty-nine plants located throughout the United States and twenty-two plants of foreign subsidiaries and affiliates. Armstrong is likely to be one of the companies poised to take advantage of the Mexican economy in the free trade environment of the 1990s.

Dana Corporation was incorporated in Virginia, October 12, 1916 as Spicer Manufacturing Corporation, with the present name adopted on July 12,1946. Dana Corporation operates worldwide principally in three business segments: automotive, industrial, and financial services. The automotive segment consists of the manufacture and marketing of a wide variety of components, primarily for use on trucks and, to a lesser extent, other highway vehicles. Its products include drive and trailer axles, frames, transmissions, power take-offs, universal joints, clutches, filters, engine parts, and other miscellaneous products. During 1989, Dana had worldwide sales of $5.2 billion and net income of $132 million. Dana's international operations contributed 26 percent of revenues and 37 percent of operating income in 1989. Ford, one of GISSA's largest customers, is responsible for 15 percent of Dana Corporation's world-wide sales. Dana Corporation affiliates include Spicer S.A. of Mexico.

Textron Inc. was incorporated in Delaware on July 31, 1967 as American Textron Inc. The present name was adopted on January 2, 1968. Textron operates in three business sectors. The sectors are: aerospace technology, commercial products, and financial services. The business segments of the aerospace technology sector are helicopters, propulsion, and systems. The business segments of the financial services sector are finance and related insurance.

In the commercial products sector, Textron has a substantial position in selected areas of the automotive, specialty fasteners, and outdoor products markets. In each of the three markets, the company strives to be a leader in the development of new products. In 1989, Textron had revenue of $1.9 billion from its commercial products. Sales from domestic automotive products approximated $777 million in 1989.

THE MEXICAN ECONOMY

Prior to the 1970s, Mexico's economic development policies focused on maintaining stable growth and controlling its level of foreign debt. Between 1958 and 1970, Mexico's Gross Domestic Product grew at an average of 6.8 percent per year while inflation averaged 3 percent. During the 1970s, discovery of massive oil fields near the southern border caused the administrations of Presidents Luis Echevertia Alvarez and Jose Lopez Portillo to shift the focus of economic development from moderate levels to rapid growth through expansionary policies, assuming substantial amounts of foreign debt. Prosperity was short lived as the demand for and price of oil declined sharply in the 1980s.

The Mexican economy was near a state of crisis when President Miguel de la Madrid took office in 1982. Total external debt amounted to $86.7 billion or 51 percent of GDP. The annual inflation rate hovered near 100 percent. Despite measures such as debt restructuring and the promotion of access to international competition taken by the de la Madrid administration, the economy continued its decline. The situation was worsened by a disastrous earthquake in 1986. In that year inflation rose to 160 percent and GDP declined by 3.8 percent. One of the prime initiatives of de la Madrid was to devalue the Mexican peso, helping to stimulate a mild recovery in 1987. Exports increased 29 percent over the previous year.

In 1988, President Salinas took office inheriting an economy that had experienced tough times. During his first two years, President Salinas implemented economic reforms raising business confidence and making the Mexican economy more competitive. Inflation declined from 160 percent in 1987 to an estimated 25 to 27 percent in 1990. Mexico's GDP grew 3 percent in 1989, outpacing population growth for the second year in a row. Far-reaching changes have improved many areas important to business such as investment regulation, transportation, privatization of owned enterprises, and Mexico's debt position, but his goal to control it seems to be incompatible with his exchange rate goals; the peso is expected to continue depreciating against the dollar to 3600 pesos/$ by the end of 1993.

Capital Markets

Government policies closely regulate financing within Mexico. Past policies have led to the nationalization of many important sectors of industry and have restricted the entry of foreign investments in Mexico. With so many nationalized firms competing for capital from the central government, there is little additional financing available to the private sector. Foreign investors are reluctant to do business in Mexico because of doubtful repayments. The Mexican government had been reluctant to provide long-term guarantees preventing nationalization of foreign-owned operations.

During 1982, a presidential decree nationalized and consolidated all private banks in Mexico, turning them into national credit companies. The Casa de Bolsa or brokerage house is also expanding in arranging and coordinating the movement of money in parallel credit markets. The insurance industry is another important source of long-term capital and is pushing for legislation to allow greater project financing.

There are nineteen domestic commercial banks in Mexico. Most are multi-service banks, allowing deposit savings, mortgages, and investments under the same roof. Banamex is the largest domestic bank, with 60 percent of all the nation's bank deposits. In Mexico, a firm cannot borrow more than 30 percent of its net worth, nor can a bank lend any single customer more than 2 percent of the bank's total net capital. If a firm wishes to borrow in excess of the 30 percent limit, it typically does so through bank syndication.

A 1978 amendment to the banking laws allows offshore banks to operate in Mexico. CitiBank is the only foreign-owned bank in Mexico, with 5 branches in Mexico City. Limitations placed on foreign borrowing by Mexican firms resulted in closing many foreign banks. Activities are now limited to securitization, trade finance, and customer service.

Another important source of capital financing is NAFINSA, the only government development bank in Mexico. NAFINSA acts as an intermediary between foreign credit sources and Mexican borrowers, or between the Mexican government and foreign lending institutions. NAFINSA performs no regular commercial banking. Rather, financing is accomplished through NAFINSA's access to development funds made available by foreign banks for new Mexican ventures and business operations. The bank specializes in priority development projects, particularly in the capital goods sector, and guarantees medium and long-term credit for industrial undertakings.

Investments by insurance companies are strictly regulated in Mexico. Portfolio investments are restricted to certain preferred and long-term bonds and real estate. By law, 30 percent of capital and revenues must be in government paper and 50 percent in urban real estate. Pension funds are another important source of capital. Casas de Bolsa (brokerage houses) have argued that they might achieve higher returns than banks, and have convinced some businesses to withdraw their funds from banks.

The Export-Import Banks of the U.S.A. and Japan are the main sources of foreign financial aid. These funds are approved between the governments, earmarked for development projects, and tied to specific agreements. The Mexican stock exchange is contemplating the introduction of an expanded futures market. At present petrodollars and futures for fourteen Mexican companies are sold. No options market exists. There are, therefore, no provisions open to GISSA in the Mexican market to introduce hedging strategies for any contract negotiated with foreign countries.

THE AUTOMOTIVE MARKET

The Mexican government has heavily regulated the automotive industry for the past thirty years. In 1989, President Salinas enacted automotive decrees that deregulated the domestic truck market and reversed the history of protectionism of the car industry. At the heart of every attempt to regulate Mexico's auto industry is an overriding concern with the country's balance of payments. Automakers showed a combined foreign trade deficit of $5.3 billion between 1978 and 1982. This deficit was reversed from 1983 to 1987. The Mexican government's intention is to convert this deficit into a net generator of foreign exchange contributing to the balance of payments. The Mexican market is mature, and production of Mexican automobiles in 1990 continued to be limited by government regulation.

The automotive industry is divided into two segments, manufacturers, and suppliers. The domestic auto industry has been predominantly owned by foreigners (U.S., Japan, and Europe) since Ford invested in 1925. The Mexican government has controlled car lines and models to avoid excessive production in an environment where economic circumstances do not justify oversupply. Today there are five foreign automakers and five truck assembly companies located in Mexico sharing a Mexican market with enormous growth potential. Mexican suppliers supply over 70 percent of all automakers' needs and contribute 56 percent of Gross Domestic Product attributable to the auto industry. The Mexican automobile market has performed erratically over the past ten years. Approximately 570,000 vehicles were sold in 1981, dropping by 18 percent in 1982 and 44 percent in 1983. Approximately 400,000 vehicles were sold in 1985 and only 250,000 vehicles were sold in 1989.

GISSA supplies domestic automakers including Ford, General Motors, Chrysler, and Renault. In 1990, GISSA gained large automobile manufacturer supply contracts with

Volkswagen and Renault. Auto supply exports from Mexico between 1983 to 1987 represent $6.6 billion compared to auto exports for the same period of $1.8 billion. In 1990, auto exports represented 25 percent of all of Mexico's non-oil-related exports.

PROSPECTS FOR A U.S.–MEXICO FREE TRADE AGREEMENT (NAFTA)

Mexico is the United States' third largest trading partner after Canada and Japan. U.S.–Mexico trade reached an estimated $59 billion in 1990 (up 35 percent from 1988). U.S. exports of goods and services to Mexico amounted to $30 billion in 1989, roughly 70 percent of Mexico's imports. This is one of the fastest growing export markets for the U.S. with U.S. exports increasing 95 percent since 1987. Bilateral investment flows are expected to increase under NAFTA; U.S. investment in Mexico reached $7.1 billion in 1989.

Mexico's population grew nearly 10 percent between 1984 and 1989 to eighty-five million and its overall GDP amounted to $201 billion. Per capita GDP was $2,375. Thus, Mexico's recovery ranks fifteenth among the nations of the world. For U.S. producers to gain better access to a market of that size is comparable to a 33 percent increase in gross foreign product (GFP).

NAFTA would create a North American market with a total output of $6 trillion, 25 percent larger than the European Community. Three hundred sixty-five million consumers live in North America compared to 320 million in Europe and 122 million in Japan. On a per capita basis, Mexico currently imports $295 from the U.S. versus $266 from the EC.

Geographic proximity is expected to make exports to Mexico easier and thus more profitable. NAFTA tariff elimination will raise the competitiveness of U.S. goods relative to other countries' goods, to which Mexican tariffs will still apply. Free trade can result in expanded bilateral trade and more predictable rules for doing business across the border. Comparative advantage involves more than labor costs. Because such advantage also entails managerial skill, proximity to the purchaser, and intangibles like sense of style, it is not clear that U.S. consumers will flock to Mexico, but the opposite may be true.

President Bush formally notified the U.S. Congress of his intentions to enter negotiations with Mexico on September 25, 1990, allowing sixty legislative days for Congress to consider the request. Negotiations began in the spring of 1991. The negotiated package was submitted to Congress the summer of 1992 and is expected to be considered by Congress in early 1993.

CONCLUSION

The dynamic economic and political context poses several questions that influence the future of GISSA. Can GISSA achieve its growth and quality aspirations given its closely-held status and the current state of Mexican markets? How diversified can GISSA remain if NAFTA is established and new competitors enter GISSA's markets? What relative emphasis should GISSA give to its production for domestic markets and export markets? What outsiders or partners, if any, should GISSA seek to help prepare for increased competition? Can the del Bosque family simultaneously retain control of the firm and expand as rapidly as it desires? These other challenges confront GISSA as the del Bosque family considers how to survive in an economy on the brink of massive change.

23

The GE Energy Management Initiative (A)

In August 1992, Raj Bhatt, Business Development Manager for GE Canada, met with executives from GE Supply, a U.S.-based distribution arm of GE. The purpose of the meeting was to discuss new business opportunities in energy efficiency, an industry that focused on the reduction of energy usage through the installation of energy-efficient technologies. Bhatt had recently gained prequalification for GE Canada to bid in a $1 billion program to install energy-efficient technologies in all Federal Government buildings. He was confident that GE's expertise in lighting, motors, appliances, and financing was sufficient to win at least some of the contracts. Furthermore, he saw the program as a stepping-stone to building a new GE business to service the energy efficiency needs of a range of clients.

   The GE Supply executives informed Bhatt that they had already established a position in the U.S. energy efficiency industry, through a joint venture with a new energy service company (ESCo), and had retained the services of a full-time consultant to develop the business. They were interested in the Federal Buildings Program that Bhatt had been working on, but felt that it would be more efficiently run through a division of GE Supply, rather than as a locally-managed Canadian venture. The meeting posed a dilemma for Bhatt. He was encouraged by the level of interest that already existed for energy efficiency within GE, but at the same time held certain misgivings about folding the Federal Buildings Program into GE Supply's nascent business. Specifically, he was concerned that a lot of interesting energy efficiency opportunities existed in Canada which a U.S.-focused business would not be in a position to exploit. Bhatt left the meeting uncertain how to proceed.

GENERAL ELECTRIC (GE)

GE, with $60 billion dollars in revenues in 1991, was among the top ten industrial corporations in the world. From the early days of Thomas Edison, it had grown to be a diversified fifty-four-business corporation by the early eighties. With 400,000 employees and a very strong corporate planning division, it exemplified the traditional strategic planning oriented corporation of the 1970s.

   In 1980, Jack Welch, the incoming CEO, made a series of sweeping changes. The corporate planning department was eliminated, layers of management were eliminated, and the concepts of empowerment and customer focus became the new drivers behind GE's activities. Of the fifty-four businesses that Welch inherited, some were sold and others were amalgamated, leaving just thirteen. Welch's stated position was that the major criterion for holding on to a business was that it was number one or number two worldwide in its chosen industry.

The corporate structure under Welch was simplified and decentralized. Each division was autonomous, and was further subdivided into a number of operating companies. The head office for each division was in the U.S., but on average, 25 percent of GE's revenues came from its non-U.S. operations. International operations, including Canada, were structured under the Vice Chairman, International Operations, but operating authority was held by the relevant division of GE. Thus, the lighting plant in Oakville, Ontario reported to GE Lighting in Cleveland, Ohio, with only a secondary line of reporting through GE Canada.

Welch was committed to creating a more open and candid management style at GE. A central thrust of this commitment was the 'Work-Out' program, which he described as follows:

> "The ultimate objective of Work-Out is clear. We want 300,000 people with different family aspirations, different financial goals, to share directly in this company's vision the decision-making process and the rewards. We want to build a more stimulating environment, a more creative environment, a freer work atmosphere, with incentives tied directly to what people do." (*Harvard Business Review*, Sept 1989: 112–120)

Through a series of workshops and facilitated sessions, Work-Out's objective was to challenge the accepted practice at every level in every business. Work-Out sessions had already realized large cost savings by identifying non-essential practices that had gone undetected for years, but equally important, they had created a new level of creativity and enthusiasm among employees.

GE Canada

GE Canada was the longest-established international subsidiary of GE, with operations in twelve of the company's thirteen businesses. In the 1970s, GE Canada operated as a "miniature replica" of its parent company: all functions were represented in Canada, and typically a full line of products was made, primarily for the Canadian market but with some exporting possibilities. The Canadian CEO was fully responsible for the profits of the Canadian operating divisions, and separate financial statements were prepared (GE held a 92 percent stake in GE Canada).

In the eighties, Jack Welch embarked on a major structural change to GE's North American business. Consistent with the increasingly global business environment that was taking shape, Welch recognized that maintaining separate country organizations could not be justified. Instead, an integrated organizational model emerged that became known as "direct-connect." Essentially, this meant creating thirteen strategic business units, and organizing them according to the global demands of the business rather than national interests. Typically, the general manager's role was eliminated in Canada, so that business leaders or functional managers reported directly to their business headquarters in the U.S., rather than through the Canadian organization. For example, the marketing manager for GE Lighting's Canadian operations reported directly to the GE Lighting marketing manager in Cleveland, Ohio.

Exhibit 23.1   GE Structure (North America)

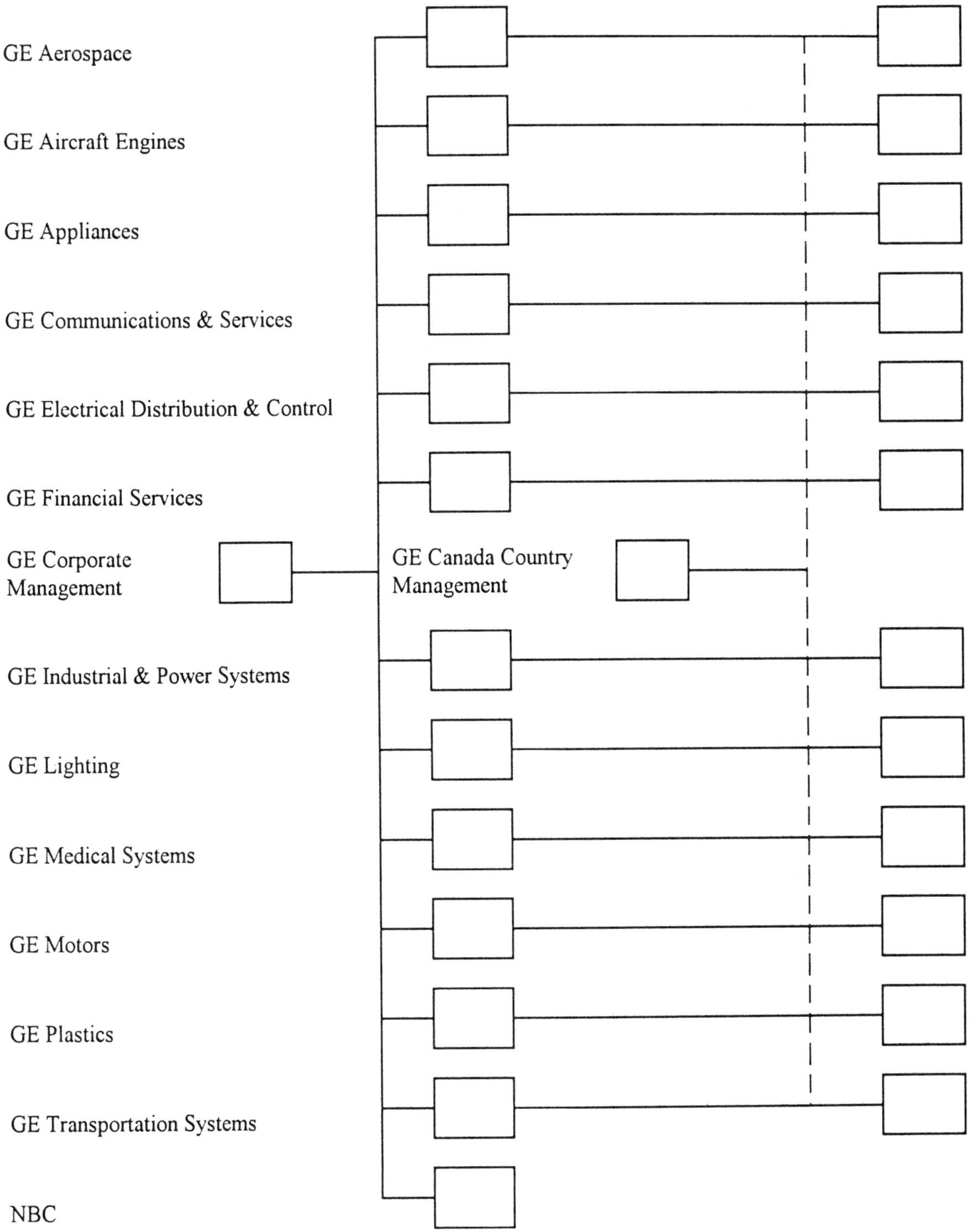

GE Aerospace

GE Aircraft Engines

GE Appliances

GE Communications & Services

GE Electrical Distribution & Control

GE Financial Services

GE Corporate Management

GE Canada Country Management

GE Industrial & Power Systems

GE Lighting

GE Medical Systems

GE Motors

GE Plastics

GE Transportation Systems

NBC

Profit responsibility was held by the global business unit. This arrangement ensured that business activities were effectively coordinated on a global basis. It also furthered Welch's objective of removing layers of management and empowering employees.

Matthew Meyer, CEO of GE Canada, had a vastly different role from his predecessors. With all operations reporting straight to their U.S. divisional bosses, Meyer was directly responsible only for the activities of a very small number of employees. He had vice presidents in finance, environmental affairs, legal, human resources, and government affairs. These managers were responsible for all the uniquely Canadian issues that cropped up, such as new legislation, tax accounting, government grants, and so on. In addition, there was a small business development group, consisting of three managers. Traditionally, this group had been involved in feasibility studies and new market development for the business units in Canada. Following the shift to a "direct-connect" structure, the role had become primarily one of looking for opportunities to leverage the strengths of Canadian activities on a global basis. They were also concerned with identifying new business opportunities in Canada. Bhatt, one of the business development managers, explained:

"Canada is a relatively small marketplace. Consequently, most U.S.-based business leaders have a limited awareness of the opportunities here because they have either a U.S. or a global focus. The role of business development is to attempt to identify investment or market opportunities here that they might find valuable."

There was some discussion among business development managers over the extent to which they should actively "sell" business opportunities to the GE businesses. Some felt that a proactive strategy of promoting Canadian opportunities was appropriate; others preferred to investigate only those cases where business development's involvement had been solicited. The recent decision to promote the VP, Business Development, but not replace him, added further to the uncertainty over the group's role.

Raj Bhatt

Bhatt was only twenty-nine. He had worked at GE for just one year, following a successful period at Northern Telecom and an MBA at the University of Western Ontario.

"Business development is quite a challenging experience. There are lots of good opportunities in Canada, but it is sometimes difficult to achieve the level of interest and buy-in necessary to attract the appropriate attention. The Oakville lighting plant, a global manufacturing mandate, is a planned $144 million investment and is certainly our biggest success so far, but there have been a lot of ideas that failed to materialize."

The business development manager typically held that post for only two years, after which he or she was expected to take a line position in one of the businesses. Bhatt had been given a number of attractive options, but had turned them down because he was afraid that his involvement was critical to a number of projects. Specifically, he was concerned that the energy efficiency business opportunity he had championed up to now would die because no one else had the knowledge of, or the enthusiasm for, that particular opportunity.

ENERGY EFFICIENCY

Energy efficiency covered the multitude of ways that energy usage could be optimized, including conservation, use of efficient appliances, and off-peak usage. Energy Efficiency was originally conceived in the early 1970s as a response to rising oil prices. It recently saw a resurgence due to the environmental movement and the increasing need for cost competitiveness in the late eighties. Although strongly motivated by public opinion and government pressure, energy efficiency initiatives were usually sponsored by the energy supply utilities. They recognized that they could more effectively keep their investment down by reducing demand than by building expensive new power stations. There were also obvious benefits to consumers (in reduced costs) and to the environment.

The growth in utility-sponsored programs for energy efficiency was responsible for the formation of many energy service companies (ESCos). These companies aimed to meet the demands and needs of their customers by utilizing these programs. Under the most common arrangement (called a performance contract), the ESCo would install energy efficient technologies at no upfront cost to the client. The costs would be recouped from the savings realized. Such an arrangement could be very lucrative, but the ESCo bore all the risk in the event that the promised savings never materialized.

The ESCo Industry in Canada

The Canadian ESCo industry was among the most advanced in the world. Both Federal and Provincial governments had active energy-management programs to promote "green" issues, and had targeted energy efficiency as a critical industry. Ontario Hydro and Quebec Hydro had budgets for energy efficiency of $800 million and $300 million, respectively, in comparison to the CDN$1.5 billion budget for all U.S. utilities combined.

As a result of the utilities' involvement, the Canadian ESCo industry was growing very rapidly; 1989 revenues of $20 million had grown to $100 million by 1992, and one estimate put the total market potential in the billions of dollars. Three major segments could be identified, each accounting for approximately one third of the total volume. They were: commercial, which consisted primarily of office buildings, hospitals, and other public buildings; industrial, which consisted of factories and production plants; and residential, which consisted of single-family dwellings. So far the commercial sector had been the most rewarding to ESCos, largely due to the similarities between (for example) one hospital and another. Industrial also had potential, but required knowledge of the specific process technology used in each case.

Over the past decade, the ESCo industry in Canada had experienced mixed fortunes, as companies struggled to understand the dynamics of the market. Lack of technical and risk management experience, flawed contracts, lack of financial strength, and energy price collapses had all led to very low levels of profitability among major players. The recent upsurge of interest in energy efficiency, however, had pushed the industry onto a more steady footing. Furthermore, a shake-out had occurred, leaving between five and ten serious competitors in Canada.

ESCo Strategies

ESCos saw themselves as undertaking three useful functions with commercial and industrial customers. First, they could undertake energy audits of client sites and advise what forms of energy management were most appropriate. Second, they could engineer and provide access to a wide range of energy-efficient technologies that would normally be hard to get hold of. Third, they could install new energy-efficient equipment, under a performance contract. In the Canadian industry, there were several hundred consulting engineers that participated in energy audits, but only seven "full-service" ESCos that undertook all three functions.

Of the three functions, programs such as performance contracting offered the greatest potential return to ESCos, but also the highest degree of risk. Following an installation, it took between five and ten years before the financial benefits were realized. ESCos were paid at the time of installation by their financing partners, who recovered their costs over the lifetime of the project, but in the event that the project was badly estimated, the shortfall in revenue would have to be made up by the ESCo. Access to capital at a reasonable cost was thus critical. Some ESCos had parent companies with deep pockets. The audit and supply functions, while less lucrative, were important elements of the ESCo's business because they established legitimacy in the eyes of the customer. Many commercial clients were extremely skeptical of the estimated energy savings provided by ESCos, but if they agreed to an energy audit, there was a greater likelihood they could be sold on the merits of an installation. The credibility of the guarantee provided by the ESCo was thus of great importance.

THE GE ENERGY MANAGEMENT INITIATIVE

The Initial Opportunity

As GE Business Development Manager, Raj Bhatt received a communication from the Federal Government inviting ESCos to seek to be prequalified for the implementation of performance contracts in 50,000 federal buildings in Canada. The program had a potential total value of $1 billion, which was to be split into a number of smaller contracts. Bhatt was struck by the potential fit between GE's areas of expertise and the requirements of the program. ESCos had to be able to provide energy-efficient lighting, motors, and controls and provide financing for the project; GE was a leading supplier of many of the required products and had a large financing division. Unlike rival firms that would have to form consortia between electrical and financing companies, GE could do many things in-house.

Bhatt submitted a proposal for the Federal Buildings program and, along with a number of other consortia, achieved "prequalification," meaning the right to bid on subsequent contracts that fell under the federal buildings umbrella. This success underlines the magnitude of the opportunity that GE was facing in the ESCo industry. Rather than limiting GE's involvement to the on-off Federal Buildings Program, Bhatt thought there was potential for an ongoing GE business to meet the expected surge in demand for energy management services. He began to think through the best way of proceeding.

The GE Canada Executive Meeting

Bhatt's first move was to meet with the GE Canada executive group and get their reaction to his idea for an energy management business. Attending were Matthew Meyer, Chairman & CEO; Mike Kozinsky, VP Finance; and Scott Larwood, VP Government Relations. Larwood had already been heavily involved in the Federal Buildings Program and was in favor of Bhatt's proposal.

Bhatt: GE Canada is very well-positioned to start an energy management business. We have a broader range of relevant products and services than any other ESCo, and the Ontario and Quebec Hydro programs are among the most advanced in the world.

Kozinsky (Finance): But this is a systems business. We have never been very good at systems implementation.

Bhatt: I realize that we may have to find partners. We are working with a small ESCo on the Federal Buildings project which will do all the installation work. We can identify suitable future partners as things progress.

Kozinsky (Finance): But what is our experience in being a prime contractor? This seems to be very different from any business we have been involved with before.

Larwood (Government Relations): That's not quite true. The Apparatus Technical Service (ATS) business in Power Systems manages service contracts, and there is a lot of project experience in the States.

Meyer (CEO): But there seems to be a considerable risk here. What happens if we pull down a load of asbestos when we're changing a lighting system? GE is an obvious target for legal action.

Kozinsky (Finance): And you stated earlier that there is some downside financial risk if the performance contract does not yield the expected savings.

Bhatt: True, but the estimates are conservative. The overall financial projections are very promising, and involve very little up-front cost. Apart from the salaries of three or four employees, most costs are on a contract-by-contract basis.

Meyer (CEO): Have you given any thought as to how this business would fit into the GE structure?

Bhatt: One of the strengths of GE Canada is that it already taps into all the different businesses. I would like to see the energy management business based in Canada, and drawing from the other GE businesses as required.

Bhatt received a lot of questioning and cautioning on various aspects of the proposal, but there was consensus at the end that the project was worth pursuing. Meyer recommended that Bhatt investigate the level of interest in the U.S. businesses and at the corporate level before any formal proposal was put together.

The GE Supply Opportunity

In discussion with U.S. colleagues, Bhatt discovered that three U.S. divisions were attempting to establish their own ESCo-like initiatives. Two of them were at about the same stage of development as Bhatt. The third, GE Supply, which was a division of GE Industrial and Power Systems, was more advanced. They had been working with an ESCo for a number of months, and had retained a well-connected consultant to advise them. Up to now, the ESCo had assumed all the risk, with GE providing their name, their products, and some servicing expertise, but the division was planning to create a joint venture with the ESCo in the near future.

On hearing about the GE Supply initiative, Bhatt went to Connecticut to visit the GE Supply executives to discuss their respective plans. Present at the meeting were Bhatt, Doug Taylor, CEO of GE Supply, and Fred Allen, manager of the Energy Management business.

Taylor (CEO): Last week we signed a formal alliance agreement with Wetherwell Inc. to run for 18 months. We are now actively looking for contracts.

Allen (Energy Management): But the U.S. market requires some education. How is the market in Canada?

Bhatt: There is a very promising opportunity that we are working on right now. Basically, the Federal Government is looking for bidders on a $1 billion program, and we have already gained pre-qualification.

Allen (Energy Management): That beats anything we've got down here. I think there could be some real opportunities for us to work together. We have gained quite a lot of experience over the past twelve months, and combined with your market, we could have a winning combination.

Bhatt: I am certainly interested in exploring opportunities. How do you see a Canadian energy management business fitting with your business?

Taylor (CEO): We could manage the Canadian business out of our office here.

Bhatt: That causes me some concern. The business relies on close coordination with utilities and government bodies, and a strong local presence would definitely be necessary. I must admit, we considered that management of at least part of the business should be in Canada. The opportunities in Canada are unmatched.

Taylor (CEO): Well, there is some strength to your argument, but I don't see why this business should not fit the normal model.

Bhatt had some misgivings when the meeting came to a close. The business depended on close ties with government bodies, provincial utilities, and local contractors to be really successful, and he felt that these would be lost if there was not a strong Canadian presence. Under the "direct-connect" system, he felt that would be more difficult to achieve.